Macroeconomics

Macroeconomics
A European Text

FOURTH EDITION

Michael Burda
and
Charles Wyplosz

OXFORD
UNIVERSITY PRESS

OXFORD
UNIVERSITY PRESS

Great Clarendon Street, Oxford OX2 6DP

Oxford University Press is a department of the University of Oxford.
It furthers the University's objective of excellence in research, scholarship,
and education by publishing worldwide in

Oxford New York

Auckland Cape Town Dar es Salaam Hong Kong Karachi
Kuala Lumpur Madrid Melbourne Mexico City Nairobi
New Delhi Shanghai Taipei Toronto

With offices in

Argentina Austria Brazil Chile Czech Republic France Greece
Guatemala Hungary Italy Japan South Korea Poland Portugal
Singapore Switzerland Thailand Turkey Ukraine Vietnam

Oxford is a registered trade mark of Oxford University Press
in the UK and in certain other countries

Published in the United States
by Oxford University Press Inc., New York

British Library Cataloguing in Publication Data

Data available

Library of Congress Cataloging in Publication Data

Data available

ISBN 0-19-926496-1

1 3 5 7 9 10 8 6 4 2

Typeset in OUP Swift by Graphicraft Limited, Hong Kong
Printed in Great Britain by Ashford Colour Press Limited, Gosport, Hampshire

Foreword to the Fourth Edition

As always, our new edition features updated tables and figures as well as new boxes with new and exciting applications of macroeconomics to the European policy debate. It also includes deeper changes. Drawing on a poll of textbook users, kindly organized by our editor, we have taken a number of extremely useful comments and suggestions on board. The main message that we heard was that the text was sometimes a bit too involved. With this in mind, we have revised the whole book, streamlining and simplifying the vocabulary, relying less on equations while emphasizing graphical and verbal reasoning. We have eliminated some maths and moved much of the rest to boxes and footnotes that can be ignored by students uncomfortable with formality. The text is now more accessible without sacrificing rigour.

While many teachers have long found the mathematical appendices an important asset, others felt that they were intimidating for students, even if they were told to ignore them. Fortunately, the IT revolution offers a convenient solution: we have moved all appendices—some of which have been expanded and extended—to our dedicated OUP website, where they are available free of charge. Hopefully, the more advanced or ambitious students will not be deterred from using this material. We have moved the 'recommended readings' to our website, which will allow for more flexible and frequent updates. Many exercises have been changed and they are now presented in order of increasing difficulty. In addition, we have included essay-type questions.

More importantly, perhaps, we have rewritten the core chapters. There was considerable overlap between Chapters 10 and 11, those that present the short-run Keynesian analysis, the *IS-LM-BP* framework, which remains at the heart of macroeconomics, if only to deliver initial intuition.[1] In the new Chapter 10, which is based on the old Chapter 11, we emphasize up-front the open economy Mundell–Fleming model. The new Chapter 11, based on the old Chapter 10, now develops this model to explain the distinction between Keynesian and neoclassical models. Some instructors may wish to skip this chapter, which goes deeper in the theory of macroeconomic general equilibrium and prepares the analysis of the neoclassical long run.

Chapters 12 and 13, the two other key chapters that present the *AD-AS* model, have also been substantially rewritten. As in the earlier 'foundations' chapters, as well as in the later 'policy' parts of the book, we have simplified the arguments and added new interesting material.

Finally, in response to numerous requests, we have added a short Epilogue, with the idea of providing readers with a sense of the evolution of the field of macroeconomics. We present the history of ideas and debates and their main contributors.

An important consequence of this profound rewriting and restructuring is to offer several alternative fast tracks for relatively short courses:

◆ Essentials: the core material of traditional macroeconomics can be covered by adopting, without loss of continuity, the following sequence: Chapters 1, 2, 4, 6, 8, 9, 10, 12, and 13.

---

[1] To align ourselves with a common—if misleading—tradition, we now call the line of international financial market integration the Balance of Payments (*BP*) line.

- Emphasis on international macroeconomics: carry on with Chapters 7, 19, and possibly 20.

- Microeconomic foundation: insert in sequence or after the core material Chapters 5 and 11.

- Emphasis on growth: insert in sequence or after the core material Chapters 3 and 18, possibly 14.

- Policy developments: follow up the core material with Chapters 15, 16, and 17.

In preparing this new edition, we have benefited from the support of our editor at OUP, Tim Page. We are grateful to Olya Andrejeva, Sebastian Braun, Nadia Ivanova, Kang Long, Aileen Lotz, and Fang Yao for essential research assistance. Silke Anger and Bud Collier made a number of editorial comments and stimulating suggestions along the way. Claudia Keidel provided useful help in preparing the manuscript.

Contents

List of Figures *xi*

List of Tables *xvi*

List of Boxes *xviii*

PART I
Introduction to Macroeconomics *1*

1 What is Macroeconomics? *3*

1.1 Overview *4*

1.2 Macroeconomics as a Discipline *10*

1.3 The Methodology of Macroeconomics *14*

1.4 Preview of the Book *17*

2 Macroeconomic Accounts *21*

2.1 Overview *22*

2.2 Gross Domestic Product *22*

2.3 Flows of Incomes and Expenditures *30*

2.4 Balance of Payments *36*

Summary *40*

PART II
The Real Macroeconomy *43*

3 Economic Growth *45*

3.1 Overview *45*

3.2 Stylized Facts and Steady States *47*

3.3 Capital Accumulation *49*

3.4 Population Growth *58*

3.5 Technological Progress *61*

3.6 Putting It All Together: Growth Accounting *62*

3.7 Endogenous Growth: A Primer *65*

Summary *67*

4 Labour Markets and Unemployment *71*

4.1 Overview *72*

4.2 Demand and Supply in the Labour Market *73*

4.3 A Static Interpretation of Unemployment *82*

4.4 A Dynamic Interpretation of Unemployment *90*

4.5 The Equilibrium Rate of Unemployment *94*

Summary *97*

5 Borrowing, Lending, and Budget Constraints *101*

5.1 Overview *102*

5.2 Thinking about the Future *103*

5.3 The Household's Intertemporal Budget Constraint *104*

5.4 The Firm and the Private Sector's Intertemporal Budget Constraint *108*

5.5 Public and Private Budget Constraints *113*

5.6 The Current Account and the Budget Constraint of the Nation *120*

Summary *122*

6 Private Sector Demand: Consumption and Investment *125*

6.1 Overview *126*

6.2 Consumption *127*

6.3 Investment *138*

Summary *148*

7 The Real Exchange Rate *151*

7.1 Overview *152*

7.2 The Real Exchange Rate and the Primary Current Account Function *153*

7.3 The Real Exchange Rate as the Relative Price of Non-traded Goods *156*

7.4 The National Intertemporal Budget Constraint and the Equilibrium Real Exchange Rate *161*

Summary *168*

PART III
Money *171*

8 Money and the Demand for Money *173*

8.1 Overview *174*

8.2 Technical Definitions of Money *174*

8.3 Why Is this Money? *177*

8.4 Money: A Balance Sheet Approach *179*

8.5 The Demand for Money *181*

8.6 Equilibrium in the Money Market: The Short Run *186*

8.7 Equilibrium in the Money Market: The Long Run *188*

Summary *194*

9 The Supply of Money and Monetary Policy *199*

9.1 Overview *200*

9.2 Objectives, Targets, and Instruments *201*

9.3 Money Creation *203*

9.4 Controlling Monetary Conditions *209*

9.5 Monetary Policy in an Open Economy *216*

9.6 Monetary Financing of the Government: A Slippery Objective *217*

9.7 Bank Regulation and Monetary Control *220*

Summary *223*

PART IV
Macroeconomic Equilibrium *227*

10 Aggregate Demand, Output, and the Interest Rate *229*

10.1 Overview *230*

10.2 Aggregate Demand and the Goods Market *232*

10.3 The Goods Market and the *IS* Curve *237*

10.4 The Money Market and the *LM* Curve *241*

10.5 International Capital Flows and Macroeconomic Equilibrium *243*

10.6 Output and Interest Rate Determination under Fixed Exchange Rates *246*

10.7 Output and Interest Rate Determination under Flexible Exchange Rates *252*

10.8 Fixed and Flexible Rates: A Wrap-Up *255*

Summary *256*

11 Output, Employment and Prices *261*

11.1 Overview *262*

11.2 The *IS-LM* Model *263*

11.3 General Equilibrium *264*

11.4 General Equilibrium with Flexible Prices:
The Neoclassical Case *268*

11.5 General Equilibrium with Sticky Prices:
The Keynesian Case *272*

Summary *276*

PART V
Inflation and Business Cycles *279*

12 Aggregate Supply and Inflation *281*

12.1 Overview *282*

12.2 The Phillips Curve: Chimera or a Stylized
Fact? *283*

12.3 Accounting for Inflation: The Battle of
the Mark-ups *288*

12.4 Inflation, Unemployment, and Output *294*

Summary *299*

13 Aggregate Demand and Aggregate Supply *303*

13.1 Overview *304*

13.2 Aggregate Demand and Supply under
Fixed Exchange Rates *305*

13.3 Aggregate Demand and Supply under
Flexible Exchange Rates *315*

13.4 How to Use the *AS-AD* Framework *319*

Summary *327*

14 Business Cycles *331*

14.1 Overview *332*

14.2 Stylized Facts about Business Cycles *333*

14.3 Deterministic and Stochastic
Interpretations of the Business Cycle *341*

14.4 Sticky Price Business Cycles *346*

14.5 Real Business Cycles *349*

14.6 Taking Stock of the Two Theories *352*

Summary *355*

PART VI
Macroeconomic Policy *359*

15 Fiscal Policy, Debt, and Seigniorage *361*

15.1 Overview *362*

15.2 Fiscal Policy and Economic Welfare *363*

15.3 Macroeconomic Stabilization *365*

15.4 Deficit Financing: Public Debt and
Seigniorage *373*

15.5 Three Ways to Stabilize the
Public Debt *376*

Summary *379*

16 The Limits of Demand Management *383*

16.1 Overview *384*

16.2 Policy Activism and Demand
Management: What are the Issues? *385*

16.3 Macroeconomic Policy and
Expectations *393*

16.4 The Institutions of Policy-Making *394*

16.5 Politics and Economics *402*

Summary *404*

17 Supply-Side Policy *407*

17.1 Overview *408*

17.2 Market Efficiency and Equilibrium
Output *409*

17.3 Improving the Effectiveness of Goods
Markets *414*

17.4 Improving the Efficiency of Labour
Markets *420*

Summary *432*

18 Economic Growth: Theory and Policy *435*

18.1 Overview *436*

18.2 Growth and Complementary Inputs *437*

18.3 Growth, Knowledge, and Innovation *441*

18.4 Growth and the Economic Environment *446*

18.5 Growth and Politics *452*

Summary *454*

PART VII
Asset Markets and International Financial Architecture *457*

19 Asset Markets and Macroeconomics *459*

19.1 Overview *460*

19.2 How Asset Markets Work *460*

19.3 Linking Asset Markets and Macroeconomics *470*

19.4 Exchange Rate Determination in the Short Run *479*

Summary *486*

20 The Architecture of the International Monetary System *491*

20.1 Overview *492*

20.2 History of Monetary Arrangements *493*

20.3 The International Monetary Fund *504*

20.4 Currency Crises *506*

20.5 The Choice of an Exchange Rate Regime *514*

Summary *521*

21 Epilogue *525*

21.1 The Keynesian Revolution *526*

21.2 The Monetarist Revolution *528*

21.3 The Rational Expectations Revolution *531*

21.4 Microfoundations of Macroeconomics *532*

21.5 Institutional and Political Economics *533*

21.6 Labour Markets *534*

21.7 Growth and Development *536*

21.8 Conclusions *537*

References *539*
Glossary *541*

List of Figures

1.1 Gross Domestic Product (GDP), Germany, France, and the UK, 1870–2001 *4*

1.2 Quarterly Gross Domestic Product, UK, 1962: 1–2002: 4 *6*

1.3 Unemployment Rates in the European Union, Switzerland, and the USA, 1970–2003 *7*

1.4 Labour Share of Income in Manufacturing and Stock Prices, Four Countries, 1951–2002 *8*

1.5 Capacity Utilization Rates and Inflation, USA, 1962–2003 *9*

1.6 Price Levels and Inflation Rates, France and the UK, 1870–2002 *12*

1.7 Endogenous and Exogenous Variables *14*

2.1 GDP Deflator and the Consumer Price Index Inflation Rates: Italy, 1985–2001 *27*

2.2 The Circular Flow Diagram *31*

2.3 From Expenditure to Income to Personal Disposable Income *34*

3.1 The Output–Labour and Capital–Labour Ratios in Three Countries *48*

3.2 The Production Function: Diminishing Marginal Productivity *51*

3.3 The Production Function in Intensive Form *52*

3.4 The Steady State *53*

3.5 Investment, GDP per capita, and Real GDP Growth, 115 Countries, 1950–2000 *54*

3.6 An Increase in the Savings Rate *55*

3.7 The Golden Rule *56*

3.8 Raising Steady-State Consumption *56*

3.9 Was Centrally Planned Poland Dynamically Inefficient? *57*

3.10 Population Growth *58*

3.11 The Steady State with Population Growth *59*

3.12 Population Growth and GDP per capita, 1960–2000 *60*

3.13 The Steady State with Population Growth and Technological Progress *62*

3.14 Growth Rates along the Steady State *62*

3.15 Multifactor Productivity in the USA *63*

3.16 Endogenous Growth with Non-Declining Marginal Productivity *66*

4.1 Household Preferences *73*

4.2 The Household Budget Line and Optimal Choice *74*

4.3 Reaction of the Household to a Wage Increase: Labour Supply *75*

4.4 Individual and Aggregate Labour Supply *77*

4.5 The Production Function and the Labour Demand Curve *77*

4.6 An Increase in Labour Productivity *78*

4.7 Equilibrium in the Labour Market *78*

4.8 Shifting Labour Demand and Supply *80*

4.9 Involuntary Unemployment *83*

4.10 Trade Unions' Indifference Curves *85*

4.11 The Collective Labour Supply Curve *86*

4.12 Labour Market Equilibrium with a Trade Union *86*

4.13 Minimum Wages *88*

4.14 A Map of Labour Markets *90*

4.15 Long-Term Unemployment Rates and the Duration of Unemployment Benefits, 1999–2000 *94*

4.16 Employment and Real Wages: Europe and the USA *96*

4.17 Actual and Equilibrium Employment *97*

5.1 Endowment, Wealth, and Consumption *105*
5.2 Inheriting Wealth or Indebtedness *108*
5.3 The Production Function *109*
5.4 Productive Technology *110*
5.5 Unproductive Technology *110*
5.6 Investment Increases Wealth *111*
5.7 Corporate and Household Saving, 1981–1987 *112*
5.8 The Government Budget Line *114*
5.9 Primary Budget Surpluses, Four Countries, 1974–2000 *115*
5.10 Ricardian Equivalence *116*
5.11 Borrowing Constraints *118*
5.12 Ricardian Equivalence in Denmark, 1981–2001 *119*

6.1 Variability of GDP Components, 1970–2001 *126*
6.2 Indifference Curves *128*
6.3 Optimal Consumption *129*
6.4 Life-Cycle Consumption *129*
6.5 Temporary and Permanent Income Changes *130*
6.6 Real GDP and Retail Sales Growth in the Czech Republic, 1997–2002 *132*
6.7 Real Price of Crude Oil, 1956–2002 *133*
6.8 Current Accounts in Europe, 1956–2002 *133*
6.9 The Effect of an Increase in the Interest Rate *134*
6.10 Consumption, Disposable Income, and Wealth in France, 1980–2002 *135*
6.11 Credit Constraints *136*
6.12 GDP, Domestic Demand, and the Current Account: Poland and East Germany *137*
6.13 The Optimal Capital Stock *139*
6.14 Technological Progress *140*
6.15 The q-theory of Investment *142*
6.16 Investment and Tobin's q, Inter-war and Modern Germany *143*
6.17 Tobin's q *146*

7.1 Nominal and Real Exchange Rates, Four Countries, 1975–2002 *153*
7.2 The Primary Current Account Function *156*
7.3 The Production Possibilities Frontier (PPF) *157*

7.4 Price Lines *159*
7.5 Optimal Production *159*
7.6 Indifference Curves *160*
7.7 Optimal Production and Consumption *160*
7.8 The Equilibrium Real Exchange Rate *162*
7.9 Net External Position and the Real Exchange Rate: The Case of Sweden, 1986–1998 *164*
7.10 The Real Equilibrium Exchange Rate and Productivity in the Traded Goods Sector *164*
7.11 Real Exchange Rates in Transition Countries, 1991–2002 *166*

8.1 Balance Sheets of the Central Bank, the Commercial Banks, and the Non-bank Sector *180*
8.2 Narrow and Wide Monetary Aggregates, Four Economies, 1980–2002 *182*
8.3 Money Demand and Prices, when GDP is Constant *185*
8.4 Equilibrium in the Money Market *186*
8.5 Expansionary Monetary Policy *187*
8.6 An Increase in Real Economic Activity *187*
8.7 A Decline in Transaction Costs *187*
8.8 Money Market Disequilibrium *188*
8.9 Money, Inflation, and Exchange Rate Appreciation in the Long Run: OECD Countries, 1970–1998 *189*
8.10 Money and Long-Run Growth *189*
8.11 Nominal Interest Rates, UK and the Netherlands, 1870–2002 *190*
8.12 Money Demand and High Inflation in Bulgaria, 1991–2002 *192*

9.1 Instruments, Targets, and Objectives in Monetary Policy *201*
9.2 Monetary Policy Procedures *202*
9.3 The Balance Sheets, Again *204*
9.4 The Reserves–Money Stock Link *206*
9.5 The Reserves–Money Stock Link with Currency *207*
9.6 The Money Market *210*
9.7 ECB Interest Rates *212*
9.8 The Letter and the Fan *215*
9.9 Foreign Exchange Market Intervention and Sterilization *217*
9.10 Reserve and Capital Adequacy Ratios *222*

10.1 Cyclical Fluctuations *230*
10.2 General Macroeconomic Equilibrium *231*
10.3 The 45° Diagram *234*
10.4 The Multiplier *235*
10.5 Deriving the *IS* Curve *237*
10.6 An Exogenous Increase in Aggregate Demand *239*
10.7 GDP Growth and Tobin's *q* in the USA, 1995–2003 *240*
10.8 Deriving the *LM* Curve *241*
10.9 An Increase in the Money Supply Shifts the *LM* Curve Outward *242*
10.10 The Balance of Payments Line *244*
10.11 General Equilibrium *244*
10.12 Monetary Policy under Fixed Exchange Rates *246*
10.13 Demand Disturbances under Fixed Exchange Rates *248*
10.14 Argentina 1993–2003 *250*
10.15 Policy Mix *251*
10.16 A Financial Disturbance *251*
10.17 A Devaluation *252*
10.18 Demand Disturbance under Flexible Exchange Rates *253*
10.19 Monetary Policy under Flexible Exchange Rates *254*

11.1 Goods and Money Market Equilibrium *264*
11.2 Output and Employment *265*
11.3 General Equilibrium *267*
11.4 The Role of the Price Level *268*
11.5 Monetary Neutrality *270*
11.6 Sticky Price Equilibrium *274*
11.7 Monetary Neutrality Fails when the Price Level is Fixed *275*

12.1 Phillips Curves: The UK, 1888–1975, and a Sixteen-Country Average, 1921–1973, excluding 1939–1949 *283*
12.2 The Phillips Curve and Aggregate Supply *284*
12.3 The Output Gap and Unemployment in Germany, 1966–2004 *285*
12.4 Okun's Law *285*
12.5 The Long Run *287*
12.6 Phillips Curves: The Recent Experience, Euroland and the UK, 1961–2004 *287*

12.7 The Augmented Phillips Curve and the Aggregate Supply Curve *295*
12.8 From the Short to the Long Run *297*
12.9 The Oil Shocks and the DM, 1965–2003 *298*

13.1 Aggregate Demand and Aggregate Supply *304*
13.2 *IS-LM-BP* and Aggregate Demand under Fixed Exchange Rates *307*
13.3 Shifts in the Aggregate Demand Curve *308*
13.4 Aggregate Demand and Supply under Fixed Exchange Rates *308*
13.5 Fiscal Policy under Fixed Exchange Rates *310*
13.6 A Devaluation *313*
13.7 Expansionary Monetary Policy under a Fixed Exchange Rate Regime *313*
13.8 The Real Exchange Rate Franc/Deutschmark, 1975–1998 *314*
13.9 *IS-LM-BP* and Aggregate Demand under Flexible Exchange Rates *315*
13.10 Aggregate Demand and Supply under Flexible Exchange Rates *316*
13.11 Monetary Policy under Flexible Exchange Rates *317*
13.12 GDP in Hungary and Poland, 1989–2004 *320*
13.13 The Oil Shocks: A Turning Point for Six Countries, pre- and post-1973 *321*
13.14 An Adverse Supply Shock *322*
13.15 An Adverse Demand Shock *323*
13.16 Short-Term Interest Rates in Euroland and in the USA, 2000–2004 *324*
13.17 Disinflation *325*

14.1 Actual and Trend GDP and Detrended GDP, UK, 1963–2002 *334*
14.2 Burns–Mitchell Diagrams for Real GDP, 1964–2002 *336*
14.3 Leading and Lagging Indicators, 1968–2002 *338*
14.4 Components of Aggregate Spending, Eight Countries, 1968–2002 *340*
14.5 Deterministic Cycles in the Multiplier-Accelerator Model *342*
14.6 The Impulse-Propagation Mechanism *344*
14.7 Impulses and Propagations: An Example *345*

14.8 The Propagation Framework in the *AS-AD* Model *346*

14.9 A Demand Shock: The Effect of German Unification on West Germany, 1990–1994 *347*

14.10 A Supply Shock: The Oil Price Shock of 1973–1974 *348*

14.11 The Solow Residual and GDP, Germany, 1961–1993 *350*

14.12 A Productivity Shock *350*

14.13 Intertemporal Substitution of Leisure *351*

14.14 Cyclical Patterns in the Labour Market, G8 Countries, 1965–2003 *353*

15.1 Historical Evolution of Public Debts in Four Countries *368*

15.2 Stabilization Policies *369*

15.3 Cyclical Behaviour of Net Taxes in the UK, 1972–2003 *369*

15.4 Endogenous and Exogenous Components of Budgets *371*

15.5 Changes in Actual and Cyclically Adjusted Budget Balances from 2000 to 2003 *372*

16.1 The Neoclassical Case *386*

16.2 The Keynesian Case *386*

16.3 Unemployment in the UK and Germany, 1890–2003 *388*

16.4 Lags and Demand Management Policy *389*

16.5 Variability of Inflation, Real Wages, and Unemployment: All OECD Countries, 1960–2003 *391*

16.6 The Effect of a Reduction in Corporate Taxes *394*

16.7 Inflation, Growth, and Central Bank Independence *398*

16.8 Political Business Cycles *403*

16.9 Partisan Politics *404*

17.1 The Macroeconomics of Supply-Side Policies *408*

17.2 The Supply-Side Economics of Immigration *412*

17.3 The Effect of Taxation *416*

17.4 The Laffer Curve *417*

17.5 Beveridge Curves in the UK, Germany, and the USA, 1960–2000 *422*

17.6 Incentives and the Social Safety Net *427*

17.7 Real Wages and Unemployment in the UK, the Netherlands, Germany, and the USA, 1960–2002 *431*

18.1 The Convergence Hypothesis in Reality *438*

18.2 Public Investment Spending, 2004 *440*

18.3 Long Waves in Technological Progress *444*

18.4 Human Capital and Growth, 1950–1995 *445*

18.5 Growth Performance under Central Planning *448*

18.6 Real GDP per capita in Sub-Saharan Africa *449*

18.7 Rule of Law and Growth, 1960–1998 *450*

18.8 Life Expectancy and Income *451*

18.9 The Kuznets Curve *452*

19.1 Trading Hours of Stock Markets around the World, Greenwich Mean Time *461*

19.2 Spatial Arbitrage: DM Offshore and Onshore Three-Month Interest Rates, 1978–1998 *466*

19.3 Triangular Arbitrage *466*

19.4 Ostmark–DM Rate and Bid–Ask Spread, August 1989–June 1990 *470*

19.5 The Term Structure of Interest Rates *471*

19.6 An Increase in the Domestic Interest Rate *475*

19.7 Possible Stock Price Paths *477*

19.8 Tulipmania, 1637 *478*

19.9 The Rise and Fall of NASDAQ Stocks, 1996–2003 *479*

19.10 Daily Changes of the Dollar/Euro Exchange Rate in 2003 *480*

19.11 General Equilibrium *482*

19.12 Overshooting *483*

19.13 Overshooting and Undershooting in the *IS-LM* Framework *484*

19.14 Overshooting over Time *485*

19.15 Nominal and Real Effective Exchange Rates: Euro-area, Japan, and USA, 1980–2003 *486*

20.1 Monetary Gold Stock and Cumulative Gold Production, 1840–1980 *496*

20.2 The Decline of World Trade during the Great Depression *498*

20.3 The Three Layers of Bretton Woods *499*

20.4 US Official Liabilities and Gold Reserves, 1950–1970 *500*

20.5 Inflation Rates: USA, UK, Germany, and Italy, 1960–1976 *501*

20.6 The Thai Boom and Bust *507*

20.7 First Generation Crisis *508*

20.8 British Foreign Exchange Reserves and Domestic Credit: The 1992 Crisis *510*

20.9 Self-Fulfilling Crises *511*

20.10 Currency in Crisis *512*

20.11 The $N - 1$ Problem *519*

List of Tables

1.1   Real Income per Capita *5*
1.2   Openness *10*
1.3   Forecasting the Year 2002 *16*

2.1   Growth Rates of Nominal GDP, Real GDP, and GDP Deflator: Euro-area 1990–2002 *26*
2.2   Estimates of the Size of the Underground Economy *28*
2.3   Unpaid Work: The Netherlands in 1990 *28*
2.4   Estimates of German GDP in 1999 *29*
2.5   Components of GDP by Expenditure, 1970–2001 *33*
2.6   GDP and Household Disposable Income, 2003 *34*
2.7   The Accounting Identity in 2002 *35*
2.8   Balance of Payments *36*
2.9   Balance of Payments, Various Countries, 2001 *38*

3.1   The Growth Phenomenon *47*
3.2   Capital–Output Ratios, 1913–1998 *48*
3.3   Growth of Real Gross Fixed Capital Stock, 1913–2001 *64*
3.4   Population, Employment, and Hours Worked, 1900–2001 *64*
3.5   The Solow Decomposition *65*

4.1   Annual Total Hours Worked and Average Wages, 1870–2000 *76*
4.2   Weekly Hours Worked per capita *81*
4.3   Female Labour Force Participation Rates, Unemployment Rates, and Employment Ratios, 2002 *82*
4.4   European Trade Unions: Membership and Coverage, 1950–2000 *84*

4.5   Standardized Unemployment Rates *87*
4.6   Minimum Wages and Youth Employment and Unemployment, 2000 *89*
4.7   Unemployment: Average Stocks and Annual Flows in 2002 *91*
4.8   Inflows into Unemployment and Unemployment Rates in the UK, March 2004 *92*
4.9   Unemployment Insurance: Conditions for Eligibility and Benefits, 1999 *93*
4.10   Estimates of Equilibrium Rates of Unemployment *95*

5.1   Public and Private Borrowing Rates, March 2004: Long-Term Bonds *117*

7.1   Price Level Comparison, 2000 *167*

8.1   Money in Three Countries, December 2003 *176*
8.2   Currency Substitution in Central and Eastern Europe, 1993 *178*
8.3   Assets of Central Banks in Selected Countries, Year-End 2002 *181*
8.4   Elasticities of Money Demand *184*
8.5   Inflation and Money Growth in the Long Run: A Rule of Thumb *191*
8.6   Prices of IKEA Mirrors across Europe, 1998 *194*

9.1   Consolidated Balance Sheet of the Eurosystem, 30 April 2004 *203*
9.2   M0, M2, Money Market Multipliers, and Currency, 2003 *207*
9.3   Theoretical Values of the Money Multiplier *208*

9.4 Seigniorage around the World *219*
9.5 Deposit Insurance in Europe, 2004 *220*

10.1 Openness and Size *231*
10.2 Demand Multipliers: Five Examples *236*
10.3 Sterilized and Unsterilized Foreign Exchange Market Interventions *247*
10.4 The Mundell–Fleming Model: A Summary *256*

12.1 Wage Share of Value Added by Country and Selected Industries, 2001 *289*
12.2 Variability of Inflation, Unemployment, and Imported Commodity Prices in Britain, 1888–2003 *295*

14.1 Descriptive Statistics of Business Cycles, 1963–2002 *335*
14.2 Business Cycle Correlations of Macroeconomic Variables with Output, 1968–2002 *337*
14.3 Variability of Key Macro Variables over the Cycle, 1964–2002 *339*
14.4 Decomposition of the Variance of GDP, 1979:1–1993:4 *349*

15.1 General Government Spending and Finances: EU, USA, and Japan, 2004 *362*
15.2 Government Transfers, Various Countries, 1960 and 2004 *364*
15.3 Budget Balances, Various Countries, 1975–2004 *365*
15.4 Fiscal Implications of German Reunification *367*
15.5 Expected and Realized Budgets in 2003 *370*
15.6 Gross Public Debt, Various Countries, 1970–2004 *373*

15.7 Net Debts and Primary Budget Balances, 2004 *374*
15.8 Public Finances in Italy, 1918–1928 *379*

16.1 Inflation Targets Set by Inflation-Targeting Central Banks in 2003 *392*
16.2 Episodes of Expansionary Fiscal Consolidations in the European Union *396*
16.3 Central Bank Independence Reforms *397*
16.4 Terms of Central Bank Governors and Boards *399*
16.5 German Hyperinflation: Money, Prices, and Inflation, January 1922–October 1923 *400*

17.1 Telecommunications Prices in Germany, 1995–1999 *418*
17.2 Subsidies in Various Countries *420*
17.3 Scandinavian Labour Market Programme Expenditure, 2002 *424*
17.4 Measures of the Strictness of Labour Market Regulation *425*
17.5 Labour Taxation in 2003 *428*

18.1 Non-rivalrousness and Excludability: A Taxonomy of Goods *442*
18.2 What Drives Growth? Some Estimates *454*

19.1 Bond Prices and Yields *472*

20.1 Inflation Rates in Five Countries, 1900–1913 *495*
20.2 Beggar-thy-Neighbour Depreciations, Various Countries, 1931–1938 *498*
20.3 IMF Votes in January 2004 *506*
20.4 The Impact of a 0.1% Tobin Tax and the Holding Period of Investments *516*

List of Boxes

1.1 Forecasting the Year 2002 *16*
1.2 Macroeconomic Schools of Thought:
A Primer *18*

2.1 Value Added and Value Subtracted:
Two Examples *24*
2.2 What GDP Measures *25*
2.3 Price Deflators and Price Indexes *27*
2.4 The Underground Economy and Unpaid
Work *28*
2.5 How National Accounts Estimates Vary
over Time *29*

3.1 For the Mathematically Minded:
The Cobb–Douglas Production Function *50*
3.2 Dynamic Inefficiency in Poland? *57*
3.3 Population Growth and GDP per capita *60*
3.4 The New Economy: Another Industrial
Revolution? *63*

4.1 Technical Change and Unemployment *79*
4.2 Market Hours at Work: Europe versus
the USA *81*
4.3 The European Unemployment Problem *87*
4.4 Minimum Wages and Youth Employment and
Unemployment, 2000 *89*
4.5 'Eurosclerosis' and 'EU-phoria' *96*

5.1 Neither a Borrower nor a Lender Be:
The Economics and the Sociology of
Credit *106*
5.2 Discounting and Bond Prices *107*
5.3 Gross Investment, Depreciation, and
the Capital Stock *109*
5.4 Productive and Unproductive
Investments *111*

5.5 The Modigliani–Miller Theorem *112*
5.6 Pyramids: Is it Possible to Outrun the Budget
Constraint? *121*

6.1 Indifference Curves and Intertemporal
Substitution *128*
6.2 Permanent Income and Life-Cycle
Consumption *129*
6.3 Boom and Bust in the Czech Republic,
1997–2000 *131*
6.4 Oil Shocks and European Current
Accounts *132*
6.5 Current Income and Spending in East
Germany and Poland *136*
6.6 Looking beyond the Next Period and Taking
Account of Capital Depreciation *140*
6.7 The User Cost of Capital and the Price of
Investment Goods *146*

7.1 Computing and Comparing Effective
Exchange Rates *155*
7.2 The Shape of the Production Possibilities
Frontier *158*
7.3 Norway's Oil Fund *165*
7.4 The Balassa–Samuelson Effect *167*

8.1 The Vision of Wicksell: A Moneyless
Society *176*
8.2 Parallel Currencies *178*
8.3 The Many Reasons for Holding
Money *185*
8.4 The Algebra of Long-Run Inflation *190*
8.5 The Demand for Money in a High-Inflation
Episode: Bulgaria, 1991–2002 *192*
8.6 The Law of One Price and Absolute
Purchasing Power Parity *194*

9.1 The Money Multiplier with Currency *208*
9.2 Where are the Greenbacks? *208*
9.3 How the ECB does it *211*
9.4 The Bank of England's Plan and its Fan *214*
9.5 Bank Runs and Lender of Last Resort: A Double-Edged Sword *221*
9.6 Capital Adequacy Ratios *222*

10.1 When the US Stock Market Bubble Burst in 2000 *239*
10.2 Exchange Rate Regimes in Europe, 2004 *245*
10.3 Capital Controls and Monetary Independence *248*
10.4 Argentina's Fixed Exchange Rate Regime *250*

11.1 The Euro and Monetary Neutrality *272*
11.2 The Keynesian Assumption *273*

12.1 When and How Firms Set Prices *288*

13.1 The Arithmetics of the Real Exchange Rate and of Money Growth under a Fixed Exchange Rate Regime *306*
13.2 Fiscal Policy with Rational Expectations *311*
13.3 Peaceful Coexistence with Different Inflation Rates: France and Germany *314*
13.4 The Oil Shocks of the 1970s and 1980s *320*
13.5 Transatlantic Differences in 2000–2004 *324*
13.6 Wage Negotiations: The Time Dimension *326*

14.1 Famous Cycles *335*
14.2 The Multiplier-Accelerator Model in More Detail *343*
14.3 Computers, Scientists, and Business Cycles *344*

15.1 Tax Smoothing after German Reunification *367*
15.2 The Budgetary Process *370*
15.3 Debt-Deficit Arithmetic *375*
15.4 Euroland and the Stability and Growth Pact *377*
15.5 Mussolini and the Public Debt *379*

16.1 Optimal Inflation *392*
16.2 Non-Keynesian Effects of Fiscal Consolidation *396*
16.3 The Nuts and Bolts of Central Bank Independence *399*
16.4 Fiscal Austerity and Stopping Hyperinflations *401*

17.1 EU Competition Policy and National Preferences *411*
17.2 The Supply-Side Economics of Immigration *412*
17.3 The Deadweight Loss from Taxation *416*
17.4 Privatization, Deregulation, and the European Telecommunications Boom *418*
17.5 Active versus Passive Labour Market Policies *424*
17.6 Crusoe Caught in the Safety Net *427*
17.7 Taxes and the Labour Market in Europe *429*
17.8 Bust 'em or Trust 'em? Trade Unions and Reform in the UK and the Netherlands *430*

18.1 Protecting and Punishing Monopolists *443*
18.2 Growth in Communist Countries *447*

19.1 Risk Diversification *463*
19.2 The Price of Risk *464*
19.3 The Short-Lived Market for Ostmarks *469*
19.4 The Term Structure of Interest Rates *471*
19.5 Tulipmania *478*
19.6 Mussa's Stylized Facts and the Asset Behaviour of Exchange Rates *481*
19.7 Overshooting and Undershooting in the *IS-LM* Framework *484*

20.1 Bimetallism and Gresham's Law *493*
20.2 How the IMF is Managed *506*
20.3 The South-East Asian Crisis of 1997–1998 *512*
20.4 The Tobin Tax *516*
20.5 Exchange Rate Regimes in the Transition Countries *518*
20.6 The *N* – 1 Problem *519*
20.7 Optimum Currency Area Theory *521*

PART I

Introduction to Macroeconomics

1 **What is Macroeconomics?** *3*
2 **Macroeconomic Accounts** *21*

Part I of this textbook sets the stage for macroeconomics as a subject.
Chapter 1 explains the objectives and methods of macroeconomics, its history and usefulness, as well as its controversies and open questions. It provides a number of essential definitions and offers a preview of what will follow.
Chapter 2 introduces the national income accounts, the language economists use to describe and communicate the economic activities of a region or a nation, as well as the balance of payments, which summarizes its dealings with the rest of the world.

What is Macroeconomics? 1

1.1 Overview *4*
   1.1.1   Income, Economic Growth, and Business Cycles *4*
   1.1.2   Unemployment *6*
   1.1.3   Factors of Production and Income Distribution *7*
   1.1.4   Inflation *7*
   1.1.5   Financial Markets and the Real Economy *9*
   1.1.6   Openness *10*

1.2 Macroeconomics as a Discipline *10*
   1.2.1   The Genesis of Macroeconomics *10*
   1.2.2   Macroeconomics and Microeconomics *11*
   1.2.3   Macroeconomics and Economic Policy *13*
   1.2.4   Demand and Supply *13*

1.3 The Methodology of Macroeconomics *14*
   1.3.1   What is to be Explained? *14*
   1.3.2   Theory and Realism *14*
   1.3.3   Positive and Normative Analysis *15*
   1.3.4   Testing Theories: The Role of Data *15*
   1.3.5   Macroeconomic Modelling and Forecasting *15*

1.4 Preview of the Book *17*
   1.4.1   Structure *17*
   1.4.2   Controversies and Consensus *17*
   1.4.3   Rigour and Intuition *17*
   1.4.4   Data and Institutions *17*
   1.4.5   Europe *18*

1.1 Overview

Whether we like it or not, economic themes tend to dominate the news. A day seldom passes when we do not hear about unemployment, inflation, economic growth, stock markets, interest rates, or foreign exchange rates. We hear and read so much about these phenomena because, directly or indirectly, they affect our well-being. It is perhaps mostly for this reason that macroeconomics, the study of these economy-wide phenomena, is so exciting. Macroeconomics is more than just headlines, however; it is a fascinating intellectual adventure. The breadth of issues it covers is evidence enough of its inherent complexity. All the same, we will see that simple economic reasoning can take us a long way. And it is often surprising how well a few simple ideas fit complex situations.

Macroeconomics can also be useful. The economic well-being of all consumers, rich or poor, is affected by movements in interest rates, exchange rates, and the rate of inflation. Businesses stand to gain or lose considerable amounts of money when their economic environment changes, regardless of how well they are managed. Being prepared for such changes in fortunes can have considerable value; more generally, it makes us all better citizens able to grasp the complex challenges that our societies face. Macroeconomics is relevant to voters who wonder what their governments are up to, and can also help governments avoid the worst economic crises that have afflicted modern industrial societies in the past century—depressions, when overall economic activity is very far below average, and hyperinflations, when prices are increasing at monthly rates of 50% or more. These extreme situations can tear at a society's social fabric, yet can be prevented when policy-makers apply sound economic principles.

1.1.1 Income, Economic Growth, and Business Cycles

The most frequently used measure of a nation's economic well-being is its output and income, the **gross domestic product (GDP)**. Figure 1.1(a) displays the evolution of GDP for France, Germany, and the UK since 1870. A positive long-run general tendency or **trend** dominates shorter-run fluctuations. The trend rate of growth has been fairly stable, perhaps with an increase after the Second World War. Another way of seeing this is to plot the natural logarithm of

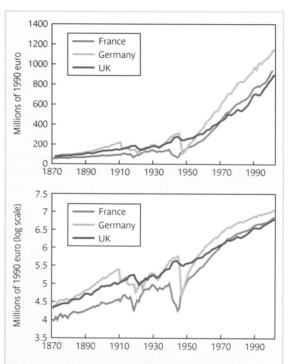

Fig. 1.1 Gross Domestic Product (GDP), Germany, France, and the UK, 1870 – 2001

National output and income, as captured by the gross domestic product, exhibits a robust growth trend. Growth tends to be exponential; that is, annual percentage increases are reasonably stable in the long run. This does not preclude significant year-to-year variations. When the data are displayed on a logarithmic scale instead (panel b), the slope of the curve measures the annual rate of growth.

Source: **www.eco.rug.nl/~Maddison.**

Table 1.1 Real Income per Capita (GDP in euros, 1990 prices)

	1900	1913	1929	1950	1987	1992	1999	2002	Av. growth rate
Austria	2,155	2,592	2,766	2,772	11,458	12,932	14,631	15,428	1.9
Belgium	2,087	3,156	3,780	4,085	11,624	13,231	14,947	15,694	2.0
Denmark	2,256	2,926	3,796	5,193	13,480	14,089	16,765	17,126	2.0
Finland	1,248	1,579	2,032	3,181	11,505	11,309	14,289	15,164	2.5
France	2,151	2,606	3,523	3,943	12,380	13,710	15,033	15,875	2.0
Germany	2,232	2,729	3,030	2,903	11,744	12,601	13,520	14,028	1.8
Italy	1,335	1,917	2,314	2,619	11,179	12,444	13,660	14,312	2.4
Netherlands	2,561	3,028	4,255	4,485	11,770	13,274	15,701	16,238	1.8
Norway	1,449	1,870	2,597	4,086	13,615	14,555	17,907	19,135	2.6
Sweden	1,915	2,316	2,894	5,041	12,702	12,728	14,678	15,983	2.1
Switzerland	2,867	3,191	4,736	6,779	14,801	15,548	16,036	16,737	1.7
United Kingdom	3,360	3,680	4,116	5,190	11,513	12,033	14,428	15,308	1.5
Japan	882	1,037	1,515	1,437	12,155	14,532	15,431	15,490	2.8
Canada	2,177	3,326	3,789	5,454	13,723	13,613	16,043	17,415	2.1
USA	3,060	3,965	5,160	7,151	16,296	17,329	20,490	21,692	1.9
India	448	503	544	463	841	1,003	1,377	1,421[a]	1.1
Argentina	2,061	2,840	3,266	3,730	5,459	5,607	6,515	6,058[a]	1.1
Bangladesh	488	519	521	463	517	576	712	782	0.5

[a] 2001 data.

Source: **www.eco.rug.nl/~Maddison**.

GDP against time, as in panel (*b*). With this so-called logarithmic scale the slope of the curve is a direct measure of the annual growth rate: a constant growth rate would yield a straight line.[1] In the long run, on average, we are not far from the trend.

For the large majority of countries, this trend growth in total output coincides with remarkable increases in living standards. Table 1.1 shows that per capita or average income increased by a factor of more than sixfold in Belgium since 1900, by sevenfold in Sweden, and by almost a factor of 17 in Japan. In contrast, real income per capita rose by only 60% over the same period in Bangladesh. Some countries have faced serious setbacks, such as wars and famines, while others have grown rapidly. Some, like India, stagnated for many decades before suddenly entering a period of rapid increase in living standards.

For this reason, **economic growth** is one of the most exciting issues in macroeconomics. Chapter 3 explores the list of reasons why economies grow. One of them is population increase, since more people can produce more output. Another is the accumulation of means of production: plant and equipment, roads, communication networks, and other forms of infrastructure make workers more productive. Most important is the development and harnessing of knowledge to economic ends. The sharp acceleration of scientific discoveries towards the end of the eighteenth century is thought to have triggered the industrial revolution, and some believe we are now witnessing the onset of a new

---

[1] For mathematically inclined readers, if $x(t)$ grows at the constant rate $g \equiv (1/x)dx/dt$, then $x(t) = A \exp(gt)$ and $\ln x(t) = \ln A + gt$, where A is a constant and t stands for time.

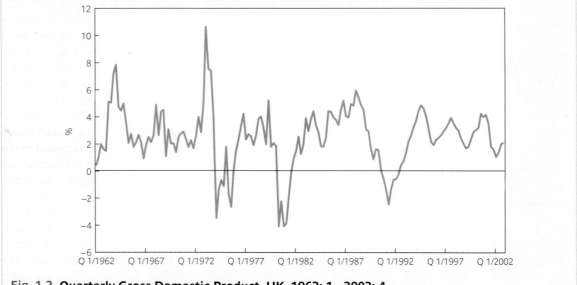

Fig. 1.2 Quarterly Gross Domestic Product, UK, 1962: 1 – 2002: 4

With quarterly data, fluctuations of economic activity around trend become more apparent.

Sources: IMF; OECD.

wave of advances related to information and tele-communications technology.

While output and income have increased by staggering amounts over many decades, this growth is by no means constant or even steady. A second important message that we can take from Figure 1.1 is that real output tends to fluctuate around its trend. This is even more apparent in Figure 1.2, which focuses on the quarter-by-quarter evolution of GDP in the United Kingdom and magnifies the relative importance of short-run fluctuations. These sustained periods of ups and downs are called **business cycles**. One important challenge of macroeconomics is to explain such deviations of GDP from its underlying trend: why they occur and persist over anywhere from one to five years, and what can be done, if anything, to avoid the disruptions that are associated with them. This is the common theme of Parts III, IV, and V of this book.

1.1.2 Unemployment

One important phenomenon associated with cyclical fluctuations is **unemployment**, the fact that people seeking work cannot find it, even when the economy

is growing rapidly. The **unemployment rate** is the ratio of the number of unemployed workers to the size of the **labour force**. The labour force consists of those who are either working or are actively looking for a job. In comparison with the total population, it leaves out young people who are not yet working, the old who are retired, and those who do not wish to work—or have given up hope of working.

There are many reasons why we are concerned about unemployment. It is natural to associate idle workers with a loss of output and income to the economy. We need to ask, at the same time, whether unemployed are receiving offers of work, whether they are turning down job offers, if so, for what reason. Are the jobs that workers are searching for available at all, or are their aspirations unreasonable? The answers to these questions will help us better understand this complex phenomenon.

Unemployment is generally not a pleasant affair. Even with well-developed and efficient unemployment assistance programmes, long-term jobless workers can experience emotional stress and their skills may deteriorate. Even if they are not measurable, the social and psychological costs of

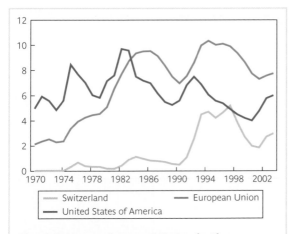

Fig. 1.3 Unemployment Rates in the European Union, Switzerland, and the USA, 1970–2003

The unemployment rate, measured as the proportion of workers who do not have a job but are looking for one, varies considerably across countries. In the USA, the unemployment rate fluctuates according to business cycles. In contrast, the experience of the European Union has been a marked increase over the last three decades, signalling a key specificity of the continent. Not all countries of Europe, however, have suffered from massive unemployment, as Switzerland shows.
Source: OECD.

unemployment are high for the affected individuals and for society as a whole. By that criterion, Europe has not done well over the last decades, as Figure 1.3 shows. The average rate of unemployment has grown inexorably to reach double-digit numbers. In the USA, in contrast, unemployment has closely followed the business cycle, rising in periods of slowdown, declining when growth returned. At the same time, not all European countries have shared this misery, as the case of Switzerland shows. Chapter 4 and later, Chapter 17, present explanations for these varying experiences.

1.1.3 Factors of Production and Income Distribution

The output of an economy, its GDP, is by and large the result of work effort by men and women combined with equipment—'machines', but also buildings and other structures. **Labour** and **capital**

are the technical names given to the two main **factors of production**, or inputs.[2] The distribution of total income between these two factors of production is often a political issue, with important economic aspects. Understandably, wage-earners wish to enlarge their share of the pie. Figure 1.4 shows the share of income in manufacturing that goes to labour, the **labour share**. It also plots the evolution of the stock market **index** over the same period, which tracks the value of shares in companies traded on the stock exchange or bourse. An index is a number set to take a simple value (e.g. 1 or 100) on a particular date for easy comparison, and is primarily designed to show relative changes. In stock markets, shares in companies are traded and valued on the basis of their profitability. The figure shows an inverse relationship between the labour share and the stock price index. When the share of income going to labour is high, less is available for the firms' owners, and stock prices are depressed. While it would be premature to assert that one causes the other, it is valid to conclude that both are driven by common economic phenomena. In Chapter 6, we will see that depressed stock prices may adversely affect the accumulation of productive equipment and, ultimately, the growth and size of the economic pie itself.

1.1.4 Inflation

Inflation refers to the rate of change of the average level of prices. For comparability, the inflation rate is usually stated in terms of percentage change per year, even when it is measured more frequently, such as every quarter or every month. Most of the time, inflation is low or moderate at rates ranging from just above 0% to 4%. In the 1970s many European countries experienced double-digit inflation, with rates rising to 10%, 20%, or more. In a number of countries, for example in Latin America or in the transition countries of Eastern Europe, inflation rates of several hundred per cent were quite common in the 1980s. When inflation is very high it is usually measured on a monthly basis; the term **hyperinflation** describes situations when this

---

2 Land, energy, intellectual property, and many other inputs also matter, but will be neglected as a first approximation.

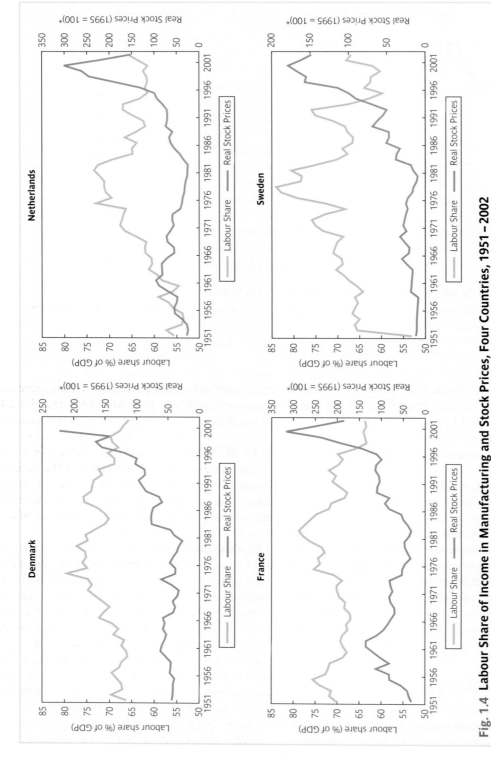

Fig. 1.4 Labour Share of Income in Manufacturing and Stock Prices, Four Countries, 1951–2002

Labour and capital share the fruits of the economic activity of a nation. The labour share is the fraction of economic output which accrues to workers in wages and other forms of compensation. The valuation of firm assets reflected in stock prices is negatively associated with the labour share.

Sources: OECD; IMF; US Department of Labour.

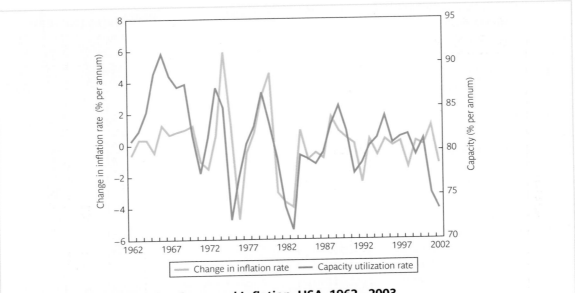

Fig. 1.5 Capacity Utilization Rates and Inflation, USA, 1962–2003

When measures of the utilization of capacity indicate a high level of activity in factories, the rate of inflation tends to increase. Conversely, low levels of activity are accompanied by declining rates of inflation.

Sources: IMF; OECD Main Economic Indicators.

monthly inflation rate exceeds 50%. A sign of exceptional economic distress, hyperinflation has been observed in Central Europe in the early 1920s, in Latin America in the 1980s, and in many countries born out of the collapse of the Soviet Union in the early 1990s.

In normal times, inflation is related to the business cycle. Figure 1.5 shows how the rate of inflation changes when the rate of capacity utilization varies. The rate of **capacity utilization** measures the degree to which companies use available plant and equipment, and it serves as a good indicator of cyclical conditions. The inflation rate is generally **procyclical**: it tends to rise in periods of high growth and declines in periods of slow growth. In contrast, the behaviour of unemployment is **countercyclical**. The behaviour of inflation is investigated in Parts IV and V of this book.

1.1.5 Financial Markets and the Real Economy

Financial markets play a central role in modern economies. Literally or with the help of sophistic-

ated communications technologies, they represent arenas where buyers and sellers of financial assets such as bonds, stocks, currencies, and other financial instruments meet to trade. Together with banks and other financial institutions, financial markets gather resources from households in the form of savings and lend them out to others who will spend them. One specific feature of these markets is the extreme day-to-day variability of prices at which financial instruments are traded.

Physical investment, the accumulation of productive capital, is intimately related to financial conditions. It is one channel through which financial markets affect the **real economy**. The other channel is consumption. Stocks—shares in corporations—represent one form of private wealth. When share prices rise, people feel richer and consume more. The real economy is contrasted with the financial or **monetary economy**: the former concerns the production and consumption of goods and services, and the incomes associated with productive activities; the latter deals with trade in assets, i.e. monetary and financial instruments. Chapter 10 brings the real and the monetary spheres of the economy together to understand short-run determination of output, interest rates, and exchange rates. Chapter 11 explores these short and long-run linkages in more detail. Chapters 12 and 13 bring together the issues of inflation and exchange rates.

1.1.6 Openness

Every country engages in trade, exporting and importing goods and services to and from other partner countries. An increasing number of countries—sometimes called emerging market countries—are also connected through trade in financial assets. One measure of a country's openness, or exposure to the influences of the rest of the world, is the ratio of its exports to its GDP. Table 1.2 shows that openness has considerably increased over the past decades, as part of the process of globalization. Smaller countries tend to be more open than larger countries, and indeed the USA and Japan are fairly closed by international standards. This is also the case of the European Union vis-à-vis the rest of the world, even though considerable trade integration has taken place among its member countries, as the table clearly shows. On 1 May 2004, the European Union expanded by ten nations and 75 million inhabitants, an event which will further accentuate the importance of international trade, financial, and policy links between these countries.

As a consequence, no country is truly from influences of events that occur elsewhere, sometimes far away. A good example is the financial crisis that started in Thailand in June 1997 and

Table 1.2 Openness (ratio of exports to GDP, %)

	1960	2001
European Union	6.1	11.8
United States	5.2	11.2
Japan	10.7	10.8
Belgium	38.3	84.4
Denmark	32.7	45.6
Germany	19.0	35.0
Hungary	—	60.6
Ireland	30.6	95.4
Netherlands	46.3	65.1
Poland	—	19.4
Portugal	16.0	31.6
Russian Federation	—	36.3
Spain	8.9	29.9
Sweden	22.7	46.5
Switzerland	27.7	45.5
Ukraine	—	55.5
United Kingdom	20.9	27.1

Source: World Bank; Eurostat.

spread to the rest of South-East Asia. It didn't stop there, moving on to Russia, affecting Hungary and Poland along the way, before hitting Brazil and finally, with some delay, Argentina. Chapters 19 and 20 look at these issues.

1.2 Macroeconomics as a Discipline

1.2.1 The Genesis of Macroeconomics

Why do we observe cyclical fluctuations in the level of activity, for example the movements of GDP around its trend? Why is unemployment generally countercyclical, while changes in inflation appear procyclical? For a long time, economists paid little attention to such phenomena. In fact, it was believed that properly functioning markets would deliver the best possible outcome, to a good approximation at least, and that there was no point in looking into their aggregate behaviour. This principle was called 'laissez-faire'. Laissez-faire was opposed by proponents of interventionism, who advocated government support for particular markets and industries, including subsidies and protection from foreign competition.

This does not mean that business cycles were ignored completely. In fact, cycles of varying lengths were identified and studied, ranging from inventory cycles of one or two years' duration to long-wave cycles lasting half a century. Such cycles were seen as the cumulative outcomes of disturbances such as discoveries, inventions, exceptionally good or bad crops, wrong bets by firms on goods that customers want to buy, or even changing tastes of consumers at home and abroad. Inflation was seen as the consequence of rapidly growing money stocks, first because of gold discoveries in the nineteenth century, afterwards because of reckless paper money creation by central banks. As will be seen in Chapter 14, much of this wisdom remains valid today. Yet the Great Depression of the 1930s, which spread worldwide sending millions into unemployment and misery, seemed too severe to be simply bad luck. Reflecting upon the Great Depression in 1936, British economist John Maynard Keynes published *The General Theory of Employment, Interest and Money*, a book that is often said to have started the field of macroeconomics. Keynes stressed the role of aggregate demand in macroeconomic fluctuations. His followers later persuaded policy-makers to engage in aggregate demand management, that is, to manipulate government demand in order to smooth out fluctuations, mainly to avoid protracted recessions.

An evaluation of the success of demand management policies—which is the subject of Chapters 15 and 16—is not conclusive. There have been both benefits and costs. Since the Second World War, the amplitude of the business cycle appears to have diminished considerably, as can be seen in Figure 1.1. While earlier generations assumed that favourable periods of growth were inevitably followed by periods of declining activity, today we worry mostly about slowdowns of growth. At the same time, economists have also begun to think hard about the supply side—meaning the productive capacity of an economy—and more efficient

utilization of labour and capital resources. This applies especially to unemployment, which remains a big problem in Europe. These topics are the subject of Chapter 17.

Another remarkable change in the behaviour of the post-war economy concerns the general price level, or the cost of goods in terms of money. Until the Second World War, prices were as likely to rise as they were to fall, as can be seen from Figure 1.6. Apart from war periods, the price level was trendless; over long periods of twenty to fifty years, the cost of living—a measure of the average price level—seemed just as likely to fall as to rise. One interpretation of the post-war era—a controversial one, as we shall see—is that macroeconomics has led to more stable growth rates at the cost of inflation. In the mid-1980s, concern with high inflation triggered a change of heart. In particular, most central banks have given up Keynesian policies and refocused their energy on keeping inflation low.

1.2.2 Macroeconomics and Microeconomics

The macroeconomy is just the sum of hundreds or thousands of markets, each of which is explained by microeconomic principles. Microeconomics is devoted to the study of prices of individual goods and of the markets where these goods are produced and sold. Why do we need two separate disciplines? To a great extent they are linked. Microeconomics is dedicated to the analysis of market behaviour of individuals. Macroeconomics is concerned with collective behaviour, the outcome of individual decisions taken without full knowledge of what others do. Keynes stressed the notion of coordination failures, which arise in decentralized markets as illustrated in the following example.

A consumer wants to purchase a car, but his income is insufficient for him to do so. A car manufacturer could actually hire him to build cars, and with his salary he would then be able to buy one. That one sale, however, would not suffice to pay his salary, so other buyers would need to be found. In order to generate sufficient demand for his employment, several other individuals would need to be hired, perhaps in different industries. For this scheme to work, a considerable amount of coordination

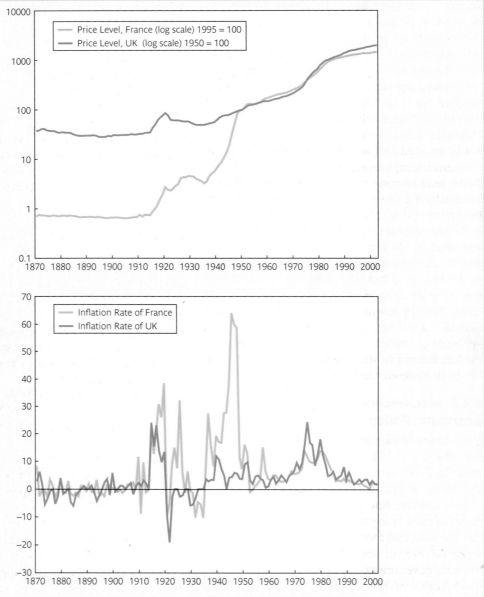

Fig. 1.6 Price Levels and Inflation Rates, France and the UK, 1870 – 2002

Until the outbreak of the First World War, the price level was stable, and inflation was close to zero on average. Since the Second World War, the price level has risen secularly, average inflation has been positive, high in the late 1970s and much of the 1980s, declining over the 1990s.

Source: Maddison (1991), OECD.

among producers and consumers would be required. The laissez-faire principle is that prices and markets automatically and perfectly perform this coordinating role. Keynes' view was that sometimes they fail to do so. Then, there may be many consumers wishing to buy goods and willing to work to produce them, and many firms that would benefit from hiring them if only they could be persuaded that their sales would increase. But this potential may not be realized and we have both recession (fewer sales) and unemployment (fewer jobs). Even if market forces tend to correct this imbalance (which they eventually do), the period of time necessary may be long enough to involve significant social costs.

Macroeconomics started with the idea that prices and markets do not continuously resolve all the coordination requirements of a modern economy. As microeconomics has moved in this direction too, the sharp distinction between the two fields has faded. Modern macroeconomics starts from sound microeconomic principles, and we follow this approach in the early chapters. We then focus on market failures to study business cycles and what can be done about them.

1.2.3 Macroeconomics and Economic Policy

Early macroeconomists argued that governments have the means and the duty to correct market failures. The experiences of the past decades have shown that governments too may fail. Indeed, one major dividing line among macroeconomists is between those who primarily fear market failures on the one side, and those who primarily fear government failures on the other. Yet, in nearly every country, governments are held responsible for the good health of the economy. At election times incumbent governments are judged, first among many other issues, on their economic performance. This is largely a consequence of the **Keynesian revolution**. It explains why the study of macroeconomics is so intertwined with policy and politics. Part V is devoted to these issues.

1.2.4 Demand and Supply

In its most concentrated form, macroeconomics boils down to separating events into two categories: those that affect the demand for goods and services, and those that affect the supply of those goods and services. The **demand side** relates to spending decisions by **economic agents**—households, firms, and government agencies—both at home and abroad. The principle of aggregate demand management policies is that the government can take actions to offset or smooth out those of private agents—firms and households—in order to dampen or eliminate fluctuations in total spending. The idea is to take the edge off recessions as well as booms. Two traditional demand management instruments are fiscal and monetary policy. **Fiscal policy** manipulates government expenditures or taxes in an attempt to affect the volume of national spending. This subject is studied in detail in Chapter 15. **Monetary policy** is directed at influencing interest and exchange rates, and more generally conditions in financial markets; this in turn affects spending on goods and services. Chapters 8 and 9 provide an in-depth analysis of money and monetary policy.

The **supply side** relates to the productive potential of the economy. The choice of hours worked by households, the productivity of their labour, and in general the efficiency with which resources are allocated in generating a nation's output, all influence an economy's aggregate supply. Accordingly, supply-side policies represent government's effort to increase an economy's long-run capacity as well as its overall efficiency. Frequently, this effort is about reducing or eliminating government-induced inefficiencies, which were introduced before the importance of the supply side was understood, or as the result of successful lobbying by interest groups. It is also about bringing idle or underutilized resources into productive uses. Unemployment policy—designed to fight the scourge of market economies—occupies a key role in the supply side. Chapter 17 explores these issues and shows how the government can improve or worsen the economic climate.

1.3 The Methodology of Macroeconomics

1.3.1 What is to be Explained?

Macroeconomics is concerned with aggregate activity, the level of unemployment, interest rates, inflation, wages, the exchange rate, and the balance of payments with other countries. As a scientific undertaking, macroeconomics deals with phenomena which have highly complex channels of causation. Consider a relatively simple example: in this book you will learn that inflation affects the determination of the rate at which foreign money is traded for domestic money, the **exchange rate**. You will also learn that the inflation rate is also affected *by* the exchange rate. Before beginning to think about these questions, it is essential to be clear about what we want to explain and what we take as given, or outside the realm of analysis. The variables to be explained using economic principles are called **endogenous** variables. The other variables—those we do not try to explain—are called **exogenous** variables. This distinction is represented in Figure 1.7. Examples of variables considered exogenous are policy instruments (the tools of fiscal and monetary policies), economic conditions abroad (foreign levels of activity and interest rates), the price of oil, and sometimes even domestic social conditions such as business optimism or trade union militancy.

The distinction between endogenous and exogenous variables is necessarily arbitrary. Many exogenous variables are not strictly independent of the endogenous variables. Because the analysis occurs in steps, many variables first considered exogenous or given at the outset are later made endogenous, or endogenized. For example, fiscal and monetary policy decisions are often responses to the course of inflation or unemployment. While it is convenient to take policy variables as exogenous, it is sometimes illuminating to endogenize them. Chapter 16 takes some steps in this direction.

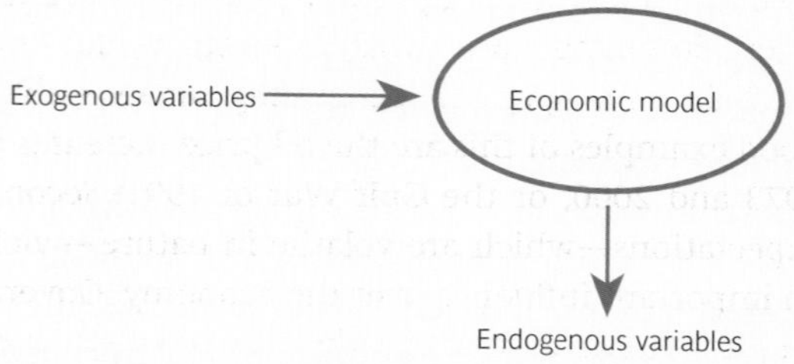

1.3.2 Theory and Realism

Macroeconomics proceeds by making simplifying assumptions. We never literally believe in our assumptions, but we need them in order to see through the vast complexity of an economy. This is why the distinction between endogenous and exogenous variables is artificial. Truly exogenous variables are rare: two examples are climatic conditions (and even these may be affected by economic events, such as the greenhouse effect) and scientific discoveries and inventions (which also may result from economic decisions). The task of systematically linking the behaviour of endogenous variables to changes in exogenous variables is accomplished by specifying relationships between all the variables of interest.

All these relationships, when brought together, constitute a theory. Almost by definition, theory departs from realism. If the real world could be understood without simplifying assumptions, theories would be unnecessary. The problem is not with economics, but rather with the world's inherent complexity. Progress is made by weeding out those assumptions and theories that lead us to false conclusions. As time passes, some theories prove to be

Fig. 1.7 Endogenous and Exogenous Variables

Endogenous variables are the object of analysis in an economic model. Exogenous variables are determined outside the economic model. The weather, political decisions, and the onset of time are examples of variables usually considered exogenous.

unfounded, while others gain acceptability. This process is long and complex, and far from complete. Because macroeconomics is a young discipline, a number of controversies continue to dominate, and this aspect is discussed in Section 1.4 below.

1.3.3 Positive and Normative Analysis

Macroeconomic analysis and policy are closely linked. Because a number of exogenous variables are under the control of government, it makes sense to ask what is good and what is bad policy. At its best, macroeconomics can explain the economy; for example, it can link particular events to exogenous events or policy decisions. This is **positive economics**: it refrains from value judgements. **Normative economics** takes a further step and passes judgement or makes policy recommendations. In so doing, it must specify what criteria are used in arriving at particular conclusions. This inevitably implies a value judgement. Economists generally like to make policy recommendations. As long as they reveal their criteria, this is part of their professional activity. In this textbook, we will generally refrain from normative economic analysis.[3] At the same time, we believe and hope that many readers will make use of their newly acquired knowledge to indulge in the normative side of macroeconomics: this is what makes it fun.

1.3.4 Testing Theories: The Role of Data

The generally accepted way of evaluating theories is to subject them to scientific testing. In macroeconomics, this means looking at the facts, i.e. at data. This is easier said than done, and there are a number of unusual difficulties. First, data correspond to sometimes elusive concepts, as Chapter 2 will show. Second, constructing aggregate data implies enquiring into the behaviour of millions of individuals, who sometimes have good or bad reasons to misrepresent the truth. Third, economics shares the predicament common to other social sciences

that experimentation is not really possible—when observed, people often change their behaviour. Not only is it possibly immoral—no macroeconomist would wish to start a hyperinflation just to test a theory—but more importantly, many important variables simply are not observable. This is the case of expectations, for example. Macroeconomists are forced to conduct empirical tests with the data that they have. They develop statistical techniques, often sophisticated ones, to deal with observation and measurement errors. They refine the techniques they use to gather and analyse data. This allows the elimination of some theories and the modification of others. The surviving theories will be those that withstand the test of time in this scientific process.

1.3.5 Macroeconomic Modelling and Forecasting

Economists are frequently asked to make forecasts. Governments, international organizations, and large financial institutions frequently employ large teams of economists to prepare forecasts. If macroeconomics were to be judged by the performance of forecasts, the verdict would not be unkind. The respectable track record of forecasters has however been sullied by some large historical errors. Box 1.1 illustrates this fact by examining the accuracy of forecasts, after the fact, for the year 2002.

There are several reasons why economic forecasting is inherently difficult. First and foremost, even an excellent understanding of an economy's structure —how its endogenous variables interact—does not preclude misjudging changes in exogenous variables. Good examples of this are the oil price increases of 1973 and 2000, or the Gulf War of 1991. Second, expectations—which are volatile in nature—wield an important influence over the economy. Governments sometimes react to their own forecasts by implementing policies designed to prevent those forecasts from happening. Political changes occur quickly and can disrupt the economic environment. Finally, it takes time—often several months—to know what has really happened at any given point, so forecasts are always based on provisional information which becomes more precise only with time.

---

[3] Many are motivated by 'social conscience' to study economics. Much like medical doctors who want to cure the sick, economists are often eager to provide relief to the disadvantaged and suffering.

Box 1.1 Forecasting the Year 2002

Economic forecasts can be wrong, and often significantly so. Table 1.3 presents forecasts of GDP growth and inflation published every six months by the Organization for Economic Cooperation and Development (OECD), an organization of industrialized countries. With the exception of South Korea, both economic growth and inflation in 2002 turned out to be considerably lower than first expected from the perspective at year end 2000. Several factors contributed to this development. First, a sharp drop in stock prices associated with the collapse of the internet boom was followed by sharply lower investment spending by firms around the world. This contributed directly to the slowdown in growth as well as inflation. Second, the terrorist attacks on the United States in September 2001 reduced investment as well as consumer spending in most industrial countries. Finally, a rise in oil prices is generally associated with a slowdown

in economic activity. From the perspective of 2000, these were all unforeseen events, with a large negative impact on the economy all the same.

Table 1.3 also shows how being wrong can change over time. This is frequently the case, as forecasters tend to underestimate large changes, and are usually cautious to modify their forecasts unless new evidence is compelling. Only in the case of the US economy was the OECD quick to expect a major slowdown in 2002, and only as of mid-2001—well before 11 September. These expectations were later revised significantly *upward*, as the US responded by cutting income taxes sharply and increasing defence spending, measures which generally increase economic growth. These policies could not have been fully anticipated at mid-2001, since they were largely a result of the terrorist attacks which occurred later on.

 Table 1.3 Forecasting the Year 2002

	France	Germany	Japan	Korea	UK	USA
Economic Growth (annual increase in real GDP, % per annum)						
Forecast (December 2000)	2.5	2.5	2.0	5.6	2.3	3.3
Forecast (June 2001)	2.7	2.4	1.1	5.5	2.6	3.1
Forecast (December 2001)	1.6	1.0	−1.0	3.2	1.7	0.7
Actual Outcome	1.2	0.2	0.3	6.3	1.8	2.4
Inflation (rate of change in average prices, % per annum)						
Forecast (December 2000)	2.0	1.6	−0.1	2.8	2.3	2.2
Forecast (June 2001)	1.5	1.5	−0.5	3.5	2.2	1.6
Forecast (December 2001)	1.4	1.0	−1.5	3.3	2.3	1.0
Actual Outcome	1.5	1.4	−1.5	3	0.8	1.4

Source: OECD, *Economic Outlook*.

Most forecasts are generated by computer-based models. These models resemble those that we present in this book. They are made of hundreds, sometimes thousands, of equations. Constructing these equations is a long and difficult task. The exogenous variables must be guessed by forecasters before they can ask their computers for an answer. This introduces many margins of error. The models can never be fully reliable, and the exogenous variables may be difficult to pinpoint. For these reasons, the forecasters themselves take their results with a grain of salt, and often, when the outcome is not completely satisfactory, 'drop in' their own subjective factor to the results.

1.4 Preview of the Book

1.4.1 Structure

The book proceeds in steps. Parts I–IV build up an understanding of the measurement and the behaviour of the underlying economy. Part I is concerned mostly with defining terms and constructing a macroeconomic vocabulary. Part II elaborates the behaviour of the real economy. It focuses on the motivations of consumers and producers, abstracting from the influences of money and financial aspects of the economy. Part III studies money and its central role in macroeconomics, as well as the financial system that creates it. Part IV studies macroeconomic equilibrium in the short, medium, and long run. Part V examines inflation and its evolution, and pins down its determinants over a longer horizon. It introduces a framework for thinking about inflation and the business cycle. Part VI then uses this framework to explore policy issues facing governments: fiscal policy, demand management, and supply policy. The focus then shifts in Part VII to more specialized topics, financial markets and foreign exchange rates, as well as the world international financial system.

1.4.2 Controversies and Consensus

Economists often make a bad name for themselves by quarrelling in public. Visible disagreements among economists frequently have to do with finer points, if not outright hair-splitting. This discourse is intellectually healthy, but misleading to outside observers, whose opinions are often based on accounts in the popular press and more apt to recall sensational talk-show appearances rather than sober analysis of theory and data. It is unfortunate that many disagreements have important policy implications. Perhaps as a result, politicians often see economics as a sort of debating event, with economists acting as advocates for one particular ideology or another. Getting a stamp of approval for a particular policy means simply finding the right economist with the right theory.

In this textbook we do not shy from presenting some of the most important disagreements among economists along the way, leaving the reader free to judge. Yet we do not dwell upon these controversies either, choosing to focus rather on the common ground. Because there is so much that is not controversial, it is best first to understand the broad areas of consensus. Box 1.2. provides more details.

1.4.3 Rigour and Intuition

The only possible scientific approach to the complexities of the real world is the rigour of reasoning. However, to be useful, macroeconomics must be versatile and easily put to work when we want to understand particular events. This is why a great deal of macroeconomics simply amounts to accumulating intuition about particular phenomena. Our objective is, therefore, to leave readers with an intuitive understanding of how the economy functions. We do this by trying to draw robust yet simple conclusions from the various and often intricate principles presented. Such intuition is never completely rigorous, but can be useful in practice. Rigour plays its crucial role in reminding us when intuition is correct, and when it should be used with caution.

1.4.4 Data and Institutions

Macroeconomics is fascinating because it tells us a great deal about the world in which we live. It is not merely a set of abstract principles with interesting logical properties. Many theories will look odd at first sight, yet they capture key aspects of the real world. This is why at each important step we pause to look at facts. Facts can be data or particular episodes. Studying them carefully shows how theories work and shape our understanding of macroeconomic phenomena. It broadens our knowledge of important events that have shaped the lives of millions of people.

On the other hand, a graph or a table is no substitute for more rigorous analysis of the data. Merely

Box 1.2 Macroeconomic Schools of Thought: A Primer

Almost from the beginning, macroeconomics has been divided into two main schools of thought. Keynesians (and their neo-Keynesian heirs) and monetarists (and neo-monetarists) continue to pursue the old debate between laissez-faire and interventionism. Keynesians are often characterized by the view that markets function imperfectly and that governments can and should use economic policy actively to combat recessions. Monetarists[4] tend to reject this view, seeing politics and the power of bureaucracies as barriers to government efforts to steer the economy away from business cycles and more generally market failures, which they see as either unavoidable or of lesser importance. Given these premises, each school uses theories and data to build and support its case.

These labels are not exclusive. In the United States, where much of the debate takes place, reference is sometimes made to salt-water versus freshwater macroeconomists. Salt-water economists come from univer-

sities located on the two US seaboards (Harvard, MIT, Yale, Stanford, Berkeley) and tend to defend the Keynesian legacy. Freshwater economists are more frequently associated with Monetarism and laissez-faire and hail from universities located near the Great Lakes, e.g. Chicago, Rochester, or Minnesota. In Europe, similar controversies characterize national, and increasingly European debates. National traditions tend to make British and French economists more Keynesian, while German or Swedish economists more Monetarist. Dutch, Italian, and Spanish economists are hard to classify, having as many exceptions as examples for any rule. In recent years, older Keynesian ideas have enjoyed a renaissance among politicians in France and Germany, primarily, who endorse more active fiscal and monetary policy. Later on in this book, we will see how this new emphasis on activist policy is a consequence of the common European currency, the Euro, which was introduced in 1999.

demonstrating that two economic variables move closely together is a far cry from proving that one causes the other. Our motive in using data to illustrate economic phenomena is to give readers a feel for economics itself. At the end of each chapter we give a list of suggested reading—which is by no means meant to be exhaustive—for those who want to learn more about the theory and practice of macroeconomics.

Finally, good economic theories must be valid under different conditions. At the same time, the response of different countries to exogenous economic stimuli are often shaped by their particular economic and political institutions. These include their form of government, the existence of labour unions and employers' associations, and regula-

tions. The interplay of macroeconomic principles and institutions is an essential part of a proper understanding of the field, and this is why we spend a lot of time reviewing them. The economics of these institutions is, however, far beyond the level of this textbook.

1.4.5 Europe

Our textbook bears the subtitle 'A European Text'. Does this mean that we think that macroeconomics in Europe is fundamentally different from macroeconomics elsewhere, say in the USA, Japan, or Latin America? Most certainly not! On the contrary, we take the view that macroeconomics is sufficiently global in scope to apply to economies around the world. This includes the transforming economies of Central and Eastern Europe as well as the newly emerging economies of southern and eastern Asia. On the other hand, we do wish to send a more subtle signal: we believe strongly that European economies have important distinguishing features that make them hard to study through the lens of, say, the leading textbooks from North America.

---

[4] The term 'monetarist' derives from the Latin 'moneta' signalling their original emphasis on excess money growth as the sole cause of inflation. Now the term is more generally applied to those who generally advocate unregulated markets and criticize government intervention at both the microeconomic and the macroeconomic level.

There is much in Europe that warrants such a European emphasis. Rather than a collection of states under a federal government, Europe is a mosaic of nation-states, each with a sovereign macroeconomic policy-maker, but also with distinct preferences and endowments. Surely, the completion of the Single European Market, the creation of a monetary union, and the recent significant enlargement of the European Union will increase the pressure towards integration, raising specific new challenges along the way. In addition, to varying degrees, European countries share a common view of the relationship between market forces and social justice. The attachment to fairness and economic solidarity is deeply ingrained in Europe's traditions and history, which explain why our labour markets differ so much from those in the USA. This observation alone warrants a markedly different look, even if the underlying theory is the same.

Key Concepts

- macroeconomics
- gross domestic product (GDP)
- trend
- economic growth
- business cycle
- unemployment rate
- labour force
- labour
- capital
- factors of production
- labour share
- index, index number
- inflation
- hyperinflation
- capacity utilization
- procyclical and countercyclical

- real economy, monetary economy
- laissez-faire versus interventionism
- aggregate demand management
- price level
- co-ordination failures
- Keynesian revolution
- demand side
- economic agents
- fiscal policy
- monetary policy
- supply side
- exchange rate
- endogenous
- exogenous
- positive and normative economics

📖 Suggested Further Reading

On economics as a science, and the process of scientific discovery, see:

Friedman, Milton (1953), 'The Methodology of Positive Economics', in his *Essays in Positive Economics*, University of Chicago Press.

Kuhn, Thomas S. (1982), *The Structure of Scientific Revolutions*, University of Chicago Press.

On the state of macroeconomics and its controversies, see:

Dornbusch, Rudi (2000), *Keys to Prosperity*, MIT Press.

Greenwald, Bruce C., and Stiglitz, Joseph E. (1988), 'Examining Alternative Macro-economic Theories', *Brookings Papers on Economic Activity*, 1: 207–70.

Solow, Robert M. (1980), 'On Theories of Unemployment', *American Economic Review*, 70: 1–11.

The symposium 'Forecasts for the Future of Economics', *Journal of Economic Perspectives*, Winter 2000.

➔ Media

Students can greatly benefit from reading daily the economic section of their newspaper. Some publications with high-quality analyses (but not free of prejudices) are (in English): the *Financial Times* and *The Economist*. There is also a wealth of information on the internet. See our website for directions.

Data are produced by national statistical institutes and central banks. Some international institutions produce comparable data and are of easy access: the IMF's *International Financial Statistics* and its biannual survey *World Economic Outlook*, the OECD's biannual *Economic Outlook*, the World Bank's *World Development Report* and *Global Economic Prospects*, the European Commission's *European Economy*, and the EBRD's annual *Transition Report*. All maintain websites, more or less generous in allowing access to their publications.

Macroeconomic Accounts 2

2.1 Overview 22

2.2 Gross Domestic Product 22

   2.2.1   Three Definitions of Gross Domestic Product 22

   2.2.2   Real versus Nominal, Deflators versus Price Indices 23

   2.2.3   Measuring and Interpreting GDP 26

2.3 Flows of Incomes and Expenditures 30

   2.3.1   The Circular Flow Diagram 30

   2.3.2   Summary of the Flow Diagram 32

   2.3.3   More Detail 33

   2.3.4   A Key Accounting Identity 35

   2.3.5   Identities versus Economics 35

2.4 Balance of Payments 36

   2.4.1   Commercial Transactions 36

   2.4.2   Financial Transactions 37

   2.4.3   Errors and Omissions 38

   2.4.4   The Meaning of the Accounts 39

Summary 40

Facts and theories meet in analysis. The combination of the two is essential if economics is to progress, since it is neither a pure subject, like mathematics, of which one does not ask that the theories should be applicable to actual phenomena, nor is it a collection of facts, like the objects on a junk heap, of which one does not ask how they are related.

—Richard Stone[1]

2.1 Overview

Every science has a language of its own: not to exclude non-experts, but rather to make discussion more meaningful and precise. In this chapter we will learn how to talk about the macroeconomy. We first provide a macroeconomic description of the economy and some definitions of more frequently used concepts. As a natural point of departure, the chapter begins with a discussion of the national income accounts and a number of **accounting identities**—how magnitudes we are interested in relate to each other, by definition. The national income accounts play a central role throughout the study of macroeconomics.

Thus, Chapter 2 will be limited to a description of what happens in an economy. It is essential for the overall goal of macroeconomics, which is ultimately to understand the underlying behaviour of these aggregate magnitudes. The distinction between description (this chapter) and analysis (the rest of the book) is similar to that found in biology. While it is essential to understand that living organisms consist of a collection of different cells, this biological description is only a first step. Vastly more important is to learn how cells function and affect each other; this constitutes the analysis. In a similar way, decomposing the gross domestic product into its components, or looking at the external accounts, describes interactions and relationships without explaining how or why. That is the job of subsequent chapters. It is an unavoidable step, and it is essential to be clear about these definitions which may be trickier than meets the eye.

2.2 Gross Domestic Product

2.2.1 Three Definitions of Gross Domestic Product

The **gross domestic product** (GDP) is defined for a particular geographic area—usually a country, but possibly a region or a city, or a group of countries such as the European Union (EU). It is also defined over a time interval, usually a year or a quarter; this is because the GDP is a **flow variable**, much like the amount of water flowing down a river. Flow variables differ from **stock variables**, which are always defined with reference to a particular point in time, such as the quantity of water held back by a dam.[2]

---

[1] Sir Richard Stone (1913–1991) of Cambridge University received the Nobel Prize in Economics in 1984 and is generally regarded as the father of national income accounting.

[2] Another example of a stock variable is a company's balance sheet, which measures its financial state at a single point in time, say 31 December; in contrast, an income statement records the profit or loss attributed to the firm over a time period, say 1 January to 31 December, and is a flow variable.

A country's GDP is a measure of its productive activity. A first definition is the sum of all final sales of goods and services:

Definition 1:
GDP = the sum of all net final sales within a geographic location during a period of time, usually a year.

This definition refers specifically to **final sales**, i.e. goods and services sold to the consumer or firm that will ultimately use them. For example, the purchase of a loaf of bread or a motor car by a household is a final sale. In contrast, a car sold to a dealer which is subsequently resold during the measurement period, or a loaf of bread purchased by a grocery store which is later sold to a household are not final but **intermediate sales**. Intermediate sales are excluded from GDP to avoid double counting. For this reason, GDP should never be confused with total sales, or turnover. Consistent with this approach, exports are always counted as final sales regardless of how the foreigners use them, because they leave the national economy.

Our second definition of GDP recognizes that each final sale of a good or service represents the ultimate step that validates all the efforts that have gone into producing and making it available to the buyer. It encapsulates a chain of economic activities which are each seen as **value added**:

Definition 2:
GDP = the sum of value added occuring within a given geographic location during a period of time.

A firm creates value added by transforming raw materials and unfinished goods into products it can sell in the market place. The firm's value added is the difference between its sales (turnover) and the costs of raw materials, unfinished goods, and imports from abroad. If the firm produces intermediate goods, its sales are costs to its customers who themselves are producers. This value added is not counted twice, because it is deducted from those customers' own sales in computing its own value added. When the final consumer purchases a good or a service in the market, the price includes all the value added created at each stage in the production process, hence the consistency between Definitions 1 and 2. Box 2.1 uses a concrete example to show how various productive activities contribute to a country's total value added.

GDP includes all incomes earned within a country's borders—by residents and non-residents alike. Because one person's final spending must be someone else's income, the third definition of GDP is also consistent with the first:

Definition 3:
GDP = the sum of factor. Incomes earned from economic activities within a geographic location during a period of time.

GDP statistics are quoted daily in the financial and political press. The GDP is generally considered to be the most important indicator of an economy's health, and its evolution is closely watched by managers, economists, and politicians. Yet the definition of GDP contains a fair amount of arbitrariness, and it is open to debate whether every positive movement in GDP constitutes an improvement in national well-being. More details on this controversial issue are provided in Box 2.2.

2.2.2 Real versus Nominal, Deflators versus Price Indices

Real and nominal GDP

Now that we know what GDP is and how GDP data are constructed, we can understand how the national income statisticians have solved the problem of adding up apples and oranges: the solution is to use *prices* to convert volumes (the numbers of apples and oranges) into values (sales of apples and oranges). Suppose an economy produces these two goods and requires no imports. Final sales of apples and oranges are obtained by multiplying the quantities of apples and oranges sold, Q^a and Q^o, by their respective prices, P^a and P^o, yielding **nominal GDP**, or GDP at current prices:

$$\text{(2.1)} \qquad \text{GDP} = P^a Q^a + P^o Q^o.$$

Yet there is always a catch. If the price of oranges increases from one year to the next, nominal GDP rises even if the volume of final sales remains unchanged! An increase in nominal GDP can result from either higher prices *or* more output. To separate the effects of output and price movements, national income accountants distinguish between nominal and **real GDP**. Increases in real GDP correspond to

Box 2.1 Value Added and Value Subtracted: Two Examples

Consider the following example of value added. A keg of beer is produced and sold for final use by consumers at the price of €100. It is useful to break up this final sale into the steps of value added which were involved in its production. First, a brewery bought barley from a farmer, paying €10, used and paid for energy in the brewing process with a value of €20, and bought a keg from a key manufacturer at a cost of €5. (For simplicity, the intermediate inputs of the farmer, energy producer, and keg manufacturer are assumed to be zero.) The beer is sold to a wholesaler for €80, so the brewery's own contribution to value added per keg is €45, given by his sale price (€80) less costs of inputs (€10 + €20 + €5 = €35). Next, the wholesaler sells the keg for €90 to a retailer, contributing value added of €10. The retailer sells the keg for €100, generating €10 of value added on his own. Summing up, the final price can be broken down into value added at each stage of production and delivery of the final good:

Value added contributed by the:

Farmer	€10
Energy producer	20
Keg manufacturer	5
Brewery	45
Wholesaler	10
Retailer	10
Sum	**€100**

Each step in the value added chain represents a source of income for factors of production involved. Suppose for example that the brewer had labour costs of €35 (wages and salaries as well as social security contribu-tions) and €5 in beer taxes. Then the brewery's activity led to €5 profits, which are the income to the owners —assuming there were no further costs such as interest on loans, royalties for brands or trademarks, or rent. Similarly, if the wholesaler had no costs (employees, rent, or interest), the €10 of value added would represent his income, which can also be thought of as his profit which he receives as owner of the business. The example shows how the division of the value added is arbitrary and potentially separate from the issue of whether value added is generated at all.

Because value added is essential for generating income, it is reasonable to think that few economic activities could survive very long if they *subtracted* value i.e. if sales did not even cover material input costs. Not only would labour and capital receive no income for their efforts, but also someone would have to pay for the operating loss on each unit of output sold. Yet there are many examples of value subtraction. One is automobile production in Eastern Germany immediately following the fall of the Iron Curtain in 1989. Under communism, many citizens of the German Democratic Republic waited years to pay up to 15,000 Marks for the mediocre Trabant car produced by the people's combine VEB Sachsenring. After the wall came down, demand disappeared and price of Trabants dropped so sharply that production represented value subtraction at world prices for inputs. For a while, production continued, with workers' wages paid by western German taxpayers. It became clear that this was not a sensible option, and Trabant production was stopped in 1991.

---

increases in physical output, the number of apples and oranges produced and sold. Whereas nominal GDP is computed as in (2.1) using the actual selling prices, real GDP is computed by using prices observed in some agreed base year.[3] In our example, if prices of apples and oranges were P_0^a and P_0^o in the base year, the real GDP in year t, when net final sales of apples and oranges are Q_t^a and Q_t^o, is:

$$(2.2) \qquad \text{Real GDP}_t = P_0^a Q_t^a + P_0^o Q_t^o.$$

This distinction is very general and applies to all macroeconomic variables: nominal variables represent values at current prices; real variables represent volumes at constant prices. As an example, Table 2.1 reports growth rates of nominal and real GDP for the Euro-zone.

Price deflators and indices

The distinction between nominal and real GDP can be used as a measure of the general price level, or the price of goods in terms of money. The **GDP**

---

[3] Problems arise when new goods are introduced, or existing goods improve in quality. National income accountants have devised procedures to deal with such effects.

Box 2.2 What GDP Measures

The GDP concerns only recorded market transactions. This leaves out many activities which are not carried out through legal channels or which do not reach the market place, like growing vegetables in the garden. Furthermore, since goods and services are measured by their sale prices, two identical goods may enter the GDP differently if one of them is sold at a discount. Finally, it is not a measure of happiness: painful expenses (having a tooth removed, for example) enter the GDP in the same way as pleasurable ones. When someone dies, GDP rises: the funeral service, the hospital expenses, and the execution of the will by lawyers and bankers all represent additional final sales of goods and services. Pollution and other forms of environmental damage are ignored in the GDP, since they are not traded in markets.

Services enter the GDP exactly like goods. Services include medical doctors' fees or an estate agent's commission when an existing house is sold. In the latter case, if the house's value has increased since it was purchased, the previous owner enjoys a capital gain, but this form of income does not enter GDP. Used-goods sales, such as cars or antique furniture, do not enter the GDP either. Such transactions represent a transfer of ownership rather than production; these goods entered GDP when first sold, but the fees of the dealers represent a service which is accounted for. Sales by retailers from inventory accumulated in earlier periods actually reduce GDP, as they represent a depletion of stocks.

Public services are part of GDP, even if they are not really sold. Their price is simply measured by their cost of production. For example, public education enters GDP as the sum of teachers' salaries, operating costs such as electricity or heating costs, and equipment including rents. Similarly, the national defence enters the GDP as total expenditure on armed forces.

A related measure is **Gross National Product** (GNP). Unlike the location-based GDP, the GNP is *ownership based*. It is the value added attributable to all factors of production owned by a country's residents, regardless of where those factors are employed. It thus includes value added or income earned abroad and repatriated by residents. For example, an Italian living in Como and commuting to work in Lugano in Switzerland contributes to the Italian GNP and to the Swiss GDP, but not to the Italian GDP or Swiss GNP. Because GNP is harder to measure, economists tend to follow GDP and we will do the same.

To see how important distinction between GDP and GNP can be, consider the case of Ireland. After several years of high economic growth, Ireland's GDP per capita now exceeds that of the UK. Nevertheless, many of Ireland's factories are owned by foreigners or were purchased with money borrowed abroad. The investment income and interest paid to those foreigners is significant enough that Irish per capita GNP is lower than the UK's.

---

deflator, one way of measuring the price level, is simply the ratio of nominal to real GDP:

(2.3) GDP deflator = nominal GDP/real GDP.

In the chosen base year, nominal and real GDP coincide and the GDP deflator equals 1.0. (Sometimes it is multiplied by 100 for ease of comparison over the years.) It can be thought of as an average of all prices of final goods in terms of money, where each price is implicitly weighted by the proportion of the corresponding good in the GDP. As these proportions change over the years, so do the weights.

The inflation rate can be measured by the rate of increase in the GDP deflator, which in turn can be approximated by the following formula:

(2.4) GDP deflator inflation
= nominal GDP growth rate
– real GDP growth rate.

For example, Table 2.1 shows that in 2002 the nominal GDP of the Euro-zone rose by 3.4% while the real GDP increased only by 1.5%. On average, therefore, prices rose by roughly 1.9%.[4]

An alternative measure of inflation is based on an average of prices with fixed weights, called a **price index**. A basket of goods is selected and the amount

---

[4] To see why this formula is an approximation, suppose real GDP increased at rate g and inflation at rate π. The rate of nominal growth must be $(1 + g)(1 + \pi) - 1 = g + \pi + g\pi$. For g and π small, $g\pi \cong 0$, so the rate of growth of nominal GDP is approximately equal to $g + \pi$.

Table 2.1 Growth Rates of Nominal GDP, Real GDP, and GDP Deflator: Euro-area 1990–2002 (% per annum)

	Nominal GDP growth	Real GDP growth	GDP deflator growth
1990	7.7	3.0	4.7
1991	9.6	1.7	7.9
1992	4.2	1.2	3.0
1993	0.3	−0.4	0.7
1994	4.8	2.8	2.0
1995	4.0	2.4	1.6
1996	5.0	1.6	3.4
1997	5.3	2.5	2.8
1998	4.7	2.9	1.8
1999	5.1	2.7	2.4
2000	6.4	3.4	3.0
2001	3.3	1.6	1.7
2002	3.4	1.5	1.9

Source: Eurostat, EU Wirtschaftsdaten Pocketbook.

of each good, or category of goods, in the basket is used to weight the corresponding prices. An example is the **consumer price index (CPI)**. This is based on a basket of goods consumed by a representative or average individual.

Figure 2.1 shows the growth rates of the GDP deflator and of the CPI in Italy. Differences between the two measures of inflation are usually not very large, but they can become significant when the price of imports changed relative to output produced domestically. In the late 1970s and in 1991 for example, the price of crude oil increased faster than prices of goods and services produced in Italy, as measured by the GDP deflator. Since Italians consume many goods which involve petroleum products (gasoline, diesel fuel, heating oil, plastics, paints, etc.) the CPI increased at a faster rate than the GDP deflator. In contrast, when oil prices fell in the 1980s and late 1990s, imports became cheaper and CPI inflation fell behind, as can be seen from Figure 2.1.

Price indexes can be tailored to describe the prices of certain types of goods, of certain types of consumers, or for certain sectors of the economy.

Along with price deflators, there is a large menu to choose from, each price index or deflator having its own special emphasis. Box 2.3 presents some frequently used deflators and indexes.

2.2.3 Measuring and Interpreting GDP

The GDP, which represents the economic performance of an entire economy, is not easy to measure. The task is generally carried out by official statistical offices which draw on various sources of information. One natural source is the tax authorities. Firms report sales (first definition of GDP), individuals report incomes (third definition), and in most countries (all EU countries, but not the USA) value added taxes (VAT) are collected by intermediate and final sellers who then report their value added when they pay the tax (second definition).

The fact that GDP figures are collected through tax returns immediately raises the suspicion that individuals and firms may misrepresent their finances to the fiscal authorities. Such unreported income is frequently referred to as the **underground economy**. Box 2.4 presents estimates of how large it could be. It also alerts us to the importance of **unpaid work**.

Box 2.3 Price Deflators and Price Indexes

The price index closest to the GDP deflator is the producer price index (PPI), with fixed weights corresponding to a basket representative of national production. Similarly, the CPI is closely tracked by the consumption deflator, the ratio of nominal and real aggregate consumption expenditures by households. A price index like the CPI or the PPI is an example of a fixed-weight, or *Laspeyres index*. The consumption deflator, which is based on the actual share of goods in the corresponding year's consumption, is called a variable weight or *Paasche index*. The CPI and the consumption deflator include goods and services produced abroad and imported, while the PPI and the GDP deflator do not, but these latter measures include goods and services locally produced and exported. Figure 2.1 suggests a growing divergence between the PPI and the CPI in Italy over the 1980s. The reason is that imported goods prices increased by less than those of domestically produced goods.

Other frequently used deflators are related to exports, imports, investment goods, and government purchases. The wholesale price index (WPI) measures the average price of goods at the wholesale stage, and various commodity price indexes track the evolution of raw materials prices. The dizzying diversity of indexes and deflators simply reflects the fact that there is no absolute 'average' price. Different price levels are used for different purposes. For example, wage-earners wish to tie their wages to their cost of living; in this case, the relevant index is the CPI or the consumption deflator. In the case of Italy, linking wages to the CPI rather than to the PPI resulted in higher profits for firms whose incomes are better described by the PPI. Because the CPI and other Laspeyres indexes are easier to compute, they tend to be used most often in practice.

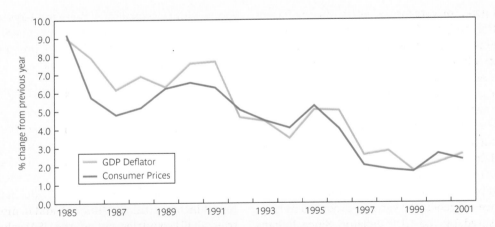

Fig. 2.1 GDP Deflator and the Consumer Price Index Inflation Rates: Italy, 1985 – 2001

Both the GDP deflator and the consumer price index (CPI) measure the price level, or the price of goods in terms of money. They are used to compute the inflation rate. The figure shows that both inflation rates tend to move together over time, with occasional exceptions when the difference in the underlying 'baskets' makes a difference. In the late 1980s, world oil prices went down sharply. Since gas and heating oil are part of household consumption, inflation measured by the CPI declined. Since oil is imported, it does not contribute value added directly in Italy, and has only a small impact on the GDP deflator.

Source: International Financial Statistics Yearbook, 2002.

Box 2.4 **The Underground Economy and Unpaid Work**

Who hasn't taken advantage of a carpenter's, car mechanic's, or painter's offer to do some work 'without a receipt'? Agents engage in the underground, or informal economy for straightforward reasons. First, they want to avoid taxes (the value added tax, employment and social security charges, profit taxes). Another reason is that criminal activities, such as drug-dealing, prostitution, or racketeering, are obviously better kept underground. By definition, the size of the underground economy is unknown, but national income statisticians often attempt to guess its importance. They use various approaches such as monitoring electricity use, which tends to be higher in economies where unreported

market activity is more significant, or looking at the amount of large-denomination currency in circulation since underground transactions do not use bank accounts and profits are held in large bills. The sale of intermediate inputs related to final production often indicates underground economy activities. For example, a large discrepancy exists between the purchase of construction materials and reported construction activity. Table 2.2 shows the extent of the underground economy in a number of countries.

Another serious drawback of GDP as a measure of economic activity is unpaid work. Minor repairs around the house, caring for children, cooking for the family

 Table 2.2 **Estimates of the Size of the Underground Economy (% of GDP)**

Africa		**Central Europe**	
Nigeria, Egypt	68–76	Hungary, Bulgaria, Poland	20–8
Tunisia, Morocco	39–45	Czech Republic, Romania, Slovakia	9–16
Latin America		**Former Soviet Union**	
Mexico, Peru	40–60	Belarus, Georgia, Ukraine	28–43
Chile, Brazil, Venezuela	25–35	Baltic States, Russia	20–7
Asia		**OECD**	
Thailand	70	Belgium, Greece, Italy, Spain, Portugal	24–30
Philippines, Malaysia, Korea	38–50	All others	13–23
Hong Kong, Singapore	13	Austria, Japan, USA, Switzerland	8–10

Source: Schneider and Enste (2000).

and cleaning up take up much time and effort. Wealthier people hire help for these chores, in which case it becomes part of GDP (if reported to the tax authorities). Most people do it themselves, and it is unrecorded. Table 2.3 presents estimates for the Netherlands of the size of this 'lost output'. The first part shows that women perform much unpaid work. The second part shows that unpaid work represents a sizeable part of official GDP. The estimates depend on which salary we impute to this activity, the lowest figure corresponds to the minimum wage, the highest to the average wage.

 Table 2.3 **Unpaid Work: The Netherlands in 1990**

Hours per week	Average paid work	Average unpaid work
Men	32.6	17.5
Women	9.4	39.8
% of GDP		36–58

Source: Marga Bruyn-Hundt, *The Economics of Unpaid Work*, Thesis Publishers, Amsterdam (1996).

Box 2.5 **How National Accounts Estimates Vary over Time**

Because governments, firms, and investors require timely information about the economy, national statistical institutes in advanced economies have devised ways of quickly producing preliminary estimates of GDP. The procedure is based on the knowledge that the value added of, for example, the 100 largest corporations represents a given proportion of GDP. If the proportion were 10%, as these firms fill in VAT tax reports or respond to specially designed questionnaires, multiplying by 10 their combined value added provides a rough early estimate of GDP. A few months later, revised estimates can be based on data provided by a larger sample of firms.

Waiting still longer will allow the incorporation of estimates based on an early and partial analysis of tax returns. Detailed analysis of all tax returns data—using procedures to reconcile differences between measures based on the three definitions—leads to a final figure. Table 2.4 shows successive estimates of German GDP in the year 1999. The first estimate, published just three months after year end, fell short of the latest figure by €8.6 bn. or by almost 0.5% of the initial estimate. This may not seem like much, but it represents about a quarter of the actual growth rate recorded that year (2.0%).

 Table 2.4 **Estimates of German GDP in 1999**

Date of publication	German GDP in 1999 (bn. € in 1995 prices)	% difference from previous estimate	% difference from Mar. 2000
Mar. 2000	1,906.2	—	—
Jun. 2000	1,908.3	0.11	0.11
Sep. 2000	1,907.5	−0.04	0.07
Jun. 2001	1,911.1	0.19	0.26
Sep. 2002	1,914.8	0.19	0.45
Jun. 2003	1,914.8	0.00	0.45

Source: Deutsche Bundesbank.

Another shortcoming associated with the magnitude of the task is the time it takes to get reasonably accurate numbers. Data from tax returns are usually processed with delay. Usually at the end of the first month of each quarter, figures for the preceding quarter are released. Box 2.5 explains how such flash estimates are produced and updated several times over the following years. The inaccuracy of these estimates is unsettling because they are frequently used by governments when deciding on economic policies, by investors when valuing their assets, and by firms deciding on hiring or firing workers and on acquiring new plant and equipment. This is why other indicators are often used to supplement the GDP figures.[5] It is also why analysts

tend to concentrate on growth rates rather than levels. As long as the distortions do not change much over time, measured GDP growth rates offer a good picture of average economy performance.

It is tempting to compare GDPs across countries. Most often we look at GDP per capita, or the average income earned within a country's boundaries. Such data must be regarded with caution, however. First, GDP is a measure of income, not wealth. Income is a flow, while wealth is the stock of assets accumulated over longer periods of time. For example, the average income earned in the UK is lower than that of

---

5 Ch. 14 provides a description of the most frequently used indicators.

Abu Dhabi; yet average British wealth is likely to be much higher, as Britain has been accumulating wealth for centuries, in the form of private assets (e.g. houses, factories, jewels, stocks) and national assets (e.g. the London Bridge, paintings in the British Museum, railroads, highways and telecommunication networks, and much more).

The second caveat is that a large number of transactions are not recorded, especially in developing countries. They belong to what is sometimes called the informal economy. For example, much food can be produced within the extended family (a non-market activity), or exchanged for other food (a non-reported market activity). Very low reported per capita income levels in developing economies underestimate true value added and income. Finally, GDPs are measured in the country's local monetary unit, or currency and are then converted into a common currency using the exchange rate. But local costs are often much lower in poor countries, for reasons presented in Chapter 7. To correct for this effect, economists often use GDP figures which have been adjusted for differences in purchasing power.

2.3 Flows of Incomes and Expenditures

2.3.1 The Circular Flow Diagram

From final expenditures to net taxes and factor income

Each individual's expenditure necessarily contributes to some other individual's income. The simplified **circular flow** diagram represented in Figure 2.2 is based on this simple truth and goes a long way in tracking the functioning of an economy. Based on the first and third definitions of GDP, it shows how income from sales goes from firms to individuals and back to the market place. The GDP appears in the left part of the figure. It represents the final net sales of firms.

Since firms are owned by households, the GDP represents the gross income of factors of production employed in the geographic region under consideration. Technically, GDP also includes 'sales' of labour services by the self-employed. It also includes all sales of households' labour and capital services abroad. In order to keep things simple, we will ignore these components of GDP in what follows, so that all value added in the economy represents income to residents.

To see what firms do with revenues coming from their final sales, we move clockwise. The government, shown as the circle inside the flow diagram, takes (in the form of taxes) and gives (in the form of various transfers). Because it needs to pay for its purchases of goods and services, the government will almost always take in more than it gives away in transfers. The difference between taxes and transfers is called **net taxes** and is represented by T. These taxes are taken in at several points of the value added chain—as indirect taxes such as value-added taxes, or as direct taxes on different types of income. Here we consolidate them for simplicity. What is left of GDP after these taxes and transfers are subtracted is called **private income**, Y-T.

From private income to absorption plus net exports—GDP

Private income is ultimately earned by those households which own the factors of production involved in creating the value added. The largest part of private income is wages and salaries paid to workers plus payments for rent and royalties, as well as net interest on loans from banks. The residual which remains after firms pay all these other factors is known as gross profit. This profit can either be saved by the firm or redistributed back to firm owners as income.[6] Since all factors of production are

---

[6] The other production costs are mainly land and buildings, financial costs (borrowing from banks and bondholders), and raw materials and intermediate goods which, for the country as a whole, are frequently imported.

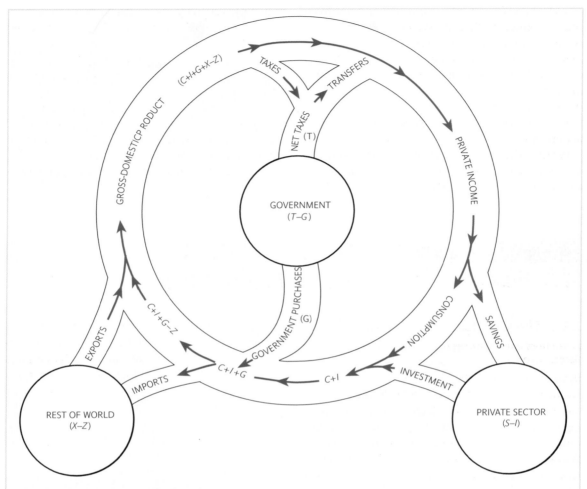

Fig. 2.2 **The Circular Flow Diagram**

The lower left part of the wheel represents sales of domestically produced goods and services, the sum of consumption spending (C), investment spending (I), government purchases (G), and exports (X) less imports (Z). In the upper left part of the wheel this is interpreted as income to residents. This income is taxed by the government, which also pays out various types of transfers to households and firms. What is left, private income, may be saved (S) or spent (C). The private sector borrows to invest in productive equipment (I). The balance S − I is the private sector's net saving behaviour. The balance T − G is the public sector budget surplus. X − Z represent the country's net exports

ultimately owned by some households, households receive income as employees, as owners of land and patents, as bondholder, or as shareholders. Households can either save this income, or spend it on **consumption**.

The consolidation of households with firms they own comprises the private sector. The flow diagram shows how the aggregate savings of the private sector (S) are deposited with the financial sector. The financial sector includes banks, financial institutions, and stock markets whose function is to collect savings and channel them to firms seeking to invest, that is to purchase productive equipment. This activity, called **financial intermediation**, is represented by the lower-right circle. In the aggregate, the private sector uses its **savings**—what it does not consume—to finance the acquisition of new productive equipment by firms. Productive equipment, including structures, is referred to as **physical capital**, and purchases of new equipment is called **investment**. The excess of private saving over investment $(S - I)$ is called net private saving. Net private saving can be positive or negative. Firms and households spend their income—part of it borrowed—to consume (C) and to invest (I).[7]

To private sector expenditures on goods and services $(C + I)$ the government adds its own demand (G). Governments purchase goods (roads, military equipment, newly built buildings, and stationery for the bureaucracy) and services (of civil servants and other employees). In addition, governments distribute various subsidies to firms and households, and pay interest on the public debt. Total national spending, sometimes called **absorption**, is the sum $(C + I + G)$ of private and public spending on goods and services. Part of absorption includes the purchase of imported goods and services (Z). This is shown as the branch going into the leftmost circle which represents the rest of the world; it should not be thought of merely as merchandise purchases, but as covering all kinds of services, including labour and capital services. Similarly, while some domestic income thus leaks abroad, foreigners buy domestically produced goods and services, the country's exports (X). Netting these two flows with the rest of the world gives net exports $(X - Z)$. When positive, net exports increase demand for domestic production above that originating with domestic residents; when negative, demand for domestic production less than total domestic demand.

The sum of absorption and net exports represents the total final sales that occur within the geographic area: that is, the GDP. The circular flow of income is closed. This circularity is the essence of economic activity: we (collectively) earn to (collectively) spend.

---

[7] It is important to stress the difference between this terminology and that used in the business or popular press, in which 'investment' includes the acquisition of existing assets or financial instruments. Although stocks and bonds are often issued by firms to finance the purchase of productive equipment, their simple acquisition or sale does not necessarily give rise to what is called 'investment' in economics, i.e. the creation of new productive capacity.

2.3.2 Summary of the Flow Diagram

The flow diagram can be summarized using the first and third definitions of GDP, which is represented by the symbol Y. As net final sales, the GDP is broken down into four main categories: final sales of consumption goods and services (C), final sales of investment goods and additions to inventory stocks (I), final sales to the government (G), and sales to the rest of the world (X). Since part of domestic income leaks abroad to pay for imported goods, imports (Z) must be subtracted, which gives the first decomposition of GDP by final expenditures:

$$(2.5) \qquad Y = C + I + G + X - Z.$$

The flow diagram also shows that GDP can be viewed as net incomes earned by factors of production. What do they do with this income? The three possibilities are given by the right-hand side of the flow diagram: they pay taxes net of transfers (T), they save (S), and they consume (C). Hence the second decomposition by uses of income:

$$(2.6) \qquad Y = C + S + T.$$

Table 2.5 presents the components of the first decomposition as a percentage of GDP for a few countries. Consumption typically amounts to about 60% of GDP. The investment rate—the ratio of investment expenditures to GDP—ranges from 16 to 30%. Because investment corresponds to the accumulation of productive equipment, it matters for future economic growth. Since governments also invest in infrastructure equipment (roads, bridges, public utilities), what is considered investment in some countries may be undertaken by the government in others. The 'size of government' is considerably greater than the share of government expenditures (14–23%) since transfers must also be included. It varies considerably, even among advanced economies. When total spending is considered, adding transfers to expenditures, the government often 'handles' more than half of GDP: many goods and services that are privately produced elsewhere are delivered freely as public goods in many countries of Europe; these include medical services, schools, child care, and public transport.

The flows of incomes and spending captured by the diagram constitute the real, as opposed to financial,

Table 2.5 Components of GDP by Expenditure, 1970–2001 (% of GDP)

	Consumption (C)	Investment (I)	Government purchases (G)
Australia	59	24	19
Germany[a]	57	23	20
France[a]	56	21	23
UK	63	18	20
Italy[a]	58	21	19
Japan	55	30	14
Canada	57	20	20
Switzerland	60	24	14
USA	66	16	19
Euro-area[b]	57	22	20

[a] 1970–98.
[b] 1999–2001.
Source: IMF.

side of an economy. Parts of these flows leak out to the financial side in the form of corporate and household savings; others leak out to the government in the form of tax payments or social security contributions; others to foreigners as imports. To the extent that withdrawals of resources from the circular flow due to a particular sector is not matched exactly by inflows in the form of spending, then that sector's net asset position must be changing, by definition.[8] If savings of the private sector exceed investment spending, for example, this means that net accumulation of assets in the private sector was positive. The same holds for the consolidated government if net taxes exceed government purchases of goods and services, or for the nation if net export of goods and services, broadly defined, is positive. Asset accumulation or de-cumulation has economic consequences. How the financial side of the economy functions, and how the real and financial sides are linked, is studied in Part III of this book.

2.3.3 More Detail

While GDP represents the collective income earned within a nation's boundaries, not all of it ends up in the hands of individuals. What households actually receive to spend or save is called **personal disposable income**. Table 2.6 shows that some 25–55% of GDP does not reach individual households. It either goes to the government (net taxes) or is saved by firms (retained earnings).

Figure 2.3 starts with GDP and, moving right, decomposes it by its ultimate recipient. The first item is **depreciation**: in the process of producing GDP, productive equipment is subjected to wear and tear and obsolescence. Properly measured, this depreciation should be subtracted from GDP to give a clearer picture of the output that is actually available as income. Subtracting depreciation from GDP gives us the **net domestic national product (NDP)**.[9] Moving further to the right, national income is what is left for firms once indirect taxes

[8] If the net outflow is positive, net assets owned by the sector must be increasing; if the net outflow is negative, net assets are decreasing. Technically, increasing net assets can occur either by increases in gross financial assets (claims on other sectors), or by reducing gross liabilities (i.e. paying off existing debt to other sectors).

[9] In practice, financial accounting of depreciation is determined by tax regulations. Firms are allowed to subtract from their revenues a given proportion of the book value of equipment for computing taxable profits. It may under- or overstate actual economic depreciation by a wide margin.

Table 2.6 GDP and Household Disposable Income, 2003

	GDP (billions national currency)	Household disposable income	
		Level	% of GDP
Germany	2,170.8	1,253.5	**57.7**
France	1,559.8	867.3	**55.6**
Sweden	2,353.5	1,077.7	**45.8**
Switzerland	431.6	284.8	**66.0**
United States	10,840.3	8,161.2	**75.3**
United Kingdom	1,083.1	744.4	**68.7**

Source: OECD, *Economic Outlook* Database.

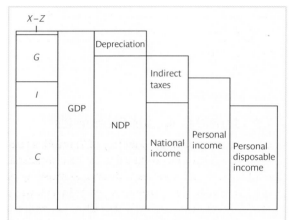

Fig. 2.3 From Expenditure to Income to Personal Disposable Income

Depreciation is stripped away from GDP to obtain net domestic product (NDP). When net factor income from abroad is zero, we can subtract indirect taxes from, and add firm subsidies to, NDP to obtain national income (NI). (If net factor income from abroad is not zero, it must then be added at this stage.) National income can be distributed in a number of ways: firms' savings (retained earnings), taxes on businesses, and contributions to social security are subtracted from national income, leaving various forms of income paid in the end to households. The government also transfers income to households (social security, unemployment insurance, etc.). This results in personal income (PI). After income taxes and some miscellaneous fees, we are left with personal disposable income (PDI), that is, resources available to households for spending or saving.

are paid out. Indirect taxes vary from country to country, and include the value added tax (VAT) and excise taxes (on petrol, tobacco, alcohol). They are collected by sellers on behalf of the government.

After indirect taxes, firms dispose of the value added they generate in four ways. First, they pay wages and salaries and other compensation to their employees. This includes contributions to social insurance. Second, they pay interest to bondholders and banks. Third, they pay corporate or business income taxes. What remains is profits to the firms' owners, or shareholders. These profits are either distributed as dividends or held back as retained earnings, sometimes called net corporate saving.[10]

To summarize, what is not paid as corporate taxes or saved by firms is ultimately paid out to households as the firms' employees, their owners, or indirectly as their creditors. When government transfers (e.g. unemployment benefits, disability payments, health care reimbursements, family allowances) are added to labour incomes and distributed profits, the result is personal income. Households cannot freely dispose of their personal income: they must first pay personal income taxes, as well as non-tax payments like parking fines and other governmental fees. The result is personal

---

[10] Adding net corporate savings to depreciation gives gross corporate savings. It represents the resources that firms set aside to replace used equipment and generally to strengthen their financial position.

disposable income, which can either be consumed or saved.

2.3.4 A Key Accounting Identity

The two decompositions of GDP, (2.5) and (2.6), are accounting identities: they hold by definition. Therefore it is always the case that:

$$C + S + T = C + I + G + X - Z.$$

Consumption C appears on both sides of this equality and can be eliminated. When this is done and terms are rearranged, the two accounting identities yield a third one:

(2.7) $(S - I) + (T - G) = (X - Z).$

The last term, $X - Z$, is the balance of exports over imports, not only of goods and services, including the services of factors of production employed outside the national borders. Parentheses highlight the fact that the corresponding expressions appear in Figure 2.2 as net flows of the private sector (household and business), government, and the rest of the world, respectively. Each of the three net flows can be thought of as a form of saving, a leakage out of (if positive), or an injection into (if negative) the circular flow of income and expenditure. If $S > I$, the private sector as a whole is a net saver. If $S < I$, the private sector is a net borrower. Similarly, if $T > G$ the government is saving, and if $G > T$ it is borrowing by issuing public debt to domestic or foreign residents. The identity (2.7) shows how these leakages are linked, by definition.

Table 2.7 presents the accounting identity (2.7) for several countries in 2002. In the USA both private and public sectors are spending more than they take in; the country as a whole is running an external deficit of 4.8% of GDP. In Japan, the private sector's massive surplus swamps the public sector's deficit, leaving the country with an external surplus of almost 3% of GDP. The European Union as a whole looks more like Japan, but the internal imbalances are smaller and nearly cancel each other to deliver near-external balance. At the same time, the EU's individual member countries display different and varied situations.

Table 2.7 The Accounting Identity in 2002 (% of GDP)

	$S - I$	$T - G$	$X - Z = CA$
USA	−1.4	−3.4	−4.8
Japan	9.9	−7.1	2.8
Belgium	4.7	0.0	4.7
Denmark	1.1	1.8	2.9
France	5.3	−3.2	2.1
Germany	6.1	−3.6	2.5
Italy	2.0	−2.5	−0.5
Netherlands	3.2	−1.1	2.1
Spain	−2.5	−0.1	−2.6
Sweden	3.0	1.1	4.1
UK	0.5	−1.3	−0.8
European Union	2.9	−2.0	0.9

Source: OECD, *Economic Outlook* 2003/1.

2.3.5 Identities versus Economics

In a manner of speaking, identity (2.7) implies that all goods and services produced must be purchased. The total demand for goods and services must equal supply. For example, if private savings in a country exceed private investment ($S > I$), either net exports must be positive or the government budget must be in deficit, or both. At the same time, identities tell us little or nothing about causation. Without knowing more, it is impossible to know whether (i) the government deficit is at the origin of positive net private savings, (ii) high exports are generating income that is simply saved by residents, or (iii) low domestic investment spending is coinciding with a domestic recession, in which both imports and tax revenues are low and putting current account surplus and/or government budget into deficit. This is the difference between measuring data and interpreting them. This is also the difference between accounting and economics. The identity (2.7) is not only a requirement that accounts be correctly measured: we will later see that it can also be seen as a market equilibrium condition which implies that adjustment mechanisms are at work.

2.4 **Balance of Payments**

The **balance of payment** accounts record all transactions between a country and the rest of the world. The presentation in Table 2.8 separates out international transactions on goods and services (upper part) from financial transactions (lower part). The balance of payments obeys the following simple rule: transactions involving outflows of our money are recorded as deficit (–) items; items leading to inflows of our money are considered as surplus (+) items. The rest will become clear as we move along.

2.4.1 **Commercial Transactions**

The first accounts to consider in Table 2.8 record exports and imports of goods, imports entered with

Table 2.8   Balance of Payments

1. Exports of Goods	
2. Imports of Goods	
3.	**(Merchandise) Trade Balance = (1) – (2)**
4. Exports of Services	
5. Imports of Services	
6. Net Royalties	
7. Net Investment Income	
8.	**Invisible Balance = (4) – (5) + (6) + (7)**
9.	**Balance on Goods and Services = (3) + (8)**
10. Net Foreign Workers' Remittances	
11. Net International Aid	
12.	**Unilateral Transfers = (10) + (11)**
13.	**Current Account Balance (CA) = (3) + (8) + (12)**
14. Gross Inward Direct Investment	
15. Gross Outward Direct Investment	
16. Gross Inward Portfolio Investment	
17. Gross Outward Portfolio Investment	
18.	**Long-Term Financial Account Balance = (14) – (15) + (16) – (17)**
19. Short-Term Inward Capital Flows	
20. Short-Term Outward Capital Flows	
21.	**Short-Term Financial Account Balance = (19) – (20)**
22.	**Financial Account Balance (FA) = (18) + (21)**
23. Errors and Omissions	
24.	**Overall Balance = (13) + (22)**
25. Balance on Official Intervention Account (net sales of foreign exchange) (OFF)	

Memo: Balance of Payments: CA + FA + OFF = 0.

a minus sign. The net result is the **merchandise trade balance**. The balance of trade on goods and services is equal to the merchandise trade balance plus the balance on **invisibles**, which include investment income, royalties, and other services. The most important item is undoubtedly the **current account**. It is obtained by adding to the balance of goods and services the balance of unilateral transfers, that is payments not related to commercial or financial transactions (public transfers, foreign aid, payments to and from the EU budget, and what guest workers remit to their home countries). All current account items may be broadly interpreted as transactions describing purchases and sales of goods and services, including the services of foreign workers, capital, and know-how, or goodwill (of countries receiving aid). This is how to interpret net exports $(X - Z)$ in the previous sections.

The importance of the current account is best seen by returning to the GDP decomposition (2.5) which can be rewritten as:

$$(2.8) \qquad CA = Y - (C + I + G) = Y - A,$$

where $A = C + I + G$ is referred to as absorption, or total domestic spending on goods and services, both domestic and foreign, by households, firms, and government agencies. By definition, the current account is the excess of income (GDP) over spending. It signals whether the country is a net borrower or a net lender. When a country earns more than it spends (that is, $CA = Y - A > 0$), it is a net lender vis-à-vis the rest of the world. Conversely, a country running a current account deficit spends more than it earns ($CA < 0$ and $A > Y$) and must match the difference by borrowing abroad.

Table 2.9 provides a few examples. Turkey is one country whose citizens work as guest workers abroad. This explains its positive transfers balance, as is the case for Mexico. Sweden is in the opposite situation; many foreign workers live there and remit money to their home countries. This is also the case of the EU and the USA.

2.4.2 Financial Transactions

The rest of the balance of payments describes financial transactions. As any exercise in accounting, all items in the balance of payments must add up to

zero. This is not only accounting, this is a consequence of (2.8): current account surpluses must be matched by net financial outflows because the country is lending to the rest of the world, or, put differently, is acquiring assets abroad. Current account deficits imply borrowing from abroad, so financial capital is flowing into the country. Accordingly, the remainder of the balance of payments, representing financial transactions, must be equal to, and of opposite sign to, the current account. The remaining question is: who actually performs balancing act?

The answer is given by two accounts: the **financial account**, which indicates the balance of purchaser of net sales of foreign assets by private domestic residents, and the **official account**, the net transactions performed by the monetary authority, usually the central bank. The first thing to note is that there are two main distinctions among financial transactions. The first concerns private and official accounts. The official account captures the fact that the monetary authorities also contribute to the balancing process. If this account is in deficit, it means residents have sent more money abroad than they received, through either commercial transactions—the current account—or financial transactions—the financial account—or any combination of both. This was the case of the Euro-zone in 2001, as can be seen in Table 2.9. In that case the monetary authorities absorb the difference, bringing domestic money back home; hence the positive surplus entry in the table. This means that the monetary authorities have sold some of their **foreign exchange reserves** (foreign currencies that they hold) and received domestic currency for it in return.[11] Such actions are called **foreign exchange market interventions**. When a monetary authority buys back its own currency, it necessarily spends some of the foreign currencies that it holds. The distinction between private and official financing is further taken up in Section 2.4.4.

The second distinction is between long-term and short-term financial transactions. Long-term

---

[11] Note that this follows the rule of thumb mentioned above for thinking about the sign of an entry in the balance of payments: ask yourself whether it means that domestic money comes in (a plus) or goes out (a minus).

Table 2.9 Balance of Payments, Various Countries, 2001($US bn.)

	Euro-area	USA	Sweden	Turkey	Mexico
Current account	**−12.32**	**−393.39**	**6.70**	**3.40**	**−17.71**
Trade balance	67.59	−424.23	13.83	−4.54	−9.96
Balance on goods and services	68.14	−358.29	12.81	4.59	−14.45
Balance on goods, services and income	32.74	−343.92	9.96	−0.41	−27.02
Unilateral transfers	−45.06	−49.47	−3.26	3.80	9.32
Capital account[a]	**7.99**	**0.83**	**0.51**	**NA**	**NA**
Financial account	**−51.21**	**386.79**	**1.82**	**−14.20**	**22.27**
Direct investment abroad	−228.64	−127.84	−6.96	−0.50	0.00
Direct investment inward	138.06	130.80	13.09	3.27	24.73
Portfolio investment assets	−258.29	−94.66	−23.04	−0.79	3.86
Portfolio investment liabilities	290.08	426.06	10.34	−3.73	0.99
Financial derivatives: Assets	0.00	0.00	33.68	0.00	0.00
Financial derivatives: Liabilities	−3.51	0.00	−38.89	0.00	0.00
Other investment assets	−219.21	−143.54	0.93	−0.16	−3.59
Other investment liabilities	230.30	195.97	12.69	−12.30	−0.01
Net errors and omissions (balancing item)	**38.65**	**10.70**	**−10.08**	**−2.09**	**2.32**
(Overall balance)	**−16.89**	**4.93**	**−1.05**	**−12.89**	**6.88**
Reserves and related items	**16.89**	**−4.93**	**1.05**	**12.89**	**−6.88**

[a] Recently, IMF has used the term 'capital account' transactions as those transfer of funds linked to acquisition of fixed assets and the sales of non-produced, non-financial assets such as real estate.

Source: IMF.

accounts concern the sales or purchases of assets of more than one year to maturity. Examples are foreign direct investment, acquisition of foreign companies, portfolio investment, or the establishment of subsidiaries abroad. Short-term transactions involving assets of less than one year of maturity—including bank accounts—are often associated with 'hot money', motivated by the expectation of quick returns rather than by long-term business strategies.

2.4.3 Errors and Omissions

There is a final item in Table 2.9, 'Errors and Omissions', which requires some explanation. By definition, the total of the balance of payments should be zero:

$$(2.9) \quad \underset{\substack{\text{current} \\ \text{account}}}{\text{CA}} + \underset{\substack{\text{financial} \\ \text{account}}}{\text{FA}} + \underset{\substack{\text{official} \\ \text{interventions}}}{\text{Off}} = 0.$$

While accounting guarantees the consistency of current and financial accounts in theory, the nature of data gathering for payments statistics virtually guarantees discrepancies. Trade data originate with customs authorities. Financial data come from the banking system, since international transactions are mediated by financial organizations. Official interventions, of course, are known by the monetary authorities, which are often responsible for collecting the data and producing the balance of payments accounts. Because these data come from different sources, relationship (2.9) will never hold in practice. This is why an additional account is needed called 'Errors and Omissions'; this balancing item is necessary to arrive at zero at the bottom of the table. While there are genuine mistakes—the sheer volume of data to be treated is an invitation for errors—there may also be omissions which are less than innocent.[12] Table 2.9 shows some that deficits on errors and omissions can be quite large.

2.4.4 The Meaning of the Accounts

A current account imbalance must be matched, or financed, one-for-one by either the private financial account or official interventions by the monetary authorities. What is the difference between the two mechanisms? A country with a current account deficit is making more payments abroad than it receives. More domestic money must be flowing out than is entering the country. If the private financial account is in balance, the imbalance between inflows and outflows will translate into excess supply of the domestic currency on exchange markets worldwide. Now two things can happen. First, the excess supply tends to depreciate, or reduce the value of, the domestic currency.[13] If the monetary authorities want to avoid a depreciation, they must relieve the pressure by selling the 'missing' foreign currency for their own currency—hence a positive entry in the official financial account (Off) in (2.9). The country's current account deficit is thus financed by sales of foreign exchange reserves.[14]

Suppose the central bank refused to intervene (Off = 0). In this case the domestic currency would be in excess supply on world markets. With an excess of sellers, it would tend to depreciate, or lose value. This exchange rate depreciation works towards reducing the current account deficit, as domestic goods become more expensive and foreign goods become cheaper. It will also prompt capital inflows as foreigners take advantage of the low exchange rate to acquire domestic assets. In the accounting identity (2.9), either the current account deficit disappears or the private financial account is positive, or both. Similarly, a current account surplus can be financed privately (a negative financial account), publicly (purchases of foreign exchange reserves), or both.

The monetary authorities determine if, and to what extent, a current account imbalance translates into a change in the exchange rate. At one extreme, the monetary authorities may be committed to maintaining a fixed exchange rate and they must intervene. If they do so, they must purchase or sell foreign exchange to whatever extent necessary. At the other extreme, the monetary authorities never intervene and the exchange rate is determined solely by the market. This is why the sum of the current and financial accounts (including errors and omissions) attracts special attention: it is the mirror image of interventions by the monetary authorities and reveals their behaviour. It is called the **overall balance**, and most often somewhat improperly the balance of payments (BoP):[15] ignoring errors and omissions,

$$(2.10) \qquad \text{BoP} = \text{CA} + \text{FA} = -\text{Off}.$$

A balance of payments surplus means that the authorities have acquired foreign exchange reserves. Put differently, they have sold the domestic currency to match an excess demand for the domestic currency, thus preventing or reducing pressure for an exchange rate appreciation (Off < O). Accordingly, the official account is in deficit. A balance of payments deficit corresponds to a loss of reserves as the monetary authorities buy back the domestic currency to prevent a depreciation (Off > O); the official account would then be in surplus.

---

[12] By definition, the sum of the current accounts of all countries in the world should equal zero. In fact, it is systematically negative, as receipts are 'omitted' more often than expenditures.

[13] Later chapters will explore this process in much greater detail. A currency appreciates when its value in terms of other currencies increases. Conversely, if its value decreases, we speak of a depreciation.

[14] Technically, this can be thought of as an official credit from foreign monetary authorities, or calling in of loans made to them in previous periods.

[15] Strictly speaking, this is incorrect because the balance of payments represents the whole document. The official balance is its bottom line and the one that attracts the most attention.

❗ Summary

1 The gross domestic product (GDP) can be defined in three equivalent ways: as the flow of final sales, the flow of factor incomes, or the flow of value added.

2 Because nominal GDP measures final sales at market prices, an increase in the price level leads to an increase in GDP even if quantities sold are constant. Real GDP is computed by pricing current output with constant prices, corresponding to a chosen base year.

3 The GDP deflator is the ratio of nominal to real GDP. It is one measure of the price level. Inflation is approximately equal to the difference between the nominal and real GDP growth rates. Price indexes, also used to compute inflation rates, use constant-weights baskets of goods and services.

4 Measurement of GDP is imperfect, costly, and time consuming. A large amount of economic activity is unmeasured, such as household services and the underground economy. Yet year-on-year comparisons, such as annual growth rates, are less affected by measurement problems.

5 GDP is equal to the sum of consumption, investment, government spending, and the current account $(Y = C + I + G + CA)$. At the same time, GDP is equal to consumption, plus private sector savings, plus net taxes (gross taxes less public transfers received by the private sector) $(Y = C + S + T)$. It follows as an identity that the current account surplus is equal to the surplus of the government plus the surplus of the private sector $(CA = (T - G) + (S - I))$.

6 The balance of payments is a record of current account transactions and their financial counterparts, the financial account. The current account is the sum of the merchandise, invisibles, and transfer accounts; any surplus or deficit must be matched by an equal and opposite sum of private long-term capital, short-term financial errors and omissions, and official intervention accounts.

7 When the monetary authorities undertake to maintain the value of their country's exchange rate, they must intervene on exchange rate markets to match any possible balance of payments imbalance. Conversely, the exchange rate floats freely when the monetary authorities refrain from intervening; then all adjustment for balance of payments equilibrium occurs within the private sector, as a result of changes in the market-determined exchange rate.

🔑 Key Concepts

- accounting identities
- gross domestic product (GDP)
- flow versus stock variables
- final versus intermediate sales
- value added
- gross national product (GNP)
- nominal and real GDP

- GDP deflator
- price index, consumer price index (CPI)
- underground economy
- unpaid work
- circular flow
- net taxes
- private income

- consumption
- financial intermediation
- savings, net private saving
- physical capital
- investment
- absorption
- personal disposable income
- depreciation
- net domestic national product (NDP)
- balance of payment

- merchandise trade balance
- invisibles
- current account
- official account
- financial account
- foreign exchange rate reserves
- foreign exchange market intervention, official account
- overall balance

❷ Exercises

1 You are given the following data:

GDP	5,000
depreciation	500
before-tax corporate profits	1,000
social security contributions	700
transfers to households and firms	1,000
net interest to foreigners	200
proprietary income	70
net corporate saving	600
indirect taxes	1,000
subsidies to enterprises	400
fines and fees	100
net remittances to rest of world	500
corporate taxes	100
consolidated government deficit	100
personal taxes	1,500
household savings	200
investment expenditure	1,200

Compute: NDP, national income, personal income, personal disposable income, consumption, government purchases, GDP, the current account balance. State your assumptions clearly.

2 What happens to GDP when an electrician divorces his wife and bills her for his next repair job that he had previously done for free? What

happens when a housewife becomes self-employed as her own day-care centre?

3 'Services do not contribute to GDP as much as industry because industry produces tangible goods.' Comment.

4 I bought my house for €100,000. I have just sold it for €200,000, and the estate agent received a 10% commission from the buyer. What is the effect on GDP?

5 Suppose you have the following data on prices and quantities:

Prices (€)

	Apples	Pears	Petrol
2003	1.0	2.0	5.0
2004	1.0	3.0	6.0

Quantities

	Apples	Pears	Petrol
2003	300	100	50
2004	400	150	40

(a) If the economy produced all three (and only these three) goods, compute the nominal GDP in both periods, and real GDP at 2003 prices. What is the rate of inflation in 2004, as measured by the change in the GDP deflator?

(b) Suppose a CPI is constructed using weights corresponding to quantities produced in 2003. What is the rate of inflation measured by the CPI?

6 Over the past five years taxes were about 60% of GDP in Sweden. Yet disposable income over the past five years also amounted to 60% of GDP. How can these numbers be reconciled?

7 How would the following transactions be recorded in the French balance of payments?

A French resident buys an Austin Mini produced in the United Kingdom.

A French resident purchases stocks in a German corporation from a German bank.

A French national living in Switzerland buys stock in a French company from a bank in Switzerland.

A French resident builds a house in Italy, paying Italian residents to do the job.

A French resident gives money to Greenpeace located in Hamburg, Germany.

A French banker sends a wire transfer of euros to his daughter at the Humboldt-University in Berlin. The same French banker wires euros from his bank account in Berlin to his account in Paris.

A Tunisian worker in Marseilles sends money to his family in Tunis.

Peugeot SA, a French concern, pays dividends to a resident of Finland.

Profits of Owen Corning, a US company, are reinvested in capacity expansion of a factory in Fontainebleau, France.

The Banque de France (a part of the European Central Bank) purchases Danish kroner to prevent the exchange rate (in Euro) from falling in Copenhagen.

A French resident of Colmar, a town in Alsace near the German border, smuggles home a stereo purchased in Freiburg (Germany).

8 'Commuters reduce the GDP because they send home a large fraction of their earnings.' Comment.

➔ Essay Questions

1 'Legalizing drugs would increase the GDP and tax receipts, but worsen the balance of payments.' Comment.

2 In recent years firms in Europe as well as in the United States have begun to 'outsource' or divest themselves of many traditional service functions, purchasing them on the market instead. Companies are increasingly obtaining computer, catering, legal, consulting, and other business services by ordering them from outside, independent companies. What is the effect of outsourcing on GDP? (Think of the example of a firm which turns its cafeteria into an independent contractor.) How does your answer depend on what the new firm does with its independence?

3 GDP mixes up everything. It includes 'goods' such as apples we eat and theatre shows we enjoy, but also 'bads' such as petrol burnt in traffic congestion and burial costs. It ignores many 'goods' as well, the value of a good neighbour or the free time that we can spend watching a sunset. Comment and explore how you would compute Gross Domestic Happiness?

PART II

The Real Macroeconomy

3 **Economic Growth** *45*
4 **Labour Markets and Unemployment** *71*
5 **Borrowing, Lending, and Budget Constraints** *101*
6 **Private Sector Demand: Consumption and Investment** *125*
7 **The Real Exchange Rate** *151*

Part II focuses exclusively on the real side of the macroeconomy: the demand for and production of goods and services. For a time, we will set aside discussion of monetary, or nominal aspects of the economy and focus on the behaviour of households, firms, and the government, and how these different decision-makers interact in various markets. We begin with the phenomenon of economic growth, the most fundamental of all issues facing modern economies. As the ultimate determinant of the poverty or wealth of nations, economic growth will help anchor our understanding of the long run. Next, we look at the labour market, one of the most important markets of all: the supply of labour by households, the demand by firms, and how to think about unemployment. We then consider spending decisions by households, firms, and governments. How are these economic actors constrained by available resources, and how should they make the best of what they have? The last chapter introduces the real exchange rate, which defines a country's competitiveness as well as its terms of trade, or the command of resources its own output yields over foreign goods and services.

Economic Growth

3.1 Overview *45*

3.2 Stylized Facts and Steady States *47*
  3.2.1   Thinking about Economic Growth: Kaldor's Five Stylized Facts *47*
  3.2.2   Steady States *49*

3.3 Capital Accumulation *49*
  3.3.1   The Aggregate Production Function *50*
  3.3.2   Savings and Capital Accumulation *52*
  3.3.3   Depreciation and the Steady State *52*
  3.3.4   The Role of Savings for Growth *53*
  3.3.5   The Golden Rule *55*

3.4 Population Growth *58*

3.5 Technological Progress *61*

3.6 Putting It All Together: Growth Accounting *62*

3.7 Endogenous Growth: A Primer *65*

Summary *67*

The consequences for human welfare involved in questions like these are simply staggering: Once one starts to think about them, it is hard to think about anything else.

—R. E. Lucas, Jr.[1]

3.1 Overview

It seems almost like an immutable law of nature: over decades and centuries, more and more goods are produced and standards of living continually improve, and we have come to expect more of the same. Indeed, in spite of occasional setbacks arising from wars, natural disasters, or epidemics, **economic growth** has been responsible for staggering changes in the way the world lives. The upper part of Table 3.1 shows the evolution of GDP per capita, most commonly employed measure of standard of living, in Western Europe and China over the past six centuries. On this measure, standards of living increased by twenty-five-fold in Western Europe compared with sixfold in China, which in 1500 was by far the world's most advanced economy.

Such enormous changes are the cumulative result of seemingly small, annual steps. Consider the advanced economies of the world, which grow by roughly 2–4% per year. These apparently limited advances should not be taken lightly: a 2% difference compounds into 49% after twenty years, and 170% after half a century. The recent phenomenal growth successes of China and India and troubling slowdowns in Germany and Japan in recent years prove that growth is not an unchanging constant. For this reason, politicians are concerned about persistent differences in growth rates between countries.

The lower part of Table 3.1 presents more detailed information covering nearly two centuries. It is well worth looking carefully at it for it raises a host of intriguing questions. Is economic growth a universal phenomenon? Why are national growth rates so similar? Why do some countries exhibit periods of spectacular growth, as Japan in 1950–73, the USA in 1820–70, or much of Europe after the Second World War? Why do nations sometimes experience long periods of stagnation, as did China until the last two decades of the twentieth century? Is there a tendency for growth rates to converge, so that periods of above-average growth compensate for periods of below-average growth? What does this imply for levels of GDP per capita? These questions are among the most important ones in economics, for growth determines the wealth and poverty of nations.

In this chapter, we will learn that there are four main reasons why economies grow. First, investment adds to the stock of equipment, the capital stock. More equipment enables workers to produce more. Second, the **population** often tends to grow, which means that more workers are potentially available for market production. In Europe, indigenous population growth has given way to immigration and the entry of a higher proportion of women into the labour force. The third reason is **technological progress**: as knowledge accumulates and techniques improve, workers and the machines they work with become more productive. Finally, advances in productivity are influenced by a host of factors, including rewards to innovation, quality of education, or the size of a country. These four explanations are not mutually exclusive. In this chapter, each source of growth will be considered, step by step, using a framework known as the **Solow**

---

[1] Robert E. Lucas, Jr. (1937–   ) , Chicago economist and Nobel Prize laureate in 1995, is generally regarded as one of the most influential of contemporary macroeconomists. Among his many fundamental contributions to the field, he has researched extensively the determinants of economic growth.

Table 3.1 **The Growth Phenomenon**

(a) GDP per capita in Western Europe and China, 1500–2001 (1990 international Geary Khamis dollars)

	1500	1820	1950	2001
Western Europe	771	1,204	4,579	19,256
China	600	600	439	3,583

Source: www.eco.rug.nl/~Maddison

(b) Average Annual Real GDP Growth Rates 1820–2001

	1820–70	1870–1913	1913–50	1950–73	1973–2001	Overall growth 1820–2001
Belgium	2.2	2.0	1.0	4.1	2.1	2.1
Denmark	1.9	2.7	2.6	3.8	2.2	2.5
Finland	1.6	2.7	2.7	4.9	2.6	2.7
France	1.4	1.6	1.2	5.1	2.2	2.0
Germany	2.0	2.8	0.3	5.7	1.8	2.3
Italy	1.2	1.9	1.5	5.6	2.3	2.2
Netherlands	1.7	2.2	2.4	4.7	2.5	2.5
Norway	1.7	2.1	2.9	4.1	3.3	2.6
Sweden	1.6	2.2	2.7	3.7	1.8	2.3
Switzerland	1.9	2.6	2.6	4.5	1.2	n.a.
United Kingdom	2.1	1.9	1.2	2.9	2.1	2.0
Japan	0.4	2.4	2.2	9.3	2.7	2.7
United States	4.2	3.9	2.8	3.9	2.9	3.6

Source: Maddison (2003). The World Economy, Historical Statistics, OECD, Paris.

growth model,[2] which incorporates the first three explanations. Because it is such an extensive topic, discussion of the fourth source of growth will be postponed until Chapter 18.

3.2 Stylized Facts and Steady States

3.2.1 Thinking about Economic Growth: Kaldor's Five Stylized Facts

It is common and useful for economists to reason abstractly about economic growth. To do so, they usually think of an economy producing a single output (real GDP) using various inputs, or ingredients. These inputs are the factors of production discussed in Chapter 2. First there is labour; there is physical capital, which is equipment and structures; to a less important extent there is land and other measurable factors of production. Growth theory—the study of economic growth across nations and over

[2] Robert Solow (1924–), MIT economist and recipient of the Nobel Prize in 1987, pioneered the study of economic growth in the 1950s.

time—asks whether we produce more because we employ more inputs, or whether the inputs become more productive over time, or both. It also asks what is the contribution of each factor. Yet even at this modest level of abstraction, there is little to restrict a theory of economic growth without looking at the facts, i.e. how have inputs and outputs grown over time?

In 1961, the British economist Nicholas Kaldor (1908–86) identified several **stylized facts** about economic growth.[3] Stylized facts are empirical regularities which may not be rigorously exact always and everywhere, but seem to capture some important features in the economies we observe. We will frequently use stylized facts to help organize our ideas, just as a detective looks for clues before undertaking a thorough investigation. The first of the stylized facts we will examine is:

Stylized Fact No. 1: output per capita and capital intensity keep increasing

The most remarkable aspect of the growth phenomenon is that real GDP, the volume of goods and services produced, seems to grow without bound. Yet labour input, measured in man-hours (L), grows more slowly than capital (K) and output (Y). This means that the production process becomes increasingly more capital intensive or, equivalently, that the ratio of capital to labour (K/L) increases secularly. It also means that the ratio of output to labour (Y/L) rises. Because output per hour of work is closely related to income per capita, economic growth is desirable, since it implies a continuing increase in standards of living. Figure 3.1 presents the evolution of the output–labour and capital–labour ratios for three countries.

Stylized Fact No. 2: the capital–output ratio is trendless

As they grow in a seemingly unbounded fashion, the capital stock and output tend to track each other. As a consequence, the ratio of capital to output (K/Y) shows no systematic trend. This is apparent from Figure 3.1, but Table 3.2 shows that it is only

[3] Kaldor (1961: 177–222).

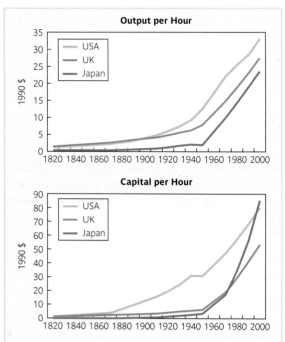

Fig. 3.1 The Output–Labour and Capital–Labour Ratios in Three Countries
Output–labour and capital–labour ratios are continuously increasing. Growth accelerated in the USA in the early twentieth century, after 1950 in Japan and the UK.
Source: Maddison (1991), Groningen Total Economy Database (**www.ggdc.net**), chained.

Table 3.2 Capital–Output Ratios (K/Y), 1913–1998

	1913	1950	1973	1998
France	n.a.	1.4	1.1	2.1
Germany	n.a.	1.4	1.3	2.0
Japan	0.9	1.0	2.6	2.4
UK	0.8	0.8	1.3	1.1
USA	3.3	2.4	1.5	1.3

Sources: Maddison (1995); 1998 data for France and Germany is from Groningen Total Economy Database (**www.ggdc.net**), chained; 1998 data for Japan, USA and UK is from 'Growth Accounts, Technological Change and Role of Energy in Western Growth' (A. Maddison).
Note: Capital is fixed non-residential capital stock.

approximately true. Yet, even if the capital–output ratio is not exactly constant, it does not display the steady, unrelenting increases seen in Stylized Fact No. 1.

Stylized Fact No. 3: hourly wages keep rising

The trend increase in the ratios of output and capital to labour (Y/L and K/L) means that an hour of work uses ever more equipment to produce ever more output. As workers become productive, they are entitled to higher hourly wages (this link will be shown more formally in the next chapter). And, indeed, hourly real wages grow secularly, which means ever-increasing living standards for workers.

Stylized Fact No. 4: the rate of profit is trendless

The absence of a clear trend for the capital–output ratio (K/Y) implies that the same amount of equipment delivers about the same amount of output. It is to be expected therefore that the rate of profit does not exhibit a trend either (this is the same logic as in the previous stylized fact, to be confirmed in subsequent chapters). Income flowing to owners of capital has increased, but only because the stock of capital itself has increased.

Stylized Fact No. 5: the relative shares of GDP going to labour and capital are trendless

It has already been shown that total incomes deriving from labour and capital have increased secularly. It turns out that they also tend to increase at about the same rate, so that the distribution of total income (GDP) between capital and labour has been relatively stable.

3.2.2 Steady States

Even though they are not literally true at all times, stylized facts fix our attention on certain central tendencies in the data. As we study growth, we are tracking moving targets, variables that keep increasing all the time, without bound, going towards infinity! Our work is made easier if we can identify relationships which are stable even if the economy is constantly growing. The simplest example is GDP: could it be that its growth rate is constant, despite apparently boundless growth? The answer is yes, but only on average of five or ten years or more. In Chapter 1, we noted the important phenomenon of business cycles, periods of fast growth followed by periods of slow growth. Here we are not interested in business cycles; in fact in the analysis of economic growth, we will disregard shorter-term fluctuations—compare Figures 1.1 and 1.2—to concentrate on the long run.

This is why it is convenient to imagine how things would look if there were no business cycles. Such a situation is called a **steady state**. It never happens, much as the stylized facts are never exactly observed. We never reach the long run: looking at today ten years ago, we thought of it as the long run, but now that we are there, we can see all the details that were indistinguishable back then. Still, when we consider GDPs that double up every ten to twenty years, a temporary boom or recession which shifts today's GDP by one or two percentage points amounts to little in the greater order of things, the powerful phenomenon of continuous long-run growth. Steady states—and stylized facts—are not just convenient ways of making our lives simpler, they are essential tools for distinguishing the forest from the trees.

3.3 **Capital Accumulation**

This first of our three explanations focuses on savings and investment. To keep things simple, we start by assuming that the size of the population, the labour force, and the number of hours worked remain constant. The central intuition is delivered by the now-familiar circular flow diagram in Figure 2.2. Households and firms save part of their income. Savings flow into the financial system (banks, stock

Box 3.1 For the Mathematically Minded: The Cobb–Douglas Production Function

The various properties of the production function can be easily established by using a special form, the Cobb–Douglas production function:

(B3.1) $$Y = K^\alpha L^{1-\alpha}.$$

where α is a constant parameter which represents the technology in use, which can take values between 0 and 1, and has the interpretation of the percentage change in output resulting from a 1% increase in the capital input.[4] We can now reproduce formally all the results in the text.

Diminishing marginal productivity

The marginal productivity of capital is $\partial F/\partial K = \alpha K^{\alpha-1} L^{1-\alpha} = \alpha(L/K)^{1-\alpha}$. Since $\alpha < 1$, we see that this expression is a decreasing function of K and an increasing function of L. A similar analysis can be applied to the marginal

productivity of labour $\partial F/\partial L = (1-\alpha)(K/L)^\alpha$, which is increasing in K and decreasing in L.

Constant Returns

The Cobb–Douglas function has the constant returns to scale property: for a positive scaling factor t,

(B3.2) $(tK)^\alpha (tL)^{1-\alpha} = t^\alpha t^{1-\alpha} K^\alpha L^{1-\alpha} = tK^\alpha L^{1-\alpha} = tY.$

The intensive form

Divide both sides of (B3.1) by L, which is like setting $t = 1/L$ in equation (B3.2), to obtain:

(B3.3) $Y/L = y = (K^\alpha L^{1-\alpha})/L = K^\alpha L^{-\alpha} = (K/L)^\alpha = k^\alpha,$

where $k = K/L$ and $y = Y/L$ as in the text. The figure is indeed well represented by Figure 3.3.

---

markets, etc.), where they are channelled to borrowers, firms, and households. Here, the relevant part is that which goes to firms which want to invest, i.e. to increase their productive capacity by purchasing capital goods. This expansion of productive capacity, in turn, raises output, which then raises future savings and investment, and so on. But this simplicity conceals some issues which turn out to be interesting and important: is this process of **capital accumulation** never ending? Does more saving necessarily mean faster growth? And since saving can be thought of as deferred consumption, is it a good idea?

3.3.1 The Aggregate Production Function

To answer these questions, we need a number of tools. The first, and most important tool we will use, is the **aggregate production function**. It describes how an economy's capital stock K and employed labour L produce the total output of an economy, or its GDP:

(3.1) $$Y = F(K, L).$$
$$+\ +$$

The production function is meant to capture the simple fact that goods and services are produced using (at least) two factors of production, equipment and manpower. The production function is a powerful short-cut widely used in microeconomics to study the output of individual firms; here instead we use it to study the output of the entire economy. Box 3.1 provides one particularly popular example of a production function. The total stock of capital, which includes plants and machinery as well as roads and railroads, electricity and telephone networks, is represented by K; the symbol L stands for the total number of hours worked, or man-hours. Thus L combines the numbers of workers (N) and the average hours (h) that they work per year ($L = Nh$).[5] The plus ('+') signs shown underneath the production function in (3.1) signify that output rises with either

---

4 To see this, note that the elasticity of output with respect to capital is defined as $(dY/dK)(K/Y)$ and is given by $(\alpha K^{\alpha-1}L^{1-\alpha})(K^{1-\alpha}L^{\alpha-1}) = \alpha$. Similarly, $(1-\alpha)$ is the elasticity of output with respect to the labour input.

5 Since output and labour inputs are flows, they could also be measured per quarter or per month, but should be measured over the same time interval. Note that capital is a stock, usually measured at the beginning of the current, or end of the last period. The important distinction between stocks and flows was introduced in Ch. 1.

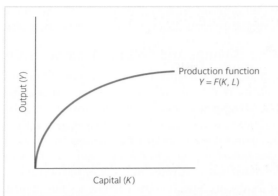

Fig. 3.2 The Production Function: Diminishing Marginal Productivity

Holding labour input L (the number of hours worked) unchanged, adding to the capital stock K (available productive equipment) allows an economy to produce more, but in smaller and smaller increments.

more capital or more labour.[6] How this happens is related to two basic assumptions which are central to understanding production and growth.

Diminishing marginal productivity

Consider a country with workers and a stock of capital. Then imagine that one machine is added and the capital stock rises by the amount ΔK, with the number of workers constant. Output will also rise, by ΔY. The ratio $\Delta Y/\Delta K$, the amount of new output per unit of incremental capital, is called the economy's **marginal productivity**. Now, imagine that we continue again and again to add capital, while continuing to hold labour input constant. Should we expect to see output increasing by the same amount for each increment of capital? It turns out generally not to be the case. As more and more equipment is brought into the production process, it works with less and less of the given labour input, and the increases in output become smaller and smaller. This is the principle of **diminishing marginal productivity**. It is represented in Figure 3.2 which describes how output rises with capital, holding the use of labour unchanged. The flattening of the curve illustrates

the assumption. In fact the slope of the curve is equal to the economy's marginal productivity.

It turns out that the principle of diminishing marginal productivity applies also to the labour input. Increasing the employment of man-hours will raise output; but output from additional man-hours declines as more and more labour is being applied to a fixed stock of capital.

Returns to scale

Output increases when either inputs of capital or labour increases. But what happens if both capital and labour increase in the same proportion? Suppose, for example, that the inputs of capital and labour were both doubled. If output doubles as a result, the production function is said to have **constant returns to scale**. If output more than doubles, we observe **increasing returns to scale**. **Decreasing returns** is the case when output increases by less than 100%. It is believed that decreasing returns to scale are unlikely. Increasing returns, in contrast, cannot be ruled out, but we will ignore this possibility until Section 3.7, and later in Chapter 18. In fact, the bulk of the evidence points in the direction of constant returns to scale.

With constant returns we can think of the link between inputs and output—the production function—as a zoom lens: as long as we scale up the inputs, so does the output. It should be intuitive that, under this condition, an attractive property of the production function emerges: output per hour of work—the **output–labour ratio** (Y/L)—depends only on capital per hour of work—the **capital–labour ratio** (K/L). This permits a great simplification as the production function can be written in the following intensive form:[7]

$$(3.2) \qquad y = f(k),$$

where $y = Y/L$ and $k = K/L$.

---

[6] Formally, this means that the two partial derivatives $F_K(K, L) \equiv \partial F/\partial K$ and $F_L(K, L) \equiv \partial F/\partial L$ are positive.

[7] Formally, things are a bit harder. The definition of constant returns is that if we scale up K and L by a factor t, Y is scaled up by the exactly same factor; mathematically, $tY = F(tK, tL)$ for all $t > 0$. In the text we use the case where $t = 2$, we double all inputs and produce twice as much. Now we can choose any value for t, for instance $t = 1/L$. This yields $y = F(k, 1)$, which we rename as $f(k)$ because $F(k, 1)$ depends on k. The intensive production function $f(k)$ is so called because it expresses output produced per unit of labour (y) as a function of the capital intensity of production (k).

The intensive form representation is convenient for three reasons. First, it allows us to track per capita values of output and the capital stock (y and k) which, according to Stylized Fact No. 1, grow secularly together. Second, as long as average hours worked per person do not change, output per hour and GDP per capita increase at the same rate: total hours worked $L = Nh$ grows at the same rate as the number of workers N when the number of hours worked per person h remains constant. Consequently, the intensive form which describes output per hour Y/L allows us to study the rate of growth of output per capita Y/N, the standards of living. We will freely use these two expressions as equivalent.[8] Third, income per capita does not depend on the absolute size of the economy, but what the average person has to work with. Put differently, the size of a country does not matter for its growth performance. The intensive-form production function is depicted in Figure 3.3. Because

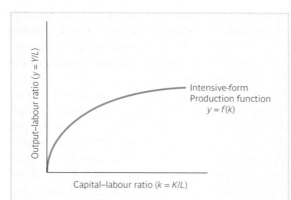

Fig. 3.3 The Production Function in Intensive Form

The production function shows that the output–labour ratio y grows with the capital–labour ratio k. Its slope is the marginal productivity of labour since with constant returns to scale $\Delta Y/\Delta K = \Delta y/\Delta k$. The principle of declining marginal productivity implies that the curve becomes flatter as k increases.

[8] In Ch. 4 we will see that this is not always the case; increases in the rate of labour force participation (L/N) or hours worked (h) can represent significant sources of growth for extended periods of time.

of diminishing marginal productivity, the curve becomes flatter as the capital–labour ratio increases.

3.3.2 Savings and Capital Accumulation

The national accounts of Chapter 2, more precisely identity (2.7), captures all potential sources that can be tapped to finance private investment, i.e. additions to the capital stock. Investment (I) can be financed either by private savings by firms or households (S), by government savings (the consolidated budget surplus, or $T - G$), or the net savings of foreigners (which is the current account deficit, $Z - X$):

$$(3.3) \qquad I = S + (T - G) + (Z - X).$$

For the time being, suppose that the government budget is in balance, so $T = G$. Similarly, for simplicity, let us also ignore deficits or surpluses in the current account, so $Z = X$. Then it follows that $I = S$; increases in the stock of capital are entirely financed by domestic saving. This is the first explanation of the growth phenomenon: we save, we invest, we grow. To make things more precise, we now assume that a constant fraction s of GDP is saved to finance investment:

$$(3.4) \quad I = sY \quad \text{and therefore } I/L = s(Y/L) = sy = sf(k).$$

3.3.3 Depreciation and the Steady State

New physical capital is accumulated through investment, but the old capital **depreciates**: some of it wears out, some becomes obsolescent. The proportion δ of capital thus routinely lost is called the **depreciation rate**. The depreciation rate for the overall economy is fairly stable and will be taken as constant: the more capital is in place, the more proportionally depreciates. Depreciation is represented in Figure 3.4 as the **depreciation line**, with a slope δ.

If investment exceeds depreciation, the capital stock rises. The capital stock could even shrink if investment were smaller than depreciation, a phenomenon not uncommon in declining industries. The net effect of gross investment and depreciation on the capital stock can be expressed in the following way:

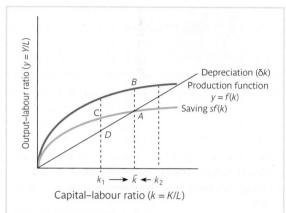

Fig. 3.4 The Steady State

The capital–labour ratio stops changing when investment is equal to depreciation. This occurs at point A, the intersection between the saving schedule $sf(k)$ and the depreciation line δk. The corresponding output–labour ratio is determined by the production function $f(k)$ at point B. When away from point A, the economy moves towards its steady state. Starting with below the steady state at k_1, investment (point C) exceeds depreciation (point D) and the capital–output ratio will increase until it reaches its steady-state level $\bar{k}$.

(3.5) $\Delta K = sY - \delta K$

or equivalently, in intensive form:

$$\Delta k = sy - \delta k,$$

where the Greek letter Δ stands for a change over some defined period of time, such as a year.

Let us take stock of our results up until now. The production function (3.2) relates the output to inputs, capital and labour. Its intensive form, presented in Figure 3.3 and Figure 3.4, relates the output–labour ratio to the capital-labour ratio. According to (3.5), capital accumulation is also driven by the output–labour ratio. Since, for the moment, population and hours per worker are held constant, saving and investment are a fixed fraction of output (sY). They are also a fixed fraction of output per capita $(sY/L = sy = sf(k))$. Depreciation is proportional to capital stock per capita, and given by δk. Putting the two pieces together, we find that, at any moment of time, capital accumulation (Δk) is determined by the existing, previously accumulated stock of capital (k):

(3.6) $\Delta k = sf(k) - \delta k.$

In Figure 3.4, Δk is the vertical distance between the savings investment schedule $sf(k)$ and the depreciation line δk, so we can see where the economy is heading. When $\Delta k > 0$, the capital stock per capita is rising and the economy is growing, since more output can be produced; when $\Delta k < 0$, the capital stock per capita is falling and the output per capita is declining.[9] At the intersection (point A) of the saving-investment schedule and the depreciation line, investment and depreciation are equal, so the capital–labour ratio (point B) no longer changes. The newly accumulated capital stock exactly compensates the older one that is lost to depreciation— the water flows into the bathtub at the same speed as it leaks out. This is the steady state, where the capital–output ratio is neither rising nor falling.

The analysis predicts that the economy will automatically gravitate to its steady state and then stay there. Suppose the economy is to the left of the steady-state capital–output ratio $\bar{k}$, say at the level k_1.[10] Figure 3.4 shows that investment $sf(k_1)$ at point C exceeds depreciation δk_1 at point D. As can be seen from (3.6), the distance CD represents the increase in the capital–labour ratio, which now rises towards its steady-state level $\bar{k}$.

Could the capital stock proceed beyond $\bar{k}$, going all way to, say, k_2? It turns out that it can't; the adjustment towards point A from below always proceeds in the same direction. To see how the economy behaves when capital is above its steady state, consider $k_2 > \bar{k}$. Investment $sf(k_2)$ is less than depreciation δk_2, the capital–labour ratio must decline, and we move leftward towards $\bar{k}$, the economy's stable resting point. Later we shall see that the stability of capital and output per capita carries over when we account for population growth.

3.3.4 The Role of Savings for Growth

The last section established that the more a country saves, the more it invests; the more it invests, the

---

[9] This situation is similar to filling up a bathtub when the drain is slightly open: investment is like the tap, while the role of depreciation is played by the drain.

[10] In general, steady-state values of variables will be indicated here with a upper bar, e.g. $\bar{k}$, $\bar{y}$, etc.

higher is its capital–output ratio; and the larger its capital–output ratio, the higher its output–labour ratio. As a long-run proposition, we should expect to find that countries with high savings and investment rates have high per capita incomes. Is this true? The first panel of Figure 3.5 looks at the whole world and indeed detects such a link. The poor countries of Africa typically invest little, in contrast with the richer countries of Europe and Asia.

Yet, the link is not strong enough to explain even most of the differences between countries; much more must be going on. Indeed, we soon proceed

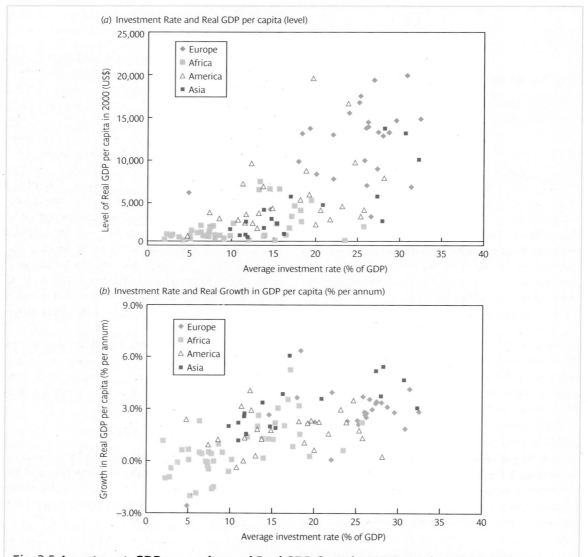

Fig. 3.5 Investment, GDP per capita, and Real GDP Growth, 115 Countries, 1950–2000
For a sample of 115 countries over the period 1950–2000, the correlation coefficient between the investment rate (the ratio of investment to GDP) and average per capita GDP over the period is significant at 0.69. The correlation of the investment rate in the countries with the growth rate of real GDP growth is also high (0.65).
Source: Penn World Tables Mark 6.1 (**http://pwt.econ.upenn.edu/php_site/pwt_index.php**).

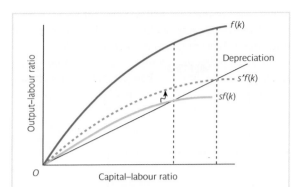

Fig. 3.6 An Increase in the Savings Rate

An increase in the savings rate raises capital intensity (k) and the output/labour ratio (y).

to put more flesh on the bare bones we just put together. But one aspect should be recognized immediately: savings and investment in the Solow model affect the steady-state level of output, but not the steady-state growth rate. To see this consider Figure 3.6, which shows the effect of an increase in the savings rate from s to s'. The savings function shifts upwards, but the production function remains unchanged. The steady-state output–labour and capital–labour ratios are both higher, indicating more capital-intensive production. Adjustment to the new steady state will not be immediate, meaning higher growth for some time. This will frequently give the impression that higher investment rates cause higher economic growth, as the second panel of Figure 3.5 shows. Yet, theory is clear: once the steady state has been reached, no further growth effect can be expected from a higher savings rate. We still need a story to explain growth in per capita output: this is the story told in Sections 3.4 and 3.5.

It may be surprising that increased savings does not affect long-run growth. Why can't higher savings allow capital and output to grow forever? Initially, the capital stock rises, but as more capital is put into place, more capital depreciates and thus needs to be replaced. So we need more investment to keep the capital stock constant. Yet the resources for that increased investment are not there because the marginal productivity of capital decreases. As a result, further additions to the capital–labour

ratio yield smaller and smaller increases in income, and therefore in savings. Depreciation, however, rises proportionately. Put simply, the decreasing marginal productivity principle implies that saving more and more pays off less and less. The last section of this chapter confirms that the outcome is very different when the marginal productivity of capital is not decreasing.

3.3.5 The Golden Rule

Figure 3.5 seems to convey an important message: to become richer, you need to save and invest more. But is being richer always necessarily better? Besides the philosophical doubts one might have about growth—which are not the subject of this chapter—one can also question whether more thriftiness (saving) always makes us happier, even if it always increases GDP per capita. Savings represent a sacrifice; from the perspective of the household, it is income which is not spent on consumption. Once we remember that savings come at the expense of consumption, we need to ask whether it is worth it. Savings are income put aside for later consumption, and consumption is responsible for economic satisfaction. So when we ask what is the best that can be achieved, we ought to be aiming for the highest possible level of per capita consumption.

To see this more concretely, note that in the steady state when the capital stock per capita is $\bar{k}$, savings equal depreciation, so steady-state consumption $\bar{c}$ (the part of income that is not saved) is given by:

(3.7) $$\bar{c} = \bar{y} - s\bar{y} = f(\bar{k}) - \delta\bar{k}$$

In Figure 3.7, consumption is given by the vertical distance between the production function and the depreciation line.[11] If we could choose the saving rate, we could effectively pick any point of intersection of the savings schedule with the depreciation line, and therefore any level of consumption we so desired. The figure shows that the highest

[11] Note that everything, including consumption and saving, is measured as a ratio to the labour input, man-hours. As already noted, if the number of hours worked does not change, the ratios move exactly as per capita consumption, saving, output, etc.

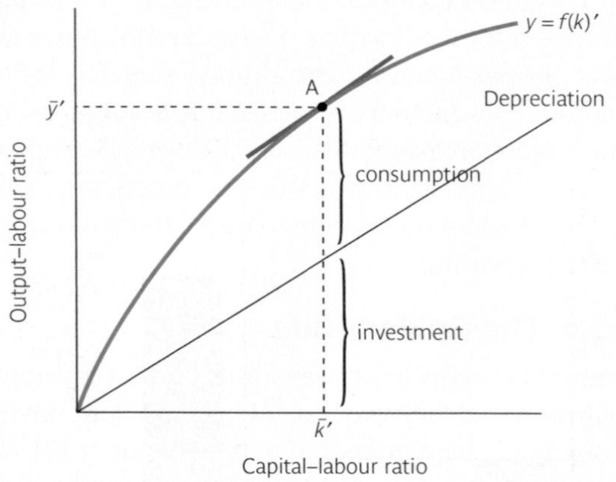

Fig. 3.7 **The Golden Rule**

Steady-state consumption $\bar{c}$ (as a ratio to labour) is the vertical distance between the production function and the depreciation line δk. It is at a maximum at point A corresponding to $\bar{k}'$, where the slope of the production function, the marginal productivity of capital, is equal to δ, the slope of the depreciation line.

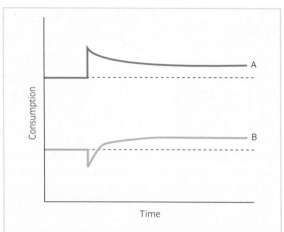

Fig. 3.8 **Raising Steady-State Consumption**

In a dynamically inefficient economy (A), it is possible to permanently raise consumption by reducing saving. In a dynamically efficient economy (B), higher future consumption requires early sacrifices.

consumption level is achieved where the slope of the production function is parallel to the depreciation line.[12] The corresponding optimal steady-state capital–output ratio is $\bar{k}$. Since the slope of the production function schedule is the marginal productivity of capital (MPK), the most desired situation can be characterized by the following condition:

$$(3.8) \qquad \text{MPK} = \delta.$$

This condition is called the **golden rule**, and can be thought of as a recipe for achieving the best use of existing technological capabilities. In this case—with no population growth and no technical progress—the golden rule states that the economy maximizes its per capita consumption in the steady state when the marginal gain from an additional unit of GDP saved and invested in capital (MPK), equals its marginal cost (the periodic future depreciation that will be necessary to maintain capital per capita at that level).

What are the consequences of 'disobeying' the golden rule? If the capital–labour ratio exceeds $\bar{k}'$, too much capital has been accumulated, and the MPK

[12] An exercise asks you to prove this assertion.

is lower than the depreciation rate δ. By reducing savings today, an economy could actually *increase* consumption, both today and in the future. This looks like a free lunch, and indeed, it is one. We say that the economy suffers from **dynamic inefficiency**. Dynamically inefficient economies simply invest too much and consume too little.

In contrast, if the economy is to the left of $\bar{k}'$, steady-state income and consumption may be raised by saving more, but not immediately; consumption only in the long run. The economy is called **dynamically efficient** because there is no free lunch readily available. Indeed, moving towards $\bar{k}'$ from a position on the left requires the current generation to give up some consumption—that is, save now—so that future generations can enjoy more consumption which results from more capital and income. The difference between dynamically efficient and inefficient savings rates is illustrated in Figure 3.8, which shows how we move from one steady state to another one with higher consumption.

Dynamic inefficiency arises when savings are too high. We must keep saving a lot for ever to make up for the depreciation of an excessive amount of capital. Dynamic inefficiency may have characterized the centrally planned economies of Central and

Box 3.2 Dynamic Inefficiency in Poland?

The upper part of Figure 3.9 compares centrally planned Poland with Italy, one of the countries with the highest saving rates in Europe. The first graph shows the increase in GDP per capita between 1980 and 1990 (the GDP measure is adjusted for purchasing power to take into account different price systems): while Italy's income grew by 63%, Poland's only increased by 36%, about half. The second graph shows the average proportion of GDP dedicated to saving over the same period. Clearly, Poland saved a lot, and received little for it in terms of income growth. And, as the lower part of the figure shows, the situation was reversed after 1991, when Poland dropped central planning: from 1991 to 1997, its per capita GDP increased by 40%, while it grew by 17% in Italy, with the same saving rate. However, our theory predicts that savings affect the steady-state level of GDP per capita, not its growth rate. If we look at GDP per capita, in 1980 it stood at $3,250 in Poland, and at $5,790 in Italy, with the difference only deepening thereafter. Is this proof of dynamic inefficiency, i.e. that a significant part of savings was used merely to keep up an excessively large stock of capital? Anecdotal evidence would suggest so. Stories about centrally planned economies are replete with examples of wasted resources: uninstalled equipment rusting in backyards, new machinery prematurely discarded because of lack of spare parts, tools ill-adapted to factory needs, etc. One important factor behind this wastage was that factory managers were rewarded for spending on equipment and their promised plans, not for the actual output. An alternative interpretation is that the investment was in poor quality equipment, which could not match Western technology. No matter how we look at it, savings were not put to their best use in centrally planned Poland.

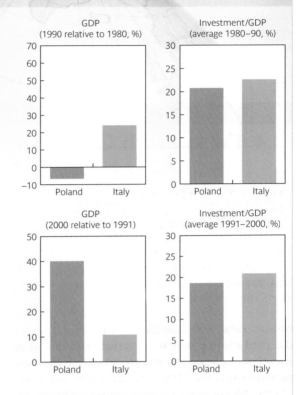

Fig. 3.9 Was Centrally Planned Poland Dynamically Inefficient?

Despite a higher rate of saving, Polish per capita GDP grew only about half as fast as Italy's over the period 1980–90. Afterwards, during the transition period, Poland grew much faster, with about the same saving rate as Italy.

Source: Penn World Tables Mark 6.1 (http://pwt.econ.upenn.edu/php_site/pwt_index.php).

Eastern Europe. We say 'may' because the proof that an economy is inefficient lies in showing that its marginal productivity of capital is lower than the depreciation rate, and neither of these is easily measurable. What we do know is that Communist leaders were rather proud of their economies' high investment rates, which were in fact considerably higher than in the capitalist West. Yet it is also well documented that overall standards of living were considerably lower, and consumer goods in notoriously short supply. Box 3.2 presents the case of Poland.

In dynamically efficient countries, future generations would benefit from raising saving today, but those currently alive would lose. Should governments do something about it? Since it would represent a transfer of revenues from current to future generations, there is no simple answer, it is truly a deep political choice with no solution since future generations don't vote today. Anyway, can it be done? Savings depend on a host of factors such as taxation, the existence of health and retirement systems, cultural aspects affecting family links. Most importantly, perhaps, saving and investment

are influenced by political conditions. Political instability and especially wars, civil or otherwise, can lead to destruction and theft of capital, and hardly encourage thrifty behaviour. Indeed, in many of the poorest countries in the world property rights are under threat or non-existent.

3.4 Population Growth

We have found that, when decreasing marginal productivity sets in, capital accumulation cannot sustain permanent growth. The result that output and the capital stock are constant grossly violates the evidence, so we must be missing some crucial ingredients. This section takes a first step and shows that growth can be permanent once we introduce population growth.

Labour input grows either when more people are at work, or when each worker works more hours. In the next chapter, we will see that the number of hours worked per person has declined secularly over the past century and a half. At the same time,

the number of workers has been rising, as illustrated in Figure 3.10, either because of natural demographic forces (the balance between births and deaths) or immigration. Overall, the balance of effects is ambiguous. In order to make the general point, we will simply assume that the number of man-hours is growing and look at the data afterwards.

Fortunately, the reasoning of Section 3.3 remains valid: the economy will gravitate to a steady state at which the capital–labour and output–labour ratios ($k = K/L$ and $y = Y/L$) stabilize. With L growing at the rate n, this means that output Y and capital K will also

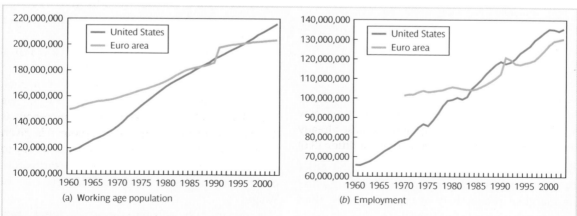

Fig. 3.10 **Population Growth**
Population of working age (between 15 and 64) has been growing both in the USA and Europe (the data refer to EU11, i.e. the European Union less Denmark, Greece, Sweden, and the UK). Employment has also been growing, albeit less fast in Europe. Note the jump in Europe in 1991, the year after German unification.
Source: OECD, *Economic Outlook.*

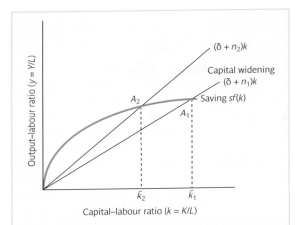

Fig. 3.11 The Steady State with Population Growth

The capital–labour ratio remains unchanged when investment is equal to $(\delta + n_1)k$.

This occurs at point A_1, the intersection between the saving schedule $sf(k)$ and the capital widening line $(\delta + n_1)k$. An increase in the rate of growth of the population from n_1 to n_2 is shown as a counter-clockwise rotation of the capital widening line. The new steady-state capital output ratio declines from $\bar{k}_1$ to $\bar{k}_2$.

grow at rate n. The increase in the labour input is a source of growth. Quite simply, if income per capita is to remain unchanged in the steady state, income must grow at the same rate as the number of people.

The role of saving and capital accumulation remains the same as in the previous section, only the details change. For the capital–labour ratio to remain unchanged in the steady state, investment must not only compensate for capital depreciation, but also for labour growth, providing new workers with the same equipment as those already employed. The capital accumulation condition (3.6) now becomes:[13]

(3.9) $\Delta k = sf(k) - (\delta + n)k.$

Figure 3.11 summarizes the Solow model with population growth. The only difference from Fig-

ure 3.4 is that the depreciation line δk has been replaced by the **capital widening line** $(\delta + n)k$. The term 'capital widening' captures the notion that the capital stock must now also increase to equip the newly arrived workers. The steady state is at point A_1, the intersection of the saving-investment schedule and the capital widening line where $\Delta k = 0$.

The role of population growth is best illustrated by asking what is the effect of an increase in the rate of population growth, from n_1 to n_2. In Figure 3.11 the capital widening line becomes steeper and the new steady state at point A_2 is characterized by a lower capital–labour ratio $\bar{k}_2$. Thus the higher is the rate of population growth, the lower is the sustainable steady-state capital–labour ratio. Since the output–labour ratio is $f(\bar{k})$ we find that it also declines with population growth. Put differently, the Solow model implies that, all other things being equal, countries with rapidly growing population will tend to be poorer than countries with lower population growth. More investment is needed to keep the capital–labour ratio steady when more workers are arriving each year. Investment which is forthcoming at the constant savings rate will be insufficient to do the job; capital intensity must decline, and so will the output–labour ratio. Box 3.3 examines whether it is indeed the case that high population growth lowers GDP per capita. The complete story turns out to be somewhat more complicated, but the Solow model is a good starting point for organizing our thoughts on this issue.

Since a growing population increases continuously the number of people who are able to consume, it requires us to modify the golden rule. Following the same reasoning as before, we note that steady-state investment per man-hour is $(\delta + n)\bar{k}$, so consumption per man-hour $\bar{c}$ is given by $f(\bar{k}) - (\delta + n)\bar{k}$. Proceeding as before, it is easy to see that consumption is at a maximum when:

(3.10) $MPK = \delta + n.$

The 'modified' golden rule equates the marginal productivity of capital with the sum of the depreciation rate δ and the population growth rate n. The intuition applied above continues to apply: the marginal returns of an additional unit of capital (per capita) is set to its marginal cost, which now

[13] To establish this result formally, note that $\Delta k = \Delta(K/L) = (\Delta K/L) - (\Delta L/L)(K/L) = [(\Delta K/L) - (\Delta L/L)]k$ by the law of differentiation, and substitute $\Delta K = I - \delta K$ and $\Delta L/L = n$. Then set $I = sY$ and rearrange, yielding $\Delta k = sy - nk = sf(k) - nk$.

Box 3.3 Population Growth and GDP per capita

Figure 3.12 plots GDP per capita in 2000 and the average rate of population growth over the period 1960–2000. The figure could be seen as confirming the negative relationship predicted by the Solow growth model. Taken at face value, this result would support the hypothesis— associated with English economist and philosopher Thomas Malthus—that population growth impoverishes nations. Malthus's reasoning was not based on the Solow model, however. He thought that a fixed land area could not feed a constantly increasing population and that population growth would result in starvation. He ignored technological change, in this case the green revolution which significantly raised agricultural output in the last

half of the twentieth century. As we confirm in Section 3.5, technological change can alter the outlook radically.

But the Malthusian view is sometimes taken seriously in some countries which attempt to limit demographic growth, the most spectacular example being China's one-child-only policy. Several European countries, in contrast, currently view demography as a source of growth. Anyway, what should one make of the evidence displayed in Figure 3.12? Probably that one should exercise caution when interpreting such diagrams. The figure could be read as saying that as people become richer, they have fewer children. There exists a great deal of evidence in favour of this alternative interpretation.

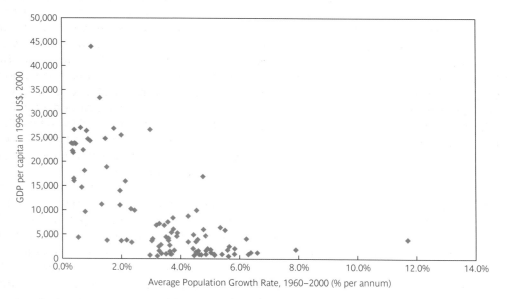

Fig. 3.12 Population Growth and GDP per capita, 1960–2000
The figure, which reports data for 98 countries, plots real GDP and indicates a discernible negative association between GDP per capita and the rate of population growth.
Source: Penn World Table Mark 6.1 (Summers, Heston, Aten).

includes not only depreciation, but also the commitment to equipping future generations with the same capital per head as the current generation. When the population is growing, the marginal

product of capital must be higher; the principle of diminishing marginal productivity implies that the capital–labour ratio must be lower. Consequently, output per head is also lower.

3.5 Technological Progress

Having taken population growth into account, we have found one good reason why output—and the capital stock—can grow permanently. Yet the picture remains incomplete: in the steady state of the modified Solow growth model just considered, the capital–labour and output–labour ratios are constant, which means that the standards of living are not rising. This is grossly inconsistent with Kaldor's first stylized fact and the data reported in Table 3.1. What other sources of growth are there? An obvious candidate is technological progress. It stands to reason that over time, increased knowledge and better, more sophisticated techniques make workers and the equipment they work with more productive.

It turns out that with a slight alteration, our framework readily shows how technical progress works. To do so, we need to extend the aggregate production function introduced in (3.1) to allow for the same quantity of equipment and labour to yield more output. The most convenient way to do this is to introduce a measure of the state of technology, A:

(3.11) $$Y = F(A, K, L).$$
$$\quad\quad + \;\; + \;\; +$$

Along with the production function itself, A captures the state of technology. When it increases, even if K and L remain unchanged, Y rises. It should be emphasized that A is *not* a factor of production, it is not paid for, each firm just benefits from it. We will assume that A increases regularly at a constant rate a, without trying to explain so far precisely how and why. Technological progress, which is the increase in A, is therefore exogenous.

In order to connect immediately to previous results in this chapter, we take two steps. First we modify (3.11) in the following way:

(3.12) $$Y = F(K, AL)$$

and we refer to AL as **effective labour**, to capture the idea that, with the same equipment, one hour of work today produces more output than before because A is higher. Effective labour AL grows for two reasons: more labour L, and greater effectiveness A. For this reason, the rate of growth of AL is $a + n$.

Next, we redefine y and k as ratios relative to effective labour: $y = Y/AL$, $k = K/AL$. Once this is done, we recover the now-familiar production function in intensive form, $y = f(k)$. Not surprisingly, the ratio of capital to effective labour k accumulates as follows:

(3.13) $$\Delta k = sf(k) - (\delta + a + n)k.$$

The reasoning is the same as when we introduced population growth. The ratio $k = K/AL$ rises with K and declines with A and L. So k will increase if saving $sf(k)$, and hence investment, exceeds capital accumulation needed to make up for depreciation δ, population growth n, and increased effectiveness a. From there on, it is a simple matter to modify Figure 3.11 to Figure 3.13. The steady state is now characterized by constant ratios of capital and output to effective labour ($y = Y/AL$ and $k = K/AL$). As a consequence both output Y and capital K will grow at the rate $a + n$, the sum of technological progress and population growth.

An increase in the rate of technological progress, a, steepens the capital widening line and reduces the ratios of capital and output to effective labour. Does this mean that technological change reduces capital and output per capita? Intuition says that it should not be the case, and it is not. While more progress means a decline in y and k, recall that these are measured not in labour units, but in effective units, Y/AL and K/AL. In the steady state, these ratios are constant, but if we look at the more meaningful ratios per hour (or per capita if we ignore changes in hours worked) $Y/L = Ay$ and $K/L = Ak$, we do find that they increase, both at the rate a, the rate of technological progress.[14] Figure 3.14 shows this evolution

---

[14] Note that everything, including consumption and saving, is measured as a ratio to the labour input, man-hours. As already noted, if the number of hours worked does not change, the ratios move exactly as per capita consumption, saving, output, etc.

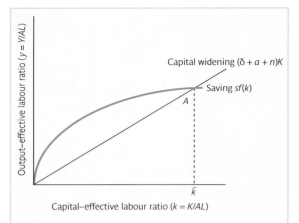

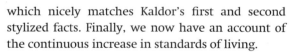

Fig. 3.13 The Steady State with Population Growth and Technological Progress

In an economy with both population growth and technological progress, inputs and output are measured in units per effective labour input. The intensive form production function inherits this property. The slope of the capital accumulation line is now $\delta + a + n$, where a is the rate of technological progress. The steady state occurs when investment is equal to $(\delta + a + n)k$ (point A), which is the intersection of the saving schedule $sf(k)$ with the capital widening line $(\delta + a + n)k$. At the steady-state $\bar{k}$, output and capital increase at rate $a + n$, while GDP per capita increases at rate a.

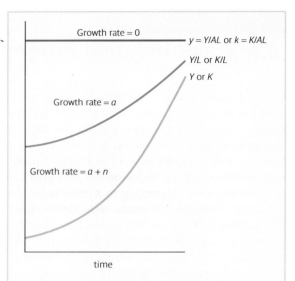

Fig. 3.14 Growth Rates along the Steady State

While output and capital measured in effective labour units (Y/AL and K/AL) are constant in the steady state, output–labour and capital–labour ratios (Y/L and K/L) grow at the rate of technological progress a, and output and the capital stock (Y and K) grow at the rate $a + n$, the sum of the rates of population growth and technological progress.

which nicely matches Kaldor's first and second stylized facts. Finally, we now have an account of the continuous increase in standards of living.

Finally, how is the golden rule affected? Redefining c as the ratio of total consumption to effective labour C/AL, in the steady state the following modified version of (3.7) will hold:

$$\bar{c} = f(\bar{k}) - (\delta + a + n)\bar{k}.$$

Now the golden rule requires that the marginal productivity of capital be the sum of the rates of depreciation, of technological change and of population growth:

(3.14) $$MPK = \delta + a + n.$$

3.6 Putting It All Together: Growth Accounting

In its fully developed form, the Solow model identifies three sources of GDP growth: capital accumulation, population growth, and technological progress. Because of diminishing marginal productivity, capital accumulation alone cannot sustain growth.

Population growth explains GDP growth, but not the continuous increase of standards of living which is so striking in most parts of the world. Technological progress, therefore, is the key to better economic conditions.

Box 3.4 The New Economy: Another Industrial Revolution?

The fantastic changes brought about by innovations in computer technology, and the associated wonders of IT (information technology) such as the internet, wireless telecommunications and conspicuous use of electronic equipment, have led many observers to conclude that a new industrial revolution is upon us, of the dimensions of the fantastic acceleration of growth that started towards the end of the nineteenth century. Figure 3.15 reports estimates of increases in A (multifactor productivity) in the USA, computed as annual averages over four periods. A difference of 1% per year cumulates to 28% after 25 years. The figure shows a formidable acceleration in the period 1913–72, and again over 1995–9, hence the case for a second industrial revolution.

In reviewing this evolution, however, Gordon (2000) notes that what is really extraordinary is the collapse of productivity growth in the period 1972–95. In his view, we are now only recovering from this unusual period of decline, related to the two oil shocks and associated increases in inflation and unemployment. To buttress his case, Gordon lists the great inventions that brought the first industrial revolution—the discovery of electricity, the combustion engine (cars, planes, tools), electronics (including radio, telephones, television),

and sanitation (including the discovery of germs and bacteria)—and claims that computers (already invented in 1950) pale in comparison. Time will tell.

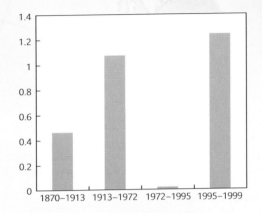

Fig. 3.15 Multifactor Productivity in the USA (average annual growth, %)
The average annual increase in A (multifactor productivity) has accelerated sharply after 1913, came to a near stop over 1972–95, and seems to have vigorously bounced back at the end of the 1990s.

Source: Gordon 2000.

How big is it? Unfortunately, it is very difficult to measure technological progress. Computers, for instance, probably raise growth, but by how much? Some people believe that the 'new economy', borne by the information technology revolution, is going to push standards of living faster than ever; others are sceptical that the effect is any bigger than the other big discoveries which mark economic history. Box 3.4 provides some details on this exciting debate.

One approach to put numbers on technological progress is to start with the things we know and can measure: GDP growth, capital accumulation, and man-hours worked. Going back to (3.11), we can measure Y and two of its inputs, K and L. The remaining input A, sometimes called **multifactor (or total factor) productivity**, has to be inferred or imputed. In practice, once we know how much

GDP has increased, and how much of this increase is explained by capital and hours worked, we can interpret what is left over as the increase in A, i.e. $a = \Delta A/A$. This unexplained part of output growth is called the **Solow residual** and it is computed as follows:

$$\text{Solow residual} = \frac{\Delta Y}{Y} - \text{contributions of capital accumulation and man-hours worked.}$$

The contributions of factor inputs, capital and labour depend on their growth and income shares in GDP.[15]

[15] The formula commonly applied is $\frac{\Delta Y}{Y} = (1 - s_L)\frac{\Delta K}{K} + s_L\frac{\Delta L}{L} +$ residual, where Y is real GDP, s_L is the share of labour in GDP and $(1 - s_L)$ is the share of capital. It uses the assumption, standard in microeconomics, that each factor receives a reward equal to its marginal productivity. See the WebAppendix for more details.

Table 3.3 Growth of Real Gross Fixed Capital Stock, 1913–2001 (% per annum)

	1913–50	1950–73	1973–87	1987–2001
France	1.2	6.4	3.7	3.3
Germany	1.1	7.7	2.7	2.5
Netherlands	2.4	6.9	2.2	2.6
UK	1.6	5.7	2.3	3.9
USA	1.7	3.8	2.6	3.3

Source: Maddison (1991), Marcel P. Timmer, Gerard Ympa, and Bart von Ark, *IT in the European Union: Driving Productivity Divergence*? GGDC Research Memorandum GD-67, University of Groningen, Appendix Tables.

Table 3.4 Population, Employment, and Hours Worked, 1900–2001 (average annual growth rates)

Country	Population	Employment	Hours worked per person
France	0.4	0.2	−0.6
Germany	0.9	1.0	−0.6
Netherlands	1.1	1.4	−0.7
UK	0.4	0.5	−0.5
Japan	1.1	1.0	−0.4
USA	1.3	1.6	−0.5

Source: Maddison (2001), Groningen Growth and Development Centre and the Conference Board, Total Economy Database.

Capital accumulation

Table 3.3 shows that, typically capital has been growing at about 2–2.5% per year over most of the twentieth century in the developed countries. Capital accumulation accelerated sharply in the 1950s and 1960s as part of the post-war reconstruction. Many European countries accumulated capital considerably faster than the USA and the UK up until the mid-1970s; the reason is that continental Europe was poorer at the end of the Second World War. These sustained periods of rapid capital accumulation fit well the description of catch-up, when the capital stock is below its steady-state level.

Labour input

The most appropriate measure of labour input is total number of hours worked. For several reasons,

growth in population or the number of employees does not necessarily translate into increased man-hours. Even if unemployment is ignored, the number of employed people at work differs from the size of the population, and the relationship between employment and hours worked is constantly changing. People live longer, study longer, and retire earlier—or later. At the same time, women have increased their labour force participation over the past three decades.[16] Table 3.4 shows that these effects have roughly cancelled each other out as employment and population size have increased by similar amounts in our sample of developed countries.

[16] Ch. 4 explores these various issues in more detail.

Second, employment and the number of hours worked may grow at different rates. Table 3.4 documents the sharp decline in the number of hours worked per person in the developed world, as people put in shorter days, shorter weeks, and fewer weeks per year. Indeed, the number of man-hours has grown much more slowly than population and employment, even declining in Austria, Belgium, France, and the UK. Overall, European labour input has increased between nil and 0.3%, while immigration lifted it well above 1% in North America and Australia. The dramatic decline in hours worked per person (an average annual reduction of 0.6% per year means a total reduction of 68% over the period 1900–86) is a central feature of the growth process. As societies have become richer, demand for leisure has increased. In the UK, for example, the average number of hours worked per year has declined from 2,725 in 1900 to 1,720 in 1999.

The Solow residual

Table 3.5 presents the Solow decomposition in two different contexts. The first employs historical data collected by Angus Maddison for the period 1913–87. The second examines the same countries over the last two decades. As already suspected, growth in inputs of labour and capital can account for only one-half to two-thirds of total economic growth in these economies. The rest is the Solow residual, and confirms the importance of technological progress. A puzzling observation is the apparent slowdown in technological change during the 1970s and the 1980s, which contrasts with reports of an acceleration since the late 1990s. In the table, only the USA and Germany exhibit higher growth in technical progress (the Solow residual) in the second decade, which is generally thought to be a period associated with technological acceleration.

Table 3.5 The Solow Decomposition

(a) 1913–1987[a] (average annual growth rates)

Country	GDP	Contribution of inputs	Residual
France	2.6	1.1	1.5
Germany	2.8	1.4	1.4
Netherlands	3.0	2.0	1.0
UK	1.9	1.2	0.7
Japan	4.7	3.0	1.7
USA	3.0	2.0	1.0

[a] An adjustment is made to account for the modernization of productive capital.

(b) 1981–1990 (average annual growth rates)

Country	GDP	Contribution of inputs	Residual
France	2.5	1.4	1.1
Germany	2.3	1.7	0.6
Netherlands	2.3	1.3	1.0
UK	2.7	1.4	1.3
Japan	4.1	2.9	1.2
USA	3.2	2.2	1.0

(c) 1991–2000 (average annual growth rates)

Country	GDP	Contribution of inputs	Residual
France	2.1	1.4	0.7
Germany	1.9	0.8	1.1
Netherlands	2.9	2.2	0.7
UK	2.3	1.4	0.9
Japan	1.5	1.4	0.1
USA	3.2	2.1	1.1

Source: Authors' calculation from data in Maddison (1991) and OECD, *Economic Outlook*.

3.7 Endogenous Growth: A Primer

According to the Solow growth model, technological change is the engine that pushes the output–labour ratio—or GDP per capita—ever higher. But what generates technological change? So far, we have assumed that it is exogenous, rising at a rate a. Is it as simple as that? Could it not be that technological progress itself is driven by man-made decisions? For example, technological progress seems likely to depend on investment in education and science, on research and development (R&D), and on millions of discoveries, small and large. Opening up this box makes the rate of growth endogenous. This is the exciting task assigned to Chapter 18. Here, for the sake of completeness, we briefly sketch the theory of **endogenous growth**, leaving out most of the substantial issues for later.

In a nutshell, the Solow growth model predicts that the capital–output ratio will converge to a value in the steady state which is predetermined by the economy's characteristics. The principle of declining marginal productivity is responsible for this result, as represented in Figure 3.13 by the flattening of the aggregate production function schedule. As the stock capital in an economy increases, the marginal output and income that additional investment yields will fall. As income falls, savings falls, as does investment: the economy grows less and less.

But if marginal productivity does not decline, the schedule no longer flattens as capital is accumulated. In fact, it becomes a straight line, which is in fact consistent with output increasing at the same rate as new capital is being accumulated. The same property also applies to the saving schedule since savings are a constant proportion of output. Figure 3.16 shows how things change radically. If the capital–labour ratio is initially at k_1, investment corresponds to point A and the ratio of capital to effective labour ratio $k = K/AL$ increases by the distance AB. As this ratio grows to reach the level k_2, saving is determined by point C and the capital–effective labour ratio keeps rising even faster as indicated by the distance CD. There is no end to this process.

What is happening? Because the marginal productivity of capital does not decline, more of it produces more income and therefore more saving. Growth of the income-effective labour and capital-effective labour ratios never ends.[17] This contrasts sharply with the case of declining marginal productivity, in which a unique steady state is always reached with $y = K/AL$ constant and GDP per capita Y/L grows at constant rate a. Now y itself is rising

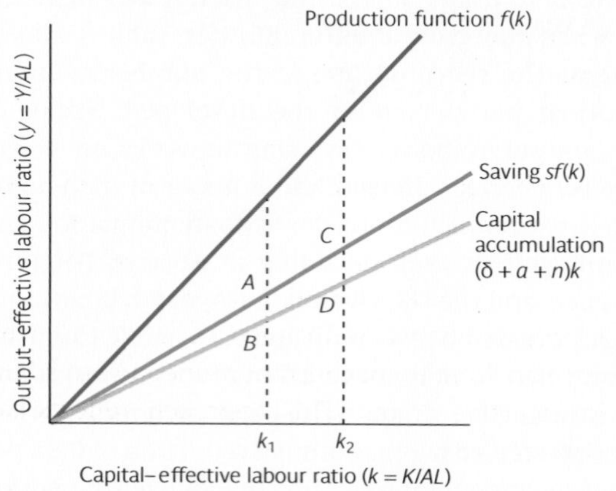

Fig. 3.16 Endogenous Growth with Non-Declining Marginal Productivity

Here we look at the case of constant marginal productivity of capital: the production function is now represented by a straight line. If saving is large enough to exceed depreciation and the need for capital widening, the capital stock will increase without bound. For example, starting from k_1, AB represents new capital being installed, which takes the economy to k_2. There CD corresponds to a further increase in the capital stock. And so on.

secularly, and Y/L rises even faster.[18] Another implication of non-declining marginal productivity of capital is that an increase in the saving rate makes the saving schedule rotate upward, leading to faster accumulation of the capital stock and permanent growth in GDP per capita.

We have thus found an example in which growth can be determined endogenously. In the absence of diminishing returns, policies which accelerate growth become feasible, because these effects are permanent. Among other things, it may pay handsomely to subsidize education, research, and development, other innovative activities, and even certain types of investment spending. This and related aspects of economic growth are the subject of Chapter 18.

---

[17] Formally, if the production function in intensive form is $y = Ak$, then $\Delta k = sAk - (\delta + a + n)k$, which implies a permanent growth rate of k given by $\Delta k/k = sA - (\delta + a + n)k$.

[18] Note that in this case we need the saving line to be above the capital accumulation line. If the configuration were the opposite, the capital–effective labour ratio would instead shrink to zero over time.

❶ Summary

1 Economic growth refers to the steady expansion of GDP over a period of a decade or longer periods. Growth theory is concerned with the study of economic growth in the steady state, a situation in which output and capital grow at the same pace and remain in constant proportion to labour in effective terms. This approach reflects key stylized facts.

2 The aggregate production function shows that output grows when more inputs (capital and labour) are used, and when technological progress increases the effectiveness of those inputs.

3 The capital stock, the sum of productive equipment and structures, is accumulated through investment, and investment is financed by savings. When savings are a stable proportion of output, the steady-state capital stock is determined by the net effect of savings and capital depreciation. The assumption that the marginal productivity of capital is declining implies that output, and therefore savings, grow less than proportionately to the stock of capital, in contrast to depreciation, which rises in proportion to capital. Eventually, the size of the capital stock exhausts the potential of savings to raise it further.

4 In the absence of population growth and technological change, the steady state is characterized by zero output and capital growth. Adding population growth provides a first explanation of secular output growth, but standards of living —measured as output per capita—still do not increase. It is only when we allow for technological progress that permanent growth in per capita output and capital is possible.

5 Savings represent deferred consumption: less is consumed today, but the capital stock will increase in the future, which will raise income and consumption. The golden rule looks for the situation in which consumption in the steady state is as high as possible. In the complete Solow model, it occurs where the marginal productivity of capital is equal to the rate of depreciation (replacing worn out capital) plus the rate of population growth (providing new workers with equipment) plus the rate of technological change (adjusting capital to enhanced labour effectiveness): $MPK = \delta + n + a$.

6 An economy is dynamically efficient when steady-state consumption can be raised in the future only at the expense of lower consumption today. An economy is dynamically inefficient when both current and future steady-state consumption can both be raised. In the former case, the capital stock is lower than the golden-rule level, calling for additional accumulation. In the latter case, the capital stock is above the golden-rule level.

7 In the Solow model, saving does not affect the steady-state growth rate, but only the level of output per capita.

8 Removing the assumption of diminishing marginal productivity allows output to grow forever, even in the absence of population growth and technological change. It implies that changes in saving and/or productivity can have permanent growth-enhancing effects. This is the basis for the theory of endogenous growth.

🔑 Key Concepts

- economic growth
- technological progress
- Solow growth model
- stylized facts
- steady state
- capital accumulation
- aggregate production function
- diminishing marginal productivity
- returns to scale (constant, increasing, decreasing)
- output–labour ratio
- capital–labour ratio

- depreciate, depreciation rate
- depreciation line
- golden rule
- dynamic inefficiency, dynamically efficient
- capital widening line
- effective labour
- Solow decomposition
- Solow residual
- multifactor (or total factor) productivity
- endogenous growth

❓ Exercises

1 Draw production functions $f(k)$ with decreasing, constant, and increasing returns to scale.

2 Discuss what a steady state is in the context of the Solow growth model. Is it a useful concept? Why do you think stylized facts are necessary to organize the discussion of economic growth?

3 Suppose K/Y is constant at 2. (a) Assume first that there is no population growth and no techno-logical progress. What is the steady-state saving–output ratio consistent with a rate of depreciation of 5%? (b) Now allow for population growth and technological progress. What is the steady-state saving–output ratio consistent with a rate of depreciation of 5% and 3% real growth?

4 Consider a country with zero technological progress and $K/L = 3$. Its population grows at the rate of 2% per year. What is the steady-state rate

of growth of its GDP per capita if the saving rate is 20%? If it is 30%? How do your answers change if depreciation occurs at a rate of 0.05% per year?

5 Suppose the aggregate production function is given by $Y = \sqrt{KL}$. Does it have increasing, decreasing, or constant returns to scale? Are the marginal products of capital and labour declining?

6 Why is the golden rule in Figure 3.7 achieved at $\bar{k}'$? To establish this result, imagine that you start to the left of $\bar{k}'$ and explain why moving to the right increases consumption. Similarly show that consumption decreases when moving rightwards from a position to the right of $\bar{k}'$.

7 The golden rule (3.14) is MPK $= \delta + a + n$. In comparison with the no-technological change case, we now require a higher marginal

productivity of capital. With diminishing marginal productivity, this means a lower capital stock per effective unit of labour. Is that not surprising? How can you explain this apparent paradox?

8 How can the Solow model explain that nowadays workers use a vast array of highly efficient equipment such as powerful machinery or computers?

9 Draw a graph showing the evolution of Y/L in the catch-up phase and then in the ensuing steady state when the economy starts from a capital–effective labour ratio below its steady-state level. Draw a picture showing investment (not the capital stock).

10 Why is the proper measure of technological progress the rate of increase of the Solow residual, and not labour or capital productivity?

⊙ Essay Questions

1 Japan in the 1960s, Korea in the 1980s, China in the 1990s, and many other countries have undergone a period of rapid growth, in effect catching up on the richer and more developed countries. How can you explain this phenomenon, and why did it not happen earlier?

2 Many wars and colonial expeditions were launched to increase a country's land and population. Can wars indeed make a victorious country richer?

3 'Outsourcing is the normal evolution for a country that is reaching non-increasing returns.' Comment.

4 Examining the panels of Figure 3.5, one immediately notices that African countries are bunched in the lower left-hand part of the diagram, while the European countries are clustered in the upper right-hand region. What explanation of this fact is offered by the Solow growth model? Do you think this is a sufficient explanation? Explain.

5 As countries become richer, they produce less goods and more services. How can you explain this?

Labour Markets and Unemployment

4

4.1 Overview *72*

4.2 Demand and Supply in the Labour Market *73*
- 4.2.1 Labour Supply and the Consumption–Leisure Trade-off *73*
- 4.2.2 Labour Demand, Productivity, and Real Wages *76*
- 4.2.3 Labour Market Equilibrium *78*
- 4.2.4 The Interpretation of Unemployment *80*

4.3 A Static Interpretation of Unemployment *82*
- 4.3.1 Involuntary Unemployment and Real Wage Adjustment *83*
- 4.3.2 Collective Bargaining and Real Wage Rigidity *83*
- 4.3.3 Social Minima and Real Wage Rigidity *87*
- 4.3.4 Efficiency Wages and Real Wage Rigidity *88*

4.4 A Dynamic Interpretation of Unemployment *90*
- 4.4.1 Labour Market States and Transitions *90*
- 4.4.2 Stocks, Flows, and Frictional Unemployment *90*
- 4.4.3 Job Finding and the Duration of Unemployment *92*

4.5 The Equilibrium Rate of Unemployment *94*
- 4.5.1 The Concept *94*
- 4.5.2 The European Experience *95*
- 4.5.3 Actual and Equilibrium Unemployment *95*

Summary *97*

Labour is the source of all value.

—Karl Marx[1]

In our present day complicated economic life we are likely to be confused by the many industrial operations and money transactions. But net income remains exactly what it was to primitive Robinson Crusoe on his island—the enjoyment from eating the berries we pick, so to speak, less the discomfort or the labour of picking them.

—Irving Fisher[2]

4.1 Overview

In the last chapter, output was shown to be a function of an economy's **endowment** of factors of production—its capital and labour—as well as its technical sophistication. The evolution of the capital stock and of technology were examined in some detail, but the supply of labour was simply taken as given, regardless of the wage or other variables. Even in storybooks, life is not so simple. In the famous novel by Daniel Defoe, the shipwrecked castaway Robinson Crusoe was blessed with a stock of capital (coconut trees) to produce output (coconuts), but needed to expend time and effort to gather and transport the fruits that he would eventually consume. Like most people, Crusoe had to choose whether or not he would work, and how much effort he would put into it. Presumably, the rewards to work played a role in his decision. And the decision how much to work determined how many coconuts in the end could be harvested.

Thus, while Karl Marx may be out of favour these days, he was certainly right to see labour as the most important factor of production. Virtually everything stems directly or indirectly from labour. Raw materials are brought forth from the earth by human hands; equipment used in this and other forms of economic activity is made using labour and previously manufactured equipment, itself the output of labourers and capital in a more distant past. Even the knowledge embodied in people—human capital—comes from our own efforts at mastering skills and techniques, as well as the time our teachers spent trying to educate us.

In order to introduce the labour market into the macroeconomy, we study the decisions of households and firms to supply and demand hours of work. Households work so that they can consume, but they also want to spend some of their time not working and enjoying **leisure** or free time. The supply of labour is seen as a trade-off between consumption and leisure. At the same time, someone must be willing to employ and pay for the hours of work that workers want to supply at the going wage; labour must also be demanded. For firms to demand labour, it must have some value to them in production. How the markets value labour and how demand and supply interact is the subject matter of this chapter. Most importantly, we will learn how **unemployment** emerges—when labour goes unutilized in an economy.

We begin by studying the behaviour of the supplier of labour—a representative household that can choose its working time. Next, we look at demand

---

[1] Karl Marx (1818–83) was a German economist and political philosopher whose theories predicted the immiseration of the working class and the ultimate crisis and collapse of market (capitalist) economies. Although he clearly got all that wrong, his empirical observations on the plight of the working class and his focus on issues relating to product and labour markets—and his influence on the lives of millions of people who lived and worked under communism and socialism—earn him a central place in the history of economic thought.

[2] Irving Fisher (1867–1947) was an American economist who is often described as one of the greatest mathematical economists of all time. Among other subjects, he contributed to the theory of investment, capital, and interest rates; monetary economics and the theory of inflation; and most notably to the theory and practice of price index numbers. He was founder and first president of the Econometric Society.

for labour by a representative firm. This naturally leads to the standard confrontation of demand and supply. Yet we will see that labour is not a standard 'commodity'. Workers are not identical, and the quality of labour services is difficult to ascertain and harder to monitor. Unlike machines or raw materials, workers can decide whether they would like to work for a particular employer and under which conditions to sell their labour services. In fact, the employment relationship involves explicit and implicit contractual arrangements which are highly specific to both firm and employee. The functioning of labour markets is also influenced by country-specific institutions, such as labour law or collective bargaining, and is the object of complex legal and customary rules. Finally, the labour market is a dynamic market, with suppliers of labour entering and exiting unemployment at a remarkable rate. We show how these interactions help us to understand the concept of equilibrium unemployment, which may differ from actual unemployment observed at a particular point in time.

4.2 Demand and Supply in the Labour Market

4.2.1 Labour Supply and the Consumption–Leisure Trade-off

In modern societies, consuming requires income. Earning income most often means working, or supplying labour to firms in return for a wage or salary.[3] But labour has a cost, too: every hour of work means an hour less of free time. Because households value both consumption and leisure, they balance the two the best they can, given the possibilities available to them. This trade-off is known as the **consumption–leisure trade-off**. In a parable which should be familiar, we consider the choice of Robinson Crusoe, who was forced to make do with the limited resources of his island.[4]

We see Crusoe as consuming all that he earns from work, the coconuts that he picks up, leaving aside issues related to saving and investment. These will be treated in detail in Chapters 5 and 6. Crusoe's preferences with regard to consumption and leisure are summarized by indifference curves

in Figure 4.1. Each indifference curve shows combinations of consumption and leisure which make Crusoe equally happy. Higher indifference curves correspond to higher levels of utility or happiness. The steepness of each curve at any given point shows how readily Crusoe substitutes consumption for leisure, holding his level of satisfaction constant. The shape of Crusoe's indifference curves tells us that the greater his consumption relative to his

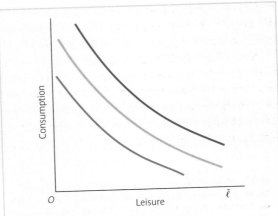

Fig. 4.1 Household Preferences

An indifference curve shows how readily a household is willing to substitute consumption C for leisure ℓ, holding its level of satisfaction or utility constant. Curves further out from the origin correspond to higher levels of utility.

---

3 Here 'firms' are understood in a broadest sense, including public as well as private enterprises, national, regional, and local governments, or even oneself, in the case of self-employment. In what follows we will focus on firms which strive to maximize profits, or the income which remains after costs (including labour) are subtracted.

4 The use of this character, based on the classic novel by Daniel Defoe (1660–1731), is traditional in economics and will be seen again in Chs. 5 and 6, in which goods are distinguished by the point in time that they are consumed.

leisure, the more of that consumption he is willing to give up for an additional unit of leisure, or the higher is the **marginal rate of substitution** of consumption for leisure. It is an important principle in economics that the more scarce a good becomes relative to others, the more of those other goods one is willing to give up for it.

Crusoe is limited by natural circumstances in the total amount of time, denoted $\bar{\ell}$, available over any given period (a day, a month, a year, or more). All scarce resources have a price, and time is no exception. The price of an hour of leisure is its opportunity cost: how much could one otherwise earn in that hour by working in the market? For this reason, the price of leisure is called the **real (consumption) wage**. In practice, it is measured as the ratio of nominal wages (W) to the consumer price index (P). With $\bar{\ell}$ hours at his disposal and facing an hourly real wage $w = W/P$, the value of Crusoe's total time endowment valued in terms of consumption is $\bar{\ell}w$. This endowment can be allocated between C units of consumption and ℓ hours of leisure, with value ℓw, according to the following equation:[5]

(4.1) $$\bar{\ell}w = \ell w + C.$$

Equation (4.1) can be thought of as a time budget line, since it stipulates various combinations of leisure and consumption which are possible without additional resources.[6] It is depicted in Figure 4.2 as the negatively sloped line AB. The horizontal distance OA is equal to $\bar{\ell}$, Crusoe's endowment of time, or the fixed number of hours at his disposal. The distance OB measures the value of that endowment in terms of consumption goods. It is the total amount of consumption attainable when leisure is zero—when Crusoe is working all the time.[7]

The negative slope of the budget line ($-w$) measures the trade-off of consumption for leisure offered by the market: how much consumption must be given up to get an additional unit of leisure, or how much consumption can be 'purchased' with an additional hour of work. It explains why the real wage is often referred to as the **relative price** of leisure in terms of consumption. If the real wage changes, the budget line rotates around point A, which measures his fixed time endowment $\bar{\ell}$.

Optimal choice and the individual labour supply schedule

Crusoe maximizes his utility by choosing the highest possible indifference curve without violating his budget line. This is achieved at point R in Figure 4.2, where the indifference curve is tangent to the budget line. At this point, the marginal rate of substitution of consumption for leisure is equal to the market wage w. Given the terms of trade offered by the market, he cannot make himself any better off (reach a higher indifference curve) by further swapping leisure for consumption. This property is a defining characteristic of an optimum.

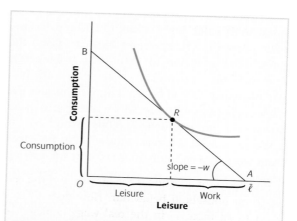

Fig. 4.2 The Household Budget Line and Optimal Choice

The household has a total of $\bar{\ell}$ hours at its disposal (measured by the distance OA) for either leisure or work. For every unit of leisure that it gives up, it can earn w consumption goods. The real wage w determines the slope of the budget line AB. Given the budget line, the highest possible utility is achieved at point R, where an indifference curve is tangent to the budget line.

---

[5] The nominal budget constraint is $\bar{\ell}W = \ell W + PC$. To write it in terms of consumption goods as in (4.1), we simply divide by P, the price of consumption goods.

[6] Alternatively, the budget constraint can be expressed in terms of 'cash flow': when Crusoe takes ℓ hours of leisure, he works $\bar{\ell} - \ell$ hours and earns $w(\bar{\ell} - \ell)$ coconuts. Since Crusoe does not save, this income $w(\bar{\ell} - \ell)$ is spent on consumption; so $w(\bar{\ell} - \ell) = C$, which is simply a rearranged version of equation (4.1).

[7] If Crusoe possessed some initial wealth to begin with, the budget line would be shifted upwards (vertically) by that amount. This represents the consumption he could attain without having to work at all.

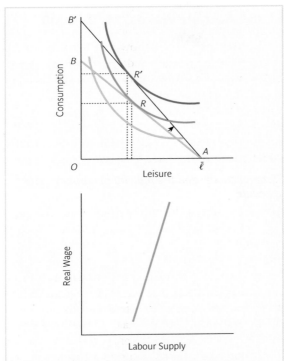

Fig. 4.3 Reaction of the Household to a Wage Increase: Labour Supply

When the real wage increases, the budget line rotates around point *A* (the endowment of time remains unchanged) and becomes steeper, because a unit of leisure is exchanged for more units of consumption. This allows both consumption and leisure to increase at the same time (income effect). Because leisure is more expensive, however, some is given up (substitution effect). In the case depicted here, the substitution effect dominates.

An important question is the influence of the real wage on household behaviour. How does Crusoe react to an increase in the real wage depicted in the left panel of Figure 4.3? At any level of leisure and labour supplied, a higher wage increases the amount of consumption that can be afforded (i.e. *OB* increases) and the budget line rotates clockwise. This change has two effects. First, the relative attractiveness of leisure declines, since its relative price has risen. This alone would encourage Crusoe to take less leisure, work harder, and consume more. This is the **substitution effect**. At the same time, Crusoe's labour is better paid so that, holding leisure constant, he earns and consumes more. His reaction to this increase in income should be to work a bit less and enjoy both more consumption and more leisure. This incentive to work less in response to a wage increase is called the **income effect**.

So, will he work more (substitution) or less (income)? This question cannot be answered unambiguously without knowing more about Crusoe's preferences. In Figure 4.3, the substitution effect dominates, so the net effect is positive: an increase in the wage leads to a decline in leisure and an increase in labour supply. This is depicted in the second panel of Figure 4.3 as an upward-sloping **household labour supply curve**.

In practice, the response to rising wages varies widely across individuals, depending on tastes, family circumstances, age, etc. It also depends on the time horizon under consideration.[8] In the short run, most individuals do not seem to react much to changes in the real wage. In the long run, the labour supply decreases as the income effect dominates. Indeed, Table 4.1 shows that, over the last 100 years, real wages have increased five- to fifteen-fold, while working hours have declined by one-half. Labour supply behaviour also varies according to sex. For men, the average work-week, the retirement age, and the **labour force participation rate** have fallen secularly since 1900.[9] In contrast, labour force participation and hours per week of women have risen. One possible interpretation is that the income effect of higher wages dominates for men, whereas the substitution effect dominates for women. Another interpretation is that customs and sociological factors change, and that services such as child care and schooling have made it possible for more women to take up paid jobs.

The aggregate labour supply curve

We have studied a representative household's decision to work. The next step economists usually take is to add up the supplies of individual households

---

8 The reader is invited to look at the WebAppendix for details.
9 The labour force participation rate is defined as the proportion of working-age people either working or registered as unemployed.

Table 4.1 Annual Total Hours Worked and Average Wages, 1870 – 2000

	1870	1913	1938	1973	1992	2000
Annual hours worked per person						
France	2,945	2,588	1,848	1,771	1,542	1,517
Germany	2,941	2,584	2,316	1,804	1,563	1,469
UK	2,984	2,624	2,267	1,688	1,491	1,491
USA	2,964	2,605	2,062	1,717	1,589	1,660
Sweden	2,945	2,588	2,204	1,571	1,515	1,588
Real Wage (index: 1870 = 100)						
France	100	205	335	1,048	1,417	1,434
Germany	100	185	285	944	1,178	1,222
UK	100	157	256	439	640	733
USA	100	189	325	596	659	737
Sweden	100	270	521	1,228	1,493	1,727

Source: Hours worked are from Maddison (1991) for years 1870 – 1992 and from Groningen Growth and Development Centre and The Conference Board, Total Economy Database for the year 2000; wages are from Mitchell (1978, 1983), and OECD, *Main Economic Indicators* and *Economic Outlook*; German wage data 1913 – 38 are approximated using average labour productivity growth.

across the economy, while noting the special aspects of labour and labour markets. In many instances, individuals cannot vary the hours of work that they supply; at best, they can choose between working or not working at all. Most labour contracts specify a standard working time (length of the work week, days of holiday leave per year). It is a matter of 'take it or leave it'. Sometimes workers are better off not working at all. In cases such as these, small wage increases may not be sufficient to motivate households to take up jobs, although large ones might.[10] In any case, the aggregate labour supply remains the sum of many individual decisions (to work or not work, and how many hours to work). While individual labour supply is measured in hours during some period of time (for example, per year as in Table 4.1), aggregate supply is measured in **man-hours**, the total amount of hours supplied by all workers during that same period (men and women, of course).[11] When wages rise, even if those who

already work do not modify their supply of labour (the benchmark case), others who had preferred not to work may now decide to join the labour force. Figure 4.4 shows how it is then possible for a steep or even vertical (inelastic) individual supply curve to coexist with a flatter aggregate supply curve.

4.2.2 Labour Demand, Productivity, and Real Wages

Labour demand and the extended production function

Firms use both capital and labour to produce goods and services. As discussed in Chapter 3, the capital stock at any particular point in time is best thought of as given; from month to month firms vary their

---

[10] These important cases are taken up in detail in Chs. 14 and 17.

[11] Aggregate employment is sometimes measured as the number of people who have a job. Generally, we will use the first definition (man-hours), and make explicit mention when referring to the number of employed workers. Under any definition, when more workers enter the labour force, the labour supply curve shifts to the right independently of the wage level.

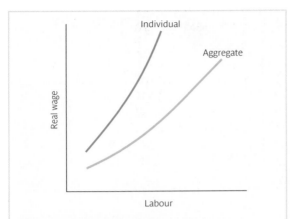

Fig. 4.4 Individual and Aggregate Labour Supply

The aggregate labour supply curve is less steep than that of individual households for two important reasons. First it represents the summation of a great number of upwardly sloped individual supply curves. Second, new workers choose to enter the labour force as wages rise.

the production function measures the **marginal productivity of labour** (MPL), the quantity of additional output which results from one more unit of labour input (an hour). The shape of the curve reflects the principle of decreasing marginal productivity: all else held constant, the MPL in a representative firm is declining as the amount of labour employed increases.

In deciding how much labour to employ, the representative firm seeks the highest possible profit given the cost of labour, the real hourly wage w. The capital stock is assumed fixed. The line OR represents the total cost of labour to the firm at different levels of employment. Because L hours of work cost wL, its slope is w. For each level of employment, profit is measured as the vertical distance between the curve depicting the production function and the labour cost line OR. Profit is at a maximum at point A, where the production function is parallel to OR. At this point, the MPL, the slope of the production function, is equal to the real wage, the slope of OR. If the MPL exceeds the real wage, hiring one more hour of work raises revenues by MPL and raises costs only by w, implying an increase in profits. The firm would therefore hire the extra hour, and will continue to hire extra hours until the MPL has

output by adjusting employment of labour (man-hours). The link between output Y and employment L holding capital constant is captured by the production function shown in Figure 4.5. The slope of

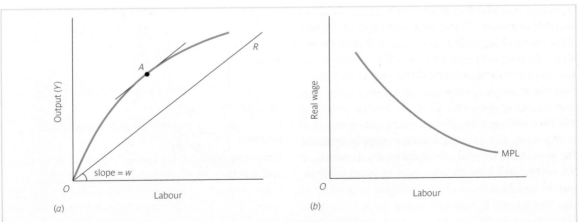

Fig. 4.5 The Production Function and the Labour Demand Curve

When labour input increases, output increases, but at a declining rate. This additional output is the marginal productivity of labour (MPL). In panel (a), the ray OR represents the labour cost of producing when the hourly real wage is w. The vertical distance between the production function and the cost line represents the firm's profit. The firm maximizes its profit at point A, where the curve is parallel to OR, i.e. where MPL = w. Its demand for labour is given in panel (b) by the declining marginal product of labour (MPL) curve.

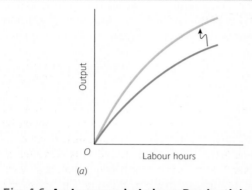
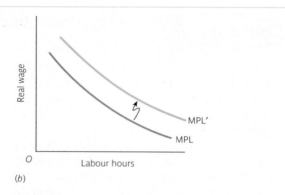

(a)   (b)

Fig. 4.6 An Increase in Labour Productivity
Labour can become more productive either because more capital is put in place, or because technological progress makes labour more productive using the existing stock of equipment. In panel (a), at any level of labour input, more output is produced and the production function is everywhere steeper. The MPL increases and the demand for labour schedule shifts up in panel (b).

declined to the point where it is equal to the real wage. In the opposite case, in which the real wage exceeds the MPL, the firm can increase its profit by reducing its demand for labour. Because it is optimal to set labour such that MPL = w, the MPL schedule in panel (b) of Figure 4.5 is also the firm's **labour demand curve**.

Shifts in the demand for labour

We now consider reasons for the labour demand curve to shift—to change position. One possible reason is an increase in the capital stock K, which until now was assumed constant. Panel (a) of Figure 4.6 shows that this raises MPL—the production function becomes steeper at every level of production. The labour demand curve shifts out in panel (b). Another shifter of labour demand is a technological improvement that makes labour more productive at any given level of input, yielding a similar effect. This helps account for the fact that wages have grown secularly over time. Similarly, a decline in the capital stock, brought about by war, natural disasters, or technical obsolescence, will cause the labour demand curve to shift inwards, i.e. down and to the left. In the case of labour-saving technical change, it is possible for labour demand to decline, even as total output is increasing. Box 4.1 explains the important phenomenon of technical change in more detail.

4.2.3 Labour Market Equilibrium

We now have the building blocks for understanding the labour market: a supply curve derived from household behaviour, and a demand curve derived from firm behaviour. The interaction of supply and demand for labour is depicted in Figure 4.7.

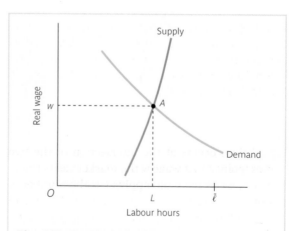

Fig. 4.7 Equilibrium in the Labour Market
Labour market equilibrium occurs at point A where demand and supply are equal. The real wage w clears the market at employment level L. Since total labour endowment is given by $\bar{\ell}$, the distance $(\bar{\ell} - L)$ is voluntary unemployment.

Box 4.1 Technical Change and Unemployment

What is the effect of technological progress on jobs? It is often claimed that technology destroys jobs by making people less important for the production of goods and services. Don't computers reduce the need for secretaries? Isn't the internet replacing mail and jobs in the post office? It would be hard to deny that technological advances kill some jobs, and even whole professions. From the dawn of the industrial revolution in the early nineteenth century, the Luddites in Britain or the 'soyeux' in France agitated against mechanized weaving machines and went as far as to incite mobs to destroy them in large numbers. And indeed, weaving cloth by hand has disappeared as a trade, as have many other technically backward activities. Nevertheless, overall productivity of labour has increased roughly tenfold in the nations of Western Europe in the past 120 years, and if anything, unemployment is somewhat lower now than it was a century and a half ago, so the story must be more complicated than simply technology killing jobs. Technological progress does mean that more can be produced with fewer man-hours, i.e. labour productivity (Y/L) rises. Yet employment L must not necessarily decline, because output Y can, and usually does rise as a result. And if output rises as fast as labour productivity, employment must have increased (since $L = Y/(Y/L)$). In the end, the key question is: how are increases in labour productivity split between Y and L? A correct answer requires much more knowledge about the macroeconomy, in order to trace everything that affects the net outcome. That is the task of macroeconomics.

We note first that higher productivity of labour leads to higher real wages w. For demand for labour to decline and unemployment in the aggregate to rise, it is usually the case that real wage rises faster than productivity. In fact, there are two good reasons why the effect should be one for one: first, it implies a constant share of labour in income (wL/Y), one of the stylized facts presented in Chapter 3. At the same time, labour supply is at work. Table 4.1 suggests that over the long haul, increasing wages leads to a voluntary decline in hours supplied by individuals. But this still does not tell us what happens to the number of people at work, since L is measured in man-hours: if hours worked per person decline, there is no need for employment to decline. This is indeed what has happened.

So what about the disappearance of some jobs, and the decline of whole regions? Here we face the 'fallacy of composition': what applies to a particular industry will generally not apply to the economy as a whole. The demand for secretaries may have fallen, but who builds and maintains the computers that make secretaries redundant? New jobs replace old jobs. Of course, these are not the same people. At the aggregate level, old skills are replaced by new skills, but some individuals must be retrained, which takes time, and some are sidelined. That some people become unemployed does not mean that total employment declines. Economic progress may be painful for some, but it is by no means a systematic job-killer. And it is the most important way of bringing about increases in the standards of living.

Equilibrium occurs at the intersection of the two curves (point A). At wage w the market clears (there is no excess demand or supply): L is the number of hours firms want to hire and households want to work. Both the real wage rate and employment are endogenously determined in the labour market.

This simple characterization of the labour market is an important part of an economist's toolkit, and its predictions serve as the benchmark for the rest of the chapter. Figure 4.8 provides two examples of its usefulness. Panel (*a*) shows the outcome of an increase in labour productivity result-

ing from capital accumulation or technological advances. The labour demand curve shifts outward; the supply curve remains unaffected. The result is an unambiguous increase in real wages. In the figure, employment increases, but if the labour supply curve is vertical, employment remains unchanged and labour income wL would rise proportionally with the real wage. If the supply curve is backward bending, employment (man-hours) would even decline, as Table 4.1 suggests has been the case over the past century. The second panel of Figure 4.8 shows that an exogenous increase in the supply of

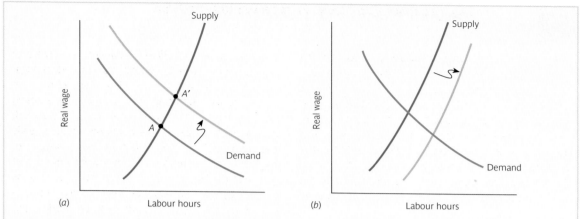

Fig. 4.8 Shifting Labour Demand and Supply

When labour demand increases (panel (a)), for example because of additional capital or technological progress, the real wage and the employment level both increase. When labour supply increases instead (panel (b))—because of new entries into the labour force, for example—employment rises but the real wage declines.

labour leads to an increase in employment, but also to a reduction in real wages.

4.2.4 The Interpretation of Unemployment

While the supply-and-demand apparatus allows us to evaluate the effect of various changes on equilibrium employment and real wages, it is disappointing in one crucial respect. At point A in Figure 4.7, labour supplied is equal to labour demand and denoted by L. Any unemployed labour—literally, labour not employed—reflects the voluntary decisions of households and firms. If total potential labour supply is $\bar{\ell}$, unemployment (measured as hours of work not employed) is simply $\bar{\ell} - L$. Since point A is on the labour supply curve, it reflects the optimal behaviour of households. The standard interpretation of Figure 4.7 is that the equilibrium real wage w is too low to persuade all workers to give up leisure: some may wish to work only part-time, others may not want to work at all. In Figure 4.7, there are no hours which are involuntarily unemployed at the wage w.

It might be disturbing to think that unemployment could be chosen freely. Yet **voluntary unemployment** is an important phenomenon. It is not

only the very wealthy who can afford not to work: those who receive an income from other sources (from a spouse or from the state, for example) may also find that the net wage they can earn does not compensate for lost leisure or non-market activities, including working at home or raising children. Voluntary unemployment is likely to be more widespread among low-skilled people who cannot hope to earn much, or in countries where taxes are so high that working yields little net gain. The most obvious costs are faced by families with children. The high cost of child care—or simply the unavailability of such services—explains why two-earner families are not as common in some countries as in others. Box 4.2 presents more general evidence on how very different patterns of household labour supply can emerge, suggesting that labour market institutions may have a more important role for explaining differences across countries than preferences themselves.

The decision for women to enter and remain in the labour force is of central importance for an economy's productive potential. Table 4.3 displays the labour force participation rate (the proportion of women of working age in the labour force, whether employed or not), the female unemployment rate,

Box 4.2 Market Hours at Work: Europe versus the USA

International comparisons should always be taken with a grain of salt, because data from different countries—especially labour market data—are frequently difficult to compare. Yet often differences are just too large to be measurement error. Table 4.2 compares hours worked per week, on average, per adult of working age (in general, aged 15–65). It is clear that most Europeans spend considerably less time at work than Americans or Britons do, 20–5% less in some cases. Yet there are clearly different trends in the data, reflecting the outcome of changing

Table 4.2 Weekly Hours Worked per capita (all adults of working age)

	1990	2000
Denmark	17.9	18.1
France	15.8	14.9
Germany	—	14.5
Italy	14.1	13.9
The Netherlands	14.6	16.0
Sweden	21.7	20.5
Switzerland	—	19.5[a]
United Kingdom	20.3	19.7
United States	22.2	21.9

[a] 2001.

Source: International Labour Office, authors' calculations.

labour supply at two different margins: a decrease in average hours worked by those already in work as documented in Table 4.1 (the so-called intensive margin), versus a trend of increasing labour supply at the extensive margin (labour force participation). Thus, in Denmark and the Netherlands, weekly hours per capita actually rose from 1990 to 2000, reflecting recent successful reactivation of long-term unemployed and rising entry of women in the labour force. In other countries, such as France, Italy, and Germany, hours per capita continue to decline, as the negative trend in hours worked per employee dominates the participation trend.

Does this mean that continental Europeans are lazy? Despite such striking international differences, underlying economic behaviour is remarkably similar, refuting the laziness hypothesis. Two labour economists, Richard Freeman and Ronald Schettkatt, compared time use by women in US and German households and discovered that the amount of leisure time enjoyed by both was remarkably similar on average—39 and 38 hours per week respectively, which is consistent with a benchmark case of inelastic household labour supply discussed in the text. The most important difference between the two countries was time spent in the market versus home production—that is, unpaid work in the household. Here German women logged 36 hours per week in home production, versus only 27 hours per week for American women. Differences in market opportunities and the net rewards to work are the best candidates for explaining the difference between the two countries.[12]

and the proportion of women of working age actually employed. The variation of these indicators across countries is significant, and points to differences in both cultures and institutions. Female participation in the labour force is very high in countries like Denmark and Sweden, which have

a highly developed and subsidized child care system.

[12] See Freeman and Schettkat (2002). In an exercise, you are asked to explain the different decisions of US and German households by appealing to different rates of labour taxation.

Table 4.3 Female Labour Force Participation Rates, Unemployment Rates, and Employment Ratios, 2002

	Participation rate	Unemployment rate	Employment ratio
Belgium	55.4	7.8	39.3
Canada	71.9	7.1	56.4
Denmark	75.9	4.3	57.6
Finland	72.8	9.1	58.2
France	62.1	10.1	43.6
Germany	55.4	8.3	45.4
Ireland	57.3	3.7	46.9
Japan	59.7	5.1	46.1
Luxembourg	53.5	3.6	41.9
The Netherlands	67.1	3.6	53.2
Norway	76.6	3.7	67.1
Portugal	65.0	6.1	50.7
Spain	53.7	16.4	35.0
Sweden	77.1	4.7	65.0
United Kingdom	69.4	4.4	53.1
United States	70.1	5.6	56.3

Source: OECD.

4.3 A Static Interpretation of Unemployment

Our first attempt at defining unemployment in the last section was somewhat unsatisfactory. Surely, unemployment is more than simply labour withheld voluntarily from the market. The International Labour Organization (ILO) and the Organization for Economic Cooperation and Development (OECD) define an individual as unemployed if he or she does not have a job during the reference period and is actively looking for one and is ready to work. Let us begin anew by defining the **labour force** as the part of the population that is either working (*L*) or unemployed (*U*). The labour force mainly excludes young people in school, the retired, and those who are not looking for work. It corresponds closely to the amount of labour supplied to the market, given current conditions, including the level of real wages. Denoting the labour force as L^S, we can write:

$$\textbf{(4.2)} \quad \underset{\text{labour force}}{L^S} = \underset{\text{employment}}{L} + \underset{\text{unemployment}}{U}.$$

The unemployment rate *u* is then given by the fraction of the labour force which is out of work, or $u = U/L^S$. Perhaps it is now clear why the picture of unemployment in Figure 4.7 is incomplete: according to the ILO definition, it is zero! In the rest of this chapter, we examine alternative reasons for unemployment as well as its implications for the well-being of society.

4.3.1 Involuntary Unemployment and Real Wage Adjustment

One interpretation of unemployment is the failure of markets to clear. Figure 4.9 considers the important case where the real wage is fixed at $\bar{w}$, which is higher than the level which equates supply and demand, w. At $\bar{w}$, firms are willing to hire $\bar{L}$ labour, while workers supply L^S. Since firms cannot be forced to hire more than they wish, actual employment is $\bar{L}$, and $L^S - \bar{L}$ is labour supplied but not demanded by the market. This is **involuntary unemployment**. Involuntary unemployment occurs when an individual is willing and able to work at the wage $\bar{w}$ but cannot find a job, no matter how hard he or she tries. At point B, the marginal product of labour (MPL) exceeds the valuation of leisure time by households which are out of work.

In Figure 4.9, it is the failure of the wage to decline that perpetuates unemployment. If the real wage were to fall to w at point A, demand would increase, supply would decrease, and unemployment would be eliminated at L. This is a key result: the existence of involuntary unemployment must be explained by **real wage rigidity**, which we examine next.

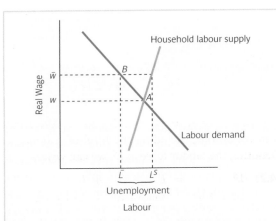

Fig. 4.9 Involuntary Unemployment

At the real wage rate $\bar{w}$ workers supply L^S of labour but firms demand, and hire, only $\bar{L}$. The quantity $L^S - \bar{L}$, which is supplied by households but not demanded by firms, represents involuntary unemployment. If the real wage were to adjust to the level w, the market would clear at point A.

4.3.2 Collective Bargaining and Real Wage Rigidity

For sustained real wage rigidity to occur, involuntarily unemployed workers must be unable to supply their labour services at wages below $\bar{w}$, or firms must be unwilling to take up such offers, or be unable to make their own. What important institutional features of labour markets have been overlooked so far? **Labour (or trade) unions** are one of the most fundamental and universal institutions that operate in modern economies. Unions are employees' organizations which advocate interests of labour in a number of dimensions, most importantly wages. They are matched by often equally powerful **employers' associations**, such as the CBI in the UK, the MEDEF in France, the BDA in Germany, or the SAF in Sweden. Bargaining between employers and unions contrasts sharply with the perfect-competition description of labour markets described in Section 4.2. We need to study the motives of negotiators, and how they impact on wage determination. In doing so, we discover how unemployment can be voluntary from the perspective of trade unions, and nevertheless be involuntary from the viewpoint of the individual household.[13]

The rationale for labour unions

The employer–employee relationship has inherently conflictual aspects. One is the distribution of income; while economic principles assert that income should be split according to marginal productivity, in practice marginal productivity is difficult to measure and economic principles are not always adhered to. Another more subtle reason is that firms need to monitor effort at work, a key element of productivity, which is under the control of each individual employee. Individual workers facing a large employer are in a poor bargaining position. They have little influence over their own wage rate and may not even feel safe discussing working conditions, fearing reprisals in the form of a salary cut or dismissal. They may even feel pressure to accept

---

[13] It should be stressed that we limit ourselves strictly to the economic significance of trade unions. As the history of the labour movement amply demonstrates, unions have had an enormous influence on modern society, which goes beyond economics.

Table 4.4 European Trade Unions: Membership and Coverage, 1950–2000

Country	Structure	Union membership (%)				Union coverage (%)
		1950	1970	1990	2000	2000
Sweden	Umbrella (ILO, TCO, SACO/SR)	67	67	82	86	92
Finland	Umbrella (SAK)	30	51	73	85	97
Denmark	Umbrella (LO)	56	63	75	74	70
Norway	Umbrella (LO, AF, YS)	45	50	56	50	70
Belgium	Party, religious (FGTB, CSC, CGSLB, CNC)	43	42	50	65	90
Ireland	Mostly along occupational/craft lines, umbrella ICTU	42	59	59	n.a.	90
Austria	Umbrella/industrial (ÖGB)	62	57	47	33	96
Italy	Party, religious (CGIL, CISL, UIL)	45	37	39	28	91
United Kingdom	Mostly along occupational/craft lines (96 in TUC, fragmented)	45	50	43	29	30
Germany[a]	Umbrella/industrial (DGB, DAG)	38	32	36	22	82
Portugal	Local and plant-level bargaining; 'social pacts' at national level	—	—	40	32	85
The Netherlands	Party, religious (FNV, CNV, RMHP, AVC)	43	37	24	19	81
Switzerland	Mostly plant level (SGB)	40	30	27	21	46
Greece	Mostly along occupational/craft lines, umbrella GSEE	—	—	34	n.a.	96
Spain	Industrial, company level (CC.OO, UGT, CIGA)	—	—	12	13	87
France	Party, religious (CGT, CFDT, CFTC, GGC, FO)	30	20	14	8	94
Memo: USA	Mostly local plant level (AFL–CIO)	x	x	16	14	14

[a] West Germany until 1990.

Source: Density rates from Ebbinghaus and Visser (2000); EIRO (**www.eiro.eurofound.eu.int/2002/12/study/tn02121202s.html**) and European Commission (2000).

conditions that would not be acceptable under competitive conditions.

Workers organized themselves into unions to help resist such pressures, but especially to achieve higher pay levels and a voice in the day-to-day operation of the workplace. How big and influential are they? As Table 4.4 shows, union organizations vary considerably from country to country. Scandinavian countries have a tradition of centralized unionization; workers in Britain are organized according to craft; France, Italy, and Spain have unions with ties to political parties. These differences reflect social history as well as the costs and benefits associated with union membership. The costs are dues

that members must pay. The benefits vary, ranging from higher wages and protection from arbitrary employer decisions to more specific advantages, including priority for certain jobs and income supplements when unions are on strike. In some countries, many advantages accrue to all workers, so there is little point in paying union dues. This is the case in France, for example.[14] In other countries, such as Belgium and Scandinavia, unions help manage funds that hand out some social benefits,

[14] This is an example of the so-called free-rider problem. If no workers pay dues, the union disappears and no one is protected. So some workers must pay the dues for all to have a union.

Fig. 4.10 Trade Unions' Indifference Curves
When a trade union values both higher wages and more employment, its preferences are described by indifference curves. A 'hard-line' union is not willing to give up much in lower wages to raise employment. A union mainly preoccupied with employment is represented by steep indifference curves.

including unemployment insurance. In the USA, some unions even issue credit cards and provide other financial services to their members. In the end, the influence of unions is usually much stronger than simple membership statistics would suggest, and is partly related to labour laws which institutionalize their role. This is evident from the last column in Table 4.4, which shows the fraction of all workers working under contracts negotiated by unions, whether or not they are union members.

The economics of labour unions

Simplifying somewhat, we can think of two primary economic objectives which motivate unions: higher real wages, and more jobs.[15] It is helpful to think of union preferences in terms of indifference curves shown in Figure 4.10. The slope of the indifference curve represents the willingness of the union leadership to trade off employment for wages. It is flat for 'hard-line' unions which are unwilling to trade wages against employment, steeper for unions which care relatively more about jobs than wages.

[15] Unions care about many other aspects of labour markets, such as safety at work, working time, employees' rights, and influence over working conditions and organization. To simplify the analysis, these aspects are not considered here.

In contrast to Section 4.2, we now describe a labour market in which union indifference curves replace those of the representative individual as the relevant preferences, capturing the fact that the active agent in the labour market is not the individual, but his or her trade union or, more generally, the collective bargaining process. The 'budget line' faced by the union is the demand for labour. From Section 4.2.2 we know that labour demand is given by the MPL (either a firm's MPL, or that of an industry or the entire economy: if firms are all alike, their individual demand does not differ from the collective one represented by an employers' association).

Given the demand for labour that it faces, the optimal choice for the union is the tangency point of the highest indifference curve with the current demand for labour. When the demand for labour shifts, the union's menu of options shifts as well. Capital accumulation or technological progress which shifts out the labour demand curve, for example, will increase the wage that can be paid at a given employment level, or increase the sustainable employment that can be engaged at given wages. Inward shifts of labour demand are also possible, attributable to destruction or obsolescence of the capital stock—e.g. due to wars, earthquakes, the lack of new investment, or new inventions—and have the opposite effect, shrinking available options to the union. As the labour demand schedule shifts, successive tangency points map out the **collective labour supply curve** depicted in Figure 4.11. The curve describes the most desired joint evolution of real wages and employment from the union's viewpoint.

The slope of the collective labour supply curve thus reflects the preferences of the union for employment and wages as well as its economic environment.[16] Union members who are currently employed or who enjoy seniority or job protection tend to fight for a hard-line union: if their influence is high, the slope of the collective labour supply

[16] Note that the collective labour supply curve depends on the successive shifts in the demand for labour that we imagine. Different shifts can change both the position and the slope of the labour demand curve. A number of outcomes are possible; they are described in more detail graphically in the WebAppendix to Chapter 4.

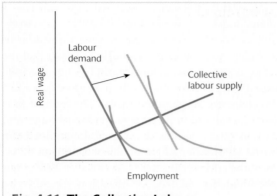

Fig. 4.11 The Collective Labour Supply Curve

The collective labour supply curve is obtained by connecting the points of tangency between the indifference curves and a shifting labour demand schedule.

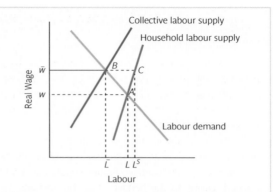

Fig. 4.12 Labour Market Equilibrium with a Trade Union

When a labour union represents workers at wage negotiations, labour market equilibrium occurs at point B. If the union collective labour supply curve is above the individual labour supply curve, the real wage $\bar{w}$ is higher and employment $\bar{L}$ (hours or number of workers) lower than at point A, which would be the outcome if individuals were negotiating individually. The result is the existence of union-voluntary, individual-involuntary unemployment ($L^S - \bar{L}$): it is the difference between actual employment $\bar{L}$ and the amount of work L^S that workers are willing to supply individually at the real wage rate $\bar{w}$ (point C).

curve will be steep. In contrast, a 'jobs-first' union accepts to moderate real wage increases and supply more labour: it will tend to exhibit a flat collective labour supply curve. More details on different possible shapes of the collective labour supply curve are discussed in the WebAppendix.

Employment effects of collective bargaining

The collective labour supply curve resembles the individual supply curve of Figure 4.3, but has different origins. Collectively, through their unions, workers increase their bargaining power and accordingly aim at better outcomes. In particular, for a given amount of labour supplied, they ask for higher real wages: the union-driven collective labour supply curve can only lie above the individual labour supply curves. Without the union's influence on wage setting, equilibrium would occur in Figure 4.12 at point A: individuals would be willing to work up to L at wage w. They cannot, however, because the wage H is set through negotiations between the firms and the trade union, and individuals cannot simply underbid their employed colleagues. Unemployment ($L^S - \bar{L}$) is involuntary for affected individuals, but voluntary from the union's point of view.

Why do unions enforce wage rigidity, apparently against the will of unemployed workers? One reason

is that the leadership is typically elected by the employed, sometimes called the **insiders**. Unemployed workers are almost always a small minority of the membership, even at record high unemployment rates of 10% or even 20%. Furthermore, unemployed workers often give up their membership or lose interest in union affairs. They are called the **outsiders**. Unions end up representing the insiders, who have jobs, not the outsiders, who are unemployed. Employed workers look for high real wages (for themselves) at the cost of some unemployment (for others). Box 4.3 illustrates how the relentless rise of unemployment in Europe after the two oil shocks can be explained by this effect.

The split between unions and unemployed workers cannot go too far, though. Since unemployment increased to high levels in Europe in the 1970s and 1980s, unions have become more employment conscious and real wage growth has moderated. One reason is that members become worried

Box 4.3 The European Unemployment Problem

Two major negative shifts to the demand for labour have occurred during the past thirty years. Both were associated with the sudden oil price increases of the mid-1970s and early 1980s and are called the oil shocks. By all accounts, they corresponded to a significant inward shift of the aggregate labour demand curve. If trade unions react to a smaller membership by demanding higher wages, the collective labour supply curve shifts upward. Owing to the behaviour of the 'insiders' who have jobs, employment prospects for 'outsiders' are reduced. After the oil shocks are absorbed, the employ-ment level is permanently reduced. That such an effect —dubbed the 'hysteresis effect'—has been observed in several European countries is suggested by the step-wise increase in the unemployment rate following each oil shock (Table 4.5). In contrast, unemployment rates in the USA increased at the time of each oil shock but then reverted towards earlier levels. As unemployment rises, pressure to do something does as well; in a number of countries, measures have been taken, as will be seen below.

 Table 4.5 Standardized Unemployment Rates (% of labour force)

	1960–9	1970–9	1980–9	1990–9	2000–3
France	2.0	3.8	9.0	11.2	9.1
Germany	0.8	2.4	6.8	8.0	8.5
Italy	3.8	4.7	8.4	10.7	9.8
Spain	2.5	4.4	17.5	19.6	11.8
Sweden	1.7	2.1	2.5	6.2	5.0
United Kingdom	1.8	3.6	9.5	8.0	5.3
USA	4.8	6.2	7.3	5.8	5.1

Source: OECD *Economic Outlook* Database. Rates are adjusted from national data for comparability.

that they too might become unemployed. A second reason is criticism from the non-unionized component of society. Yet another is that the loss in membership revealed in Table 4.4 has meant lower income for the union from dues as well as less overall influence.

It would be unfair to assert that unions are solely responsible for real wage rigidity. The employers' associations represent the collective interests of firms. They represent an additional mechanism for policing collective bargaining agreements reached with unions. In the end, employers' associations do not control the demand for labour: this is the prerogative of the individual companies. While it is in firms' interest to keep wages low—trade unions were often created to prevent employers from exer-cising rather ruthlessly their power and imposing very low wages—it is also in their interest to keep the wages of their competitors high, or at least to prevent them from hiring cheap labour. In this way, employers' associations can also contribute to real wage rigidity.

4.3.3 Social Minima and Real Wage Rigidity

Beyond trade unions and employers' associations, several other institutional and economic factors can contribute to wage rigidity, and therefore involuntary unemployment. Frequently mentioned in the European context are social minima, or minimum standards for income and earnings mandated by the government for reasons of social equity or protection. One example of social minima are **minimum wages**, which are legal limits below which wages may not fall.

Many countries legislated minimum wages long ago for a variety of reasons. One was to prevent employers with too much market power from depressing wages artificially. Another reason was to protect young people from exploitation. With schooling rudimentary and poverty endemic, for many youngsters on-the-job training was the only way to get started; unscrupulous employers would offer very low wages, sometimes below minimal survival needs. Social protection was and often still is justified. Even in countries without statutory or legal minimum wages, it is frequently the case that collective agreements are extended to uncovered workers, and contract wages assume the characteristics of a legal minimum wage. With occasional exceptions, this is currently the case in Austria, Belgium, Denmark, Finland, Germany, Greece, Italy, Norway, and Sweden.

The primary economic[17] effect of minimum wages is to discourage firms from hiring workers with low MPL, which tend to be the young, the unskilled, those with little training, or those with the wrong skills. Figure 4.13 illustrates the effect of minimum wages. To serve any purpose at all, the minimum wage w_{min} must be higher than the wage $\bar{w}$ that would obtain otherwise, and which is itself higher than what individuals would accept with market clearing (w). The result is unemployment ($L^S_{min} - \bar{L}_{min}$) even higher than the level implied by the wage set in collective bargaining ($L^S - \bar{L}$).

Some evidence on the effect of minimum wages is discussed in Box 4.4. Those most likely to be hurt by the existence of minimum wage legislation are poorly educated young people with no job experience and older workers with obsolete skills. The effect is quite widespread, because, once a floor is set, it pushes up the lower echelons of the wage pyramid, possibly affecting better qualified workers as well. The range of qualifications for which the MPL is below the real wage is wider than just the very lowest echelons.

---

[17] Emphasis is put here on the economic effects of minimum wages. Other important considerations include equity and social norms which reject the existence of 'working poor'.

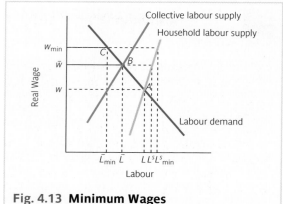

Fig. 4.13 Minimum Wages
Minimum wages reduce the demand for labour below the level that would result with either union-negotiated wages or individual-supplied labour.

4.3.4 Efficiency Wages and Real Wage Rigidity

Another reason why real wages may not decline in the presence of involuntary unemployment is that firms do not wish to lower them. The phenomenon is often called **efficiency wages**, and it is related to another special aspect of labour. In contrast with other factors of production, work effort is not easily observed by firms, and yet it matters a lot. By paying a worker a wage in excess of his marginal productivity, firms may attempt to elicit more work of better quality. A worker who is dismissed for lack of effort is unlikely to obtain such a good deal elsewhere, especially if dismissals are interpreted as a sign of poor work effort. Firms may also pay efficiency wages to obtain a better selection of applicants and to keep workers from quitting too often.

In capital-intensive industries, where shirking could seriously disrupt the production process and where a high-quality workforce is of primary importance, firms may have a strong incentive to pay efficiency wages. In this case, the function of real wages goes beyond simply equilibrating demand and supply in labour markets. Generally, wages will not be able to satisfy both functions, and will tend to be rigid and lie above the market-clearing level, as in Figure 4.12.

Box 4.4 Minimum Wages and Youth Unemployment

It is striking that teenagers in the USA often work during the summer when their European counterparts go on vacation. One reason might be that wages that must be paid for young, unskilled labour are too high in Europe. The US minimum wage amounts to about a third of the average manufacturing wage, while in many European countries it well exceeds 50%. This is one reason why filling station attendants and grocery shop assistants have all but disappeared in most European countries. Table 4.6 shows non-employment and unemployment rates for young people in a number of countries as well as the average minimum wage as a fraction of the average overall wage. In interpreting the table, it is important to note that youth in Denmark younger than 18 receive a deep discount from collectively bargained minimum wage as they do in the USA, while in France, Belgium, and the Netherlands, the minimum wage as a fraction of the median wage is high, meaning that a great many jobs are paid the minimum wage.

In France the minimum wage, called the SMIC (Salaire Minimum Interpersonnel de Croissance), is an important element of the collective bargaining system. It is set by a council on which both the government and unions are represented. Many government employees receive the SMIC. In recent years, 10–15% of workers in industry, commerce, and services earned the SMIC or near it, a much higher proportion than in the USA (about 3%). While the minimum wage in general has a negative effect on youth employment, it may lead to a substitution of adults for youths, at the same time increasing the employment of the former. Recent evidence from Portugal's experience with the minimum wage supports this hypothesis.

Table 4.6 Minimum Wages and Youth Employment and Unemployment, 2000

Country	Minimum wage as a fraction of the average wage	Youth employment – population ratio	Youth unemployment rate (%)
Italy	n.a.	0.26	29.7
France	0.62	0.23	20.7
Australia	0.58	0.61	12.3
Germany	n.a.	0.48	7.7
Ireland	0.56	0.48	6.4
Denmark	n.a.	0.67	6.7
Greece	0.51	0.27	29.5
Sweden	n.a.	0.46	11.9
Belgium	0.49	0.30	15.2
Luxembourg	0.49	0.32	6.4
The Netherlands	0.47	0.68	6.6
UK	0.46	0.55	13.2
Canada	0.42	0.56	12.6
Portugal	0.38	0.42	8.6
USA	0.36	0.60	9.3
Japan	0.33	0.43	9.2
Spain	0.32	0.36	25.5

Source: Neumark and Wascher (2003).

4.4 A Dynamic Interpretation of Unemployment

4.4.1 Labour Market States and Transitions

Any person in the working-age population is either employed, unemployed, or out of the labour force. Figure 4.14 displays these three states and how flows occur between them. A striking aspect of labour markets in developed economies is the sheer size of these flows. Table 4.7 shows that the flow of individuals moving into and out of unemployment per year is a multiple of the stock of unemployment at any given time. In contrast to the static picture painted in Section 4.3, labour markets are remarkably dynamic, even when unemployment is stuck at high levels.

There are three ways of becoming unemployed. First, new entrants to the labour market may join the labour force before they have found work, but are unsuccessful, at least initially. Second, **separations** of workers from jobs may lead to unemployment. Voluntary separations from the employee's viewpoint (called quits) account for roughly 50% to 66% of all separations from employment in the UK, and up to 70% in the USA. Yet quits rarely lead to unemployment: most workers who quit take up another job immediately (transition from employment to

employment). Most of those who quit but do not start a new job leave the labour force, usually for family reasons (maternity leave for example), return to school, retirement, etc. Finally, job losers—those who are involuntarily separated—tend to flow into unemployment. Job loss may occur when short-term contracts expire (common in France and Spain), factories close or relocate, or because of unanticipated redundancies or lay-offs (more common in Denmark, the UK, and the USA).

4.4.2 Stocks, Flows, and Frictional Unemployment

No two positions and no two persons are the same. Pairing a worker and an unfilled job opening or vacancy is not always easy and may take time. The matching of skills, occupation, industry, and geographical location requires a large amount of information. The more efficient the labour markets are, the faster the match is achieved. In the meantime, **frictional unemployment** occurs. This is an unavoidable result of the dynamics of labour force movements, and the normal process of job creation and destruction.

In addition to the efficiency of the job-matching process, frictional unemployment depends on the

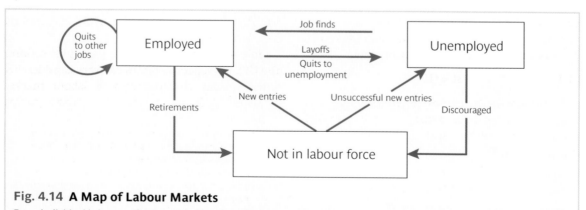

Fig. 4.14 A Map of Labour Markets

Every individual is in one of three states: employed, unemployed, or out of the labour force. Over any period of time, large numbers of workers are flowing from one state to another.

Table 4.7 **Unemployment: Average Stocks and Annual Flows in 2002**

	Unemployment stock, (annual average, millions of persons)	Unemployment flows:	
		Inflows (millions of cases per year)	Outflows (millions of cases per year)
Germany	4.06	7.41	7.20
Austria	0.23	0.82	0.88
UK	0.96	2.80	2.81
France	2.26	4.68	4.26
USA	8.19	37.5	36.9

Sources: Bundesanstalt für Arbeit (Germany), Claimant Account, Dept. of Employment (UK), Bulletin Menusuel de Statistique, INSEE (France), Arbeitsmarktservice Österreich (Austria), US Department of Labor (USA).

number of job separations and the number of vacancies. If we ignore the flows from and to 'Not in the labour force' in Figure 4.14, the number of workers who become unemployed (per month or per year) represents a fraction s, called the **separation rate**, of existing jobs (L). While sL workers flow into unemployment each period, a number of unemployed workers find jobs. If we use f to denote the job **finding rate**, i.e. the fraction of the unemployed (U) who find employment during the period, the change in unemployment in a given period is given by

(4.3) $\Delta U = sL - fU.$

Frictional unemployment can be understood as the stock U^f of unemployment that is expected to occur, on average, when unemployment remains steady. Equality of flows into and out of unemployment occurs when $\Delta U = 0$ in (4.3), or when

(4.4) $sL = fU.$

It is convenient to express unemployment as a proportion of the labour force $L^S = L + U$. Then (4.4) can be used to write the frictional rate of unemployment u^f as[18]

(4.5) $u^f = U^f/N = \dfrac{s}{s + f}.$

[18] Since $L^S = L + U$ (see (4.2)), $1 = (L/L^S) + (U/L^S)$. Dividing (4.5) by L^S, and substituting $(L/L^S) = 1 - u$ gives (4.5).

We can think of the proportion s of workers separated from their jobs as the probability of losing a job when currently employed and, similarly, the proportion f of unemployed workers represents the probability of finding a job when unemployed.[19] (4.5) says that frictional unemployment is larger, the less frequent are job finds and the more frequent are job separations.

The separation rate s has two components: structural and cyclical. The structural aspect is linked to the ease with which firms dismiss workers. It is lower in countries where legal and social restrictions exist (as in most European countries) than in countries where redundancies are more acceptable (e.g. the UK and the USA).[20] The cyclical aspect simply refers to the fact that during recessions the probability of losing a job rises and so, therefore, does frictional unemployment.

Table 4.8 shows that in one particular country (the UK), job separation rates can vary considerably across various characteristics of labour market participants. Those specific labour force groups

[19] These figures hide a large degree of heterogeneity in the labour market: some individuals find a job readily after becoming unemployed, whereas others may have very low probabilities of exiting unemployment.

[20] It is, however, usually the case that outflow rates in countries with employment protection are also lower, because firms are more reluctant to hire new workers. For that reason the effect of employment protection on unemployment is ambiguous.

Table 4.8 **Inflows into Unemployment and Unemployment Rates in the UK, March 2004**

	Inflow rate into unemployment (monthly, as % of employment)	Unemployment rate (% of relevant labour force)
By region: Britain		
East Midlands	0.7	2.9
Eastern	0.5	2.3
London	0.8	3.6
North-East	1.0	4.6
North-West	0.8	3.3
Northern Ireland	0.7	4.0
Scotland	0.9	3.9
South-East	0.5	1.8
South-West	0.5	1.9
Wales	0.8	3.5
West Midlands	0.8	3.6
Yorkshire and the Humber	0.8	3.4
Total	0.7	3.1
By demographic group: UK		
Aged 16–17	1.0	21.1[a]
Aged 18–24	2.2	9.9[a]
Aged 25–49	0.6	3.9[a]
Aged 50 and over	0.4	2.5[a]
Male	0.9	4.3
Female	0.4	1.7

[a] Average from Dec. 2003 to Feb. 2004.

Source: UK Labour Market Trends (March 2004).

that exhibit higher separation rates of inflow into unemployment indeed tend to have higher unemployment rates.

4.4.3 Job Finding and the Duration of Unemployment

The job-finding rate f depends on the effectiveness of the matching process. It depends on how hard the unemployed look for jobs, how many job openings are available, and how easy it is to spot an opportunity (and how many opportunities are available). It may also depend on incentives to remain unemployed, and unemployment insurance may therefore slow down the exit rate out of unemployment.

Table 4.9 shows that unemployment benefit systems vary considerably from country to country, with respect to eligibility criteria, income replacement, and the period over which they are paid. At the same time, unemployment benefits have adverse side-effects. While **unemployment benefits** or assistance reflect a widely perceived need for solidarity and social conscience, they may encourage unemployed workers in declining industries to wait for an unlikely recovery rather than to retrain and change sectors. They also act as a disincentive for looking for

Table 4.9 Unemployment Insurance: Conditions for Eligibility and Benefits, 1999

	Eligibility conditions		Maximum duration: benefit	Replacement rate of net earnings/ Benefit level[c]	Restrictions
	Employment	Period			
Austria	26 weeks	12 months	30(50) weeks	50%	according to wage class
Belgium	312 days	18 months	∞	60%	of max. earnings
Denmark	52 weeks	3 years	5 years	90%	of average earnings with maximum
Finland	43 weeks	24 months	50 weeks	121 marks	per day
France	registered employment		27 months	57.4%	
Germany	360 days	3 years	2.5 years ∞	60%	of net earnings
Greece	200 days	2 years	max. 12 months	40%	
Ireland	39 weeks	last 1 year	max. 15 months	£70.50	per week
Italy	52 weeks	2 years	max. 180 days	30%	
Japan	6 months	12 months	max. 300 days	80%	of daily wages
The Netherlands	26 weeks	39 weeks	7 years	70%	of minimum wage
New Zealand	resident for 24 months		∞	NZ$147.89	per week
Norway	registered employment		78 weeks	0.2%	of annual income per day
Spain	12 months	last 6 years	180 days	70%	of average earnings
Sweden	450 hours	6 months	max. 450 days	240 kr	per day
Switzerland	6 months	2 years	max. 520 days	70%	of last earnings
UK	a		6 months	£51.40	per week
USA	15–20 weeks[b]	1 year	max. 26 weeks (with extension, 39 weeks)	50%	of last earnings, taxable

[a] 25 times the weekly lower earnings level in one of last two complete tax years (April to March).
[b] Different in various states. [c] Single household without children.

Source: 'Social Security Programs throughout the World'; Social Security Administration, Office of Policy, Office of Research, Evaluation and Statistics, SSA Publication No. 13-11805; August 1999.

a job, or as an incentive for being 'choosier'.[21] If the benefits are generous, and particularly if they are long-lasting, unemployed workers may take more time to find an acceptable job, a time in which their skills and re-employability may deteriorate. This

phenomenon is called the unemployment trap. This is especially true for unemployed low wage-earners who face loss of benefit upon taking on a new job. As can be seen in Figure 4.15, there is a tendency for people to remain unemployed longer in countries where unemployment benefits are more generous, paying more income over longer periods. As the finding rate declines, frictional unemployment rises. This confirms an uncomfortable trade-off between social concern and economic efficiency.

[21] Strictly speaking, this applies only to those who already qualify for benefits. Prior work experience is often required before one can draw unemployment insurance benefits. In this case, individuals will be more willing to accept the first job. This is often called the 'entitlement effect'.

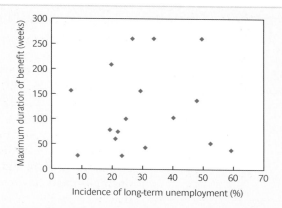

Fig. 4.15 Long-Term Unemployment Rates and the Duration of Unemployment Benefits, 1999 – 2000

The generosity of unemployment benefits can be measured in a number of ways: eligibility conditions, the fraction of net wage replaced by benefit, as well as the period of time over which they are available. In this figure the percentage of unemployed who have been unemployed for more than twelve months is plotted against the maximal duration of unemployment benefits (both unemployment insurance and unemployment assistance). The fraction of long-term unemployed in the total population of unemployed tends to be higher in countries where benefits are available for a longer time, although this clearly represents only one of many potential causes. Countries are: Austria, Belgium, Denmark, Finland, France, Germany, Greece, Ireland, Italy, Japan, the Netherlands, Norway, Spain, Sweden, Switzerland, United Kingdom, and the USA.

Source: OECD, US Social Security Administration.

4.5 The Equilibrium Rate of Unemployment

4.5.1 The Concept

If all unemployment were voluntary, it would hardly attract any attention. The existence of high and evidently involuntary unemployment means that labour markets do not function like other markets. A large number of market imperfections, arising from both economic and institutional factors, requires that we qualify the pure-competition paradigm of Section 4.2 and consider an alternative definition of equilibrium to the equality of demand for labour by firms and the supply of labour by households.

Labour market equilibrium attempts to capture the unemployment rate that would occur in the absence of cyclical disturbances. Because of imper-fections, labour markets may be in equilibrium and yet unemployment may not be limited to voluntary unemployment. **Equilibrium unemployment** can be viewed as the sum of frictional and structural unemployment:

(4.7)   **Equilibrium unemployment
= frictional unemployment
+ structural unemployment.**

Frictional unemployment occurs because it takes time for a match to occur between a worker seeking a job and a vacancy needing to be filled. It depends on the efficiency of the labour market, including the eagerness of both parties to find a match quickly. The frictional unemployment rate may well vary over time, not just because the market's

Table 4.10 Estimates of Equilibrium Rates of Unemployment

	1970–9	1980–9	1990–9	2001–4[a]
Germany	2.4	6.8	9.2	7.2
Italy	4.7	8.4	10.9	9.0
Japan	1.7	2.5	3.1	3.9
Spain	4.4	17.5	19.7	11.2
UK	3.6	9.6	8.0	5.3
USA	6.2	7.3	5.6	5.1

[a] 2003/2004 are projections.

Source: OECD, *Economic Outlook* Database.

efficiency changes but because economic conditions make it more or less likely for people to find jobs or to become unemployed.

Structural unemployment has many causes. The common thread is that the supply of labour is influenced by a number of institutions and regulations. Collective labour supply, which is brought into balance with labour demand in equilibrium, does not quite match individual supply behaviour. Some workers are involuntarily unemployed even when real wages equate the collective supply of labour with the demand of firms.

Estimates of equilibrium rates of unemployment are provided in Table 4.10. The contrast between Europe and North America is striking. The equilibrium unemployment rate was generally very low in Europe in the 1960s. Since then it has risen considerably while remaining stable in the USA. A comparison of Table 4.10 with Table 4.4 shows that actual unemployment has followed the same pattern. To begin to understand this dramatic evolution, we return to the two components of the equilibrium rate of unemployment.

4.5.2 The European Experience

The evidence suggests that European unemployment rose when large numbers of workers lost their jobs at the time of the oil shocks. The expected subsequent return to pre-oil-shock levels has been thwarted in many European countries by a fall in

the finding rate, so exit from unemployment has become increasingly harder. Is the development of the social safety net to be blamed for having provided workers with the incentive to wait out their unemployment? Circumstantial evidence—for example Figure 4.15—points in that direction when based on a comparison between Europe, where the safety net has become extensive, and the USA. Yet there is some disturbing counter-evidence. The social safety net is even more developed in Denmark, Sweden, and Norway, where long-term unemployment has remained lower. This implies that what really matters is not the safety net itself, but the disincentives that it may generate. Unemployment benefits, for example, provide an alternative to finding a job, and help transform temporary unemployment into permanent—structural—unemployment. Long-term unemployment has become increasingly widespread, and as workers gradually lose their human capital and contact with the active labour force, they become unsuitable for any vacancy.

The strikingly different evolution of the equilibrium unemployment rate across countries also points to the importance of institutions in influencing wage levels. This concerns the process of wage bargaining. The comparison between Europe and the USA in Box 4.5 shows that high unemployment in the EU is related to steep real wage increases, amounting to what has been dubbed the European 'wage shock'. Labour costs consist not only of wages: in many European countries, labour taxes and contributions elements of the social security system have also been allowed to rise steeply. Of importance too is the regulation of the use of labour (length of the work-week, dismissal restrictions, part-time work, etc.). We return to these issues in Chapter 17.

4.5.3 Actual and Equilibrium Unemployment

It can take a long time, often years, before real wages actually adjust to their long-run values shown in Figures 4.7 and 4.12. In the meantime, actual unemployment can deviate from equilibrium unemployment. Actual employment is below, and actual unemployment above, equilibrium when

Box 4.5 'Eurosclerosis' and 'EU-phoria'

With a few exceptions, European economies have experienced high rates of unemployment since the mid-1970s. Most of us grew up with high rates of unemployment in Europe. Yet it may be surprising that in the 1960s and early 1970s, Europe had lower unemployment rates than the United States. A number of things happened in the 1970s which were not particularly favourable for countries with an important role for collective wage setting. First the two oil price shocks, which acted like large negative productivity shocks, shifted labour demand to the left. This shift was reinforced by a slowdown in investment by firms in response to low profitability. Second, a slowdown in the rate of total factor productivity growth shrank the pie over which unions could bargain. Third, the late 1960s and early 1970s were a particularly militant period for European trade unions, with a number of general strikes and labour unrest across the continent and the UK. 'Hard-line' unions succeeded in pushing real wages higher and increasing their downward rigidity. The term 'Eurosclerosis' was coined by German economist Herbert Giersch of the Kiel Institute of World Economics to characterize this period of gloom and doom. Facing this rising tide of unemployment, many leaders simply accepted unemployment as beyond any influence of policy.

The experience of the 1980s and 1990s in some European countries teaches us that it is possible to restore low rates of unemployment. In the United Kingdom, the Tory government of Lady Thatcher used legislation to weaken significantly the power of trade unions, while reducing the level of social welfare and unemployment benefits. In contrast, the Netherlands chose a more cooperative path: unions and employers reached a historic agreement on wage moderation (the Wassenaar Accord) in 1982, to which the government responded with tax cuts and more favourable fiscal treatment of part-time work. It is significant that the union leader at the time, Wim Kok, later became prime minister and guarantor of the agreement, which is generally regarded as an unparalleled success. While radically different,

both UK and Dutch success stories do share the element of persistent wage moderation as a common ingredient. The lesson is that Euro-pessimism is unfounded: unemployment can be brought down, but it takes time, and political will.

Fig. 4.16 Employment and Real Wages: Europe and the USA

Over the period 1970–2000, real wages more than doubled in the Euro-area, while employment stagnated. At the same time, as real wages stagnated in the USA, employment rose more than 70%. (Real wages = total compensation per employee deflated by the GDP deflator.)
Source: OECD.

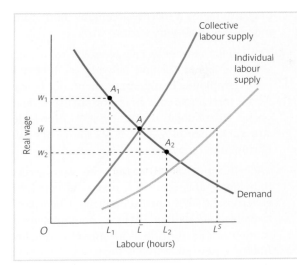

Fig. 4.17 Actual and Equilibrium Employment
When unions negotiate on behalf of workers, market equilibrium occurs at point A, and equilibrium unemployment is $L^S - \bar{L}$. Actual employment and unemployment may differ if the real wage is slow to move to its equilibrium level $\bar{w}$. If it is above the market equilibrium level ($w_1 > \bar{w}$), firms reduce employment to L_1 and actual unemployment exceeds equilibrium unemployment. Conversely, below-equilibrium real wages ($w_2 < \bar{w}$) enable firms to connect with structurally unemployed workers willing to work at lower wages than the union-set level. The resulting unemployment rate is lower than the equilibrium level.

the real wage is above the equilibrium level, as at point A_1 in Figure 4.17. When the real wage is low, firms may be able temporarily to move away from the union-set collective labour supply curve towards the individual labour supply curve (point A_2), for example by using agencies specializing in temporary jobs or overtime work. Workers may have overestimated the real wage by underestimating

the rise in the price level. Firms may be willing to hire more workers at the going wage. In such situations employment is above, and unemployment below, the equilibrium level. These deviations, while short-term in nature, tend to be associated with fluctuations of the economy associated with the business cycle. We revisit this important topic in Chapter 12.

⚠ Summary

1 Households trade off leisure against consumption (more generally, labour income). An increase in wages can induce more labour supply if the substitution effect dominates, that is, labour supply is relatively elastic. It will supply less labour if the income effect dominates, or no change at all if the labour supply is inelastic and the two effects offset each other.

2 Individual labour supply seems to be inelastic in the short run, but in the long run is more likely to be backward bending as the higher incomes afforded by higher real wages allow households to enjoy both more leisure as well as

more consumption. Aggregate labour supply is more responsive to real wage changes than that of households in the short run, as real wage increases draw new individuals into the labour force.

3 The demand for labour by firms depends on its (marginal) productivity which is determined by the available technology and the capital stock. Firms hire labour to the point where the marginal productivity of labour is equal to the real wage. The labour demand schedule is shifted outwards by an improvement in technology or an increase in the capital stock.

4 Equilibrium employment and the wage level are given by the intersection of labour demand and labour supply. Improvements in technology or increases in capital will be reflected in higher wages if labour supply is inelastic, and in higher employment if labour supply is elastic.

5 Involuntary unemployment arises when real wages do not decline to clear the market so that not all labour supplied by households is hired.

6 Labour unions care about real wages and employment. In determining their target wage, given the demand for labour firms, they ask for higher real wages than if the labour market were perfectly competitive. While the resulting unemployment rate is (optimal and) voluntary for unions, it may be involuntary for individuals.

7 Very centralized or decentralized wage negotiations deliver lower real wages and less unemployment than negotiations taking place at intermediate levels of centralization (industry by industry, or by craft).

8 Because firms cannot easily monitor work effort or wish to elicit lower turnover or improve worker quality, they may offer efficiency wages. This is yet another reason why real wages may be set above market-clearing levels.

9 Labour markets are also characterized by widespread government interventions. Minimum wages, designed to protect workers, can actually cause unemployment. Despite this, governments may see minimum wages as an effective means of guaranteeing a socially acceptable minimum income for those who want to work.

10 The labour market is characterized by a considerable amount of flow between its different states (employment, unemployment, not in the labour force). Search is an important aspect and results in frictional unemployment. Alongside structural unemployment, it is a source of equilibrium unemployment.

11 The efficiency of job search can vary across individuals and countries, and is affected by government labour market policies. Unemployment benefits, designed to make unemployment more bearable, provide disincentives to quickly finding a new job, thereby increasing frictional unemployment. Other programmes, such as training and relocation subsidies, can reduce frictional unemployment.

12 Because of distortions and regulations, equilibrium unemployment is never zero or entirely voluntary. Individuals may be willing to work at lower wages than those prevailing in equilibrium, but may not be able to underbid in the market. This is the sense in which real wages are downwardly rigid.

13 Real wages are slow to adjust to disequilibria, if only because they fulfil many other roles. This speed of adjustment will depend on labour market institutions, among other things. As a result, actual and equilibrium unemployment may differ for some time.

🔑 Key Concepts

- endowment
- leisure
- unemployment
- consumption – leisure trade-off
- marginal rate of substitution
- real (consumption) wage
- relative price
- substitution effect
- income effect
- household labour supply curve

- ◆ labour force, labour force participation rate
- ◆ man-hours
- ◆ marginal productivity of labour
- ◆ labour demand curve
- ◆ voluntary unemployment
- ◆ involuntary unemployment
- ◆ real wage rigidity
- ◆ labour (or trade) unions
- ◆ employers' associations
- ◆ collective labour supply curve

- ◆ insiders and outsiders
- ◆ minimum wages
- ◆ efficiency wages
- ◆ separations
- ◆ frictional unemployment
- ◆ separation rate
- ◆ finding rate
- ◆ unemployment benefits
- ◆ equilibrium unemployment
- ◆ structural unemployment

❓ Exercises

1 Suppose that the household in Figure 4.3 receives an inheritance. What is the effect on its decision to work and to consume? According to this result, do rich people work more or less than poor people? Does your answer make sense? Why or why not?

2 Suppose Robinson Crusoe is paid a higher wage ('overtime') if he works more than eight hours a day, but only has sixteen hours at his disposal.

(a) Draw his budget line in this case.

(b) Does the existence of overtime necessarily make him better off?

(c) Show Crusoe's optimal behaviour for 'normal' indifference curves. Under which conditions will he choose to work overtime? Under which conditions will he refuse?

3 What is the effect on the labour market of a minimum wage that is actually lower than the equilibrium wage? Show in your graphical answer the new equilibrium wage and the level of employment.

4 It is frequently claimed that Europe's unemployment problem is due to high labour taxes in the form of employer and employee contributions to social security, which are proportional to wages for

some range. Assume that individuals care about after-tax wages.

(a) Using the diagram in Figure 4.3, depict the effect of a high-tax versus low-tax environment on labour supply. What is the effect on labour supply and equilibrium wages? State your assumptions carefully.

(b) What is the effect on equilibrium employment levels resulting from the increased tax for the case of the utility function $U = c^{\alpha} \ell^{1-\alpha}$ (ignore labour demand)

(c) What changes in your answer to (b) if the tax revenues are rebated to the households as a lump-sum payment, i.e. unrelated to their income tax payments? Given that high labour taxation (social security charges and income taxes) in France, Germany, and Italy coincides with high rates of transfers to households (as opposed to Britain and the US), how could you explain the observed pattern of market labour supply in Table 4.2?

5 Derive the collective labour supply curve graphically. Show how different union preferences can interact with the same shift of labour demand and lead to (a) rigid wages around some 'target

level' with flexible employment; (b) flexible wages around some target level of employment; (c) flexible wages when employment is rising, but rigid when employment is declining.

6 One of the immediate consequences of opening the borders between East and West Germany was the potential for migration between the two regions. Because of a more productive capital stock and more know-how, wages in the West were about three times as much as those in the East. Consequently many East Germans moved to the West. What are the consequences for this migration for real wages (a) in West Germany? (b) in East Germany? (c) for employment in the two regions? Can you explain why West German trade unions were eager to organize their comrades in the East?

7 It is often the case that unemployment benefits are paid out of a fund financed by taxes levied on the firms proportionately to their wage bill. How might this affect equilibrium unemployment?

8 In Japan the bonus system is widespread. Workers often receive 30% of their pay in the form of a profit-contingent payment, which can go up or down depending on the fortunes of the enterprise in which they work. What are the implications of such a system for real wage rigidity and equilibrium employment?

9 It is sometimes said that the massive influx of women into the labour force is a cause of unemployment.

(a) Draw the effect on the labour market as described by Figure 4.10. What does it mean for real wages and employment?

(b) Using Chapter 3, note that more available labour raises the MPK. Assuming that, as a result of more investment, the capital stock increases: how does your answer to (a) change?

→ Essay Questions

1 Severance regulations—laws that impose costs on firms when they fire workers—are universally thought to influence labour markets, but it is hotly disputed whether they increase or decrease unemployment. Discuss.

2 Despite evidence that they are a source of unemployment, social minima remain widespread in Europe. Why?

3 European workers work fewer hours per week, fewer weeks per year, and fewer years in their lifetimes than Americans and Asians. Why? And what are the implications?

4 Typically, workers are not given the choice of the number of hours that they work; the length of the work week is standardized. Why? What difference would it make for employment to organize work à la carte?

5 'It is preposterous to accuse trade unions of being responsible for unemployment.' Comment.

Borrowing, Lending, and Budget Constraints 5

5.1 Overview *102*

5.2 Thinking about the Future *103*
5.2.1   The Future Has a Price *103*
5.2.2   The Rational Expectations Hypothesis *103*
5.2.3   The Parable of Robinson Crusoe *104*

5.3 The Household's Intertemporal Budget Constraint *104*
5.3.1   Consumption and Intertemporal Trade *104*
5.3.2   The Real Interest Rate *105*
5.3.3   Wealth and Present Discounted Values *105*

5.4 The Firm and the Private Sector's Intertemporal Budget Constraint *108*
5.4.1   Firms and the Investment Decision *108*
5.4.2   The Production Function *108*
5.4.3   The Cost of Investment *109*
5.4.4   The Intertemporal Budget Constraint of the Consolidated Private Sector *110*

5.5 Public and Private Budget Constraints *113*
5.5.1   The Public Budget Constraint *113*
5.5.2   The Consolidated Public and Private Budget Constraint *114*
5.5.3   When Ricardian Equivalence Can Fail *116*

5.6 The Current Account and the Budget Constraint of the Nation *120*
5.6.1   The Primary Current Account *120*
5.6.2   Enforcement of International Credit Contracts and Sovereign Borrowing *120*

Summary *122*

In matter of fact, as everyone knows, a price is paid for the use of capital. This is proof enough that in our real-world economic life capital is in short supply. Were there not a scarcity of capital, it would be certainly available for use for free. The widely-held view that an overabundance of capital has been created by exaggerated savings behaviour in modern societies is thus wrong in any case . . . The price, which is paid for the use of capital, we shall call the capital interest rate or simply the interest rate.

—Gustav Cassel[1]

5.1 Overview

Each of the three sectors identified in the circular flow diagram of Chapter 2—the private sector, the government, and the rest of the world—can borrow and lend. In doing so, they shift income and spending between the present and the future. Borrowing brings future income forward to be spent today. Lending or, more generally, saving defers the use of current income to some later date. This link between the present and the future takes the form of **intertemporal budget constraints**: the liabilities of each sector must eventually be repaid, while accumulated assets will eventually be spent. In this chapter we will learn more about intertemporal trade—how households, firms, government, and the nation as a whole can move resources through time.

Lending and borrowing decisions are inevitably driven by expectations about future economic conditions. The importance of expectations for current behaviour cannot be overemphasized. Those who reasonably expect their incomes to grow rapidly will want to borrow now and raise their current standards of living instead of waiting. In contrast, the lucky winner of a lottery will probably save a large fraction of the prize, because it is unlikely to occur again. Firms' investment decisions, too, are a gamble on future demand. Not the present, not the past, but expectations of the future exert the greatest influence on firms' capital budgeting decisions.

The shifting of spending over time involves trade. One could think of a lender as a seller of money today, the borrower as a buyer. Because people are impatient, time has a price. This price is determined by the interest rate. The intertemporal budget constraint provides the rules of the game. It may be a surprising way of thinking about things that we do every day, but it will provide a powerful framework for understanding some fundamental features of economics. Because the future is unbounded, it can be rather overwhelming to think about it in simple terms. So we adopt two simplifying devices. First, we will reduce the course of time to just two periods, called today and tomorrow, the present and the indefinite future. Second, we will continue to employ Robinson Crusoe, introduced in the last chapter, as a parable for consumer, producer, and his own government, all at once. These steps will make pretty abstract considerations a bit easier to handle.

---

[1] Gustav Karl Cassel (1866–1945), professor at the University of Stockholm and founding member of the Swedish school of economics, is widely regarded as one of the greatest Swedish economists of the twentieth century. He is the father of the purchasing power parity theory of exchange rates, which we will see shortly in Chs. 7 and 8.

5.2 Thinking about the Future

5.2.1 The Future Has a Price

It is a basic economic principle that anything of value must have a price. This includes money and goods delivered at future dates. In fact, markets exist for the sole purpose of pricing future deliveries of primary commodities: London's Commodity Futures, New York's Mercantile Exchange, or Rotterdam's Oil Futures deal in such futures contracts. Markets for financial resources are conspicuous: in most countries, markets for loans determine the interest rate—the price for borrowing and the return from lending. More advanced countries have stock markets which constantly place a value on companies, primarily on the basis of expected future earnings (profits).

Microeconomic principles can be readily used to understand how the future is priced. There is a direct parallel between *intertemporal* consumption choices (between present and future goods) and *intratemporal* consumption choices (among goods at a particular point in time). When we choose between consuming now or in the future, we effectively decide whether to save or to borrow. As rational households plan spending over time, they take into account their future incomes and needs, and balance these against the interest rate at which they can borrow or save. Similarly, rational firms forecast the profitability of plant and equipment in which they invest; they compare the return from investments with the interest rate, which represents either the cost of funds or, if funds are available, the best alternative use for them.

5.2.2 The Rational Expectations Hypothesis

Expectations about the future are crucial to all this. But how exactly do people form expectations? Do they get it right or wrong? This book takes the view that agents' forecasts are correct *on average*. This is the **rational expectations hypothesis**. It does not imply that individual agents forecast the future perfectly; it does imply that they do not make systematic errors. Alternative assumptions about expectations are presented formally in the WebAppendix to this chapter. These alternatives are logically weak, either because they rule out forward-looking behaviour, or because they assume that agents do not use all the available information about the future in a rational manner. The rational expectations hypothesis takes the opposite position, assuming that agents do use all available information in a way that reflects its costs, and use it in a skilled enough way to be right, on average. Some claim that this is unrealistic, because it assumes too much rationality.

We adopt the rational expectations hypothesis for two reasons. First, economics itself is based on the hypothesis that agents behave rationally. If we accept this as a description of consumption and production, why not about expectations formation? Second, even if most people are not fully rational all the time, alternatives are no closer to realism because they assert that people are repeatedly and systematically wrong. If they are, they must suffer losses. Isn't it natural to expect them to take steps to avoid such errors in the future? In the end, there are no good alternatives to assuming that economic agents are at least as clever as we economists are.

There is an even better justification for rational expectations. We are ultimately interested in how prices, interest rates, incomes, and spending interact on the market place. It is enough that a few well-informed agents behave rationally to drive the markets. If unions act on behalf of their members, it suffices that their expectations be correct on average. In financial markets, all that is required is that a number of professional traders be well informed with sufficient resources at their disposal. If they perceive that prices are too low compared with their valuation, they will buy, forcing prices upwards; if prices are too high to be consistent with their expectations, they will sell. Less well-informed customers end up accepting the market prices because they are on average right, even if never quite right.

5.2.3 The Parable of Robinson Crusoe

The analysis of private sector behaviour proceeds in two steps. This chapter sets up the intertemporal budget constraint facing households, firms, the government, and the nation as a whole. Chapter 6 will use these constraints to study behaviour. Because there are millions of agents, a difficulty arises: how can we account for so many actions? One simplifying assumption is to focus on opportunities and behaviour of a representative household, or a representative firm. This step is by no means absurd; at the macroeconomic level, agents do face common price levels, interest rates, and macroeconomic conditions; consumers share many aspects of tastes or preferences. This simplification allows us to study the behaviour of a single consumer and or firm as a stand-in for the average behaviour of the economy. The representative consumer and a representative firm should be understood as a parable, a way of capturing key aspects of economic life. It is a good example of an economic model.

Following a long tradition in intertemporal economics and the shorter tradition of the previous chapter, we will work with Robinson Crusoe as our representative agent, stranded on an island and forced to fend for himself. As already mentioned, it is convenient to collapse time into two periods, 'today' and 'tomorrow',[2] where tomorrow is a metaphor for the future. Effectively, the day after tomorrow, Crusoe will be rescued and will no longer need to concern himself with the economics of his island.

5.3 The Household's Intertemporal Budget Constraint

5.3.1 Consumption and Intertemporal Trade

Robinson Crusoe was forced to survive using a single available resource, coconuts. In fact, we initially imagine that the island does not even have coconut trees: rather, the coconuts simply wash up on the beach. The number of coconuts that he (rationally) expects to have today and tomorrow is called his **endowment**.[3] It is exogenous because, until Robinson learns how to plant coconuts, he has no choice but to consume what nature gives him. His endowment of Y_1 coconuts today and Y_2 coconuts tomorrow is represented by point A in Figure 5.1. Since coconuts are perishable, Crusoe's consumption is also given by point A. This is the **autarky** point. A household or a country operates in autarky when it does not trade and consumes its endowment.

If, however, there is a not-too-distant island which is inhabited by other economic agents, trade is possible. Because Crusoe's coconuts are just as good as his neighbours', we might not expect to observe any trade between them. Yet Crusoe may well be interested in **intertemporal trade**, or trade across time. He might lend his neighbours some coconuts today, if he expects to find only a few tomorrow. On the contrary, if today's 'harvest' is abnormally low, he may borrow coconuts now and repay later when times are better. Generally, borrowing and lending are associated with a price,

---

[2] The two-period version is the workhorse of intertemporal economic analysis and is attributable to the American economist Irving Fisher (1867–1947).

[3] For now, we will ignore uncertainty and assume that Crusoe has a perfect foresight with respect to the future. Perfect foresight is the equivalent of rational expectations when there is no uncertainty. Second, we will neglect issues of labour supply in this chapter to focus on other issues; effectively we will assume that Crusoe's labour supply is perfectly inelastic (constant). Ch. 4 has already considered the important case when Crusoe enjoys leisure and puts a price on working (picking up coconuts) albeit in an intratemporal setting.

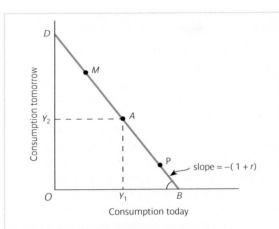

Fig. 5.1 Endowment, Wealth, and Consumption

Resources available today and tomorrow—the endowment—determine wealth and available consumption choices along the budget line BD. In the figure, the same level of wealth (OB) is attainable by a professional athlete (point P) or a university student (point M).

the interest rate, which we will describe below in more detail.

The rest of the chapter will explore, in very simple terms, the rules of this very fundamental activity in market economies—borrowing and lending. The activity of credit markets is of great importance in macroeconomics. Seen as a way of moving away from autarky, it would seem obvious that borrowing and lending—and credit and capital markets more generally—are natural events in economic life, just as obvious as the trade of goods and services. Yet banking and credit markets have long suffered reputation problems. Box 5.1 explores these reservations and possible reasons for them.

5.3.2 The Real Interest Rate

Crusoe and his neighbours must agree on the terms of repayment: how much should he pay (or receive) tomorrow for one coconut borrowed (lent) today? These terms are the **real interest rate**. If the neighbours are already conducting intertemporal trade among themselves, and offer him the same rate of interest, then from Crusoe's point of view the

interest rate, denoted by r, is exogenous. If he lends 100 coconuts today, he will receive $100(1 + r)$ coconuts tomorrow. Equivalently, to receive 100 coconuts tomorrow he must save $100/(1 + r)$ coconuts today. We say that a coconut tomorrow is worth $1/(1 + r)$ coconuts today.

The price of tomorrow's consumption in terms of today's consumption, $1/(1 + r)$, is called an **intertemporal price**. As the real interest rate r is positive, it says that goods tomorrow are less valuable than goods today. The real interest rate measures the cost of waiting. Valuing future goods in terms of goods today (here, dividing by the interest factor, 1 plus the real interest rate) is called **discounting**. Box 5.2 presents the important concept of discounting more generally. It can be used for example to explain the inverse relationship between bond prices and interest rates, among other things.

Intertemporal trade allows Crusoe to choose consumption combinations represented by the line BD in Figure 5.1. This line must go through his endowment point A, since he can always choose not to trade at all. At point B Crusoe could forgo consumption tomorrow completely: he borrows against his future endowment Y_2, receives $Y_2/(1 + r)$ coconuts, and consumes $Y_1 + Y_2/(1 + r)$ coconuts today. At point D he would fast today and lend all his current endowment Y_1 in order to consume $Y_1(1+r)+Y_2$ coconuts tomorrow. The line BD represents all the possibilities open to Crusoe, in between the extremes just described. It is called the **budget line**; its slope[4] is given by $-(1 + r)$. If the rate of interest increases, the budget line becomes steeper: for a given amount of saving today, more will be available tomorrow.

5.3.3 Wealth and Present Discounted Values

If Crusoe's income 'from nature' in the first period is Y_1 and he consumes C_1 in the same period, his saving is $Y_1 - C_1$. If $Y_1 - C_1$ is positive, he is lending; if $Y_1 - C_1$ is negative, he is borrowing. In the second period, his maximal consumption C_2 will equal the

---

4 The slope of the budget constraint is negative and is given by -1 times the ratio OD/OB. From the text we know that $OD/OB = [Y_1(1 + r) + Y_2]/[Y_1 + Y_2/(1 + r)] = 1 + r$.

Box 5.1 Neither a Borrower nor a Lender Be: The Economics and the Sociology of Credit

In a well-known scene from Shakespeare's *Hamlet*, Polonius gives his son Laertes some parting advice: 'Neither a borrower, nor a lender be: For loan oft loses both itself and friend, and borrowing dulls the edge of husbandry.' In other famous plays, such as *The Merchant of Venice*, Shakespeare gives lenders a pretty tough time. Is it morally wrong to borrow (or to lend)? And what is wrong with charging interest, if borrower and lender freely agree to it? Although the economic arguments against autarky are convincing, many great religions of the world—including Islam, Christianity, and Judaism—have banned lending at a positive interest rate at one time or another in their histories. Why the ambivalence?

Perhaps it is because lenders have an unconditional claim on the resources of individual borrowers in a risky world. If the fortunes of a borrower go south, those of the lender do not—that is, unless the borrower declares bankruptcy. Perhaps it is because borrowers appear to be in a poor bargaining position, often seeking credit when all else has failed. Perhaps it is because individuals are frustrated when their bank won't give them the loan they think they deserve, because the credit officer deems us 'too risky'. And the market has ways of dealing with individual risks which are distasteful to many. One is charging higher interest rates, which appears opportunistic since the poorest risks pay the highest premiums. Yet loan-sharking, with its illegal enforcement mechanisms, as well as 'payday loans' which amount to selling one's own wage packet in advance, at effective annual interest rates often in excess of 600%, are

accepted by many economic agents as a legitimate means of improving their well-being.

From the macroeconomic perspective, economies have little problem moving resources from the future to the present and vice versa. In 2004, UK consumers owed debt equal to roughly 135% of GDP to finance their purchases. Financial institutions—in all their different forms—borrow from their depositors, issue securities, and borrow from the central bank, in order to lend to their customers, firms as well as households. Securitization of loans—the pooling of many different loans and their resale on the capital markets—has proven an excellent way of averaging out individual risk associated with automobile, home, and college education loans.

Even when lending at interest is prohibited as in many Islamic countries, the market finds ways around the ban, for example declaring loans to be 'equity stakes' which participate in profits and losses of the enterprise. Irving Fisher wrote in 1930 that 'interest taking cannot be prevented by prohibiting loan contracts. To forbid the particular form of sale called a loan contract would leave possible other forms of sale, and the mere act of valuation of every property right involves an implicit rate of interest . . . Indeed as long as buying and selling of any kind were permitted, the virtual effect of lending and borrowing would be retained.' In the end, the fundamental truth is that the market for loans exists because there are gains from trade: different degrees of patience, different wants, different opportunities, different information.

sum of income Y_2 and $(1+r)(Y_1-C_1)$, the interest and principal on his savings from period 1. If saving was negative in the first period, this means paying back principal plus interest. Formally, we have

(5.1) $C_2 = Y_2 + (Y_1 - C_1)(1 + r).$

This fully describes Crusoe's intertemporal budget constraint. Dividing both sides by $(1 + r)$ and rearranging,

(5.2) $C_1 + \dfrac{C_2}{1 + r} = Y_1 + \dfrac{Y_2}{1 + r}.$

The left-hand side is the **present discounted value** of consumption: it is the sum of today's and tomorrow's consumption valued in terms of goods today. The right-hand side is equal to the present discounted value of income (his endowment). It is the maximum consumption that Crusoe could enjoy today given his resources today and tomorrow, and is represented by point B in Figure 5.1. Put differently, OB is the present discounted value of Crusoe's total endowment, in fact it represents his wealth, denoted by the symbol Ω:

Box 5.2 **Discounting and Bond Prices**

Discounting is used in economics and finance to evaluate the value of future incomes or expenditures in terms of resources today. It is frequently used to value financial assets. Discounting asks: what is the amount required today, given an interest rate, to generate some payment or payments in the future? By valuing a coconut tomorrow only as worth $1/(1 + r)$ coconuts today, Robinson Crusoe has successfully applied discounting to a practical problem.

Let us apply discounting to a financial problem, and consider a simple bond which pays €100 in one year's time. (This type of bond is called a *pure discount* bond.) If the interest rate is 5%, what is the value of this bond today? It is the amount, which if invested now, yields €100 next year. If that amount is B, then it must be true that

$$B(1 + 0.05) = 100,$$

so $B = 1/(1.05) \approx €95.24$. Similarly, the value of a two-year discount bond is given by $B = 100/(1 + 0.05)^2 = €90.70$. The further into the future the payback is, the more heavily any amount is discounted, and the lower the discount bond price is.

Conversely, given discount rate r, the present value of a stream of payments a_t over n years, for $t = 1, \ldots, n$ has present value

$$\frac{a_1}{1 + r} + \frac{a_2}{(1 + r)^2} + \frac{a_3}{(1 + r)^3} + \ldots + \frac{a_n}{(1 + r)^n}.$$

Now consider the case of a consol, a bond that promises to pay a fixed amount a for ever. Is it possible to put a price on that income stream, even though the payments are infinite? As long as the interest rate is strictly positive, the answer is yes! The price of a consol p which pays a each period is simply the present discounted value of its payments:

$$p = \frac{a}{1 + r} + \frac{a}{(1 + r)^2} + \frac{a}{(1 + r)^3} + \ldots + \frac{a}{(1 + r)^n} + \ldots$$

$$= \frac{a}{1 + r}\left[1 + \frac{1}{(1 + r)} + \frac{1}{(1 + r)^2} + \ldots\right]$$

$$= \frac{a}{1 + r}\left[\frac{1}{1 - \frac{1}{1 + r}}\right] = \frac{a}{r}$$

where we have applied the formula for a sum of a geometric series to the term in brackets. The price of a consol is clearly inversely related to the interest rate. Other bonds have a finite maturity so the formula is more complicated, but the general principle continues to hold that higher real interest rates imply lower bond prices.[5]

$$(5.3) \qquad \Omega = Y_1 + \frac{Y_2}{1 + r}.$$

If lending and borrowing is available without restriction, the same menu of possible consumption over both periods can be financed by individuals with very different income profiles. It doesn't matter whether Crusoe is a university student with low current and high future income, as represented by point M in Figure 5.1, or a professional athlete with high current and low future income (point P). As long as these points are on the same intertemporal budget constraint, the present discounted value of income is the same and intertemporal trade allows income to be shifted across time by borrowing and lending.

If Crusoe has initial tradeable wealth B_1 (an initial cache of coconuts), his wealth will increase by this amount and the budget constraint will be modified as follows:[6]

$$(5.4) \qquad C_1 + \frac{C_2}{1 + r} = Y_1 + \frac{Y_2}{1 + r} + B_1.$$

Naturally, this means that he can consume more in both periods. If he started with a debt, then B_1 is

---

5   In fact, the interest rate is *determined* or implied by the bond price, which is set in the course of bond market trades. More details on bond valuation and interest rates can be found in Ch. 19.

6   This is obtained by noting that today's available resources are $Y_1 + B_1$ so that (5.2) is changed to $C_2 = Y_2 + (B_1 + Y_1 - C_1)(1 + r)$.

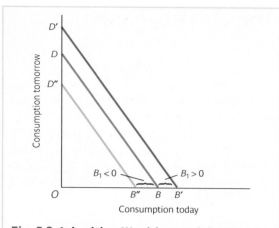

Fig. 5.2 Inheriting Wealth or Indebtedness
When wealth $B_1 > 0$ is inherited, the budget line shifts from BD to $B'D'$. Debt $B_1 < 0$ shifts the budget line to $B''D''$. The lines are parallel because the real interest rate is unchanged.

negative and he will have to consume less in order to repay the debt with interest. In general, total wealth is the sum of inherited wealth or indebtedness B_1 and of the present value of income. This is shown in Figure 5.2, where the inherited wealth or indebtedness is added to the present value of income. At a given real interest rate, it implies shifting the budget line BD to $B'D'$ or $B''D''$.

5.4 The Firm and the Private Sector's Intertemporal Budget Constraint

5.4.1 Firms and the Investment Decision

Up until now, Crusoe's income was considered exogenous. In fact, income mostly comes from carefully chosen productive activities. Production normally requires that resources are diverted from consumption and used to acquire productive capital. Crusoe could plant coconuts today which would grow into trees bearing coconuts tomorrow. Naturally, once planted, a coconut cannot be consumed: it is useful only for its future production. The use of valuable resources to produce more goods later is called **investment** or **fixed capital formation**. Indeed, a large quantity of goods produced in modern economies have no consumption value whatsoever; they are designed solely to make future production possible.

Like consumption, the investment decision has a fundamentally intertemporal aspect. Firms decide to accumulate capital when it is profitable to do so, and profitability depends on expected future outcomes. In order to pay for—we often say, in order to finance—their investments, firms obtain resources from the capital market (stock exchanges, bond markets, or banks) or use their own funds (retained earnings).

5.4.2 The Production Function

The investment decision depends upon the amount of output that can be produced with the available equipment (the number of coconuts to be obtained from a tree). The **production function** $F(K)$ captures this relationship between capital input and output and is depicted in Figure 5.3. It can be thought of as a special case of the production function of

Box 5.3 Gross Investment, Depreciation, and the Capital Stock

When previously accumulated capital exists, the situation is somewhat more involved than in the case of Crusoe's bare island. The stock of capital may differ in the future from the accumulated stock K_1 in two ways. First, new capital I_1 may be invested. Second, depreciation may remove some of the value of the capital stock. Depreciation occurs because of wear and tear or obsolescence. It is a proportion δ of the capital stock. The new capital stock is:

$$K_2 = K_1 + I_1 - \delta K_1$$

new capital = old capital + gross − depreciation
stock   investment

$$= (1 - \delta)K_1 + I_1.$$

The realized change in the capital stock, $\Delta K = K_2 - K_1$, is equal to $I_1 - \delta K_1$, the difference between gross investment and depreciation of previously accumulated capital. For the capital stock to grow, new investment spending must exceed depreciation.

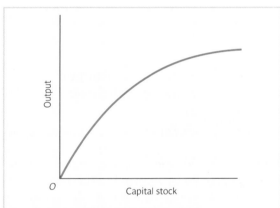

Fig. 5.3 The Production Function

As more input is added, output increases, but at a decreasing rate. This is the principle of declining marginal productivity.

Chapter 3, in which labour input is exogenous.[7] The shape of the curve implies that, as more capital is accumulated, the additional or marginal yield declines. That marginal output decreases when more input is put in place is the principle of **diminishing marginal productivity** already encountered in Chapter 3.[8]

5.4.3 The Cost of Investment

Starting with no capital stock (we assume that there are no coconut trees on the island at the outset), today's investment represents the total stock of capital available for production tomorrow. (Box 5.3 considers the more realistic case when previously accumulated capital already exists.) Crusoe understands that he can either invest K in productive equipment, or lend K to his neighbours. In the first case, he will have an output $F(K)$ tomorrow. In the second case, he will receive $K(1 + r)$. The real interest rate represents the **opportunity cost** of the resources used in investment. Because of the option of lending at rate r, the investment must yield at least $1 + r$ to be worth undertaking.[9]

Figure 5.4 shows the opportunity cost of invested capital K as the ray OR from the origin, which is given by $(1 + r)K$. As long as the resulting output exceeds the cost, the technology is sufficiently productive and investment is worthwhile. At point A, investment just covers its cost; there is no economic profit possible. To the right of A, investment uses up more resources than it produces. Positive economic profits occur only to the left of A.

The interest rate r is evidently a central determinant of the profitability of investment. Changes in the interest rate can change the set of investment levels that are productive. If the rate of interest

---

7 Suppose the supply of labour is exogenous and normalized so $L = 1$, and $Y = F(K, L)$ as in Chapter 3. Then $Y = F(K, 1)$.

8 The reason behind this principle is that, given the existing amount of labour used to man the equipment (here, Crusoe's time), adding new equipment is less and less effective in raising output.

9 Alternatively, Crusoe could borrow coconuts for investment purposes. The interest rate then is the cost of investment. This is discussed in Box 5.5 and in the WebAppendix.

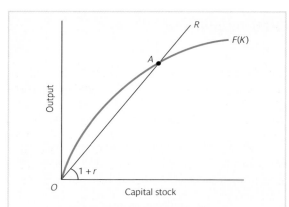

Fig. 5.4 Productive Technology
The cost of borrowing to finance investment is given by
OR. As long as output exceeds the cost of borrowing, the
technology is productive and the producer makes profit.
Beyond A, she makes losses.

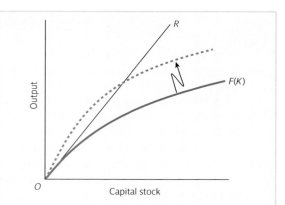

Fig. 5.5 Unproductive Technology
Given the interest rate, no firm will operate with the
production function shown in the figure. A technological
innovation which shifts the production function upwards
can make an unproductive technology productive again.

were to increase, the OR line would rotate upward,
pushing point A to the left, reducing the return
from any investment level, and thus narrowing the
range of productive investments. Another angle on
the problem is to compute the net return V from
investing K. It is the difference between the present
value of output tomorrow and investment today:[10]

(5.5)
$$V = \frac{F(K)}{1 + r} - K.$$

An investment project is economically justifiable
only if it has a positive present value. In terms of
(5.5), that means $V > 0$ or if $F(K) > K(1 + r)$. Figure 5.5
illustrates a case when the technology is not productive enough given the real interest rate. In that
case it does not pay to invest: it is more profitable
to lend at the rate r. It would require either an
improvement in technology (the production function schedule shifts upward) or a lowering of the
interest rate (the ray OR rotates downward) for
investment to be worthwhile. Box 5.4 gives a discussion of what productive and unproductive
investments can mean in practice.

[10] By assumption the trees are assumed not to have resale
value; they die after the second period. If they didn't, one
would need to add back the resale value of the depreciated
trees in the second period, which would increase the value
of the investment activity. This modification is described in
detail in the next chapter.

5.4.4 The Intertemporal Budget Constraint of the Consolidated Private Sector

The budget constraint of Section 5.3 takes endowments as given. Once investment and production
are taken into account, income tomorrow is no
longer simply given by nature. The budget constraint now depends on the amount that is invested
and on its profitability. As long as it is profitable,
investment increases wealth. Figure 5.6 shows how
this happens. Starting from point A, Crusoe can save
either by lending to his neighbours or by investing
an amount I_1 up to a maximum of his endowment
Y_1. If all his savings are invested, the capital stock
available for tomorrow's output production is the
difference between today's endowment Y_1 and
consumption C_1:

(5.6)
$$K_2 = I_1 = Y_1 - C_1.$$

The more he invests—the more we move to the
left—the larger will be tomorrow's production. This
is why the production function is now the mirror
image of the one shown in Figure 5.4: as we move leftward from the endowment point A, investment
increases and tomorrow's output becomes larger.
Tomorrow's income is the sum of the endowment Y_2
(the coconuts lying on the beach) plus output $F(K_2)$:

Box 5.4 **Productive and Unproductive Investments**

Macroeconomics teaches us that investment is the way of creating more resources tomorrow by giving up resources today. This is clearly sensible when thinking about the aggregate economy: in 2003 about £175 billion was spent in the UK on capital goods in the form of private and public equipment and structures. Those billions can be thought of as the sum of thousands, if not millions of efforts to move resources productively into the future, just like the sum of Robinson Crusoe's many individual coconut trees. It is natural to expect that this aggregate effort will look like the project in Figure 5.4. Individual investment projects however, like individual trees on Crusoe's island, do not have certain outcomes. In fact, many such projects are risky; while they are likely to look like Figure 5.4, there is always a positive if small probability that they will be unproductive and will end up looking like Figure 5.5. Investments are like bets on the future, and betting is a risky business.

There are many examples of projects which looked promising on the drawing board which later didn't pay off. One example is the famous Channel Tunnel connecting England and France, which had been discussed since the days of Napoleon as a way of improving transport

infrastructure between the two countries; the project was not undertaken until the 1980s. UK Prime Minister Thatcher insisted that the 38-km tunnel, which was then projected to cost £7.4 billion, be financed by a private stock issue, and it was: 300,000 investors in France and the UK paid about €5.30 per share in 1987 for a piece of the 'Chunnel'. In the end, the project cost £15 billion and, despite its technological success, met stiff economic competition from improved ferry services and cheap air travel across the English Channel. The investment has not yielded the profits that its investors expected, and the stock price in mid-2004 stood at about 40 European cents.

And of course there are good investments. An investor who purchased a *single share* in Microsoft Corporation at a price of $21 when it was first offered on 13 March 1986 and held it for the next eighteen years would have done quite well, ending up in mid-2004 (after stock splits) with 288 shares valued at roughly $25 each—a total value of $7,200! This represents a compounded annual rate of return of 38.3%. Had the investor sold at the peak of the high-tech market in 2000 at a price of 60, she would done even better. Now *that's* a good investment.

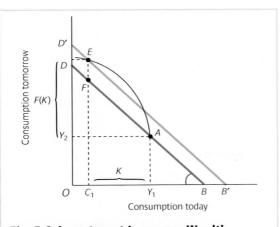

Fig. 5.6 **Investment Increases Wealth**

Investing I_1 (which becomes K_2) in a productive technology allows a household to increase its wealth over and above that corresponding to the initial endowment A. Here wealth increases by BB' as FE additional goods become available in the second period.

(5.7) $$C_2 = Y_2 + F(K_2).$$

The intertemporal budget constraint determines the present value of consumption $C_1 + C_2/(1 + r)$. With $C_1 = Y_1 - I_1$ given by (5.6) and C_2 given by (5.7), the present value of consumption is equal to wealth Ω:

(5.8) $$C_1 + \frac{C_2}{1 + r} = \Omega,$$

where wealth Ω now consists of the sum of the present discounted value of income plus the value of the firm:[11]

[11] To see this, write wealth as the present discounted value of net income: $\Omega = Y_1 - I_1 + \dfrac{Y_2}{1 + r} + \dfrac{F(K_2)}{1 + r}$. Rearrange using

$$V = \frac{F(K_2)}{1 + r} - I_1 = \frac{F(K_2)}{1 + r} - K_2 \text{ to obtain}$$

$$\Omega = \left[Y_1 + \frac{Y_2}{1 + r} \right] + \left[\frac{F(K_2)}{1 + r} - I_1 \right] = \left[Y_1 + \frac{Y_2}{1 + r} \right] + V.$$

Box 5.5   The Modigliani–Miller Theorem

One of the implications of the consolidation of household and firm accounts is that households ultimately own the firms. The activity of firms thus affects the value of household wealth. In practice, firms may be owned directly by households (we speak of stocks or shares in the firm, or equity ownership), or firms may borrow resources with a promise to repay in the future (they issue debt or obtain loans from banks). Shareholders are often called **residual claimants**, since they have a claim to whatever remains after firms have incurred their costs, serviced their debt (outstanding bonds and borrowing from banks), and paid taxes. Similarly, if a firm is declared bankrupt, those who have lent to the firm (bondholders, banks, and other creditors) have priority over equity holders. Under ideal conditions, it does not matter whether a firm uses debt or equity to finance an investment project. This result is known as the Modigliani–Miller Theorem.[12]

In the same vein, there is no difference between firms' savings and household savings lent to firms, at least to first approximation. Firms save when they retain earnings instead of distributing them to shareholders. In that case, shareholders are entitled to the future earnings generated by non-distributed profits. The number of shares does not change, but each share is worth more. In the second case, the shareholders provide the firm with additional resources in return for future earnings associated with the new investment: they now hold more shares but the value of each share remains approximately unchanged. In both cases, for a given investment project, the shareholders' wealth is the same. In the first case, they implicitly lend to the firm the equivalent of undistributed earnings.

The firm is thus best thought of as an agent which acts on behalf of its owners (its shareholders). It is irrelevant whether the firm or the shareholders do the saving. In practice, there is some evidence to support this view. While relative shares of saving by firms and households vary considerably from one country to another, the sum of the two sources of saving appears more similar. For example, as seen in Figure 5.7, the bulk of saving is done by households in firms in Italy and Germany. In contrast, corporations account for a larger share of total savings in Japan, the Netherlands, and the UK. One reason for this variation is the difference in the tax treatment of dividends, retained earnings, and capital gains. When the capital gains associated with retained earnings are taxed less heavily than dividend income, for example, shareholders are better off when firms save on their behalf.

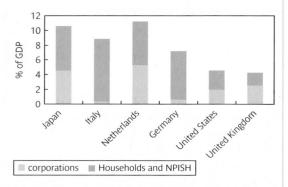

Fig. 5.7 Corporate and Household Saving, 1981–1987

Total saving rates differ across countries, but not as much as the share of saving of the corporate and household sectors. Tax treatment of income from saving largely explains the latter difference.

Source: OECD National Accounts.

(5.9)
$$\Omega = \left[Y_1 + \frac{Y_2}{1 + r} \right] + V$$

Total wealth = endowment + value of the firm

[12] It is named after the two Nobel Prize laureates, Franco Modigliani of MIT (1918–2003) and Merton Miller (1923–2000) of the University of Chicago.

Wealth now consists of two parts. The first part is the present value of the endowment as before in (5.3). The second part is the increase in wealth by V, the net value of the investment activity, as in (5.5). In Figure 5.6 the outcome of investment I_1 is shown as point E. Note that E lies above the initial budget line; this is because the production technology is productive at the rate of interest r. The distance

OB still represents the present value of the endowment. But now, for a choice of investment I_1 which brings Crusoe to point E, new total wealth is the distance OB'. Since the value of future output is discounted at the same rate r, the new budget line is parallel to BD. The distance BB' is the net return on investment.[13]

In the parable, Crusoe represents the private sector as a whole, which consists of individuals and firms. Firms ultimately belong to their shareholders, and the net return from investment raises their wealth. In effect, the firm is simply a veil. It should be valued as the present value of net income from all its activities. If shareholders anticipate that a firm will become more profitable in the future—because of a technological advance, as represented by the shift in Figure 5.6—then net expected returns rise and they are richer. This wealth gain takes the form of an increase in the value of the firm. In the real world, this would be reflected in the value of a firm on the stock market.

Does it matter how this increase in wealth occurs —whether firms borrow to finance the investment or use their own savings? In Crusoe's world the answer is simple: it doesn't. This is easy to see from Figure 5.6: if borrowed coconuts can be planted, Crusoe could bring forward the present value of his endowment to point B. Yet as long as he invests as in Figure 5.6, the value of his wealth is the same! It does not matter whether a firm uses debt (borrowing) or equity (own saved funds) to finance the investment plans. This result, known as the **Modigliani–Miller Theorem**, is discussed in more detail in Box 5.5.

5.5 Public and Private Budget Constraints

5.5.1 The Public Budget Constraint

There was no government on Robinson Crusoe's island. In the real world, there is a public sector which collects taxes, purchases goods and services, and transfers incomes. Yet the government is little different from other economic agents. It can borrow and lend, but must repay its debt with interest or be repaid by its debtors. The government spends G_1 and G_2 today and tomorrow, and raises net taxes T_1 and T_2.[14] We will consider a government that has debt outstanding at the beginning of the period in the amount D_1. This debt must be serviced (interest must be paid) at interest rate r_G.

If Crusoe's government spends more than its income today, then it is running a deficit in the amount $G_1 - T_1 + r_G D_1 > 0$, and must borrow to finance that deficit. Following a convention of the OECD, the government's total borrowing requirement can be broken down into two parts: the **primary deficit** $(G_1 - T_1)$, the amount by which non-interest expenditures exceed revenues, and interest payments $(r_G D_1)$.

In this example, a government obeys its intertemporal budget constraint when the primary surplus $(T_2 - G_2)$ is sufficient to repay not only today's deficit $(G_1 - T_1)$ plus interest on that deficit $r_G(G_1 - T_1)$, but also the inherited debt from the past D_1, plus interest $r_G D_1$:

$$\textbf{(5.10)} \quad T_2 - G_2 = (1 + r_G)(G_1 - T_1) + D_1 + r_G D_1$$
$$= (1 + r_G)(D_1 + G_1 - T_1).$$

The government budget constraint can be rearranged as:

---

[13] Note that the production schedule cuts the new budget line $B'D'$, suggesting that this result might be improved by investing a little bit less than I_1. Ch. 6 shows that, when Crusoe behaves optimally, he will invest to push out his new budget line as far as possible.

[14] It should be stressed that G represents government purchases of goods and services. It is not the same as total government outlays, which include transfer payments. In our notation, transfer payments are deducted from taxes to give net taxes T. Although interest payments are treated like transfers in the national income and product accounts, they are such a central component of the intertemporal budget constraint that we will always distinguish them from other transfers throughout this book.

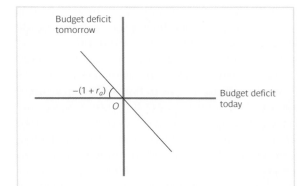

Fig. 5.8 The Government Budget Line

A deficit today must be matched by a budget surplus tomorrow, or vice versa, if the government is to obey its intertemporal budget constraint.

(5.11) $\qquad D_1 = (T_1 - G_1) + \dfrac{T_2 - G_2}{1 + r_G}.$

For the government to obey its intertemporal budget constraint, the sum of the present value of primary budget surpluses is equal to initial outstanding debt. The government budget constraint is illustrated in Figure 5.8 for the case of no initial debt or assets. The budget line passes through the origin. The slope of the line is $-(1 + r_G)$. As with the household, it is possible to rearrange (5.11) slightly, to get

(5.12) $\qquad D_1 + G_1 + \dfrac{G_2}{1 + r_G} = T_1 + \dfrac{T_2}{1 + r_G}$

The government's intertemporal budget constraint can be expressed as the equality of present values of spending on goods and services and income (net taxes).

Do governments really obey their budget constraints? To be sure, there are spectacular examples of government defaults, or repudiation of past debts. Most were associated with sharp political upheavals: the turbulent years of the French Revolution, the October 1917 revolution in Russia, the end of the Weimar Republic in 1933, Castro's revolution in Cuba.[15] In most cases, however, it

---

[15] The public debt must be carefully distinguished from the external debt, although in some instances the public debt is held by foreigners and represents the bulk of the external debt. This chapter assumes that the public debt is held by domestic residents.

is politically difficult for a government to default. Latin American defaults in the 1980s, or Russia's in 1998, were traumatic events.

In order to avoid defaults, today's primary deficits require primary surpluses later, and conversely. Given spending plans, lower taxes today are followed by higher taxes tomorrow. Alternatively, for a given path of taxes, more spending today requires spending cuts tomorrow. How long does 'today' last before a government is hit 'tomorrow' by the budget constraint? Governments that start with little debt can run deficits for many years. Figure 5.9 presents examples of primary budget balances relative to the size of the economy (GDP). Some countries (the UK) show a succession of primary deficits and surpluses. In other cases (Ireland, Italy, the USA) deficits have been sustained over many years, yet eventually the budget constraint has prevailed and the primary budgets were corrected, sometimes moving into spectacular surpluses.

5.5.2 The Consolidated Public and Private Budget Constraint

If private agents are capable of understanding the logic of the previous section, might it not be the case that they can see through the public sector veil, just as the corporate veil was pierced when we consolidated the household and firm budget constraints? Could the private sector understand that it is they who ultimately pay the taxes anyway? Consider the budget constraints of the private and public sectors, ignoring the existence of firms, and setting initial debt to zero:

(5.13) $\qquad C_1 + \dfrac{C_2}{1 + r} = Y_1 - T_1 + \dfrac{Y_2 - T_2}{1 + r}.$

(5.14) $\qquad G_1 + \dfrac{G_2}{1 + r_G} = T_1 + \dfrac{T_2}{1 + r_G}.$

In the first budget constraint, the private citizens pay the taxes, while in the second, the government receives them. Note that the government and the private sector do not necessarily face the same interest rates when they engage in borrowing or lending activities: the government sector borrows and lends at rate r_G, the private sector at rate r. Suppose however for the moment, that interest rates are the same, so $r = r_G$. It is possible to add

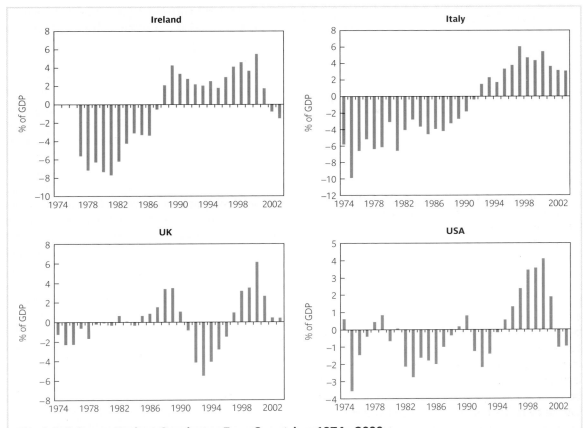

Fig. 5.9 Primary Budget Surpluses, Four Countries, 1974–2000

Over time, primary budget balances must add up, in present-value terms, to initial public debt. Some governments, like the UK, have maintained primary budget balances on average over many years. Those that have allowed deficits to cumulate into large indebtedness eventually have to run surpluses, as has been the case in Ireland, Italy, and the USA. *Source*: OECD.

up the private and public budget constraints, obtaining the following expression:

(5.15) $\quad C_1 + \dfrac{C_2}{1+r} = (Y_1 - G_1) + \dfrac{Y_2 - G_2}{1+r}.$

This looks very much like the private sector budget constraint (5.13), except that taxes have been replaced by public spending. In fact, it appears that the private sector has fully internalized the public sector's budget constraint, so that the taxes no longer appear in the budget constraint at all.

The result, that the private sector fully internalizes the public sector's budget constraint, is known

as the **Ricardian equivalence proposition**.[16] In Figure 5.10, point A represents Crusoe's endowment measured before taxes. Once public spending is taken into account as in (5.16), the private endowment is represented by point A'. The government reduces Crusoe's private wealth by an amount represented by the distance BB', which is either the present value of taxes or the present value of public spending—the

[16] Named after English economist David Ricardo (1772–1823), who first formulated this idea, only to dismiss it as unlikely. The idea has been revived and championed by Harvard economist Robert Barro.

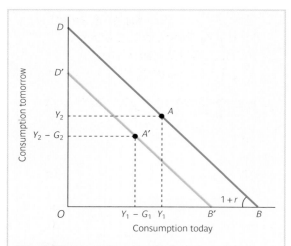

Fig. 5.10 Ricardian Equivalence

The government's spending and taxing activities reduce private wealth. Given government purchases, the precise scheduling of taxes does not matter.

two are equal because of the government budget constraint. Public spending can be financed either by current taxes or by borrowing. If the government reduces taxes today without changing its expenditures, it borrows today and will raise taxes tomorrow. For the private sector, this means more net-of-tax income today and less tomorrow. As long as the public and private sectors borrow and lend at the same rate $(r = r_G)$, these intertemporal shifts are equivalent and the public borrowing can be matched one for one by private saving along the same private budget line.

There are three ways of interpreting this important result. First, as seen by reorganizing (5.15), total national spending—the sum of private and public spending on goods and services—cannot exceed the country's wealth. The country can borrow or lend abroad, but it must respect its (national) budget constraint.[17]

Equation (5.15) has a second interpretation. Private sector wealth—which can be spent on private consumption—is the difference, in present-value

terms, between private endowments and public spending on goods and services. It is as if the government had simply confiscated resources equal, in present value, to its expenditures, and the private sector kept the remainder. Given public spending decisions, taxes can be levied today or tomorrow: the pattern of taxation over time has no effect on private wealth. What matters is public spending, which represents resources taken away from the private sector and which must be financed by taxation at some point, today or tomorrow.

The third interpretation of (5.15) concerns private wealth. When a government borrows from its own citizens to cover its deficit, it issues bonds which are a promise to repay interest and principal. Do households that own the debt consider it as part of their wealth? In this interpretation, they do not: government's indebtedness does not appear as part of private wealth in the right-hand side of (5.15). The reason is that the private sector pierces the veil of government: it recognizes that the government's promises to pay—the principal and interest on public debt—are matched by taxes levied to service the debt, today or tomorrow. Public bonds are an asset to households which is exactly offset by the value of their tax liabilities. Ricardian equivalence asserts that government debt does not represent net wealth to the aggregate private sector.

5.5.3 When Ricardian Equivalence Can Fail

The Ricardian equivalence result is highly controversial. It means that the path of taxes is irrelevant for the behaviour of the private sector. It implies that the stock of government debt does not, on net, contribute to the wealth position of households. Holding government purchases of goods and services (G) constant, budget deficits do not matter. It drives home the point that governments are net drains on an economy's resources without leaving open the possibility of effects of tax and spending policies. This section considers the many assumptions, implicit or explicit, required to reach the Ricardian equivalence result. In the end, the result of this discussion is that budget deficits probably do matter, and that at least some fraction

---

[17] This can be seen by rewriting (5.15) as

$$(C_1 + G_1) + \frac{C_2 + G_2}{1 + r} = Y_1 + \frac{Y_2}{1 + r}.$$

of public debt is regarded by the private sector as wealth.[18]

Mortal or new citizens

The citizens are not all alike when they face the tax-man: some pay a lot more taxes than others. So the burden of public debt service is not equally borne by all citizens. Similarly some hold government debt, and some don't. Yet, this does not imply that the aggregate household sector can escape the implications of equations (5.14)–(5.15). In the *aggregate* future tax burdens are the same.

On the other hand, citizens are certainly mortal. If they are not alive in period 2, they will not fully incorporate the intertemporal budget constraint of the government into their own budget constraints. If the current private sector fails to factor in *all* future tax liabilities, it is possible that government debt represents private wealth to some agents, and bond-financed deficits increase their wealth.

Different interest rates

We have assumed that the government and the private sector face the same interest rate as they engage in intertemporal trade ($r = r_G$). Is that realistic? Table 5.1 displays interest rates for two categories of borrowing. Interest rates on Treasury bonds represent the cost of borrowing faced by the public sector. The corporate bond rate is the interest rate charged by the bond market for firms with the best reputation; most private borrowers face significantly higher rates (by some 1–2% more for businesses, and much more for households). In many but not all cases, private borrowing rates exceed the comparable public borrowing rate. This is probably because the government is considered a less risky borrower.

The table shows that these rates can differ. When they do, government debt can have important effects on the private budget constraint. Combining the private and public budget constraints yields[19]

Country	Government bonds	Corporate bonds
Australia	5.30	6.23
Britain	4.65	5.53
Canada	4.15	5.69
Denmark	3.97	5.12
Japan	1.30	1.44
Sweden	4.12	2.61
United States	3.71	5.42
Euro-area	3.81	3.64

Table 5.1 Public and Private Borrowing Rates, March 2004: Long-Term Bonds (% per annum)

Source: *The Economist*, 27 March 2004.

$$(5.16) \quad C_1 + \frac{C_2}{1+r} = (Y_1 - G_1) + \frac{Y_2 - G_2}{1+r} + \left[\frac{r - r_G}{1+r}\right](G_1 - T_1)$$

This result is distinctly different from (5.15). The left-hand side is the private sector's present value of consumption, discounted at the rate of interest r at which private citizens can engage in intertemporal trade. The right-hand side must therefore represent private wealth. It includes the present discounted value of net private income (GDP less public spending) as before, plus an additional term. This term shows that when $r > r_G$, a fraction of the deficit $G_1 - T_1$, public borrowing in period 1, increases private sector wealth.

How can a tax cut which holds current and future spending constant increase private wealth? Because the government access to lower borrowing costs is equivalent to a subsidy to the private sector, as if the government were 'lending' the tax reduction

---

18 Other potential failures of the Ricardian equivalence proposition are related to the behaviour of agents under uncertainty, and go beyond the scope of this book.

19 To derive this result, multiply both sides of (5.14) by $(1 + r_G)/(1 + r)$, and rewrite as

$$G_1 + \frac{G_2}{1+r} + \frac{r_G - r}{1+r}G_1 = T_1 + \frac{T_2}{1+r} + \frac{r_G - r}{1+r}T_1$$

so that

$$T_1 + \frac{T_2}{1+r} = G_1 + \frac{G_2}{1+r} + \frac{r_G - r}{1+r}(G_1 - T_1).$$

Substitution in (5.13) yields (5.16).

today and demanding repayment tomorrow—through taxes—at the lower interest rate r_G. The government indirectly allows the private sector to borrow on its own, more favourable terms.[20]

Restrictions on borrowing

Many households cannot borrow as much as future expected income would justify. They may be unable to convince lenders—typically banks—of their creditworthiness. Lenders do not have the means of fully investigating customers' statements on a credit application form. In addition, future incomes are never really certain; so lending to households is risky. Borrowing rates exceed lending rates to compensate for this risk. In the worst case, no lending is extended and individuals are said to be credit rationed. The case of credit rationing is represented in Figure 5.11. With a net private endowment represented by point A, the agent can only move along her budget line on the segment AD. The segment AB is not attainable through private borrowing. If the government runs a deficit today, the agent may reach point A' as she consumes $Y_1 - T_1$, which is larger than $Y_1 - G_1$ since $T_1 < G_1$.

Most often individuals face higher and rising costs of borrowing. Lending institutions frequently demand higher interest rates from individuals to compensate for additional risk. The situation is similar to the case studied in the previous section and is also illustrated in Figure 5.11. When lending, the constrained agent can move along AD, but for borrowing she moves along AB'. The budget line is now kinked at the endowment point. In this case, public debt contributes to citizens' wealth, and the time profile of taxes affects the private sector budget constraint. At point A' the constrained citizen is better off than anywhere along AB'. As in the previous section, the government borrows on behalf of its citizens, increasing the wealth of those who cannot borrow on those terms.

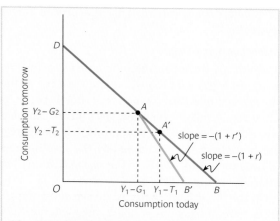

Fig. 5.11 Borrowing Constraints

When the household cannot borrow at all, its budget line is restricted to the segment AD, because it cannot consume today more than what is left of the endowment after public spending $(Y_1 - G_1)$. If the government reduces taxes and borrows instead (abroad), the household's borrowing line extends to the segment $A'D$. When borrowing constraints take the form of a higher private borrowing rate r', the budget line is the kinked line $B'AD$. A budget deficit at A' relaxes the private household's budget constraint.

Distortionary taxation and unemployed resources

Ricardian equivalence can fail because people change their behaviour in response to taxes. Most taxes are said to be distortionary. For example, taxation on labour income or wages may lead some to work less, and this will reduce output. In the parable of Crusoe, the endowments of coconuts are exogenous, so increasing taxes on them does not affect their supply. In the real world, taxes can reduce wealth because they reduce output. This is especially important in the presence of under-utilized resources, like unemployment. If a tax cut increases the level of economic activity and generates additional income, then the associated fiscal deficit will be associated with higher wealth.

Evidence

Given the long list of qualifications, it would seem quite unlikely that Ricardian equivalence could ever hold in practice. Yet, it receives some empirical backing, especially when the public budget moves

---

[20] Contrary to appearances, there is no 'free lunch' here: the government is simply borrowing more cheaply than the private sector can. In doing so, it effects a transfer from lenders to the beneficiaries of the tax cut, who experience an increase in the present value of their resources. In reality, lenders could be foreigners, but are more likely to be wealthier domestic residents.

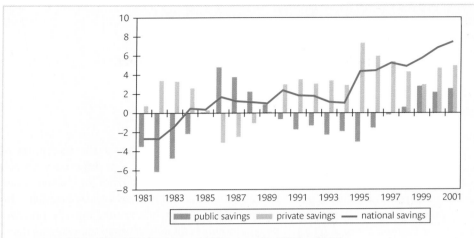

Fig. 5.12 Ricardian Equivalence in Denmark, 1981 – 2001

In the mid-1980s the Danish government put an end to a long period of budget deficits. The private sector's net saving decreased nearly one from one (not quite, since the country's current account improved). The opposite happened in the early 1990s. Both episodes conform partially with the predictions of the Ricardian equivalence hypothesis. In contrast, when the USA increased its government budget deficit dramatically in the early 1980s, the current account worsened in parallel.

Source: OECD National Accounts.

by large amounts that are clearly perceptible to the private sector, possibly signalling fundamental policy shifts. Figure 5.12 illustrates one such case. In Denmark, over the period 1981–94, the budget went from deficit to surplus and back to deficit. The private sector went exactly in the opposite direction. The country's overall balance (an issue taken up in Section 5.6 below) followed the public sector's changes, but in a muted way as the private sector partially offset the budget. A key aspect of this 'test' is the assumption that expectations of government purchases (*G*) remained roughly constant (as a fraction of GDP). This seems, *ex post*, to have been a defensible assumption: government consumption in Denmark at the beginning and the end of the 1990s represented about 26% of GDP.

A case that is difficult to explain using Ricardian equivalence is the Netherlands in the last quarter-century. The government deficit as a fraction of GDP declined from an average of 4.4% in the period 1975–87 to 1.9% in the period 1988–2000. More impressively, the share of all government spending (including transfers) in GDP fell over the period from 58.3% to 51.7%, while government purchases of goods and services declined from 16.4% to 13.8%. According to the theory, this spectacular rollback of government borrowing should have been associated with a sharp decrease in private sector savings. Yet the private sector balance hardly budged over the two periods, declining from 6.6% to 6.5% of GDP. To explain this outcome, we need to move beyond the simple Ricardian approach.

5.6 The Current Account and the Budget Constraint of the Nation

5.6.1 The Primary Current Account

The budget constraint of the nation shown in (5.17) results from the consolidation of the budget constraints of the private and public sectors. The country's net saving vis-à-vis the rest of world occurs through the balance on the current account. Much like the public sector budget surplus, it can be decomposed into a **primary current account** (PCA) and net external investment income, rF:

(5.19)
$$CA = PCA + rF,$$

where F represents the country's net asset position vis-à-vis the rest of the world, and r, as before, is the average real interest rate paid on F. Net investment income is positive when the country holds more assets than liabilities ($F > 0$), or negative, in the case of an indebted country ($F < 0$).

It should not be surprising that the consolidation of the public and private intertemporal budget constraints can be expressed in terms of primary current accounts. In the two-period framework, ignoring any initial asset position, the budget constraint of the nation requires that the present value of a country's primary current accounts equal zero:

(5.20)
$$PCA_1 + \frac{PCA_2}{1 + r} = 0.$$

Primary current account deficits in the first period must be repaid by primary current surpluses (in present value) in the second. Symmetrically, surpluses in the first period enable a nation to spend more than it produces in the future. It would seem wasteful for a country not to do this; otherwise it is literally giving away resources for claims on the rest of the world which it will never use.

Condition (5.20) can be suitably modified if there is an initial net asset position F_1:[21]

---

[21] For convenience, as earlier for the private sector, F_0 represents here both principal and interest inherited from the past. Later in Ch. 17 we will deal with the two explicitly and separately.

(5.21)
$$PCA_1 + \frac{PCA_2}{1 + r} = -F_1.$$

If a country has net wealth at the beginning of period 1 (F_1 is positive), it can draw on it to run future current account deficits in present-value terms. If there is external debt (F_1 is negative) the present value of current accounts must be positive, by an amount sufficient to repay the external debt.

The implication for the country as a whole is the same as for the private and public sector: primary current account deficits today must be eventually matched by surpluses, and conversely. If a country fails to satisfy its budget constraint, eventually it will face a tough situation. Many of the crises of the 1990s can be traced back to growing fears that some countries were not going to meet their budget constraints.

5.6.2 Enforcement of International Credit Contracts and Sovereign Borrowing

We have seen in this chapter that private households, firms, and governments face an intertemporal budget constraint which limits their ability to borrow at any point in time to the present value of lifetime resources. 'Lifetime' has a clear definition for individuals; for firms and governments less so, since the existence of firms and governments is never guaranteed. Nevertheless, within a legal jurisdiction, private borrowers and lenders will generally be able to rely on special institutions to enforce the budget constraint. Firms or individuals which simply walk away from debts face bankruptcy and possibly jail. Of course there are always exceptions, but they generally involve fraud, either via outright default ('take the money and run') or more complicated schemes such as pyramids described in Box 5.6; these tricks are usually declared illegal as soon as they are detected. In principle, these rules should also apply to governments, regardless of

Box 5.6 Pyramids: Is it Possible to Outrun the Budget Constraint?

Failure to understand the budget constraint can be costly to ordinary citizens and governments alike. The view that debts must be repaid is frequently lost on gullible gamblers who invest in 'pyramids'. These arrangements function as follows. A dubious financier offers depositors huge returns. When the time comes to repay, he uses freshly deposited money to pay principal and interest to the earliest investors. For this to work, he must attract ever more depositors. And it works. Word of mouth spreads news of the wonderful opportunity and when the first depositors get their money back the sceptics are silenced by the 'evidence'. More and more people want their share of the pie. So the scheme grows and grows, and grow it must to simply pay back maturing deposits. But it cannot grow indefinitely, simply because there is not an infinity of people in a country, or even in the world. Pyramids must eventually collapse and the people who set up such schemes know it. So they wait until they think that they have enough deposits at hand, and they suddenly disappear with the money, and thousands of investors discover that they have just lost their life savings.

Pyramids are often called Ponzi-schemes, after Charles Ponzi, an Italian immigrant to the USA who operated a grand-scale scheme in the early twentieth century. Poor Ponzi did not run away fast enough; he went to jail, was later released, deported, and died a pauper in a Rio de Janeiro hospital.[22] Most countries ban pyramid schemes, but they flourished in the early years of transition in several former communist countries (with huge ones in Bulgaria, Romania, Russia). Apparently, most ordinary citizens were unable to learn about the mathematics of intertemporal trade and budget constraints, or were convinced by smooth-talking salesmen that they as individuals could escape in time. The collapse of the Albanian variety in late 1996 impoverished tens of thousands of already poor people, many who had sold their cattle and houses in response to promises of 300% return and more. Massive street demonstrations sub-sequently brought down the government, which had failed to close down the pyramids after they had collected an estimated €1 billion in a country with a GDP of €2.3 billion.

whether they borrow at home or abroad. As soon as they try to violate their budget constraint, the source of credit should dry up rapidly.

It is important, however, to distinguish between international borrowing by private entities and **sovereign borrowing**, or international borrowing by national governments. A country cannot be bankrupted or jailed, of course. Unlike private lending within a country, enforcement of sovereign loan contracts is legally difficult. What happens when a country's government is unable to serve its debt? The first reaction is that foreign lending immediately stops, and this often affects would-be private borrowers. The country must at least balance its current account, since it cannot borrow, which forces painful adjustments in private and public budgets. Thereafter negotiations start with the creditors to try to arrange a rescheduling of debt service. Rescheduling means that the terms of

repayment are changed from the original loan agreement, but without changing the present value of those repayments. Debt forgiveness, in contrast, involves a reduction in the present value of the loan burden to the borrowing country, and a loss to the creditor.

Two institutions have been set up to deal with troubled sovereign borrowers: the Paris Club which brings together official lenders (countries which lend to countries) and the London Club which brings together private lenders (banks, large financial institutions). As long as an agreement is not reached, a delinquent country is frozen out of international lending, and this may last many, many years.

[22] For more details on Charles Ponzi's life see
  http://en.wikipedia.org/wiki/Charles_Ponzi.

❗ Summary

1 Because households may borrow or lend, their budget constraint is fundamentally intertemporal. It incorporates all current and future spending on the one hand, and all current and future income on the other. Future spending and incomes are discounted using the interest rate at which households can borrow or lend.

2 Wealth is the sum of the present value of current and future income and inherited assets less debts. The intertemporal budget constraint requires that the present value of spending be less than, or equal to, wealth. It applies to all economic agents, households, firms, the public sector, and the nation as a whole.

3 When firms invest, they forgo—on behalf of their shareholders—current consumption for future output. The profitability of investment depends both on the technology and on the rate of interest. The rate of interest is the opportunity cost of capital that investors apply to investment projects because it is available on other assets.

4 Budget constraints can be added together, or consolidated. Consolidating the households' and the firms' budget constraints gives the budget constraint of the private sector. As a first approximation, corporations are a veil: they provide their owners or shareholders with a means of increasing their wealth.

5 The public sector intertemporal budget constraint implies that, for a given time profile of government purchases, tax reductions today imply tax increases later on, and conversely. Alternatively, given a tax profile, more government spending today implies less spending later on, and conversely.

6 The Ricardian equivalence proposition asserts that the private sector internalizes the public sector budget constraint. Public debt is not considered as private wealth, and the time profile of taxes does not affect the private sector budget constraint. If the private sector can freely borrow at the same rate as the government, public dissaving (saving) is matched one for one by private saving (dissaving): the private sector pierces the veil of the government budget to keep total national saving unchanged.

7 Ricardian equivalence is unlikely to hold for several reasons. For example, individuals may expect that some current public debt will be repaid after they die; also, private interest rates typically exceed the rate at which the government borrows. Many households face borrowing constraints. Yet there is some evidence that the private sector internalizes part of government debt.

8 The national budget constraint is the consolidation of the private and public sector budget constraints. It states that the present value of primary current account deficits cannot exceed the nation's net external wealth. It also implies that, all things being equal, higher primary current account deficits today will require primary current account surpluses in the future.

9 Although it must also obey an intertemporal budget constraint, sovereign borrowing by a nation may differ from private international borrowing by its residents. One difference is that governments and countries cannot be bankrupted, and the assets of defaulting governments are hard to seize.

🔑 Key Concepts

- intertemporal budget constraints
- rational expectations hypothesis
- endowment
- autarky
- intertemporal trade
- real interest rate
- intertemporal price
- discounting
- budget line
- present discounted value
- investment

- fixed capital formation
- production function
- diminishing marginal productivity
- opportunity cost
- residual claimants
- Modigliani – Miller Theorem
- primary deficit
- Ricardian equivalence proposition
- primary current account
- sovereign borrowing

❓ Exercises

1 Suppose that Crusoe cannot trade with his native neighbours, but coconuts no longer spoil completely, so he can store them for consumption tomorrow. Suppose that 10% of the stored coconuts are lost because of spoilage. Represent this situation graphically.

2 Draw the government budget line in Figure 5.8 when there is an initial public debt D_1.

3 In the text, Robinson Crusoe does not want to leave any wealth beyond tomorrow, presumably because he knows he will be rescued. The situation would be different if he wanted to leave his friend Friday a gift of fixed amount B_3 in the second period. (B_3 might also be thought of as a bequest.) Write down Crusoe's budget constraint and represent it graphically.

4 The real interest rate is 5%. What is the value of a new firm which invests €100,000 and expects to have returns net of costs of €40,000 next year,

€52,000 the year after, €56,000 the third year, and then to close down with equipment valued at zero? How does your answer change if the equipment is instead sold for €20,000?

5 If a firm decides not to distribute dividends to its shareholders, its share price often increases. Can you explain why? Are the shareholders necessarily wealthier? Under what conditions would you expect such an action to have no effect at all?

6 What is the present value for Crusoe of 100 coconuts tomorrow if the real rate of interest is (a) 5%? (b) 10%?

7 Suppose the production function has the Cobb–Douglas form: $Y = AK^{\alpha}L^{1-\alpha}$, and assume labour input is fixed at $L = 1$. Let $\alpha = 0.5$ and $A = 1$. At an interest rate of 5% and no depreciation, what is the level of the capital stock K for which the project is just profitable? How does your answer change when the interest rate is 10%?

When the depreciation rate is 5% per annum? When $A = 2$?

8 Write down the value of the firm when the production function is $Y_2 = F(K_2, \bar{L})$ and the capital stock in the second period is given by $K_2 = I_1 + (1 - \delta K_1)$. How does the initial and given stock of capital in the first period affect the firm's value? The depreciation rate? The rate of investment?

9 Why do you think the interest rate is positive? What would be the consequence of a negative interest rate?

→ Essay Questions

1 Some contend that the 'pay as you go' system of social security in many European countries, in which the currently employed pay the pension benefits of older workers currently in retirement, is a pyramid. Do you agree or disagree? Explain.

2 'Without clear property rights, an economy cannot function properly.' Discuss this statement, using examples to back up your view.

3 For the governement to fulfil its budget constraint, it is sufficient but not necessary that its budget be balanced every year. Why? Why might a balanced budget law not be a good idea? What conclusions do you draw?

4 Financial institutions seek to impose the budget constraint on individuals and firms by refusing to lend when they fear a bankruptcy. Yet, they do not know what will happen to their clients in the future, and they are bound to know less about it than their clients themselves. What are the consequences of this case of 'information asymmetry'? Can you imagine ways of alleviating these effects?

5 When a country defaults on its external debt, a frequent controversy concerns whether the country is unable or unwilling to honour its debt. Discuss this distinction and why it is impossible to resolve the controversy.

Private Sector Demand: Consumption and Investment

6

6.1 Overview *126*

6.2 Consumption *127*

    6.2.1   Optimal Consumption *127*

    6.2.2   Implications *130*

    6.2.3   Wealth or Income? *134*

    6.2.4   The Consumption Function *136*

6.3 Investment *138*

    6.3.1   The Optimal Capital Stock *138*

    6.3.2   Investment and the Real Interest Rate *139*

    6.3.3   The Accelerator Principle *141*

    6.3.4   Investment and Tobin's *q* *141*

    6.3.5   The Microeconomic Foundations of Tobin's *q* *144*

    6.3.6   The Investment Function *147*

Summary *148*

There is often misconception in reasoning about spending [consumption] and investing. For example, Henry Ford's remark has been widely reported: 'No successful boy ever saved any money. They spent it as fast as they got it for things to *improve themselves.*' In this remark Mr. Ford drew no hard and fast line between spending for personal enjoyment and investment for improvement. And there is no hard and fast line . . . Spending merely means expending money primarily for more or less *immediate* enjoyment. Saving or investing is spending money for more less *deferred* enjoyment.

—Irving Fisher (*Theory of Interest* (1930), 114)

6.1 Overview

Defined as final goods expenditures, the GDP consists of consumption, investment, government purchases, and the net exports of goods and services. These components represent demands for goods and services by various sectors—households, firms, the government, and foreigners. Their sum is often called aggregate spending, or aggregate demand.[1] This chapter focuses on explaining the behaviour of the most important private elements of aggregate spending: consumption and investment.

Figure 6.1 shows that the variability of these private components (as a share of GDP) is quite different, suggesting that they are driven by different motives; in particular, private consumption is much more stable than investment. This pattern can be seen in both the USA and the Euro-area; at the same time, public spending on goods and services is more volatile in the USA. Among other things, this chapter will contribute towards explaining this strikingly different behaviour of consumption and investment.

As in previous chapters, our point of departure is a parable of a representative consumer and a representative firm. Both are taken to be rational: they strive to do the best they can given their available resources and opportunities. We often say that they take decisions to optimize, or achieve the best possible outcome. Although optimizing behaviour is sometimes understood as implying extraordinary intelligence or the ability to perform elaborate

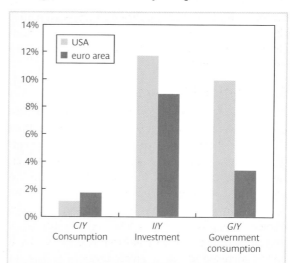

Fig. 6.1 Variability of GDP Components, 1970–2001

The coefficient of variation measures how much some variable fluctuates relative to its average value. Technically, it is defined as the ratio of the variable's standard deviation to the mean. The chart shows that the fraction of GDP represented by consumption is much more stable than investment or government spending. This pattern is common to both the Euro-area and the USA.
Source: OECD.

---

[1] Naturally, these goods and services are also supplied (i.e. sold) voluntarily by domestic firms, so they also represent aggregate *supply* too. In later chapters, we will see how the role of demand is more important for the determination of short-run macroeconomic developments, with only a passive role for aggregate supply. In the medium to long run, in contrast, the supply side becomes the most important determinant of economic output.

calculations, in fact it simply means that agents are rational and, possibly through trial and error, behave in a logically consistent fashion.[2] The end product of the chapter is a **consumption function** and an **investment function**, two key building blocks of macroeconomic analysis.

6.2 Consumption

Households receive income from their labour or their asset holdings and have to decide what to do with it. The decision to consume is a decision not to save, and saving is a decision to postpone consumption. It is fundamentally intertemporal: now or later, which is better? *Micro*economics focuses on how households decide *what* to consume, e.g. apples or oranges. For *macro*economics, the emphasis is on *when* to consume. For this reason, we make the simplifying assumption that there is only one good to consume (Robinson Crusoe's coconuts) and the focus is the choice between now and later.

6.2.1 Optimal Consumption

As Robinson Crusoe considers consuming the coconuts that he finds on the beach, he realizes that he can borrow or lend some of them through intertemporal trade with his neighbours. In fact, he may choose any combination of consumption today and consumption tomorrow as long as he remains on, or inside, his budget constraint. His choice depends on his preferences, which are described in Figure 6.2 by **indifference curves**. Each curve corresponds to a given level of **utility**, or well-being. A particular indifference curve represents combinations of consumption today and consumption tomorrow that leave Crusoe indifferent.

Higher indifference curves correspond to higher levels of utility.

Two central aspects of indifference curves are their slope and their curvature. For a particular consumption combination, the slope of an indifference curve shows Crusoe's willingness to swap consumption tomorrow for consumption today, holding utility constant. Where the curve is steep, for example, he is willing to give up a lot of future consumption to increase today's consumption. A flat curve indicates reluctance to give up consumption tomorrow for consumption today. The second aspect, the curvature, shows how the willingness to substitute depends on the relative abundance of consumption in the two periods. The more abundant consumption tomorrow is relative to today's, the greater the willingness to swap tomorrow's consumption for today's. Moving along an indifference curve upwards and to the left, Crusoe is less and less willing to give up coconuts today as the expected consumption of coconuts tomorrow relative to today's grows larger and larger. Box 6.1 provides more details on the phenomenon of intertemporal substitution.

Naturally, Crusoe wants to consume as much as possible in both periods, but he is limited by his intertemporal budget, which is the straight line in Figure 6.3. The best that he can do is point R, where the highest possible indifference curve just touches the budget line. A more desirable indifference curve like IC_3 is beyond his means, as it lies above his budget line. He can afford the utility level corresponding to IC_1 because this curve cuts the budget line, but can attain the higher utility level associated with IC_2, which is tangent to his budget line. Box 6.1 provides a more detailed interpretation.

---

[2] Introspection often makes us sceptical about such assumptions. Who hasn't given in to the temptation of buying a pastry when not really hungry or a stereo system when short of cash? Such departures from rationality are in fact infrequent enough to be outweighed by a majority of well-thought-out decisions. This is why rationality in economics is the right way to approximate reality.

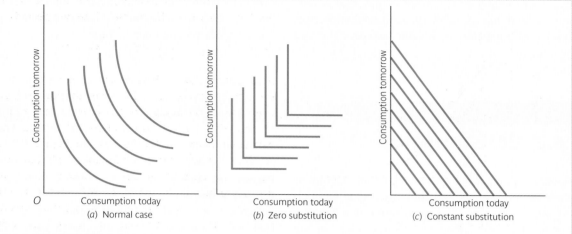

Fig. 6.2 Indifference Curves

Along any indifference curve, utility is constant. In panel (*a*), consumption tomorrow can be substituted smoothly for consumption today, but, as consumption today increases, at a decreasing rate. In (*b*), the consumer can be made better off only by increasing consumption today and tomorrow in fixed proportions. In (*c*), consumption today and consumption tomorrow are always substituted at the same rate. In all cases, indifference curves further up in the north-east direction correspond to higher utility levels.

 ## Box 6.1 Indifference Curves and Intertemporal Substitution

Each indifference curve holds utility or satisfaction constant. Moving to the right along a given indifference curve, today's consumption increases while tomorrow's declines. At any particular point, the slope of the indifference curve shows how many units of goods tomorrow we are willing to give up for an additional unit of goods today. The technical term for this willingness to trade goods tomorrow for goods today is the **marginal rate of intertemporal substitution**.

In most cases, this willingness to substitute consumption across time reacts to moving along the indifference curve. The curve becomes flatter because we are willing to give up increasingly less consumption tomorrow for consumption today. The opposite occurs as we move up and to the left. The curvature of the indifference curve captures the sensitivity of the marginal rate of intertemporal substitution to relative consumption, as examples can help illustrate. In Figure 6.2, panel (*a*) describes the normal situation, but it is worth thinking about two opposite extremes. At one end of the spectrum, there can be no substitutability at all: the consumer is better off only if consumption is increased in fixed proportion in both periods. The indifference curves would look like the letter L in panel (*b*) of Figure 6.2. At the other extreme, the marginal rate of substitution is constant: the consumer is always willing to substitute the same amount of consumption today for consumption tomorrow, regardless of how much is consumed. The indifference would be a straight downward-sloping line, as in panel (*c*).

Consider Figure 6.3, which characterizes optimal consumption. The key feature of point *R* in Figure 6.3 is that the marginal rate of substitution is just equal to the slope of the budget line, or $1 + r$. To see why, suppose that Crusoe obeys his budget constraint but has a marginal rate of substitution of 1; he is willing to exchange one coconut today for one tomorrow. By lending 1 today, he gets $(1 + r)$ tomorrow—a good deal for him—and can make himself better off, i.e. move towards *R*. If he goes too far, the marginal rate of substitution will exceed $(1 + r)$; he then prefers to shift consumption back to the present, increasing his utility by doing so. Only when the marginal rate of substitution is equal to the intertemporal price of consumption has Crusoe exhausted all gains from intertemporal trade.

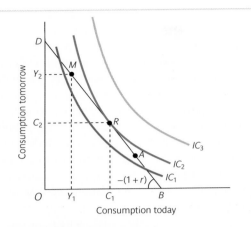

Fig. 6.3 Optimal Consumption

The budget line shows how much can be consumed today and tomorrow for given endowment (represented by point M) and real interest rate (the slope). Optimal consumption is achieved at point R. In this case the consumer borrows today $C_1 - Y_1$ and repays $Y_2 - C_2$ tomorrow. Consumption at R is also possible for an individual with endowment A, who lends today and dissaves tomorrow.

When Crusoe is on his budget line, he spends his total wealth (OB) in the course of the two periods:

$$(6.1) \qquad C_1 + \frac{C_2}{1 + r} = Y_1 + \frac{Y_2}{1 + r} = \Omega.$$

If he can borrow or lend as much as he wants at the going interest rate, his consumption pattern over time depends only on the present *value* of his income—his budget constraint—and not on the particular *timing* of his income. In Figure 6.3, a 'student Crusoe' (with endowment M) borrows because his current income Y_1 is low relatively to his future income Y_2, while a 'professional athlete Crusoe' (endowment point A) with high current and low future income will save. Since both individuals lie on the same budget line, they have the same wealth OB. If both have identical tastes as described by their indifference curves, saving and borrowing allows them to have identical consumption patterns. The associated principles of life-cycle and permanent income consumption are presented in Box 6.2.

 Box 6.2 Permanent Income and Life-Cycle Consumption[3]

Most individuals or households do not expect a constant flow of income over their lifetimes. Typically, young people earn less than older people. The principle of optimal consumption implies that they should borrow when young and repay debts or even save when older in order to *smooth* the time profile of consumption. This is an application of the same principle which was used to explain why winners of lotteries do not spend all their income at once, or why people who become unemployed try to maintain (approximately) the level of consumption they enjoyed while employed.

Figure 6.4 displays a typical pattern of rising expected income and shows how **life-cycle consumption** would be chosen. To maintain a constant flow of consumption, the individual would spend an amount corresponding to his or her **permanent income** each year. Permanent income is that income which, if constant, would deliver

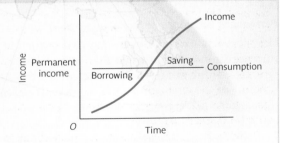

Fig. 6.4 Life-Cycle Consumption

When income is expected to increase over a lifetime, consumption smoothing implies borrowing when young and paying back when older.

the same present value of income as the actual expected income path. It is a good measure of sustainable consumption over the time horizon of an individual.

---

[3] The permanent income hypothesis was developed by Chicago economist Milton Friedman (1912–) and was cited as his main contribution when he was awarded the Nobel Prize in 1976. The life-cycle theory of consumption was also recognized by the Nobel Prize committee as an important contribution of MIT economist Franco Modigliani (1918–2003).

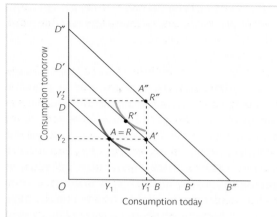

Fig. 6.5 Temporary and Permanent Income Changes

The shift from A to A' describes a temporary increase in income. Consumption rises both today and tomorrow. (The household moves from R to R'.) Part of today's income windfall is saved to sustain higher spending tomorrow. The shift to point A" represents a permanent increase in income. It does not require consumption smoothing through saving or borrowing. The best course of action is permanently to increase consumption (to point R").

6.2.2 Implications

Permanent versus temporary changes in income

How does Robinson Crusoe respond to a temporary increase in income? Imagine that today's harvest is unusually plentiful, rising to Y_1' in Figure 6.5, while next period's harvest Y_2 is expected to remain unchanged. For simplicity, the figure represents the case where, initially, consumption was exactly matching income in both periods so that there was no need to borrow or lend (points A and R overlap). The endowment point now shifts from A to A', on the new budget line B'D', which is parallel to the initial line BD since the real interest rate remains unchanged. It is natural to expect that Crusoe will consume more. However, the key insight is that his consumption (point R') will rise in *both* periods. Consumption today increases less than the windfall, as he saves some of it to spread over time. A temporary increase in income is accompanied by a permanent, but smaller, increase in consumption.

What if, instead, the increase in income is permanent, in the sense that both Y_1 and Y_2 rise by equal amounts? (Think of a lasting improvement in the harvest outlook, or an enduring improvement in Crusoe's coconut technology!) The new endowment point is A" and the corresponding budget line is B"D". Optimal consumption moves to point R". As a first approximation, points A" and R" coincide and consumption rises in both periods.[4] Being equally better off in both periods, Crusoe sees no reason to save or borrow. A permanent increase in income is absorbed in a permanent increase in consumption of similar size.

Finally, consider the case when income is unchanged today, but is correctly expected to increase tomorrow. If Robinson knows that his future crop will be more plentiful, he will borrow today against his future income to afford a better standard of living immediately. This type of behaviour, far from being thriftless or incautious, actually makes him better off.

An implication of this reasoning is that only new information should alter consumption behaviour. If future incomes are correctly anticipated, they will be incorporated into current wealth and current consumption will fully reflect this information. The only reason why consumption will change is if unexpected disturbances affect income, either current or future, so that wealth is changed. Since all that is known of the future is already taken into account in the evaluation of wealth, only true surprises can alter wealth and therefore consumption. Put differently, changes in consumption must be unpredictable. This is known as the **random walk** theory of consumption, because changes in consumption should be random.[5]

Consumption smoothing and the current account

The common theme behind the three cases examined above is that people generally dislike highly variable

---

[4] This is only an approximation. Impatient consumers may bring forward some of tomorrow's windfall, whereas more patient agents would save some of today's windfall for tomorrow's consumption. The exact answer will depend on the shape and position of their indifference curves.

[5] The random walk theory of consumption was formulated by Robert E. Hall of Stanford University. It is surprisingly difficult to reject empirically.

consumption patterns. When faced with a temporary change in income, rational consumers save or borrow to spread the effects on consumption over time. In bad times, this may take the form of dissaving (spending from accumulated savings) or borrowing (from the bank, from relatives, or using a credit card). In good times, consumers accumulate assets or repay their debts. This phenomenon is known as **consumption smoothing**. It explains why consumption is less variable than GDP in Figure 6.1, and is in general the most stable component of aggregate demand.

This does not mean that consumption is *always* more stable than GDP. Since the evolution of actual GDP is a mixture of permanent and temporary disturbances, consumption will on average reflect the nature of this mixture, responding more to permanent than to temporary changes. Indeed, there are times when consumption is more unstable than GDP. A good example is the case when income is expected to fall in the future: consumption spending declines immediately although current income remains stable. The subsequent fall in GDP is often seen as being caused by the consumption shortfall, while in fact it is simply an event which was

correctly anticipated by consumers. Box 6.3 presents an example where consumption seems to have preceded GDP as the Czech Republic was entering into a recession.

Consumption smoothing means that Crusoe borrows when facing a temporary loss of income today or a windfall tomorrow, and saves when benefiting from a temporary gain or expected future bad times. Saving and borrowing play the role of a buffer in the presence of transitory income disturbances. Moving from a particular individual to the country as a whole, the logic remains the same but the mechanics are slightly trickier. Net borrowing or lending is possible only vis-à-vis the rest of the world. In this case, saving or borrowing takes place through the primary current account. One important consequence of aggregate consumption smoothing, therefore, is that temporary imbalances in the primary current account reflect the efforts of domestic households to smooth consumption. From the fundamental identity of macroeconomics, the primary current account is GDP less domestic spending:

(6.2) $$PCA = Y - (C + I + G).$$

Box 6.3 Boom and Bust in the Czech Republic, 1997–2000

After an initial period of successful transition, the Czech economy slowed down in late 1996. Investors began to sell the Czech currency, the koruna, and the Czech central bank was forced to devalue it, meaning to lower its price in other currencies. Confidence in the Czech miracle faded. Figure 6.6 shows that real GDP growth turned negative in early 1997 and was not positive again until 1999. There is very little evidence that consumption was being smoothed during this period. In fact, the sharp decline from mid-1996 seemed to contribute to the downward spiral of GDP, just as its sudden recovery in early 1999 preceded the resumption of GDP growth.

Were Czech consumers busy disproving economic principles? Not necessarily—but the example shows how the simple model needs help to explain all the facts. Two likely interpretations run as follows. In 1996, the government implemented policies designed to reduce

the growing budget deficit, including raising taxes, which undoubtedly both reduced disposable income and hurt consumer confidence. More importantly, the Czech Republic—seen as one of the most successful transition countries—had enjoyed a large inflow of foreign capital in the early 1990s. Much of this capital inflow financed a consumption boom in 1994–5, just as one would expect an optimistic Robinson Crusoe to react when first exposed to the capital market. The capital inflow quickly reversed itself when the economy slowed, as expectations of a miracle became more realistic. Anticipating bad times, consumers cut back on spending. An interesting question indeed is how much the Czech slump in consumption anticipated the bust, and how much it actually *caused* it. To answer it, we will need to know much more about the way income is determined—and that is the material of later chapters.

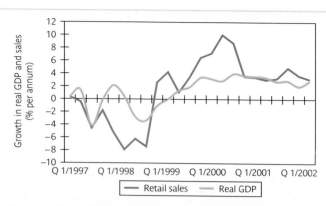

Fig. 6.6 Real GDP and Retail Sales Growth in the Czech Republic, 1997–2002

In the mid-1990s, growth of consumption—here represented by retail sales—in this relatively successful transforming economy slowed sharply. This slowdown was followed by a downturn in GDP. Similarly, late in 1998, an upturn in retails sales seems to anticipate the general improvement in economic conditions observed from 1999 onward. Deciding whether the swings in consumption 'caused' the output fluctuations or simply 'anticipated' them is an important and recurrent question posed in macroeconomics.

Source: OECD.

If GDP declines while investment and public spending remain unchanged, consumption smoothing implies a worsening PCA. Similarly, a temporary increase in GDP would lead to a temporary surplus. For most countries, primary current accounts are typically small and oscillate around zero. To some extent these may be regarded as an optimal response to temporary shifts in incomes. A specific example reviewed in Box 6.4 is the reaction to the oil price increases that occurred in the 1970s.

 Box 6.4 Oil Shocks and European Current Accounts

Oil prices have increased abruptly four times in the past quarter-century. At the end of 1973 they quadrupled. They doubled in several instalments over 1979–80, increased again by 50% in 1990 after a marked decline of about 75% over the 1980s, and then by 50% again in 2000 (Figure 6.7). For those European countries which are heavily dependent on oil for their energy needs, an oil shock can be thought of as a reduction in income.[6] Even if the price increase is permanent, the short-run impact will always be larger than in the long run because conservation can reduce dependence over time. Oil-importing countries should respond by running current account deficits, while oil and energy exporting countries would be expected to show large surpluses. Figure 6.8 shows that in the 1970s, the UK and Denmark reacted just as theory predicts, with current accounts going into deficit. In contrast, the current account of the Netherlands, which exported natural gas at the time, was the mirror image of most oil-importing countries, moving into surplus. Later, when oil prices fell dramatically in the mid-1980s, the current account of the UK—now an oil producer—deteriorated, while that of Denmark and the Netherlands—no longer a gas exporter—moved into surplus.

---

[6] At the time, it was not obvious whether these shocks were temporary or permanent. Fig. 6.7 strongly suggests that they were temporary, but back in the mid-1970s or early 1980s this information was not available to economic agents, and the oil price increases were generally regarded as permanent. Milton Friedman was a lone voice in the wilderness when he wrote in 1975: 'Almost regardless of our energy policy, the OPEC cartel will break down. That is assured by a world-wide reduction in crude-oil consumption and expansion in alternative supplies in response to high prices. The only question is how long it will take' (*Newsweek*, 17 Feb. 1975).

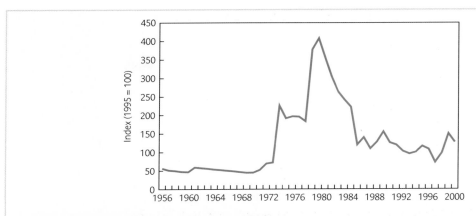

Fig. 6.7 Real Price of Crude Oil, 1956 – 2002

The real price of oil is computed as the ratio of the US dollar price of crude oil to the consumer price index of all industrialized countries. In 1973 – 4 and 1979 – 80 the price of oil jumped by 100 – 200%. After falling sharply in the 1980s, it rose again in 1990 and 2000.

Source: IMF.

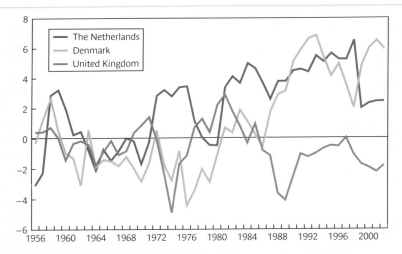

Fig. 6.8 Current Accounts in Europe, 1956 – 2002

As importers of oil, most European economies suffered large income losses when oil prices rose sharply. Denmark is typical in this regard. Consumption smoothing calls for temporary borrowing now (current account deficit) and repayment later (current account surplus). The Netherlands, a gas exporter in the 1970s, experienced in contrast a temporary windfall which was saved abroad through current account surpluses. The current account of the UK, an oil producer since the late 1970s, seems to move with both windfall gains and losses due to fluctuating oil prices over the period.

Sources: OECD, *Economic Outlook*; IMF.

Consumption and the real interest rate

When the real interest rate rises, so do the rewards to saving. Put differently, the price of consumption tomorrow in terms of consumption today declines. Will saving always increase and consumption always decline? The question is harder to answer than it first appears. Figure 6.9 shows that the effect on consumption today depends on whether Crusoe

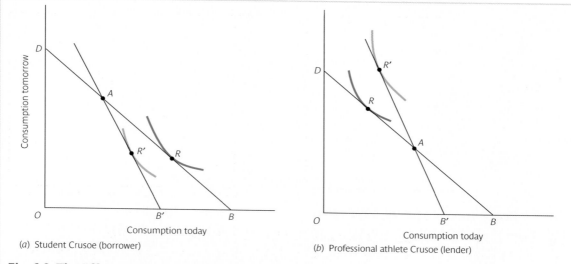

(a) Student Crusoe (borrower) (b) Professional athlete Crusoe (lender)

Fig. 6.9 The Effect of an Increase in the Interest Rate

As the interest rate increases, the budget line becomes steeper and rotates about the endowment point A. The response of the consumer depends on whether she is a borrower or a lender. The borrower (a) will tend to consume less today because the interest rate at which resources are brought forward has increased. The lender (b) consumes more today, since the same amount of lending can increase the amount of consumption possible tomorrow without reducing today's.

is a net borrower (e.g. a student) or a net lender (e.g. a professional athlete). Since endowments today and tomorrow are unchanged in both panels of the figure, the budget line rotates around point A. Optimal consumption shifts from point R to point R'. Net lenders gain from higher interest rates, moving to a higher indifference curve and consuming more in both periods. The borrower who faces higher interest costs is in the opposite situation, as he must devote more resources to debt service, and his current consumption declines. Increases in interest rates have important redistributive effects between borrowers and lenders: an increase hurts the former and benefits the latter.

The effect of the interest rate on consumption is ambiguous because it works through two channels. First, it increases the cost of goods today relative to those tomorrow. An increase in the interest rate makes the budget constraint steeper, since it determines the slope of the intertemporal budget constraint. Second, it reduces the value of wealth Ω, which is the present discounted value of all income. This effect will depend on how much of our wealth stems from future, as opposed to current, income.

6.2.3 Wealth or Income?

An old tradition in macroeconomics, which can be traced back to John Maynard Keynes, links consumption spending by households to current income—which we have called disposable income Y^d and defined as GDP less net taxes. Keynes argued that most people simply set aside a fraction of disposable income for saving, and consume the rest.[7] The evidence seems to support this hypothesis: Figure 6.10 shows the evidence for France, plotting consumption expenditures in each year in the period 1980–2002 against disposable income and a measure of household wealth, which includes liquid financial assets of families as well as the value of fixed assets and real estate. The link between consumption and disposable income is strong, in fact stronger than that between consumption and wealth.

This evidence challenges a key implication of the theory developed in the previous sections: that consumption is driven by wealth, not current income,

---

[7] This assumption regarding saving and consumption is central to the Solow growth model studied in Ch. 3.

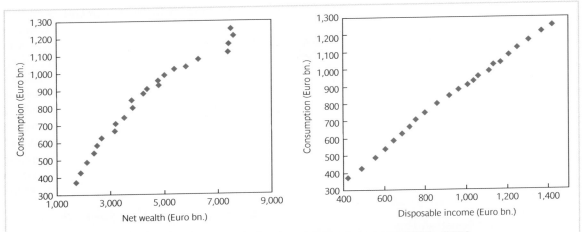

Fig. 6.10 Consumption, Disposable Income, and Wealth in France, 1980–2002

The link between consumption and wealth is strong, but less tight than the link between consumption and disposable income.

Source: OECD.

and that households strive to smooth their consumption relative to income. One possible explanation is that income and wealth grow in tandem, so that the observed consumption–income relationship may reflect a common dependence on wealth. Yet wealth appears more volatile than disposable income, partly because of fluctuations in share prices on stock markets. It is likely that households regard short-term stock market gains and losses as temporary and pay attention only to long-term increases in wealth. In addition, private wealth is not well known, in part because people are very reluctant to provide information about their assets, in part because expected future income—an important component of wealth—is not measurable and therefore left out.

A second, more fundamental explanation is related to a household's ability to borrow and lend. The Crusoe parable assumes that the representative household can borrow freely at a given interest rate. This might be the case if present and future incomes of individual households—against which borrowing is pledged—were known with certainty to lenders. In real life, banks and other lending intermediaries cannot know the repayment prospects of all individual borrowers with certainty. A

common banking practice is to demand collateral —the borrower pledges tangible wealth such as a house in case of non-payment. This option is not available to all households. Banks charge higher interest rates to customers who appear riskier and sometimes refuse to lend at any rate, or place ceilings on the amount that can be borrowed. Consumers who cannot obtain credit in spite of future earnings potential are said to be **credit rationed**.

In the presence of credit rationing, spending is governed by current disposable income, not wealth.[8] This is shown in Figure 6.11, which uses Figure 5.11 as its point of departure. Because Robinson Crusoe is prevented from borrowing, his consumption possibilities are limited to the kinked line *CAB*. In particular, he cannot reach the segment *AD* of his intertemporal budget constraint, and his preferred consumption plan *R* is not possible. In that case, the best option for him is point *A*, where

---

[8] Ch. 5 provides a detailed treatment of interest rates and credit rationing. It also shows that with credit rationing, Ricardian equivalence will not hold for those who would like to borrow, so that current taxes affect current consumption as well, hence the relevance of disposable income as opposed to GDP.

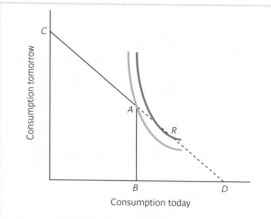

Fig. 6.11 Credit Constraints

If Crusoe cannot borrow, his budget constraint shrinks from *CD* to *CA*. He would like to be at point *R*, however, borrowing today and paying back tomorrow. The best outcome for him under the circumstances is to consume at point *A*, with consumption equal to income both today and tomorrow.

he consumes exactly his income in both periods. If a significant proportion of households is rationed in credit markets, disposable income also will influence consumption, along with wealth, which only matters for non-rationed households. Box 6.5 illustrates the importance of national borrowing constraints in the early phase of the process of economic transformation in Eastern Europe. But even in advanced countries, credit rationing affects a substantial proportion of households. It is therefore not surprising to observe the tight link between consumption and disposable income in Figure 6.10.

6.2.4 The Consumption Function

Let us now summarize the results set out thus far. Consumption is driven primarily by wealth, and wealth is based on current and discounted future incomes of households. In practice, many people are unable to borrow even though their expected future income is higher. For them, disposable income is the effective determinant of consumption.

 Box 6.5 Current Income and Spending in East Germany and Poland

The swift conversion of East Germany (the former German Democratic Republic) and Poland to market-based economies in 1990 provides a unique example of an anticipated increase in permanent income. In both countries, the adoption of market-based institutions implied that income levels would eventually reach Western Europe's. The transition to a market economy however is painful, possibly leading to an initial fall in income as inefficient production capacity is shut down and workers change occupations and industries. While current observable income falls, wealth is rising because future incomes are so much larger than before. Faced with an expected windfall, optimal consumption rises, both now and in the future. Actual current consumption can increase only if people are able to borrow or receive transfers. As part of German unification, the citizens of the Eastern Länder had access to a well-developed

domestic financial market. For the former East Germany, borrowing 'abroad' meant becoming customers of West German banks, or recipients of credits or grants from the government. On the other hand, Poland started with a large external debt preventing its government from further borrowing, and its citizens and firms certainly did not have access to foreign bank credit despite high growth. Figure 6.12 shows the dramatic difference. While GDP fell in East Germany after 1990, private consumption there rose to equal total East German GDP. Public spending and private investment also rose, bringing the current account deficit to nearly 100% of GDP. In credit-constrained Poland, on the other side, spending tracked income. Because of its large external debt, Poland actually had to run a primary surplus. In contrast, East Germany's large external debt was assumed by West Germany.

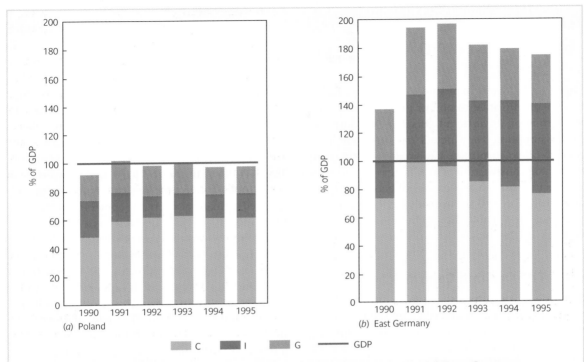

Fig. 6.12 GDP, Domestic Demand, and the Current Account: Poland and East Germany

Spending in East Germany rose after unification as firms, citizens, and authorities were able to borrow against higher expected future income. There is no link between consumption and spending as 'foreign' borrowing is almost as large as income. In Poland, which has similar long-run growth prospects, spending follows income because of the impossibility of borrowing large amounts abroad.

Sources: DIW Wochenbericht; World Bank; CSO; DGII.

This, along with the fact that income and wealth tend to grow together, means that consumption seems to be better explained by disposable income. In fact, both matter, as can be seen from the example in Box 6.5 and as is apparent in Figure 6.10. Section 6.2.2 also notes that the real interest rate affects consumption, but its direct role is ambiguous. In all likelihood, a negative effect of interest rates on consumption is most likely to occur indirectly through wealth: a rise in interest rates reduces wealth and consumption. In the end, we capture these various effects by writing down the consumption function, a compact notation linking consumption to its two main determinants

$$(6.3) \qquad C = C(\,\Omega,\, Y^d).$$
$$\qquad\qquad\qquad + \quad +$$

The plus signs underneath the arguments of the function reminds us that consumption increases with both wealth Ω and disposable income Y^d. This is the fundamental formulation that will be used in the rest of this textbook.

6.3 Investment

The second category of private spending decisions to be explained is investment, or gross domestic capital formation. Investment goods are not intended for consumption. They include machine tools, computers, office furniture, land-moving equipment, buses, and construction of new factory buildings, as well as increases in inventories of goods to be sold at a future date. All these goods have the common trait that they enable the production of goods and services in the future. The decision to invest is therefore an intertemporal decision.

6.3.1 The Optimal Capital Stock

The amount of output that can be produced by a representative firm is described by the production function $Y = F(K)$, which gives output of coconuts Y available tomorrow when Crusoe plants K coconuts today on his bare desert island. The production function is depicted in panel (a) of Figure 6.13.[9] A related concept is the **marginal productivity of capital (MPK)**. This is the amount of extra output that can be obtained when an additional unit of capital is installed ($\Delta Y/\Delta K$), and can be measured as the slope of the production function.[10] Because of the principle of declining marginal productivity, the MPK declines as more capital is put in place, as is shown in panel (b).

We looked at the return from capital; what about the costs? When he decides to save a coconut, Crusoe can always choose between planting it or lending it to inhabitants of neighbouring islands. In the latter case, he can expect 'tomorrow' to receive the coconut plus interest. Or else, if he does not have enough savings, he can borrow a coconut, and pay back principal and interest tomorrow. The same is true for any firm. If the investment is financed by resources that could instead be invested in financial assets, the **opportunity cost** of the investment is $(1 + r)$. If the investment is financed by borrowing, the **marginal cost** of investment is $(1+r)$.[11] In both cases, the cost is the same: it is shown in panel (a) of Figure 6.13 as the ray OR. The ray represents the total cost, $(1+r)K$, of capital installed today and productive tomorrow, the sum of the principal and the interest charged. (The cost of equipment here is unity because it takes one coconut to start a tree.) The marginal cost of capital, or the cost of one incremental unit of productive capacity, is simply $(1 + r)$. It is represented in panel (b) by a horizontal line.

The firm's profit in the second period is the difference between what it produces and the cost of production:

(6.4) $\text{Profit} = F(K) - K(1 + r).$

In panel (a), this is measured as the vertical distance between the curve depicting the production function and the ray OR. To maximize profit, the manager chooses the **optimal capital stock** $\bar{K}$ such that the distance between the two schedules is as large as possible. This occurs where the slope of the production schedule (given by its tangent) is equal to the slope of the cost-of-capital schedule OR. Then the marginal productivity of capital (MPK) is equal to the marginal cost, here the opportunity cost equal to $1 + r$:

[9] This paragraph summarizes the exposition of the firm's budget constraint in S. 5.4 of Ch. 5. Think of $F(K)$ as a shorthand version of the production function introduced in Ch. 3, $Y = F(K, L)$, with labour supply constant ($L = 1$).

[10] To see why, imagine a point on the curve. An increase ΔK in the stock of capital is represented as a horizontal move from the initial point. How much output ΔY is available? It is measured as the vertical distance which brings us back to the production function. The ratio $\Delta Y/\Delta K$ is the slope of the line connecting the point of departure and the point of arrival back on the production function. As the initial step ΔK is made shorter, this slope becomes the slope of the curve itself. (Formally, the line becomes tangent to the curve.)

[11] Some precision is required for the careful reader. Presumably, capital can be resold. Here we assume that Crusoe abandons his coconut grove upon rescue. If he could sell it, the expected resale value comes as a deduction of the cost of investment. Box 6.6 elaborates on this point.

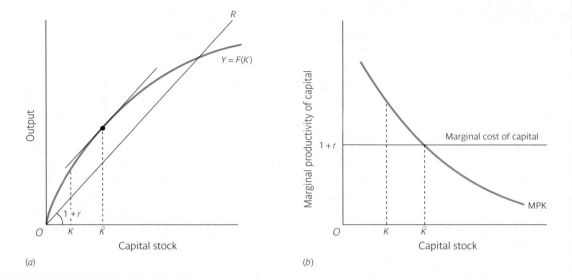

Fig. 6.13 The Optimal Capital Stock
The optimal stock of capital $\bar{K}$ is achieved when the firm's production function is furthest from the line OR, which represents the cost of capital. There the marginal productivity of capital is equal to its marginal cost (MPK = $1 + r$). Investment is the difference between the desired capital stock $\bar{K}$ and the previously accumulated capital stock K.

(6.5) $$\text{MPK} = 1 + r.$$

marginal   marginal cost
productivity   of capital
of capital

In Figure 6.13(*b*), the optimal capital stock $\bar{K}$ corresponds to the intersection of the MPK and marginal cost curves. Box 6.6 provides an extension of this result to the case when capital does not depreciate completely and can be resold after the second period.

If each and every firm behaves optimally, the same principles can be applied to the economy as a whole. Two conclusions follow. First, the optimal capital stock depends positively on the expected effectiveness of the available technology, captured by the marginal productivity of capital. An improvement in technology or technological progress means that more output can be produced with the same capital stock. In Figure 6.14, the production function in panel (*a*) and the MPK schedule in panel (*b*) both shift upward. The optimal stock of capital increases from $\bar{K}$ to $\bar{K}'$. Second, the optimal capital stock depends negatively on the real interest rate.

If the real interest rate increases, the cost schedule OR rotates counter-clockwise in Figure 6.14(*a*) and the marginal cost schedule shifts upward in panel (*b*). The intuition behind this important result is that, for a given state of technology, higher opportunity costs of capital reduce the amount of capital that can be optimally employed and still be more profitable than simply 'lending' the resources in the financial markets.

6.3.2 Investment and the Real Interest Rate

Investment occurs for two reasons: to bring the capital stock to its desired level, and to make up for capital lost through physical or economic depreciation.[12] In Figure 6.13, we can find the optimal stock of capital $\bar{K}$ and the stock of capital inherited from

---

[12] From Box 5.3 we know that $\Delta K = I - \delta K$, where ΔK is the increase in the stock of capital, δ is the rate of depreciation, and therefore δK is the amount of capital that was used up. This decomposition can be rewritten as $I = \Delta K + \delta K$, which shows that I—gross investment—must cover ΔK—net investment—as well as replacing depreciated capital.

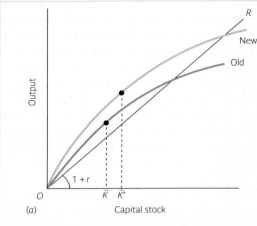
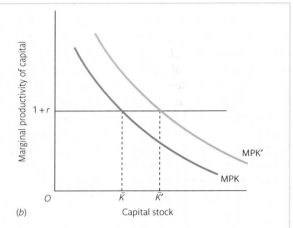

(a)   Capital stock   (b)   Capital stock

Fig. 6.14 Technological Progress

Technological progress makes more output possible with the same stock of capital. In panel (a) the production schedule shifts upward. In panel (b) the MPK schedule moves up to the right. The optimal stock of capital is now $\bar{K}'$, which is larger than initial value $\bar{K}$.

 Box 6.6 Looking beyond the Next Period and Taking Account of Capital Depreciation

The two-period approach implicitly assumes that when Crusoe is rescued at the end of the second period he abandons his capital stock. But what if he sells it to Friday, who chooses to stay on the island? If there is a 'resale market', the results will change in an important way. When stating, as in (6.5), that the marginal cost of capital equals its marginal product, we need to include the resale value of capital as part of the firm's income. For simplicity, suppose the price of trees is equal to one (coconut). Then the optimal condition is

(6.7) $\underset{\substack{\text{marginal product} \\ \text{of capital}}}{\text{MPK}} + \underset{\substack{\text{resale value} \\ \text{of capital}}}{1} = \underset{\substack{\text{marginal cost} \\ \text{of capital}}}{1 + r}.$

The cost of capital is 1, the same as the value of output since these are all coconuts. This condition can be rewritten more simply as:

(6.8) $\text{MPK} = r.$

The marginal product of capital need only be equal to the real interest rate, rather than $1 + r$ when Crusoe needed to recoup the principal of his investment. In practice, firms can usually resell their equipment at some price, so they will require a lower productivity because they

take into account the value of their equipment. So equation (6.8) rather than (6.5) is more likely to be relevant in practice. It is important to note that this does not invalidate the investment function (6.6).

But the story continues. In reality, installed capital is being worn out over time, or becomes economically obsolete. This loss of productive equipment is captured by a **rate of depreciation** δ. Tomorrow's value of today's capital is not 1 but $1 - \delta$. Taking this into account, (6.8) becomes

(6.9) $\underset{\substack{\text{marginal product} \\ \text{of capital}}}{\text{MPK}} + \underset{\substack{\text{resale value} \\ \text{of capital}}}{1 - \delta} = \underset{\substack{\text{marginal cost} \\ \text{of capital}}}{1 + r}$

which simplifies to

(6.10) $\text{MPK} = r + \delta.$

The optimal capital stock is reached when the marginal product of capital is equal to the sum of the interest rate r and the depreciation rate δ. Because depreciation can be thought of as an additional cost of capital, the right-hand side is often called the **user cost of capital**. The original rule for the optimal capital stock (6.5) can be regarded as a special case of complete depreciation ($\delta = 1$).

past investment K—perhaps there were already some coconut trees around when Crusoe came to his island. Ignoring depreciation, optimal investment is simply the difference $\bar{K} - K$. Thus, given the accumulated stock of capital so far and the rate of depreciation, the determinants of optimal investment are the same as those of the optimal stock of capital. An increase in the real interest rate which lowers the optimal stock of capital also lowers optimal investment, since the capital stock brought forward from the last period as well as the rate of depreciation remain unchanged. Accordingly, the investment function could be expressed as

$$(6.6) \qquad I = I(\underset{-}{r}).$$

6.3.3 The Accelerator Principle

In contrast to Crusoe's treeless island, in the real world some capital stock already exists. It is reasonable to expect that, for the capital stock to reach its optimal level derived in Section 6.3.1, investment would have to move in roughly the same proportion. This idea gives rise to a simple way of thinking about investment. Suppose the optimal capital stock is proportional to the expected output level:

$$(6.11) \qquad \bar{K}_2 = vY_2,$$

which can be justified both theoretically and empirically.[13] Then, with firms investing to keep the capital stock at its optimal level, an increase of GDP from Y_1 to Y_2 requires a change from $\bar{K}_1 = vY_1$ to $\bar{K}_2 = vY_2$. Ignoring depreciation, this means an investment of:

$$(6.12) \qquad I_1 = \bar{K}_2 - \bar{K}_1 = v(Y_2 - Y_1) = v\Delta Y_2.$$

This relationship captures the **accelerator principle**. It is called the accelerator because in order for investment to remain constant, output must

increase. Increases in investment are therefore associated with an *acceleration* of output. In practice, the capital–output ratio v is between 2 and 3 in most economies; put differently, annual GDP represents between one-third and one-half of the installed capital stock. GDP movements therefore are associated with much larger swings in investment.[14] This provides one reason why investment is more volatile than GDP: it is based on expectations of the future. In the following sections we will develop this idea in greater detail.

6.3.4 Investment and Tobin's *q*

Why do observers of the economic scene continuously monitor the evolution of stock markets? Prices of shares often move in erratic ways which may not seem particularly related to economic activity. In fact, stock prices are intimately related to macroeconomics. Aggregate economic activity affects stock prices, and stock prices are important determinants of aggregate economic activity. One important link is via wealth: when stock prices rise, shareholders become richer and spend more. Another link, which is our focus here, is investment.

Shares in publicly traded companies are titles of ownership. They represent claims on firms' present and future profits. Profits are the difference between firms' sales and their costs, which are mostly wages when the economy as a whole is considered. Share prices can be thought of as the market's best estimate of the value of those present and future profits. This value may differ from the price of the capital goods that constitute the firm itself, which is sometimes called the replacement cost of a firm's capital stock.

For a number of reasons, it is likely that the market value of a firm will differ—sometimes significantly—from the replacement cost of its physical capital. One such reason is the existence of intangible assets which include such factors as the firm's know-how, its network of distributors and retailers, its reputation among customers, etc. A more important reason, from the point of view of

---

[13] The long-run stability of the capital–output ratio was stressed in Ch. 3. Consider the case of the Cobb–Douglas production function with constant employment equal to 1, so $Y = AK^\alpha$. Here marginal productivity is $MPK = \partial Y/\partial K = \alpha AK^{\alpha-1} = \alpha AK^\alpha/K = \alpha Y/K$. The optimal capital stock is K^* such that $MPK = 1 + r$, so $\alpha Y/K^* = 1 + r$, and $K^* = \alpha Y/(1 + r)$. Setting $v = \alpha/(1 + r)$ gives (6.11).

[14] To account for depreciation, (6.12) is simply changed to $I_1 = v\Delta Y + \delta K_1$. The same conclusions apply.

macroeconomics, is the fact that 'Rome wasn't built in a day'. Establishing a new firm from scratch requires time and resources. These costs are greater, the more rapidly an investment project is undertaken. To summarize this, we define a ratio, called **Tobin's q**, which is defined as follows:[15]

(6.13)   Tobin's q

$$= \frac{\text{market value of installed capital}}{\text{replacement cost of installed capital}}.$$

The numerator of Tobin's q is the firm's value as priced by the stock market, the total value of all existing shares. The denominator is the amount that would have to be spent to replace the capital goods incorporated in existing firms.

The **q-theory of investment** relates the behaviour of aggregate investment to Tobin's q. When Tobin's q is greater than one, installed capital in the existing firm is more valuable than what it would cost to purchase it new and start a new firm from scratch. For this reason, entrepreneurs (people who start and run businesses) should take the hint and purchase new plant and equipment. Investment is then positive. For example, a Tobin's q of 1.2 would imply that a firm that spends 100 on new investment in plant and equipment increases its market value by 120. Installation adds a value of 20 to uninstalled equipment. Given the principle of declining marginal productivity, investment reduces the return on the capital over time and therefore reduces Tobin's q. Firms will continue to invest, increasing the capital stock and reducing the marginal product of capital, until Tobin's q has returned to unity.

Alternatively, when q is lower than 1, selling off equipment at replacement cost is profitable and therefore desirable from the point of view of the firm's shareholders, so net investment should be negative. In the aggregate economy, this can occur

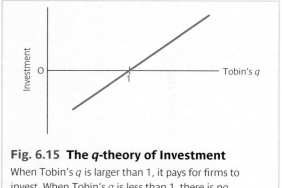

Fig. 6.15 The *q*-theory of Investment

When Tobin's q is larger than 1, it pays for firms to invest. When Tobin's q is less than 1, there is no incentive to invest, but rather an incentive to disinvest, or to dismantle or abandon productive capacity.

only if gross investment is exceeded by depreciation or capital is dismantled, sold, or scrapped. The dependence of investment on Tobin's q is displayed in Figure 6.15.

How is the q-theory related to the previous section, which showed that the interest rate is a key determinant of investment? The stock market values firms by discounting future earnings using the real interest rate. Any increase in the interest rate leads to heavier discounting and therefore to a decline in stock prices. Thus, the negative effect of the real interest rate on investment is actually incorporated into Tobin's q.

But Tobin's q does more than just take the interest rate into account; it also incorporates two other factors in the investment decision. First, gains in productivity of capital raise future income, and thereby increase share prices and q. An excellent example of how this can occur was the massive rise (and later, decline) in stock prices in the wake of the internet and new communications technologies. Second, q incorporates the role of expectations. Inevitably, investment is a bet on the future: firms buy equipment now to produce output for several years under uncertain conditions. How they will be able to take advantage of the equipment is not known when the investment occurs. Uncertainty ranges from the general economic situation, to competition in domestic and foreign markets, to the evolution of technology and even political

---

[15] It is named after US economist and Nobel laureate James Tobin (1918–2002), who pointed out in 1969 that investment should be positively related to the ratio of a firm's market valuation to the replacement value of its capital stock. In the meantime, more sophisticated analyses have shown the conditions under which this 'average q' concept is equal to the marginal concept presented in the text. For our purposes, we will simply assume that these conditions are met.

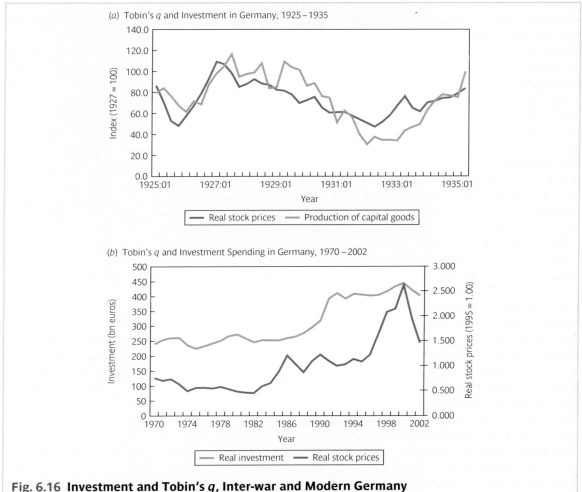

Fig. 6.16 Investment and Tobin's *q*, Inter-war and Modern Germany

Both in historical and more modern contexts, investment has consistently followed movements of Tobin's *q*, as proxied by a stock price index divided by the consumer price index.

Source: IMF, Ritschl (2004).

developments. All these aspects are continuously evaluated by the stock markets. Forward-looking share prices are volatile because these factors are volatile, and in the end this explains why investment is the most volatile component of GDP. It was Keynes who linked the high variability of investment to the **animal spirits** of entrepreneurs, that is, their fickle and volatile expectations of the future profitability of investment. It is precisely this volatility that can be seen so clearly in Figure 6.1.

To see how Tobin's *q* works as a predictor of investment expenditures, consider Figure 6.16, which presents data for Germany 1970–2002 as well from a much earlier period, the late 1920s and early 1930s, which included the Great Depression.[16] The link is quite strong, with a variable but

[16] Here we present rates of change in real investment spending.

relatively short lag. This is true despite the fact that not all companies are publicly traded; frequently, firms are too small to issue shares, and many larger ones are reluctant to 'go public'. It is often cheaper for firms to draw on their own savings (retained earnings) because profits are usually taxed less when reinvested than when distributed. Some firms prefer to finance investment by borrowing rather than by issuing shares; especially in continental Europe, bank lending plays an important if not dominant role. Despite these limitations, Tobin's q still does a pretty good job measuring the incentive to invest for these firms: it reflects both expected profitability—the numerator—and the real cost of borrowing through the discount factor and the cost of capital—the denominator.

Tobin's q explains the link between the stock market and the state of the economy. The economic function of stock exchanges is to evaluate the future profitability of firms and to place a value today for the whole stream of future earnings from capital ownership. For the macroeconomy as a whole, average stock prices represent the value of the capital stock in place. (Financial markets also assess the degree of riskiness related to unavoidable uncertainty, and this is factored into share prices— the subject of Chapter 19). Present and especially future economic conditions affect stock prices. Conversely, we should expect stock markets to affect economic conditions since stock prices influence investment through Tobin's q.

6.3.5 The Microeconomic Foundations of Tobin's q[17]

Installation costs

We now have two ways of thinking about the firm's investment decision. The first is that the firm invests to reach its optimal capital stock. The second approach sees investment as taking advantage of the difference between the value of capital already in place (installed) and its replacement cost—the cost of new capital goods. From either perspective, one might expect firms to seize such opportunities quickly. In practice, however, they do not adjust the capital stock instantaneously to its optimal level. For this reason q can and will differ systematically from unity for a long time. One reason for this is that firms face **installation costs** in addition to the direct costs considered so far.

The idea behind installation costs is simple. With adequate resources, it could have been possible to dig the Eurotunnel in just six months. Doing so, however, would have been enormously 'costly' in many ways, so it was completed over several years instead. Intuitively, the bigger the investment per unit of time, the more costly it is to install it. Examples of installation costs include the fact that each addition of new equipment in a factory disrupts existing production and that workers must be trained to operate new equipment.

Installation costs explain why Tobin's q is not always equal to unity. In the absence of installation costs, firms would promptly bring capital to its optimal stock level, equating marginal productivity and marginal cost as in equation (6.6), which can be rewritten as

$$(6.14) \qquad \frac{\text{MPK}}{1 + r} = 1.$$

$\text{MPK}/(1 + r)$ is the present value of the return on investment: it is next period's return on the latest addition of capital discounted back to today.[18] It must be equal to the marginal cost of equipment which is unity. When installation is costly, however, the cost of investing is not just the price of equipment: it now includes an additional cost, the marginal cost of installing new equipment, φ. This installation cost can be thought of as equipment which is 'eaten up' in the installation process. Furthermore, φ is an increasing function of the investment undertaken.[19] The optimal investment decision is to invest until the present value of the

---

[17] This section is a more advanced presentation of the q-theory of investment based on the notion of installation costs. It shows the similarity with the reasoning used to establish the optimal stock of capital. It can be skipped without any loss of continuity. The WebAppendix to this chapter presents a formal analysis.

[18] Remember, there are just two periods, so 'tomorrow' is a shorthand for the indefinite future. Otherwise we would have to discount all future MPKs.

[19] For example, the investment costs associated with a 10% increase in the capital stock could be four times the costs implied by a 5% increase.

MPK of new equipment is equal to the augmented marginal cost of equipment:

(6.15) $$\frac{MPK}{1 + r} = 1 + \varphi.$$

Comparing (6.14) and (6.15), we see that installation costs raise the MPK required to justify the investment. This can be achieved by taking a smaller step towards capital stock $\bar{K}$, since marginal productivity is higher the lower is the stock of capital. Since installation costs increase with the amount of investment each period, the next round of installation is cheaper, φ is lower, so firms will engage into more investment, and so on until φ is driven down to zero and (6.14) holds. That way firms break the path towards $\bar{K}$ into small steps which entail smaller costs.

Installation costs and Tobin's q

The stock market should value the return on an additional unit of investment by the present value of its marginal return, MPK/(1 + r). In the case of Robinson Crusoe, the replacement cost of capital is simply the cost of coconuts (uninstalled equipment) which is 1. Tobin's q is therefore[20]

(6.16) $$q = \left(\frac{MPK}{1 + r}\right)\Big/1.$$

Equation (6.16) establishes the link between the two investment principles. The optimal capital stock of capital is reached when (6.14) is satisfied, that is when Tobin's q is equal to 1. When q is above 1, the MPK exceeds $1 + r$, and investment is warranted. When q is lower than 1, the MPK is low given the replacement cost of physical capital. As new capital is put in place, the MPK declines, as does q. Investment becomes smaller and installation costs φ decline until they become negligible. At that stage $q = 1$, MPK $= 1 + r$, and the stock of capital is at its optimal level. Installation costs cause firms to move towards the optimal capital stock incrementally;

along the way the return on investment in present-value terms exceeds the replacement, or user, cost of capital.[21] Box 6.7 provides more details on both the user cost of capital as well as its relationship to Tobin's q.

The geometry of installation costs

Installation costs have two particular properties. First, they increase with the size of the investment. Big steps are more than proportionally more expensive than small ones. Second, they are transitory. Once the equipment is in place, the only relevant cost is the interest rate and depreciation—the opportunity cost of resources employed in production. Figure 6.17 modifies panel (b) of Figure 6.14 in two ways. First, investment is measured on the horizontal axis as the investment rate I/K, which gives a better indication of the intensity of disruptions which give rise to installation costs.[22] Second, on the vertical axis, marginal costs and returns are expressed in today's present discounted values. The marginal cost of capital in present value is equal to 1, because one unit of capital implies giving up one unit of consumption good today. The horizontal schedule represents the cost of investment in the absence of installation costs. With installation costs, the cost of investment exceeds the cost of capital. The more equipment is put in place, the higher is the marginal cost; hence the upward-sloping marginal cost of investment curve. The marginal return on investment is MPK/(1 + r); it is downward sloping because of the principle of declining marginal productivity.

Firms invest until the marginal cost equals the marginal return at point A in panel (a) of Figure 6.17, where the two curves intersect. The value of an additional unit of capital installed—Tobin's q— exceeds the replacement cost of capital. Without installation costs, the firm would choose point C instead and invest more. It may be surprising that the

---

[20] We cheat a bit here. The definition of Tobin's q is based on the market value of firms, while what matters in theory is the *marginal* return on investment. The market value of firms depends on the *average* return on all capital, not just the latest addition. We overlook the difference between these two definitions of average and marginal q.

[21] A related approach, pioneered by Professors Finn Kydland of Carnegie Mellon and Edward Prescott of Arizona, stresses that it takes time to design, acquire, and put in place new equipment. The implications are similar to those of installation costs.

[22] In the absence of depreciation, $I/K = \Delta K/K$. Focusing on the investment rate is justified by the idea that a given amount of investment is more disruptive in a small firm (or economy) than in a large one.

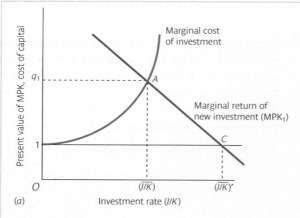
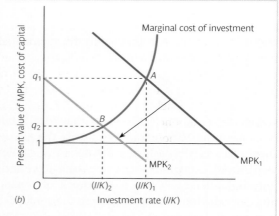

Fig. 6.17 Tobin's q

In panel (a) profits are maximized at point A, where the marginal return of investment in present-value terms is equal to its marginal cost. The marginal cost of capital is 1 (unit of forgone consumption). The optimum rate of investment is $(\overline{I/K})'$. Tobin's q corresponds to point A: it is the ratio of the marginal return on new investment to the cost of new capital. In the absence of installation costs (point B), the optimum rate of investment $(\overline{I/K})$ brings the capital stock immediately to its optimum level. In panel (b) investment starts at point A as before. With a higher stock of capital, the MPK then declines as represented by the shift from MPK_1 to MPK_2. With Tobin's q still above unity, investment continues but at the lower rate $(I/K)_2$. The process continues until q is equal to 1, and no further investment is warranted.

Box 6.7 The User Cost of Capital and the Price of Investment Goods

In Robinson Crusoe's world, coconuts were used for both consumption and investment. In the real world, investment and consumption goods are different and have different prices. This complicates slightly, but does not invalidate, the main line of reasoning. Let p^K be the relative price of investment goods, defined as P^K/P, where P is the price of consumption goods (in euros) and P^K the price of capital goods (in euros). If p^K is constant, profit for the firm expressed in units of the consumption good is:

(6.17)
$$\text{profit} = \frac{F(K)}{1+r} - p^k K.$$

Comparing this expression to (6.5), the optimal stock of capital fulfils a slightly modified version of (6.6):

(6.18)
$$MPK = p^K(1+r),$$

and the definition of Tobin's q becomes

(6.19)
$$q = \frac{MPK/(1+r)}{p^k}.$$

The only difference is that Tobin's q now compares the marginal product of capital with its replacement cost, the price of investment goods. With installation costs, optimal investment must obey

(6.20)
$$\underset{\substack{\text{present value}\\\text{of MPK}}}{MPK/(1+r)} = \underset{\substack{\text{marginal cost}\\\text{of capital}}}{(1+\varphi)p^K}$$

or, in terms of Tobin's q,

(6.21)
$$q = \frac{MPK/(1+r)}{p^k} = (1+\varphi)$$

The analysis can be extended in a straightforward way to several periods and to allow the price of investment goods to vary over time. If Crusoe buys investment goods at p_1^K and sells back $(1-\delta)$ at price p_2^K, he would maximize

(6.17')
$$\text{profit} = \frac{F(K)}{1+r} - p_1^k K + \frac{(1-\delta)p_2^k K}{1+r}.$$

and optimal capital stock would satisfy

(6.18')
$$MPK = (1+r)p_1^K - (1-\delta)p_2^K$$
$$= [(1+r)-(1-\delta)(1+\pi^K)]p_1^K,$$

where π^K is the rate of change in the price of capital goods $(p_2^K/p_1^K - 1)$. For sufficiently small values of r, δ, and π^K, this can be approximated as $MPK \approx (r+\delta+\pi^K)p_1^K$. This version of the user cost of capital thus allows for the possibility that the relative price of investment goods may change over time.

marginal return is higher with than without installation costs. Rather than reducing the long-term profitability of investment, installation costs simply induce firms to invest at a slower rate. In the long run, firms achieve the same desired capital stock as in the absence of adjustment costs.

Panel (b) shows how the investment rate moves over time. With q above 1, investment first occurs at rate $(I/K)_1$ corresponding to point A. Each MPK schedule is drawn for a given stock of already installed capital. Moving along the schedule, we find the profitability of further additions to the existing capital stock.

Once the capital stock has increased as a result of investment, however, these additions become less productive—because of the principle of declining marginal productivity. So, as further investment accumulates, the MPK schedule shifts downwards, in the figure from MPK_1 to MPK_2.[23] Investment continues as long as Tobin's q is greater than unity, but will do so at a declining rate, here at rate $(I/K)_2$ corresponding to point B. The process will continue until q is driven down back to 1 and the capital stock has reached its long-run, optimal level.

6.3.6 The Investment Function

The investment function summarizes compactly all the ideas that have been developed until now. First, investment is inversely related to the interest rate because it measures the opportunity cost of those resources. Higher interest rates imply lower invest-ment spending. Second, the accelerator mechanism captures the stable long-run relationship between the capital stock and output. Since the rate of proportionality is greater than 1, increases in output lead to magnified increases in investment expenditures. Finally, Tobin's q reflects the fact that some firms finance their expenditures by issuing shares on the stock market. High stock prices mean that the market places a high value on installed capital, so firms can raise more resources per share issued, and this encourages investment. They provide a central indicator of the market's assessment of the profitability of new investment. Tobin's q also incorporates some, but not all, of the effect of real interest rates on investment, because a higher interest rate discounts future profits more heavily and reduces q. (For firms that raise money not on the stock market, but by issuing bonds or borrowing from banks, it is the interest rate alone that represents the cost of investment.) These results can be summarized by the following investment function, which will be used in various forms throughout the book:

(6.22) $I = I(r, \Delta Y, q).$
                     $\quad\; -\;\; +\;\; +$

This function states that investment depends negatively on the real interest rate r, positively on the change in GDP, and positively on Tobin's q.[24] Holding interest rates constant, an increase in Tobin's q increases investment.

[23] The observant student will note that for linear curves, and in the absence of depreciation, the intercept of each successive MPK curve with the vertical axis is determined by the value of q in the preceding period.

[24] In theory, Tobin's q should contain all information necessary to infer the profitability of investment. Since many firms finance investment through borrowing and retained earnings, the interest rate also matters directly. In addition, as with households, many firms are rationed on the credit market, so they have to rely upon current income to finance spending on productive equipment. This would rationalize a third term related to the discussion of the accelerator in S. 6.3.3.

❶ Summary

1 Rational consumers attempt to smooth consumption over time, borrowing in bad years, saving in good ones. Consumption is driven primarily by wealth, the present discounted value of current and future incomes, and initial net asset holdings. Over a life cycle, income typically increases. To smooth out consumption, agents typically borrow when young and pay back later.

2 Individual consumption smoothing means that, in the aggregate, temporary disturbances are met by current account imbalances (national saving or dissaving) to reduce the need to adjust consumption abruptly. In contrast, permanent disturbances lead to immediate consumption adjustment rather than to borrowing or lending.

3 Financial market imperfections, arising from uncertainty about future incomes and the inability of banks to assess individual future prospects, prevent households from borrowing against future expected income. As a result, current disposable income also affects aggregate consumption.

4 The effect of changes in the real interest rate on current consumption is ambiguous. Lenders tend to increase, while borrowers decrease, consumption in response to increases in the interest rate. In the aggregate, however, higher interest rates are likely to reduce consumption by reducing wealth.

5 The consumption function relates aggregate consumption to wealth (positively) and disposable income (positively).

6 The optimal capital stock equates the marginal productivity of capital to the marginal cost of capital. The optimal capital stock increases when the real interest rate declines and when technological gains raise the marginal productivity of capital.

7 Investment over and above capital depreciation increases the capital stock. As the optimal capital stock, investment is driven by the real interest rate.

8 The accelerator mechanism links investment to changes in output. This is both a mechanical relationship (in the long run the capital output ratio is constant) and a symptom of credit rationing.

9 The ratio of the market value of installed capital to the replacement cost of installed capital is called Tobin's q. It is an approximation of the ratio of the present discounted value of the marginal return of investment to the marginal cost of capital. This ratio is equal to unity when the capital stock has reached its optimal level. When Tobin's q is larger than unity, the capital stock is below its optimal level and firms benefit from further investment.

10 The market value of installed capital, the numerator in Tobin's q, is priced in the stock market. In setting this price, stock markets look ahead. The forward-looking nature of Tobin's q mirrors how firms take into account expected future earnings when they make investment decisions.

11 Because of various installation costs, firms do not acquire their optimal capital stock immediately. Rather, they spread investment over time, gradually bringing capital up to the optimal level.

12 The present discounted return to investment exceeds the marginal cost of capital to compensate for installation costs. Investment proceeds until the present value of its return, at the margin, equals the marginal cost of investment, the sum of borrowing and installation costs.

13 The investment function states that aggregate investment depends upon: (i) the real interest rate (negatively); (ii) GDP growth (positively); (iii) Tobin's q (positively).

☯ Key Concepts

- consumption function
- investment function
- indifference curves
- utility
- marginal rate of intertemporal substitution
- life-cycle consumption
- permanent income
- random walk
- consumption smoothing
- credit rationed
- marginal productivity of capital (MPK)

- opportunity cost
- marginal cost of capital
- optimal capital stock
- rate of depreciation
- user cost of capital
- accelerator principle
- Tobin's q
- q-theory of investment
- animal spirits
- installation costs

❓ Exercises

1 Consider a household whose income is £5,000 today and £10,000 tomorrow.

(a) If the real interest rate is 5%, what is its wealth (i) in terms of today's consumption, (ii) in terms of tomorrow's consumption? Compute the household's permanent income (see Box 6.2).

(b) If today's income unexpectedly increases by £200, what is the change in permanent income?

(c) If income goes up by £200 permanently, what is the effect on permanent income?

(d) Answer the same questions with a 10% real interest rate.

(e) Suppose the utility of the household is given by $\sqrt{C_1 C_2}$, where C_1 and C_2 are consumption today and tomorrow. Derive optimal consumption today and tomorrow for (a), (b), (c), and (d).

2 Show, graphically, the effects on current and future consumption of an income windfall gain expected in the future. Applied to the national level: how would the current account of a country full of rational consumers react to a windfall?

3 Define the permanent income hypothesis. How does it relate to the more general theory of consumption derived from intertemporal utility maximization?

4 Suppose you expect to live for six decades. Your income is £15,000 in the first, £300,000 in the second, £350,000 in the third, £450,000 in the fourth, £200,000 in the fifth, and £100,000 in the last. What is your permanent income if the interest rate is 3%? If it is 5%? If you desire to consume your permanent income each year, what does your savings pattern look like? Do you think this is feasible? How does your answer

change if you decide to bequeath £50,000 to your favourite charity?

5 Should a temporary increase in taxes to finance a temporary increase in public spending reduce the current account deficit? What about a permanent increase in both taxes and public spending? What is the effect on the current account in an open economy?

6 Latin American countries have long suffered from high interest rates on international borrowing. Using the Fisher diagram, trace out the theoretical effect of lower world interest rates on consumption and investment in these borrowing countries. What do you expect the effect to be on the (primary) current account? State your assumptions carefully.

7 There is evidence that spending on durable goods increases faster than spending on non-durables

during a temporary boom expansion. Can you give some economic reasons why? (Hint: think of durable goods expenditure as a form of saving.)

8 In Figure 6.5 it is assumed that initially there is no borrowing or lending.

(a) If the consumer was initially a net borrower, what is the effect of (i) a temporary increase in income, (ii) a permanent increase? Contrast your results with the case treated in the text.

(b) Apply the same question for the case where the consumer was initially a net lender.

9 Governments that wish to speed up investment by firms offer a temporary tax credit, which works as follows. Firms that invest before a deadline will be allowed to pay current taxes later, say five years later. Why should such a trick work?

Essay Questions

1 A great deal of debate has arisen in Germany on the financing of the expenditure necessary to improve the much neglected infrastructure in its new eastern states. One side favours increased taxes, which would fall largely on households. The other side favours an increased budget deficit. Which side is right? How important to your answer is your assumption of whether the spending increase is permanent or temporary?

2 In 2000, the consensus among US economists was that an additional dollar of household wealth would lead to about $0.05 of additional consumption. Between 2000 and mid-2002, the value of the stock market fell by close to 25%. Yet US consumption did not fall by the amount forecast. How can you explain this, using the concepts

developed in the chapter? (Hint: in the five years previous to 2000, US stock markets rose in value by more than 100%!)

3 In poor countries, people hardly save. One explanation is that there are few banks and that the banks are not interested in lending to households because they never know whether they will be repaid. Another explanation is that with earnings barely at the subsistence level, people have nothing to save. Evaluate these views.

4 The ageing population problem is affecting old Europe but not dynamic Asia. Why do some observers expect Europe to run large primary current account surpluses, with the opposite happening in Asia?

The Real Exchange Rate 7

7.1 Overview *152*

7.2 The Real Exchange Rate and the Primary Current Account Function *153*

    7.2.1   The Real Exchange Rate Defined *153*

    7.2.2   Measuring the Real Exchange Rate in Practice *154*

    7.2.3   How the Real Exchange Rate Affects the Primary Current Account *155*

7.3 The Real Exchange Rate as the Relative Price of Non-traded Goods *156*

    7.3.1   Traded versus Non-traded Goods *156*

    7.3.2   The Production Possibilities Frontier *157*

    7.3.3   The Case of a Balanced Primary Current Account *159*

    7.3.4   The Case of a Non-zero Primary Current Account: The Role of the Real Exchange Rate *160*

7.4 The National Intertemporal Budget Constraint and the Equilibrium Real Exchange Rate *161*

    7.4.1   The Long Run and the Primary Current Account: A Review *161*

    7.4.2   The Equilibrium Real Exchange Rate and the Primary Current Account in the Long Run *162*

    7.4.3   The Fundamental Determinants of the Real Exchange Rate *163*

Summary *168*

Suppose a man climbs five feet up a sea wall, then climbs down 12 feet. Whether he drowns or not depends upon how high above sea-level he was when he started. The same problem arises in deciding whether currencies are under- or over-valued.

—*The Economist*, 26 August 1995

7.1 Overview

This chapter completes the analysis of the real side of the economy by opening up the economy to trade in goods and assets across national borders. From the macroeconomic perspective, we are mostly interested in how international trade enables nations to borrow and lend by importing or exporting more than they produce at a particular point in time. In the language of Chapter 5, we explore more deeply how the current account balances the intertemporal budget constraint.

Until now, production and consumption at a given point in time consisted of a single good, called 'output'. An important innovation in this chapter is to expand the analysis to two goods. This important modification allows us to study relative prices, or prices of goods in terms of others (e.g. how many cakes can be exchanged for a car). This is not our first encounter with **relative prices**: the real wage (the ratio of nominal wages to a price index) or the real interest rate (the price of today's consumption in terms of tomorrow's consumption) fall in that category. Relative prices are the essence of a market economy.[1] They act as signals and provide incentives to producers and consumers to adapt their behaviour to changing market conditions.

In the international context, the **real exchange rate** performs this important function. The real exchange rate is the relative price of our goods (domestic goods and services) in terms of foreign goods (goods and services produced abroad). It is related to the **nominal exchange rate**, the price of domestic money in terms of foreign money. In fact, the real exchange rate is the nominal exchange rate which has been adjusted for the prices of domestic and foreign goods.

The central message of this chapter is twofold: the real exchange rate affects the primary current account by shifting both production and consumption choices between the home and foreign goods. The second message is that the real exchange rate is itself an endogenous variable. As in Chapter 3, we focus on the long run when all markets are in equilibrium, so the **equilibrium real exchange rate** is such that the intertemporal budget constraint for the country as a whole (presented in Chapter 5) is satisfied.

Because there are many possible definitions of home and foreign goods, the real exchange rate can be defined in a number of ways. This chapter looks at two important ones. The first is simply the ratio of prices at home to those abroad, expressed in a common currency. The second definition distinguishes between those goods and services that are traded internationally and those that are produced at home and are not subject to international competition.

---

[1] It is a fact that the crucial first step in the transformation of Eastern European countries to market economies was to free up prices so that they could play this fundamental role.

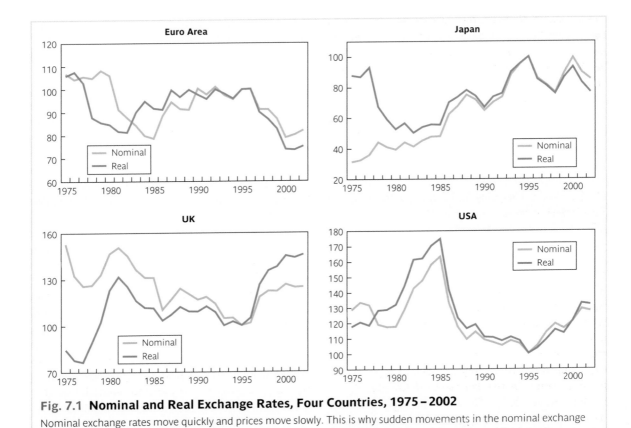

Fig. 7.1 Nominal and Real Exchange Rates, Four Countries, 1975–2002

Nominal exchange rates move quickly and prices move slowly. This is why sudden movements in the nominal exchange rate are reflected in the real exchange rate. Over the longer run, different evolutions of domestic and foreign prices— i.e. different inflation rates—may break the co-movements between the two exchange rates.

Source: IMF.

7.2 The Real Exchange Rate and the Primary Current Account Function

7.2.1 The Real Exchange Rate Defined

To compare prices of goods produced at home with those of goods produced abroad, we need to express them in a common currency. For that purpose, we use the nominal exchange rate. Nominal exchange rates are set on the foreign exchange market.[2] Exchange rates can be quoted in either of two ways: either as the number of foreign monetary units per domestic unit (this is called **British terms**, e.g. $1.5 per £1 from the perspective of UK residents, or $1.1 per €1 from the point of view of European Monetary Union) or as the number of domestic

---

[2] Exchange markets and the nominal exchange rates are studied in detail in Ch. 19. A quick look at that chapter may be useful.

monetary units per foreign unit (which used to be called **European terms**, e.g. CHF1.6 per $1 for Switzerland). This text adopts the convention of British terms since it is commonly used for quoting the euro and the pound. With this convention, a currency **appreciation** corresponds to an increase in its value in terms of foreign currencies, so the exchange rate rises (e.g. from $0.9 to $1.1 for €1). Conversely, a loss of value, or a **depreciation**, would imply a decline in the exchange rate.

If S denotes the exchange rate (say, US dollars per Euro) and P^* is the price of foreign goods expressed in foreign currency (say, $), then the domestic price of foreign goods is P^*/S (measured in euros). Conversely, if P is the price of domestic goods in domestic currency, their price in foreign currency is SP (in this case, measured in dollars).[3] The real exchange rate, the relative price of domestic goods in terms of foreign goods, is the ratio of those two price levels:

(7.1)
$$\sigma = \frac{P}{P^*/S} = \frac{SP}{P^*}$$

both prices in domestic currency   both prices in foreign currency

As long as we compare goods prices in the same currency we arrive at the same definition. The real exchange rate can be thought of as the nominal exchange rate 'doubly deflated' by foreign and domestic goods prices. Like their nominal counterparts, real exchange rates are said to appreciate (σ increases) or depreciate (σ declines).

As long as goods prices P^* and P remain unchanged or move closely together, the nominal and real exchange rates move together. As Figure 7.1 illustrates, over short horizons, the nominal and real exchange rates tend to fluctuate in tandem. This is so because typically nominal exchange rates are quite volatile, while prices tend to be sticky. Over the longer run, however, nominal and real exchange rates seem to have independent lives of their own, which justifies studying separately the

real exchange rate in the long run (this chapter) and the nominal exchange rate (Chapter 19).

In order to grasp better the distinction between the nominal and real exchange rates, it is useful to ask: when do the two move together? Clearly from (7.1), when domestic and foreign price levels change by the same percentage amount, their ratio will remain constant. But this only occurs when inflation is the same at home and abroad. If, on the contrary, inflation pushes foreign prices (P^*) faster than domestic prices (P), the real exchange rate depreciates (σ decreases) as long as the nominal exchange rate S does not appreciate enough to offset fully the decline in P/P^*. In the special case when the nominal exchange rate is fixed, real exchange rate changes can only occur when domestic and foreign prices rise at different rates.

It is also possible for the nominal exchange rate to appreciate without the real exchange rate changing at all. This would occur, for instance, if inflation is lower at home than abroad (P/P^* declines), while S is rising at a rate equal to the difference in the two inflation rates. This was the case in Germany, on average, over the period 1975–90. A general feature, visible in Figure 7.1, is that real exchange rates are more stable in the long run than in the short run, and also more stable than nominal exchange rates. This relative long-run stability makes it easier to first study the real exchange rate in the long run, and then to study the nominal exchange rate in the long and short run.[4]

7.2.2 Measuring the Real Exchange Rate in Practice

Measuring real exchange rates in practice poses two problems. The first concerns the definition of 'foreign'. The rest of the world comprises a large number of countries. With each country the home country has a bilateral exchange rate. How should one go about aggregating these individual rates? The solution consists in computing an 'average foreign price level' P^* as a weighted average of prices in a large number of trading partner countries (ideally, all of them), and 'an average nominal exchange rate' S as a weighted average of our nominal exchange rate

---

[3] To see this: P is measured in euros, P^* is measured in dollars, and S is expressed in terms of dollars per euro. Then P^*/S is measured in euros (since ($) / ($/euro) = euro). Similarly, SP is measured in dollars.

[4] This is why Ch. 7 comes before Ch. 19!

Box 7.1 Computing and Comparing Effective Exchange Rates[5]

Effective exchange rates are computed using a number of partner-countries. Each partner-country receives a weight typically representing its importance in trade for the country in question; for example, its share of our exports or our imports, or the average of both. Geometric averaging is applied to price indices in these countries and to our bilateral exchange rates vis-à-vis their currencies. If n countries are selected and S_i is the bilateral nominal exchange rate vis-à-vis country i with trade weight w_i, our effective nominal exchange rate is:

$$S = (S_1)^{w_1} (S_2)^{w_2} (S_3)^{w_3} \ldots (S_n)^{w_n},$$

where the weights sum up to 1 ($\sum w_i = 1$). The effective foreign price level P^* is computed by applying the same weights to each partner-country's price index P_i:

$$P^* = (P_1)^{w_1} (P_2)^{w_2} (P_3)^{w_3} \ldots (P_n)^{w_n},$$

Then the effective real exchange rate is simply the average of our real exchange rates vis-à-vis each partner-country:

$$\sigma = \left(\frac{S_1 P}{P_1}\right)^{w_1} \left(\frac{S_2 P}{P_2}\right)^{w_2} \left(\frac{S_3 P}{P_3}\right)^{w_3} \ldots \left(\frac{S_n P}{P_n}\right)^{w_n} = \frac{SP}{P^*}$$

This approach can be applied to other classes of goods. A frequently used measure of the real exchange rate is the ratio of export to import prices. It differs from the ratio of non-traded to traded good prices in two ways: it ignores the existence of non-traded goods, and it distinguishes among the traded goods those which are produced domestically and exported from the imported goods produced abroad. In this view the 'home' goods are exports instead of non-traded, and the 'foreign' goods are imports instead of all traded goods lumped together. The choice between this or that measure really depends on the characteristics of the country at hand and on the question of interest.

vis-à-vis each of them. The weights assigned to each country are chosen to represent its importance to us. Box 7.1 explains how this is accomplished. The corresponding values of S and σ are called respectively the nominal and real **effective exchange rates**. 'Effective' means that it accounts for the fact that not all exchange rates matter equally. The result is an index—we can no longer express the nominal exchange rate in value terms, e.g. dollars per euro—computed to take a simple value, e.g. 1 or 100, in some base year. The indices presented in Figure 7.1 take on the value 100 in 1995.

A second problem arises when deciding which prices to compare. A real exchange rate is the price ratio of two baskets of goods and services. Because so many baskets are possible, there is no one real exchange rate that answers all the questions one may wish to consider, so several definitions are possible. One of them is the ratio of domestically produced exports to foreign-produced import prices, sometimes called the **external terms of trade**. Another definition is the ratio of non-traded to traded goods prices, sometimes called the **internal**

terms of trade. The merit of the first definition is to be more precise about where the traded goods are produced. The advantage of the second definition is that it separates out the sectors open to foreign competition (which produce traded goods) from those that are sheltered (and produce non-traded goods). Broader-based real exchange rates compare consumer price indices or GDP deflators. Other indices are designed to measure a country's competitiveness by focusing on production costs, chiefly labour costs.

7.2.3 How the Real Exchange Rate Affects the Primary Current Account

What is the link between the real exchange rate and the primary current account (PCA)? Consider, for instance, a real depreciation: domestic goods

---

[5] Nominal and real effective exchange rates are computed and published by various sources. Among them, *International Financial Statistics*, a monthly publication of the International Monetary Fund, presents a variety of real exchange rates (using GDP deflators, export prices, CPIs, labour costs) computed using a sample of eighteen advanced economies.

become cheaper relative to foreign goods. In general, there will be two reactions. The first is on the consumers' side: an increase in foreign prices reduces domestic spending on foreign goods and makes domestic goods more attractive. This improves the primary current account. The second reaction is related to production. The depreciation makes firms more interested in producing substitutes for now-higher priced foreign goods, possibly even towards goods for export, and less interested in producing domestic goods which just became cheap. This, too improves the primary current account. The **primary current account function** formally summarizes these observations:

(7.2) $PCA = PCA(\sigma, \ldots).$

                         $(-)$

As usual, the minus sign indicates that an increase in the real exchange rate σ has a negative effect on the primary current account.[6] All other things equal—which is represented by the dots in (7.2)[7]—a real appreciation leads to a worsening (decline) in the primary current account, which can either mean a reduction in the primary current deficit or an increase in the primary current account surplus.

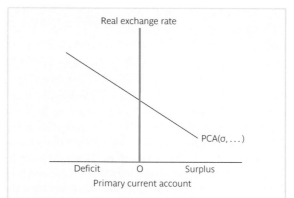

Fig. 7.2 The Primary Current Account Function

The primary current account function shows the relation between the real exchange rate and the primary account balance. It is downward sloping because a more depreciated real exchange rate, everything else unchanged, leads to an improvement in the primary current account.

This function is represented by the downward-sloping schedule in Figure 7.2. The rest of this chapter analyses this important macroeconomic relationship.

7.3 The Real Exchange Rate as the Relative Price of Non-traded Goods

7.3.1 Traded versus Non-traded Goods

Among the many possible definitions of the real exchange rate, we will work primarily with the second one presented in Section 7.2: the ratio of **non-traded** to **traded goods** prices. Losing the distinction between exports and imports is acceptable for developed countries, which in fact trade among themselves in very similar goods: the UK exports cars to France and France exports cars to the UK, etc. For those developing countries which export natural resources and import industrial products, the distinction between exports and imports would be much more important.

How do we tell the difference between traded and non-traded goods? There is no clear boundary between the two, but common sense can take us a

---

[6] Some students may wonder if a depreciation couldn't in fact worsen the current account. In rare cases it is indeed possible, if consumers cannot substitute away from more expensive imports, their value might actually rise; if exports do not react strongly enough, the current account could worsen when measured in terms of the domestic good. This case is sufficiently rare to be ignored in a textbook like this one.

[7] The other variables that affect the PCA are specified further in Ch. 10.

long way. Examples of goods or services that cannot be physically traded are housing, construction, and transportation. The most important obstacle to trade is transportation costs: haircuts, medical services, car repair, or cement are good examples. Other goods and services could be traded but are not because country-specific regulations limit their usefulness elsewhere or prevent their exchange (e.g. standards: why are washing machines in the United States so different from European ones?). Many goods may be non-traded but are nevertheless tradable: if protection were removed or transportation costs were to fall, they might become traded.[8] In the end, the distinction is useful and important for one good economic reason: non-traded goods do not face the same competitive pressure as traded goods. When trade is relatively free, traded goods cannot differ much in price and quality. Non-traded goods, on the other side, are purely local.

Denoting by P^T and P^N the home currency prices of traded and non-traded goods, measured in euros, the relative price of non-traded goods in terms of traded goods is

$$(7.3) \qquad \sigma = \frac{P^N}{P^T}$$

Under pressure from world trade competition, the domestic price of traded goods P^T will align itself with foreign prices P^{T*} when expressed in the same currency, so $P^T = P^{T*}/S$, where P^{T*} is the price of foreign-produced traded goods expressed in foreign currency. This is a rather extreme way of recognizing the constraint that international competition imposes on the domestic pricing of traded goods. It is roughly correct for 'small' countries which do not much influence world prices and must take P^{T*} as given. The real exchange rate can therefore be expressed as

$$(7.4) \qquad \sigma = \frac{SP^N}{P^{T*}}$$

i.e. the relative price of non-traded goods in terms of traded goods. As given by (7.4), the real exchange

rate represents an internal term of trade because it is the price ratio of the two categories of domestically produced goods. It measures how many traded goods must be given up to obtain one unit of locally produced, non-traded goods. When non-traded goods are costly in terms of traded goods, the real exchange rate is said to be appreciated relative to a situation in which they are cheaper.

7.3.2 The Production Possibilities Frontier

When resources are not wasted, producing more of one good in an economy implies producing less of the other. This is the proper way of thinking about the production possibilities of an economy in the medium to long run; there is no free lunch. Producing lots of automobiles means that there are fewer workers and machines around to produce other things, say haircuts. Applied to the distinction between tradable and non-tradable goods, this trade-off can be represented in Figure 7.3 by the **production possibilities frontier (PPF)**. The curve

Fig. 7.3 The Production Possibilities Frontier (PPF)

The production possibilities frontier (PPF) summarizes maximal combinations of different goods that an economy can produce, given its available resources and, perhaps, its markets institutions and regulations. Its slope is the marginal rate of transformation or, here, how many units of tradable goods must be given up to produce a unit of the non-tradable good.

---

[8] Financial services were long considered a non-traded good, until the information technology revolution sharply reduced the costs of providing and transporting such services.

Box 7.2   The Shape of the Production Possibilities Frontier

The shape of the PPF describes how an economy's available resources can be used to produce various combination of two goods. As we move down the curve to the south-east, the production of traded goods declines while that of non-traded goods increases. The negative slope of the PPF reminds us that we cannot produce more of one good without producing less of the other one—since factors of production are in fixed supply and must be reallocated between competing uses. The rate at which one good is 'transformed' into the other (called the marginal rate of transformation) is measured by the slope of the PPF at any particular point. The steeper the slope, the more traded goods must be given up to produce one more unit of the non-traded good. The PPF is bowed-out with respect to the origin, meaning that this sacrifice of traded goods for additional increments of the non-traded goods increases with the quantity of non-traded goods already produced. One reason is that some factors of production are fixed—the stock of capital at any time, management skills, land, and natural resources. For example, given the stock of capital, as labour is shifted towards the non-traded goods sector, the MPL declines in the non-traded goods sector and rises in the traded goods sector: moving workers is increasingly costly in terms of lost traded output, and is less and less effective in producing more non-traded goods. Other reasons for decreasing returns are: labour is specialized, as some workers enjoy a comparative advantage in producing particular goods; there are costs of moving from one pattern of production to another; and technologies differ across sectors. If both sectors use the same technology, with constant returns to scale, if no particular skills are required, and if the movement of inputs across sectors is costless, the PPF becomes a straight line and the marginal rate of transformation is constant.

describes the whole range of combinations of traded (Y^T) and non-traded goods (Y^N) that can be produced in an economy, given existing resources and technology. Moving along the PPF reveals how production can be shifted from one sector to the other by transferring resources. Box 7.2 explains why the PPF is concave or bowed out from the origin.

The PPF shifts outwards over time, primarily for two reasons. First, more inputs (capital, labour) may become available. Second, technical progress in either or both of the two sectors allows more production with the same inputs. In a market economy, the PPF must also account for existing imperfections and distortions in goods, labour, and capital markets. For example, if a reduction in the generosity of unemployment benefits leads workers to supply more labour, such a policy would shift the PPF outwards.

For any chosen combination of production of tradable and non-tradable goods, nominal GDP in euros is given by

(7.5)   nominal GDP $= P^T Y^T + P^N Y^N$.

The nominal GDP is the sum of the nominal value added in both sectors. The real GDP is obtained by deflating the nominal GDP. This can be done by using an aggregate price index (the GDP deflator, the average of P^T and P^N) or else by choosing one good as **numeraire**. A numeraire is simply a good in which other goods prices are quoted. Choosing the traded good as numeraire, the real GDP, expressed in units of traded goods, is obtained by dividing the nominal GDP by P^T, the price of traded goods:

(7.6) $Y = Y^T + \sigma Y^N$ with $\sigma = P^N/P^T$.

A particular value of real GDP could correspond to any number of different combinations of the two goods. These combinations are shown in Figure 7.4 as the **price line** AB. The slope of the price line ($-\sigma$) is given by the real exchange rate. The intersection with the y-axis represents the value of GDP in terms of the numeraire (traded goods). If the real exchange rate appreciates (non-traded good prices rise relatively to traded goods prices), a given real GDP (measured by OA in terms of traded goods) corresponds to less of the more valuable non-traded good (from OB to OC); the new price line AC is

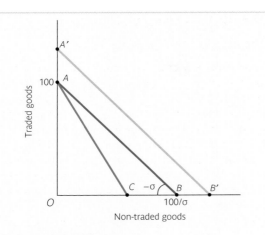

Fig. 7.4 Price Lines
A price line corresponds to a particular value of real GDP evaluated in terms of traded goods. Given the relative price s of non-traded goods, a real GDP of 100 can be attained by producing 100 traded goods (point A) or $100/\sigma$ non-traded goods (point B), or any combination of both goods along the line AB. $A'B'$ represents a higher real GDP with the same relative price. If non-traded goods become more expensive (σ rises) the price line becomes steeper, with the intercept moving from point B to point C. The intersection of the price line with the y-axis (point A) is the real value of total GDP in terms of the traded good.

Fig. 7.5 Optimal Production
Given technology and resources, the highest real GDP is achieved at point P, where the price line (which is as high as possible) is tangent to the production possibilities frontier. If the relative price of non-traded goods rises, maximum GDP is reached at a point like P', where more of the more highly valued non-traded good is produced.

steeper. A higher real GDP with the same corresponds to a higher price line, like $A'B'$.

Figure 7.5 shows that, for a given value of the real exchange rate, the most-preferred outcome is attained at point P where a price line is tangent to the PPF. At this point there is no incentive to shift production in favour of either of the two goods: given relative prices, this output mix maximizes real GDP. When relative prices change, so does the optimal output mix. For example, when the relative price of non-traded goods rises (a real exchange rate appreciation), the price line becomes steeper and the tangency point moves to P'. Quite reasonably, production shifts towards the more valuable non-traded good and away from the less valuable traded good. A decline in the relative price of non-traded goods (a real exchange rate depreciation) triggers the opposite shift of resources and production.

7.3.3 The Case of a Balanced Primary Current Account

The real exchange rate determines the optimal production mix, but what determines the real exchange rate? The answer is that the market does. Technology, resources, and consumer tastes meet each other in the market place. Technology and resources are summarized by the PPF. Once we know about tastes and the budget constraint of consumers, we can find the real exchange rate that delivers equilibrium between demand and supply for both traded and non-traded goods simultaneously. This equilibrium real exchange rate is relevant for the long run, when resources are not idle and all markets have reached equilibrium.

Figure 7.6 depicts tastes of households in the usual way. Much like the preferences between consumption today and consumption tomorrow (intertemporal choice), preferences between traded and non-traded goods (intratemporal choice) can be summarized by indifference curves, with the

Fig. 7.6 Indifference Curves
Consumers' intratemporal preferences are described
by indifference curves. Each curve becomes flatter
towards the right because as more non-traded goods are
consumed the willingness to give up more traded goods
for one more non-traded good declines. Curves to the
north-east correspond to increasing levels of satisfaction.

**Fig. 7.7 Optimal Production and
Consumption**
Available technology and resources constrain efficient
production to points on the PPF. The highest satisfaction
is attained at point A, where one indifference curve
is tangent to the PPF. The common slope of the PPF
and the indifference curve at this point represents the
relative price that will lead markets to achieve optimality:
the production mix reflects what consumers want.

same shape for the same reasons. And as usual,
moving outward gives higher utility levels.

Free choice in the market place permits consumers to achieve the highest possible utility
given the available technology and endowment of
productive resources.[9] In Figure 7.7 this occurs at
point A, where the PPF and the indifference curves
are tangent to each other. Their common slope at
the tangency point is the relative price that makes
both producers and consumers aim at precisely
that point. At this market-clearing relative price,
producers maximize value added and consumers are
happy to buy both goods exactly in the proportion
produced. The PPF plays a role similar to a budget
line: it describes the country's available resources,
except that a relative price is needed to value these
resources. The interaction between technology (the
PPF) and tastes (the indifference curves) in the market place determine the equilibrium relative price.

7.3.4 The Case of a Non-zero Primary Current Account: The Role of the Real Exchange Rate

An important feature of Figure 7.7 is that at point A
the primary current account is balanced. Aggregate
income and total spending are equal, as are production and spending in each of the two sectors. But in
reality the current account is not always balanced;
in fact, it is almost never balanced! How should we
think of primary current account imbalances? Put
briefly, surpluses or deficits break the link between
production and spending at any point in time.
When nations run current account deficits or
surpluses, they are taking advantage of their intertemporal budget constraint.[10] The full geometry
of this case is treated on the website, and we outline
only the key ideas here.

[9] Technically, the relative prices reflect simultaneously
the marginal rate of substitution for consumers and the
marginal rate of transformation of traded for non-traded
goods.

[10] Remember that Chapter 2 establishes that the primary
current account is the difference between income (from
production) and spending. This is the same point again.

First, it is important to remember that market equilibrium has a very different meaning for traded and non-traded goods. Traded goods are produced and consumed at home and abroad so that market equilibrium is achieved at the world level. At home, it is possible to have a situation where, for example, spending exceeds production. In that case, the difference is met through imports. (These are paid for by an increase in foreign debt or a decrease in domestic holdings of foreign assets.) Similarly, exports absorb the excess of local production over local consumption. Non-traded goods, on the other side, are produced and consumed locally. The market is local and equilibrium requires that production be equal to consumption at home. Graphically, the production point P shown in Figure 7.5 and the absorption point A shown in Figure 7.7 need not coincide. Trade offers freedom, but it is not the case that 'anything goes':

- The budget constraint imposes that the primary current account deficit today be matched by surpluses later on, and conversely.
- Point A must be vertically above or below point P, since production and absorption of non-traded goods must be equal.
- The slopes of the PPF and the indifference curves at points P and A must be the same, since the relative price does not differ between sellers and buyers within the country (this ignores, of course, tariffs and taxes, such as VAT).

Changes in the real exchange rate will lead both producers and consumers to revise their behaviour in a consistent way. For example, a real appreciation leads producers to reallocate resources towards producing less traded goods, and consumers to spend more on traded goods.

The result is a worsening of the primary current account. Two conclusions follow:

First, the PCA function is indeed downward sloping, as already depicted in Figure 7.2. An increase in the real exchange rate σ, all other things equal, reduces the primary current account surplus or increases the primary account deficit. The exchange rate affects the primary current account by shifting production and spending between traded and non-traded goods in opposite directions.

Second, if the primary current account needs to change to reach a particular value—to meet the intertemporal budget constraint—the real exchange rate will have to change accordingly. For example, it will have to depreciate sufficiently to induce producers and consumers to change their behaviour in a way consistent with a required improvement in the current account.

7.4 The National Intertemporal Budget Constraint and the Equilibrium Real Exchange Rate

7.4.1 The Long Run and the Primary Current Account: A Review

The nation's intertemporal budget constraint introduced in Chapter 5 states that a nation cannot borrow beyond its means and that accumulated assets can and should be eventually spent.[11] In present-value terms, the country meets its external constraint when the current and future primary current account deficits match the initial net asset position of the country (or the surpluses must at least match the initial debt). In the simplified two-period framework, this statement was written formally as:

$$(7.7) \qquad PCA_1 + \frac{PCA_2}{1 + r} = -F_1$$

where F_1 is the net external position of the country at the beginning of the period. F_1 is positive when the

[11] This section presents a review of the two-period framework developed in Ch. 5. When an infinite horizon is considered, the problem becomes somewhat more complicated; see Ch. 15 for details.

country was a net lender previously, and negative when the country is a net debtor.

As long as it meets its intertemporal budget constraint, the country is free to choose the pattern of its primary accounts over time. This degree of freedom evaporates in the second and 'last' period. Tomorrow's primary account must match the accumulated net external position. As in Chapters 5 and 6, 'tomorrow' is a metaphor for the long-run steady state: on average, short-run fluctuations simply cancel out. Then the primary current account must be such that, by the end of period 2 (the proverbial end of time) the country repays its accumulated debt, or spends its assets, principal and interest, inherited from period 1:

(7.8) $PCA_2 = -(1 + r)(F_1 + PCA_1) = -F_2$

where F_2 is the net external position of the country at the beginning of the second period. A positive asset position $(F_2 > 0)$ allows a deficit in the second period, while a position of external indebtedness $(F_2 > 0)$ requires a surplus.

7.4.2 The Equilibrium Real Exchange Rate and the Primary Current Account in the Long Run

The requirement that the long-run primary current account be consistent with the country's external budget constraint defines the **equilibrium, or long-run, real exchange rate**. The primary current account function depicted in Figure 7.2 shows the real exchange rate needed to achieve a given primary current account. The second period's budget constraint given by (7.8) requires that the primary current account be equal to the negative of the country's net foreign asset position, plus interest: it means paying off the debt (when F_2 is negative) through a surplus, or running down accumulated assets (when F_2 is positive) through a deficit. The constraint is shown as the vertical schedule $-F_2$ in Figure 7.8. If a country is indebted, then $F_2 < 0$, and the schedule $-F_2$ will lie to the right in the figure. If on the other hand a country is a net creditor with $F_2 > 0$, the vertical schedule will lie to the left in the figure. For the budget constraint to be satisfied in period 2, the economy must be at the intersection of the primary current account schedule and this

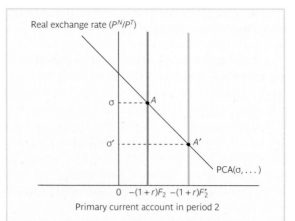

Fig. 7.8 The Equilibrium Real Exchange Rate
Long-run equilibrium requires that the future primary current account match the net asset position, F_2. To point A corresponds the equilibrium real exchange rate σ. A less favourable net asset position $F_2' < F_2$ implies a lower primary current account deficit (or a larger current account surplus) in the future. The vertical schedule is shifted to the right. This requires a lower real exchange rate to generate a larger primary current account surplus to serve the external debt if $F_2 < 0$, or a smaller deficit as net foreign repayments are reduced if $F_2 > 0$.

vertical line. At point A, the equilibrium exchange rate can be read off the vertical axis. Quite simply, the downward-sloping primary current account schedule shows how the real exchange rate affects the primary current account, the long-run budget constraint shows how the required primary current account determines the equilibrium real exchange rate.[12]

As it represents the long run, the equilibrium real exchange rate is unlikely to correspond to the observed real exchange rate at any point in time. Indeed, Figure 7.1 shows that the real exchange rate varies quite a bit, much more than would be warranted by the evolution of the net external position. When the real exchange rate is above its equilibrium level it is **overvalued**; it is **undervalued** in the opposite case. In the long run, however, it must

---

[12] The same result can be reached with the help of Figure 7.7, and is presented in the WebAppendix.

return to its equilibrium value to ensure that the budget constraint is not violated.

7.4.3 The Fundamental Determinants of the Real Exchange Rate

The result that the net external investment position drives the equilibrium real exchange rate is a very powerful one. It means that, eventually, market forces will take the real exchange rate to where it should be. The time required to get there can be considerable, however, taking several years or longer. A **misaligned exchange rate** implies either that the country is living beyond its means, which it can do only as long as it can continue to borrow, or that it is consuming and investing below its potential, and can keep doing so only as long as its households, firms, and government are willing to save. The concept of an equilibrium real exchange rate looks beyond such transitory phases to focus on the steady state. It is the beacon that shows where the real exchange rate is headed.

Graphically, this conclusion looks deceptively simple: the equilibrium exchange rate is determined by the PCA schedule and the initial net foreign asset position. It is possible, however, to go beyond the curves and ask which variables, known as the **fundamental determinants**, or **fundamentals** for short, are responsible for the evolution of the real exchange rate. While the analysis is motivated by Figure 7.7, which shows the special case of a balanced current account, it is consistent with the more general case treated on the website: the real exchange rate must be such that production and consumption decisions are consistent with the primary current account required by the budget constraint and, conversely, that any change in the real exchange rate is associated with changes in the relative production and consumption of traded and non-traded goods. What follows is a list of the most important fundamentals.

Net external position

The net external investment position is a fundamental determinant of the real exchange rate. All other things equal, the more positive the external investment position, the more appreciated the equilibrium exchange rate will be. Similarly, indebted countries will require depreciated real exchange rates in order to generate the resources for debt service. Figure 7.8 depicts the latter case: if foreign indebtedness grows from F_1 to F_1', the net asset position schedule shifts to the right, and the equilibrium real exchange rate must depreciate. In order to satisfy its budget constraint, a country that has been borrowing abroad must generate primary current account surpluses to service its debt. Productive resources have to be shifted towards the traded goods sector, and local demand must be curtailed. The real exchange rate depreciation provides the incentives needed for these changes to occur.

The net external position of a country is determined by history and is difficult, if not impossible, to change at any point in time. Examples abound of countries such as Indonesia and Nigeria which were made fabulously wealthy by oil discoveries, but then squandered their wealth and even became highly indebted as a result. Sometimes a sudden change in asset prices can bring about a change in the external position: a good example here is Sweden, shown in Figure 7.9. Note that an increase of the real interest rate paid on the external debt has the same effect as an increase in the debt itself.

Production: resources and structure

The PPF summarizes a country's resource endowments, productive capacities, and sectoral structure. These characteristics differ across countries and vary over time within a country. One general tendency is that the more productive a country is in traded goods, the higher is its equilibrium exchange rate. The reasoning is as follows: more productive countries produce more traded goods at the expense of non-traded goods, so the less of the latter are available for domestic consumption. But domestic consumption is met by domestic production. To induce the economy to produce and consume in this way, *ceteris paribus*, the relative price of non-traded to traded goods, the real exchange rate σ must appreciate to shift spending away from non-traded goods.

The best way to demonstrate this point is to ask the following question: what would happen if the traded goods sector suddenly became more productive? Figure 7.10 shows how the PPF would

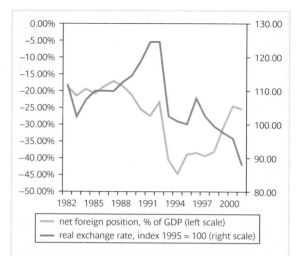

Fig. 7.9 Net External Position and the Real Exchange Rate: The Case of Sweden, 1986–1998

In the early 1980s, Sweden enjoyed a moderate current account surplus, hence a nearly stable net external position, with an indebtedness of about 20% of GDP. Then the real exchange appreciated and became overvalued as witnessed by a severe deterioration of the current account and the associated external debt build-up. In the early 1990s the real exchange rate started to depreciate. By the mid-1990s it had reached an equilibrium level as the debt stabilized.

Source: IMF.

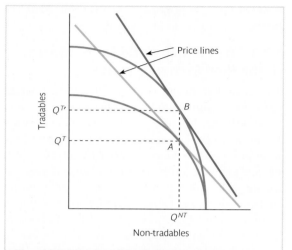

Fig. 7.10 The Real Equilibrium Exchange Rate and Productivity in the Traded Goods Sector

An increase in the productivity of the traded goods sector, which may also represent an exogenous tradable resource discovery, shifts the PPF upwards in a biased fashion. A real exchange rate which maintains constant non-tradable production (point *B*) must be appreciated relative to the original position (point *A*), as can be seen in the steeper price line.

react, shifting upwards so that more tradable good output is feasible at any given output of non-tradable goods. Keeping production of non-tradables constant and continuing to assume external balance, the equilibrium exchange rate must appreciate (σ must rise) and the slope of the price line becomes steeper.

Why could such a shift occur? There are many good reasons associated with ideas found in Chapter 3; technological progress and steady capital accumulation are two good examples. Another is a discovery of natural resources which are tradable. When oil was discovered in the UK's North Sea in the mid-1970s, sterling's real exchange rate soon appreciated by more than 30%. Ironically, the result was a shift away from 'traditional' industry (other traded goods besides oil) towards services, with

massive plant closures and unemployment as industrial workers could not be immediately absorbed by the oil industry or the non-traded goods sector. This striking process of de-industrialization is called the **Dutch disease**, ever since it was first diagnosed in the 1960s when gas was discovered in the Netherlands' side of the North Sea.[13] The Dutch disease explains why resource-rich countries typically find it more difficult to develop and maintain an industrial sector, as can be seen in contemporary Russia. This should not be a source of long-term concern though: why produce industrial goods when mother Nature provides easy exports? In the short run, however, the adjustment can be rather painful. Box 7.3 explains how Norway,

---

[13] The website presents the phenomenon in more formal detail; you are asked to study the issue in more depth in one of the problems at the end of this chapter.

Box 7.3 Norway's Oil Fund

No matter how you look at it, Norway is a wealthy nation. GDP per capita in 2002 was $42,000 (based on current exchange rates) which compares with an EU average of $22,600 (EU-15) and the wealthiest nation in the EU, Luxembourg, which was $47,200 per person. (Norway is not a member of the EU.) Moreover, Norway has accumulated substantial financial assets over the years, roughly 603 billion Norwegian kroner (73 billion euros) in 2002, or about 39.6% of GDP.[14] Most of this wealth can be linked to large discoveries and subsequent production of crude petroleum in the North Sea. Over the years, Norway has produced and sold more than 17 billion barrels of oil. Where did all that money go? The Finance Ministry gives the following answer:

The Government Petroleum Fund was established in 1990. Its construction aims at helping the management of fiscal policy by making the petroleum revenues more visible. The Fund has two main purposes. First, it acts as a buffer to smooth short-term fluctuations in the oil revenues. This will make the Norwegian economy more robust and allow greater room to manoeuvre in economic policy. Second, it will serve as a tool for coping with the financial challenges from the ageing population and the expected decline in oil revenues, by transferring wealth to future generations. The process of transforming physical petroleum reserves into financial assets in the Petroleum Fund will reduce future dependence on the oil revenues. By the end of the first half of 2003, the

Government Petroleum Fund amounted to 775.5 billion Norwegian Kroners (~93.5 billion Euro). Projections indicate that the Fund will have grown from 49 per cent of GDP today to about 90 per cent by the end of 2010. The income of the Fund consists of the net cash flow from petroleum activities plus the return on the Fund's assets. The expenditures of the Fund are the transfers to the Fiscal budget to finance the non-oil budget deficit.[15]

Like a rational consumer, Norwegians seem to have understood that this income from oil production is finite and thus represents a windfall, just as in the analysis of Section 6.2.2. Not only does the petroleum fund buffer the government budget against fluctuations in the price of oil and its production volume, it also provides a means of spreading the windfall over many generations of Norwegians, thereby smoothing private and public consumption. Moreover, it delivers extra resources to support sectors threatened by the real exchange rate appreciation which generally accompanies a windfall gain of this magnitude—the Dutch disease. To use the phrasing of a large Norwegian bank: 'The Petroleum Fund makes it possible . . . to avoid abrupt shifts in the industry structure, such as we have seen in many other countries with substantial revenues from natural resources, and contributes to sustainable business and industry in the long term.'[16]

which has experienced a substantial windfall in the form of North Sea oil, has dealt with the Dutch disease.

Another example is the kind of restructuring which has followed the end of central planning in Eastern and Central Europe. Under the previous regime, much emphasis had been placed on heavy industrial output which, while normally tradable, was in fact rarely sold outside the Soviet block. At the same time, services were deliberately kept underdeveloped. The transformation process led to the rapid emergence of a new service sector and

the gradual restructuring of the industrial sector toward producing goods which are effectively tradable. The result has been a strong trend towards appreciation, as seen from Figure 7.11.

Absorption: preferences and wealth

Changes in consumption patterns also affect the equilibrium real exchange rate. For example, as we grow richer we spend more on non-traded

[15] *Source*: Norwegian Ministry of Finance, Economic Policy Department, 'The Norwegian Government Petroleum Fund': **http://odin.dep.no/filarkiv/192293/fakta.pdf**.
[16] Norges Bank [**www.norges-bank.no/english/petroleum_fund/**].

[14] *Source*: Statistics Norway **www.ssb.no/en/indicators/dsbb/**.

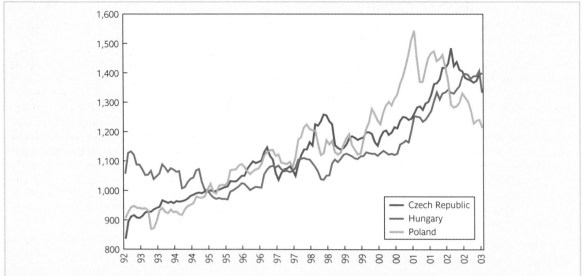

Fig. 7.11 Real Exchange Rates in Transition Countries, 1991 – 2002 (Index: Jan. 1995 = 100)
The figure depicts the evolution of the ratio of the price of services to the producer price index, a measure of the real exchange rate. All three successful transition countries show a strong upward trend, with accumulated real appreciation of 100% over a decade in the case of Poland.
Source: IMF.

goods. Non-traded services such as leisure (movies, restaurants, etc.), education, and medical services may even take an increasing importance in our budgets. Since non-traded goods must be produced domestically, an increased demand must be accompanied by a higher relative price to elicit more production. Anything which increases the wealth of resident households—a real estate or stock market boom, the repatriated earnings of foreign relatives, or foreign aid—can have similar effects.

The size of government, a big consumer, may also affect the real exchange rate. Governments spend a large part of their budgets on non-traded goods and services (public services, roads, and other utilities). Since such spending is financed by taxes levied on people who tend to spend more on traded goods, an increase in the size of government tends to shift domestic absorption towards non-traded goods, and thus to raise their relative price, i.e. the real exchange rate.

In the end . . .

Any change that reflects 'deep' or structural changes is likely to affect the current account and therefore the equilibrium real exchange rate. In practice, however, disturbances large enough to produce significant changes in the equilibrium real exchange rate are rather rare events. This is why it is often a good rule of thumb to consider that the equilibrium real exchange rate remains roughly unchanged. But then one must be always on the watch for the possibility that a major change is under way. A point in the case is the catch-up process whereby poorer countries successfully enter a take-off growth phase. As they accumulate capital, import advanced technology, and become more productive their economies undergo a systematic transformation. The result is a continuing appreciation of the real exchange rate. This is known as the **Balassa – Samuelson effect**, which is described in Box 7.4.

Box 7.4 The Balassa–Samuelson Effect[17]

Travellers frequently observe that wealthier countries are systematically more expensive than poorer ones. This is documented in Table 7.1, which shows the GDP deflators in various countries converted into a common currency. The GDP deflator is a weighted average of traded and non-traded goods prices. If the prices of internationally traded goods are roughly equalized in a common currency,[18] then differences in average price levels reflect differences in non-traded goods prices— such as haircuts, hotel rooms, transport, bread, and so on. The table then suggests that non-traded goods are cheaper in poorer countries. Why is that so? Many services which constitute a large share of non-traded goods are 'luxury' goods: restaurants, legal services, household services, child care, medical services. In poor countries, demand for services is limited and, as a result, their prices are low.

A second reason is related to the supply of services. Poorer countries are characterized by lower stocks of physical and/or human capital (Chapter 3), which implies lower productivity in the traded goods sector. When productivity in traded goods is low, the marginal product of labour is low, and the wage is commensurately low. (Otherwise this sector will not competitive in world markets!) Wages will also be low in the non-traded sector, since worker mobility, customs (demands for fairness), and trade union activity typically prevent wages from differing much from one sector to another. With lower wages, prices in the non-traded goods sector will be lower in poorer countries.

 Table 7.1 Price Level Comparison, 2000 (USA = 100)

Europe		Asia	
Austria	93.7	China	23.1
Belgium	89.2	Bangladesh	19.6
Denmark	106.8	India	17.1
France	90.7	Israel	92.5
Germany	95.0	Japan	144.8
Iceland	113.1	Pakistan	19.9
Ireland	92.6	Singapore	80.1
Italy	81.3		
Netherlands	90.1	**Africa**	
Norway	112.4	Chad	19.1
Spain	73.8	Egypt	34.4
Sweden	104.8	Mozambique	19.3
Switzerland	118.1	Nigeria	39.3
UK	98.5		
		Central and South America	
North America and Oceania		Brazil	45.1
Canada	79.3	Chile	44.6
USA	100.0	Mexico	60.8
Australia	74.6	Peru	43.5
New Zealand	66.2	Venezuela	69.0

Source: Penn World Tables Mark 6.1 (Summers, Heston, Aten).

[17] Named after Bela Balassa (1928–1991), Hungarian-born economist at Johns Hopkins University, also known as gourmet and author of a confidential restaurant guide, and after Paul Samuelson (1915–), the 1970 Nobel laureate from MIT. A formal derivation of the Balassa–Samuelson effect is available in the WebAppendix.

[18] The assumption that prices of internationally traded goods are equalized is sometimes called the Law of One Price. Reasons for and exceptions to this rule are developed in Ch. 8.

❶ Summary

1 Real exchange rates measure the price of domestic goods in terms of foreign goods. A variety of prices can be used (export price index, CPI, WPI, GDP deflator, labour costs) to 'double-deflate' the nominal exchange rate and address different questions. A convenient definition is the ratio of non-traded to traded good prices.

2 Effective nominal and real exchange rates are weighted averages of a country's exchange rates vis-à-vis the rest of the world, in practice its main trading partners.

3 Regardless of the definition, the real exchange rate affects the primary current account. A decrease in the real exchange rate (a depreciation) will tend to improve the primary current account. Indeed, relatively lower non-traded good prices encourage producers to shift to the traded good sector away from the non-traded good sector, and encourage consumers to substitute non-traded for traded goods.

4 While the production and consumption of non-traded goods must be equal, the primary current account is the difference between the production of and spending on traded goods.

5 The primary current account is driven in the long run by the nation's budget constraint. So the equilibrium long-run real exchange rate depends on the country's inherited net external position. Countries that accumulate large external indebtedness will tend to have depreciating real exchange rates, and countries with large external asset positions will tend to have appreciating real exchange rates.

6 The equilibrium real exchange rate changes in response to disturbances that affect a country's structure: productivity, tastes, other relative prices. These are generally rare events.

7 Increases in wealth and productivity, especially in the traded goods sector, are associated with more appreciated real exchange rates. This explains why price levels measured in a common currency are lower in poorer countries.

❍━ Key Concepts

- relative prices
- real exchange rate
- nominal exchange rate
- equilibrium real exchange rate
- British/European terms
- appreciation/depreciation
- effective exchange rates
- external/internal terms of trade
- primary current account function
- production possibilities frontier (PPF)
- numeraire
- non-traded and traded goods
- price line
- over- and undervalued
- misaligned exchange rate
- fundamental determinants/fundamentals
- Dutch disease
- Balassa – Samuelson effect

❓ Exercises

1 Are the following goods and services traded or non-traded? On what assumptions do your answers depend?

(*a*) Personal computers

(*b*) Bread

(*c*) On-line medical counselling

(*d*) Newspapers

(*e*) Insurance

(*f*) Car rentals

(*g*) Tourism

2 What happens to the real exchange rate between two countries if the price level at home doubles, all other things given? If the price of foreign goods doubles? If the nominal exchange rate doubles?

3 Explain why it is optimal to produce along the PPF and not inside it. Picking a point on the PPF in Figure 7.7 that is not at the tangency with the price line, explain why it is desirable to move towards the tangency point.

4 You have the following data on net foreign investment position of the following countries, estimated by the International Monetary Fund and expressed in US dollars:

1990	1997	2002
Austria	−6.87	−32.78	−50.46
Finland	−39.32	−48.61	−37.7
France	−21.68	269.37	191.17
Germany	348.9	74.99	230.08
Italy	−84.69	2.16	−100.68
Netherlands	63.8	25.85	−127.43
Japan	329.36	958.73	1,462.16
Spain	−61.86	−99.06	−178.94
Switzerland	217.89	308.6	420.9
United Kingdom	13.32	−136.63	−40.98
United States	−166.84	−1,076.13	−3,508.4

Choose five countries. How would you go about seeing whether the countries you chose are violating their intertemporal budget constraints? What other information might you need to make a better judgement? (One hint: it would be a good idea to divide the investment position by GDP. Why? To do this, you can obtain GDP figures in US dollars by visiting the IMF website **www.imf.org/external/pubs/ft/weo/2003/02/data/index.htm**, where the data are available for free.)

5 Redraw Figure 7.7 to show the case of a primary current account surplus. How does your diagram change when the primary current account is in deficit?

6 In the European Monetary Union, there is a single monetary policy which aims at the area-wide inflation. Are there good reasons to expect inflation to differ systematically across countries?

7 Debt relief can be thought of as the reduction of a nation's debt in present-value terms. What effect would you expect debt relief to have on the real exchange rate of a highly indebted country?

8 Estonia has tied its nominal exchange rate to the DM (and to the euro). Yet, inflation is significantly higher than in Germany. Why? Does it mean that its exchange rate is becoming overvalued?

9 The real exchange rate of the Russian rouble appears to be positively related to the price of oil on world markets. Given that Russia is one of the world's most important oil producers, explain how this might be the case. What are the possible effects of a sudden rise in oil prices on manufacturing industry in Russia?

→ Essay Questions

1 It is often claimed that foreign food aid promotes patterns of dependency for recipient developing countries, in particular, that it reduces local food production and slows development. Show how the model of the real exchange rate as the price of non-tradable goods could explain this. Would the argument change if instead richer countries simply purchased more of developing countries' agricultural output? Explain your answer carefully.

2 Over 1999–2002, the dollar rose and the euro fell, both in real terms. Market commentators explained this evolution by the advances achieved in the USA in the information technology sector and by the difficulties of adopting a common currency in Europe. Evaluate these arguments.

3 'Being an oil-rich country is a blessing and a curse.' Comment.

4 Imagine that a poor country, where wages are a pittance, will start growing and catching up. Describe the evolution of wages, various prices, and the composition of its exports and imports over the next five decades.

5 'The quality of government is the most important exchange rate fundamental'. Comment.

PART III
Money

8 **Money and the Demand for Money** *173*
9 **The Supply of Money and Monetary Policy** *199*

We have focused our attention on the real side of the economy until now, but in doing so we ignored the existence of money and the fact that goods we buy and wages we earn are measured in units of money, or in nominal terms. In Part III of this textbook, we correct this important oversight. We also show that it is possible to separate out the real from the nominal side in the long run. In the shorter run, however, the real and monetary sectors are intertwined. This interaction—among other things—gives rise to the phenomenon of business cycles, the succession of periods of rapid economic growth and recession.

The main objective of Part III is to establish what money is, how it is created, and what role it plays in a modern, open economy. We also study how central banks operate and see that they are often torn between conflicting objectives: setting the interest rate, the exchange rate, the rate of money growth, and ultimately the rate of inflation.

Money and the Demand for Money

8

8.1 Overview *174*

8.2 Technical Definitions of Money *174*
   8.2.1   A Narrow Definition *175*
   8.2.2   Broader Aggregates *175*
   8.2.3   Liquidity versus Yield *175*

8.3 Why Is this Money? *177*
   8.3.1   Economic Functions of Money *177*
   8.3.2   A Dominated Asset *177*
   8.3.3   A Public Good *178*

8.4 Money: A Balance Sheet Approach *179*
   8.4.1   Consolidated Balance Sheets *179*
   8.4.2   Currency as a Liability of the Central Bank *180*
   8.4.3   Sight Deposits as a Liability of Commercial Banks *180*

8.5 The Demand for Money *181*
   8.5.1   The Price Level as a Determinant of Money Demand *181*
   8.5.2   Real Income as a Determinant of Money Demand *182*
   8.5.3   Nominal Interest Rates as a Determinant of Money Demand *183*
   8.5.4   The Money Demand Function *183*

8.6 Equilibrium in the Money Market: The Short Run *186*
   8.6.1   Money Supply Effects *186*
   8.6.2   Cyclical Fluctuations *187*
   8.6.3   Transaction Costs *187*
   8.6.4   The Equilibrating Role of the Interest Rate and Asset Prices *188*

8.7 Equilibrium in the Money Market: The Long Run *188*
   8.7.1   Long-Run Inflation *188*
   8.7.2   Inflation and the Fisher Principle *191*
   8.7.3   The Exchange Rate in the Long Run: Purchasing Power Parity *193*

Summary *194*

Money is not, properly speaking, one of the subjects of commerce; but only the instrument which men have agreed upon to facilitate the exchange of one commodity for another. It is none of the wheels of trade: it is the oil which renders the motion of the wheels more smooth and easy.

—David Hume[1]

The invention of a circulating medium, which supersedes the narrow, cumbrous process of barter, by facilitating transactions of every variety of importance among all sorts of people, is a grand type of advance in civilization.

—Chambers's *Encyclopedia*, 1870

8.1 Overview

Virtually every civilization has used one form of money or another, and money has been at the centre of attention in civilizations since the beginning of recorded history. Money is certainly a form of wealth—it represents a means of transporting resources into the future—but has a number of special qualities. Its return is typically very low—banknotes yield no interest at all—and yet it is perceived as desirable, even the ultimate form into which all other assets can be transformed. The reason is that money facilitates transactions between economic agents. It is indispensable to the proper functioning of a modern economy. To be convinced of this, we need only imagine the costs a barter economy would impose on our daily lives.

Yet, the definition of money is far from clear. Banknotes and coins are money. What about chequebook balances? Travellers' cheques? Savings accounts? Other financial instruments? There are indeed various forms of money, some of them even produced by different economic agents. This chapter therefore starts with several definitions of money. It also focuses on the demand for money. Since money is not an ideal way to hold wealth, we need to understand why it is held at all. This is the first step towards understanding money's role in the macroeconomy: its effect on prices, interest rates, and, eventually, real economic activity. The question of how the supply of money is determined is left to the next chapter.

8.2 Technical Definitions of Money

The definition of money has been an issue of dispute for a long time, and the difficulties have been compounded recently by the computer and internet revolution. Once upon a time, gold, silver, and other commodities served as money. Slowly but surely, paper money (banknotes) edged out these **commodity monies**. Next came the widespread use of sight deposits, or bank deposits which can be con-

verted into cash on demand. Nowadays, the speed, ease, and low cost of converting one type of asset into another have blurred conventional distinctions between money and other related forms of wealth. Plastic cards are a familiar sight and e-money is on the rise. A proper definition must capture the enduring qualities that characterize money, while abstracting from those that are transient, arbitrary, or country specific. We will begin with several technical definitions which are commonly used by central banks, national governments, and international agencies, and see how adequate they are in capturing what money is.

---

[1] David Hume (1711–76) was arguably Scotland's greatest moral philosopher and economist (although Adam Smith is pretty strong competition). Hume's most noteworthy contribution to economics was his essay *Of Money* (1752), from which this quotation is taken.

8.2.1 A Narrow Definition

Currency (banknotes and coins) is undoubtedly a form of money, even though a century ago there were doubts that these forms were as trustworthy as coins made from precious metals. Yet the use of currency to settle transactions is relatively limited; economic agents often use bank deposits instead. This is the rationale for a first definition of money: currency in the hands of the public (households, firms, and governments) plus sight deposits (bank accounts that are payable on demand, often called demand deposits or current accounts). This **monetary aggregate** is denominated as M1:

M1 = currency in circulation + sight deposits.

This measure is open to different interpretations which highlight the danger of rigid definitions. For example, should travellers' cheques be counted as money? They do not fit the bureaucrat's definition, but they seem to function much like the other stuff. Some countries do include travellers' cheques in M1. What about credit cards or even prepaid telephone cards, or foreign currency, which in some countries, such as post-communist Eastern Europe, is used alongside domestic currency? Practices differ, and changing circumstances and technology can call any definition into question.

8.2.2 Broader Aggregates

Sight or demand deposits at banks have three main characteristics: (1) they may be converted into cash on demand at the issuing bank, (2) cheques can be written or bank transfers can be made against them, and (3) the interest paid is either nil or lower than that offered by other assets. This is why banks often offer more attractive accounts that bear interest, but cannot be drawn on with cheques. Yet such funds can often be transferred into regular sight deposits—often a phone call, a series of key-strokes on a telephone handset, or an internet connection is enough. The ease of transfer renders these assets very similar to sight deposits. This is why they are included in our second definition of money, M2:

M2 = M1 + time (or savings) deposits at banks with unrestricted access.

An even broader measure includes instruments such as large certificates of deposit, or time deposits with a longer term and possibly restricted access, foreign currency deposits, and deposits with non-bank institutions. The precise meaning of 'larger' and 'longer maturity' depends on local rules and regulations. The distinction is one of degree: these instruments are less liquid, meaning that they are more costly or difficult to convert into cash or current accounts. This is called M3:

M3 = M2 + larger, fixed-term deposits
+ accounts at non-bank institutions.

8.2.3 Liquidity versus Yield

Beyond currency and M1, all definitions are inevitably arbitrary and vary from country to country. This is why monetary aggregates like those presented in Table 8.1 are not directly comparable across countries. Still, all the aggregates measure the 'liquid wealth' of the non-banking sector. M1 is considered perfectly liquid, whereas M2 and M3 are not suitable for transactions and must generally be converted into M1 for that purpose.

Beyond the definitions, differences across countries reflect the stage of development of banking services as well as national regulations. Banks and financial institutions (savings banks, unit trusts, investment management firms, and life insurance companies) compete for customers' wealth. In some countries banks are able to offer interest on current accounts; in others they have to compete through different means (free bank accounts, proximity of branches, computerized services). Competition and technical change force banks and financial institutions to invent new types of accounts that are not part of M1 but are better remunerated and yet easily transformed into a form suitable for transactions. The computer revolution has made complex transfer agreements virtually costless and has thereby rendered money definitions increasingly arbitrary. Many believe we are not far from the moneyless society that the Swedish economist Knut Wicksell once imagined and which is described in Box 8.1. As a simplification, we will generally think of money in terms of its narrower definition, M1.

Table 8.1 Money in Three Countries, December 2003

		Currency	M1	M2	M3
UK	(£ bn.)	39.9	597.8	956.7	1,141.5
	as % GDP	3.6	54.3	86.9	103.7
Euro-zone	(€bn.)	398.1	2,647.6	5,225.5	6,142.5
	as % GDP	5.5	36.5	72.0	84.6
USA	($ bn.)	644.2	1,293.0	6,071.0	8,819.5
	as % GDP	5.9	11.8	55.3	80.3

Source: IMF, central banks' bulletins.

Box 8.1 The Vision of Wicksell: A Moneyless Society

Once upon a time, money was gold or silver, or seashells, or large stones on South Pacific islands. Such commodity money has an intrinsic value, since it is made of goods that can be used for other purposes. These goods are 'wasted' when used as money, and this is one reason why paper and cheap metal have replaced silver or gold. A century ago, the Swedish economist Knut Wicksell (1851–1926) went further. He asked: why have money at all? He envisioned a central record keeper who would keep a tally of all credits and debits. Whenever an individual worked, his balance would be credited; whenever he spent, the balance would be debited. In principle, it would be possible to run a negative balance, i.e. to borrow from the system. In the end, instead of producing currency, the central bank would operate and guarantee this record-keeping system and determine the value of the unit of account.

At the time, Wicksell's moneyless society was dismissed as impractical science fiction. A century later, the technical problems of establishing such a 'moneyless society' have been largely solved. Large powerful computers can keep accurate, up-to-date records and investigate the creditworthiness of households and businesses. The year 2003 was a watershed: for the first time, US consumers paid more for goods and services using credit and debit cards than with cheques or cash. The biggest increase from 1999 to 2003 was seen in the use of debit cards, rising from 21% of all retail purchases in 1999 to 31% in 2003. Similar increases are expected soon in Europe, especially in France and the UK, where credit and debit cards are commonplace.

In Swindon, a community near London, a widely noted, large-scale experiment with electronic cash cards conducted by Mondex and NatWest Bank from 1995 to 1998 pointed up a number of hurdles which still remain for an economy without cash. Could there be a demand for money, as we have defined it, in a 'moneyless society'? If the system were perfect and all transactions could be recorded at point of sale, probably not. Yet the amount of trade that occurs in informal settings is still large, and often convenient. It may be a long time before the local newspaper kiosk installs such a system. More importantly, a significant portion of society may have something to hide from a system like Wicksell's. Anyone trying to evade taxes, work in the underground economy, or engage in other illicit activity will always desire a means of payment that is not necessarily traceable to the transacting party. Right or wrong, the very intrusiveness of Wicksell's system might be its most objectionable trait.

8.3 Why Is this Money?

Technology makes the search for a definition of money very difficult indeed. Perhaps it would make more sense to look for defining characteristics of money. Why is M1 money? Why do businesses and individuals use it? On the surface, both questions seem trivial. Good business sense would say that money is whatever is generally accepted in payment, and it is used because others will accept it. The reasoning is circular: money is money because it is accepted, and it is accepted because it is money! In a perplexing way, this circularity is one of money's most intrinsic and durable aspects, despite its other rapidly changing attributes over the centuries. In the end, the best definition of money is: an asset that is generally accepted as a means of payment.[2]

8.3.1 Economic Functions of Money

An alternative, and widely used, approach is to define money by its attributes, that is by what money does for us and why we use it. This section presents several key ideas from this rich tradition.[3]

A medium of exchange

Money is a **medium of exchange**. People use it to settle accounts, regardless of what is being bought or sold. In a remarkably convenient way, money solves the **double coincidence of wants**. The double coincidence of wants can be illustrated by the following problem. Thomas is selling apples. François is interested in purchasing apples, but he is selling tomatoes which Thomas does not want. (In fact, Thomas is looking for potatoes.) Direct trade may not take place between the two of them. They would need to find Vittorio, who happens to be selling potatoes and is interested in buying tomatoes. If Vittorio

doesn't show up, trade doesn't occur. Money admirably solves this problem.

A unit of account

In a moneyless or barter economy, all goods would be traded according to their relative prices (tomatoes versus apples versus potatoes versus tomatoes). As the number of goods grows, the number of relative prices rises rapidly. With two goods there is a single relative price; with three goods, there are three relative prices; with five goods, ten. If there are fifty goods, the number of relative prices rises to 1,225; and so on.[4] The need for a 'common denominator' or **unit of account** is obvious. Money serves as a numeraire or a benchmark in which all other goods are priced.

A store of value and standard of deferred payment

We have already noted that money is an asset and therefore one way of holding wealth. Wealth transfers resources from the present to the future, for later consumption or further wealth accumulation. The value of money may change over time, but that is also true of any other **store of value**. Similarly, money can be used as the numeraire in which debt contracts are written: it serves as a **standard of deferred payment**.

8.3.2 A Dominated Asset

Money is a **dominated asset**. It bears a lower rate of return than assets of comparable riskiness, such as Treasury bills (short-term government bonds), which are also backed by the state. This yield disadvantage can be seen as the cost of 'staying liquid' and is the reason for the systematic inverse relationship between liquidity and returns: the larger the yield on a monetary instrument, the more restrictions are attached to it. Examples are the need to maintain a minimum (and often substantial) balance, limitations on the minimum amount that can be settled

---

[2] In a way, we know about as much as a US Supreme Court Justice knew when asked to define pornography: I can't tell you what it is, but I know it when I see it.

[3] This tradition starts with the work of British economist William Jevons (1835–82), especially his *Money and the Mechanism of Exchange* (1875).

[4] The mathematical formula for the number of relative or bilateral prices is $n(n-1)/2$, where n is the number of goods.

Box 8.2 Parallel Currencies

There have been a number of episodes in history when private money has circulated alongside, or even in lieu of, fiat money created by the state. Examples of such 'free issue' environments are Scotland in the eighteenth century, the USA in the nineteenth century, and Hong Kong today. In these episodes banknotes privately issued by local banks circulated along with gold, silver, or national banknotes. Even assuming its authenticity, however, it was often difficult for those presented with such banknotes to know their true value, since this involved information about the quality of the bank in question, as well as what others thought of the notes. Generally, banknotes were sold at a discount from face value. (In nineteenth-century USA, it was related to the distance from the issuing bank.) Banknotes were treated as the senior debt of the issuing bank: their holders were the very first to be paid off in the event of bankruptcy. All the same, bank failures often meant that the money became worthless. It was common for 'banknote reporters' to publish regular listings of counterfeit banknotes as well as discounts or premiums in terms of gold, so that transacting parties might agree on an exchange value.

Nowadays, parallel currencies are observed in countries with extreme economic instability and mistrust of the government, but they usually circulate in the form

of foreign exchange rather than private issue. US dollars and Deutschmarks circulated freely in many Eastern European and Latin American countries, as well as in Israel during the hyperinflation of the early 1980s. This phenomenon of dollarization became very widespread in the former communist countries early on in their process of economic transformation; Table 8.2 shows the extent of currency substitution that occurred at the time. Dollarization usually comes to an end as soon as conditions stabilize and public trust is restored.

Table 8.2 Currency Substitution in Central and Eastern Europe, 1993[a]

Albania	18	Poland	28
Bulgaria	30	Romania	35
Estonia	5	Russia	35
Latvia	25	Slovenia	42
Lithuania	25	Ukraine	28

[a] Currency substitution is defined as the ratio of foreign currency deposits to broad money.

Source: Sahay and Végh (1995).

per cheque, charges on cheque writing or transfers to other accounts, and so on. As a rule, the more liquid an asset is, the lower is its yield; the price of liquidity is forgone interest.

8.3.3 A Public Good

Money compensates for its inferiority in terms of interest by serving as the means of payment. In other words, it is so generally accepted that it can be used as payment without asking. But why is it so generally accepted? The following example can illustrate this very special feature of money.

Suppose a shopkeeper accepts a written promise from a trustworthy customer to pay his grocery bill at some future date. This promise, or IOU,[5] represents

the shopkeeper's claims on his customer's future resources, and is simply a loan. This loan has value; if the customer in question is particularly trustworthy, the shopkeeper might be able to use this IOU to pay for his own purchases. The IOU could be used as a means of payment by parties completely unrelated to the shopkeeper or his customer; that is to say, it could become money. For this to happen, the public usually requires significant information about the creditworthiness or credibility of the initial customer—the originator or issuer of the money. And yet, if they simply assume that the customer is creditworthy, the money could circulate as a means of payment without any difficulty. In the end, the reputation of the initial issuer of the IOUs determines the acceptability of this type of money. Yet it is very unlikely that the shopkeeper himself, much

---

[5] IOU = I owe you.

less third parties, will ever know, or care to know, enough about individuals to accept their IOUs as money. Private IOUs are a victim of **information asymmetry**: the fact that others know less about the customer than he himself does. As a result, if his IOUs were widely accepted, he could very well one day succumb to the temptation of issuing more IOUs than he is able to repay. Since this potential misbehaviour is easily suspected, no one will accept these IOUs.

Money is accepted either because it has intrinsic value (gold, for example), or because it is an IOU from an institution with a solid reputation. The creditworthiness of the state is essential for **fiat money**[6]—non-commodity money—to circulate. Confidence emerges as the key characteristic of money. Other institutions may attempt to acquire sufficient reputation to issue their own parallel currencies, and Box 8.2 reports on some historical experiences with them.

For IOUs to circulate in the above example, several costs are incurred. The value of the IOUs must be ascertained at each transaction, and in case of default the shopkeeper may be required to guarantee the bad debt. The safety of money is a **public good**, meaning that it is enjoyed simultaneously by many different people. The social benefit (the gains to all members of the community) from this activity exceeds its private cost (to the shopkeeper). Unfortunately, the shopkeeper or the creditworthy customer cannot charge others for providing this service and so he has little incentive to supply private money, even if it is desirable from a social point of view. It is a general result that, if left to the market, public goods are undersupplied, no matter how useful they are. This is where governments have a special responsibility. Because they are easily recognized and enjoy more credibility than the average citizen, governments generally establish the monetary standard and supply the medium of exchange, declaring it to be legal tender and requiring that it be accepted in exchange for goods. In the end, this is probably the most efficient way of satisfying the definition given at the beginning of this section.

8.4 Money: A Balance Sheet Approach

8.4.1 Consolidated Balance Sheets

Money is an asset for those who hold it. With the exception of commodity money, however, it is also someone else's liability. This can be seen by examining the **balance sheets** of the banking system displayed in Figure 8.1. A balance sheet is a snapshot of an entity's financial status. **Net worth** is the difference between the value of its assets—listed on the left side of the balance sheet—and its liabilities—listed on the right side. We consider three big players: the central bank, the commercial banking sector, and the non-banking sector, which includes households, corporations, and the government.

The balance sheets depicted in Figure 8.1 are consolidated: the assets and liabilities belonging to the same sector cancel. For example, within the non-bank sector, borrowing by the government or corporations from private citizens cancel out and do not appear. The money stock M1 is represented by the tinted area, the sum of currency held by the public and sight deposits. It can be found on the asset side of the non-financial sector's balance sheet.[7] It appears simultaneously in the balance sheet of the consolidated banking sector as a liability.

---

6 Fiat comes from the Latin 'let there be', or 'let it be'.

7 Following common practice, we have excluded government deposits at the central bank from M1. Government accounts tend to be quite volatile and are not really under the control of the private sector. Volatility is a problem because the aggregates often move too much to be used as a gauge of monetary conditions. In some countries (for example the USA), as a result of a sharp distinction between the Treasury and the central bank, the Treasury actually refrains from using the central bank for the bulk of its transactions, preferring accounts at commercial banks.

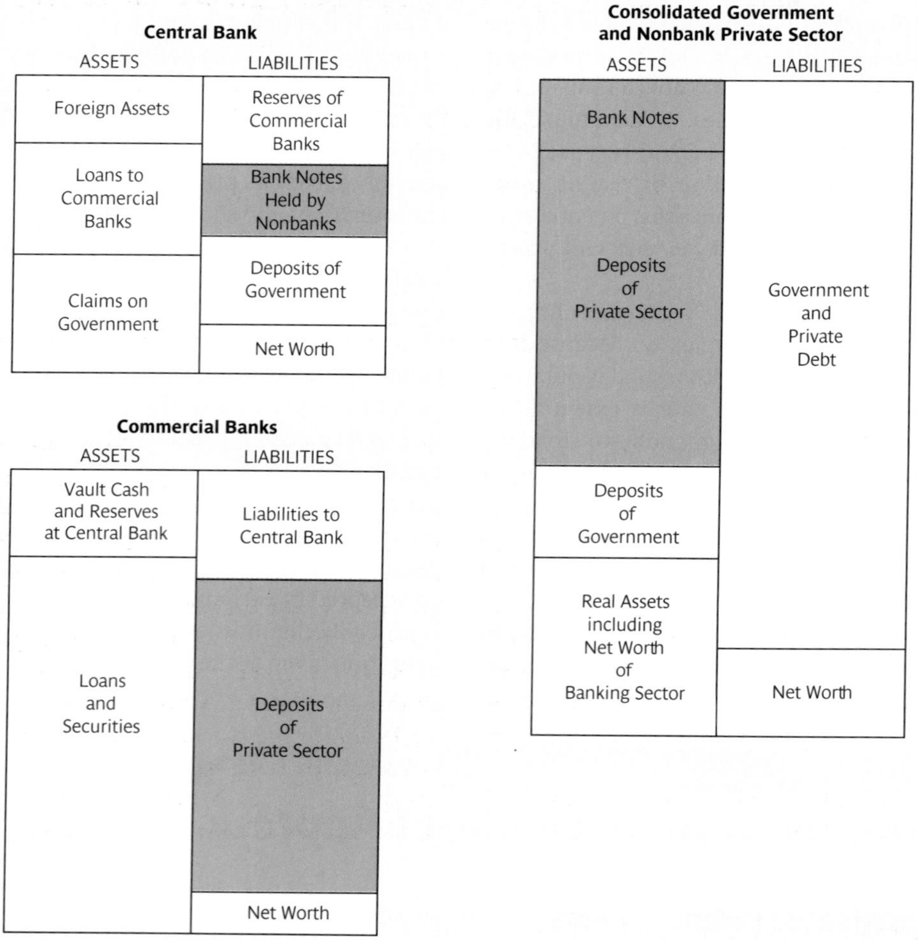

Fig. 8.1 Balance Sheets of the Central Bank, the Commercial Banks, and the Non-bank Sector

8.4.2 Currency as a Liability of the Central Bank

Cash held by the public is a liability of the central bank. When central banks first began issuing paper money, or currency, in the nineteenth century, they committed themselves to exchange these banknotes against gold on demand. This is how the public eventually came to trust paper money and regard it as being as good as gold or silver. Today, the gold backing is no longer explicit; and gold holdings represent of small and dwindling fraction of central banks' assets, and silver has all but disappeared from their vaults. Table 8.3 shows that precious metals have been replaced in most balance sheets of central banks by debt of the government, private financial institutions, or foreign central banks. These assets have become the 'backing' for currency.

8.4.3 Sight Deposits as a Liability of Commercial Banks

Sight deposits, the larger part of M1, are liabilities of the commercial banking sector. Figure 8.1 shows that sight deposits are backed by three types of asset. First, banks hold some currency and deposits

Table 8.3 Assets of Central Banks in Selected Countries, Year-End 2002 (bn. euros)

	Gold	Foreign assets	Claims on deposit banks	Claims on government
Euroland	144.64	374.80	399.00	110.20
USA	11.68	83.54	—	685.60
UK	3.66	12.59	—	25.87
Japan	1.24	427.58	24.18	72.23
Sweden	0.30	18.41	3.35	—
Poland	1.20	0.30	0.14	0.17

Source: IMF.

with the central bank; both of these are the central bank's liability. (We ignore here their holdings of foreign currency.) Second, banks may own government debt. Third, banks hold debt of households and firms. If we consolidate the liabilities of the central bank and commercial banks, we arrive at M1 and the government's own deposits. Money is thus as good as the consolidated assets of the central bank and the commercial banks, and that is the indebtedness of the government and of the private sector.

This is why, in the end, modern money—in contrast to gold or silver money—ultimately rests on the trust of agents in their own economies. To bolster this trust, regulations are designed to enhance the creditworthiness of the banking sector. Yet, banking panics may occur in troubled times, when the value of such regulation may be called into question. Acting out of concern for their wealth, people withdraw their deposits to acquire foreign currencies or other non-financial assets such as gold or durable goods. To honour these withdrawals, banks are forced to convert other assets on their balance sheets to cash, often at a loss. When one single link in the chain of confidence breaks, the whole fragile edifice can come tumbling down.

8.5 The Demand for Money

It is the exceptional individual indeed who derives pleasure from owning and holding money for its own sake. For most households and firms, money is only useful because it facilitates transactions. Since money is a dominated asset, however, most people will not hold a significant fraction of their wealth in that form. Figure 8.2 shows the evolution of M1 and M2, scaled by nominal output (M/PY). Because the money stocks are nominal, it is natural to measure them relative to nominal rather than real output. Recent innovations in payment technologies have provided a convenient means of shifting resources from non-interest-bearing, or low-interest, sight deposits (M1) to better remunerated accounts (M2). This may explain the upward trend in M2 although the expected downward trend in M1 is at best modest. In fact, the figure suggests that where a downward trend occurred it was reversed after 1985. Both ratios also fluctuate quite sizeably. This section is devoted to explaining these movements in money demand.

8.5.1 The Price Level as a Determinant of Money Demand

Money demand is largely motivated by the need to carry out transactions, that is, by its command

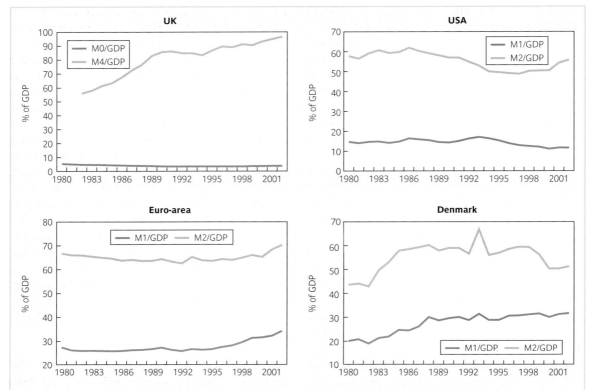

Fig. 8.2 Narrow and Wide Monetary Aggregates, Four Economies, 1980 – 2002

Changing definitions over time and across countries makes it difficult to track down the evolution of monetary aggregates. For the United Kingdom, we display the monetary base M0, a very narrow aggregate defined in Chapter 9, and M4, a very broad aggregate. In Euroland and the United States, M1 and M2 share fairly similar definitions, and the level of the two series is comparable, although EU Europe tends to hold more cash and liquid deposits that US or UK residents. Possible economies of scale may encourage a downward trend in the narrow aggregates. In Denmark, a small open economy which does not currently use the euro, similar patterns of money holdings can be observed; the unusual upward blip in 1993 is associated with a wave of mortgage refinancing which took place in that year.

Source: IMF; OECD.

over goods and services. Money is valued for its purchasing power, and this purchasing power is measured by the price level—effectively the cost of goods in terms of money. The implication is that the demand for money is a demand for real rather than nominal balances. The real value of money can be represented as:

$$\text{Real money stock} = M/P,$$

where M is the nominal stock of money and P is the consumer price index (CPI). The real money stock remains unchanged when the nominal stock increases exactly by the same proportion as the price level. All other things being equal, if the money supply and the price level (and the nominal value of all other assets in the economy) were to double, there would be no effect on the real economy. This property is called the **neutrality of money**. Its importance for macroeconomics cannot be exaggerated.

8.5.2 Real Income as a Determinant of Money Demand

The main reason for holding money (M1) is to facilitate transactions. The real volume of economic activity must therefore be an important factor in determining the demand for money, and we should expect a positive relationship between real GDP and the real money stock. Is this relationship proportional? The WebAppendix shows that **transaction costs** (bank commissions, or time and effort spent converting money from and into other assets) lead people to use money more efficiently. If we ignore this effect, however, the demand for money should be positively related to the level of economic activity, approximated by the GDP.[8]

The elasticity of money demand with respect to GDP is defined as the percentage increase in money demand resulting from a 1% increase in the GDP.[9] If it is equal to unity, money demand is proportional to GDP. The presence of scale economies would correspond to elasticities less than unity. Table 8.4 presents elasticities of money demand for a number of countries, separating the short run (within one quarter) from the long run. For the long run, when adjustment of money balances is complete, the elasticities are as often above as they are below unity, the average being 1.2. Bearing in mind the lack of precision inherent in obtaining such estimates, it is acceptable, as a rule of thumb, to consider that money demand is about proportional to income, all other things equal.

8.5.3 Nominal Interest Rates as a Determinant of Money Demand

The **nominal interest rate** is the rate actually paid by borrowers for loans or bonds that are denominated in money terms. By contrast, real interest rates—which until now were the only interest rates considered—would apply to loans in terms of goods, or loans based on a price index. The difference between nominal and real interest rates arises because lenders in money terms expect inflation, that is, for the price of goods to rise over the period of the loan. Without compensation, repayment of a loan in money rather than in goods at the same interest rate would penalize the lender. If he expects to receive money that has lost value in the future,

he will require a higher nominal interest rate as compensation: the nominal rate increases with the expected rate of inflation (see Section 8.7.2).

The nominal interest rate matters for the demand for money because it is the **opportunity cost** that households and firms face for holding wealth in this form. Money bears a zero nominal interest rate—and a negative real interest rate, as explained below—which must be compared with the nominal rate available for other assets. Holding money implies forgoing that nominal interest rate. For firms which work with large cash balances, these costs can be significant, so cash management, the art of keeping these balances low, is very serious business. Table 8.4 shows estimates of the elasticity of money demand vis-à-vis the interest rate. The negative signs confirm that money demand declines when interest rates rise. The average long-run effect means that, when the nominal interest rate rises by one percentage point, real money demand falls by 3.7%.[10]

8.5.4 The Money Demand Function

Summarizing, we have found that the demand for nominal money is proportional to the price level, or, equivalently, the demand for money is a demand for real money. Real money, in turn, is demanded to facilitate real transactions and therefore increases with the real GDP. Holding money, though, has a cost that is measured by the nominal interest rate. Higher interest rates discourage the holding of wealth in the form of money. On the other hand, if it is costly to turn other assets into liquidity, real money holdings are larger. The **money demand function** is a compact way of describing these various effects:

$$\textbf{(8.1)} \qquad M/P = \mathscr{L}(Y, i, c),$$
$$\qquad\qquad\qquad + \; - \; +$$

where M is the nominal stock of money, P is the price level, Y is real GDP, i is the nominal interest rate, and c is the average cost of converting other forms of wealth into money. The signs underneath

---

[8] GDP is not an ideal measure of transactions; total sales, as opposed to final sales, might be preferable.

[9] The formal definition is $\dfrac{\Delta(M/P)/(M/P)}{\Delta Y/Y}$

[10] There is a subtle difference between the income elasticity of money demand (the percentage effect of a 1% increase in income) and the semi-elasticity of a one-percentage-point increase in the interest rate. Formally, the elasticity of y with respect to x is $(\Delta y/y)/(\Delta x/x)$ and the semi-elasticity is $(\Delta y/y)/\Delta x$.

Table 8.4 Elasticities of Money Demand (effect of a 1% increase in income (GNP) or of a 1 percentage point increase in the nominal interest rate)

	Real income		Nominal interest rate	
	Short run	Long run	Short run	Long run
Belgium	0.06	0.41	−0.50	−3.57
Denmark	0.27	1.67	−0.30	−1.88
Finland	0.64	1.13	−0.77	−1.57
France	0.10	0.36	−0.19	−0.70
Germany	0.35	1.19	−0.53	−1.83
Greece	0.16	1.25	−0.13	−1.00
Ireland	0.07	1.48	−0.45	−9.00
Italy	0.11	1.88	−0.31	−5.17
Netherlands	0.41	0.71	−0.86	−1.51
Norway	0.09	1.74	−0.23	−4.60
Portugal	0.18	0.95	−0.51	−2.68
Sweden	0.49	1.40	N.A.	N.A.
Switzerland	0.04	0.36	−0.79	−7.18
UK	0.12	1.70	−0.43	−6.14
Japan	0.05	1.76	−0.44	−6.29
USA	0.06	1.18	−0.12	−2.40
Unweighted av.		1.20		−3.70

Note: The short-run effect is measured within a quarter. The long-run effect corresponds to a complete adjustment of indefinite duration. The demand concerns the real stock of money.

Source: Fair (1987).

remind us of the effect of each variable on the demand for money. The WebAppendix shows how (8.1) can be formally justified by inventory management principles. Other justifications are summarized in Box 8.3.

The effect of the price level on money demand thus depends on whether we are looking at a once-and-for-all change, or at an anticipated movement in the rate of change in the price level (inflation). This important distinction is made more clear in Figure 8.3, where it is assumed for simplicity that real GDP is constant. Under these conditions, as long as the inflation rate ($\Delta P/P$) is constant, the real demand for money remains unchanged. Panel (*a*) shows the case of zero inflation ($\Delta P/P = 0$). The price level is constant, except for a single jump which is perceived by agents as one-off (for example,

an increase in sales tax or VAT). Panel (*b*) shows the case of a non-zero but constant inflation rate ($\Delta P/P > 0$). Real money demand is constant, but lower than with zero inflation, and the nominal money demand rises in proportion to the price level. Panel (*c*) shows the case where inflation is rising. Real money demand declines while nominal money grows increasingly faster, yet more slowly than the price level.

The **velocity of money** measures how many times on average a unit of money is spent during the measurement period (usually a year). It is defined as $V = PY/M$, and is the inverse of the ratio shown in Figure 8.2. For example, if $V = 3$, the money stock M is spent on average three times on the GDP, or the money stock 'turns round three times' over the year. Given the money demand function, velocity is:

Box 8.3 The Many Reasons for Holding Money

Until now, the demand for money had been explained by its role in facilitating transactions. This is often called the inventory theory of money because it comes from the trade-off between the cost of holding that inventory —interest costs—and the transaction cost of converting interest-bearing assets into money. The inventory explanation may also be expanded to account for uncertainty and the perceived risk of being caught without liquidity in emergencies. This behaviour towards risk is called the precautionary motive and generally predicts that the demand for money rises when economic conditions become more uncertain.

A very different approach emphasizes that money is one asset among several. The portfolio balance or speculative demand for money view argues that agents spread their wealth so as to diversify their assets, considering not only the returns (zero for currency, the nominal yield on bonds) but also the risk characteristics of each asset. The corresponding demand-for-money function includes the interest rate and transaction costs as before, but is related to wealth instead of transactions or the real GDP. One particular aspect of the portfolio approach is the speculative motive. In fast-moving financial markets, traders must be ready to buy or sell quickly very large amounts of assets. When interest rates are low and expected to rise, bond prices are expected to fall. (It is a good idea to take another look at Box 5.2, which explains the inverse relationship between bond prices and the interest rate.) It is then considered better to 'stay liquid', meaning to hold more money and fewer bonds, avoiding capital losses on the bonds. In contrast, when interest rates are high and expected to decline, traders want to acquire bonds and take advantage of capital gains when their prices rise: the speculative demand for money declines.

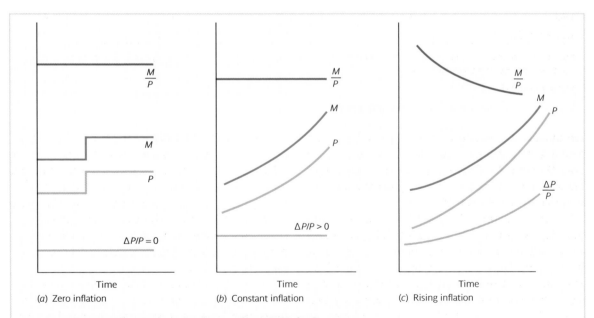

Fig. 8.3 Money Demand and Prices, when GDP is Constant

When expected inflation is constant, real money demand is constant and nominal money demand just moves with the price level. This is true for both panels (a) and (b). In panel (a) there is a one-shot unexpected price increase. In panel (c) prices rise at an increasing rate. As inflation increases, real money demand declines, which means that the nominal money demand grows less quickly than prices.

(8.2) $V = Y/\mathcal{L}(Y, i, c)$

In the particular case where real money demand is proportional to real GDP, velocity is independent of GDP.[11] In the short run, transaction costs do not change much so that velocity simply moves as the interest rate changes. When the interest rate rises, holding money becomes more expensive and people save on cash balances; the money turns round faster, and velocity increases. Over the longer run, if transaction costs decline, people will hold less money and velocity will show a rising trend.

8.6 Equilibrium in the Money Market: The Short Run

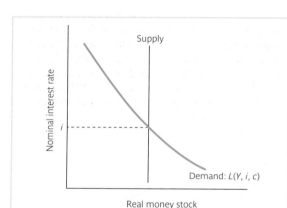

Fig. 8.4 Equilibrium in the Money Market
Given the level of economic activity and the cost of converting funds, the negative slope of the money demand curve reflects the effect of the opportunity cost of holding money. When the central bank sets the money supply (the vertical supply schedule), the interest rate adjusts to clear the money market.

The real money demand function is depicted in Figure 8.4. Its negative slope reflects the opportunity cost of holding money. Its position corresponds to a particular GDP level. If the GDP increases, so does the demand for money at any nominal interest rate. The schedule shifts to the right.

In Chapter 9, we examine how central banks control monetary conditions: the money supply and interest rates. Here we simply assume that the central bank fixes the nominal money supply which, for a given price level, renders the real money supply exogenous, hence the vertical line in Figure 8.4. Money market equilibrium is described by the intersection of both schedules. This simple apparatus can be used to explain the short-run relationship between money and interest rates. It is only a short-run view because it takes as exogenous the real GDP, the price level, and the inflation rate: over the short run (say, a quarter) these variables normally change very little. With a constant inflation rate, the results that follow apply to both the nominal and real interest rates.

8.6.1 Money Supply Effects

Figure 8.5 shows the effect on interest rates of an increase in the real money supply, represented by a rightward shift in the vertical schedule. The demand curve does not shift, since its other determinants (real GDP and transactions costs) are assumed to remain unaffected.[12] As the equilibrium moves from A to A', the interest rate declines. This illustrates the power of the central bank to influence interest rates. A restrictive or 'tight' monetary policy occurs when the central bank contracts the real money supply, which would be represented by a leftward shift of the vertical supply schedule. In that case nominal and real interest rates rise.

---

[11] When money demand is proportional to real GDP, it can be rewritten as $\mathcal{L}(Y, i, c) \equiv Y\,\ell(i, c)$ so $V = 1/\ell(i, c)$.

[12] Chs. 10 and 11 examine directly the effect of money supply and interest rates on GDP.

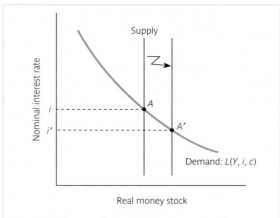

Fig. 8.5 Expansionary Monetary Policy

An increase in the real money supply lowers the nominal interest rate. A decline in interest rates induces a higher demand so as to match the higher supply.

8.6.2 Cyclical Fluctuations

An increase in real GDP increases money demand, and the demand schedule shifts to the right as shown in Figure 8.6. If the real money supply remains unchanged, the interest rate must rise until the increased demand induced by the higher GDP is entirely offset by the higher opportunity cost of holding money. This is one reason why interest rates are procyclical, rising in booms and declining in recessions.

8.6.3 Transaction Costs

If the nominal cost of converting wealth between interest-bearing assets and money decreases, more wealth is held in the form of interest-bearing assets and less in the form of money. The money demand curve shifts to the left, as in Figure 8.7, and interest rates fall to the point where the opportunity cost is low enough to persuade agents to hold the existing money supply. An example of a decrease in transaction costs is the development and introduction of internet banking, which make it easier to convert savings accounts and other assets into current deposits. On the other hand, transaction costs might *increase* if banks charged more for this service, or if an increase in wages made individuals' leisure time spent in line at the bank or on-line in front of a computer more valuable.

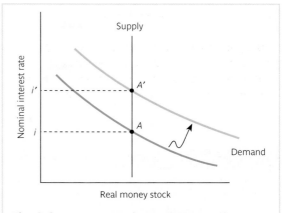

Fig. 8.6 An Increase in Real Economic Activity

An increase in real economic activity increases the demand for money and the schedule shifts to the right. Starting at point *A*, the new equilibrium occurs at point *A'* and the nominal interest rate increases from *i* to *i'*. With supply unchanged, demand cannot increase in equilibrium. The interest rate must rise until its negative effect on demand exactly offsets the positive effect of the increase in GDP.

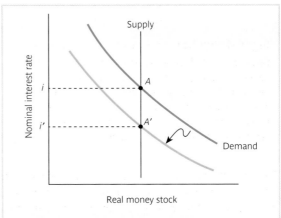

Fig. 8.7 A Decline in Transaction Costs

A decline in the cost of converting assets from money to interest-bearing forms reduces the demand for money and shifts the demand schedule to the left. Since the supply does not change, the interest rate must fall to reduce the opportunity cost of holding money until demand is restored to its initial level.

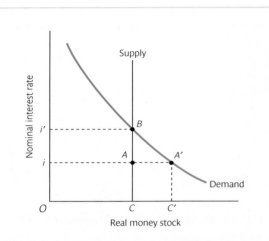

Fig. 8.8 Money Market Disequilibrium

Point *A* to the left of the demand curve describes a situation of excess demand for money. At the relatively low interest rate *i*, agents want to hold more real money balances (at point *A'* on the demand curve). They attempt to sell other assets or borrow money, but with unchanged supply the interest rate rises until equilibrium is restored at point *B* at interest *i'*.

8.6.4 The Equilibrating Role of the Interest Rate and Asset Prices

How is equilibrium achieved in the short run? Point *A* in Figure 8.8 is to the left of the demand curve: it depicts the case of an excess demand for money. At interest rate *i*, agents would like to hold real balances (point *A'*) in excess of the available supply (point *A*). To obtain additional liquidity, they attempt to sell other assets such as bonds or to borrow funds from each other. With a fixed money supply *OC*, however, these efforts cannot be successful in the aggregate. The interest rate increases as the result of competition for more money, and bond prices fall as more bonds are offered for sale.[13] Equilibrium is restored at point *B* at interest rate *i'*.

Financial markets react extremely quickly to disequilibria. This is because large losses can be incurred by holding bonds when their prices are falling. Similarly, very large capital gains are available to those who buy bonds before their prices increase. Any disequilibrium in the money market is eliminated by swift interest rate and bond price changes, and the economy promptly returns to its money demand schedule.

8.7 Equilibrium in the Money Market: The Long Run

The money market equilibrium condition also settles the long-run link between money, prices and inflation, and the exchange rate. Two very simple and powerful results emerge. First, in the long run, inflation is determined by the rate of money growth. Second, in the long run, the rate of nominal exchange rate depreciation is determined by the rate of inflation. Figure 8.9(*a*) presents long-run averages of money growth and inflation rates for all the OECD countries. Panel (*b*) does the same for exchange rates and inflation (relatively to the dollar and US inflation). While not perfect, the positive relationship between all three variables is unmistakable.

8.7.1 Long-Run Inflation

As the economy grows, more money is needed to facilitate more transactions. In Figure 8.10, this means that the demand schedule continuously shifts to the right. If the real money stock were held constant, the interest rate would grow from point *A* to point *A'* and then continuously further up as the demand schedule moves rightward. But we know that nominal interest rates do not grow without bounds over the long run. The two examples in

[13] The link between interest rates and bond prices is presented in Box 5.2.

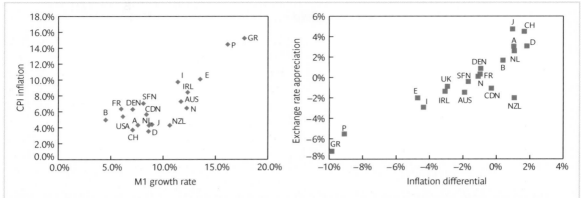

Fig. 8.9 Money, Inflation, and Exchange Rate Appreciation in the Long Run: OECD Countries, 1970–1998

Averaging over many years eliminates short-run effects. Panel (*a*) shows that countries that have experienced high inflation rates are those where nominal money has grown faster. Panel (*b*) shows that the rate of exchange rate depreciation vis-à-vis the USA is about equal to the inflation differential exchange vis-à-vis the USA, as suggested by purchasing power parity.

Source: IMF.

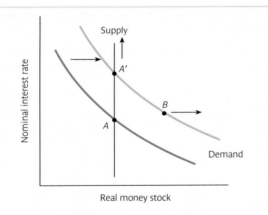

Fig. 8.10 Money and Long-Run Growth

As real GDP increases, so does the demand for real money. The demand schedule shifts to the right. If the real money supply did not respond, the interest rate would rise, as shown by the move from point *A* to point *A'*. Continuous growth would result in an ever-shifting demand schedule and an ever-rising interest rate. The absence of long-run trend in the nominal interest rate means that, somehow, the supply curve must shift over time to move from *A* to *B*, and further to the right.

Figure 8.11 show that the British and Dutch nominal interest rate rose at times of sustained inflation (after the Second World War, and then in the 1970s). But they seem to have returned to lower levels, rather than continuing to rise. What must happen in Figure 8.10 is that the supply schedule eventually moves rightward until it passes through a point like *B* where the real money supply matches the long-run growth in its demand. How can that be?

In the long run, the central bank controls only the nominal money stock. It can affect neither prices, nor inflation, nor the real money supply. The only possibility of reconciling any discrepancy between real money demand (*M/P*) and nominal supply (*M*) growth is for prices and inflation to play the balancing act as endogenous variables. Inflation is the channel through which, in the long run, money market equilibrium is ultimately achieved. (See Box 8.4 for details.)

Consider the case shown in Table 8.5, where economic growth implies a 3% average annual increase in real money demand. If the central bank allows the nominal money stock to grow at the same 3% per year, demand and supply will coincide when the average inflation rate is 0%. Were the nominal

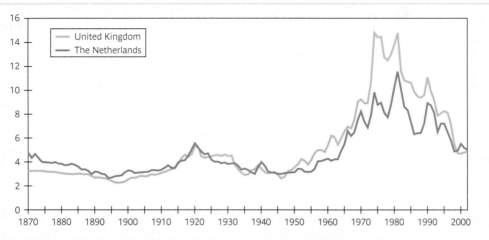

Fig. 8.11 Nominal Interest Rates, UK and the Netherlands, 1870–2002

Over very long periods the nominal interest rate is trendless, despite shorter-run fluctuations and possible 'staircase behaviour' reflecting the higher inflation rate of the 1970s and 1980s.

Source: Homer (1963); IMF.

 Box 8.4 **The Algebra of Long-Run Inflation**

The money demand function $\mathcal{L}(Y, i, c)$ identifies three determinants of the real money stock. As long as the transaction cost c is constant in real terms, it can safely be ignored. Similarly, when the interest rate does not exhibit any long-term trend, despite considerable variability, it does not affect real money in the long run. This just leaves the real GDP. If η is the elasticity of the demand for money with respect to GDP, an annual GDP growth rate of g translates into an annual growth rate ηg in money demand. Noting that the growth rate of the real money stock is the difference between the growth rates of the nominal money stock and the price level, we have the equilibrium condition:

$$(8.3) \qquad \Delta(M/P)/(M/P) = \mu - \pi = \eta g$$

where $\mu = \Delta M/M$ and $\pi = \Delta P/P$. Given the real growth rate g, this expression shows that the long-run inflation rate

is the difference between the nominal money growth rate and the rate of growth of real GNP, up to the elasticity factor η:

$$(8.4) \qquad \pi = \mu - \eta g.$$

Looking ahead, the relationship (8.4) can be combined with relative purchasing power parity (PPP) in equation (8.9) to yield the long-run rate of exchange rate depreciation:

$$(8.5) \qquad \Delta S/S = (\mu^* - \mu) - (\eta^* g^* - \eta g).$$

Faster money growth abroad than at home ($\mu^* > \mu$) leads in the long run to an appreciation. Faster output growth at home than abroad ($g > g^*$) also leads to an appreciation, if the faster demand for money is not accommodated by a faster growth in the money supply.

money stock to grow at an average annual rate of 8%, inflation would have to be 5%: only then would the real money stock grow at the same 3% rate (8% nominal less 5% of inflation) as real money demand.

This is why in the long run inflation is a monetary phenomenon. It is due to money growth in excess of that of real money balances demanded by the public. Figure 8.9 confirms the strength of this conclusion.

Table 8.5 Inflation and Money Growth in the Long Run: A Rule of Thumb (assuming that real money demand grows at 3% p.a.)

Nominal money supply (%)	Inflation rate (%)
0	−3
3	0
8	5
50	47
103	100

8.7.2 Inflation and the Fisher Principle

Section 8.5.1 looked at the role of the price level in the demand for money. The rate of inflation, i.e. the rate of increase in the price level, has an independent effect on money demand. The distinction is subtle and is illustrated in Figure 8.3 above. A once-and-for-all and unexpected increase in the price level raises nominal money demand proportionately. In contrast, continuous price increases—inflation—erode the purchasing power of money. For example, with a 10% annual inflation rate, a given stock of money in real terms is worth 10% less a year later.

The effect can be understood by the distinction between nominal and real interest rates. By definition, the real interest rate (r) is the difference between the nominal interest rate (i) and the expected rate of inflation (π^e):

$$(8.6) \qquad r \quad = i \quad - \quad \pi^e.$$

real interest rate | nominal interest rate | less | expected inflation

For decisions such as consumption and investment, we have seen that the real interest rate is the one that matters. In principle, no one would lend money at a nominal interest rate lower than expected inflation because the interest payment does not compensate for the loss of purchasing power. Implicitly, at least, borrowers and lenders agree that a positive real interest rate should remunerate the lender. Over long periods, real interest rate shows no trend. The nominal rate can therefore be seen as the sum of

the reward to the lender, or the cost of borrowing (the real interest rate), and expected inflation. This is just (8.6) rewritten as

$$(8.7) \qquad i = r + \pi^e.$$

This relationship (8.7) linking the nominal interest rate, the real interest rate, and the expected rate of inflation is called the **Fisher principle** or the **Fisher equation**.[14] It shows that the negative effect of expected inflation on real money demand works itself through the nominal interest rate. The nominal rate includes both the forgone real opportunity cost (r) and the expected capital loss on the nominal value of the loan (π^e). The long-run stability of the real interest rate—which we know from Chapter 5 is related to the marginal product of capital—implies that the nominal interest rate fully reflects expected inflation. The store-of-value and standard-of-deferred-payment properties of money are eroded when its value in terms of the goods it can buy is deteriorating because prices keep increasing.

There are many ways that lenders and borrowers enforce the Fisher principle. In countries with chronically high inflation, nominal interest rates are often indexed: loan contracts include a clause that stipulates that the interest rate be adjusted for inflation of some price index over the lifetime of the loan. Another way of limiting the damage from unexpected inflation is to lend only over short periods of time, sometimes not longer than a week. Because these loans are rolled over at the new prevailing interest rate, they are roughly equivalent to indexed lending. As inflation rises, borrowers and lenders attempt to keep the real interest rate unchanged, and the nominal interest rate rises along with inflation.

The best laboratory available for testing the theory of the demand for money is a **hyperinflation**—when inflation reaches rates in excess of 50% per month. In Central Europe, a wave of hyperinflations occurred in the early 1920s, and again early in the recent economic transformation in Russia, the Ukraine, and Serbia, to mention just a few examples. Inflation rates as high as 10% per hour were observed for brief periods. Under such circumstances,

---

[14] Named after Irving Fisher, the Yale economist referred to in Chs. 4 and 5.

lending occurs at astronomically high interest rates, over short periods or not at all. Domestic money holdings fall dramatically, as people fear ever-increasing losses on the real value of money and, with nominal interest rates rising, hold increasingly smaller amounts of cash, sometimes just enough for the day's shopping. The velocity of money increases. People convert their wealth into assets immune to inflation, including precious metals as well as durable goods such as TVs and refrigerators. Foreign currency begins to circulate openly, with goods prices quoted and traded in both local and

Box 8.5 The Demand for Money in a High-Inflation Episode: Bulgaria, 1991–2002

Figure 8.12 shows how, in the case of Bulgaria, real money balances (M/P) declined dramatically when inflation picked up speed, even in advance of the actual increase. After sharp increases in the wake of price liberalization in the early 1990s, relatively moderate inflation was maintained until 1995. Yet the first half of the 1990s in Bulgaria was characterized by a significant budget deficit, high monetary growth, and flagging confidence in government policy, which led to steadily rising inflation. By the first quarter of 1997, the inflation rate reached almost 400% per annum; in the same period real money balances had fallen to 10% of their 1991 value. As subsequent reforms ultimately defeated inflation, Bulgarians became convinced they could return to the domestic currency, the leva, although this process was slow.

In general, when high inflation or hyperinflation is beaten, nominal interest rates decline, and the demand for money rises again in real terms. This effect is called reliquification. It is a signal that people believe the inflationary episode to be over. Yet, Figure 8.12 shows that a sceptical public needs time to be convinced. Temporary successes are often followed by relapses, so even after a successful battle against inflation, nominal interest rates remain high and real cash balances low, increasing only gradually over time. Another way of stating this is that during the late 1990s, the expected rate of inflation in Bulgaria was much higher than the observed rate.

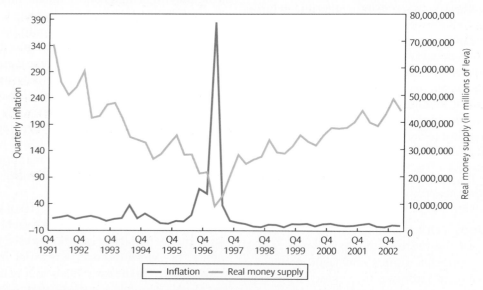

Fig. 8.12 Money Demand and High Inflation in Bulgaria, 1991–2002

The demand for real money balances declines when the expected rate of inflation rises. When hyperinflation is credibly eliminated, money demand should return to normal levels. Bulgaria, a small open economy undergoing a painful transition after the collapse of the Soviet Union and the end of central planning, confirms this theoretical prediction.
Source: IMF.

more stable foreign currencies (e.g. dollars), a phenomenon called currency substitution (see also Box 8.2). Once shattered, confidence is not easily restored when inflation returns to low levels, as people expect a return to the old regime. Box 8.5 provides some details on the recent experience of high inflation in Bulgaria in the course of its transition to a market economy.

8.7.3 The Exchange Rate in the Long Run: Purchasing Power Parity

The real exchange rate (σ) is defined in Chapter 7 as the ratio of domestic to foreign prices, expressed in same currency ($\sigma = SP/P^*$). Its rate of change is the sum of the rate of nominal appreciation plus the domestic inflation rate less the foreign inflation rate:

$$(8.8) \qquad \frac{\Delta\sigma}{\sigma} = \frac{\Delta S}{S} + \frac{\Delta P}{P} - \frac{\Delta P^*}{P^*}$$

In Chapter 7 we also saw that the long-run real exchange rate is driven by real factors—tastes, relative productivity, accumulated external net asset position—and the need to meet the nation's budget constraint. When these real factors remain unchanged, the equilibrium real exchange rate is constant. The real exchange rate is constant when the nominal exchange rate appreciates at a rate ($\Delta S/S$) equal to the difference between the foreign ($\pi^* = \Delta P^*/P^*$) and domestic ($\pi = \Delta P/P$) inflation rates, the **inflation differential**:

$$(8.9) \qquad \Delta S/S = \pi^* - \pi.$$

To keep the real exchange rate unchanged—that is to maintain external competitiveness—a country with a higher rate of inflation than the rest of the world (when $\pi^* < \pi$) must have a depreciating currency ($\Delta S/S < 0$), whereas a low-inflation-rate country will have an appreciating currency. This principle is called **relative purchasing power parity (PPP)**. Figure 8.9 provides strong evidence for PPP. As predicted by (8.9), for each country the link between the average depreciation of its currency vis-à-vis the dollar and the inflation differential vis-à-vis the USA is tight.

Bringing together PPP and the explanation of long-run inflation, we see that the long-run rate of exchange rate depreciation depends on the difference between the rate of money growth at home and abroad. This reasoning is formalized in Box 8.4. Countries with fast money growth have more inflation than those with slow money growth. If the real exchange rate is constant, their nominal exchange rate must depreciate. On the other hand, the demand for real money rises rapidly in fast-growing economies. Given the rate of growth of the nominal money supply, the nominal exchange rate tends to appreciate.

A much stronger version of this idea is **absolute purchasing power parity**, which asserts that price levels are equalized across countries when converted into the same currency. This implies not only that σ is constant, but is equal to unity. Put differently, $P^* = SP$. The evidence on absolute PPP is rather spotty; Box 8.6 provides one convincing piece of evidence on the failure of absolute PPP to hold.

 Box 8.6 **The Law of One Price and Absolute Purchasing Power Parity**

A key ingredient in the logic behind absolute PPP is the law of one price. This 'law' asserts that the same good should trade everywhere at the same price, when prices are expressed in the same currency. If prices were to differ significantly, it is asserted, enterprising traders would buy the goods where they are cheapest and sell them where they fetch a higher price. This process would push prices towards each other until all profit opportunities have disappeared. In practice, the law of one price is known to be grossly violated. Table 8.6 provides an

example, using prices of a standardized good (mirrors) sold by the same firm in different (international) markets. More examples and some of the reasons behind the results were presented in Chapter 7. Yet in the long run, if countries have access to similar technologies and converge to similar wealth levels, absolute purchasing parity becomes a much more reasonable proposition—not good by good, but across broad baskets of goods. This might well characterize price-level convergence in Europe.

Table 8.6 Prices of IKEA Mirrors across Europe, 1998 (US$)

| | Mirrors | | |
	Alg (square mirror tiles)	Guldros (round mirror)	Krabb (wavy mirror)
Austria	24	113	48
Belgium	22	111	28
Denmark	13	119	34
Finland	15	107	21
France	21	100	33
Germany	22	97	51
Italy	23	79	44
Netherlands	20	101	20
Norway	12	82	27
Spain	32	112	34
Sweden	15	94	24
Switzerland	19	67	27
United Kingdom	25	115	30

Source: Jonathan Haskel and Holger Wolf, 'Why does the "Law of one Price" Fail?', CEPR Discussion Paper, No. 2187 July 1999 .

❶ Summary

1 Money is an asset that is generally accepted as a means of payment. This definition leaves some room for interpretation, especially as payment technologies change over time.

2 Money has four attributes: it is a medium of exchange, a unit of account, a store of value, and a standard for deferred payment. Bearing no or low interest, it is dominated by other assets. Its desirability stems from its unique ability to resolve the problems of the double coincidence of wants and of information asymmetry.

3 Money is a public good. The fact that it is easily recognized and generally accepted generates benefits for the community. This is why there is a role for the government in issuing and guaranteeing money.

4 Money is simultaneously an asset of the private non-banking sector and a liability of the banking system. Currency is a liability of the monetary authority (central bank), while sight deposits are a liability of commercial banks.

5 The demand for money is a demand for real money. Agents are interested in the purchasing power of money, not in its nominal or face value.

6 The demand for real money depends positively on the volume of transactions, approximated by the real GDP. It depends negatively on the nominal interest rate, the opportunity cost of holding money. The demand for money increases with transaction costs because agents have an incentive to limit the number of transactions between money and other assets.

7 An unexpected and once-for-all increase in the price level does not affect the real demand for money. It affects the nominal demand for money, which increases in proportion with the price level.

8 Inflation reduces the purchasing power of money. An expected increase in inflation leads agents to reduce their real demand for money. This effect is captured by the nominal interest rate, the sum of the real interest rate, and the expected rate of inflation.

9 In the short run, money market equilibrium occurs rapidly through changes in the interest rate and bond prices. In the long run, money market equilibrium is achieved through changes in the price level and/or the rate of inflation.

10 In the long run, in the absence of real disturbances and relative purchasing power, parity holds. Then the rate of nominal exchange rate depreciation is equal to the inflation differential.

🔑 Key Concepts

- commodity monies
- monetary aggregates (M1, M2, etc.)
- medium of exchange
- double coincidence of wants
- unit of account
- store of value
- standard of deferred payment
- dominated asset
- information asymmetry
- fiat money
- public good
- balance sheet

- net worth
- neutrality of money
- transaction costs
- nominal interest rate
- opportunity cost
- money demand function
- velocity of money
- Fisher principle, Fisher equation
- hyperinflation
- inflation differential
- purchasing power parity (PPP), absolute and relative

❓ Exercises

1 If inflation is positive, simply maintaining the nominal money supply at some constant level amounts to a contractionary monetary policy. True or false? Explain.

2 In many economies—especially smaller, open economies—it is possible to hold bank sight deposits denominated in a foreign currency.

(a) Should these deposits be included in measures of the money supply? Give arguments for and against.

(b) How important is the openness of the economy concerned?

(c) Suppose these deposits are not included. How does a withdrawal from such a deposit, paid out in cash, affect the money supply, all things equal?

3 Real GDP increases by 1% and the real demand for money rises by 1.2%. The nominal interest rate and all other determinants of money demand are assumed constant.

(a) The income elasticity of money demand is defined as the percentage effect of an increase of 1% of real GDP on real money demand. Calculate the income elasticity of money demand in this example (at least as an approximation).

(b) Armed with your answer to (a), you later observe a similar situation, in which simultaneously real GDP increases by 1%, and the interest rate rises by 1% (e.g. 5% to 6%). All other determinants of money demand are constant. What is the (semi-)interest elasticity of money demand?

4 In the consolidated balance sheet of the government and non-bank private sector, suppose we know the following:

(a) Deposits of the government and the private sector amount to 1,500.

(b) Total net worth is 300.

(c) The net public debt of the government is 600 and its gross debt 750, the difference being in bank deposits. (The government has no real assets.)

(d) The gross private debt is 1,200.

(e) Private real assets total 450.

What is the value of banknotes and currency in circulation? What is M1? State your assumptions clearly.

5 The percentage effect on real money demand of an increase of one percentage point of the interest rate (say, from 5% to 6%) is sometimes called the interest rate semi-elasticity of the demand for money. Suppose it takes the value −0.1. The income elasticity of money demand (the percentage effect of an increase of 1% of real GDP on real

money demand) is 0.8. Find the increase in the interest rate required to maintain money market equilibrium, at unchanged real money supply, when output increases by 1%, 2%, and 5%.

6 Debit cards allow bank customers to pay for purchases 'instantly' with their current account balances, without the intermediate step of borrowing (as with credit cards) or writing a cheque.

(a) Does the existence of debit cards affect the technical definition of money?

(b) Do you think the introduction of debit cards affects the demand for money? How?

(c) How would introducing debit cards which access savings accounts affect your answers to (a) and (b)?

7 Suppose a country is hit by an earthquake which destroys a significant amount of the productive resources available (capital, labour, infrastructure). What would you expect to happen to the demand for money? What is likely to happen to prices if the nominal money supply is kept constant? How would your answer change if the earthquake destroyed the infrastructure of the banking system as well, making it much more difficult to conduct transactions with the bank and to convert different forms of deposits?

8 Suppose the inflation rate in Turkey is expected to be about 10% per year over the next year.

(a) What does the Fisher principle predict for the nominal interest rate if the real interest rate for low-risk loans is 5%.

(b) Suppose the inflation rate turns out to be 15% over the year. Were borrowers or lenders the winners if they had made contracts according to your answer to (a)?

(c) Suppose the inflation rate in Euroland is 2% per year. What does relative purchasing power parity theory predict for the evolution of the exchange rate of the lira, the Turkish currency, vis-à-vis the euro when the inflation rate in Turkey is 10%?

⮑ Essay Questions

1 Suppose Poland adopts the euro in 2010, and adopts the exchange rate 6 zloty/euro. Under these conditions, all payments and contracts in zloty would be converted without exception to euros. If this is expected and understood by all economic agents, what does the neutrality of money imply for the real economic effects of this action? Comment.

2 A currency area is defined as the region which employs a particular money. Why do currency areas almost always coincide with boundaries of nations?

3 An increase in Value Added Taxes (VAT) mechanically increases the price level. What does it mean for inflation in both the short and the long run?

4 Over the period 2000–4, the nominal money supply has grown very fast in the European monetary union. The European Central Bank has repeatedly expressed fear that inflation could increase, but this has not happened. How can you explain this?

5 Explain carefully the relationship between the law of one price and absolute and relative PPP. Which property(ies) do you expect to observe? Under which conditions?

The Supply of Money and Monetary Policy 9

9.1 Overview *200*

9.2 Objectives, Targets, and Instruments *201*

9.3 Money Creation *203*

   9.3.1   The Roles of Central and Commercial Banks *203*

   9.3.2   The Money Multiplier *205*

9.4 Controlling Monetary Conditions *209*

   9.4.1   Derived Demand for Base Money *209*

   9.4.2   Open Market Operations *210*

   9.4.3   The Practice of Monetary Policy *211*

   9.4.4   Reserve Requirements as a Tool of Monetary Policy *212*

   9.4.5   Monetary Policy Targets *213*

9.5 Monetary Policy in an Open Economy *216*

   9.5.1   Foreign Exchange Market Interventions *216*

   9.5.2   Sterilization *216*

9.6 Monetary Financing of the Government: A Slippery Objective *217*

   9.6.1   Direct Credit to the Government *218*

   9.6.2   Indirect Credit: Seigniorage and the Inflation Tax *218*

   9.6.3   Independence of the Central Bank *219*

9.7 Bank Regulation and Monetary Control *220*

   9.7.1   Central Bank Oversight *220*

   9.7.2   Lender of Last Resort *221*

   9.7.3   Capital Adequacy Ratios *221*

   9.7.4   Technological Innovation in Banking and Monetary Control *223*

Summary *223*

By playing upon the reserves of the bank, the note-issuing authority can induce an expansion or a contraction of credit at will. But in order to do so, it must have at its disposal some machinery for issuing and withdrawing notes easily and promptly. A Government which can only withdraw notes by raising the necessary funds from the public by taxes or loans does not fulfil this condition. The best instrument for the regulation of the supply of paper money is a State Bank or else a Central Bank which, while not itself a part of the Executive Government, is willing regularly to co-operate with it.

—R. G. Hawtrey[1]

9.1 Overview

In Chapter 8 we studied the demand for money. It is now time to study the other side of the market, the supply of money, in more detail. Money in the narrow sense—banknotes and demand deposits—is supplied jointly by the commercial banks and the **central bank**, the bankers' bank. While commercial banks supply most of the money, control of the process rests solely with the central bank. The following four broad questions are addressed in this chapter: (1) What are the central bank's objectives, and how does it meet them? (2) How does the central bank exert control over the money supply process, given that money is generated primarily by commercial banks? (3) What are the links between domestic and foreign monetary conditions? (4) How can the central bank help safeguard the integrity of the financial system, given its inherent fragility?

Central banks are typically required to deliver low and stable inflation. In Chapter 8, we learned that this requires a low rate of money growth in the long run. Yet the link between money growth and inflation is usually slow to emerge. In the meantime, the central bank needs additional guideposts. It typically focuses its energy on intermediate targets, which may either be the money supply, market interest rate levels, or even the exchange rate. Achieving targets requires careful use of instruments under direct control of the central bank, which will be explained later in great detail. Some targets are difficult if not impossible to manipulate using some instruments.

The choice of a target has been changing, partly in response to prevailing conditions, partly as new techniques are developed. A particular difficulty that has arisen in recent decades is that the central bank can only control M1, M2, or wider monetary aggregates indirectly, mostly through cost of money, the interest rate. In recent years, a number of central banks have begun to target inflation directly, instead of targeting money growth, the standard strategy used in the 1980s to bring inflation down. Exchange rate targeting, which has also proved useful for reining in inflation, has lost popularity because of conflicts that arise between the central bank's domestic and foreign monetary policy objectives, which can occasionally result in serious crises.

While the guiding principles of monetary control are fundamentally the same across countries, institutions and procedures differ widely. These differences may appear important in the day-to-day operation of a national central bank, but they tend to cloud and confuse discussion of the unifying aspects of monetary policy. For that reason we downplay them, stressing instead aspects of a monetary system that should be thought of as a common denominator of various arrangements observed in developed economies.

---

[1] Ralph G. Hawtrey (1879–1971) was a successful British economist who avoided universities almost completely, working his way up through the civil service. A friend and critic of Keynes, Hawtrey is best known for developing the concept of the multiplier, which appears in this chapter. He also articulated one of the earliest pure monetary theories of the business cycle based on bank credit.

9.2 Objectives, Targets, and Instruments

Most central banks are responsible for establishing and maintaining price stability. For instance, the Maastricht Treaty provides an explicit mandate for the ESCB (European System of Central Banks or **Eurosystem**):

The primary objective of the ESCB shall be to maintain price stability. Without prejudice to the objective of price stability, the ESCB shall support the general economic policies in the Community with a view to contributing to the achievement of the objectives of the Community. (Article 105)

The European Central Bank (ECB) defines price stability as 'an annual increase in the price level below 2% over the medium run', i.e. an inflation rate between 0% and 2%. In 2004, the Bank of England had an inflation objective of 2%. The US Federal Reserve does not have an explicit quantitative objective and seems to adapt to current conditions, but leaves no doubt that it wants inflation to remain low.[2]

Inflation may be the **objective**, but central banks cannot control it directly. In Chapter 8, we saw that inflation is determined in the long run by the growth rate of money, more precisely by the confrontation of the real demand for money with a nominal money supply. Real demand is driven by the (non-bank) public; the nominal supply is the responsibility of the central bank. The 'art of central banking' is to match the supply of money today with its ultimate, long-run impact on inflation. Thus achievement of the inflation objective is indirect. To that effect, central banks rely on targets and instruments. Figure 9.1 is a schematic representation of the most commonly used targets and instruments available to central banks.

[2] Inflation has become the objective of central banks only since the 1980s. In the 1960s, many central banks were more preoccupied with economic growth and unemployment. The general increase in inflation rates in the late 1970s and early 1980s prompted a re-examination of central banks' objectives and led to important changes. Some central banks have not fully repudiated the growth objective, e.g. the US Federal Reserve.

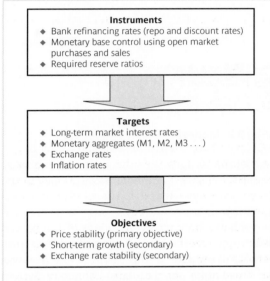

Fig. 9.1 Instruments, Targets, and Objectives in Monetary Policy

The distinction between instruments, targets, and objectives is an important one when analysing monetary policy. Instruments and targets are means to an end rather than ends in themselves. Instruments and targets differ inasmuch as the former are under the direct control of the central bank—such as bank lending rates or open market operations—while the latter are usually more relevant for achieving a given objective.

Targets are intermediate objectives which, while closely related to the ultimate inflation objective, are more easily controlled by the central bank. Three main targets are often mentioned. The first is the rate of growth of monetary aggregates (M1, M2, M3, M4, etc.), which determine the subsequent rate of inflation once demand is taken into account. The ECB, for instance, once identified M3 growth as the first 'pillar' of its monetary policy strategy. Another frequently mentioned target is the exchange rate. Like the nominal money supply, the nominal exchange rate is closely associated with the rate of inflation, as was shown in Chapter 8. The ECB lists

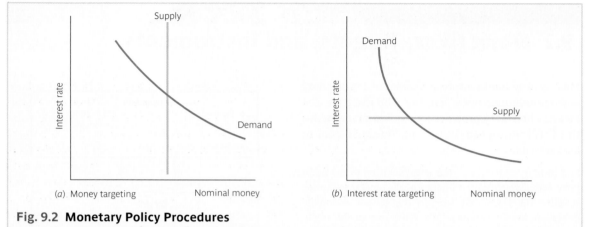

Fig. 9.2 Monetary Policy Procedures
The central bank could try to set a monetary aggregate such as M2 as its policy target, leaving the market to determine the interest rate (panel (a)). Conversely it can set the interest rate; in that case it must provide the market with whatever volume of money is demanded at the chosen rate (panel (b)).

the exchange rate as a component of the second 'pillar'. Some central banks may try to fix or stabilize market interest rates or the exchange rate. This was the case within the European Monetary System which existed from 1979 to 1998. Many Eastern and Central European countries have also relied on the exchange rate target to stabilize prices. More recently, inflation has become a popular target. The question of a choice of a target is addressed in Section 9.4.5.

Unfortunately, targets are not under the direct control of the central bank, either. Central banks use **instruments**, which they control with precision and which influence the targets. Nowadays, interest rates set directly by the central bank have become the instrument of choice. In the past, central banks sometimes worked primarily with narrow monetary aggregates, like the supply of central bank liabilities (currency plus deposits of commercial banks at the central bank).

The tensions between instruments and targets can be seen in Figure 9.2 which depicts the public's nominal demand for money as a function of the interest rate i. Chapter 8 showed that the demand for money is based on what it can purchase with it. Its demand for nominal money therefore depends on both the price level P and real money demand $\mathcal{L}(Y, i, c)$:

(9.1)   Nominal demand for money
$$= M^d = P\mathcal{L}\,(Y, i, c)$$

Given the price level, the central bank faces the demand schedule shown in Figure 9.2. The schedule is downward sloping because the real demand for money declines when the interest rate rises. It summarizes the tastes and preferences of the non-bank public.

The central bank cannot do anything about the public's preferences; it can only decide where to be on the demand schedule. Its policy target can focus primarily on quantities—meaning it will take action to set the quantity of money, as shown in the left panel of the figure. In this case, it must accept whatever interest rate is compatible with the public's behaviour. When it operates with an interest rate instrument or less direct target, as shown on the rightmost graph, it gives up the possibility of controlling the money supply. In short, the central bank can aim at the price or the quantity of money, not both. Today, most central banks in fact focus on the price of money, i.e. the interest rate.[3]

---

[3] Note that the interest rate i is the price of one period loans repaid in money, and therefore represents the opportunity cost of holding money; the price level P refers to the price of goods and services in terms of money.

9.3 Money Creation

This section makes two main points. First, most of what we have defined as money is actually created by commercial banks in the process of lending to private customers. Direct money creation by the monetary authorities only involves cash (banknotes and coins) and **bank reserves** held by commercial banks at the central bank (a bank's own deposits drawn against the central bank). Second, the central bank exerts indirect control on private money creation by commercial banks by limiting the volume of their reserves. The instruments that a central bank ultimately uses are those that influence the bank's lending behaviour and demand for reserves.

9.3.1 The Roles of Central and Commercial Banks

The central bank and the monetary base

The central bank is a public or quasi-public agency with an explicit, exclusive legal mandate to control money and credit conditions.[4] It is the 'bankers' bank', which banks can use to settle claims against each other, and it may also serve as a clearing house of cheques or transfers written on accounts of depositors. It generally does not take deposits from the private sector but may serve as the government's bank. It may also gather, process, and analyse information about the financial and real economy. Most importantly, the central bank guarantees the value of the currency by aiming at price stability. It does so by issuing currency, one of the components of M1. It also creates bank reserves, the claims on the central bank held by commercial banks already mentioned above. The sum of currency in circulation and commercial bank reserves is known as the **monetary base**, sometimes called M0.[5] The monetary base is represented by the shaded area in Figure 9.3 and is the sum of the first two liability entries in the balance sheet of the European Central Bank shown in Table 9.1.

Table 9.1 Consolidated Balance Sheet of the Eurosystem, 30 April 2004 (€ billions)

Assets		Liabilities	
Gold and foreign reserves	310.1	Currency in circulation	435.4
Claims on governments	42.6	Reserves held by commercial banks	133.6
Claims on banks and financial institutions	295.1	Government deposits	62.1
Other assets	205.7	Other liabilities	20.4
		Net worth	202.0
Total	**853.5**	**Total**	**853.5**

Source: ECB Monthly Bulletin, May 2004, table 1.1.

---

4 The Bank of England was a private institution from its founding in 1694 until its nationalization in 1946, much like the Banque de France, founded in 1800 and nationalized in 1945. The Bundesbank was established in 1949 as a successor to the Deutsche Reichsbank founded in 1876. The oldest central bank is the Swedish Riksbank, founded in 1668, while other dates of foundation are: Bank of Japan, 1882; Banca d'Italia, 1893; Austrian National Bank, 1816; Swiss National Bank, 1905. The Federal Reserve of the USA was founded in 1913 and is owned by the member banks, although profits above a statutory maximum are remitted, as in most countries, to the government (Goodhart 1988).

5 Other expressions used are 'high-powered', 'base money', or 'central bank money'.

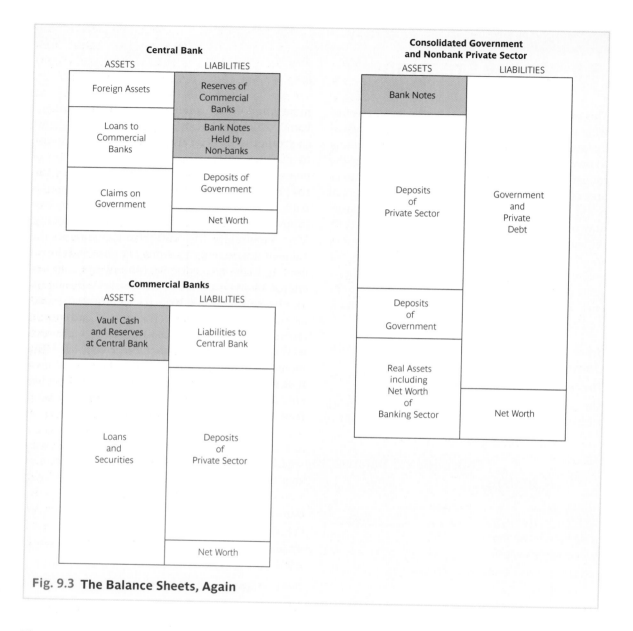

Fig. 9.3 The Balance Sheets, Again

The role of commercial banks in money creation

As **financial intermediaries**, commercial banks collect funds from depositors and lend them to customers, channelling resources from savers to borrowers. They also perform a payment-clearing role in settling accounts among their customers and with those of other banks. Much more important, however, is their role in the money supply process. Were it not for banks, the only circulating medium of exchange would be currency. In fact, the bulk of the money supply used in modern economies is bank deposits, and these deposits are actually created by the commercial banking system. The money-creating function of banks is what distinguishes them from other financial intermediaries such as savings banks, brokers, and stock markets. All of those institutions collect, lend, and invest funds, but none of them has the right to create money, because none of them may legally lend more than they have received in deposits.

By lending money that they do not directly possess, commercial banks are in effect issuing money. How do they do it? We will learn below that, by issuing a loan to a customer, a bank increases the volume of its assets, as shown in Figure 9.3. The increase is matched on the liability side by the amount of the loan credited to the customer's bank account. Quite simply put, that is how new money is created by a bank.

Prudential and legal reserves requirements

There is a catch, however. Banks need to have enough bank reserves—cash in their vaults and reserves—on the asset side of their balance sheets. Bank reserves can be thought of as the 'money' that commercial banks use to conduct transactions among themselves and with the central bank. The reserves pay little or no interest, so commercial banks would rather keep them at a minimum. What determines this minimum, then? First, banks must have enough currency at hand to meet everyday withdrawals by customers. For that purpose, they use vault cash or draw on their deposits at the central bank which are immediately convertible into cash. In addition, banks require a means of settling payments among themselves and on behalf of their customers. Settlements between banks are usually made by transfers from the central bank account of one bank to another.

Suppose, for example, that a customer of Bank A receives some payment in the form of a cheque drawn on Bank B.[6] He deposits the cheque in his current account at Bank A. Bank A simultaneously

credits its customer's account and deposits the cheque with the central bank. The central bank then debits Bank B's reserves account and credits Bank A's reserve account. For such transactions, a positive reserve balance is obviously necessary at the central bank. During a given period, any commercial bank may receive large amounts in deposits and face large withdrawals. If the two about balance, which is normally the case, they actually need very limited amounts of reserves; but sometimes withdrawals may exceed deposits by a large amount. This is why commercial banks always find it prudent to hold some fraction of their assets in the form of either vault cash or deposits at the central bank.

A second reason for banks to hold reserves can be legal. In many countries, deposit-taking banks are required by law to hold a fraction of outstanding deposits in the form of bank reserves at the central bank. These so-called **reserves requirements** are one of many regulations that are imposed on banks, and are normally set as a proportion of deposits. This proportion is called the **reserve ratio**. In the Euro-area, the reserve ratio is set at 2% of banks' deposits. It is 3% in the USA (rising to 10% for large deposits). There are no reserve requirements in a number of countries (e.g. Canada, the UK, and Switzerland), which rely solely on prudential behaviour. Reserve requirements are not always binding, and banks sometimes hold reserves in excess of the legal amount. Except under extraordinary conditions, however, excess reserves holdings by commercial banks are usually kept to a minimum because of the associated opportunity costs—forgone lending business.

9.3.2 The Money Multiplier

Whether compulsory or prudential, a linkage has been established between current deposits at banks, which are liabilities of commercial banks to their customers, and bank reserves, which are assets of the commercial bank and liabilities of the central bank. This linkage is the central bank's source of control over the money supply. Whenever a bank makes a loan to a customer, it creates a new deposit, and it will need to hold more reserves at the central bank. This link implies a relationship, known as the **money multiplier**, between the monetary base and

[6] A cheque is a piece of paper, issued by a payer, which entitles its bearer (payee) to payment drawn on the payer's current account at a commercial bank, thereby making current accounts a means of payment. In many European countries, cheques are no longer the payment mechanism of choice, going the way of the phonograph player and the tape recorder. Electronic debit cards now allow payers to transfer their balances directly, bypassing the need for writing cheques and worrying about their acceptance. Despite this technological advance, the need for a central bank remains: at the end of any given day, some bank may come up short and will need extra liquidity to cover its obligations. In the aggregate, only the central bank is capable of satisfying this demand for liquidity.

each monetary aggregate. The multiplier process is both simple and striking. It can be presented in two different ways. The first stresses the end result, while the second, developed in the WebAppendix, tracks the relatively involved process by which money is actually created.

Reserve ratios and reserve multipliers

Note that two of the main items in a bank's balance sheet (Figure 9.3) correspond to costly activities:

- Reserves, when borrowed from the central bank, carry an interest charge. Unborrowed reserves held at the central bank yield little or no interest income, hence bear an opportunity cost.
- Customers' demand deposits require setting up and maintaining a network of branches with personnel, equipment, and office rental. In addition, depositors may even earn some interest.

So how do banks make a profit? The answer is: make sure that the asset side of the balance sheet is earning a good rate of return. Holding interest-yielding assets is one way, lending to their customers is another, usually more profitable one. Good banking practice therefore calls for lending as much as is prudently possible. This can be done easily enough: it is sufficient to credit the customer's account. As long as the interest on the loan exceeds the cost of managing the deposit, it is profitable to do so.

If this is the case, why don't banks simply increase customer credit, and the corresponding deposits, without bounds? Naturally, prudential banking means identifying good credit risks and excluding borrowers who will not repay their loans; for the moment, let us assume that there are enough good credit opportunities around. Even in this case, the reserve ratio will restrict lending by commercial banks. As illustrated in Figure 9.4, banks' reserves may not be less than the (required or prudent) reserves ratio (rr) times the volume of deposits:

(9.2)   Reserves $\geq rr \times$ deposits.

The figure may also be read in reverse: the volume of deposits cannot exceed a multiple of existing reserves. The tinted area in Figure 9.4 shows that an increase in reserves can be multiplied up into a larger volume of deposits. If reserves are a fraction

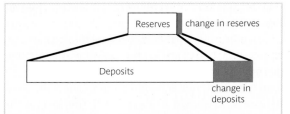

Fig. 9.4 The Reserves – Money Stock Link
When reserves are a constant proportion (rr) of deposits ($R = rrD$), deposits cannot grow without an increase in reserves. Conversely, a change in reserves ΔR allows banks to increase their deposits—by granting loans—in much larger amounts. The reserve multiplier is the inverse of the reserve ratio.

of deposits, then deposits are a multiple of reserves. Formally, rearranging (9.2) gives:

(9.3)   Deposits $\leq (1/rr) \times$ reserves.

The factor ($1/rr$) is often called the *reserve multiplier*. Equation (9.3) means that together, commercial banks cannot expand their money creation beyond a multiple of reserves. Here is the catch: in the aggregate, reserves can only be obtained from the central bank.

The monetary base multiplier

We now understand how the central bank can put a cap on the volume of bank deposits by controlling the volume of bank reserves. But two difficulties arise. The first is that the central bank can only control M0, the sum of bank reserves and currency. Second, the central bank is not just interested in controlling bank deposits, but rather the wider aggregates (M1, M2, M3, M4) which ultimately determine the rate of inflation. Both of these facts mean that monetary control may be less precise than implied by the simple reserve multiplier.

Consider first that, although the central bank is the sole (legal!) producer of M0, the sum of currency and bank reserves, it cannot control its components. It is the public that decides how much of the M2 it demands to hold in the form of currency. Effectively, the remainder is deposited at banks and can serve as bank reserves. Since the central bank is interested in controlling the aggregate money stock

(M1, M2, or broader aggregates), rather than reserves per se, more attention is paid to the monetary base multiplier, or money multiplier, which relates the monetary base to a monetary aggregate, for example M2:

(9.4)   Monetary multiplier = M2/M0.

Next, we ask what happens if some of the newly created monetary base, M0, does not entirely end up as bank reserves. Figure 9.4 does not distinguish between currency and bank deposits at the central bank, in Figure 9.5 this omission is corrected.

Table 9.2 presents actual ratios of the money supply (M2) to the monetary base (M0). They are much smaller than the inverse of the reserves ratio as predicted by formula (9.3), because of currency holdings by non-banks. To see this, imagine first a world without currency, so that all transactions are carried out using bank deposits (cheques, plastic cards, transfers). All of M2 takes the form of bank deposits and the monetary base is entirely held by commercial banks (see Figure 9.4). Now, if the public chooses to hold part of their money in the form of currency, any loan by the banking system results in some cash withdrawal. The banks lose some of their reserves, which limits their loan-making activity. The larger the share of currency is in M0, the fewer reserves which remain in the banking system, and the smaller is the multiplier. Box 9.1 shows formally that the monetary multiplier is indeed lower, the more currency the public holds. Table 9.2 confirms that countries with a predilection for currency tend to have low money multipliers.

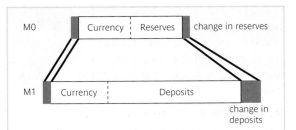

Fig. 9.5 The Reserves – Money Stock Link with Currency

The public holds currency as well as bank accounts. As reserves are a constant proportion of deposits, any increase in reserves allows an increase in deposits, with a multiplier equal to the inverse of the reserve ratio. The central bank, however, controls the monetary base M0, not the breakdown between its components, currency and reserves. If the money multiplier is defined as the effect of an increase in the monetary base on the money supply M2, it is smaller because part of the money created by the commercial banks will be converted into currency, leaking out of the banking system.

Leakages

The money multiplier is lower when conversion of bank deposits into currency acts as a drain on commercial banks' reserves. Other leakages produce the same effect and help explain the relatively low money multipliers reported in Table 9.2. Leakages occur when money is deposited in non-bank financial institutions which operate with a 100% reserve requirement. Money can also leak abroad, and this reduces the amount of reserves available for the

Table 9.2 M0, M2, Money Market Multipliers, and Currency, 2003

	M0 (% of GDP)	M2 (% of GDP)	Multiplier M2/M0	Currency (% of M2)
Euro-zone	7.2	72.3	10.1	7.4
UK	4.6	89.1	19.4	3.6
USA	6.8	58.3	8.6	10.7
Japan	20.2	135.6	6.7	11.0

Source: Central bank websites.

Box 9.1 **The Money Multiplier with Currency**

Assuming that the public wishes to hold a proportion cc of M1 in the form of currency (CU), and that the banks keep a fraction rr of deposits (D) in bank reserves (R) (for simplicity, ignore vault cash), the two aggregates M0 and M1 can be written as

(9.5) $M0 = CU + R = ccM1 + rrD$

(9.6) $M1 = CU + D = ccM1 + D.$

Then (9.6) implies $D = (1 - cc)M1$. Inserting this value of D in (9.5) gives

(9.7) $M0 = [cc + rr(1 - cc)]M1,$

so

(9.8)   Money multiplier = M1/M0

$$= \frac{1}{cc + rr(1 - cc)}.$$

The money market multiplier is $1/rr$ if the public's holdings of currency are zero (if $cc = 0$). It is equal to 1 if all

M1 is cash ($cc = 1$). Table 9.3 shows how the multiplier varies with different values of the currency-to-M1 ratio cc and the reserves ratio rr.

Table 9.3 **Theoretical Values of the Money Multiplier (M1/M0)**

Currency/M1	Reserve ratio		
	5%	10%	20%
0%	20.0	10.0	5.0
5%	10.3	6.9	4.0
10%	6.9	5.3	3.6
20%	4.2	3.6	2.8
30%	3.0	2.7	2.3

banking system. Box 9.2 shows that this leakage can be sizeable.

A variable multiplier

We assumed that commercial banks use any reserve in excess of the minimum level to make loans, and that they have no difficulty finding customers. Neither of these assumptions need always be correct. Banks manage their assets and liabilities very carefully, with an eye to the future. They may reject some loan applications as being too risky, or may keep extra reserves as an option for future business.

Box 9.2 **Where are the Greenbacks?**

In mid-July 2004, roughly $730 billion worth of US dollars were in circulation, almost double the amount in recorded in 1996. This amounts to roughly $2,500 for every man, woman, and child in the United States, or $10,000 for a four-person family! This contrasts sharply with surveys in the mid-1990s, which indicated that the average US four-person household held about $300 in cash in 1995, some $20 billion in total. Business holdings are estimated to amount to another $20 billion.

Where is the rest? The Federal Reserve estimates that two-thirds of all US currency, and most $100 bills,

circulate abroad. Why? Illegal activities are financed using dollars to avoid traceable transactions. 'Greenbacks' are also known to circulate in many countries as the sole currency (Ecuador, Liberia, Panama) or as a **parallel currency** in many countries where high inflation makes local currencies unappealing as a store of value. In recent years, significant amounts of cash have flowed to Argentina, Russia, former republics of the former Soviet Union, and the Middle East. China, with its massive and persistent current account surplus with the United States, is certainly partly responsible for the recent jump in greenbacks abroad.

As a result, banks routinely hold excess reserves. The volume of excess reserves is variable, and depends on economic conditions (which affect the risk that loans will go unpaid) and on the likely evolution of interest rates (expected future increases increase the attractiveness of holding reserves now).

The private sector's behaviour can be variable, too. For example, fears of worsening economic conditions, or the expectation of declining interest rates, may limit the amount of new credit that the public wants to borrow. As a result, the response of banks to reserve availability is less automatic than implied by the money multiplier formulae. As conditions change, or are expected to change, the actual multiplier can fluctuate.

Required or self-imposed reserves ratios?

Some countries, Switzerland and the UK, for example, have zero or symbolic reserve requirements, and yet they are considered perfectly safe places to hold banking accounts. Reserve requirements serve several purposes. Initially, they were imposed to reduce the perceived and actual riskiness of banking systems. Next, they guaranteed a role for the central bank in the business of money creation. Finally, they became the means for central banks to control the money supply. Whether reserves are required or self-imposed, as long as $rr > 0$ deposits are linked to reserves, and the central bank retains control over money supply.

Why impose reserve requirements, then? One reason is that they represent a form of taxation on the banking system or on the banks' depositors. Since reserves do not bear market interest, banks cannot afford to pay market rates on their interest-bearing bank deposits. If their customers have few alternatives, they will wind up paying the tax. At a time of globalization, reserve requirements subject the domestic banking sector to a competitive disadvantage relative to other countries with lower or non-existent minimum ratios. And indeed, as financial integration deepened in the 1990s, reserve requirements declined. The ECB now imposes the same low ratio throughout the Euro-area, but competition with outside financial centres in Europe—London and Zurich in particular—remains.

9.4 Controlling Monetary Conditions

9.4.1 Derived Demand for Base Money

Summarizing so far, we have reached three important conclusions:

- The public (households and firms) have preferences concerning the amount of nominal money (M1, M2, M3, etc.) they wish to hold. This is represented by the nominal demand for money (9.1).

- The banking system creates the money in the process of credit creation—by lending to firms and households. In doing so, they need—for regulatory or prudential reasons—to hold reserves, as represented by equation (9.2).

- In spite of the various leakages that affect money created by banks, there is a reasonably stable link between the monetary base and the money stock: this is the money multiplier m (described in equations (9.4) or (9.8), depending on what is assumed about the leakages).

Returning to the notation of the previous chapter, let us ignore the distinctions between M1, M2, etc., and simply call the public's demand for nominal money M. In money market equilibrium it is also the nominal quantity of money supplied by commercial banks. Commercial banks will require bank reserves and vault cash to supply M; we say it gives rise to a **derived demand** for the monetary base M0 by commercial banks, which we shall call $M0^d$:

(9.9) $$M0^d = M/m = P\mathcal{L}(Y, i, c)/m.$$

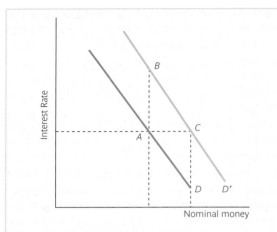

Fig. 9.6 The Money Market

The public's demand for money translates into a demand for the monetary base by commercial banks. If the public wants to hold more money, the derived demand schedule shifts to the right. The central bank may decide not to respond, in which case the interest rate rises (point B), or to keep the interest unchanged (point C), or any combination of M0 and the interest rate as long as it lies on the demand schedule.

Here m is the money multiplier derived in the previous section. This is the behaviour captured in in Figure 9.6: the downward-sloping schedule describes the derived demand for the monetary base for given price level P, real GDP Y and transaction costs c, and money multiplier m.

Now imagine that, starting at point A, the GDP of the economy grows. This will give rise to additional transactions demand for real balances. Where will households and firms find the extra money that they need to carry out an ever-increasing volume of transactions? One possibility is to borrow from banks. As the banks respond by granting loans, their need for reserves increases. Although individual banks may be able to borrow reserves from each other, viewed as a whole, the increase in the total demand for money translates into an increase in the demand for the monetary base, captured by the rightward shift of the demand schedule from D to D'. How the central bank responds is examined in the following section. At this stage we just note that any change in the demand for the overall money stock

M is transmitted to a change in the demand for the monetary base.[7]

9.4.2 Open Market Operations

Figure 9.6 represents the market for the monetary base, called the **money market**, or the **open market**, the linchpin of all financial markets. The 'commodities' traded on this market are deposits at the central bank. The market does not have a physical location, rather it operates a network complete with brokers. The players are commercial banks and financial—sometimes non-financial—institutions (e.g. insurance companies, large corporations) and the central bank. As the sole producer of base money, the central bank exercises the dominant influence on the market. Because commercial banks know that they ultimately need reserves to grant credit to their customers, they regard the interest rate charged on this market as their primary indicator of monetary conditions and tend to promptly pass on to their own customers any change in the money market rate, and all other interest rates soon follow.

Institutional details vary from country to country, but the broad features are similar. Dealers on the money market typically lend to each other over short periods of time, or with loan maturities ranging from overnight to two weeks. Market participants primarily deal with one another, which allows banks to obtain better yields on any excess reserves that they happen to hold than by keeping them in the form of deposits at the central bank. If the reserves available on the market exceed participant needs, the interest rate declines, while it rises when there is excess demand. The central bank closely monitors the situation and can intervene on the market as it wishes, conducting **open market operations**. The main features of open market operations are the following:

---

7 The transmission is not necessarily one for one because the multiplier is not perfectly constant. Here, if the commercial banks were holding excess reserves at point A, they will be able to partly satisfy their customers without needing more reserves, but if growth continues, sooner or later they will have exhausted this margin. From there on, we assume that the money multiplier is constant.

- Open market operations usually take the form of a short-term loan from the central bank to commercial banks, but can also involve outright purchases and sales of assets (typically foreign exchange or government securities).

- These loans are guaranteed by a collateral presented to the central bank by the borrower. Each central bank has a list of assets admitted as collateral, typically Treasury bills or bills issued by large corporations which are considered very safe. Indeed, it is not in the mission of a central bank to take risks in lending.

- By lending reserves, the central bank allows M0 to increase. Thereafter commercial banks step up lending to their customers, which increases M1 and the wider monetary aggregates. Calling in or not renewing loans to commercial banks has the opposite effect, i.e. dries up liquidity available to banks and tends to cause a contraction of bank lending and the money supply.

- Because these loans are short-term, commercial banks continuously need to pay back and borrow again, a procedure called rolling over. This dependence allows the central bank to influence money market conditions with great precision: it can step up lending to increase liquidity, or it can absorb liquidity and reduce the monetary base by not renewing maturing loans.

- Outright purchases and sales of assets, such as foreign exchange, have the same effect of increasing or decreasing the supply of reserves available to banks. In contrast, outright purchases involve a swap of assets and do not increase the net liabilities of the banking system.

Every central bank practises monetary policy somewhat differently. Box 9.3 describes the various open market operation procedures adopted by the ECB.

9.4.3 The Practice of Monetary Policy

On any normal business day, some commercial banks hold reserves in excess of what is required or desired, while others fall short. The money market allows participants to trade these reserves, borrowing and lending among themselves at very short maturities. As it reflects the cost of money to banks, the money market interest rate is the best gauge of monetary conditions, it determines how much banks charge their own customers. This rate is called the money market rate, with special names in

---

 Box 9.3 How the ECB does it

The ECB conducts four types of open-market operations:

- Main refinancing operations, which are weekly auctions for loans of two-week maturities. Commercial banks submit bids and the ECB chooses how much to allocate at which interest rate. This is the main source of liquidity provision to the market.

- Longer-term refinancing operations, which are monthly auctions for loans of one-month maturity. This is a limited source of financing.

- Fine-tuning and structural operations, which are occasionally conducted to deal with special circumstances.

- Standing facilities, which set a ceiling and a floor for the short-term (overnight) interest rate. These operations are undertaken by individual banks to either deposit funds at the marginal deposit rate (the floor) or borrow

from the ECB at the marginal lending rate (ceiling). These facilities are used daily at the commercial banks' initiative.

These operations generally take the form of a **reverse transaction** or **repurchase agreement** ('repo' for short), loans of limited duration. To signal its intentions, the ECB publicly announces the rate at which it will conduct its next main refinancing operations as well as the floor and ceiling rates. Figure 9.7 shows that the key short-term market rate EONIA (euro overnight index average) moves within the tunnel set by the lending and deposit rates, closely following (sometimes even anticipating) the ECB's main rate, the refinancing rate. The ECB's control of the very short-term interest rate is virtually perfect.

Source: ECB, *Annual Report*, 1999.

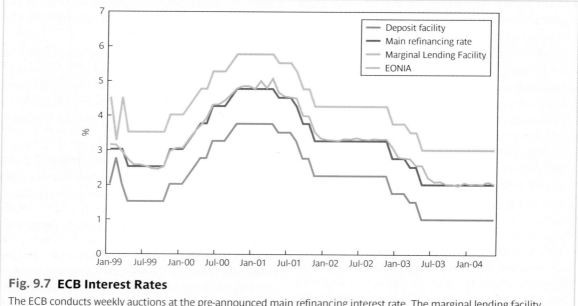

Fig. 9.7 ECB Interest Rates

The ECB conducts weekly auctions at the pre-announced main refinancing interest rate. The marginal lending facility and deposit facility rates determine, respectively, a ceiling and a floor for the interbank rate EONIA (Euro OverNight Index Average) which tends to closely follow the refinancing rate.

Source: ECB Monthly Bulletin, May 2004.

some countries, the Federal Funds Rate in the USA and EONIA in the Euro-area (see Box 9.3). As the ultimate net supplier of bank reserves—the 'commodity' being traded—the central bank orients the market on a minute-by-minute basis.

At normal times, when the economy is growing, the public's demand for money expands and the derived demand for the money base increases with it. This is represented in Figure 9.6 by the shift from D to D'. How does the central bank react? It may wish to keep the money supply unchanged, but then it must be aiming at point B, where the interest rate has increased. Instead, it may wish to keep the interest rate unchanged, aiming at point C. In that case, it must provide more monetary base by intervening on the open market. The multiplier then takes over and, eventually, the wider monetary aggregates will follow suit. What the central bank definitely cannot do is determine both the supply of monetary and the level of money market interest rates. This is why it must choose one of these two instruments.

9.4.4 Reserve Requirements as a Tool of Monetary Policy

When the central bank has imposed a reserve requirement which is binding, changing the reserve ratio can serve as an additional instrument of monetary policy. For example if the required reserve ratio is raised from 5% to 6%, with unchanged supply of reserves, deposits must contract by roughly 20%.[8] This is a drastic move, which not only stops commercial banks from lending, but might even cause them to call in (demand immediate repayment of) some existing loans. Because this move can be very costly and disruptive to banks, reserve ratios are normally changed only in small increments, and then only in emergency situations.

---

[8] When banks hold no excess reserves and currency holdings are nil, equation (9.3) implies that, if reserves are constant deposits change in the same proportion but in the opposite direction, like the reserve ratio. In the example, $\Delta rr/rr = +0.2$ implies that $\Delta D/D = -0.2$.

9.4.5 Monetary Policy Targets

A short history of monetary targeting

During much of the 1950s and 1960s, conventional wisdom was that central banks ought to maintain low and stable interest rates. This was thought to be good for investment and growth. The lesson of Figure 9.6 is that money growth cannot be controlled under such conditions. In fact, money was allowed to grow endogenously, often quite rapidly. Ultimately this policy led to high inflation rates in the 1970s.

Reminded of their duty to deliver price stability, most central banks in the OECD area opted then to target the rate of money growth explicitly. In Chapter 8, it was shown that as long as the public's demand for monetary aggregates is stable, money growth ultimately determines inflation. A low and stable rate of money growth is therefore a clear signal that inflation too will be low and stable. During the 1980s, nearly all central banks in the OECD countries operated with a money growth target, with the result that interest rates were quite volatile (to see why, look again at Figure 9.6).

Monetary targeting can be credited for the successful disinflation of the 1980s, but in the meantime disenchantment with this approach has set in. The link between money growth and inflation has become less predictable over the policy planning horizon (two to three years), much as the link between money base and wider monetary aggregates has become clouded. Widespread financial deregulation in the mid-1980s, followed by the information revolution's impact on banking and financial markets in the 1990s, have resulted in significant instability in the public's demand for money. With unexpected and poorly understood shifts in the derived demand for reserves, the link between the money supply and inflation has become unreliable and, with a variable money multiplier, control of the money base M0 does not deliver a precise handle on the wider aggregates.

Inflation targeting

A promising new approach is to target inflation directly. Initially implemented by the Bank of New Zealand in the late 1980s, **inflation targeting** has since been adopted in Canada, Chile, Israel, Mexico, Poland, Sweden, and the UK. The natural appeal of inflation targeting is that it is closest to the central bank's mandate, price stability. With a simple, verifiable target, it is easier for the central bank to communicate monetary policy actions and to reassure the public that these actions are driven by a clear and transparent commitment to achieving its objective.

The two crucial elements of inflation targeting consist of an inflation target—which may be set by the constitution of the central bank or by the government—and the central bank's own forecasts of inflation over the medium run—two to three years ahead of time. Comparing the target with forecasts provides a straightforward guide to policy action: if the forecast exceeds the target, for instance, monetary policy is tightened by raising the interest rates and slowing down money growth.

A key concern is that inflation forecasts are inherently uncertain, especially two or three years ahead. What if the central bank makes a mistake? For example, if it overestimates future inflation, it will unnecessarily raise interest rates. Naturally mistakes are possible: the great oil price increases of the 1970s would have knocked any inflation forecast off target. There is no perfect solution to this difficulty. One answer, proposed by the Bank of England, is presented in Box 9.4.

Other popular targets

Not all central banks have adopted inflation as their only target. Instead of targets, the ECB has adopted two indicators called 'pillars': one of them is the traditional money growth rate—not a target but a 'reference value' in the language of the ECB—and the other one includes numerous indicators (inflation, the output gap, the exchange rate, etc.). Still, committed to an inflation rate between 0% and 2%, the ECB is an implicit inflation-targeter. The US Federal Reserve System, the US central bank, does not have any explicit target, and operates with a high degree of pragmatism.

A number of countries aim at the external value of their currency, making the exchange rate the target of monetary policy. As will become clear in the next section, exchange rate targeting seriously constrains monetary policy. Some countries allow

Box 9.4 The Bank of England's Plan and its Fan

The Bank of England has adopted inflation targeting in monetary policy since 1993. In 1998, the Bank received formal independence from the Treasury. On both dimensions of inflation targeting and monetary independence, the Bank has strongly influenced central banking practice. Its task is not to set the inflation target; it is the political job of the Chancellor of the Exchequer to choose the appropriate rate of inflation, e.g. 2% for 2005. Figure 9.8 shows the latest order issued by Chancellor Gordon Brown.

(a) The Bank of England's inflation target: A Letter from the Chancellor

HM Treasury, 1 Horse Guards Road, London, SW1A 2HQ

10 December 2003

Mervyn King
Governor
Bank of England
Threadneedle Street
LONDON   EC2R 8AH

Dear Mervyn,

REMIT FOR THE MONETARY POLICY COMMITTEE

The Bank of England Act (1998) requires that I specify what price stability is taken to consist of and the Government's economic policy objectives at least once in every period of 12 months beginning on the anniversary of the day the Act came into force. I last wrote to the then Governor on this matter on 9 April this year.

I also wrote on 9 June to give notice of my intention to change the MPC's remit in the Pre-Budget Report to give the Bank of England a symmetric inflation target as measured by the harmonised index of consumer prices – which the National Statistician has now decided will be known as the Consumer Prices Index or CPI in the United Kingdom.

I hereby confirm that, from today, the new operational target for monetary policy will be 2 per cent as measured by the 12-month increase in the CPI. In accordance with the Act, I also confirm that the economic policy of Her Majesty's Government is to achieve high and stable levels of growth and employment by raising the sustainable growth rate and creating economic and employment opportunities for all.

I attach a copy of the new remit and an annex outlining details of the new inflation target.

Yours sincerely

GORDON BROWN

Fig. 9.8 The Letter and the Fan

The Bank of England may be free to choose the means, but the politicians choose the target. This letter dated 10 December 2003 from the Chancellor of the Exchequer, Gordon Brown, instructs the Governor of the Bank of England, Mervyn King, to target inflation based on a new price index at 2% per annum; previously it was 2.5%. The superimposed figure shows the Bank's inflation forecast as of May 2004. It spans the next two years. Rather than publishing just one number for each period ahead, the Bank of England recognizes the uncertainty inherent in the exercise and presents a 'fan', which is darker where the estimate is considered more probable, and increasingly lighter where the odds seem low. The fan thus reveals the Bank's thinking, its best guess and the size of its doubts.

Sources: Inflation Report, Bank of England, May 2004; Monetary Policy Committee (www.bankofengland.co.uk/inflationreport/); www.bankofengland.co.uk/mpc/.

(b) The Bank of England's Inflation Forecast: The Fan, 2004 – 6

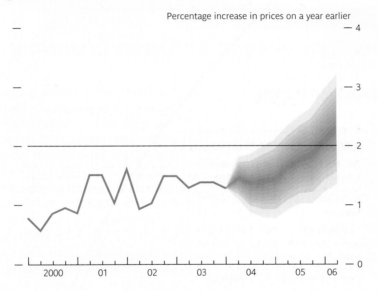

The Bank of England's task is purely technical: it simply has to achieve the target, and is fully independent in how to go about it. The Bank's operating procedure is said to be goal dependent and instrument independent. Operational decisions regarding the setting of instruments—for example, the Bank lending rate—and monetary policy are taken by the Monetary Policy Committee, consisting of the Governor, the two Deputy Governors, the Bank's Chief Economist, the Executive Director for Market Operations, plus four external members appointed by the Chancellor of the Exchequer.

If the Bank misses its target by more than 1% on either side of the 2% target, the Governor must write an open letter to the Chancellor. The Bank publishes its inflation forecast every quarter in the Inflation Report. This forecast is produced on the assumption that interest rates remain unchanged. Thus, any discrepancy between the forecast and the target can be dealt with by a change in the interest rate. Interestingly, the forecast is published as a fan, also shown in Figure 9.8.

some flexibility in the exchange rate target, either in the form of a band of fluctuation (for example within the European Monetary System), or by letting the exchange rate depreciate along a pre-specified trend (this has been the policy followed by Hungary since 1995). Others have completely linked their currency to another one, operating what is called a currency board: this is the case of Argentina,

Bosnia, Bulgaria, and Estonia.[9] The most extreme form of exchange rate targeting is the complete adoption of a foreign currency, which completely eliminates domestic monetary policy. It is called dollarization when the adopted currency is the dollar (e.g. Ecuador, Panama), or euroization when the euro becomes the national currency (e.g. in Bosnia-Herzegovina).

9.5 Monetary Policy in an Open Economy

9.5.1 Foreign Exchange Market Interventions

Monetary policy is influenced by foreign exchange markets. The link is the foreign assets that the central bank holds (see Figure 9.3), which mostly consist of deposits with foreign central banks denominated in foreign currencies, foreign Treasury bills, and some gold. Central banks use their foreign assets to intervene on the foreign exchange market to influence the exchange rate. For instance, if the central bank wishes to prevent a depreciation, i.e. a loss in the external value, it buys back its own currency on the foreign exchange markets, and pays for it by drawing on its stock of foreign assets. On the asset side of its balance sheet, foreign reserves decline; on the liability side, the monetary base is reduced since the domestic currency bought back on the foreign exchange market is effectively withdrawn from circulation. At this point, the money multiplier comes into play and the wider aggregates decline as well. Similarly, to prevent an appreciation, the central bank sells its own currency and acquires foreign assets; the monetary base increases, and so do the wider aggregates. Unless something else is done, the link is direct and automatic.

There is a similarity between exchange and open market interventions. Both affect the liabilities of the central bank (monetary base) as well as its assets and in both cases the money multiplier then

amplifies the initial effect of the intervention. The difference lies in which asset holding changes. In the case of an open market operation, it is the holdings of domestic assets that are affected (repurchase agreements, bills or other private paper, Treasury bills). In an exchange market intervention, it is the holdings of foreign exchange that are affected. This similarity highlights the possibility of a conflict between monetary control and exchange rate control. Indeed, since foreign exchange market interventions directly affect the size of the monetary base, monetary policy autonomy is lost when the central bank is compelled to intervene on foreign exchange markets to fix the exchange rate. Later chapters explore this issue in detail. The next section discusses how central banks try to break the link between foreign exchange interventions and monetary conditions at home.

9.5.2 Sterilization

The similarity between money and foreign exchange market intervention suggests a 'quick fix' for the tension between monetary policy and exchange rate control. A central bank could try to offset, or sterilize, the impact of its foreign exchange intervention on the money supply by intervening on

9 For more details on the European Monetary System or currency boards, see Ch. 20.

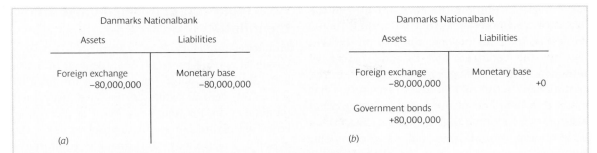

Fig. 9.9 Foreign Exchange Market Intervention and Sterilization
In panel (*a*) the central bank intervenes in the exchange market to support its currency. It sells some of its foreign exchange reserves and buys back its own currency. With some currency withdrawn from circulation, the monetary base is reduced, and the money supply will decline further through the multiplier effect. In panel (*b*) the central bank counters the money-reducing effect by sterilizing its exchange market intervention. It buys an equivalent amount of securities from commercial banks. This replaces the monetary base previously destroyed.

the open market with a transaction of the same volume, but with the opposite effect on money market liquidity.

Take a particular example of the defence of the exchange rate depicted in Figure 9.9(*a*). To support its currency, the Danish krone (DKK), the Danish central bank—Danmarks Nationalbank—sells €10 million of its foreign exchange reserves and buys the equivalent amount of its own currency, say DDK 80 million. As a result, the asset side of the central bank declines by DKK 80 million, and the monetary base shrinks by the same amount. If the central bank simultaneously purchases DKK 80 million worth of securities on the open market, it injects the same amount of monetary base that was destroyed during the foreign exchange market intervention. Panel (*b*) of Figure 9.9 shows that the end

effect of **sterilization** is a reshuffling of the asset side of the central bank's balance sheet—an increase in domestic asset holdings matched by a reduction of foreign exchange—leaving the liability side, in particular the monetary base, unchanged.

Later, we shall see that this 'quick fix' is just that —and not at all free of problems of its own. Most important, the cause of a currency's weakness, which called for intervention in the first place, is not addressed. Attempting to divorce the exchange rate from domestic monetary conditions may result in speculative attacks—crises in South-East Asia, Russia, Brazil in the late 1990s are a reminder of the limits of this strategy. At this stage, we just note that there is an automatic link between foreign exchange market interventions and the money supply, but that this link can be broken through sterilization.

9.6 Monetary Financing of the Government: A Slippery Objective

We now look more closely at the relationship between a central bank and its government. The central bank is a public institution and therefore part of the 'government', broadly speaking.

While many central banks were created by private commercial bankers, they typically ended up being nationalized and brought under government control. The proximity between an inherently cash-hungry institution (the government) and the exclusive producer of cash (the central bank) creates temptations beyond imagination. Indeed, few are the countries that in their past have refrained from including 'provider of cash' in the central bank's list of objectives. The result has most often been uncontrolled inflation, prompting institutional reforms that establish thick walls between the central bank and its government. Future chapters will look into that issue. Here we describe the various ways in which a central bank can provide resources to the government.

9.6.1 Direct Credit to the Government

A central bank can lend directly to the government by simply crediting its account (see Figure 9.3). This is monetary base (M0) creation, equivalent to printing banknotes and turning them over to the government, very much like a commercial bank creates money (M1) by lending to one of its customers. The difference is the multiplier. Indeed, as soon as the government uses its loan to purchase goods or services, the monetary base enters the commercial banking system as recipients of government payments deposit these funds in their bank accounts. At that stage, the multiplier process takes over. The effect is the same when the government borrows from commercial banks by issuing Treasury bills, which are then acquired by the central bank on the open market, another modern version of the printing press called **monetization** of the public debt.

It is often the case that governments in dire financial conditions are unable to borrow from the public or from banks. In that case, their natural tendency is to ask the central bank to do the lending. In cases of national emergencies, it may even be the most sensible thing to do. Yet if the central bank obliges—and it may be forced to if it is under direct government control—easy financing of that sort is not conducive to public budgetary rectitude. Most historical episodes of high inflation or hyperinflation are associated with direct financing of budget deficits and/or monetization of the debt.

9.6.2 Indirect Credit: Seigniorage and the Inflation Tax

Producing monetary base is virtually costless: a stroke of a pen—more precisely keying in a few zeros in the computer—or activating the printing press. Yet, central banks do not give away their monetary base for free! They use it at face value, acquiring real resources for themselves or for the national government, thus making comfortable profits. The revenue from this lucrative activity is called **seigniorage**, and can be traced back to the Middle Ages, when local lords had the monopoly of coinage on their lands and charged a fee for every coin they minted. Seigniorage is the main source of profit for central banks. As public institutions, central banks are usually required to turn over most of their profits to their governments. Although seigniorage can represent a substantial source of government revenue in times of high inflation, it has rarely done so in recent years, as Table 9.4 shows.[10]

Seigniorage should not be confused with the **inflation tax**, a related but distinctly different concept. Seigniorage income accrues as the government uses newly created money to pay its bills. The inflation tax, in contrast, erodes the value of all nominal government liabilities that are not protected against inflation, not just the monetary base. If the public debt is not indexed to inflation, and it rarely is, an unanticipated increase in inflation benefits the government by reducing the debt's real value (in general, unanticipated inflation hurts all creditors and benefits all borrowers, but within the private sector it is a redistribution of wealth and not a tax). In contrast, real assets such as property, artwork, rugs, jewels, and explicitly indexed financial

---

[10] The higher the rate of inflation, the more people must keep acquiring money to make up for its declining purchasing power, hence a seemingly endless source of revenue. In fact, when inflation rises and the value of money keeps declining, people reduce their cash balances, often drastically, thus limiting the central bank's ability to extract yet more resources.

Table 9.4 Seigniorage around the World (% of GDP)

	Seigniorage		Inflation	
	1980–91	1992–5	1980–91	1992–5
Advanced Economies	0.8	0.3	7.2	3.3
USA	0.4	0.4	5.4	2.8
Germany	0.5	0.3	2.9	3.5
Japan	0.6	0.3	2.6	0.9
Hungary	0.4	4.1	12.7	23.1
Poland	7.0	2.2	99.5	34.6
Israel	1.9	0.5	111.1	11.3
Africa	1.4	1.3	19.6	22.2
Asia	1.5	2.0	7.6	7.1
Latin America	3.2	2.4	251.4	110.1

Source: Paul Masson, Miguel Savastano, and Sunil Sahrma (1998), 'Can Inflation Targeting Be a Framework for Monetary Policy in Developing Countries?', *Finance and Development*, 35(1): 34–7.

instruments are immunized from inflation's effects. Only if inflation is correctly anticipated is the private sector protected from the inflation tax, since the nominal interest rate increases one for one with expected inflation (the Fisher principle): the capital loss on the principal is exactly compensated by the higher nominal yield (Chapter 8).[11]

9.6.3 Independence of the Central Bank

The temptation for governments to engage in inflationary finance is strong: borrowing from the central bank provides resources and, as it is inflationary, it further delivers seigniorage and the inflation tax. The benefits accrue immediately, the costs (inflation)

later. Since central banks are responsible for price stability, their instinct is to refuse to finance government budget deficits. It is no surprise that governments have a perpetual desire to control the central bank! For this reason, an increasing number of central banks have been made formally independent of their governments. Typically they are often forbidden by law from lending directly to public authorities and are explicitly required to deliver low and stable inflation rates. This is the case in the Euro-area, where central bank independence, the primacy of the price stability objective, and the prohibition of government lending are formulated explicitly in the Maastricht Treaty.

[11] Formally, seigniorage is the real value of the monetary base created: $\Delta M0/P = (\Delta M0/M0)M0/P$. In contrast, the inflation tax on the monetary base is the inflation rate π times the real stock of the base, or $\pi(M0/P)$. It turns out that when inflation is perfectly anticipated, only the monetary base cannot escape the inflation tax. Then, $\Delta M0/P = \pi(M0/P) + \Delta(M0/P)$: seigniorage is the sum of the inflation tax on the monetary base and the increase in the real stock of monetary base.

9.7 Bank Regulation and Monetary Control

9.7.1 Central Bank Oversight

The privilege of creating money conferred to commercial banks does not come without risks and restrictions. Banks are officially registered by the central bank or related agencies. They must satisfy strict operating requirements designed to deal with the risks involved in creating money. These risks reflect the **information asymmetry** problem: commercial banks have less information about their customers' creditworthiness than the customers themselves. A customer who seeks a loan from a bank has an incentive to misrepresent her situation if it is likely to lead to a refusal of credit. For this reason, bank lending may be riskier than intended. Since most of the money supply is created by commercial banks, confidence and acceptability of money is at stake.

Much as confidence in the currency (i.e. money issued by the central bank) rests on the quality of the central bank, confidence in money created by the commercial banks requires that it be freely and immediately convertible into currency at any time. The history of commercial banking is strewn with bank failures, which often turned into bank panics as worried depositors attempted to withdraw as much cash as possible, not only from the failing bank but from all financial institutions.

The reason for such chain reactions is **systemic risk**. Systemic risk arises first because banks (and, more generally, financial institutions) hold each other's assets, often in large amounts. Should one bank go bankrupt, its liabilities, held as assets by other banks, become worthless. These losses may lead in turn to more bankruptcies. In addition, if the public becomes suspicious that one bank is in trouble and could contaminate others, it will attempt to withdraw what it perceives to be endangered funds. Generalized collapses of the banking system have been observed in the 1990s, e.g. in Hong Kong, Russia, Korea, Indonesia, and Ecuador.

To reduce these risks, all countries have instituted bank regulations, and international agreements are being worked out. Regulations include the supervision of bank accounts and operations, limits on competition perceived dangerous to the stability of banks, and restrictions on asset ownership and banking activities. The purpose is to limit risk-taking by banks, to give monetary authorities advance warning in case of failure, and to guarantee the supply of good banking services. An example of protection is compulsory bank insurance: if a bank fails, the depositors are protected against loss, at least up to some limit. Table 9.5 provides examples of the extent of deposit insurance in a number of European countries.

Table 9.5 Deposit Insurance in Europe, 2004

Country	Coverage of deposits (in euros)
Austria	20,000
Belgium	20,000
Denmark	40,330[a]
Finland	25,000
France	60,000
Germany	90% up to ceiling 20,000
Greece	20,000
Ireland	90% up to ceiling 20,000
Island	20,000
Italy	103,000
The Netherlands	20,000
Norway	235,000[a]
Portugal	25,000
Sweden	28,000
Spain	20,000
UK	90% up to ceiling 47,900[a]

[a] National currency value converted into € using the exchange rate in July 2004.

Source: ECB, International Association of Deposit Insurers.

9.7.2 Lender of Last Resort

Another example of public protection of bank customers is the function of **lender of last resort**. In principle at least, the central bank is expected to provide failing banks with sufficient monetary base to avoid immediate bankruptcy and reassure depositors that they can always exchange bank deposits for currency. Bank crises occurred on a large scale in the USA during the Great Depression of the 1930s. The failure of the Federal Reserve Board (the US central bank) to act as lender of last resort at the time is widely blamed for having deepened the recession. In the wake of the first oil shock in 1974, many central banks conducted a 'lifeboat' operation to keep a number of financial institutions afloat. In view of the consequences of contagion, several central banks created the Basle Committee, described in the next section.

The lender of last resort function of a central bank represents a delicate balancing act. On the one hand, it is known and recognized that the banking system can be unstable in the face of large, sudden withdrawals, which may be based as much on irrational fears or misinformation as the truth.

Supplying liquidity in crises can spare financial systems considerable pain and suffering. On the other hand, commercial banks which know that the central bank will bail them out in emergencies will behave differently, possibly in ways which are bad for the financial system as a whole. Box 9.5 summarizes the policy dilemma faced by central banks in this regard.

9.7.3 Capital Adequacy Ratios

In the 1970s, and at an increasing rate in the 1980s, financial integration among the advanced economies brought their financial and banking systems into close contact with each other. Increasing integration had two consequences. First, systemic risk is not limited to any one country but spread across national borders, often at great speed. Even with relatively slow communication, the 1929 collapse of Wall Street quickly affected financial centres throughout the world. Modern bank regulators see an increase in global financial instability which must be met with new rules and strengthened sanctions. The crises of the late 1990s are evidence that their fears are well founded.

Second, banks compete directly with each other across borders. This calls for a level playing field to

---

 Box 9.5 Bank Runs and Lender of Last Resort: A Double-Edged Sword

When the value of commercial bank deposits becomes suspicious, bank account-holders attempt to withdraw their funds and convert them into cash. During such bank runs, it is impossible for all deposits to be paid out, because banks hold only part of their assets in cash; this is a consequence of the money multiplier. Suspicion is contagious, and can be fatal to healthy banks, indeed to the whole banking system. This is why the monetary authorities may intervene as lender of last resort. As they stand ready to create whatever money is required to honour withdrawals, it is in their power to placate depositors' anxieties and put an end to bank runs.

On the other side, lender-of-last-resort protection may encourage banks to take excessive risks, a phenomenon known as moral hazard. For that reason, central banks maintain a large degree of uncertainty as to what they would do in case of bank failure, or even deny in public

that they are ready to carry out lender-of-last-resort operations. The lender-of-last-resort function is not extended automatically, encouraging depositors to keep an eye on their banks in good times as well. The accepted procedure is to follow the Bagehot principles (named after Walter Bagehot (1826–77), a renowned British financial economist of the late 19th century):

1 lend only against marketable collateral;
2 lend in large amounts at a higher rate than the market interest rate;
3 then sell or liquidate insolvent banks, with the losses being borne by their owners and uninsured depositors.

Initially injecting cash into a bank and then letting it go bankrupt allows partly at least to protect innocent depositors while 'punishing' shareholders for their improper control over management.

Box 9.6 Capital Adequacy Ratios

Capital adequacy regulations are designed to protect the integrity of the banking system from individual bank risk, by requiring that capital (on the right-hand side) be a constant fraction of total risky assets (on the left-hand side) in their balance sheets. While a good case can be made for bank capital regulations, they sometimes put banks at a competitive disadvantage in international markets. Countries with few or no regulations may operate with lower levels of capital for a given stock of earning assets, and may earn better rates of return. In response to this problem, the Committee on Banking Regulation and Supervision (also known as the Basle Committee) has agreed on standard measures of bank capital adequacy.[12] The G-10 (the ten largest industrial countries) and the EC agreed to enforce these capital adequacy standards by end 1992 (by March 1993 in the case of Japan).

The principle is to link the amount of risky assets that banks hold with owners' equity, i.e. resources committed by the shareholders of the bank. Figure 9.10 shows the symmetry with the reserves ratios. The capital adequacy ratios cover the weak part of a bank's assets with the captive part of its liabilities, while reserves ratios cover the weak part of the liabilities with safe assets. One capital adequacy rule requires that primary or 'core' capital, consisting of paid-in equity and retained earnings, not fall below 4% of total risk assets. Secondary capital should equal at least an additional 4% of risk assets. Secondary capital is defined as hidden reserves, general loan-loss provisions, asset revaluation, and certain 'near equity' such as convertible bonds, subordinated debt, and perpetual floating rate notes. The volume of risk assets is defined by a weighting scheme that increases with the risk of the asset involved. With the growing complexity of financial instruments and the rising importance of 'emerging markets', risk classification is becoming both more arduous and less relevant. In 2001, a new agreement was reached. It aims at encouraging individual institutions to develop their own risk assessment mechanisms, but under the control of supervisory agencies.

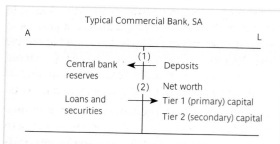

Fig. 9.10 Reserve and Capital Adequacy Ratios

Primary or 'core' capital consists of the stakes of the owners in the bank. Secondary capital includes resources close to equity, such as hidden reserves, general loan-loss provisions, asset revaluation, convertible bonds, subordinated debt. Reserve ratios (1) link safe assets to potentially volatile deposits. Capital adequacy ratios (2) link owners' equity to risky assets.

ensure fair competition. In 1989, an international agreement among most advanced economies was reached to establish minimum levels of **capital adequacy**. Banks are required to have minimum net worth as a fraction of total risky assets (see Figure 9.10). Net worth is sometimes called owners' capital or equity; it represents the owners' stake in the bank, i.e. what is left of total assets after the value of liabilities has been subtracted. Capital adequacy regulations ensure that sufficient capital (the property of the banks' owners) can act as a 'shock absorber' for the bank's balance sheet and protect depositors against bad contingencies. Details are provided in Box 9.6.

[12] The Basle Committee (established in 1975) is a permanent forum for the discussion of international aspects of bank regulation. It consists of representatives of the G-10 central banks and bank supervisory bodies. Its name comes from the fact that it is housed by the Bank for International Settlements (BIS) situated in Basle. The BIS was founded after the First World War to provide settlement, research, and other services to the world's central banks.

9.7.4 Technological Innovation in Banking and Monetary Control

Banks are constantly devising new ways of satisfying the financial needs of their customers. Many of these developments are also prompted by the banks' attempts to escape monetary policy and regulation. The central banks' objective of reining in money growth generally runs counter to individual banks' attempts to increase their profitability. Similarly, banking regulation aims at protecting customers by limiting the range of banking activities, including risk-taking. Pressed by competition and aided by continuous technological innovations—in financial instruments, computer power, and communications systems—banks often innovate by exploiting loopholes in existing legislation. As a result, monetary control is weakened and banks may become more fragile. This fragility is confirmed by continuing bank failures as well as the collapse of prestigious institutions like Barings of Britain (one of the oldest banks) or LTCM (Long-Term Capital Management, a firm created and run by several Nobel Prize winners) in the USA.

❶ Summary

1 The main objective of central banks is to achieve price stability, i.e. low and stable inflation. Some central banks may also try to stabilize output and employment. In pursuing their objective(s), central banks define one or more targets, which are related to the overall objective. To meet these targets they may have one or more instruments of monetary policy at their disposal.

2 Since most of the money stock is created by commercial banks, control of the money supply by the central bank is only indirect. The key instrument is the reserve ratio, which is either imposed by regulation or self-imposed by commercial banks themselves. This ratio establishes a link between bank reserves of the monetary base—a liability of the central bank—and bank deposits, a component of the money stock.

3 Bank reserves represent a fraction of deposits. An increase in the monetary base and in bank reserves translates into a much larger increase in deposits. This multiplicative factor is called the money multiplier.

4 The multiplier establishes a fairly stable link between the money base and the wide monetary aggregates (M1, M2, M3, M4, etc.). Thus the public's demand for money translates into a derived demand for the monetary base. This demand is expressed on the money market.

5 Facing the derived demand for the monetary base, central banks carry out open market interventions, providing commercial banks with base money. In doing so, they decide on a quantity to supply, or to supply whatever quantity is demanded to deliver the desired interest rate on the money market. An additional instrument available to the central bank is the required reserve ratio, when it exists.

6 The most popular targets in formulating monetary policy are (expected) inflation, money growth and the exchange rate. When the exchange rate is fixed, the central bank is committed to intervene on the exchange markets. There exists an automatic link between foreign exchange market interventions and the money supply. Sterilization is one way of breaking the automatic link.

7 As a public institution, a central bank can assist the government in the financing of its expenditures in three ways: (1) it can lend directly to the government; (2) it usually remits most if not all of its seigniorage profits; (3) by allowing inflation to rise, it creates an inflation tax which lowers the burden of the public debt when the latter is not indexed.

8 Because the monetary financing of public spending is a permanent temptation, an increasing number of central banks have been made independent of their governments. Independence is designed to allow central banks to refuse to jeopardize their price stability objective. It sometimes specifies that the central bank may not lend directly to the government, or sets a limit on such loans.

9 In addition to establishing the standard of payment, the central bank ultimately guarantees the value of money. This is done by a variety of regulations and the lender-of-last-resort function. Bank deposits are guaranteed—sometimes up to a certain level—through a combination of insurance schemes and implicit understanding that the central bank will create sufficient monetary base in case of bank failure. In return, the central banks may impose on banks constraints designed to reduce their vulnerability.

🔑 Key Concepts

- central bank
- Eurosystem
- objectives, targets, and instruments
- bank reserves
- monetary base
- financial intermediaries
- reserves requirements, reserve ratio
- money multiplier
- parallel currency
- derived demand
- money market
- open market

- open market operations
- reverse transaction
- repurchase agreement
- inflation targeting
- sterilization
- monetization
- seigniorage
- inflation tax
- information asymmetry
- systemic risk
- lender of last resort
- capital adequacy

❓ Exercises

1 Define and explain the distinction between objectives, targets, and instruments of monetary policy. Give some examples of conflicts between different instruments, and between different targets. Do you think it is necessarily better to have many or fewer instruments and targets?

2 Box 9.3 presents the open market procedures of the ECB. Why are lending and deposit rates the ceiling and floor for the market's interest rates? How could it be possible for the market rate to move outside the tunnel created by these interest rates?

3 Compute the multiplier when the reserves ratio is 1% and the public chooses to hold 5% of its money (M1) in cash. What should the central bank do to increase M1 by £100 million?

4 In the United States, the Federal Reserve System adjusts liquidity conditions on the open market by outright purchases and sales of government bonds for the Fed's balance sheet. Why do you think the treaty establishing the European Central Bank forbids definitive purchases of government debt? Explain why monetization of the debt (when the central bank buys Treasury bills on the open market) is equivalent to direct lending to the government.

5 Explain why and how an unstable demand for money creates problems for the central bank's objective of price stability. What does it imply for the choice of a target?

6 The central bank can control the sum of its liabilities, the monetary base, but not its breakdown between currency and banks' reserves. Explain why. Who decides, in the end?

7 In Box 9.1, the money market multiplier is computed as $1/[cc + rr(1 - cc)]$ when the public maintains a constant fraction, cc, of the total money stock in currency form. Suppose that in addition to these conditions, the private sector also holds a multiple β of its currency holdings abroad. What is the money multiplier?

8 Consider the case of a country where banks are not forced to hold reserves but do so voluntarily. How might the behaviour of commercial banks frustrate the efforts of the central bank to control the money supply? Would the same problem exist if the central bank tries to control interest rates instead?

9 We have seen two sorts of reserves: bank reserves and foreign exchange reserves. Carefully distinguish between them.

10 Using the balance sheets of Figure 9.3, explain how a government surplus—the government taking in more tax revenues than it purchases or transfers—can cause a monetary contraction. (Hint: government funds are usually held as deposits at the central bank.) How does your answer change if the government uses its surplus to retire its debt held by the public? If the debt is held by the central bank?

➔ Essay Questions

1 The mandate of the Eurosystem sets price stability as its overriding priority. In the USA, the Federal Reserve System is legally committed to pursue both 'stability of the currency' and a 'high level of employment'. Compare and discuss these mandates.

2 One of the tasks of a central bank is to intervene as lender of last resort as decribed in Box 9.5. One of the trickiest parts is to determine if a bank is insolvent (it cannot recover) or just illiquid (it has no fundamental problem but is running out of cash). Explain why it matters and how this distinction can be made.

3 Why do central banks need to have targets? Discuss and evaluate the various possible targets.

4 'Central banking is more art than science' is frequently asserted by central bankers. Discuss.

5 Does it matter whether the money multiplier is large or small?

PART IV

Macroeconomic Equilibrium

10 **Aggregate Demand, Output, and the Interest Rate** 229
11 **Output, Employment, and Prices** 261

Money is absent from Part II, the real economy is absent from Part III. This part brings the two together. The next two chapters bring the goods, money, and labour markets into a single, consistent framework. This **macroeconomic model** is then used to analyse the simultaneous determination of output, employment, the price level, and the interest rate. The outcome is called **macroeconomic equilibrium**.

Chapter 10 takes the Keynesian view as the relevant starting point for the analysis of short-run fluctuations in real economic activity and interest rates. It presents the open economy *IS-LM* model and shows the crucial role played by the exchange rate in shaping these fluctuations as well as potential policy responses. Chapter 11 clarifies the roles of output and prices in achieving equilibrium. Two competing hypotheses are presented and characterized. In the neoclassical view, price adjustments bring demand and supply into line with each other; in contrast, the Keynesian view regards prices as changing only slowly, leaving the burden of adjustment to output and employment.

Aggregate Demand, Output, and the Interest Rate

10.1 Overview *230*

10.2 Aggregate Demand and the Goods Market *232*
10.2.1 The Keynesian Description of Demand *232*
10.2.2 The 45° Diagram *233*
10.2.3 Demand Leakages and the Multiplier *235*
10.2.4 Endogenous and Exogenous Variables *236*

10.3 The Goods Market and the *IS* Curve *237*
10.3.1 From the 45° Diagram to the *IS* Curve *237*
10.3.2 The Slope of the *IS* curve and the Multiplier *238*
10.3.3 Off the *IS* Curve *238*
10.3.4 A Key Distinction: Movements along or Shifts of the *IS* Curve *238*

10.4 The Money Market and the *LM* Curve *241*
10.4.1 The *LM* Curve *241*
10.4.2 Off the *LM* Curve *242*
10.4.3 Moving along or shifting the *LM* Curve *243*

10.5 International Capital Flows and Macroeconomic Equilibrium *243*
10.5.1 Capital Flows and Interest Parity *243*
10.5.2 Macroeconomic Equilibrium and the Exchange Rate Regime *244*

10.6 Output and Interest Rate Determination under Fixed Exchange Rates *246*
10.6.1 Monetary Policy *246*
10.6.2 Real Demand Disturbances *248*
10.6.3 The Policy Mix *249*
10.6.4 International Financial Disturbances *251*
10.6.5 How to Think about a Parity Change *251*

10.7 Output and Interest Rate Determination under Flexible Exchange Rates *252*
10.7.1 Demand Disturbances *252*
10.7.2 Monetary Policy *253*
10.7.3 The Policy Mix *254*
10.7.4 International Financial Disturbances *255*

10.8 Fixed versus Flexible Rates: A Wrap-Up *255*
Summary *256*

The nature of the exchange rate regime has an important bearing not only on the relative effectiveness in influencing income and output of the two types of financial policy—monetary policy and budgetary policy—but also on their relative practicability or sustainability.

—J. Marcus Fleming

10.1 Overview

This chapter provides the first answers to the central question of macroeconomics: why do countries seem to go through recurrent business cycles, periods of fast growth and low unemployment followed by periods of slow—sometimes even negative—growth and rising unemployment?

Figure 10.1 presents a stylized illustration of these departures of real GDP from its long-run trend. In a nutshell, the answer is that business cycles originate in interactions between goods markets, financial markets, and labour markets, all of which are subject to various disturbances. These disturbances can come from home or abroad; some of them are related to the government's spending and taxing policies or to the way the central bank manages monetary conditions.

The complete answer will be clear only after several chapters. Here we go for the simplest interpretation, based on the **Keynesian assumption** that prices are constant over the short run, say a couple of years. Sometimes also called the sticky price assumption, the Keynesian assumption implies that output is determined by demand, and that production (or supply) adjusts passively to shifts in aggregate demand. The Keynesian model is too simple to capture the whole story but it is a start, and it also provides an explanation of how governments use monetary and fiscal policies to deal with macroeconomic fluctuations.

Traditionally, the Keynesian model is presented for the closed economy, sometimes followed up with an extension to the open economy. Instead, this chapter deals from the beginning with a **small open economy**. Openness refers to trade in goods, services, and assets with the rest of the world. Table 10.1 presents a standard measure of trade openness, the ratio of the average of exports and imports to GDP. It reveals an inverse relationship between size and trade openness, but even the two largest units, the Euro-zone and the USA are fairly open to trade. As for trade in assets, all developed countries and an increasing number of developing countries—called emerging market countries—are now fully integrated in the world financial markets. And the only country that is not economically small, in the sense that it is not much affected by economic conditions in the rest of the world, is the USA, and even the USA is gradually losing this status. More importantly perhaps, the small open economy behaves quite differently from the mythical closed economy. All in all, therefore, it seems natural to go straight to the small open-economy version of the Keynesian model, the **Mundell–Fleming model**.[1]

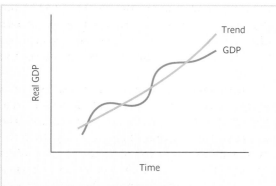

Fig. 10.1 Cyclical Fluctuations
The Keynesian assumption helps explain short-run fluctuations of real GDP around its long-run growth trend.

[1] It is named after the Nobel Laureate Robert Mundell (1932–) from Columbia University and the Briton J. Marcus Fleming (1911–1976), who worked at the IMF.

Table 10.1 Openness and Size (%)		
	Share of world GDP	Openness
Poland	0.6	29.7
Belgium	0.8	80.3
Sweden	0.7	40.2
Switzerland	0.8	40.9
Netherlands	1.3	59.1
Korea, Rep.	1.5	39.3
Brazil	1.4	14.7
Canada	2.2	14.7
China	3.9	27.4
United Kingdom	4.8	26.7
Germany	6.1	33.5
Japan	12.4	10.5
European Monetary Union	20.6	11.1
United States	32.1	11.8

Source: *World Development Indicators*, The World Bank, 2004.

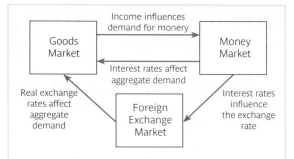

Fig. 10.2 General Macroeconomic Equilibrium

Conditions in domestic money and goods markets affect each other: interest rates and exchange rates influence the level of aggregate demand, while income affects the demand for money and, for given money supply, interest rates. General equilibrium occurs when equilibria in the three markets are consistent with each other.

For a while the Keynesian model was considered the alpha and the omega of macroeconomics. Policy-makers adopted this framework in the 1960s, paying detailed attention to the demand side of the economy while largely neglecting how the supply side sets prices. The result was inflation in the 1970s and then, when bringing inflation down became the new priority, unemployment in the 1980s. The shortcomings of the sticky price assumption are now well recognized, yet the analysis presented here is a useful 'rule of thumb' for thinking about the short run because in most countries prices change very little over a year or two. Most macroconomists and policy-makers have this framework in mind when they assess current macroeconomic conditions or make policy decisions.

The Keynesian model focuses on two markets: the market for goods and services and the money market, a shorthand for the financial markets. Here we directly study the open economy version of the Keynesian model, which allows for a third market, the foreign exchange market itself a part of international financial markets. We look at the **general equilibrium**, a key method of analysis that explores the interactions between several markets, focusing on the conditions required for their simultaneous equilibrium. This concept is summarized in Figure 10.2. Through the interest rate, the money market, described in Chapters 8 and 9, affects the goods market, and thus the level of output. The goods market, in turn, influences the demand for money and thereby the interest rate. From Chapter 7, we know that the real exchange rate influences the demand for domestic goods and we will see how the money market affects the exchange rate.

Another important step taken in this chapter is to draw attention to the crucial role of the **exchange rate regime**. We will consider two possibilities. The exchange rate may be fixed, meaning that the central bank commits to maintain the value of its currency in terms of other currencies. Alternatively, the central bank may let the exchange rate float freely. The exchange rate regime turns out to be crucial to the behaviour of the economy. For this reason, the two regimes of fixed and flexible exchange rates need to be studied separately.

10.2 Aggregate Demand and the Goods Market

10.2.1 The Keynesian Description of Demand

We start from the fundamental accounting identity of Chapter 2:

(10.1) $\qquad Y = C + I + G + \text{PCA}.$

We now move beyond the accounting identity and consider that the right-hand side represents the components of world demand for domestically produced goods and services: C is the demand of resident households for consumption goods, I represents investment spending of firms on capital goods, G is the public sector's own demand, and the primary account PCA is the net demand from the rest of the world. The PCA is the difference between the world's demand for our goods and services, exports X, and the domestic demand for foreign goods and services, imports Z. The first task, therefore, is to describe the behaviour of consumers, firms, and the PCA. The public sector will be assumed to make its choice independently of economic conditions: public spending G and tax receipts T are considered, for the time being, as exogenous. To remind ourselves of this assumption, we will denote them with an upper bar: $\bar{G}$ and $\bar{T}$.

Using the results from Chapter 6, we describe the consumers' behaviour as follows. They want to consume more, the greater their real wealth, and the higher their disposable income is. Wealth is assumed exogenous and represented by $\bar{\Omega}$.[2] Disposable income Y^d is income after tax and is given by the difference between GDP Y and tax payments $\bar{T}$. This description is summarized by the following **consumption function**, with the sign underneath a reminder of the effect of each variable on demand:

(10.2) $\qquad C = C(\bar{\Omega}, Y - \bar{T}).$
$$+ \quad +$$
$\qquad\qquad\qquad\qquad$ (consumption function)

We also saw in Chapter 6 that investment demand can be represented by the following form of the **investment function**:

(10.3) $\qquad I = I(i, \bar{q}).$
$$- \quad +$$
$\qquad\qquad\qquad\qquad$ (investment function)

The investment function states that investment expenditures increase when Tobin's q increases, and declines when the interest i rises.[3] Remember from Chapter 6 that, all other things equal, investment is driven by business expectations or entrepreneurial 'animal spirits'. This effect is captured by Tobin's q. Here we take these animal spirits as exogenous, and will assume q to be exogenous as well.

What about the last term in (10.1), the primary current account (PCA)? Remember that the primary current account surplus is defined in Chapter 2 as the difference between exports (X) and imports (Z) of goods and services:

(10.4) $\qquad\qquad \text{PCA} = X - Z.$

Consider imports first. Recall that domestic spending, or absorption, includes both domestically produced and imported goods and services.[4] It is logical, therefore, to consider that the greater overall absorption is, the more goods and services will be imported. Imports also depend on the country competitiveness, measured by the real exchange rate σ, the relative price of goods produced at home in terms of those produced abroad.[5] A real depreciation—a decrease in σ—makes foreign goods relatively more expensive, and therefore discourages imports. Conversely, a real appreciation—an increase in σ—boosts imports which are now

---

[2] As we use the model for a short-run analysis, this assumption is justified since wealth changes very slowly.

[3] Since prices are sticky and do not change, inflation can be ignored and there is no difference between the nominal interest rate i and the real interest rate r.

[4] Recall that absorption A is $A = C + I + G + \text{PCA}$.

[5] Chapter 7 presents the real exchange rate. If S is the nominal exchange rate, the real exchange rate is $\sigma = SP/P^*$, where P and P^* are, respectively, domestic and foreign price indices.

cheaper. These observations can be summarized by the **import function**:

(10.5) $$Z = Z(A, \sigma).$$
$$\quad\quad + \;\; +$$

Turning to exports, we only need to remember that they are the imports of the rest of the world, so exactly the same arguments apply but from the foreign perspective: our exports depend on foreign absorption A^* and its determinants, foreign wealth Ω^*, disposable income Y^{d*}, Tobin's q^*, etc. A real depreciation—a decrease in σ—makes domestic output cheaper to foreigners and stimulates exports. Conversely, a real appreciation—an increase in σ—depresses exports, which are more costly. The result is the **export function**:

(10.6) $$X = X(A^*, \sigma).$$
$$\quad\quad + \;\; -$$

The **primary current account function** is the difference between the export and import functions in (10.5) and (10.6):

(10.7) $$PCA = X(A^*, \sigma) - Z(A, \sigma)$$
$$\quad\quad\quad + \;\; - \quad\quad + \;\; +$$
$$= PCA(A, A^*, \sigma)$$
$$\quad\quad\; - \;\; + \;\; -$$

Those factors which boost domestic absorption A (increases in wealth, disposable income, Tobin's q, real growth, or a decline in the interest rate) increase imports and worsen the primary current account. In contrast, anything that boosts foreign spending (increases in foreign wealth, disposable income, Tobin's q, real growth, or a decline in the foreign interest rate) will increase foreign absorption A^* and therefore our exports and lead to an improvement of the primary current account. Finally, a real exchange rate appreciation (an increase in σ) leads to a deterioration of the primary account as imports rise and exports fall.

If absorption is driven primarily by GDP, we can simplify and rewrite (10.7) as:

(10.8) $$PCA = PCA(Y, Y^*, \sigma).$$ (primary current
$$\quad\quad\quad\; - \;\; + \;\; -$$ account function)

In the end, we will work with a primary current account function which states that the PCA is

negatively related to domestic real income, positively to foreign income, and negatively to the real exchange rate. This completes the picture of aggregate demand in an open economy.

10.2.2 The 45° Diagram

In Chapter 2, equation (10.1) is presented as an accounting identity which is true by definition. It can also be interpreted as the condition for equilibrium in the goods market, the right-hand side being aggregate *demand* for the nation's output and the left-hand side the *supply*. Replacing each component of demand in (10.1) by the corresponding function describing its behaviour, as specified in equations (10.2), (10.3), and (10.8), we obtain the planned or **desired demand function**:

(10.9) $$DD = C(\bar{\Omega}, Y - \bar{T}) + I(i, \bar{q}) + \bar{G} + PCA(Y, Y^*, \sigma)$$
$$\quad\quad\quad + \;\; + \quad\quad - \;\; + \quad\quad\quad - \;\; + \;\; -$$
(desired demand function)

This is a compact—and efficient—presentation of the main forces that shape aggregate demand in an open economy. GDP (Y) enters in two ways. A higher GDP increases aggregate demand via its effect on consumption, but it also exerts a negative effect via the PCA function, because it increases imports. Which effect dominates? Theory and evidence say that it is the consumption effect. The reason is that imports represent a fraction of domestic spending: when an increase in GDP causes consumption to rise, imports too rise but by less than consumption. In the end, aggregate demand rises with the GDP, a feature that is represented in Figure 10.3 by the upward-sloping DD schedule.

The schedule is flatter than the 45° line because, when income or GDP rises, demand for domestic goods and services increases by less. One reason is that part of any spending falls on imported goods, as we just saw. In addition, consumers usually save part of any additional income. They may do so because they are unsure whether any increase in income will last, a behaviour sometimes called consumption smoothing. Even if they believe that the increase in GDP is permanent, they may decide to save some of it, either for old age or for their children. Finally, part of any additional income is taxed away; as we hold public spending G constant, this extra amount of taxes is saved by the government, improving the budget balance.

This schedule only captures the effect of GDP on demand, taking all other variables as constant. If they change, the *DD* schedule will shift. For instance, an increase in the interest rate *i* reduces the demand for investment goods, which shifts the *DD* schedule downward. The same applies to the real exchange rate σ: a real appreciation reduces the country's competitiveness, resulting in lower exports, higher imports, and a deterioration of the primary current account. Changes in the other, exogenous determinants of desired demand—household wealth $\bar{\Omega}$, public spending $\bar{G}$, Tobin's $\bar{q}$, and world income Y^*—will make the *DD* schedule shift upward, while an increase in taxes and taxes $\bar{T}$ reduces disposable income and moves the schedule downward.

We now deal with the question of equilibrium in the market of goods and services. As already noted, equation (10.1) can be seen as an accounting identity, it is the way GDP is measured *ex post*; in this sense, demand always equals output. It can also be seen as the goods market equilibrium condition: output on the left-hand side must be equal to desired demand, reflecting the behaviour of consumers, firms, and the government captured by the *DD* function. The upward-sloping schedule captures the fact that, *ex ante*, demand increases with income. Market equilibrium occurs along the 45° line in Figure 10.3 at point *A*, the intersection with the *DD* schedule. This is where desired aggregate demand (measured along the vertical axis) can be satisfied since it is equal to the output (measured along the horizontal axis) that is delivered by producers to the market. This state is called **goods market equilibrium** and the corresponding output level, *Y*, is called **equilibrium GDP**.

To better grasp the meaning of equilibrium in the goods market, consider the case where GDP is *Y'*, above its equilibrium level *Y*. Output is represented by point *C*, desired demand by point *B,* so we now have a situation of excessive supply in the goods market. Since no one is forced to spend more than he wishes, sales are also represented by point *B*. Firms produce more than they sell, and the difference, represented by *BC*, goes into inventories of unsold

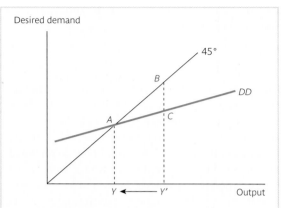

Fig. 10.3 The 45° Diagram
Desired demand *DD* increases with income (earned from output sales), but less than proportionately because part of any additional income is typically saved. Equilibrium occurs when demand equals supply, i.e. when firms deliver a level of output equal to what is being demanded, and this happens along the 45° line. The corresponding output level *Y* is called equilibrium GDP. If output exceeds its equilibrium level, for example *Y'*, supply (point *B*) exceeds demand (point *C*) so firms accumulate inventories of unsold goods. Sooner or later, they will cut production and the economy will move towards equilibrium.

goods. This is a situation that cannot last very long because firms are obviously unwilling to produce goods and services that they cannot sell. Sooner or later, they will reduce their production and the output level will decline until it reaches equilibrium. Conversely, starting below equilibrium GDP, there would be excess demand. Firms would initially satisfy demand by drawing down their previously accumulated inventories but, eventually, they would raise production until they meet the market's demands.

This analysis suggests three main lessons. First, through adjustments in the level of production, the GDP tends to return to its equilibrium level. Second, the market may be temporarily in disequilibrium. Firms use their inventories as a buffer to meet temporary changes in demand; once they realize that the change is lasting, they adjust their level of production. Finally, the accounting identity remains verified off equilibrium because inventory changes

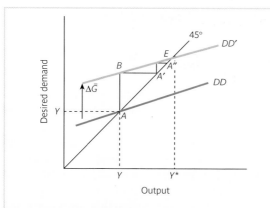

Fig. 10.4 The Multiplier

An exogenous increase in government spending shifts up the demand schedule vertically by $\Delta\bar{G}$. Supply equals demand, and the economy's equilibrium output increases to point Y^*. The multiplier effect—that $Y^* - Y$ exceeds the initial impulse $\Delta\bar{G}$—can be understood by following the staircase up from point A. The direct effect, an increase in demand and output, raises GDP to point A'. This point however is still not equilibrium, because DD lies above the 45° line. Thus, desired demand and output increases again, to point A'', and so on.

are treated as demand—positive when inventories rise, negative when they decline—and demand, and therefore sales, may differ from output.[6]

10.2.3 Demand Leakages and the Multiplier

The Keynesian model explains how output fluctuations are driven by exogenous changes in demand. Figure 10.4 provides an illustration, the case when one component of demand, say government purchases of goods and services, increases by $\Delta\bar{G}$, from $\bar{G}$ to $\bar{G}'$. The economy starts at point A with real GDP level Y.

[6] *Ex post*, when national accountants observe the situation, the accounting identity is respected because they treat the accumulation of inventories as an investment. With this accounting convention, total investment is the sum of desired investment and undesired inventory accumulation:

$$Y = C + I^{desired} + \Delta(inventories) + \bar{G} + PCA$$

The excess supply BC is the difference between *ex post* measured output and *ex ante* demand, $Y - DD$. Since desired demand is $DD = C + I^{desired} + \bar{G} + PCA$, excess demand is $\Delta(inventories)$.

The change in government expenditures increases aggregate demand by $\Delta\bar{G}$ at any level of output and the desired demand schedule shifts upward by that amount. If output remains unchanged at Y, the new situation is described by point B, with desired demand exceeding output. For a while, producers will make up the difference by drawing down their inventories but, within a few weeks, producers will raise their output to match demand, until equilibrium output is reached. In the present case, output expands by $\Delta\bar{G}$ to meet demand and the economy will move to point A' on the 45° line.

The process will not stop at point A', however. Higher sales and production means that income has risen. As some firms sell more goods and services to the government, they distribute more income (wages, profits). Those who receive this income will want to consume more, which will further raise aggregate demand. This is why at point A' desired demand again exceeds output. Inevitably, output will adjust upward to point A'', further raising demand. The process will continue until, step by step, the economy settles in equilibrium at point E, which is on both the new desired demand schedule and the 45° line. Note that, in the end, GDP increases by a *multiple* of the initial demand increase $\Delta\bar{G}$, an effect called the **Keynesian demand multiplier**. No matter which exogenous change triggers the process, and whether the disturbance is positive or negative, equilibrium output responds to demand. The overall effect, which may take several months to complete, is always larger than the initial disturbance.

The multiplier effect corresponds to the fundamental insight provided by the circular flow diagram in Chapter 2: each individual's spending is someone else's income. By raising incomes, an exogenous increase in demand generates additional income and therefore more desired demand, a never-ending process. At each stage, the effect becomes smaller, though, eventually dying out. The Keynesian multiplier is not infinite because, at each step, some fraction of income is not plugged back into further consumption.[7] The circular flow diagram shows that these

[7] If all additional income were entirely spent on domestic goods, the multiplier would be infinite.

leaks occur into taxes, savings, and imports. These three leakages represent domestic income not *automatically* respent on domestic goods and services. The word 'automatically' is important. To be sure, some if not all taxes will be used to support additional public spending, but this is an exogenous decision that the government must make regarding $\bar{G}$. Similarly, higher savings will support additional borrowing used to pay for new equipment, but this must be justified by an increase in desired investment spending, for example through improved profitability prospects captured by Tobin's q. Finally, a rise in imports will generate higher incomes abroad, triggering there another multiplier effect which might well lead to higher foreign GDP Y^* and more exports. All of these effects are plausible but, since we consider $\bar{G}$, $\bar{q}$, and Y^* as exogenous, we cannot logically treat them as responding automatically in the circular flow of income.

In the end, the larger the automatic leakages, the flatter is the DD schedule. It is easily verified in Figure 10.4 that the flatter the DD schedule, the smaller is the multiplier effect.[8] How does the multiplier look in practice? Table 10.2 presents some values of the demand multiplier for the largest economies as estimated by the German central bank, the Bundesbank. These estimates show that most of the effect occurs within one year, and that

the multiplier is indeed larger than 1 in most cases. There is still some impact left over the second year.

10.2.4 Endogenous and Exogenous Variables

It is time to recall the separation of economic variables between those which are exogenous and taken as given, and those which are endogenous and thus to be explained. The Keynesian assumption implies that the price level P is exogenous. Fiscal policy instruments such as government purchases $\bar{G}$ and taxes $\bar{T}$ are assumed to be under direct control of the government and thus are also treated as exogenous—hence the overbar symbol.[9] As in Chapter 10, household wealth $\bar{\Omega}$ is also assumed to be exogenous, as are foreign variables such as foreign GDP (Y^*) and the price level (P^*), since they are also not influenced by the small economy under consideration.

Things are not always that simple, unfortunately. Some variables are exogenous under a given exchange rate regime, and endogenous under another one. We will examine this question carefully below but an early warning is useful. When the nominal exchange rate is fixed, it is treated as exogenous ($S = \bar{S}$). Then this is also the case of the real exchange rate ($\sigma = \bar{\sigma}$) because both domestic and foreign prices P and P^* are assumed constant and therefore exogenous ($\sigma = SP/P^*$). When the exchange rate is flexible, on the other hand, both the nominal and real exchange rates must be treated as endogenous. This is quite natural, but the reasoning does not stop here. In Chapter 9, we have seen the central bank cannot set the exchange rate and the money supply at the same time. When the exchange rate is flexible and endogenously determined by market forces, the central bank can control the money supply, which is then treated as exogenous ($M = \bar{M}$). Similarly, when the central bank pegs the exchange rate, the chosen parity $\bar{S}$ is treated as exogenous, while the money supply M is endogenous.

Table 10.2 Demand Multipliers: Five Examples

	Years after change		
	1	2	3
Euro area	1.43	1.31	0.41
UK	0.75	0.33	0.01
USA	1.05	0.49	−0.38
Canada	1.24	0.52	−0.17
Japan	1.85	1.58	−0.09

Note: The numbers represent the effect of a change in government expenditure of 1% of real GDP in 2000 and 2001 in all five regions on each economy's output (as percentage deviation from baseline).

Source: Deutsche Bundesbank (2000), authors' calculations.

---

[8] The WebAppendix provides a computation of the multiplier.

[9] We treat net taxes as exogenous for simplicity, for the time being. In the WebAppendix to this chapter, more realistically, taxes are allowed to depend positively on income Y. Indeed, in practice, governments usually set tax *rates*, which implies that tax revenues tend to rise with output and income.

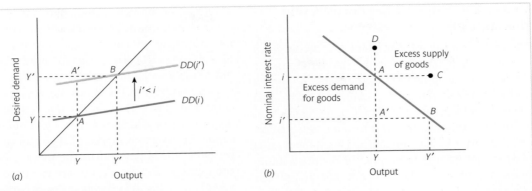

Fig. 10.5 Deriving the *IS* Curve
A reduction in the interest rate from *i* to *i'* leads to an increase in consumption and investment, which is met by an increase in output. The *IS* curve is flatter the larger is the required output increase, as measured by the distance *CB* in panel (*b*). The length of *CB* in turn depends on: (1) the responsiveness of demand to interest changes, represented by the size of the vertical shift of *DD*, or *AA'*, in panel (*a*); (2) the multiplier effect, measured by distance *A'B*. The multiplier is larger the steeper the desired demand schedule, i.e. the more sensitive is demand to changes in output.

10.3 The Goods Market and the *IS* Curve

10.3.1 From the 45° Diagram to the *IS* Curve

In Figure 10.3, the *DD* schedule depicts how desired demand varies when output changes, holding everything else (the interest and exchange rates, public spending and taxes, private wealth, foreign demand) constant. What happens if the interest rate changes? The answer is given by the first panel of Figure 10.5. The starting point *A*, where equilibrium is achieved, lies on the desired demand schedule drawn for an interest rate *i*. Suppose the interest rate declines from *i* to *i'*. From the investment function (10.3), we know that when the interest rate declines investment increases. At each level of income, desired demand is now higher, which means that the *DD* curve shifts upward. The new equilibrium is now achieved at point *B* (with a multiplier effect), which means that equilibrium output increases from *Y* to *Y'*.

The second panel of Figure 10.5 summarizes this discussion. Points *A* and *B* correspond respectively to the initial (interest rate *i* and GDP *Y*) and final (*i'* and *Y'*) outcomes. Repeating this same reasoning for other interest rate levels will produce more points like *A* and *B*. They will trace out a negative relationship between the interest rate and equilibrium output depicted by the downward-sloping schedule known as the *IS* curve.[10] *For given values of exogenous variables, the IS curve represents the combinations of nominal interest rate i and real GDP that are consistent with goods market equilibrium.* The fact that the *IS* curve is downward sloping simply captures the idea that a higher interest rate reduces private spending on investment.

---

[10] The name of this curve comes from the identity (2.6): $I - S = T - G + PCA$, and was first derived by Nobel Prize laureate Sir John Hicks. For simplicity, he assumed the government budget to be in equilibrium and no foreign trade, so the identity reduced to $I = S$. We draw the *IS* curve as a line because we do not really know, nor do we need to know, its exact shape. For a derivation of the *IS* curve using calculus, see the WebAppendix.

10.3.2 The Slope of the *IS* curve and the Multiplier

The move from point *A* to point *B* is decomposed in Figure 10.5(*b*) into two steps. The decline in the interest rate, keeping GDP constant, takes the economy from point *A* to point *A'*, off the *IS* curve. This corresponds to point *A'* in Panel (*a*) of Figure 10.5, a situation of excess demand in the goods market when the rise in the demand for equipment ΔI is not yet met by higher output. To restore equilibrium, output must increase not just by ΔI but also to meet the additional spending that additional income generates. The move from point *A'* to point *B* corresponds to the multiplier effect.

This observation explains what determines the slope of the *IS* curve.[11] The curve is flatter the longer is *A'B* relative to *AA'* in Panel (*b*). *AA'* is simply the assumed exogenous change in the interest rate, so we focus on the output response *A'B* and turn to Panel (*a*). The length of *A'B* depends on two characteristics: first, the length of *AA'*, which measures the interest rate effect on investment; second, the slope of the *DD* schedule. The steeper this schedule, the longer will be *A'B*; this is, once again, the result that the smaller are the leakages between income and spending, the steeper is the *DD* schedule and the larger is the multiplier. Summarizing, the slope of the *IS* curve is flatter (1) the greater the sensitivity of consumption and investment to changes in interest rates, as measured by the vertical shift of the desired demand schedule (*AA'*) in panel (*a*), and (2) the larger the multiplier that translates the initial exogenous change into higher total demand, as measured along *A'B*.

10.3.3 Off the *IS* Curve

What happens if, starting from point *A* in Figure 10.5(*b*), output increases holding the interest rate constant so that we move to point *C*? A higher income implies a higher level of demand, but, because of consumption smoothing, imports, and taxes, demand rises by less than output/income. At point *C*, therefore, there is not enough demand to

absorb all of the new output: this is a situation of **excess supply** on the goods market, and inventories rise. Similarly, moving vertically up from point *A* to a point like *D* corresponds to an increase in the interest rate with unchanged output. This also leads to excess supply in the goods market as aggregate demand declines. Thus the *IS* curve determines two regions: above and to the right we observe excess supply in the goods market; below and to the left, we have **excess demand** in the market for goods and services, and inventories are run down. At the boundary of the two regions, the *IS* curve represents those combinations of GDP and the interest rates which are consistent with goods market equilibrium. We have seen in Section 10.2.2 that the economy can stay temporarily off the *IS* curve, while firms use their inventories as a buffer stock, but fairly soon they will adjust their output, returning the economy to goods market equilibrium on the *IS* curve.

10.3.4 A Key Distinction: Movements along or Shifts of the *IS* Curve

It is important not to confuse *shifts* of the *IS* curve with movements *along* it. This is where the distinction between exogenous and endogenous variables comes into play. The *IS* curve describes how the two endogenous variables, the real GDP (*Y*) and the nominal interest rate (*i*), are combined to achieve equilibrium in the goods market, *everything else being held constant*. What is 'everything else'? This refers to all the variables that we treat as exogenous when we draw the *IS* schedule. Any change in any of these exogenous variables delivers another *IS* curve accordingly. Put differently, the position of the *IS* curve is determined by the exogenous variables: as long as these remain unchanged, we move *along* the *IS* curve, and whenever any of the exogenous variables change, the *IS* curve *shifts*. Figure 10.6 shows that the *IS* curve shifts up and to the right when the exogenous change is expansionary. In the opposite case of an exogenous decline in aggregate demand, the *IS* curve shifts leftwards.

Which exogenous variables are relevant? Fiscal policy is a premier source of shifts in the *IS* curve. The government is a large player in the macroeconomy, and changes in government purchases of goods $\bar{G}$

---

[11] The slope of the *IS* curve is formally shown in the WebAppendix.

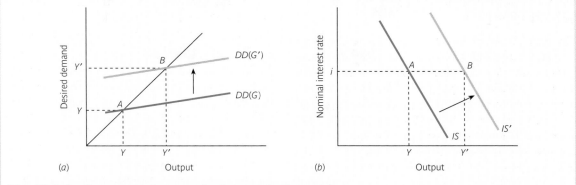

Fig. 10.6 An Exogenous Increase in Aggregate Demand

At unchanged interest rate i, an increase in any of the exogenous components of demand is represented in panel (a) by an upward shift of the aggregate demand schedule. Equilibrium occurs at point B and the new equilibrium output Y' is higher than the initial level Y. Panel (b) shows that the IS curve shifts to the right for the given interest rate.

(e.g. military procurement or road construction) or services (e.g. the wages or number of civil servants) can exert a significant influence on aggregate demand. Similarly, changes in taxation $\bar{T}$ alter disposable income available to households and consumption demand. They may also affect investment through profit taxes.

Second, changes in expectations of businessmen represent another important factor shifting the IS curve as they affect investment decisions. These expectations, which focus on the future profitability of investment, are driven as much by gut feelings as by rational calculus; this is why Keynes called them 'animal spirits'. These factors are summarized in the variable $\bar{q}$.

Third, changes in household wealth Ω, which result from fluctuations in the value of assets such as stocks (another influence of Tobin's q), bonds, housing, etc. can affect aggregate demand and thus the position of the IS curve. A classic example is the Great Depression of the 1930s, which has been traced back to the worldwide collapse of stock prices following the crash of Wall Street. Similarly, sharply falling housing prices preceded the recession of the early 1990s in the UK, Sweden, Japan, and many other countries. Box 10.1 examines the

 Box 10.1 When the US Stock Market Bubble Burst in 2000

Over the 1990s, US stock prices increased on average more than fourfold. While attention was focused and fortunes were made on developments linked to the 'information technology revolution', experts debated whether such stock increases were justified and whether such a long stretch of gains would continue. Some Cassandras started to talk openly about the emergence of a bubble, a phenomenon that propels stock prices ever higher to completely unjustified levels.[12] The Chairman of the Federal Reserve, Alan Greenspan, famously warned in 1996 against the markets' 'irrational exuberance', later reversing his opinion and becoming an enthusiastic supporter of the revolution. The market peaked in early 2000 and started a precipitous descent in the middle of year. When the dust settled in 2003, many fortunes were wiped out and a number of spectacular corporate scandals revealed how some unscrupulous businessmen and speculators had sought to magnify their gains.

[12] Chapter 19 presents this phenomenon.

Box 10.1 (*continued*)

In the meantime, the roaring US economy came to a standstill. The boom-and-bust cycle spread worldwide. Figure 10.7 illustrates these events. It shows the GDP growth rate and the evolution of Tobin's *q*. The link between growth and stock prices appears to work in both directions. During the 1990s, the boom in stock prices did reflect fundamental technological innovations of tremendous value and helped sustain the longest period of sustained growth ever recorded in the USA. As Chapter 6 showed, stock prices signalled future investment and growth. Yet, when the economy started to turn around, market participants began to debate whether the boom was 'for real' or whether they had been taken for a ride and the economy would soon undergo a hard landing. Eventually, investors concluded that a bubble had emerged and had to burst. The collapse of the bubble undoubtedly contributed to the sharpness and duration of the recession but at the end, the economy recovered long before stock prices started to rise again.

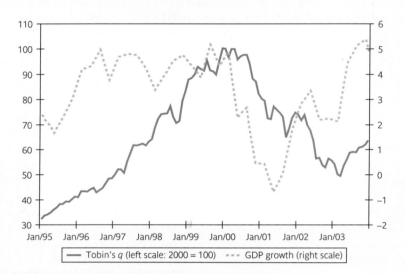

Fig. 10.7 GDP Growth and Tobin's *q* in the USA, 1995–2003

Tobin's *q* is measured as the inflation-adjusted value of the stock market index, an average of stock prices, normalized to take the value 100 in January 2000. Tobin's *q* is calculated as the stock price index deflated by the wholesale price index. Its movements sometimes precede those of real GDP, as in the mid-1990s; in this case it supports rising and high investment spending. At other times, it seems to lag real GDP, as if investors were slow to recognize the economy's turnaround.
Source: IMF and BEA.

collapse of internet- and technology-related stock prices that is regarded as an important reason for the slowdown of the US economy in late 2000, with worldwide repercussions.

Finally, foreign disturbances matter for an open economy. They affect the IS curve through the primary current account. The account is not only a source of leakage, but it also transmits foreign disturbances. Indeed, the PCA function (10.8) shows that changes in world activity Y^* can generate export-led expansions or recessions. All other things equal, an increase in Y^* will increase the PCA and cause the IS curve to shift rightward. The same applies to the real exchange rate $\sigma = SP/P^*$, which determines the economy's competitiveness. Any change in either the nominal exchange rate S or in domestic and foreign prices P and P^* must be reflected by a shift of the IS curve.

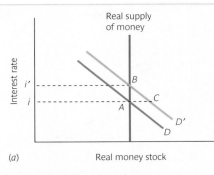
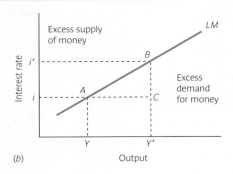

Fig. 10.8 Deriving the *LM* Curve

An exogenous increase in GDP raises the demand for money at any interest rate, hence the shift from D to D' in panel (a). At the initial interest rate i, we now have excess demand, as represented by point C in both panels. The size of the excess demand (measured by the length AC) is proportional to the responsiveness of money demand to output. The return to money equilibrium is achieved through an increase in the interest rate which reduces demand. The required increase from i to i' (measured by AB in panel (a) and by BC in panel (b)) is inversely proportional to the responsiveness of money demand to the interest rate. If money demand is very interest sensitive, a small increase in the interest rate is sufficient to eliminate the excess demand.

10.4 The Money Market and the *LM* Curve

10.4.1 The *LM* Curve

We have already studied the money market in Chapters 8 and 9. We described the demand for money by households, firms, and the government, and we showed how the central bank determines its supply through the banking system. As in Section 10.3.1, we now ask which levels of real GDP and interest rate are compatible with equilibrium in the money market, still holding the price level constant. Panel (a) of Figure 10.8 reproduces the equilibrium condition established in Chapter 8. We continue to assume that the central bank has chosen a given amount of nominal money supply $\bar{M}$. Because, for the time being, the price level P is taken as constant, the central bank also sets the real money supply $\bar{M}/P$. This is represented by the vertical supply schedule in Figure 10.8(a). The downward-sloping demand schedule captures the

idea that, given the GDP level Y and transaction costs, money demand declines as the interest rises. **Money market equilibrium** occurs at point A where supply and demand are equal:

$$(10.10) \qquad \bar{M}/P = \mathcal{L}(Y, i, \bar{c}).$$

Now consider the effect of an increase in GDP from Y to Y' in Figure 10.8, holding all else constant. The immediate consequence is that the demand for money rises. In panel (a) the money demand schedule shifts out. The new equilibrium is at point B, and the interest rate rises from i to i'. This result is summarized in panel (b) of Figure 10.8, with corresponding equilibrium points A (Y and i) and B (Y' and i'). We thus find that money market equilibrium implies a positive relationship between GDP and the interest rate. This is the *LM* curve. *The LM curve is the combination of income and interest rates for which the*

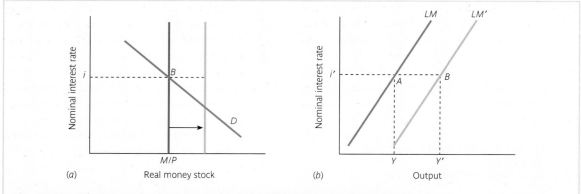

Fig. 10.9 An increase in the Money Supply Shifts the *LM* Curve Outward

An increase in the money supply at a given level of interest rates creates a situation of excess money supply. This means that all points on the original *LM* curve now represent (*i, Y*) combinations of excess supply of money. To restore equilibrium, the demand for money must be higher. To achieve this, either the interest rate must be lower or income must be higher. Thus, the new *LM* curve lies below and to the right of the old one.

money market is in equilibrium, given the price level and the exogenous variables.[13]

The *LM* curve is steeper, the longer the segment *BC* is relative to *AC*, which represents the assumed GDP increase. The length of *BC*, which represents the interest rate increase that reduces money demand by as much as it rose in response to the increase in GDP, depends on two characteristics. First, how sensitive is the demand for money to changes in the real GDP? If it is very sensitive (we say that the income elasticity of money demand is large), a given increase in output raises money demand by a large amount and the return to money market equilibrium will require a large compensating interest rate increase. This makes for a steep schedule. Second, how sensitive is the demand for money to interest rate changes? This aspect is captured by the slope of the money demand function *D* depicted in Figure 10.8(a). If the money demand function *D* is steep, the demand for money is not too sensitive to changes in the interest rate (we say that the interest elasticity of demand is low), the interest rate must move a lot to re-establish equilibrium for a given increase in GDP, hence again a steep *LM* curve; if

the money demand is flat, small changes in the interest rate are sufficient to restore equilibrium and the *LM* curve will be flat. To summarize, the *LM* curve is steeper, the more sensitive money demand is to output, and the less sensitive it is to the interest rate.

10.4.2 Off the *LM* Curve

All points *off* the *LM* curve signal conditions of disequilibrium in the money market. To see this, suppose that the economy is in equilibrium at point *A* in Figure 10.8 and that real GDP increases from *Y* to *Y'* at an unchanged interest rate, say to point *C*, holding all else constant. A higher GDP raises the demand for real money balances. Since, by assumption, the real supply of money is unchanged, the result is an excess demand for money. To restore equilibrium under these conditions, a higher interest rate is necessary. As the interest rate rises, it increases the opportunity cost of holding money, which reduces demand. The interest rate will have to rise to *i'* in order to bring demand back to equal the unchanged supply, re-establishing equilibrium at point *B*.

The region below and to the right of the *LM* curve represents disequilibrium situations of excess demand on the money market. Restoration of equilibrium requires either a rise in the interest rate, or

---

[13] The name '*LM*' originates from the fact that along the curve, the demand for liquidity (*L*) equals the money supply (*M*) in eq. (10.10). For an explicit derivation of the slope of the *LM* curve using calculus, see the WebAppendix to this chapter.

a reduction in GDP. Similarly, the region above and to the left of the *LM* curve corresponds to an excess supply of money: equilibrium can be restored with a decrease in the interest rate or an increase in income and output. The border between these two regions, the *LM* curve, is where the money market is in equilibrium, i.e. in a state of neither excess supply nor excess demand.

10.4.3 Moving along or shifting the *LM* Curve

To avoid confusion between shifts of the *LM* curve and movements along it, the same rule applies as for the *IS* curve: it remains unchanged as long as the exogenous variables do not change. In other words, a particular *LM* curve corresponds to given values of the exogenous variables: the real money supply ($\bar{M}/P$) and transaction costs ($\bar{c}$). As long as these exogenous variables remain unchanged, the economy remains on the same *LM* curve. Whenever any of the exogenous variables change, the *LM* curve shifts. For example, the *LM* curve shifts rightward when the real money supply increases (when the nominal supply increases or the price level falls) or when money market transactions become cheaper. For example, Figure 10.9 shows how changes in the nominal money supply shift the *LM* curve out. Since the price level is taken as constant, any increase in the nominal money supply is also an increase in the real supply. Then, the *LM* curve shifts to the right; conversely, when supply is reduced, the *LM* shifts to the left.

10.5 International Capital Flows and Macroeconomic Equilibrium

10.5.1 Capital Flows and Interest Parity

The primary current account function captures one link between a country and the rest of the world, through the goods market, i.e. trade in goods and services. The second link is financial: it operates through international capital movements. A convenient and usually realistic approach is to assume that the country is too small to affect financial conditions abroad. This allows us to assume that the 'foreign' rate of return i^* is exogenous. This return includes the possible expectation of a depreciation or appreciation of the exchange rate, an issue to which we return in more detail in Chapter 19.

When financial capital is freely mobile, returns on similar assets cannot differ systematically across countries.[14] To see why, think of all those financial traders who constantly scan the whole world, looking for the best possible available deals. One of their

tricks is to borrow where the rate of return is low and immediately re-lend where the return is high. They do so minute by minute and can move huge amounts of money at virtually no cost. In doing so they raise the cost of borrowing where returns are low, and lower them where they are high. Their relentless activity—sometimes called arbitrage—backed by potentially very large capital flows, means that worldwide returns for assets of similar characteristics are equalized across countries. The result is the following **interest rate parity condition**:

(10.11) $$i = i^*.$$

This condition is depicted as the horizontal **balance of payments** (BP) line in Figure 10.10.[15] Above the *BP*

[14] 'Similarity' refers to riskiness (e.g. short-term government bills and bonds are usually considered safe, as are those issued by large corporations) and the nature of the asset's payoffs, mainly its time to maturity.

[15] Why is it called Balance of Payments schedule? It is slightly misleading since, as explained in Ch. 2, the balance of payments includes the current account (CA), the financial account (FA) and the official interventions (OFF). The accounting identity is: BP = CA + FA + OFF = 0. The BP line in fact corresponds to the condition that FA not be swamped, along with the overall balance of payments by speculative flows that establish the interest parity condition.

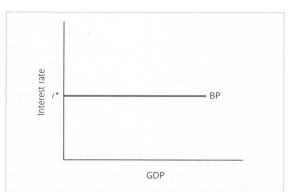

Fig. 10.10 The Balance of Payments Line

When capital can move freely across borders, assets of similar quality (in terms of maturity and risk) should yield the same return. Otherwise, unexploited profit opportunities would exist (borrowing where interest is low and lending where it is high); this is incompatible with the assumptions of free mobility. Note that i^* denotes the return on foreign assets, which includes expected capital gains or losses resulting from changes in the exchange rate.

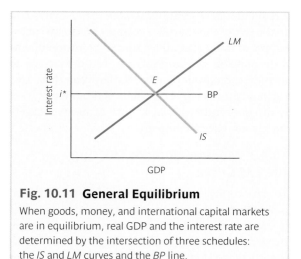

Fig. 10.11 General Equilibrium

When goods, money, and international capital markets are in equilibrium, real GDP and the interest rate are determined by the intersection of three schedules: the IS and LM curves and the BP line.

line, the domestic interest rate is higher than worldwide returns. Capital flows in as international investors seek to take advantage of better returns. The inflows can be massive and they will drive the domestic interest rate down to the world level. Conversely, below the BP line, capital flows out and its increasing scarcity drives the interest rate up.

10.5.2 Macroeconomic Equilibrium and the Exchange Rate Regime

We now summarize the previous results. We have studied three markets and, for each of them, found what combinations of real GDP and nominal interest rate are compatible with equilibrium. The IS curve captures the market for goods and services, the LM curve describes the money market and the BP line, which indicates that the interest rate of a small open economy cannot differ from the world's rate of return, corresponds to the economy's integration in the international financial markets. These schedules are drawn 'all other things equal', meaning that they remain in place as long as the corresponding exogenous variables are unchanged.

We have also seen that none of these three markets can remain off equilibrium for very long. This is why it is both convenient and realistic to consider that the economy always lies at the intersection of all three schedules. This is shown as point E in Figure 10.11. This situation is called general equilibrium because it requires that all markets be simultaneously in equilibrium. This is an example of a method of reasoning that is the essential toolkit of economics. Most non-economists can spontaneously think of a one-market equilibrium—called partial equilibrium—but become quickly lost when faced with the question of what happens simultaneously in other markets and how it affects the overall situation. An important lesson of economics in general and macroeconomics in particular is that focusing on one market and ignoring the others is the best way to make big mistakes.

The open-economy IS-LM model is an efficient way of understanding the working of an open economy in the short run, when the sticky price assumption is defensible. More precisely, it allows us to ask what happens to the model's two endogenous variables, GDP and the interest rate, when any of the exogenous variables changes. The first step is to determine which of the three schedules—IS, LM, and BP—shifts in response to an exogenous disturbance. The second step is to find out what must happen for the three schedules to go through a single general equilibrium point. The last step is to understand and interpret the result: how and why has the economy moved from the initial to the new general equilibrium?

We require that the three schedules go through the same point because powerful forces prevent any of the three markets from being out of equilibrium for very long. Inventory adjustment and output changes restore equilibrium in the goods market. A lasting disequilibrium in the goods market would manifest itself by persistent queues in front of empty stores in the case of excess demand, or by unsold goods in the case of excess supply. It is a distinguishing feature of market economies that these situations do not occur on any significant scale. Within weeks, at most months, firms are likely to adjust their production levels to meet demand. Money and international financial markets are especially known for the rapidity at which they clear, through changes in the interest rates and massive capital flows.

One important and useful feature of the Mundell–Fleming model is that it forces us to take careful account of the exchange rate regime. Section 10.6 describes the case of a country committed to a fixed exchange rate regime, which means that the monetary authorities undertake to keep their exchange rate at a publicly announced level. This is the case in many countries from Central and Eastern Europe, which peg their currencies to the euro within the European Monetary System. In fact, many small open countries have adopted fixed exchange rate regimes of various forms and shapes. Section 10.7 considers the opposite case, when the exchange rate is allowed to float freely. This corresponds to the situation of the Euro-area, Switzerland, the UK, the USA, and Japan, for instance. In between these two extremes are various degrees of managed floating, where the authorities do not commit themselves to a particular rate but nevertheless attempt to prevent large fluctuations. Box 10.2 reviews the exchange rate policies of European countries in late 2004.

Finally, it is worth recalling that the Mundell–Fleming model assumes that prices are sticky. This matters a great deal. When we found a situation of excess demand, for instance, we assumed that

---

 Box 10.2 Exchange Rate Regimes in Europe, 2004

By mid-2004, European countries could be grouped in five categories.[16] First, the twelve members of the European Monetary Union have fixed exchange rates irrevocably among themselves by the adoption of a common currency, the euro. A second group includes the new EU countries which, until they join the monetary union, are part of the Exchange Rate Mechanism (ERM) of the European Monetary System. A third group follows the euro closely. In contrast with ERM members, they do not declare any official parity but actively limit the fluctuations of their exchange rates, usually vis-à-vis the euro, but sometimes vis-à-vis the US dollar (Russia). Countries in the fourth group of 'free floaters' largely allow the market to determine their exchange rate. The countries that make up the fifth and final group have adopted currency boards: they peg to the euro and allow the money base to change only when their foreign exchange reserves change.

1 *European Monetary Union*: Austria, Belgium, Finland, France, Germany, Greece, Ireland, Italy, Luxembourg, Netherlands, Portugal, Spain.

2 *Members of the ERM*: Cyprus, Czech Republic, Denmark, Hungary, Latvia, Malta, Poland, Slovak Republic, Slovenia.

3 *Managed floaters*: Croatia, Macedonia, Norway, Romania, Russia, Sweden, Ukraine.

4 *Free floaters*: Albania, Iceland, Switzerland, UK.

5 *Currency board*: Estonia, Lithuania, Bosnia-Herzegovina, Bulgaria.

Source: IMF.

---

[16] The situation can change quickly. In fact, at the time of writing we assume that the countries that joined the European Union in May 2004 will have joined the Exchange Rate Mechanism by year's end.

supply would rise to meet the market's needs. Another possibility is for firms to raise their prices, which would discourage the excess demand. The sticky price assumption means that supply fully adjusts to demand, this is the traditional Keynesian view. If prices are flexible, it is rather demand that adjusts to supply. Chapter 11 examines these differences; Chapter 12, which deals with inflation, shows how the Keynesian model can be adapted to the realistic intermediate case where prices are slowly adjusting.

10.6 Output and Interest Rate Determination under Fixed Exchange Rates

10.6.1 Monetary Policy

The crucial role of the exchange rate regime is easy to grasp by looking at monetary policy. What happens when the central bank increases the money supply from M to M' while keeping the exchange rate fixed? In Figure 10.12, starting from initial general equilibrium at point A, the LM curve shifts down and to the right from LM to LM'. The puzzling outcome is that the three schedules describing equilibrium conditions in the three markets—goods, money, and international financial integration—no longer pass through a common intersection. Instead, we observe three pairwise intersections: the initial point A at the intersection of IS and BP, point B at the intersection of LM' and IS, and point C at the intersection of LM' and BP. At point A, above and to the left of the new LM' curve, there is an excess supply of money, which simply reflects the increase from M to M' under study. At point B, the domestic interest rate is lower than the yields available on foreign assets. At point C, off the IS curve, there is an excess supply of goods. Which of these three points, if any, is relevant?

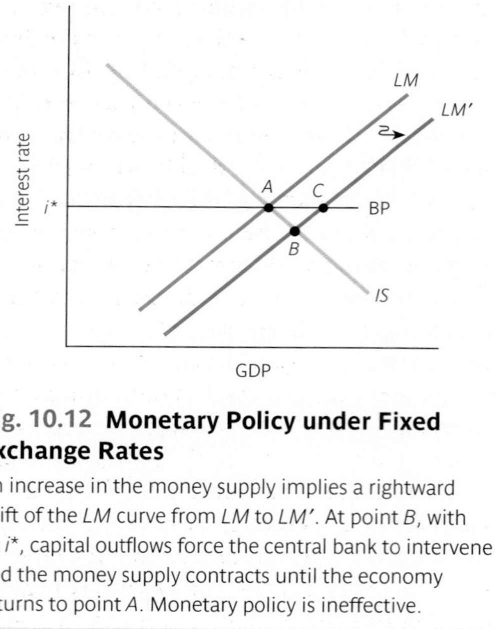

The easiest way to find out is to assume that the economy has moved to point B, at the intersection of the IS and LM curves (which corresponds to the closed economy case) and ask how market forces will react to the resulting international financial market disequilibrium. The low return on domestic assets will promptly be noted by international investors, both foreign and domestic. They will take advantage of this rare and fleeting occurrence, borrowing at home and investing abroad, and they will do so in very large amounts. In the process, they will sell on the foreign exchange markets the domestic currency that they have just borrowed, simultaneously acquiring the currencies of the countries where they wish to lend. The result will be immediate pressure on the domestic exchange rate: heavy sales of the domestic currency will push it towards depreciation.

Fig. 10.12 Monetary Policy under Fixed Exchange Rates

An increase in the money supply implies a rightward shift of the LM curve from LM to LM'. At point B, with $i < i^*$, capital outflows force the central bank to intervene and the money supply contracts until the economy returns to point A. Monetary policy is ineffective.

Remember, however, that we now consider the case of a fixed exchange rate regime. The central bank is committed to resisting the impending depreciation. Under market pressure, it must conduct an **exchange market intervention**, buying the domestic currency that is being sold on the market in excessive quantities. To do so, it spends some of its accumulated stock of **foreign exchange reserves**. But, the currency bought back by the central bank is effectively withdrawn from circulation and the money supply declines. Consequently, the *LM* curve shifts leftwards.[17] How far will it go? Quite simply, the central bank will have to intervene and reduce the money supply as long as the return on domestic assets (*i*) is less than the return on foreign assets (*i**), that is until the *LM* curve has returned to its initial position. General equilibrium will be restored at point *A*, the starting point! The important result is that monetary policy has no effect under a fixed exchange rate regime. Graphically, we find that the *LM* curve is endogenous and must always move to pass through where the two other schedules *IS* and *BP* intersect.

The result that monetary policy is ineffective under fixed exchange rates should not be surprising. Chapter 9 has already shown that monetary policy independence is lost under a fixed exchange rate regime. This can be easily seen by looking at the central bank balance sheet, simplified to the monetary base M0 on the liability side and to foreign exchange (*F*) and domestic credit or securities (*DC*) on the asset side:

(10.12) $$M0 = F + DC.$$

In order to expand the money supply, the central bank creates some additional monetary base (M0) by increasing its lending to commercial banks, or more generally, extending new credit to the economy (*DC*).[18] But we have just seen that the central bank, having increased the money supply and lowered

---

[17] Chapter 9 explains the links between foreign exchange rate market interventions and the money supply.

[18] Domestic credit is a general term describing any form of loan by the central bank to the non-bank sector (private or government). It could take the form of direct lending to the government, purchase of government debt, or refinancing of commercial lending by private banks.

Table 10.3 Sterilized and Unsterilized Foreign Exchange Market Interventions

	Unsterilized interventions			Sterilized interventions		
	M0	F	DC	M0	F	DC
Step 1	–	–	=	–	–	=
Step 2				+		+
Overall	–	–	=	=	–	+

interest rates, must then intervene on the foreign exchange market. It buys back the base (M0) and sells from its stock of foreign exchange rate reserves (*F*). In the end, what the right hand gives—more M0 and more *DC*—the left hand takes away—less M0 and *F*—and M0 must return to its initial level to keep the domestic interest rate *i* in line with the foreign rate of return *i**.

The foreign exchange market intervention procedure that follows the initial open market intervention that expanded M0 is called an **unsterilized intervention**. In principle, the central bank could, instead, conduct a **sterilized intervention**, a procedure designed to shield the monetary base from the intervention. It can be decomposed into two steps, shown in Table 10.3. The first step is as before, a purchase of domestic currency (M0) against foreign exchange reserves: this is shown with a *minus* sign in the table, as both are reduced in the central bank's balance sheet. The second step is sterilization. It consists in reinjecting the previously bought domestic currency in the domestic money market through a standard open-market operation: the central bank lends money to financial institutions, i.e. it increases both M0 and *DC*, hence the plus signs. The end result is shown at the bottom of the table: the central bank has only reshuffled its balance sheet's asset side, raising *DC* one for one as *F* declines, and has kept M0 unchanged on the liability side. A sterilized intervention fully shields the money base and, therefore, the domestic supply.

Can sterilized interventions restore the effectiveness of monetary policy? The answer is negative. Remember that the story starts with an increase in the money supply from M to M', and the underlying expansion of the monetary base from M0 to M0'. Sterilized interventions in the front of foreign exchange market pressure aim at keeping the monetary base at the level M0' and the overall money supply at the level M'. Sterilized interventions therefore keep the LM curve in its LM' position, the economy is at point B where i is below i^*, and capital flows out. As long as this lasts, the central bank must keep intervening to maintain the exchange rate as fixed. This cannot go on for ever, though, because the stock of foreign exchange reserves is being depleted along the way and it will be exhausted sooner or later. The BP line in Figure 10.1 simply says that the central bank of a small open economy must accept that the domestic interest rate cannot be moved away from the foreign rate of return.

With free capital mobility, the central bank is simply unable to reach point B: as soon as it increases M0 and M, it faces crippling pressure on the foreign exchange market and must accept a prompt return to point A, one way or another. History is strewn with examples of central banks that have tried to violate this iron law, and soon regretted it bitterly. The only feasible way to circumvent the law, is to break the link between i and i^*. This is why some countries resort to **capital controls**. These restrictions on the international movement of capital are described in Box 10.3.

10.6.2 Real Demand Disturbances

Figure 10.13 illustrates the effect of an increase in any of the exogenous components of demand for goods and services described in Section 10.3.4, such as improved business expectations, expansionary

---

 ## Box 10.3 Capital Controls and Monetary Independence

Capital controls refer to a variety of administrative measures which prevent the residents of one country from freely moving assets across borders. Some measures are designed to repel capital inflows, others to forestall outflows. When capital movements are restricted, as they were from time to time in many European countries until the late 1980s, arbitrageurs cannot equalize returns on domestic and foreign assets, and the interest rate parity condition need not hold. The domestic interest rate is decoupled from foreign returns—or at least, the link is less tight. Graphically, it is possible, at least for some time, to stay away from the BP line. In the case of a monetary expansion represented in Figure 10.12, point B is sustainable and the monetary authorities recover some independence. In practice, however, the rewards to dodging the controls—exploiting the difference between asset returns—are so high that many investors develop great skills and invest large amount of resources to circumvent the controls. Given time—sometimes a few months, more often a few days—monetary policy independence will be eroded. A similar result holds for the case of aggregate demand disturbances studied in the next section: in Figure 10.13, point B becomes possible under fixed exchange rates, at least for some time. While capital controls have fallen into disrepute, they

are occasionally invoked in crisis situations, for example in Malaysia after the crisis of 1997.

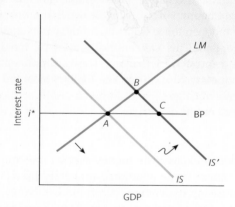

Fig. 10.13 Demand Disturbances under Fixed Exchange Rates

The demand expansion is shown as shifting the IS curve from IS to IS'. At point B, the goods and money markets are in equilibrium but the interest rate exceeds the world level. The combination of capital inflows and exchange market interventions raises the money supply, shifting the LM curve down and to the right. This proceeds until the LM curve passes through point C.

fiscal policy (an increase in public spending or tax reductions), or rising exports (following a foreign expansion). A positive demand disturbance is represented as a rightward shift of the IS curve, from IS to IS'. As in the previous section, the three market equilibrium schedules, IS', LM, and BP, no longer share a common intersection point. Since we do not have a general equilibrium, market forces will move one schedule until it intersects the two others. The question is which one and why? As before, we can note three pairwise intersection points: point A, the original position at the intersection of the LM and BP schedules, point B at the intersection of IS' and LM, and point C at the intersection of IS' and the BP line.

The method of reasoning remains the same: we consider what would happen off the BP line (as in the closed economy case) and ask what will be the reaction of the international financial markets. Note that, as the economy moves from A to B along LM, output increases to meet the higher demand, and money demand rises to finance more transactions. Since the money supply (nominal and real) is by assumption constant, the interest rate must rise to maintain equilibrium in the money market. The higher interest rate, in turn, adversely affects investment spending. This is called the **crowding-out effect**.

At point B, the domestic interest rate i exceeds the foreign rate of return, i^*. This triggers a capital inflow. International investors borrow abroad at the lower rate i^*, and sell the borrowed foreign currency to buy the domestic one, which they invest to reap the better return i. In the foreign exchange market, we observe a sudden rise in the demand for the domestic currency, the exchange rate comes under pressure and an appreciation will occur unless the monetary authorities intervene, which they do. The central bank sells its own currency to meet the higher demand, so M0 rises. The result—see equation (10.12)—is an increase in the money base by the amount of foreign exchange purchased on the foreign exchange market, and an expansion of the money supply M. This implies that the LM curve shifts rightwards. It will do so until it passes through point C where general equilibrium occurs.

The end result is that the demand disturbance does affect output. In particular, this applies to fiscal policy. In contrast with monetary policy, a fiscal expansion, for example an exogenous increase in $\bar{G}$ or a decrease in $\bar{T}$, succeeds in raising output. In fact, the expansionary effect is more powerful in a small open economy than in a closed one since point C is further to the right of point B. The crowding-out effect vanishes, simply because the domestic interest rate cannot depart from the world rate of return. The central bank is forced to expand the money supply as it intervenes on the foreign exchange market to thwart an appreciation.

The role of a fixed exchange rate regime should now be clear. The central bank is committed to intervene in the foreign exchange market whenever any discrepancy between i and i^* triggers capital flows. In doing so, it must change the money supply until domestic and foreign returns are equalized. Graphically, the LM curve passively adjusts to meet the intersection of the IS and BP schedules, restoring general equilibrium. This is simply another aspect of the fact that **monetary independence** is lost under fixed exchange rates. The money supply —and the position of the LM curve—is endogenous and beyond the control of the monetary authorities, unless they restrict capital movements as explained in Box 10.3.

10.6.3 The Policy Mix

The **policy mix** refers to the co-ordinated use of monetary and fiscal policies. An expansionary monetary policy under fixed exchange rates alone does not work, because its tendency to lower the interest rate generates capital outflows which offset the initial expansion. In contrast, an expansionary fiscal policy puts upward pressure on the interest rate and generates capital inflows. When well balanced, a joint fiscal and monetary expansion leaves the interest rate unaffected, as both the IS and LM curves move rightward to point B in Figure 10.15. This is also the point reached in the presence of a fiscal expansion because the central bank is forced to intervene on the foreign exchange market. So, what is the difference between the policy mix and a fiscal expansion? The difference can be found on the asset side of the central bank's balance sheet. On the liability side, in both cases the money base M0 rises. On the asset side, a solo fiscal expansion is

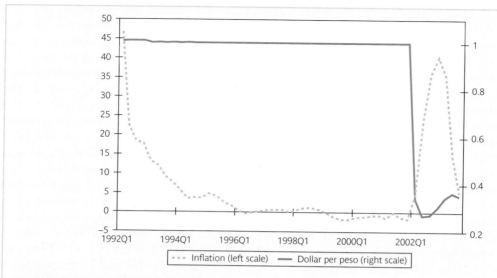

Fig. 10.14 Argentina 1993 – 2003

The exchange rate vis-à-vis the dollar was fixed at the one-for-one parity in 1991. This harnessing of monetary policy allowed a massive declined in the inflation rate, which even turned negative in several years. When the peg was abandoned in late 2001, the exchange rate collapsed and soon afterwards, inflation jumped.

Source: IMF.

accompanied by an increase of foreign exchange reserves F, while in the case of the policy mix the open market operation takes the form of an increase of central bank lending and it is DC that increases.

Thus, under fixed exchange rates, a fiscal expansion forces a monetary expansion. Either the policy mix is agreed *ex ante*, or the central bank will have to let the monetary base increase as it intervenes on the foreign exchange market, increasing its foreign exchange reserves F. Because central banks normally see it as their duty to keep inflation in check—the link between the money supply and

 Box 10.4 Argentina's Fixed Exchange Rate Regime

Throughout its history, Argentina has been crippled by high and ever-rising inflation rates, and in 1990 a high point of 10,000% per annum was reached. While the authorities have repeatedly pledged to eliminate this scourge, powerful vested interests, acting in the background, were making sure that the central bank would not impose the required discipline. In early 1991, the Menem government passed the 'Convertibility Law', tying the peso to the US dollar at the very visible rate of 1 for 1. The fixed exchange rate regime was of the hardest possible variety, called a currency board, explicitly preventing the central bank from increasing the money supply unless it acquired an equal amount of foreign exchange reserves (i.e. closing down open market operations and forfeiting sterilization). Inflation quickly declined; by 1993 it was about the same as in the USA, and stayed that way for the rest of the decade. By the end of the 1990s, however, provincial governments started to run massive budget deficits that the Federal authorities would not or could not rein in. In late 2001, facing acute economic and political instability, the government resigned. Its successor immediately abolished the Convertibility Law that ordinary citizens had viewed as immutable. The exchange rate promptly lost two-thirds of its value, output fell by more than 10%, and inflation was on the rise again.

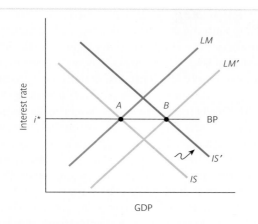

Fig. 10.15 Policy Mix

When both monetary and fiscal policies are combined in an expansionary fashion, the economy moves from point A to point B. While the outcome is the same as with just a fiscal policy expansion (Figure 10.13), in the present case the increase in the monetary supply is achieved through securities purchases by the central bank.

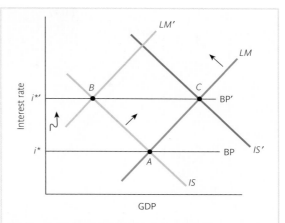

Fig. 10.16 A Financial Disturbance

The increase in the rate of return on foreign assets induces a capital outflow. Under a fixed exchange rate, the central bank intervenes to prevent a depreciation. The money supply contracts and the LM curve shifts to LM′. The new general equilibrium is at point B. Under flexible exchange rates, the exchange rate depreciates. The gain in competitiveness increases the demand for domestic goods. The IS curve shifts to IS′ and equilibrium occurs at point C.

prices is established in Chapter 12—and therefore to retain full control of the money supply, they have good reasons to feel trapped. The 2001 collapse of the fixed exchange rate regime in Argentina, presented in Figure 10.14 and Box 10.4, is a good example of this situation.

10.6.4 International Financial Disturbances

When returns on foreign assets rise exogenously from i^* to $i^{*'}$, the horizontal BP line shifts upwards, as is shown in Figure 10.16. At point A, the initial point of intersection of the IS and LM schedules, both goods and money markets are in equilibrium, but the interest rate is now too low. Capital outflows prompt a foreign exchange intervention by the central bank, the money supply contracts, and the LM curve shifts leftwards until it goes through point B, at the intersection of the IS curve, which has not moved, and the new BP line. This shows that, under a fixed exchange rate regime, the domestic economy is not shielded from international financial disturbances. If interest rates rise worldwide, they must rise at home, which provokes a recession (Y declines). This example illustrates the phenomenon

of *monetary interdependence*. Under fixed exchange rates, changes in foreign interest rates are transmitted directly to domestic interest rates.

10.6.5 How to Think about a Parity Change

We have seen that monetary policy is ineffective as long as the central bank remains committed to a specific exchange rate. That does not mean that monetary policy cannot be used. Most countries that adopt a fixed exchange *regime* allow for adjustments of the exchange rate *level*. If exchange rate changes are possible, some monetary policy independence can be restored.

Discrete, occasional changes in the exchange rate level are called **revaluations** or **devaluations**, depending on the direction on the change.[19] This is done through an official central bank declaration; the monetary authority simply changes the parity rate

---

[19] When the exchange rate floats, its changes are called appreciation or depreciation, see Section 10.7 below.

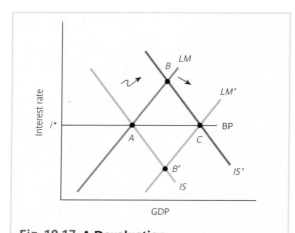

Fig. 10.17 A Devaluation

A devaluation shifts the *IS* curve out to *IS'*. At the same time, the money supply rises as central banks purchase foreign exchange, and the *LM* curve shifts downwards.

at which it stands ready to buy and sell the domestic currency against foreign exchange. Consider the case of a nominal devaluation, a lowering of the nominal exchange rate *S*. For given price levels at home and abroad, the nominal depreciation translates into a real depreciation, a decrease of the real exchange rate $\sigma = SP/P^*$. As competitiveness rises, the primary current account improves and the *IS* curve shifts outwards to *IS'*, to point B in Figure 10.17. We know that, under a fixed exchange rate regime, general equilibrium must occur at the intersection of the *IS* and *BP* schedules, here at point *C*, with the *LM* curve adjusting endogenously. In this case, the *LM* curve shifts rightward to *LM'*. The reason is very interesting. Having decided on a new lower parity, the central bank must weaken the value of its currency, which requires increasing its supply. This is readily done by selling the domestic currency on the foreign exchange market against foreign exchange. The monetary base M0 and the stock of foreign exchange reserves *F* rise, and the money supply *M* expands. This is what the rightward shift of the *LM* curve captures.

We see that a parity change is not merely a declaration of intention by the central bank, it must be backed by action. A devaluation must be accompanied by a monetary expansion, a revaluation by a monetary contraction. Monetary and exchange rate policies are just two sides of the same coin. This important observation qualifies the previous, radical conclusion that monetary policy is lost under fixed exchange rates when capital is freely mobile. A more accurate conclusion is that monetary policy can still be carried out, but through **realignments**— devaluations or revaluations—i.e. by changing the exchange rate level without abandoning the regime itself. Not too much should be made of this opportunity, however, for realignments can trigger powerful speculative attacks that may force giving up the exchange regime altogether, a topic picked up in Chapter 20.

10.7 Output and Interest Rate Determination under Flexible Exchange Rates

10.7.1 Demand Disturbances

An exogenous increase in aggregate demand under flexible exchange rates is shown as the rightward shift of the *IS* curve from *IS* to *IS'* in Figure 10.18. As is now familiar, the economy is not immediately in general equilibrium as the three schedules *IS'*, *LM*, and *BP* no longer pass through a common intersection.

The way to proceed remains the same as before: consider the closed economy equilibrium at the intersection of *IS'* and *LM*, off the *BP* line, and ask what happens to capital flows. Now, however, with a freely floating exchange rate, the central bank does not intervene in the foreign exchange market and can therefore control the money supply. Put differently, the position of the *LM* curve

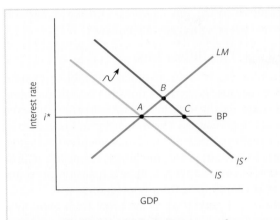

Fig. 10.18 Demand Disturbance under Flexible Exchange Rates

As real demand increases, the *IS* curve shifts rightwards. At point *B*, capital flows in and the exchange rate appreciates (*S* rises). This loss of external competitiveness leads to a fall in net foreign demand for domestic goods until the *IS* curve returns to its initial position *A*. The demand disturbance is 'crowded out'.

is exogenous, reflecting the money supply set by the monetary authorities.

In the present case, we study a pure demand disturbance: the only change is a fiscal policy expansion, the central bank keep the money supply unchanged, so the *LM* curve remains idle. At point *B* the domestic interest rate exceeds the return on foreign assets. Capital flows in and, in the absence of central bank intervention, the exchange rate appreciates (*S* rises). With domestic and foreign prices assumed constant, the real exchange rate also appreciates (σ rises), which hurts competitiveness and leads to a deterioration of the primary current account. Total demand for domestic output declines, and the *IS* curve shifts leftward. This process goes on as long as the domestic interest rate is above the financial integration line: the exchange rate continues to appreciate until the loss in competitiveness has brought the *IS* curve back to the economy's initial position at point *A*. Note, however, that the return to point *A* is not instantaneous because, in contrast to the exchange rate, which responds immediately to capital inflows, the effect

of exchange rate changes on trade and the current account takes time to complete.

We have just found that, under flexible exchange rates, aggregate demand disturbances eventually leave output and the interest rate unaffected, in sharp contrast with the fixed exchange rate case. Increases in domestic demand entirely leak abroad as a result of the loss of competitiveness. Every additional euro of demand expansion originating at home leads to a worsening of the current account by one euro.

The result applies to any of the exogenous components of demand in equation (10.9). In particular, an expansionary fiscal policy—raising public spending or reducing taxes—leads to an exchange rate appreciation and to a worsening of the current account. Similarly, a surge in business optimism and the resulting investment boom has no aggregate demand effect: it simply crowds out net demand in the foreign sector. A boom in exports, for example prompted by a foreign expansion, is matched by a loss of competitiveness which cuts into exports and raises imports, in the end keeping the PCA unchanged. The general conclusion, under flexible exchange rates, is that an economy cannot durably lift itself up via higher domestic or world demand. In the end, under floating exchange rates, *domestic demand impulses are eventually neutralized by exchange rate changes and, beyond a transitory period, the economy is insulated from foreign demand disturbances.*

Note that now it is the *IS* curve which is endogenous and moves to meet the two other schedules, *LM* and *BP*. This is because the position of the *IS* curve depends on the real exchange rate σ, as shown in Section 10.3.4. The value of a floating currency is endogenous, its exchange rate is determined in the foreign exchange market. With sticky domestic and foreign prices the real exchange rate is endogenous as well.

10.7.2 Monetary Policy

A monetary expansion is represented by the shift of the *LM* curve from *LM* to *LM'* in Figure 10.19. We focus initially on the closed economy outcome at point *B*, where the interest rate is lower than foreign returns. As capital flows out, the nominal exchange rate depreciates, which raises external

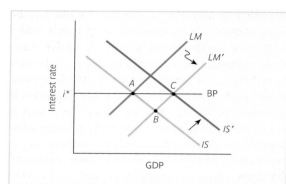

Fig. 10.19 Monetary Policy under Flexible Exchange Rates

An increase in the money supply shifts the *LM* curve to *LM'* from *LM*. At point *B*, with low domestic interest rates, the exchange rate depreciates, which leads to a current account surplus. This shifts the *IS* curve rightwards until local interest rates are equal to the foreign rate of return *i** at point *C*.

competitiveness. The result is an increase in the demand for domestic goods, and the current account improves. Graphically, the *IS* curve shifts to the right until it passes through point *C*.

In contrast to the fixed exchange rate regime, monetary policy is effective under flexible rates. As described, monetary policy works entirely through its effect on the exchange rate and the current account, rather than through the interest rate, which remains governed by foreign returns. Monetary policy is sometimes considered a **beggar-thy-neighbour policy**: it diverts world demand away from foreign goods and towards domestic goods. Beggar-thy-neighbour policies raise opposition from trade partners if the exchange rate depreciation is perceived as being unjustified, merely an attempt to achieve an 'artificial' trade advantage. It is precisely to avoid such tensions, which led to bruising trade fights in the 1930s, that many European countries have long sought to stabilize exchange rates among themselves and ended up adopting a single currency.

The impotence of monetary policy under fixed exchange rates is directly related to the fact that monetary policy is effective under flexible rates precisely because it works through exchange rate changes. In the end, monetary policy is just the other side of exchange rate policy.[20]

10.7.3 The Policy Mix

Fiscal policy is ineffective under flexible exchange rates because it exerts an upward pressure on interest rates and the resulting capital inflows lead to a currency appreciation. The monetary authorities may prevent this exchange rate movement by changing the money supply. A monetary expansion appropriately coupled with a fiscal expansion prevents the exchange rate from appreciating. This case is shown in Figure 10.15 as the move from point *A* to point *B*: the *IS* curve shifts to *IS'* as the result of the fiscal expansion while the supporting effect of monetary policy shifts the *LM* curve to *LM'*, and both schedules intersect the *BP* line at the same point. This prevents the appreciation that fiscal policy alone provokes; the additional spending generated by the fiscal expansion materializes at home instead of leaking abroad.

Comparing Figure 10.15 and Figure 10.19, we may be tempted to see no difference between a combined fiscal and monetary policy mix and just monetary policy. That would ignore what goes on in the background. When an expansionary monetary policy is used alone, the exchange rate depreciates: world demand is shifted towards domestic goods, and it is the primary account improvement that boosts demand for domestic goods. With the policy mix, the exchange rate remains unchanged; in this case, the expansionary effect originates in domestic demand while the current account deteriorates. Does it matter? In many ways, it does. To start with, the firms that benefit from a monetary expansion are those that are export oriented, while the policy mix favours firms that cater primarily to domestic customers. Then note that the depreciation, which boosts competitiveness, is good news for businesses but bad news for consumers who face higher prices for the imported goods that they purchase. Finally, while the policy mix leaves the exchange rate

---

[20] If capital controls are in place, or if financial integration is incomplete, the domestic interest rate can depart somewhat from the foreign rate of return. In particular, part of the effect of monetary policy may come through a decline in interest rates.

unchanged, the fact that a monetary policy expansion operates by making domestic firms more competitive implies that foreign competitors are hurt around the world. This is often seen as unfair and frowned upon by trade partners. We will revisit this issue in Chapter 20.

10.7.4 International Financial Disturbances

The effect of an increase in returns on foreign assets (i^*) was described in Figure 10.16 for the case of fixed exchange rates. The same diagram can be used to understand what happens under flexible exchange rates. As before, capital flows out to take advantage of better returns abroad, but now the exchange rate is free to depreciate. The country's external competitiveness and current account improve. The IS curve shifts to the right until it goes through point C.

This disturbance could correspond to a situation where the 'rest of the world' adopts a stricter monetary policy. The rest of the world can be thought of as a large closed economy (it only trades with us, a small open economy). As its LM curve shifts to the left, the interest rate i^* rises and foreign GDP declines. At home, in contrast, the GDP rises, as we have just seen. This is just another instance of the beggar-thy-neighbour effect, except that it now works in reverse: the monetary contraction abroad has an expansionary effect at home, which results from the fact that their exchange rate appreciation is our depreciation. In contrast, under fixed exchange rates, we saw in Section 10.6.4 that the domestic GDP declines following a monetary contraction abroad (point B in Figure 10.16). Foreign monetary policy has the same qualitative effect on foreign and domestic GDPs under fixed exchange rates—the transmission is said to be positive—and the opposite effect under flexible rates—a negative transmission. This feature is important for international monetary cooperation.

10.8 Fixed versus Flexible Rates: A Wrap-Up

This chapter shows just how important is the exchange rate regime for the way in which a small open economy reacts to disturbances, intended (policy measures) or not. It also shows that the exchange rate regime is best understood through the prism of monetary policy. A central bank can control the evolution of the money supply or the nominal exchange rate, not both. Table 10.4 summarizes these aspects.

A fixed exchange rate regime implies a commitment to shun the active use of monetary policy. The exchange rate anchor imposes a tight discipline on the monetary authorities, but leaves the economy vulnerable to demand disturbances, both domestic and foreign. Many countries in Europe (e.g. France and Italy) in the 1980s and in Latin America (e.g. Argentina and Brazil) in the 1990s have followed this strategy. Yet, fiscal policy too needs to be disciplined; if it is not, large budget deficits translate into large PCA deficits and the external debt eventually becomes unmanageable.[21] When this occurs, the exchange regime comes under threat, and with it its disciplinary influence. This was clearly the experience in Argentina, as Box 10.4 argues.

When the exchange rate floats freely, there is no restriction imposed on the central bank's behaviour, and monetary independence is preserved. Furthermore, the economy as a whole is shielded from real demand disturbances. Among the countries that adopt the freely floating exchange rate regime are those that have developed sufficient economic and political stability to entrust the central bank with the task of delivering price stability. This is the case of the United States, the Euro-zone,

---

[21] The link between fiscal and external deficits is clear from the accounting identity (2.7): PCA = $(S - I) + (T - G)$. The link between deficits and debt is shown in Chapter 5.

Table 10.4 The Mundell–Fleming Model: A Summary

Exchange rate regime	Fixed exchange rates	Flexible exchange rates
Effect on real GDP of:		
Fiscal policy expansion	Increase	No effect
Monetary policy expansion	No effect	Increase
Increase in foreign interest rate	Decrease	Increase
Exogenous monetary policy instrument	Exchange rate	Money supply
Endogenous monetary policy instrument	Money supply	Exchange rate

the United Kingdom, Switzerland, and many more. Other countries let their exchange rate float for the opposite reason, because inflation is so high that any peg would quickly lead to overvaluation.[22] Yet other floaters are countries that have been bruised by speculative attacks against a previous peg; this is the case, among others, of Argentina, Brazil, Chile, Russia, and many other countries.

❶ Summary

1 The Mundell–Fleming model, an extension of the *IS-LM* model to the open economy, describes the simultaneous equilibrium of three markets: the market for goods and services, the domestic money market, and the international financial market.

2 The Mundell–Fleming model adopts the Keynesian assumption that prices are sticky. In this case, output is driven by demand.

3 The primary current account improves when income and output in the rest of the world expands and the real exchange depreciates, and worsens when the domestic GDP and absorption rise at home.

4 An autonomous increase in demand for domestic goods triggers a multiplier mechanism: more demand means more output, and more output means a higher income and hence a new round of demand increases. The multiplier process is dampened by leakages in the income-demand chain: savings, taxes, and imports.

5 The *IS* curve represents the GDP level and real interest rates compatible with equilibrium in the market for goods and services. It is downward sloping because a higher interest rate reduces domestic demand and output. The *IS* curve is flatter, the more sensitive demand is to the interest rate, and the larger is the multiplier.

6 The *LM* curve represents the GDP level and real interest rates compatible with equilibrium in the domestic money market. It is upward sloping because a higher GDP level raises the demand for money. A higher interest rate is necessary to bring money demand back to an unchanged (by assumption) supply, which reduces domestic demand for goods and services. The *LM* curve is steeper the more sensitive money demand is to output and the less sensitive it is to the interest rate.

7 The *BP* line reflects the interest rate parity condition. This condition reflects the working of the international financial market which equalizes returns on similar assets. The interest rate parity

---

[22] Recall that the real exchange rate is SP/P^*. With S fixed, if P rises faster than P^*, the real exchange rate appreciates.

condition does not always hold in the case of limited international capital mobility—for example because of capital controls.

8 Bringing together the three schedules permits one to study the general macroeconomic equilibrium, when all three markets are simultaneously in equilibrium.

9 When a country's financial markets are well integrated in world markets, the domestic interest rate is tied to worldwide financial conditions. Under conditions of complete capital mobility, a third equilibrium condition requires the domestic interest rate to be equal to the world rate of return.

10 When the exchange rate is fixed, demand disturbances affect domestic GDP while monetary disturbances, including fiscal policy, have no effect on real GDP. The exchange rate is set exogenously and the money supply becomes endogenous, hence the *LM* curve moves to meet the *IS* and *BP* schedules.

11 When the exchange rate is freely floating, the economy is shielded from demand disturbances, while monetary policy is effective. The exchange rate is now endogenous while the central bank is able to set money supply exogenously. It is the *IS* curve that moves to meet the *LM* and *BP* schedules.

12 Monetary and exchange rate policies are just two side of the same coin: the central bank can control the money supply or the exchange rate, not both. Under fixed exchange rates, the central bank controls the exchange rate and must give up the control money supply, under flexible rate regime it retains control of the money supply and lets the exchange rate be determined by the market.

13 The choice of an exchange rate regime involves trade-offs. Different countries choose different regimes, and often change their regimes depending on circumstances.

🔑 Key Concepts

- Keynesian model
- small open economy
- Mundell–Fleming model
- general equilibrium
- exchange rate regime
- consumption function, investment function
- import, export, and PCA functions
- desired demand function
- goods market equilibrium
- equilibrium GDP
- Keynesian demand multiplier
- *IS* curve
- excess supply/demand
- interest parity condition
- money market intervention

- *LM* curve
- interest rate parity condition
- balance of payments (BP) line
- exchange market intervention
- foreign exchange reserves
- sterilized and unsterilized interventions
- capital controls
- crowding-out effect
- monetary independence
- revaluation/devaluation
- realignment
- policy mix
- revaluation, devaluation
- beggar-thy-neighbour policies

❓ Exercises

1 The *IS*, *LM*, and financial integration curves define six regions in Figure 10.11. Any position off a curve corresponds to market disequilibrium which can be characterized as excess demand or supply in either goods or money markets or short-term capital inflow or outflow. Define each region accordingly, e.g. excess demand in the goods market and excess supply in the money market.

2 Why do leaks out of income into spending flatten the desired demand schedule? Show graphically that, the steeper the desired demand schedule, the larger is the Keynesian multiplier.

3 Desired demand (*DD*) is represented by the following simplified function:

$$DD = 3,000 + 0.8(Y - T) + G - 100i - 500S.$$

Domestic and foreign price levels have been assumed constant and equal to one. Let $i = 5\%$ throughout. Initially $G = T = 3,000$. S is the nominal exchange rate and is assumed fixed at one.

(a) Compute the effect on GDP of an increase in T from 3,000 to 3,500. Show your result graphically. What is the value of the lump-sum tax multiplier?

(b) Compute the effect on GDP of an increase in G from 3,000 to 3,500. Show your result graphically. What is the value of the government spending multiplier?

(c) Compute the net effect on GDP when both G and T increase by the same amount, from 3,000 to 3,500. Show your result graphically. What is the value of the balanced budget multiplier? Compare your answers and discuss.

4 Suppose the demand for real money balances has the form $L(Y, i, c) = 0.5Y - 300i + 50c$. Let $P = 1$, $M = 2,500$ and $C = 10$. Plot the *LM* curve in the i, Y diagram. What is the effect of an increase in C from 10 to 20 on the *LM* curve? What is the effect of an increase in the price level from $P = 1$ to $P = 2$, holding $C = 10$? Of $M = 2,500$ to $M = 3,000$?

5 Using the *IS* and *LM* curves from Exercises 3 and 4, consider a fixed exchange rate regime with $\bar{S} = 1$ and $i^* = 10$.

(a) Find the equilibrium interest rate and real GDP. What is the equilibrium value of the nominal money supply? Explain.

(b) What is the effect of an increase in government expenditure from 3,000 to 3,500? What happens to the money supply as a result? Explain in words how the central bank allows this to occur.

6 Suppose the exchange rate in Problems 3 and 4 is fixed at 0.5, and the economy is at equilibrium $(i = i^* = 10)$. Assess the effect of an increase in the foreign interest rate i^* to 15 on equilibrium output and interest rates. If the exchange rate is allowed to float and M/P is exogenous, how will your answer change?

7 Using the *IS* and *LM* curves from Exercises 3 and 4, consider now a flexible exchange rate regime with $\bar{i}^* = 10$.

(a) Solve for the equilibrium interest rate and real GDP. Explain the differences with your answer to 4(a).

(b) What is the effect now of an increase in government expenditure from 3,000 to 3,500? How does your answer change if the money supply is increased at the same time from 3,500 to 4,000?

(c) What is the effect of an increase in taxes from 3,000 to 3,500, all other things held equal? Give your answer for both flexible and fixed exchange rate regimes, and in the latter assume $S = 1$.

8 Use the Mundell–Fleming model under flexible exchange rates to explain what happens when the demand for money exogenously declines, for instance because citizens fear economic or political instability. Same question when the exchange rate is fixed.

9 We can think of the European monetary union as a group of open countries with irrevocably fixed exchange rates. What happens if one country embarks on an expansionary fiscal policy while the central bank does not change the supply of money? Describe the effects in the country in question and in the other countries.

10 In troubled times, some currencies like the Swiss franc face a safe-haven effect whereby some international investors care less about returns than in normal times. Use the Mundell–Fleming to evaluate the impact of such a phenomenon on a safe-haven small open economy with a flexible exchange rate.

➔ Essay Questions

1 Those European countries that have joined the monetary union have delegated their monetary policies to the European Central Bank, a huge sacrifice of national sovereignty, it seems. On the other hand, they were previously members of the European Monetary System, pegging their exchange rates to each other. Evaluate the economic loss of sovereignty of Euro-area membership. [Think of both fiscal and monetary policies.]

2 Some countries seem to need to adopt a fixed exchange rate regime to discipline their monetary policies. Why might it be difficult for central banks to be disciplined on their own?

3 There are many ways of conducting an expansionary fiscal policy: raising public spending, cutting income taxes, profit taxes, or VAT. What difference does it make for different groups in the country? In your discussion, as you take a general equilibrium view of the question, look at the two possible exchange rate regimes.

4 The behaviour of inventories is a closely watched indicator of the state of the economy. Discuss under which conditions it is a valid indicator of things to come. In particular, does an increase in inventories signal an economic slowdown or a boom? (Hint: change in inventories can be either intended or unintended.)

5 Emerging market countries typically have to offer a risk premium when they borrow. This means that their domestic interest rates are higher than those abroad. What is the impact of a sudden loss of trust? Discuss the reasons why this could happen and what are, in each case, the policy options.

Output, Employment, and Prices

11

11.1 Overview 262

11.2 The *IS-LM* Model 263
    11.2.1 The Goods Market and the *IS* Curve 263
    11.2.2 The Money Market and the *LM* Curve 263
    11.2.3 Goods and Money Market Equilibrium 264

11.3 General Equilibrium 264
    11.3.1 Output and the Labour Market 264
    11.3.2 General Equilibrium Determination of Output, Interest Rates, and Prices 265
    11.3.3 Do Demand and Supply Always Meet? 266

11.4 General Equilibrium with Flexible Prices: The Neoclassical Case 268
    11.4.1 Supply-Determined Output 268
    11.4.2 Dichotomy and Money Neutrality 269

11.5 General Equilibrium with Sticky Prices: The Keynesian Case 272
    11.5.1 Demand-Determined Output 272
    11.5.2 Non-neutrality of Money 275

Summary 276

At the core of the Keynesian polemics . . . is the relationship between price flexibility and full employment. The fundamental argument of Keynes is directed against the belief that price flexibility can be depended upon to generate full employment automatically. The defenders of the classical tradition, on the other hand, still insist upon this automaticity as a basic tenet.

—Don Patinkin[1]

11.1 Overview

This chapter presents a more technical analysis of the small open-economy general equilibrium model presented in Chapter 10. The main purpose is to examine the contrast between the sticky-price version, the Keynesian model, and the flexible-price version, the neoclassical model. There are two good reasons to undertake such an analysis. First, it is not literally true that prices are sticky; this is precisely why it is called an assumption. It is helpful, therefore, to understand the implications of this assumption. Second, even though the assumption is a convenient short-cut to think about the short run, say, for two or three years, it is clearly not tenable in the long run. The flexible-price version thus provides the tool to understanding the long run. Finally, the Keynesian assumption is controversial. A number of economists argue that it is not even acceptable in the short run. In fact, Keynes himself emphasized that his intention was to challenge the then-dominant school of thought, which he dubbed 'the classics'. Today's neoclassics pursue the defence of the flexible-price assumption which, as we will see, leads to radically different conclusions concerning both the behaviour of the macroeconomy and the role of governments and central banks.[2]

Controversies can be fun, but they can also be disturbing. If macroeconomists profoundly disagree,

what good is their science? Keynesians argue that the short run extends to several years, precisely the horizon over which fiscal and monetary policy can play a useful role. Neoclassical macroeconomists argue that the short run is too brief to be worth the attention that it receives and, most importantly, too flimsy to justify policy interventions, which they see as a source of unnecessary disturbances. In fact, not too much should be made of these professional debates.[3] This chapter presents the **neoclassical synthesis**, the view that the Keynesian model is acceptable in the short run while the neoclassical model is appropriate for the long run. It implies that macroeconomic policies have a useful role to play but that their limits ought to be well recognized.

Chapters 10 and 11 partly overlap. Both use the *IS-LM* framework, but differ in important respects. In Chapter 11 the accent is on the logics of the framework, while Chapter 10 focuses on its practical use. Second, Chapter 10 considers mainly the case of the closed economy while Chapter 11 analyses the case of a small open economy, which trades goods, services, and assets with the rest of the world. Chapter 11 is self-contained as it briefly presents the *IS-LM* framework again, though skipping most of the details. It innovates in introducing a new market, the labour market. This addition is needed to deal with prices, which must now be made endogenous. This is why the international financial market—the *BP* line in Chapter 10—is dropped for

---

[1] Born and trained in Chicago, Don Patinkin (1992–95) was an Israeli economist who more than anyone else contributed to the synthesis between the work of Keynes and the classics. In a number of papers and books, Patinkin showed the conditions under which the flexibility of prices could restore the classical equilibrium and eliminate unemployment.

[2] The most recent reincarnation of the classical school of thought, called the real business-cycle approach is further studied in Chapter 14.

[3] Why 'neo' and not just 'classical'? Because the classical approach, in existence before Keynes's assault, has since been extended to allow for interactions between the goods and money market, i.e. it incorporates the *IS-LM* analysis developed by Keynes and his successors.

the sake of keeping the level of complexity under control.

This chapter establishes a number of principles. First, it shows that when all prices, including wages, are flexible, the GDP is determined by the supply side. Demand-side disturbances, the usual source of business cycles, have no effect. Second, with full price flexibility, there is a complete separa-tion between the real and the nominal sides. This dichotomy leads to the proposition that money is neutral, it does not have any real effect. Third, when prices are rigid—or sticky as often said—the dichotomy breaks down and there are numerous interactions between the real and nominal sides, which is precisely what the IS-LM model allows us to study.

11.2 The *IS-LM* Model

11.2.1 The Goods Market and the *IS* Curve

In a closed economy, the GDP consists of private consumption, investment, and government pur-chases. In the 'first period', this can be written as

(11.1) $Y = C + I + G.$

Using the assumed behaviour of the various com-ponents of private demand, presented in Chapter 10, we can derive the desired demand function which provides the right-hand side of the goods market equilibrium condition:

(11.2) $\underset{\text{supply}}{Y} = \underset{\text{desired demand}}{C(\bar{\Omega}, Y - \bar{T}) + I(i) + \bar{G}}.$

where the overbar symbol reminds us that private wealth $\bar{\Omega}$, public spending $\bar{G}$, and taxes $\bar{T}$ are taken as exogenous.[4]

How is equilibrium, the equality between demand and supply of goods and services, achieved? This is where the two approaches sharply differ. In the Keynesian approach, prices are taken to be sticky, so equilibrium is achieved when supply Y passively adjusts to demand, the right-hand side of (11.2). In the classical approach, instead, prices are flexible and can perform the equilibrating task. When desired demand exceeds supply, for instance, prices rise to whatever extent is necessary to achieve equilibrium between demand and supply. How price changes affect both supply and demand is one of the main questions studied in this chapter. This is the subject of Section 11.4.

In this section, we do not yet deal with the question of how equilibrium is achieved. We start with the sim-pler question of what the equilibrium looks like when it is achieved. More precisely, we seek values of the interest rate and output for which (11.2) holds, that is, when the goods market is in equilibrium. We do so taking the price level as given, assuming that the inflation rate is zero. With this assumption, the nominal interest rate i is equal to the real interest rate r. Later on, of course, we will relax this assumption.

In fact, using the 45° diagram presented in Chapter 10, we can define equilibrium GDP and, by changing the interest rate, we can find, as we did, that equilibrium GDP declines when the interest rate increases. This provides the downward-sloping **IS curve** in Figure 11.1.

11.2.2 The Money Market and the *LM* Curve

As in Chapter 10, we imagine that the central bank decides on the nominal money supply and we denote this level $\bar{M}$. Because, for the time being, the price level P is taken as constant, the central bank also sets the real money supply $\bar{M}/P$. Money demand is pre-sumed to rise with real GDP and to decline when the interest rate rises. **Money market equilibrium** is achieved when the exogenous supply and demand for money are equal:

(11.3) $\bar{M}/P = L(Y, i)$

---

[4]   For simplicity, Tobin's q is dropped from the investment function. The determinants of output (aggregate supply) are discussed in Ch. 3.

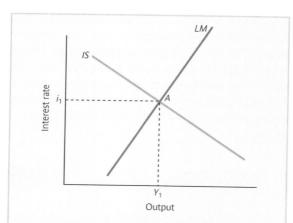

Fig. 11.1 Goods and Money Market Equilibrium

The *IS* curve describes the output and interest rate levels compatible with equilibrium in the goods market. Similarly, along the *LM* curve, the money market is in equilibrium. At point *A* both markets are simultaneously in equilibrium: there is just one such point, and just one combination of output and the interest rate.

This condition is represented in Figure 11.1 as the **LM curve**. It is upward sloping because an increase in GDP, which raises real money demand, must be matched by an increase in the interest rate sufficient to bring demand back to the exogenously set real money supply.

11.2.3 Goods and Money Market Equilibrium

Both markets are simultaneously in equilibrium at the intersection of the *IS* and *LM* curves in Figure 11.1. Given the price level and the other exogenous variables, there is *one* interest rate and *one* level of GDP compatible with equilibrium in both markets.

The *IS-LM* diagram alone describes a general equilibrium only under a number of restrictive assumptions that we made along the way. In particular, the price level was taken as exogenous and constant. The Keynesian approach stops here. It acknowledges that over time prices do change but does not deal with this question. The classical approach, which rejects the sticky price assumption, must go further. It argues that firms do not *have to* adjust supply to demand. They will do so only if it is in their interest. But then, we need to understand how firms deal with this question. Naturally, this makes things rather more complicated. This is what we now proceed to examine.

11.3 General Equilibrium

11.3.1 Output and the Labour Market

If firms are choosing how much to produce, we need to analyse their behaviour in detail. To that effect we use the usual microeconomic principles of firm theory, which have been reviewed in Chapter 3. An important input in firms' decision is the cost of labour. This brings into centre stage the labour market, which was studied closely in Chapter 4. Thus we now draw on both chapters and recall some key results in Figure 11.2.

The leftmost panel represents the labour market. Labour demand is downward sloping to reflect the fact that, given the existing capital stock—existing factories, equipment, etc.—additional labour is increasingly less productive, a manifestation of the principle of declining marginal productivity.[5] There are two labour supply schedules. The household labour supply schedule is upward sloping, to capture the labour–leisure trade-offs: people are willing to work longer hours for higher real wages and more people are willing to work when the real

---

5 Microeconomic principles state that labour demand is such that the real wage is set equal to the (marginal) productivity of labour. As productivity declines, so does the real wage that firms are willing to pay.

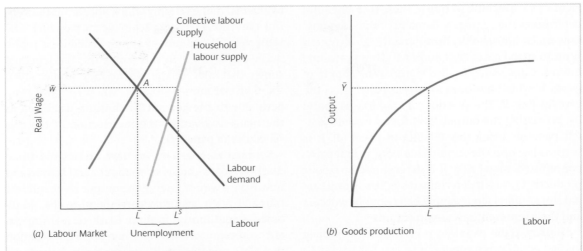

Fig. 11.2 Output and Employment

Wages adjust to establish equilibrium in the labour market at point A (panel (a)). This determines the amount of labour used by firms. Given the stock of capital, output is fully determined by employment by the production function (panel (b)).

wage rises. The collective labour supply schedule describes collective wage negotiations. It lies above the individual schedule to recognize that, collectively, workers or their representatives use their bargaining power to achieve a better deal for those employed, further trading off more jobs or longer hours against higher real wages. If real wages freely adjust to equilibrate demand and supply, the market settles at point A, with real wages at $\bar{w}$ and employment $\bar{L}$, determined by employers' demand. At this real wage level, the supply of labour is L^S, so unemployment is $L^S - \bar{L}$.

The rightmost panel of Figure 11.2 displays the production function of the economy, for a given stock of capital, which is taken as exogenous.[6] It shows that more output can be produced using more labour input, but with decreasing effects, another

implication of the principle of declining marginal productivity. At the real wage determined in the labour market (panel (a)), firms hire a level $\bar{L}$ of employment (man-hours) and produce $\bar{Y}$. The key point here is that equilibrium in the labour market determines the equilibrium level of output supplied by firms.

11.3.2 General Equilibrium Determination of Output, Interest Rates, and Prices

Figure 11.3 brings all the results of the previous sections together in a single framework. It now deals with three markets: the market for goods and services, the money market, and the labour market. The result is a more complete, and of course more complicated, general equilibrium than the one presented in Chapter 10. Panels (a) and (b) in the left part of the figure, which depicts the supply side, reproduce Figure 11.2. They show how equilibrium in the labour market determines today's output Y. This is the level of output that firms are willing to supply at current nominal wages and prices. The top centre panel (c) shows the IS and LM schedules of

---

[6] The capital stock increases over time as the result of investment spending. Thus the long-run analysis carried out here is not truly long-run. The evolution of capital over time belongs to growth theory, which is presented in Chapter 18. For the sake of simplicity, this important question is ignored here.

Figure 11.1. The intersection of these two schedules determines the aggregate demand of the economy: how much households, firms, and the government want to spend on today's output Y given prevailing interest rates. Panel (c) also features the supply of goods Ȳ, which has been drawn in panel (b) as the vertical line S. The position of this line is found by 'reflecting' the output level found in the lower left panel (b) using the 45° line in panel (d). It is vertical because the supply side here is independent of the demand side: it is determined by labour productivity—itself determined by the existing capital stock—and labour supply behaviour of workers and their representative organizations.

The top right panel (e) reproduces the money market equilibrium condition shown in Chapter 10 and links the interest rate to the real supply of money M/P. So far we have taken the price level as given and constant, but now comes the time to relax this assumption. We wish to allow the price level to vary and we need to worry about its effect. The place to start is with the real supply of money M/P. As long as the price level is constant, the nominal and real money supply behaves identically. But the central bank controls the nominal, not the real, money supply. Yet money demand is properly defined as a demand for real cash balances—we care about the purchasing power of money that we hold—and this is indeed what appears in panel (e). Now, given the nominal money stock M̄ set by the central bank, the higher the price level the lower is the real money supply M̄/P. Put differently, when prices rise the purchasing power of money declines. This inverse relationship between the real money supply and the price level is represented in panel (f) by the M̄M̄ schedule.[7]

This allows us to find the price level that is compatible with a general equilibrium in the case where it is endogenous. Panel (c) has already determined the output level and interest rates compatible with a general equilibrium in the now usual IS-LM fashion. The position of the LM curve is determined

by the real money supply which appears as the vertical real money supply schedule in panel (e). The same vertical real money supply schedule is reproduced in panel (f). In this panel, the M̄M̄ schedule shows the value of the real money supply given the nominal money stock M̄. The price level compatible with the general equilibrium described in the figure is given by the intersection of the two schedules in panel (f).

Summarizing so far, we have considered three markets (goods and services, money and labour) and now have a way of finding the output level, interest rate and price level that correspond to the simultaneous equilibrium in these markets. It is important to recognize that there has been no assertion that the price level is *explained*—or caused—by the conditions described. Causality would imply that the price level is endogenous, an assertion not made, not yet. Much as the IS-LM-BP model of Chapter 10 can be used with different assumptions of what variables are endogenous and which ones are exogenous, depending on the exchange rate regime, the general equilibrium described in Figure 11.3 will serve us to distinguish between the Keynesian case where the price level P is exogenous and the neoclassical case where it is endogenous.

11.3.3 Do Demand and Supply Always Meet?

Panels (a) and (b) in Figure 11.3 describe the supply side of the economy. They show the output level that firms wish to produce given conditions on the labour market. Panel (c) shows the level of output that is compatible with the spending patterns, the desired demand. These two output levels are derived independently from each other; there is no reason that they be equal. As drawn, the IS and LM curves intersect at point A on the supply line S that is 'projected' via panel (d) from the supply side, so that demand and supply are indeed equal. This is an instance of simultaneous equilibrium in all three markets. Is it necessarily the case?

Figure 11.4 shows an instance where aggregate demand—given by the intersection of IS and LM schedules—differs from supply Ȳ, the outcome delivered by equilibrium in the labour market *via*

[7] Mathematically astute readers will recognize the positive branch of the hyperbola $m = M/P$ linking the real money supply m given the nominal supply M.

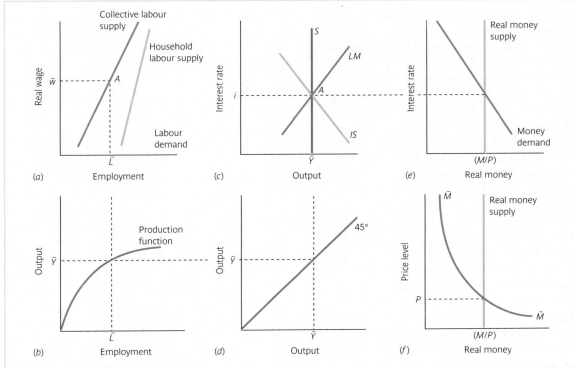

Fig. 11.3 General Equilibrium

When real wages are fully flexible, they adjust to clear the labour market at point A (panel (a)). This determines the amount of labour used by firms. Given the stock of capital, the level of output is fully determined by employment as shown in panel (b). Using the 45° line in panel (d), the level of output that firms intend to supply is shown as the economy's vertical supply schedule S in panel (c). Panels (e) and (f) show the money market and the corresponding price level. At point A in panel (c), all three markets (labour, goods, money) are simultaneously in equilibrium. This is called the general equilibrium of the economy.

the production function. This situation is represented by point B in panel (c). We find that, when we look at two of three markets, here the goods and money markets, the equilibrium output may well be different from the one that corresponds to equilibrium in the third market, here the labour market. Indeed point B lies to the left of the S curve, demand is less than supply. We could instead consider the output level that corresponds to equilibrium in the goods and labour markets, at the intersection of the IS and S schedules in panel (c). This intersection is point A, and it lies off the LM curve, a situation of excess demand in the money market. Similarly,

simultaneous equilibrium in the money and labour markets occurs at point C off the IS curve, now income $\bar{Y}$ exceeds the demand for goods.

So, do we need a lot of luck for all three markets to be in equilibrium at the same time, as in Figure 11.3? Not really. The situation just described cannot last because the market that is in disequilibrium will trigger reactions that will deliver the general equilibrium. Which reactions will be triggered depends on what variables we take as endogenous, and this is where Keynesians and neoclassics part company. This is what the rest of this chapter examines.

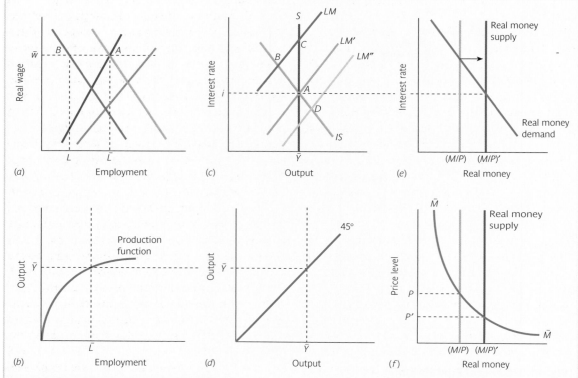

Fig. 11.4 The Role of the Price Level

When the three schedules do not go through the same point as shown in panel (c), the price level adjusts and affects the real value ($\bar{M}/P$) of a given stock of nominal money supply. The result is a shift in the LM curve until it passes through the point where the supply and IS schedules intersect. At point B demand falls short of supply, so a reduction of the price level is needed to shift the LM curve to the right. Conversely, at point D supply falls short of demand, which is curtailed when the real money supply decreases following an increase in the price level. At point A equilibrium obtains in goods, money, and labour markets.

11.4 General Equilibrium with Flexible Prices: The Neoclassical Case

11.4.1 Supply-Determined Output

In the neoclassical view, it is the price level that is endogenous and plays the equilibrating role. This section studies the role of the price level and shows that, when it is fully flexible, all three markets are always jointly in equilibrium. To see that, we start at point B in Figure 11.4, where the level of demand and income compatible with goods and money equilibrium Y is less than output $\bar{Y}$ produced and supplied by firms, given labour market equilibrium. With excess supply, it seems reasonable to imagine that a decrease in the price level can restore equilibrium.

What, then, is the effect of a reduction in the price level from P to P'? At unchanged nominal money supply $\bar{M}$, the real money supply $\bar{M}/P'$ increases, as is shown in panel (f). This means that the vertical money supply line shifts to the right in this panel and therefore in panel (e) as well. To a larger real money supply corresponds a new LM curve somewhere on the right of the initial one in panel (c). If the price decline is just right, the new LM curve is LM'. Thus we have found that there exists a price level P' low enough for the LM curve to go through point A, where general equilibrium is achieved.

That this is possible does not mean that it will happen, though. To see why it will indeed happen, go back to the initial disequilibrium point B. Firms produce $\bar{Y}$ but the market demand is weaker. For a while firms accumulate inventories, but they obviously cannot do that forever. Sooner or later, they must do something about it. The neoclassical approach assumes that they will cut prices to encourage demand. As they do, the LM curve shifts to the right—provided, of course, that the central bank does not change the money supply—and the firms will continue cutting prices until it has moved to the position LM'. Price flexibility restores general equilibrium.

The complete story is a bit more complicated, but the complication is well worth getting into. We need to wonder what happens in the labour market when the price level declines. We have assumed that nothing happens, so output remains at $\bar{Y}$ and employment stays at $\bar{L}$. For that to be the case, we also need to assume that real wages remain unchanged at $\bar{w}$, as a quick look at panels (a) and (b) readily confirm. For real wages $w = W/P$ to remain constant in the face of a declining price level P, it must be that nominal wages W decline proportionately. *This observation shows that, for the neoclassical approach to work, it is not just the price level that must be flexible, but all 'prices'.* This includes the price of labour, nominal wages, but also the price of foreign currency, the nominal exchange rate. If one of these prices is sticky, the whole process breaks down. For example, if nominal wages cannot decline—in

many countries firms cannot reduce wages—then the real wage will increase when the price level falls and labour market will no longer be in equilibrium. Similarly, if the nominal exchange rate is fixed in an open economy, a price decline will result in a real appreciation, the PCA will improve and the IS curve will shift to the right of the S line in panel (c), again preventing general equilibrium from occurring. That nominal wages are sticky, at least downward, was at the centre of Keynes's critique of classical economics. That the nominal exchange rate must adjust explains why neoclassical economists advocate the flexible exchange rate regime.

This analysis suggests two important conclusions. First, when all prices adjust freely, the economy's general equilibrium is found along the goods supply schedule S in panel (c). The S schedule represents the supply side of the economy so we find that, under full price flexibility, output is supply determined.

The second conclusion is that price adjustments restore equilibrium through the real value of money. By changing the volume of real balances, changes in the price level shift the LM curve until it goes through the intersection of the supply and IS schedules. In the case of point B, i.e. a situation where demand is weak relative to what firms are prepared to supply, a fall in the price level is needed to raise the real value of money. This in turn leads to a lower interest rate, and a higher level of aggregate demand. A similar story can be told for the case in which aggregate demand exceeds aggregate supply. If the IS and LM curves were to intersect at point D, an increase in the price level would be required to restore equilibrium, by reducing real money balances, raising the interest rate and slowing consumption and investment spending.

11.4.2 Dichotomy and Money Neutrality

The neoclassical assumption that all prices are flexible leads to the very important conclusion that nominal and real variables do not affect each other. More precisely, two results follow:

1 Real variables (real GDP, employment, relative prices, including the real exchange rate) are unaffected by the level of the money supply.

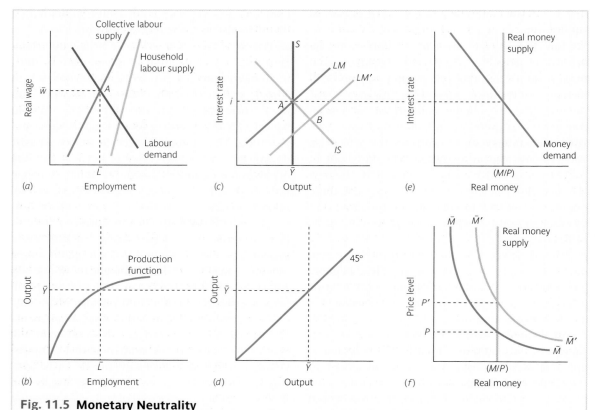

Fig. 11.5 Monetary Neutrality

An increase in the nominal money supply causes a shift from $\bar{M}\bar{M}$ to $\bar{M}'\bar{M}'$ which leads to a proportional increase in the price level. All real variables are unchanged.

2 Changes in the money supply affect *all* nominal variables (i.e. those denominated in terms of the domestic currency) by the same proportion.[8]

The reason that lies behind the first result can be seen by returning to Figure 11.4. The general equilibrium is found at the intersection of the S and IS schedules. Since the price level P is endogenous, so is the real money supply $\bar{M}/P$ and therefore the LM curve as well. Indeed, under the assumption that it

is fully flexible, the price level adjusts until the LM curve meets the two other schedules. Now note that the IS and S schedules both describe the real side of the economy, respectively the goods market and the labour market, while the LM curve describes the nominal side of the economy, the money market. The general equilibrium is entirely determined by the real side.

To understand the second result, we ask what happens if, starting from general equilibrium at point A in Figure 11.5, the central bank allows the nominal money supply to increase from $\bar{M}$ to $\bar{M}'$. What would happen if the price level were to remain unchanged? Following the increase in the nominal money supply, this would mean an

---

[8] We already encountered this property in Chapter 8 when we found that, in the long run, inflation is directly driven by the rate of money growth, the Fisher principle, and PPP. We will soon see that this is the same result.

increase in the real money supply and a rightward shift of the LM curve to LM′ in panel (c). Point B, at the intersection of the IS and LM′ implies a level of desired demand that exceeds supply $\bar{Y}$. The neoclassical assumption is that the price level will rise to eliminate the excess demand, and this requires that the LM curve returns to its initial position. This means that the real money supply, which determines the position of the LM curve, remains unchanged. The only effect of the nominal money supply increase in the six panels, therefore, is found in panel (f) where the $\bar{M}\bar{M}$ curve shifts out to $\bar{M}'\bar{M}'$. With a constant real money supply, the price level must rise by the same proportion as M, to P′ such that $\bar{M}/P = \bar{M}'/P'$.[9] Nothing else needs to change in Figure 11.5, and indeed nothing else changes.

The property that money does not affect the real side of the economy is known as **monetary neutrality**. This principle asserts that any change in the nominal money supply is met by a proportional change in all the nominal variables. This applies to the price level, as we have just seen, but also to nominal wages. Indeed since P rises to P′, nominal wages W need to rise to W′ such that the real wage remains unchanged at $\bar{w} = W/P = W'/P'$, as panel (a) shows. In an open economy, this would apply to the nominal exchange rate as well, since the IS curve cannot move from point A, which requires an unchanged primary current account.[10]

When the price level adjusts immediately in order to maintain the economy in general equilibrium, the **classical dichotomy** principle holds: nominal variables do not affect real variables. Only real disturbances, changes in technology and tastes or in public spending and taxes, can affect the real side (growth, employment, real consumption, etc.).

Monetary factors, such as the money supply and nominal interest rates, play no role.

The idea of monetary neutrality should not be too surprising. Money is a unit of account, and the unit of account should be irrelevant for the real side. A classic example is when, following a period of high inflation, a new currency is introduced, typically eliminating a few zeros. Another excellent recent example is the adoption of the euro, see Box 11.1. In fact, we have already seen in Chapter 8 that, over the long run, inflation and exchange rate depreciation are driven entirely by growth of the nominal money supply. Here, we find that this is true even in the short run under the neoclassical assumption. Whether this assumption is valid remains controversial. Evidence presented in Figure 8.9 does suggest that to a first approximation, the principles of dichotomy and money neutrality provide a good benchmark for the long-run behaviour of the macroeconomy. At the same time, the wealth of evidence suggests that strict monetary neutrality does not obtain for the short run, say from year to year. Changes in nominal money do not lead to instantaneous price changes, and appear to be related to changing rates of economic activity.

In the end, it seems reasonable to consider that, given enough time, prices are flexible. This is why there is wide agreement that the neoclassical view is an accurate description of the long run. Over horizons of several years, monetary neutrality holds and the classical dichotomy is verified. The controversy is now circumscribed over the shorter run and the evidence that prices are sticky over horizons of a few years is quite strong. Thus, in the short run, we should not expect to observe money neutrality. This is where the Keynesian approach becomes relevant.

---

9 For example, if M rises by 10%, P must also rise by 10% to keep M/P constant.

10 The real exchange is constant if the nominal exchange rate S decreases to S′ such that $\bar{\sigma} = SP/P^* = S'P'/P^*$, assuming that the foreign price level P^* remains constant. If P rises by 10%, S decreases by 10%.

Box 11.1 The Euro and Monetary Neutrality

On 1 January 1999, the euro became the currency for eleven members of the European Union: Austria, Belgium, Luxembourg, Finland, France, Germany, Ireland, Italy, the Netherlands, Portugal, and Spain; Greece joined in 2001. On 1 January 2002, for the first time, euro banknotes became legal tender for transactions but the adoption of irrevocable exchange rates three years earlier had already rendered these national currencies 'non-decimal units' of the euro. The introduction of the euro is nothing but a mere rescaling of prices, an excellent example of a purely monetary event, with no consequences for the real economy. Yet, that is not how it was promoted by most governments nor what citizens perceived when the currency was introduced.

Governments, always keen to paint their actions in the brightest colours, have promised that the adoption of the euro would boost Europe's competitiveness and raise growth. How could that be? One argument is that the adoption of a common currency eliminates transaction costs. Dutch imports from Finland are now invoiced in euros, so importers no longer have to pay banks to convert guilders into markka. This should not only lower costs but also encourage trade and competition, allowing firms to take better advantage of a now huge internal market. Indeed, there is some evidence that sharing a common currency boosts trade and, quite possibly, growth, but this effect may take years,

if not decades to materialize. (This effect has been described in A. Rose (2000), 'One Money, One Market: The Effects of Common Currencies on Trade', *Economic Policy*, 30: 7–46.) So is money non-neutral, after all? The adoption of the euro is just not a pure monetary phenomenon for it implies merging different currency areas.

What has been a purely monetary phenomenon has been the changeover from national currencies to the euro. Normally, this should not have had any impact at all. Yet, in most countries, outraged citizens have felt that prices rose in the event. This effect has been small, adding about 0.2 to 0.5% to the inflation rate, much less than what has been commonly perceived. Still, this would seem to be a case of non-neutrality. The explanation, is simple. Given the awkward conversion rates from national currencies to the euro, the change in prices has resulted in widespread rounding. In principle, producers and shopkeepers were supposed to round to the closed euro-cent, but many seem to have rounded prices up. It is this small degree of foreseeable cheating that has taken shoppers aback. It may not even been outright cheating. After all, the one-off costs associated with the changeover have not been negligible. They included the insurance, transport, and management of the currency conversion, relabelling all stickers and catalogues, etc. In the end, the costs had to be borne by the consumers.

11.5 General Equilibrium with Sticky Prices: The Keynesian Case

11.5.1 Demand-Determined Output

The Keynesian approach turns around the neoclassical view. Instead of assuming that the price level is flexible and output remains constant (ignoring the growth trend), the **Keynesian assumption** takes prices as constant and output as variable. Instead, of relying on the price mechanism to match supply and demand, it assumes that output adjusts to

demand. Is the sticky price assumption realistic? Chapter 1 offers evidence that prices are considerably less variable than output. Common day-to-day experience suggests that firms do not change prices every day. Why this is so is not entirely well understood. Discussion of these issues will be postponed until Chapter 12, but Box 11.2 presents a few good reasons why firms change prices only infrequently.

Box 11.2 The Keynesian Assumption

The assumption that the price level is insensitive to aggregate demand in the short run follows a tradition in macroeconomic analysis that began with John Maynard Keynes (1883–1946) and his *General Theory of Employment, Income and Money*, published in 1936. His purpose was to explain how the level of economic activity could fall dramatically and become stuck at such low levels as observed in the Great Depression. (Industrial production declined by 10–20% between 1929 and 1931.) Today the Keynesian assumption is a practical step towards constructing a macroeconomic framework; but Keynesians would go beyond that, claiming its validity as a good 'working assumption'. For example, Dennis Carleton of the University of Chicago found that firms in the United States change prices infrequently, often no more than once every eighteen months, even during periods of moderate inflation.

Critics of the Keynesian assumption argue that it lacks microeconomic foundations. They often ask: why don't price-setters adjust to changing economic conditions? What kind of behaviour could rationalize price rigidity? The Keynesians have three responses. First, **menu costs** might be significant. These are administrative costs associated with changing prices, relabelling packages, and advertising these changes. Surely these costs must be more than the mere relabelling of prices, since catalogue prices, which are easy to change, are not changed very often either. Similarly, modern supermarkets which use bar codes to price their goods should not find it costly to change entries in the central computer. This suggests that there must be other important reasons for nominal price rigidity.

A second explanation emphasizes *customer relationships*. To invest in consumer relations and maintain a good reputation vis-à-vis its customers, a firm may keep its price lists unchanged in the face of considerable fluctuations in demand. For example, in August 1995 VAT tax was raised by 2% in France. Many stores announced that they would not change their prices *inclusive of the tax*. Thus, to keep prices constant, they seemed willing to absorb—for a time at least—the 2% tax hike and to pay for advertisements to make this known to their customers. A third explanation of price stickiness relates to the role of *contracts*. Firms may be locked into implicit or even explicit contracts to deliver goods at a specified price for some period of time.

It is important to realize that the controversy between the neoclassical and Keynesian views does not bear on the structure of the economy. This should become obvious once we turn to Figure 11.6 for the analysis, which is just the same as all the six-panel figures used so far. The starting point is, as in Figure 11.4, a situation where the three schedules that describe the three markets (goods and services, money and labour) do not go through the same point in panel (c). This situation allows us to examine which forces bring the economy back to general equilibrium under the Keynesian assumption. As before, the money supply $\bar{M}$ is assumed to be set exogenously by the central bank. Now, however, the price level P does not change, so the real money supply, which is specified in panel (e), is also exogenous and constant. This assumption also fixes the position of the LM curve in panel (c).

The level of aggregate demand, which is indicated by point B at the intersection of the IS and LM curves, is Y, less than aggregate supply $\bar{Y}$. According to the Keynesian assumption, when they face a situation of excess supply in the goods market, firms first accumulate inventories and then reduce production. The supply schedule S in panel (c) moves to the left until it goes through point B where general equilibrium is restored. This is exactly what we saw in Chapter 10.

However, the equilibrium cannot be completely described without looking at the labour market. If firms produce less, they need less labour; reflecting the new output level Y from panel (c) through panel (d), we see in panel (b) that employment is L, below the level $\bar{L}$ corresponding to equilibrium in the labour market. Turning to panel (a), we note that the Keynesian assumption considers that all nominal prices are rigid, which includes nominal *wages* as well. Therefore, the real wage (the ratio of rigid nominal wage to the rigid price level) is also fixed at the level $\bar{w}$. What happens, then? The only possible

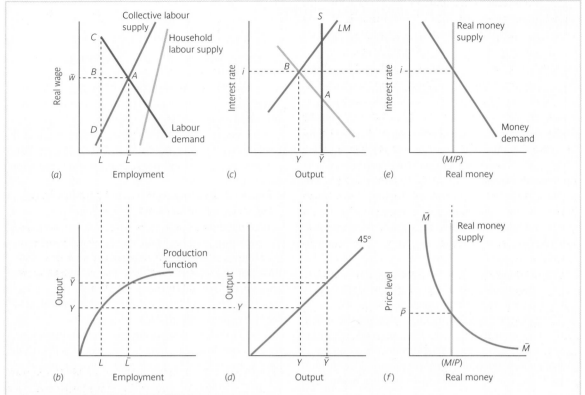

Fig. 11.6 Sticky Price Equilibrium

Starting from a situation where all three schedules do not go through the same point in panel (c), with sticky prices and a given nominal money supply, the real money stock ($\bar{M}/P$), and therefore the *LM* curve, cannot change. It is the aggregate structure of demand, and therefore the *IS* schedule, that determines the sticky price equilibrium at point *B*. Reflecting the demand-determined output level via panel (d), we find in panel (b) the level of employment *L* needed to produce *Y*. The labour market need not be in equilibrium however, and in general will be characterized by unemployment. In panel (a) it is assumed that firms pay real wages compatible with employment *M*, so that there is involuntary unemployment corresponding to *AB*.

outcome is that the new labour market situation is represented by point *B* where unemployment has increased by the distance *AB*. This is a situation of disequilibrium in the labour market: point *B* is neither on the firms' demand for labour nor on the collective labour supply schedule, much less on the individual labour supply schedule.

We find that with all prices, including nominal wages, rigid, the general equilibrium is not achieved. The labour market becomes the escape valve for disequilibria that arise in the market for

goods and services. Firms reduce production and labour demand while workers, collectively and individually do not change their supply of labour, and the real wage does not move to deal with the tension. Indeed, a key message from the Keynesian view is that unemployment, over and beyond its collectively determined equilibrium level, becomes the only available margin of adjustment.[11]

---

[11] Chapter 4 explains equilibrium unemployment as the result of the difference between the collective and individual labour supply.

The main difference between the flexible and sticky price cases can now be summarized in a convenient way. With flexible prices, the direction of causality in Figure 11.3 is counter-clockwise: moving from panel (a) to panels (b), (d), and (c), labour market equilibrium conditions determine output and panels (e) and (f) then show what price level is consistent with general equilibrium. With sticky prices, the right-hand panels (e) and (f) are no longer useful, since the LM curve already incorporates all we need to know for the money market. We now move clockwise, from panel (c) to panels (d), (b), and (a) and the labour market no longer determines conditions on the goods market, *rather is determined by it*. The case considered here, where demand falls short of supply, is the archetypal sticky-price Keynesian case.[12]

With sticky prices, the flexible-price general equilibrium does not occur, except by chance. Goods and money markets are in equilibrium, but the labour market is not. This seems realistic. We do not observe firms producing unwanted goods for very long when demand is weak, nor do we see persistent shortages when demand exceeds supply. As was noted in Chapter 8, money markets are notoriously fast to adjust. On the other side, labour markets require more time and unemployment obviously is a feature of everyday life.[13]

11.5.2 Non-neutrality of Money

An important implication of a sticky price level is that the classical dichotomy no longer holds. This can be seen in Figure 11.7 using a single diagram, panel (c)

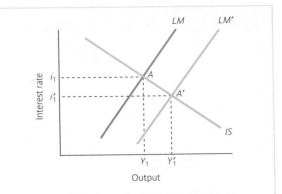

Fig. 11.7 Monetary Neutrality Fails when the Price Level is Fixed
An increase in the money supply leads to excess supply of money on points along the old LM curve. The new LM curve lies below and to the right of the old one. Equilibrium in goods and money markets implies a lower interest rate and higher real GDP than at A.

of Figure 11.6, in fact the familiar *IS-LM* diagram from Chapter 10, here in its closed-economy version. Changes in the nominal money supply shift the LM curve, and thereby affect output, employment, and all the other real variables. In the neoclassical case, monetary neutrality held because the price level moved to equate real money supply M/P with real money demand $L(Y, i, c)$ consistent with equilibrium levels of output and interest rates. In effect, the price level moved enough to bring the LM curve through the intersection of the goods supply (S) and demand (IS) schedules. When the price level is fixed, it is money demand that adjusts to money supply. This, in turn, requires changes in the interest rate and output. These changes remain compatible with goods market equilibrium: graphically, the economy moves along the IS curve from A to A'. Briefly put, since the price level does not move, changes in nominal money have real effects. The real side of the economy (GDP, employment, consumption, investment, real interest rates, etc.) are subject to influences originating in the money market.

---

[12] It is possible to consider the opposite case, where demand exceeds supply. This case, sometimes called 'repressed inflation', is rare, but was frequently observed in centrally planned economies, when prices were set low relative to market clearing values, probably for political reasons. As a result, scarcities were common.

[13] Such 'sticky price general equilibria' are sometimes called non-Walrasian, referring to Léon Walras (1834–1910), a French mathematical economist who first conceptualized the idea of general equilibrium. Walras emigrated to Lausanne in Switzerland when his theories were rejected by his French peers, who ultimately drove him to exile.

❗ Summary

1 The downward-sloping *IS* curve is the set of real GDP levels and interest rates compatible with goods market equilibrium, given the price level.

2 The money market equilibrium condition is represented by the upward-sloping *LM* curve.

3 In the labour market, there exists a real wage and a level of employment which deliver equilibrium with no involuntary unemployment, at least from the perspective of the collective bargaining parties.

4 When all three markets (goods, money, labour) clear simultaneously, the economy's general equilibrium is achieved. Whether, and how, it is reached depends very much on what is assumed about the role of the price level.

5 The neoclassical assumption is that prices are fully flexible and move to maintain equilibrium in each relevant market. Under this assumption, output is supply determined and there is no collectively involuntary unemployment. Price-level adjustments affect the real money supply and drive the *LM* curve to pass through the intersection of the supply-determined output schedule and the *IS* curve.

6 When the price level is flexible, the economy is dichotomized: real and nominal variables do not affect each other. Monetary neutrality is the absence of real effects of nominal money changes. Money affects only prices and other nominal variables.

7 The Keynesian assumption is that prices and wages are sticky, and that output is determined by demand conditions. Equilibrium occurs at the intersection of the *IS* and *LM* curves. It is possible for output to differ from the production capacity; this discrepancy leads to disequilibrium on the labour market, often resulting in involuntary unemployment.

8 With sticky prices, the classical dichotomy and monetary neutrality principles do not apply. Money matters for the real side of the economy.

9 The flexible and sticky price cases can be analysed with the same graphical apparatus. With flexible prices, GDP is supply determined and prices adjust; with sticky prices, GDP is demand determined and firms adjust output.

10 The assumption that prices are flexible is a useful way of thinking about the long run of the economy. Full price flexibility is less likely to characterize the short run.

11 The Keynesian assumption that the price level is constant and that output adjusts to achieve goods market equilibrium is a convenient shortcut for analysing the short-run determination of GDP and interest rates.

🔑 Key Concepts

- *IS* curve
- money market equilibrium
- *LM* curve
- monetary neutrality
- classical dichotomy

- menu costs
- Keynesian and neoclassical assumptions
- neoclassical synthesis
- general equilibrium

❓ Exercises

1 What is the effect on GDP, the interest rate, and employment of a one-off unexpected increase in the price level when prices and wages are rigid? When nominal wages are flexible?

2 Using the six-panel figure, show the effects on GDP, employment, the price level, and the interest rate of an increase in the transaction costs c which affects money demand. You should consider the cases of both fixed and flexible prices.

3 What is the effect on GDP, the interest rate, and employment of an expansionary fiscal policy in the neoclassical case? In the Keynesian case?

4 Imagine that a big immigration wave shifts both labour supply schedules to the right in panel (*a*) of Figure 11.3. What is the effect on GDP, the interest rate, employment, and unemployment in the neoclassical case? In the Keynesian case?

5 Consider the case where real wages are sticky and such that, in Figure 11.3(*a*), there is some involuntary unemployment. Show that, if prices are flexible, equilibrium is still possible in other markets and that output remains supply determined. Show that the economy is dichotomized and that money is neutral. (This exercise establishes that the flexible price results apply in the presence of real wage rigidity.)

6 Using the diagram in Figure 11.3, show the effect of a one-time productivity gain (an outward shift

of the production function and of the labour demand schedule) on employment, output, prices, real wages, and interest rates when prices are flexible. How does your answer change when prices are sticky?

7 Formerly planned economies emerged with an antiquated capital stock. This means that new investment will quickly raise productivity. Assuming that they start from general equilibrium as in Figure 11.3,

(a) Show the effect of investment in panels (*a*) and (*b*).

(b) Interpret the resulting situation in panel (*c*).

(c) In the case of flexible prices, what is expected to happen to GDP, the interest rate, and prices?

(d) Now answer the same question as (*c*) in the case of sticky prices.

(e) Can the outcome of question (*c*) be reached with sticky prices if the central bank changes the nominal money supply in a judicious manner?

8 Suppose that blight wiped out half of an agricultural economy's harvest. Use Figure 11.3 to predict the consequences for the general equilibrium of the economy. Assume that the nominal money supply is constant and that the productivity of investment is unchanged, meaning that the production function shifts downwards by an equal amount.

→ Essays Questions

1 Many countries outlaw reducing nominal wages, even in the presence of deflation (negative inflation, i.e. generalized price declines). This may destabilize the macroeconomy, and yet workers are unwilling to give up this legislation. Explain and comment.

2 Why are neoclassical economists in favour of laissez-faire? Why are Keynesian economists in favour of active macroeconomic policies?

3 What could bring an economy closer to the neoclassical assumption?

4 'Mature economies become increasingly unable to deal with disturbances.' Comment.

PART V

Inflation and Business Cycles

12 Aggregate Supply and Inflation *281*
13 Aggregate Demand and Aggregate Supply *303*
14 Business Cycles *331*

The next three chapters bring together the material of the first half of the book in a way that can be used in the analysis of historical episodes as well as contemporary policy dilemmas. It is the core of modern acroeconomics, and follows a tradition which distinguishes between forces of demand and supply affecting the evolution of output. Chapter 12 focuses on inflation and aggregate supply, relaxing the Keynesian fixed-price assumption and stressing the role of labour markets. Chapter 13 introduces inflation in the *IS-LM* analysis and derives the aggregate demand schedule. Bringing together the aggregate demand (*AD*) and aggregate supply (*AS*) schedules provides a powerful tool for explaining the behaviour of inflation and output. Chapter 14 then focuses on business cycles. It presents a number of stylized facts and examines how well they are explained by the *AD-AS* framework. It also introduces an alternative and competing view, the Real Business Cycle theory, which is based on an equilibrium interpretation of macroeconomic fluctuations.

Aggregate Supply and Inflation

12.1 Overview *282*

12.2 The Phillips Curve: Chimera or a Stylized Fact? *283*
12.2.1 A. W. Phillips' Discovery *283*
12.2.2 Okun's Law and a Supply Curve Interpretation of the Phillips Curve *284*
12.2.3 The Phillips Curve in Demise *286*

12.3 Accounting for Inflation: The Battle of the Mark-ups *288*
12.3.1 Prices and Costs *288*
12.3.2 The Battle of the Mark-ups: A Simple Story *290*
12.3.3 Productivity and the Labour Share *291*
12.3.4 Cyclical Effects on Mark-ups *291*
12.3.5 Completing the Picture: The Effect of Supply Shocks *293*

12.4 Inflation, Unemployment, and Output *294*
12.4.1 The Phillips Curve Rehabilitated *294*
12.4.2 Core Inflation and the Long Run *295*
12.4.3 Aggregate Supply *296*
12.4.4 From the Short to the Long Run *297*
12.4.5 Factors that Shift the Phillips and Aggregate Supply Curves *297*

Summary *299*

When the demand for a commodity or service is high relative to the supply of it we expect the price to rise, the rate of rise being greater, the greater the excess demand. Conversely when the demand is low relatively to the supply we expect the price to fall, the rate of fall being greater, the greater the deficiency of demand. It seems plausible that this principle should operate as one of the factors determining the rate of change of money wage rates, which are the price of labour services.

—A. W. Phillips[1]

12.1 Overview

A cup of tea in London that cost 5p in 1965 goes for £1.20 in 2005. The baguette in Paris which cost 40 centimes (of French franc) in 1965 fetches ten times more (in euros) forty years later. The reason for this is a general increase in the price level over the period. Whether very low or excrutiatingly high, inflation is a key feature of modern economies. It cannot be ignored, and it may matter even in the short run. After all, it is an implication of the Keynesian view that nominal variables, of which the price level is a prime example, can affect the real side. So we must look at it, and this is the main objective of this chapter.

In recent years, inflation has declined considerably, stabilizing around 2% in most developed countries and in a number of developing countries as well. In Japan, inflation has even become negative, a phenomenon called **deflation**. Yet inflation remains high and unstable in some countries. Some observers even predict a return of (very moderate) inflation in the OECD zone. Clearly, inflation is sure to remain a premier topic of macroeconomics precisely because it has a tendency to come back when most have come around to believe that it has been vanquished.

Inflation is not just about changes in the price of tea in Britain and bread in Paris. It occurs when *all* prices rise. The phenomenon does not stop there. As the price level rises, so do wages. They partly rise because of rising productivity, but they also chase prices, unless it is prices that chase wages. And the nominal exchange rate seems to be engaged in the same kind of race. Somehow, all nominal variables seem to be engaged in a process of leapfrogging. As it establishes that inflation in the long run depends on how rapid the money supply is increasing relative to output, Chapter 8 offers a first glimpse of the inflation process. In this chapter we look at the same issue in both the short and the long run.

We ask who sets prices and find that firms do, with an eye to their production costs. As we turn to the production costs, we return to the wage bargaining process encountered in Chapter 4 and find that wage negotiators worry about prices. We end up facing the puzzling result that prices drive wages and wages drive prices, in a sort of race between employers—who want large profits—and employees—who want high wages. The outcome of the analysis is an accounting of the factors that add up to a full explanation of inflation. This analysis is summarized in the **aggregate supply curve**, which will match the aggregate demand curve developed in the next chapter.

---

[1] A son of a Kiwi dairy farmer, A. W. Phillips (1914–75) started out as an apprentice electrician working in an Australian mine, then left for Britain via China and Russia in the late 1930s. After a tour of duty in the Second World War and time spent as a Japanese prisoner of war, he studied at the London School of Economics and became a lecturer and later professor there. Phillips is remembered not only for his curve relating unemployment to rates of wage change, but also for the *Moniac*, a complex hydraulic representation of macroeconomy, one of which is on display in the Science Museum in London.

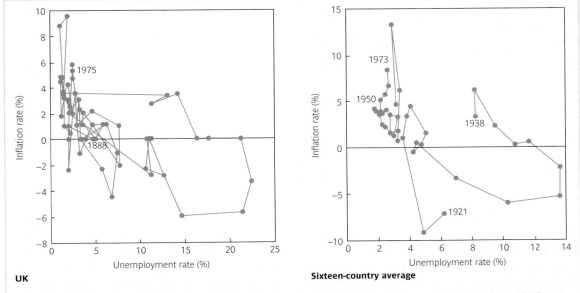

Fig. 12.1 Phillips Curves: The UK, 1888–1975, and a Sixteen-Country Average, 1921–1973, excluding 1939–1949

Sources: Maddison (1991); Mitchell (1998). Unweighted average of observations for Australia, Austria, Belgium, Canada, Denmark, Finland, France, Germany, Italy, Japan, the Netherlands, Norway, Sweden, Switzerland, the UK, and the USA. For some years, some countries are missing.

12.2 The Phillips Curve: Chimera or a Stylized Fact?

12.2.1 A. W. Phillips' Discovery

Even die-hard Keynesians conceded at the high point of their influence that they had no clue on how to incorporate inflation in their model. They referred to it as the 'missing equation'. The hunt for this equation turned up the **Phillips curve**, a negative *trade-off* observed between inflation and unemployment, the twin 'bads' of macroeconomics. It is named after the late New Zealander A. W. Phillips of the London School of Economics. In the late 1950s, Phillips plotted the annual rate of growth of nominal wages, or **wage inflation**, in Britain during the

period 1861–1957 against the rate of unemployment and found a remarkably robust negative correlation, which was confirmed for a number of other countries.[2] Figure 12.1 plots Phillips curves —using the rate of price inflation instead of wage inflation—for Britain and the average of sixteen

---

[2] Phillips was not the first to discover the Phillips curve. The American economist Irving Fischer (of Robinson Crusoe fame) published a paper in the *International Labor Review* of 1926 in which he unearthed a similar relationship in the United States.

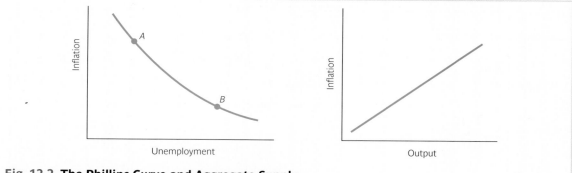

Fig. 12.2 The Phillips Curve and Aggregate Supply

The Phillips curve was once seen as a negative trade-off between unemployment and inflation, representing a set of possible options from which governments could choose. For example, it could keep unemployment down (point *A*) at the cost of some inflation, or could limit inflation (point *B*) but only by accepting unemployment. Combining the Phillips curve and Okun's law delivers the supply curve.

advanced economies for the period 1921–73 (excluding war years). While far from perfect (a number of outliers correspond to exceptional events), the Phillips curve is suggestive of an important systematic relationship: a stylized fact.

The first panel in Figure 12.2 presents the stylized version of a Phillips curve. A country could suffer from high inflation but have low unemployment (point *A*), or from high unemployment but with low inflation (point *B*). The message of the Phillips curve to policy-makers was simple and appealing: pick a point on the Phillips curve, i.e. choose a politically acceptable combination of unemployment and inflation, and then steer the economy to that point.[3] In theory, depending on the exchange rate regime, this could be achieved by moving the *IS* curve using fiscal policy (public spending and taxes) or the *LM* curve using monetary policy, or a mix of both. A country that favoured low unemployment would choose a point like *A* in Figure 12.2; a country interested in low inflation would aim at a point like *B*, accepting some unemployment. The Phillips curve was seen as a trade-off.

12.2.2 Okun's Law and a Supply Curve Interpretation of the Phillips Curve

The Phillips curve relates inflation to unemployment, but it can also be related to output. To do so, we invoke another celebrated stylized fact known as **Okun's law** that suggests an inverse relationship between output and unemployment. More precisely, we look at fluctuations of output around its long-run trend, illustrated in Figure 10.1. The distance between actual and trend output is called the **output gap**. The German output gap is shown in Figure 12.3, alongside the unemployment rate. The figure makes it clear that the output gap and the unemployment rate systematically move in opposite directions.

The inverse relationship between the gap and unemployment is known as Okun's law. It reminds us of the labour market analysis of Chapter 4, summarized in panels (*a*) and (*b*) of Figure 11.3. Under the Keynesian view, firms adapt output to demand and simultaneously adjust their demand for labour. During an expansion, for example, firms increase their production and require more labour. As they hire more workers, unemployment declines.

Formally, Okun's Law can be represented as:

(12.1) $$U - \bar{U} = -g(Y - \bar{Y}),$$

where the output gap is the deviation of real GDP Y from its trend growth path $\bar{Y}$, U is the unemployment

---

[3] This view of a trade-off was echoed by Helmut Schmidt, the ex-chancellor of West Germany, who stated in a newspaper interview in 1978 that he would prefer 5% inflation to 5% unemployment. How times have changed!

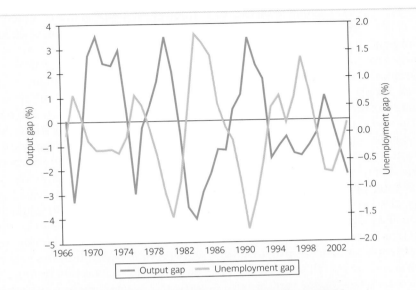

Fig. 12.3 The Output Gap and Unemployment in Germany, 1966–2004

The output gap (deviations of real GDP from its trend) is presented alongside deviations from trend of the rate of unemployment. When business conditions vary, as firms adapt the supply of goods and services, they adjust their demand for labour accordingly. For example, when the economy goes into a recession, firms use fewer workers and the unemployment rate rises.

Notes: Trend real GDP and unemployment are estimated as second-order polynomial functions of time.

Source: OECD, *Main Economic Indicators*.

rate U and $\bar{U}$ the equilibrium unemployment rate, and g is a parameter.[4] A stylized representation of Okun's law is displayed in Figure 12.4.

Summarizing so far, the Phillips curve captures an inverse relationship between inflation and the unemployment rate. Okun's Law captures an inverse relationship between the unemployment rate and the output gap. Bringing these two relationships together implies the positive relationship between the output gap and inflation shown in the second panel of Figure 12.2. This schedule is called the aggregate supply curve. Section 12.3 provides a complete interpretation of the supply curve, but

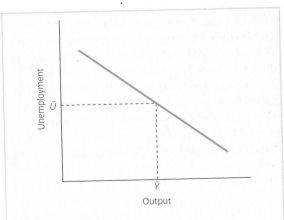

Fig. 12.4 Okun's Law

Okun's law implies that, when the economy slows down, unemployment increases; when output rises relative to trend, unemployment declines.

[4] The law is named after the US economist Arthur Okun (1928–80). In his original finding about the United States, a 1% drop in the unemployment rate was associated with a 3% increase of GDP above trend. This would imply a value for g of one-third.

the intuitive logic that lies behind it should be clear from the outset. The Keynesian assumption is that supply responds to demand, but what are the economic incentives behind it? When demand expands, for instance, under what conditions are firms willing to supply the extra output and employees willing to work more to produce that extra output? The short answer is: inflation must increase to boost wages and profits.

That the aggregate supply curve is upward sloping reminds us of the supply curve in microeconomics. This similarity is both intuitive and misleading. In microeconomics, the horizontal axis corresponds to the production of a particular good and the vertical represents that good's relative price. Here we deal with aggregate output or real GDP on the horizontal axis and the overall price index—or inflation, its rate of increase—on the vertical axis.

12.2.3 The Phillips Curve in Demise
Weak foundations

Not long after its discovery, the interpretation of the Phillips curve—that higher prices elicit more output—was perceived as standing on weak theoretical legs. In the late 1960s, Milton Friedman, the Nobel laureate of 1976 and Edmund Phelps of Columbia University[5] independently attacked the Phillips curve idea. Their challenge was to ask: how could the rate of change of nominal variables, such as nominal wages and prices, be related to real variables such as employment, unemployment, and output in the long run? If the theory of monetary neutrality as outlined in Chapter 8 and 11 is valid, then rates of change in the price level and other nominal variables should be unrelated to the real economy.[6] In particular, a simultaneous rise in prices and wages should leave relative prices—real interest rates, real wages, and real exchange rates —unchanged. Only if workers and firms suffer

from **money illusion**—that is, if they act on increases in their own prices or wages without taking contemporaneous increases in all other prices into account—will they raise output.

To understand the critique of Friedman and Phelps, it is helpful to think about the long-run behaviour of labour markets and output. The principle of monetary neutrality asserts that the economy is dichotomized in the long run: real and nominal sectors of an economy cease to influence each other. If we define the long run as the situation when the output level is on its trend growth path $\bar{Y}$ and unemployment is at its equilibrium rate $\bar{U}$, *no matter what the rate of inflation is*, then the rate of inflation is determined by the rate of money growth. Graphically, if in the long run unemployment returns to its equilibrium level, the **long-run aggregate supply curve** as well as the Phillips curve must be vertical lines, as displayed in Figure 12.5.

Wobbly evidence

The critique of Friedman and Phelps, while largely ignored in the late 1960s, proved to be right on target in the 1970s when, as Figure 12.6 shows, the Phillips curve vanished. Quite spectacularly, in the mid-1970s and early 1980s, both inflation and unemployment started to rise. **Stagflation**, as the phenomenon came to be known, was incompatible with the Phillips curve and its trade-off. A number of consequences followed. Policy-makers, now grappling to beat back inflation, became sceptical of 'Keynesian activism', as the extensive use of the *IS-LM* model. They started to put greater emphasis on long-run monetary neutrality as a guiding principle for monetary policy. German governments and the Bundesbank, never great fans of Keynesian ideas, were seen as vindicated and soon emulated. Nowhere was the shift of ideas more spectacular than in Great Britain where Mrs Thatcher invited Milton Friedman for a cup of tea soon after her election in 1979. Elsewhere, the evolution was generally slower, but there is no doubt that the vanishing of the Phillips curve had a profound effect.

Macroeconomics also underwent a profound transformation. Ironically, perhaps, the end result was to reconstruct the Phillips curve. It started as a puzzle: over nearly a century, the inverse relationship between inflation and unemployment had seemed

---

[5] This is the same Phelps who formulated the golden rule of economic growth, in Chapter 3.

[6] In his address to the American Economic Association in 1967 Friedman argued that 'there is always a temporary trade-off between inflation and unemployment, there is no permanent trade-off. The temporary trade-off comes not from inflation *per se*, but from a rising rate of inflation.' Friedman (1968: 10).

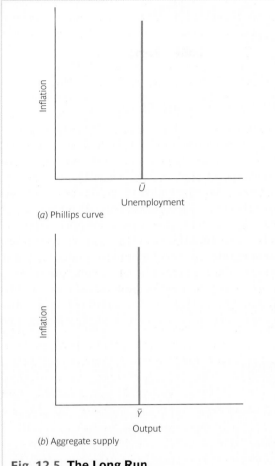

Fig. 12.5 The Long Run

In the long run, unemployment is at its equilibrium rate and output is on its trend growth path. Both the Phillips curve and the aggregate supply curve are vertical. Inflation is determined by money growth, independently of output or unemployment.

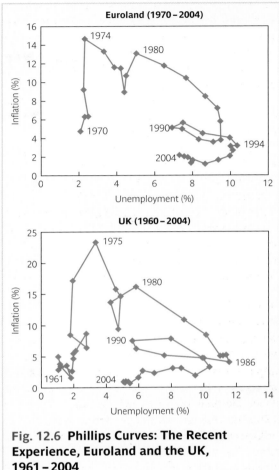

Fig. 12.6 Phillips Curves: The Recent Experience, Euroland and the UK, 1961–2004

The Phillips curve broke down at the end of the 1960s. In both Euroland and the United Kingdom, the sharpest departures occur during the years 1973–5 and 1979–81. In the most recent period the Phillips curve seems to have returned.

Sources: OECD, *Economic Outlook*.

relatively robust, so why did it break down in all countries at about the same time? That could not just be bad luck! The challenge was to explain both the existence of a Phillips curve and its disappearance, as well as the striking similarity between different countries' experiences. Nearly everywhere inflation and unemployment increased sharply, first around 1973–4, and then around 1979–80, precisely at the time of the two **oil shocks**. Indeed, oil prices increased fourfold in 1973–4 and then doubled over again in 1979–80.[7] Interestingly, in between the oil shocks, and after the second oil shock, Phillips curves re-emerged, each time further above and to the right of the previous one. These episodes are dissected in the following section.

[7] The evolution of oil prices is displayed in Figure 12.9.

12.3 Accounting for Inflation: The Battle of the Mark-ups

If we view prices as sticky in the short run but flexible in the long run, then their medium-run behaviour holds the key to understanding the disappearance of the Phillips curve. To study the medium run, we break down inflation into its most important components—an accounting exercise of sorts. We start with the observation that firms set prices. They do so with one eye on the market and the other on production costs. Focusing next on production costs, emphasis is shifted to nominal wages, labour productivity, and the cyclical state of the labour market. Consolidating price-setting and wage-setting shows not only why the Phillips curve exists, but also under which conditions it can disappear.

12.3.1 Prices and Costs

The price level is the average of individual prices, but who sets the prices of goods and services and how?[8] We see stickers in stores and catalogues, which suggest that each price is set by the producer. For producers, the higher the price, the better, provided of course that there are enough buyers, which means that competition constrains price-setters.

Box 12.1 recalls the principles that explain how competition operates and how producers try to lessen it. It describes firms as setting prices (P) as a **mark-up** above nominal production costs, aiming at a margin as large as the market will bear. Thus, behind each price decision—and therefore behind

Box 12.1 When and How Firms Set Prices

When perfect competition reigns in product markets, firms are unable to set prices. A good example is the fruit grower who sells his apples in the town market. With many other sellers around, the farmer finds it difficult to set his price very far from the average price for apples of the same variety: if he raises his price a few cents, he has no customers; if he lowers his price by a few cents, he will sell everything, but regret the forgone profits. We conclude that producers of standard products such as apples, milk, or copper have little or no **market power**.

Yet in reality, most firms *do* set prices. For this, they must have some market power. Either there is little competition among firms—generally hard to believe—or they must do something to acquire market power. In fact, they go to extreme lengths to establish it. They strive to **differentiate** their products, making them different from those of the competitors. They do so through design (similar cars always differ in many subtle ways) and through advertising to win consumer loyalty

(some people like Volkswagen, others Renault), or both. This is what marketing is all about. The payoff is some monopoly power: firms can raise prices without losing all customers. Market power allows for higher profits.[9]

Mark-up pricing is a way of describing how firms with market power set prices. Obviously, when setting a price, a firm wants to cover its production costs, and then it tries to do more. The margin over the cost of producing one more good, the marginal cost, is the mark-up. The mark-up depends on how much the market can bear, which is measured by the elasticity of demand. If the market is highly competitive, the elasticity is near-infinite as any increase will lead customers to go elsewhere. In that case the mark-up is zero and the price is equal to the marginal cost; this is the case of perfect competition. If the competition is weak, chiefly because the firm has been able to differentiate its good and build a 'niche', the demand elasticity is low and the mark-up is large.

---

[8]   Chapter 2 presents various ways of measuring the price level.

[9]   The difference between perfect competition and monopolistic pricing is explained in detail in the WebAppendix.

Table 12.1 Wage Share of Value Added by Country and Selected Industries, 2001 (%)

	Total economy	Manufacturing	Chemicals	Basic metal industries	Wholesale/ retail trade
Belgium	56.6	64.5	53.9	78.3	56.7
Czech Republic[a]	50.1	54.6	46.0	60.0	43.6
Germany[a]	58.2	74.1	69.0	75.3	63.9
Denmark	60.1	64.5	40.4	54.1	67.9
Spain	53.1	67.3	59.7	73.3	44.5
Italy	43.7	54.6	51.9	61.6	32.6
Japan	52.6	56.1	36.3	60.9	60.2
The Netherlands	56.0	59.9	45.9	78.4	60.0
Poland[a]	49.8	61.0	n.a.	n.a.	26.1
United States	58.7	66.0	49.5	70.6	55.6

[a] 2000.

Source: OECD, *National Accounts*, Volume ii.

the price level—lie two components: the profit objective, constrained by competition, and production costs.

Costs

We start with the cost of producing one good, called **average** or **unit costs**.[10] The unit cost (UC) is simply the total cost of production divided by the number of units produced. It is convenient to break down total costs into two main categories: labour and non-labour costs.

(12.2)   Unit costs in euros
= total costs in euros/number of
   units produced
= unit labour costs + unit non-labour costs

For the economy as a whole, labour costs are the single largest component of production costs. Table 12.1 shows that their share of value added ranges from 50% to 70% in developed countries, and is usually higher in labour-intensive services than

in capital-intensive industries.[11] For this reason, we temporarily ignore non-labour costs. We revisit this question in Section 12.3.5.

Labour costs and wages

A firm's labour costs are simply the product of the number of hours worked in the firm (L) and the average hourly labour cost (W). Gross hourly labour costs include not only direct wage and salary but also costs like paid vacations, direct labour taxes, social security contributions, and other benefits paid by employers on behalf of their workers. (In many European countries, these additional costs can be nearly equal to the net pay received by the worker.) Unit labour costs, therefore, are the ratio of total labour costs WL, also called the wage bill, to the number of units produced or, when many goods are produced, total production (Y). Note carefully that labour costs are in nominal terms, as they feed

[10] In theory, the relevant concept is the marginal production cost, the cost of producing another unit of output. In practice, marginal costs are difficult to measure, so we approximate them by unit costs.

[11] In interpreting these numbers, it is important to remember the distinction between value added and turnover or total sales, which was stressed in Ch. 2. As a percentage of total sales, wage shares are much lower because total turnover in an economy includes the costs of intermediate goods. The figures reported in Table 12.1 have netted out payments for intermediate inputs produced by other firms.

into prices while production is in real terms—in the aggregate, it will be real GDP.

An alternative way of thinking about the unit labour cost is to relate the cost of one hour of work to what is produced during this hour. The first component is the hourly labour cost (W), the second component is the ratio of output to hours worked (Y/L) and is called labour productivity. Unit labour cost can also be defined as the ratio of hourly labour cost and labour productivity. Summarizing:

(12.3)   Nominal unit labour costs

$$= \frac{\text{total labour costs}}{\text{output}}$$

$$= \frac{\text{gross hourly wages}}{\text{average labour productivity}}$$

or, formally: Nominal unit labour costs

$$= \frac{WL}{Y} = \frac{W}{Y/L}$$

Note yet another interpretation of unit labour costs. The firms' total income is PY, the nominal GDP. The workers receive the wage bill WL. So the labour share of output, s_L, is WL/PY, which also represents the real unit labour cost, i.e. the nominal labour costs adjusted for the price level:

(12.4)   Real unit labour costs

= Labour share of output = s_L

$$= \frac{\text{wage bill}}{\text{nominal GDP}} = \frac{WL}{PY}$$

12.3.2 The Battle of the Mark-ups: A Simple Story

Prices as mark-up on labour costs

Mark-up pricing means that firms set the price of goods as much as they can above their nominal unit costs. We have agreed to ignore non-labour costs, so we now consider that firms will aim for a price as much above their unit labour costs as the market will bear. This can be written as follows:

(12.5) $$P = (1 + \theta)\frac{WL}{Y}$$

where $\theta > 0$ is the price mark-up.

This is a simple way of thinking of the mark-up: if $\theta = 0.3$, the price is set 30% above labour costs.

Wages as a mark-up on prices

Firms mark prices above labour costs, but what determines labour costs and nominal wages? A good starting point is Chapter 4, which notes that wages are set through negotiations between employees and employers. These negotiations deal with two different issues.

First, the employees want to get as large a piece of the firm's income as they can. That means that they will aim at a labour share of output α as large as they can get away with.

Second, the negotiators can only bargain over *nominal* wages. They do not know for sure what the evolution of the price level will be. Typically wage agreements cover a period of one or more years, and the future evolution of the price level is unknown. Naturally, employees want to protect their nominal wages from inflation. Employers normally agree to incorporate inflation in wage settlements but worry about overestimating it and paying their workers 'too much'. This is why the expected rate of inflation, which is incorporated into the wage agreement, is a central part of negotiations. We denote the resulting expected price level by P^e.

In the end, both sides bargain directly over the nominal wage W and indirectly over the expected labour share $WL/P^e Y$. A simple way of describing the outcome of the negotiations is to consider that they mark up the labour share over its 'normal' level $\bar{s}_L$, with the mark-up depending on the situation at the time negotiations are held:

(12.6) $$s_L = \frac{WL}{P^e Y} = (1 + \gamma)\bar{s}_L,$$

with γ as the wage mark-up.

Note that the mark-up γ can be positive or negative, and that it is zero on average if the historical pattern of income distribution is preserved. This means that in some years the agreed-upon wage share is above its normal level, in other years it is lower.[12] Another equivalent way of describing the negotiation outcome is to note that agreeing on the expected labour share is the same thing as agreeing on unit labour costs. This can be shown by rewriting (12.6) as:

---

[12] Formally, $\alpha > \bar{\alpha}$ when $\gamma > 0$ and $\alpha < \bar{\alpha}$ when $\gamma < 0$.

(12.7) $$\frac{WL}{Y} = (1 + \gamma)\bar{s}_L P^e.$$

Putting it all together

We have described prices as a mark-up over unit costs, agreed to ignore all non-labour costs and therefore to focus on unit labour costs, and found that the expected labour share is a mark-up over its normal level. In the end, prices depend on wages and wages depend on expected prices. Formally, we can combine (12.5) and (12.7) to show that

(12.8) $$P = (1 + \theta)(1 + \gamma)\bar{s}_L P^e.$$

Isn't this a case of circular reasoning? The wage–price determination process is indeed circular: it has earned the title '**battle of the mark-ups**'.[13] The price mark-up, equation (12.1), sets the price level as a mark-up over wages, while the wage mark-up, equation (12.7), sets wages as a mark-up over the (expected) price level. Firms increase profits by reducing real labour costs through higher good prices and employees increase real wages by pushing them up relatively to expected prices. In the end, *actual* prices depend on *expected* prices. Note that the circular process has an anchor: P^e, the level of prices expected by wage negotiators to prevail over the course of the contract. We will later see that this expectation is the central determinant of inflation in the medium run.

12.3.3 Productivity and the Labour Share

Before we move on to the next and final step, two observations can clarify some ongoing debates. First, we know from Chapter 3 that labour productivity (Y/L) is growing all the time. What does this imply for the price- and wage-setting processes? Note that productivity does not appear at all in the final outcome, as represented by equation (12.8). The reasoning is important to avoid misunderstandings. An increase in labour productivity tends to reduce labour costs. Indeed equation (12.3)

implies that the rate of growth of unit labour costs is the difference between the rate of growth of hourly wages and the rate of growth of labour productivity.[14] For example, when labour productivity Y/L increases by 5%, unit labour costs decline by 5% if nominal wages W remain constant. But nominal wages do not have to be constant. If they grow at the same rate as productivity, 5% in our example, the nominal unit labour costs do not change at all. If nominal wages grow faster than labour productivity, say they grow by 8%, nominal unit labour costs increase by 3%. But then, if prices rise by 3% as well, real unit labour costs remain constant.

Figure 1.4 shows the evolution of real unit labour costs, or the labour share, in four countries over half a century. We observe some year-to-year fluctuations, but no discernible trend. This clarifies what is meant by a 'normal' labour share. It recognizes the fact that each country has a way of distributing income between employees and firms which tends to remain reasonably stable over time. The 'normal' share captures this long-run stability. It can and does change now and then, something that we consider below.

The long-run stability of labour share is easy to understand. On the one hand, productivity gains reduce real labour costs for given real wages but, on the other hand, the real wages increase with labour productivity. When these two effects just cancel each other, the labour share remains constant. Firms can afford to offer higher wages when these are paid for by higher productivity, and they can do so without facing higher labour costs. This is how technical progress continuously generates higher incomes.[15]

12.3.4 Cyclical Effects on Mark-ups

It is now time to ask what determines the two mark-ups. The brief answer is that they tend to move over business cycles. To see which side would 'win' the battle of the mark-ups, we need to separate out the two, distinctly different mark-up decisions.

[13] The battle of the mark-ups approach to understanding inflation has found empirical support in OECD countries in pathbreaking work by researchers at the London School of Economics Richard Layard, Steven Nickell, and Richard Jackman, among others.

[14] Nominal unit labour costs are defined as $W/(Y/L)$, and therefore change at the rate $\Delta W/W - \Delta(Y/L)/(Y/L)$.

[15] Not only is this a fair way of distributing productivity gains, it also matches the microeconomic principles presented in Ch. 4.

Start with the price mark-up θ. Firms naturally want it to be as large as possible, but they need to worry about competition.[16] It is quite reasonable to consider that, in good times when demand is strong, all competitors raise their price mark-ups. Turning now to the wage mark-up γ, the outcome of wage bargaining. During boom periods, rising employment generally improves the bargaining position of unions, which is reflected in a higher wage mark-up. In addition, firms may spontaneously offer higher real pay to motivate employees to work harder or longer hours, or even to encourage others to join the labour force.[17] The evidence is indeed that, together, the combined mark-ups rise during booms and decline in recessions.

Let us summarize where we stand. The battle of the mark-ups shows that the expected price level drives wages via the wage mark-up, that wages drive labour costs, which drive prices via the price mark-up. These mark-ups tend to move together over the business cycle and, the higher they are, the more the actual price level tends to rise above it expected level. This can be formalized in terms of inflation as follows:[18]

(12.9) $\qquad \pi = \bar{\pi} + \Delta(\text{mark-ups})$

where $\bar{\pi}$ is the expected rate of inflation, which we will call the core rate of inflation for reasons explained below. All that remains to do is to take into account of the previous observation that both mark-ups move with the business cycle. They both rise when the real GDP Y is above its trend $\bar{Y}$—when $Y - \bar{Y} > 0$—or, using Okun's law, when the unemployment rate U is below equilibrium $\bar{U}$—when $U - \bar{U} < 0$. Formally, this result is represented in the following fashion:

(12.10) $\quad \Delta(\text{mark-ups}) = a(Y - \bar{Y}) = -b(U - \bar{U})$

The positive parameters a and b summarize the relationship of the mark-ups to the two alternative cyclical indicators.[19]

We have now reached our destination. The circular process equation (12.8) can now be turned into an equally circular relationship between actual and **core inflation**. Taking into account the cyclical behaviour of the combined mark-ups (12.10), the relationship (12.9) can be written as:

(12.11) $\qquad \pi = \bar{\pi} + a(Y - \bar{Y}) = \bar{\pi} - b(U - \bar{U})$

This dissection of the rate of inflation shows that it depends on the core rate of inflation and the state of the business cycle. It plays a central role in macroeconomic analysis.

The core rate of inflation is a central part of the analysis that follows and is worth a little bit more thinking. Formally, it was introduced as expected inflation and it appeared when we described wage bargaining. It is meant to capture the adjustment to wages that is agreed upon by negotiators, but it is actually more than just expected inflation. It is forward looking in the sense that wage negotiators attempt to guess as correctly as possible price changes which will occur in the future over the course of the contract under discussion. It is also backward looking to correct from past mistakes: if, during the previous round of negotiations, future inflation was underestimated, the employees were penalized; if it was overestimated, wages went up too fast and profits were squeezed. This backward-looking part of wage negotiations sometimes takes the form of explicit or implicit **indexation** clauses which commit nominal wages to make up for past price increases. The risk of mistakes of this kind explains why, during periods of high inflation, wages are set for short periods because forward-looking guesses are too difficult and errors lead to very significant distortions; indexation then can become automatic. In low-inflation periods, there is little difference between the backward- and forward-looking components, and between core and expected inflation.

[16] A natural tendency is for competitors to agree on large mark-ups. Such collusion is usually strictly forbidden and competition agencies endeavour to uncover and prosecute anti-competition agreements. Fines are often huge.

[17] This reasoning is developed in detail in Ch. 4.

[18] This is an approximation that requires a little bit of work! From (12.8) we can see that the actual rate of inflation is the sum of the expected rate of inflation *plus* the rate of increase of the combined mark-ups (the term $(1 + \theta)(1 + \gamma)$). The normal labour share disappears because it is assumed constant.

[19] Using equation (12.1), we can find that $b = a/g$.

12.3.5 Completing the Picture: The Effect of Supply Shocks

It is now time to look at the non-labour costs of production, studiously ignored so far. These costs correspond to the other factors of production— capital and land, for example—as well as to inter- mediate inputs such as unfinished goods, materials, and energy. The costs of intermediate inputs to a firm are the prices charged by another firm so, at the country level, they are automatically reflected in the overall inflation rate and do not add anything to the analysis. However, this logic does not apply to imported intermediate goods and raw materials, which are set abroad and translated into domestic costs via the exchange rate. As long as PPP remains approximately true, the costs of imported inter- mediate goods simply follow domestic inflation.[20] Similarly, the cost of capital includes dividend pay- ments to shareholders and interest payments on bonds or bank loans. These costs also broadly track the inflation rate and do not change our previous results.

Does it mean that we do not need to worry about the other production costs? Most of the time, this is indeed a reasonable way of dealing with them. Now and then, however, special circumstances arise when non-labour costs do not behave so innocuously. Examples are sharp oil price rises, deep devalu- ations that move clearly way from PPP, tax hikes, or additional regulation that raises production costs. Because these events are special, we do not attempt to explain them, we treat them as exogenous shocks. Because they affect the costs of produc- tion, they are called **supply shocks**. In the end, we think of non-labour costs as generally following core inflation $\bar{\pi}$ but allow for an occasional additional component—denoted s—that captures possible supply shocks. This supply shock term can

be positive or negative: oil prices can go up, but also go down sometimes, for example. The supply shock term s is a catch-all for exogenous disturbances affecting production costs. As long as non-labour costs simply follow the core rate of inflation, the supply shock term is zero. The way to think about it is that it is close to zero most of the time, or on aver- age, with occasional significant positive or negative deviations. Under these conditions, it is possible to modify equation (12.11) to

$$(12.12) \quad \pi = \bar{\pi} + a(Y - \bar{Y}) + s$$
$$\text{or}$$
$$\pi = \bar{\pi} - b(U - \bar{U}) + s$$

actual inflation	core inflation	cyclical demand pressure	supply shock

with s taking the value of zero when non-labour costs rise at the core rate of inflation. Note that, using Okun's law, the cyclical effects are captured alternatively by fluctuations of output about trend or of unemployment about its equilibrium rate.

Beyond changes in non-labour costs, two more types of supply shocks can be important. First, we assumed that the labour share α is constant. A quick glance at Figure 1.4, however, shows that it is approximately trendless, but certainly not constant. Occasionally, it rises or declines, a process that lasts several years. Such changes are usually the outcome of deep socio-political events that strengthen or weaken trade unions. We can take care of these events by interpreting changes in the labour share as supply shocks. An exogenous increase of the labour share, for example, adds to labour costs and can be treated as $s > 0$.

Second, supply shocks may also be created by the government, especially when it changes taxes. The variety of taxes borne by the firms relate directly to production and affect the final selling price—value added or excise taxes, profit taxes, establishment and property taxes, and so on. Other costs imposed by governments are implicit, but may have a significant impact (environmental or consumer protection legislation, for example). It is important to note that all of these government-induced costs affect only the *price level*; to have an effect on the rate of inflation, they would have to increase con- tinuously, which is unlikely.

---

[20] To see this point, let P^{M*} be the foreign price of imported goods, whose rate of increase is π^{M*}. In domestic value, the price is $P^M = P^{M*}/S$ and its rate of increase is $\pi^M = \pi^{M*} - (\Delta S/S)$. If these prices, expressed in foreign currency move as the foreign price level P^*, we have $\pi^{M*} = \pi^*$. PPP predicts that $\pi = \pi^* - (\Delta S/S)$ so $\pi^M = \pi$.

12.4 Inflation, Unemployment, and Output

12.4.1 The Phillips Curve Rehabilitated

The inflation-accounting framework summarized by equation (12.12) effectively solves the Phillips curve puzzle—both its existence over decades and its apparent instability over particular periods of time. The original Phillips curve claims that inflation depends only on the level of unemployment. The inflation account (12.12) shows that cyclical labour market conditions do indeed matter, but so do core inflation, equilibrium unemployment, and occasional supply shocks. For a Phillips curve to be visible, these latter factors must be stable. When they are not, the Phillips curve vanishes. This is precisely what happened during the 1970s, when price and commodity shocks became a major source of instability. Then, as inflation rose, core inflation rose as well, and became more variable, reflecting rapidly changing expectations. In addition, in many countries equilibrium unemployment rose. The Phillips curve's demise reflects the emergence of core inflation and supply shocks as additional explanatory factors of inflation, over and beyond cyclical fluctuations.

How, then, to think of the Phillips curve if it proves to be unstable? The answer is to keep clearly in mind which variables are endogenous and which ones are taken as exogenous. As long as the exogenous variables remain constant, the curve does not move, but it will 'vanish' when they change. This is the way the reconstructed Phillips curve explains the apparent puzzle. This modern Phillips curve is sometimes referred to as the **augmented Phillips curve**, a way of drawing attention to the fact that it now pays due attention to core inflation and allows for supply shocks.

To see how to draw the curve, we start from (12.12) and note that, when supply shocks are zero ($s = 0$) and when actual unemployment equals its equilibrium level, actual inflation equals the core inflation rate:

(12.13) With $s = 0$, $\quad \pi = \bar{\pi} - b(U - \bar{U})$

thus $\quad \pi = \bar{\pi}$ when $U = \bar{U}$

This situation corresponds to point A in the left panel of Figure 12.7. This is one point on the Phillips curve. The others simply follow from allowing the unemployment rate to vary around its equilibrium level, in effect exploiting the key intuition from the old Phillips curve. For instance, at point B unemployment is below equilibrium, so the demand pressure pushes inflation above its current core rate. Conversely, point C corresponds to the case where inflation is below its core rate because the unemployment rate is above equilibrium. This traces out a downward-sloping schedule that resembles the old Phillips curve, and in fact is the same with a crucial difference: its position is determined by point A, that is, by the core inflation rate $\bar{\pi}$ and equilibrium unemployment $\bar{U}$.[21] The core rate and equilibrium unemployment are exogenous; they determine the position of the curve, giving us the location of point A. As long as they remain unchanged, the curve does not shift and we move along the curve. The supply shock s is the third exogenous variable that shifts the curve.

Table 12.2 presents the year-to-year average variability in the rate of inflation, the rate of unemployment, and commodity prices over selected historical subperiods in Britain. It turns out that, over the period surveyed by Phillips, commodity prices were quite stable. Furthermore, the general level of prices was largely trendless; inflation therefore was negligible, and core inflation was probably near zero, at least rather stable. During this period, focusing only on unemployment fluctuations in (12.12), as the Phillips curve does, makes sense. This changed in the early 1970s when unemployment was much more stable—as the result of active Keynesian policies—while somewhat more volatile commodity prices became the dominating factor affecting inflation.

---

[21] This is why the equilibrium rate of unemployment is sometimes called the NAIRU: the non-accelerating inflation rate of unemployment. At point B inflation accelerates above its core rate; at point C it decelerates. Only at A does it stabilize.

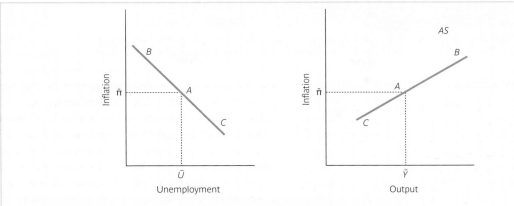

Fig. 12.7 The Augmented Phillips Curve and the Aggregate Supply Curve

By definition, point *A* represents the case where actually observed inflation π is at its core rate *u* and where unemployment is at its equilibrium rate, and output is at its trend value. When unemployment is low and output high, actual inflation is above core inflation rate (point *B*). When unemployment is high and output low, actual inflation is below core inflation (point *C*).

Table 12.2 Variability of Inflation, Unemployment, and Imported Commodity Prices in Britain, 1888 – 2003

	1990 – 2003	1969 – 82	1888 – 1965
Inflation	0.68	0.44	2.29
Unemployment	0.26	0.49	0.92
Real commodity prices	0.10	0.20	0.17

There is no presumption whatsoever that either core inflation or equilibrium unemployment are constant over time. If either changes, point *A* moves, and so does the Phillips curve. Potentially, there exists an infinity of Phillips curves, corresponding to the infinity of values that the core inflation rate or the equilibrium rate of unemployment can take. It just so happened that, over the hundred years surveyed by Phillips, the core rate of inflation and the equilibrium rate of unemployment did not change much, so there seems to have been just one Phillips curve.[22]

[22] There are good reasons for this: the period corresponds to the time of the gold standard and the Bretton Woods system, both of which constrained inflation from rising too much and kept core inflation in check.

12.4.2 Core Inflation and the Long Run

Core inflation, we saw, captures the rate of inflation agreed upon during wage negotiations. It has both a backward-looking (catching up with past inflation due to previous contracts) and a forward-looking component (what inflation is expected to be in the future). Somehow, it must be related to the actual rate of inflation. How this is so in the short run is considered in the next chapter. In this section we deal with the long run.

As negotiators consider the amount of inflation to be factored in wage settlements, they strive to guess it accurately. Of course, employees have an incentive to overstate the core rate of inflation, but employers have the opposite incentive. If there were no uncertainty and both sides always knew *ex ante* what inflation would be over the lifetime of the wage contract, core and eventual actual inflation would just be equal. Uncertainty means that core inflation must be guessed. More often than not, the guesses are wrong. Yet, the principle of rational expectations implies that wage negotiators do not make systematic forecast errors. Although forecasts are almost always incorrect, the errors are largely unsystematic and average to zero: in some years inflation is overestimated, in others it is underestimated.

These observations have two important implications. One is that there must be a link between actual inflation π and core inflation $\bar{\pi}$. Core inflation must track, albeit imperfectly, actual inflation. The backward-looking component implies that core inflation *lags* behind actual inflation, but the forward-looking component implies that core inflation *leads* actual inflation. The interplay of both components is bound to be rather murky and difficult to detect precisely. As a result, it is far from obvious how to interpret Figure 12.6. There exist statistical techniques to do so, however, and they are routinely used by economists.

The second implication relates to the long run. As business cycles unfold and GDP moves around trend, actual unemployment U fluctuates around its equilibrium level $\bar{U}$. This is Okun's law and is well illustrated in Figure 12.3. Averaging over business cycles, therefore, actual and equilibrium unemployment are equal. This allows us to think about the long run. Imagine what the economic situation will be several years ahead. There could be a boom or a recession, or just mild conditions. We don't know, and the best bet is that the economy will not be far from trend, with actual unemployment equal to core unemployment. Put differently, we now *define* the long run as the situation where the economy is back on its trend, quite possibly after having undergone various shocks, and actual unemployment is at its equilibrium level.

What about inflation? We know from Chapters 8 and 11 that, in the long run, inflation is driven by money growth and that the real side (real GDP, unemployment) is unaffected by the nominal side. This is why the long-run Phillips curve is vertical in Figure 12.5. How long is the long run? From equation (12.13), it is the time it takes for core and actual inflation to catch up with each other and stabilize at whatever rate monetary policy allows for. Views vary about how quickly this happens, and herein lie some of the most fundamental controversies in macroeconomics, already encountered in Chapter 11 and to be studied further in Chapter 16.

The vertical Phillips curve carries a crucial implication: there cannot be a long-lasting trade-off between unemployment and inflation. Demand policies cannot move the actual unemployment rate permanently away from its equilibrium level. But the equilibrium level can very well shift over time, for instance as labour markets undergo structural changes. Indeed, one of the lessons to be learned from Figure 12.6 is that equilibrium levels have shifted over the last decades. It has massively increased in the Euro-area over the 1970s and 1980s—shifting the Phillips curve to the right—and modestly declined in the late 1990s. In the UK, the decline of the equilibrium unemployment rate started earlier and has been more pronounced—a legacy of Mrs Thatcher's strong-armed supply-side policies.

12.4.3 Aggregate Supply

Focusing on the cyclical effect on the mark-ups provoked by fluctuations in unemployment about its equilibrium rate, we have interpreted (12.12) as an augmented Phillips curve. If instead the cycle is captured by fluctuations in output Y about its trend $\bar{Y}$, we obtain the aggregate supply schedule. The right panel of Figure 12.7 follows exactly the same logic as the left panel. In the absence of any supply shock ($s = 0$), when the core and actual inflation rates are equal ($\pi = \bar{\pi}$), output must be on trend ($Y = \bar{Y}$), hence point A. Point B describes a cyclical boom: output is above trend ($Y > \bar{Y}$)—and unemployment is below its equilibrium rate—and inflation, fuelled by the mark-ups, rises above its current core rate $\bar{U}$. Similarly, a recession is described by point C, and inflation falls below its core rate. The result is a short-run upward-sloping aggregate supply curve.

The aggregate supply curve conveys two messages. In the short run, it is possible for GDP to fluctuate about its trend growth path, and such fluctuations are accompanied by movements of

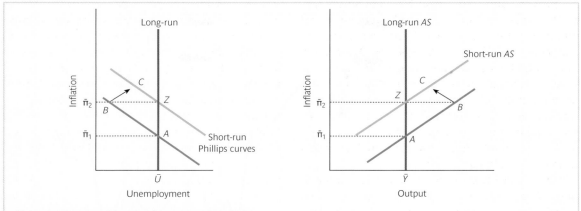

Fig. 12.8 From the Short to the Long Run
For a given core rate of inflation, the economy can sustain lower unemployment at the cost of higher inflation. This trade-off is not permanent, however. When core inflation rises to be consistent with higher actual inflation, the short-run Phillips curve shifts up. In the long run (point Z) there is no trade-off.

inflation about the core rate. In the absence of supply shocks, output and inflation move in the same direction. In the long run, GDP must return to its growth path, regardless of what the inflation rate is: real forces determine the growth of real activity and the growth of money supply determines inflation. The long-run aggregate supply schedule is vertical. It will, however, shift continuously to the right as a consequence of long-run economic growth.

12.4.4 From the Short to the Long Run

Figure 12.8 displays a short-run and a long-run Phillips curve, and the corresponding short-run and long-run aggregate supply curves. Point A, which is on both short- and long-run curves, represents the long-run equilibrium, when actual and core inflation are equal ($\bar{\pi}_1$) and actual unemployment is at its equilibrium level while output is on trend. By construction, the particular short-run curve that goes through point A corresponds to core inflation rate $\bar{\pi}_1$. Now imagine a demand expansion designed to reduce unemployment and shift the economy to a point like B: the short-run trade-off means less unemployment and more output, but also more inflation. However, at point B the actual rate of

inflation is now π_2, higher than the core rate $\bar{\pi}_1$. Sooner or later, wage negotiators will recognize that inflation has now increased to the higher level π_2. When they do so, the short-run curves shift upward, passing through point A', which corresponds to the new core inflation rate $\bar{\pi}_2 = \pi_2$. (The equilibrium rate of unemployment and trend output are assumed constant.) The unemployment–inflation trade-off worsens: any level of unemployment now requires a higher rate of inflation. If the authorities react by picking point C, both unemployment and inflation will rise, while output will decline. Yet point C is not permanently sustainable either, since inflation remains above the newer core inflation rate $\bar{\pi}_2$. Through a succession of shifts in the short-run Phillips and AS curves and associated—increasingly desperate—policy reactions, eventually unemployment and output must return to their equilibrium positions.

12.4.5 Factors that Shift the Phillips and Aggregate Supply Curves

The original position of the Phillips and aggregate supply curves in Figure 12.8 is determined by point A, that is, by core inflation and the equilibrium unemployment rate and trend GDP, respectively.

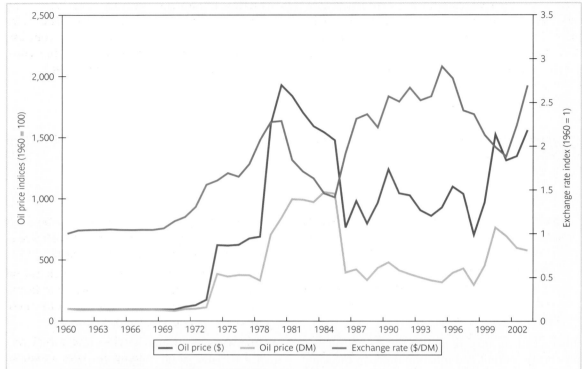

Fig. 12.9 The Oil Shocks and the DM, 1965–2003

The Deutschmark (DM) propitiously appreciated in the early 1970s when oil prices, set in US dollars, quadrupled. Valued in DM, oil prices rose much more modestly. At the time of the second oil shock in 1979–80, in contrast, the DM depreciated vis-à-vis the dollar, which worsened the supply-side effect in Germany. In 1986 the counter-oil shock was accompanied by another appreciation of the DM, and therefore an even stronger positive supply shock for Germany. In recent years oil prices have jumped up again, posing an inflation threat for Germany and the Euro-area.

Source: IMF.

This gives two reasons for the curves to shift. The first is a change in the core or underlying inflation rate: an increase in core inflation shifts the curves up. The second reason is that equilibrium unemployment and trend GDP may change. Shifts in the equilibrium unemployment rate occur occasionally. Trend output continuously rises as the outcome of long-run growth. To avoid dealing with a curve that constantly moves to the right, later chapters will draw the *AS* curves with the output gap $(Y - \bar{Y})$ on the horizontal axis.

A third reason why the supply curve may shift is the occurrence of supply shocks. Let s_{NL} be the share of non-labour costs in total production costs.

A 1% increase in real non-labour production costs—owing for example to an exchange rate depreciation or to a rise in commodity prices—raises inflation and the curve by $s_{NL}\%$. If the increase is temporary, the curve will return to its initial position, but may continue to influence inflation via core inflation. The next chapter discusses cases when this can happen.

Are commodity prices an important source of disturbances affecting the aggregate supply curve? Figure 12.9 recalls the oil shocks of 1973–4 and 1980 and also illustrates the role of exchange rates. A currency appreciation makes foreign goods cheaper when expressed in domestic prices, including imported materials and primary commodities. Exchange rate changes and commodity price changes may reinforce or offset each other. As it turned out, the well-timed appreciation of the German currency in the 1970s had the effect of cushioning the blow of the first oil shock on Germany, since it made the price of oil increase by less in Deutschmarks than in dollars. The more recent oil price surge in the year 2000, in contrast, was aggravated by the depreciation of the euro, with exactly the opposite situation in 2004.[23]

❶ Summary

1 The Phillips curve was once considered a sufficient description of the supply side. Its message was that a permanent trade-off existed between unemployment and inflation. Output could rise to meet an increase in demand but would, in the process, generate a higher rate of inflation that might or might not be acceptable.

2 From the late 1960s to the late 1980s, Phillips curves vanished. Contrary to the notion of an inflation–unemployment trade-off, inflation and unemployment both rose in the mid-1970s and early 1980s, a phenomenon called stagflation.

3 Okun's law states that the output gap—the deviation of real GDP from its trend—and unemployment—as a deviation from its equilibrium level—systematically move in opposite directions.

4 Accounting for inflation starts with the study of how firms set their prices. The result is mark-up pricing, setting prices as a mark-up over production costs.

5 Production costs are separated into two broad categories: labour and non-labour costs. Labour costs rise when wages—and related costs—increase faster than labour productivity. They often represent the most important source of cost changes.

6 Nominal wages are also set as a mark-up on the nominal price level.

7 Wages are set through negotiations that acknowledge three main factors: core inflation, productivity gains, and the state of the business cycle which largely reflects the relative bargaining strength of employees and employers.

8 Wage contracts attempt both to catch up on past inflation and to protect wages from future inflation. Core inflation captures both these backward- and forward-looking aspects.

9 Inflation accounting describes the actual rate of inflation as responding to: core inflation, demand pressure transmitted from the labour markets to goods markets, and occasional supply shocks.

10 The inflation accounts explain both why a Phillips curve may have existed for a century, and why it disappeared as the result of mounting inflation in the 1960s and early 1970s, and the two oil shocks of 1973–4 and 1979–80.

11 In the long run, unemployment returns to its equilibrium rate. Equivalently, real GDP cannot permanently stray away from the productive potential of an economy. In the long run the Phillips curve and aggregate supply schedules are vertical. The economy is dichotomized, growth and real rigidities determine the GDP and unemployment, money growth determines inflation, and there is no trade-off between inflation and unemployment.

[23] Formally, let P^* be the price of oil in US dollars, P the oil price quoted in euros, and S the exchange rate ($ per euro). Then $SP = P^*$, or $P = P^*/S$. Thus when S increases (the euro appreciates) P increases by less than P^*. Formally: $\Delta P/P = \Delta P^*/P^* - \Delta S/S$.

12 The Phillips curve describes the supply side and can be transformed into an aggregate supply curve using Okun's law. The supply curve says that, for increased output to be supplied, inflation increases because production—mainly labour—costs rise faster than anticipated, or than is reflected in core inflation. The core rate of inflation and the equilibrium unemployment rate determine the position of the short-run Phillips curve. The position of the aggregate supply curve is determined by the core rate of inflation and trend GDP. Any change in one of these variables leads to shifts in the short-run schedules.

☞ Key Concepts

- deflation supply side, demand side
- aggregate supply curve
- Phillips curve
- wage inflation
- Okun's law
- output gap
- money illusion
- long run aggregate supply curve
- stagflation
- oil shock

- mark-up
- market power
- product differentiation
- average or unit costs
- mark-up pricing
- battle of the mark-ups
- core inflation
- indexation
- supply shocks
- augmented Phillips curve

❷ Exercises

1 A Phillips curve is represented by the following relationship: $\pi = \bar{\pi} - 10(U - \bar{U}) + s$, where s is a supply shock term. Draw the curve when $\bar{\pi} = 4\%$ and $\bar{U} = 7\%$; when core inflation rises to 6%. Okun's law is $U - \bar{U} = -\dfrac{Y - \bar{Y}}{10,000}$. Draw the aggregate supply schedule when $\bar{Y} = 10,000$.

2 Why is it argued that improving the performance of the supply side of the economy is good for both inflation and employment?

3 Three types of consumer price indexes are being used in the UK: the retail price index (RPI), RPIX, which excludes the interest charge on mortgage loans, and RPIY, which also excludes indirect taxes (VAT, duties, local taxes, etc.). These distinctions have been introduced because, using the CPI, a restrictive monetary or fiscal policy might be *inflationary* in the short run. Explain why.

4 Why might an expansionary monetary policy under flexible exchange rates increase inflation? (Hint: how could a depreciation be a supply shock?) How might an expansionary fiscal policy be a source of reduced inflation in an open economy with flexible exchange rates?

5 In the 1980s, when inflation reached huge rates —more than 1,000% a year—in Brazil all prices and wages were indexed and the indexation was applied weekly. Why was indexation not only popular but generally perceived as vital?

6 What could be the effect on inflation of an increase in value added taxes (VAT)? Of an increase in corporate profit taxes? Of an increase in personal income taxes? State your assumptions carefully.

7 What are the short- and long-run effects of a sudden acceleration of productivity advances? (You may want to consider the impact on equilibrium unemployment.)

8 Show the effect on the short- and long-run Phillips curves of an oil shock, i.e. a once-and-for-all increase in the price of imported energy, assuming that core inflation remains unchanged. Does it matter whether the country is self-sufficient, or an oil importer?

9 A reform of labour market institutions reduces equilibrium unemployment to 5%. Explain the effect on inflation and unemployment in the short term and in the long term.

10 Suppose a government underestimates the equilibrium rate of unemployment and attempts to reduce the unemployment rate below the equilibrium rate by stimulating aggregate demand. Show the likely outcome of such a policy using the short- and long-run Phillips curves.

→ Essays Questions

1 It is often asserted that some central banks (e.g. the old German Bundesbank or the Swiss National Bank) have anti-inflation 'credibility': they have a reputation for keeping inflation low. How might this affect the core inflation rate? In particular, how might it influence the reaction of core inflation to commodity price shocks?

2 It is sometimes claimed in the popular press that the 'new economy' will have permanently lower inflation and lower unemployment. Can you make sense of this claim using the augmented Phillips curve? What is your assessment of its validity?

3 The information technology revolution can be interpreted as a sudden rise and sustained rise in productivity. Some see this as a source of unend-ing prosperity, others worry that many workers, whose skills become obsolete, will lose their jobs and will be unable to find new ones. Use the augmented Phillips curve to analyse the long-debated issue of how technological progress affects unemployment. You may wish to separate out the short and the long run.

4 Imagine that you are back in the 1960s, when the Phillips curve was believed to be stable. How, do you believe, were politicians arguing about where it is best to be on the curve? What mistake would each side of the debate be likely to make?

5 'Credible central banks are better able to deal with adverse supply shocks.' Explain and comment on this statement.

Aggregate Demand and Aggregate Supply **13**

13.1 **Overview** *304*

13.2 **Aggregate Demand and Supply under Fixed Exchange Rates** *305*

13.2.1 Aggregate Demand *305*

13.2.2 The Complete System *308*

13.2.3 Fiscal Policy and Demand Disturbances *309*

13.2.4 Monetary Policy and Realignments *312*

13.3 **Aggregate Demand and Supply under Flexible Exchange Rates** *315*

13.3.1 Aggregate Demand and the Complete System *315*

13.3.2 Monetary Policy *317*

13.3.3 Fiscal Policy *318*

13.3.4 Interest Rate Parity Revisited *318*

13.4 **How to Use the *AS-AD* Framework** *319*

13.4.1 Supply Shocks *319*

13.4.2 Demand Shocks *323*

13.4.3 Disinflation *324*

Summary *327*

Money influences only monetary variables and not real variables in the long run. The problem is 'how long is long?' The 'Keynesian' answer embodied in the concept of the Phillips curve was 'too long to matter!': the 'monetarist' rejoinder was 'shorter than the Keynesians think!'; extreme rationalism provides the answer 'too short for anything else to matter!'—answers that no one concerned with either the history or the practice of stabilization policy is likely to accept.

—Harry G. Johnson

13.1 Overview

This chapter presents a unified framework for thinking about business cycles and inflation. It integrates and unifies the results of previous chapters. Together with the *IS-LM-BP* diagram, the *AD-AS* framework developed here represents the 'workhorse' of macroeconomists. Its main strength lies in the distinction between aggregate demand and aggregate supply. Aggregate demand has been analysed within the *IS-LM-BP* framework under the assumption that prices are constant; the task ahead is to understand how it can be adjusted to deal with inflation.[1] The result is the downward-sloping curve *AD* in Figure 13.1: a higher inflation rate, all other things equal, reduces aggregate demand. The upward-sloping aggregate supply curve *AS* is already familiar from the previous chapter. In a market economy demand equals supply, so the position of the economy is described by the intersection of the *AD* and *AS* curves. Separating the two blades of the scissors is often the best way to approach any economic issue, and macroeconomics is no exception.

In the *IS-LM-BP* analysis of Chapter 10 the exchange rate regime (fixed or freely floating) is of crucial importance in understanding an economy's reaction to real and financial disturbances. This observation remains valid in the presence of inflation, and this chapter maintains the sharp distinction between the two regimes.

The aggregate supply curve stresses the difference between the short run, when a trade-off between output or unemployment and inflation is

possible, and the long run, when the supply curve is vertical and the trade-off has disappeared. This distinction is fundamental. In the long run, demand and monetary factors have no effect on real economic variables—for example real GDP, unemployment, or the real exchange rate—while nominal variables such as inflation and the nominal exchange rate depend only on the money supply. In the short run, however, monetary and real factors interact with each other. Understanding these interactions and linking the economy's short run to the long run is a key function of the *AD-AS* framework. The chapter concludes with examples of the framework's usefulness.

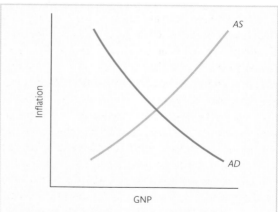

Fig. 13.1 **Aggregate Demand and Aggregate Supply**

The macroeconomy can be fully described by the intersection of the aggregate demand and supply curves. Movements of these curves help to interpret fluctuations in output and inflation.

---

[1] Ch. 11 looked at two polar assumptions, constant and purely flexible prices. As often, the real world is in between, with gradually moving prices.

13.2 Aggregate Demand and Supply under Fixed Exchange Rates

13.2.1 Aggregate Demand

A long-run restriction on domestic inflation

In this chapter, we adopt the principle of **purchasing power parity (PPP)** presented in Chapter 8. To recall, PPP asserts that the real exchange rate is constant. It is clearly not verified in the short run but it is an acceptable rule of thumb for the long run, and this is precisely the way we will use it. In the short run, deviations from PPP will play a key role in shaping aggregate demand, but *permanent* differences between domestic and foreign inflation will be ruled out because, if domestic and foreign inflation rates were to permanently diverge, the real exchange rate would appreciate or depreciate without end.

Indeed, when the exchange rate is fixed, if domestic inflation (π) exceeds the foreign inflation rate (π^*), the real exchange rate keeps appreciating (σ rises), external competitiveness worsens, the primary current account deteriorates, and demand for domestic goods decreases. Conversely, if inflation is lower at home than abroad, the real exchange rate depreciates (σ falls), competitiveness is enhanced, the primary current account improves, and demand for domestic goods rises. As long as the exchange rate is truly fixed, the assumption that PPP holds in the long run guarantees that deviations between domestic and foreign inflation can only be temporary and the current account cannot improve or worsen indefinitely. This result is formally derived in Box 13.1.

We also adopt the small open economy assumption. The country under study is too small to affect the rest of the world. In this case, the assumption means that foreign inflation is exogenous. Along with the long-run PPP assumption, this implies that, in the long run, domestic inflation is exogenous as well. This restriction is represented in Figure 13.1(b) as the horizontal long-run aggregate demand (*LAD*) line. This is a demand-induced restriction because any permanent deviation would lead to infinitely large current account deficits or surpluses, shunting world demand away or toward domestic goods and services.

This restriction may seem to contradict the conclusion, reached in Chapter 8, that long-run inflation is entirely determined by money growth. It does not. Recall that under a fixed exchange rate regime, the *IS-LM-BP* (Mundell–Fleming) framework implies that monetary policy independence is lost. This result was reached in Chapter 10 assuming sticky prices, but it remains valid in the presence of inflation. The reason is exactly the same: as the central bank intervenes on foreign exchange markets to defend the parity, domestic money supply becomes endogenous. Imagine, for example, that domestic inflation exceeds the foreign inflation rate. With a fixed exchange rate, the real exchange increases and the real appreciation undermines the economy's international competitiveness. As the IS curve shifts to the left, capital flows out, which would exert a depreciation pressure on the nominal exchange rate. The central bank must therefore intervene and buy back its currency. The money supply becomes endogenous and, instead of inflation adjusting to money growth, it is money growth that is made consistent with the requirement imposed by PPP on the domestic inflation rate. The *LAD* simply recognizes this restriction on money growth and, therefore, on the inflation rate. Box 13.1 formally derives the endogenous rate of growth of money under fixed exchange rates.

The effect of inflation on demand

Having established a long-run aggregate demand schedule, we now look at demand in the short run. Demand is captured by the *IS-LM-BP* model, but we need to allow for inflation, i.e. to dispense with the assumption that the price level is fixed. We retain the Keynesian assumption, but in a slightly modified form. The presence of inflation does not imply that prices are perfectly flexible. In fact, in a low or

Box 13.1 The Arithmetics of the Real Exchange Rate and of Money Growth under a Fixed Exchange Rate Regime

This box formally presents the long-run restriction on the domestic inflation rate. Recall that the real exchange rate is:[2]

(13.1)
$$\sigma = \frac{SP}{P^*}$$

where S is the nominal exchange rate, P the domestic price level, and P^* the foreign price level. Then, when the exchange rate is fixed, the change in the real exchange rate is equal to the inflation differential:

(13.2)
$$\frac{\Delta\sigma}{\sigma} = \pi - \pi^*$$

Applying PPP to (13.2) implies that, in the long run:

(13.3)
$$\pi = \pi^*.$$

We next establish the implication for money growth. Recall that money demand is $M/P = L(Y, i)$. If the economy grows at a rate g, and the elasticity of demand is η, then money demand, in real terms, grows at rate ηg. Next, note that the rate of growth of the real money stock is the difference between the rate of growth of the nominal stock *less* the inflation rate:

(13.4)
$$\frac{\Delta(M/P)}{M/P} = \frac{\Delta M}{M} - \frac{\Delta P}{P}.$$

Turning this equation around, we see that the nominal money growth rate is the sum of the real money growth

rate and inflation. In the long run, GDP growth g is given by real factors (the dichotomy assumption) and does not depend on money growth, while the inflation rate is determined by the rest of the world ($\pi = \pi^*$). As for the interest rate i, we know that it is also set at the world level i^*, which is assumed to be constant. Putting all this together, we find the rate of nominal money growth μ consistent with a fixed exchange rate:

(13.5)
$$\mu = \frac{\Delta M}{M} = \frac{\Delta(M/P)}{M/P} + \pi = \eta g + \pi^*.$$

It may be interesting to note that the same relation applies to the rest of the world, linking inflation abroad to the rate of money growth (μ^*) abroad and to the real growth rate of the rest of the world (g^*):

(13.6)
$$\mu^* = \eta g^* + \pi^*$$

Combining (13.5) and (13.6) we find that, for the exchange rate to be held fixed, domestic money must grow at the same rate as abroad, after due adjustment has been made for relative GDP growth:

(13.7)
$$\mu = \mu^* + \eta(g - g^*).$$

It shows that money growth at home exceeds foreign money growth if the domestic real GDP increases faster than the foreign real GDP, and conversely domestic growth is slower.

moderate inflation environment, as is the case in most countries, prices move very slowly. The Keynesian assumption that prices do not adjust instantly to establish equilibrium between demand and supply can therefore be retained, and that means that output remains demand determined in the short run—and supply determined in the long run.

We first ask what happens in the *IS-LM-BP* model when the inflation rate increases—or decreases—while nothing else changes. The first panel of Figure 13.2 shows an economy initially in general equilibrium at point A_0. For this equilibrium to be

stable, domestic inflation π_0 must be equal to foreign inflation π^*, and the rate of money growth must be consistent with the inflation rate, as just explained. It is the case at point A_0 in second panel. Now imagine that, for some unexplained reason, the rate of inflation rises from π_0 to π_1. With the foreign rate of inflation π^* unchanged—this is the small country assumption—the real exchange rate appreciates and competitiveness is eroded. The primary current account worsens and demand for domestic output declines, and the *IS* curve shifts to the left, say to IS_1.

Where is the new general equilibrium? Following the practice of Chapter 10, we know that, under a regime of fixed exchange rates with full financial

---

[2] Various definitions of the real exchange rate were presented in Ch. 7.

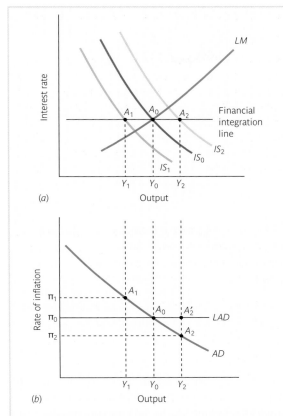

Fig. 13.2 *IS-LM-BP* and Aggregate Demand under Fixed Exchange Rates

Starting from inflation π_0 at point A_0, an increase in the rate of inflation to π_1 reduces the country's external competitiveness. The *IS* curve shifts leftward in panel (*a*). The resulting decrease in demand is reported in panel (*b*). Conversely, a reduction in inflation to π_2 improves competitiveness, shifts the *IS* curve rightward, and increases aggregate demand.

Over, say, one year, the effect of a higher inflation rate is to reduce aggregate demand.[3] Quite clearly, if instead inflation were to decline to π_2, below the foreign rate π^*, competitiveness would improve, the real exchange rate would depreciate, and the *IS* curve would shift to IS_2. The new equilibrium—after a period of one year, say—would be described by point A_2.

Connecting points like A_0, A_1, and A_2 in panel (*b*) of Figure 13.2 we trace out the **aggregate demand curve** *AD*. This curve can be seen as the transposition of the *IS-LM-BP* model in the presence of inflation. The curve is downward sloping because rising inflation weakens the country's external competitiveness, which reduces domestic and foreign demand for domestic goods. It represents aggregate demand because, anywhere along the curve, by construction the goods, money, and international financial markets are in equilibrium—or, to use the language of Chapter 8, actual and desired demand are equal. It is a short-run curve because, as long as domestic inflation differs from foreign inflation, demand continues to change (so that a year later, say, output would have moved further away from Y_0 in Figure 13.2, flattening the demand curve, eventually turning into the long-run *LAD* line).

Factors shifting the aggregate demand schedule

As usual, it is essential to be clear about when we move along the *AD* curve and when the curve shifts. The rule is always the same: the curve shifts whenever any exogenous variable changes. Since *AD* curve encapsulates the *IS-LM-BP* model, the list of endogenous and exogenous is the same, of course with the exception of the price level since the inflation rate is now endogenous. Since the *LM* curve is endogenous under a fixed exchange rate regime, so is monetary policy. On the other hand, any exogenous variable that shifts the *IS* curve also shifts the *AD* curve. For example, starting from

---

[3] Why do we need to say that point A_1 is reached after a given period of time? As long as domestic inflation exceeds the foreign rate, the real exchange rate keeps depreciating all the time. Thus, point A_1 is just a snapshot taken during a contractionary process that continues as long as inflation is higher at home than abroad. We do not elaborate on the dynamic nature of this process to keep things as simple as possible.

integration, the nominal money supply is endogenous and the *LM* curve will shift to meet the new *IS* curve and the *BP* line. Indeed, at the intersection of IS_1 and the initial *LM* curve, the interest rate has fallen below the world level, which triggers capital outflows and sales of the domestic currency on the exchange markets. To defend the parity, the central bank intervenes and buys back its own currency. The money supply declines, and the *LM* curve moves to the left until it passes through point A_1 at the intersection of the new *IS* curve and the *BP* line.

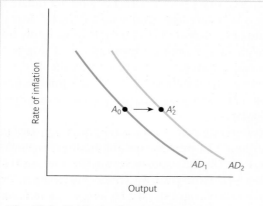

Fig. 13.3 Shifts in the Aggregate Demand Curve

Exogenous changes in demand which shift the *IS* curve also shift the short-run aggregate demand curve in the same direction. Point A'_2 corresponds to the same point in Figure 13.2, showing a demand increase at the initial inflation rate π_0.

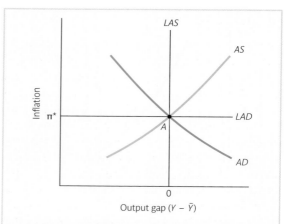

Fig. 13.4 Aggregate Demand and Supply under Fixed Exchange Rates

In the long run output is at its trend growth level, the output gap is zero, and inflation is equal to the foreign inflation rate. The short run is determined by the *AD* and *AS* curves. The figure depicts a situation of long-run equilibrium where all four curves intersect.

initial inflation rate π_0, an increase in government spending $\bar{G}$ is represented in Figure 13.2(*a*) by a shift from IS_0 to IS_2. In panel (*b*) the corresponding point is A'_2. The new demand schedule which passes through A'_2 must lie to the right of the initial schedule, as shown in Figure 13.3. The same reasoning applies to the other exogenous variables studied in Chapter 10, taxes $\bar{T}$, household wealth Ω, Tobin's q ('animal spirits'), $\bar{q}$, and foreign income Y^*. Any change in these exogenous variables that reduces aggregate demand in the *IS-LM-BP* model shifts the *AD* curve leftwards. Missing in that list is the real exchange rate, which is now endogenous because it depends on the evolution of domestic prices—which are no longer fixed—relative to foreign prices.

13.2.2 The Complete System

Figure 13.4 brings together aggregate demand and supply. The demand side comes in two parts: the downward-sloping short-run aggregate demand curve *AD*, and the horizontal long-run *LAD* line, which reflects the endogeneity of money in fixed exchange rate regimes. The supply side, derived in

Chapter 12, also comes in two parts: an upward-sloping short-run supply curve *AS*, and the vertical long-run schedule *LAS*. In the long run, on the supply side, actual and trend GDP are equal ($Y = \bar{Y}$), which requires that core and actual inflation be equal as well ($\pi = \bar{\pi}$). On the demand side, the domestic inflation rate is equal to the foreign rate ($\pi = \pi^*$). In Figure 13.4 the two long-run schedules intersect at point *A*. Note that the horizontal axis now represents the output gap $Y - \bar{Y}$, rather than real GDP *Y*. The reason for this otherwise innocuous rescaling is that trend GDP is normally continuously rising; this would require a continuous rightward shift of the *LAS* schedule, which would be quite cumbersome and, more importantly, would detract our attention from the current focus on business cycles. The long-run zero output gap reflects the principle of long-run dichotomy. The situation depicted in Figure 13.4 corresponds to a long-run equilibrium because the two short-run schedules also go through the long-run equilibrium point *A*. In the following sections, we examine several cases of short-run equilibria distinct from the long-run position and explain how the economy moves from the short to the long run.

13.2.3 Fiscal Policy and Demand Disturbances

Short run

An example of demand disturbance is a fiscal policy expansion—an increase in government purchases ($\Delta \bar{G} > 0$) or a tax reduction ($\Delta \bar{T} < 0$). It is depicted in Figure 13.5 as the rightward shift of the AD curve. Initially, at point A, the economy is in long-term equilibrium: output Y is at its trend level $\bar{Y}$, actual and core inflation are both equal to the world inflation rate π^*, and money growth is compatible with this inflation rate and with real GDP growth. The new AD' curve shows the short-run effect of fiscal policy, say after one year. At point B output has increased—as with the Mundell–Fleming framework—but now we find out that inflation has risen as well. The combination of a fixed nominal exchange rate $\bar{S}$ and an inflation rate higher than abroad (P increases faster than P^*) implies that the real exchange rate $\sigma = \bar{S}P/P^*$ appreciates. External competitiveness is being eroded and the primary current account deteriorates. Thus we find that rising inflation reduces the impact of the demand disturbance. To see why, imagine that inflation remains unchanged; in the *IS-LM-BP* fixed-price model competitiveness would have been preserved, and the outcome would have been at point B' with a larger increase in output. The horizontal distance between B and B' is a measure of the inflation-induced deterioration of the primary current account.

Long run

The long run is characterized by three observations. First, the government budget constraint rules out permanent fiscal expansions. If the initial situation is to be truly long-run, the underlying fiscal stance must be indefinitely sustainable, which requires that the public debt be stabilized. The fiscal expansion, therefore, implies that the public debt is now rising, which is not sustainable. To reach a new long-run situation, the expansionary policy must eventually be reversed and, when this is done, the aggregate demand curve will return to its initial position AD.[4] Second, output must return to its trend and the economy will stabilize on the LAS line. The logic here is that any non-zero output gap implies, by construction, that core and actual inflation differ, which again is not indefinitely sustainable. Third, inflation cannot deviate for very long from the foreign inflation rate if the exchange rate is to remain fixed. Thus, the economy must return to the LAD line. The conclusion is that in the long run the economy must return to point A, just where it started.

Transition

Summing up so far, we start from point A, move to point B and eventually move back to point A. The actual path taken by the economy from the immediate short run at point B to the long run at point A can be reconstructed using a couple of observations. We already know that the budget constraint will force at some point the government to reverse gears and either cut spending or raise taxes. When this will happen is a political decision—it could depend on the timing of elections, for instance—and we cannot say more. At any rate, the AD curve must eventually shift back to its initial position.

We can say more about the behaviour of the AS curve. Remember that its position is determined by core inflation $\bar{\pi}$, which is assumed to be initially equal to foreign inflation π^*. In Chapter 12, we saw that core inflation has backward-looking and forward-looking components. The backward-looking component reacts to actual inflation conditions, 'catching up' with current inflation. Now note that at point B, actual inflation is higher that the initial core inflation rate. Inevitably, wage negotiators—who mainly determine core inflation when they agree to raise nominal wages according to their perception of ongoing inflation conditions—will recognize that the current inflation rate is higher than it used to be assumed. They will naturally agree to push nominal wages faster, in effect bringing up core inflation, say, to equal the inflation rate observed at point B. As they do so, the short-run AS curve shifts. We know that its position is such that

---

4 In the meantime, the public debt has risen and must be paid for by a permanently higher primary budget surplus, which requires that the AD curve shifts back beyond AD. We overlook this additional complexity. It is acceptable to do so if the fiscal expansion does not last long enough to seriously increase the debt–GDP ratio. Ch. 15 returns to this issue at length.

actual and core inflation coincide when the output gap is zero. The new short-run *AS* curve is *AS′*, which cuts the *LAS* line at the current inflation rate, the one that corresponds to point *B*, i.e. at the same horizontal level as point *B*.

Where we go from point *B* depends on when the government will cancel its fiscal expansion. If it is not soon, the economy moves to point *C*, at the intersection of the *AD′* and *AS′* schedules. From *B* to *C*, inflation further rises; this means a faster erosion of external competitiveness and a deeper deterioration of aggregate demand, hence a lower GDP. This is an instance of **stagflation**.[5] If the government soon cancels the fiscal expansion, say by raising taxes, this has a contractionary effect and the *AD* schedule moves from *AD′* back to *AD* (assuming a complete policy reversal compatible with the long run). In that case, the economy moves from point *B* to point *D*. The slowdown is deeper, in fact the output gap is now negative and output has dropped below trend. Inflation may not decline, or not much, because the *AS′* schedule is based on a core rate of inflation that still incorporates the higher inflation rate that used to prevail at point *B*.

What happens next? If fiscal policy is still not corrected and the economy is at point *C*, the output gap is still positive and the new current inflation rate exceeds core inflation (remember that along *AS′* core inflation is equal to the inflation observed when the economy was at point *B*). It is just a matter of time until wage negotiators again hike core inflation, pushing the *AS* curve further above *AS′*. In that case stagflation continues as the economy moves up along the *AD′* schedule. Eventually though, the government will have to reverse the fiscal expansion and we do not pursue this case any further.

If the government has already cancelled its fiscal expansion and we have moved to point *D*, the situation is now such that the output gap is negative and actual inflation is less than core inflation.[6] Indeed, as

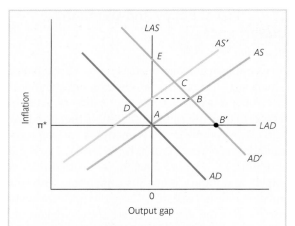

Fig. 13.5 Fiscal Policy under Fixed Exchange Rates

A fiscal expansion shifts the *AD* schedule to the right, to *AD′*. The short-run effect is shown by point *B*, an increase in real GDP accompanied by higher inflation. As core inflation catches up with actual inflation, the *AS* schedule shifts to *AS′*, whose position corresponds to a core inflation rate equal to the inflation rate observed at point *B*. If the government does not change its fiscal policy stance, the new equilibrium occurs at point *C*, where inflation has again increased above the core rate, leading to further shifts of the *AS* curve. If the government cancels the fiscal expansion, the aggregate demand curve moves back to *AD*, and the new short-run equilibrium is at point *D*, where actual inflation is now lower than core inflation. The *AS* curve starts shifting to the right and will do so until it returns to its initial position and the long-run equilibrium is restored at point *A*.

drawn in Figure 13.5, point *D* is horizontally lower than point *B*, while the *AS′* curve corresponds to a core inflation rate equal to inflation observed at point *B*. In that case, the next round of wage negotiations will recognize that inflation is ebbing and will reduce core inflation. The *AS* schedule will shift down below *AS′* and the economy will move down along the *AD* curve. At the intersection of the new *AS* curve (not shown), inflation has again declined below core inflation, prompting a new reappraisal of core inflation, a new downward shift of the *AS* curve, and a continuing movement along the *AD* curve. The process will continue until the *AS* curve

---

5   It might be useful to remember from Ch. 12 that inflation was considered as a proof that the Phillips curve—or its mirror image, the *AS* curve—'does not exist'. Here we see that it still exists, but has moved away.

6   This is a key result of the analysis of the supply curve in Ch. 12: whenever we are to the left of the long-run *AS* curve, by construction, actual inflation is below core inflation.

Box 13.2 Fiscal Policy with Rational Expectations

Chapter 5 presents the rational expectation hypothesis according to which people fully and correctly use all available information to form expectations. In effect, this amounts to assuming that core inflation is entirely driven by its forward-looking component. In this case, as soon as the policy is put in place, wage negotiators immediately realize that inflation rises when the *AD* curve shifts to *AD'* and point *B* is reached in Figure 13.5. So they embark on the following sophisticated reasoning. They immediately raise their estimate of core inflation to take into account the higher rate corresponding to point *B*, and the *AS* curve immediately shifts to *AS'*. This means that economy goes straight from point *A* to point *C*. But at point *C*, actual inflation is again higher than the core rate that determines the position of *AS'*, which is the inflation rate that corresponds to point *B*. So they now realize that *AS* should shift not to *AS'* but to an even higher position corresponding to the inflation rate observed at point *C*. To this new *AS* curve—not shown in Figure 13.5—corresponds to a new point on the curve *AD'* where, again, inflation exceeds core inflation, which requires a further upward shift of the *AS* curve. This reasoning seems unending because each time core inflation is revised upward it delivers a new higher *AS* curve which predicts an even higher observed rate of inflation. In fact, it is easy to see that the process stops when the *AS* curve has shifted all the way until it passes through point *E* at the intersection of the curve *AD'* and the *LAS* line. Realizing this, wage negotiators will immediately set core inflation to the inflation rate that corresponds to

point *E* and the fiscal expansion will bring the economy straight from point *A* to point *E*. The amazing result is that the fiscal expansion does not succeed in raising GDP above its trend; it only delivers higher inflation, which deteriorates the current account by an amount that is exactly equal to the initial fiscal impulse.[7]

The same reasoning applies when the government cancels its fiscal expansion and moves the aggregate demand schedule back to its initial *AD* position. The economy immediately jumps to point *A*, without having to go through a temporary period with a negative output gap. Thus fiscal policy, and more generally demand disturbances have no effect on output under rational expectations. The reason should be clear: along each *AS* curve, core and actual inflation rates differ except where the curve intersects the *LAS* line. Indeed the *LAS* line is constructed for the case where the output gap is zero and, in the absence of supply shock, actual and core inflation are equal; see Chapter 12. Under rational expectations, actual and core inflation cannot be systematically different, so we never depart from the *LAS* schedule and shifts of the *AD* curve only take us up or down the *LAS* line.

This illustrates the current controversies between Keynesian and neoclassical economists. The latter insist on a strict application of the rational expectation hypothesis and see no benefit from fiscal policy. Keynesians believe that the backward-looking component of core inflation is non-negligible, which slows down the shifts of the *AS* curve.

has returned to its initial position and the long-run equilibrium is achieved at point *A*.[8]

The reasoning so far has emphasized the role of the backward-looking component of core inflation. What is the role of the forward-looking component? Anticipating the future evolution of inflation, wage negotiators will reduce the lag between core and actual inflation and the *AS* curve will adjust

faster, which will speed up the return to departure point *A*; see Box 13.2.

Summarizing, we find that taking into account inflation modifies some conclusions previously drawn. First, a demand disturbance is necessarily temporary. This is simply a consequence of the government's budget constraint; it does not depend on the use of the Mundell–Fleming *IS-LM-BP* model but

---

[7] Looking at the decomposition of GDP $Y = C + I + G + PCA$, the increase in G is equal to the decrease in PCA, with no effect on Y.

[8] Actually, the economy will need to move temporarily below point *A*, because a period when inflation is lower at home than abroad is required to bring the real exchange rate back to its initial level. We do not delve into this detail.

was concealed by the model's focus on the short run. Second, a fiscal expansion initially delivers an increase in output, but this effect cannot last very long because it is accompanied by a higher inflation rate, which deteriorates the external position. This explains why the countercyclical use of fiscal policy is much less popular than it used to be in the heyday of Keynesianism, before the old Phillips curve was replaced by its expectations-augmented version. A more radical view, based on the rational expectation hypothesis, denies any fiscal policy effect.

13.2.4 Monetary Policy and Realignments

A key lesson from Chapter 10 is that monetary policy is impotent when the exchange rate is fixed. The central bank must totally dedicate the money supply to uphold the exchange rate peg. The interest parity condition requires that the domestic interest rate be equal to the foreign rate, which means that the central bank must supply money as demanded by the public at that interest rate. This pretty much happened within the European Monetary System, where all countries de facto handed over control of monetary policy to the German Bundesbank. Growing frustration with this loss of monetary policy independence has been a prime motivation for European Monetary Union.

Yet, this does not mean that monetary policy is entirely lost when the exchange rate is fixed but adjustable, in the sense that the parity can be modified.[9] Exchange rate realignments allow for some limited role of monetary policy. As shown in Chapter 10, devaluation means reducing the nominal exchange rate and expanding the money supply accordingly. This is shown in panel (a) of Figure 13.6 where the initial situation at point A is a long-run equilibrium, with domestic observed and core inflation both equal to foreign inflation. At an unchanged inflation rate, a nominal depreciation results in a real depreciation, a gain in external competitiveness, an improvement in the current account, and, therefore, a rightward shift of IS to IS'. Full equilibrium is reached at point B as the LM

curve shifts to LM' as the result of the intended monetary expansion—achieved either on the open market or through foreign exchange market interventions. In panel (b), the demand expansion is shown as the shift of the aggregate demand schedule from AD to AD', and the corresponding outcome is represented by point B. As is now becoming customary, we find that an output expansion does not come for free, it is accompanied by rising inflation.

Point B does not represent a long-run equilibrium, though, since it is neither on the LAD nor on the LAS schedules. It lies on a short-run AS curve whose position is determined by initial core inflation (equal to the world rate of inflation) while actual inflation has now risen. This means that the real exchange rate starts rising, the current account deteriorates, and the IS curve shifts leftward in panel (a), accompanied by a leftward shift of the LM curve as the central bank intervenes on the foreign exchange market to defend the new parity.[10] This movement is mirrored by a leftward shift of AD in panel (b). If nothing else is done, the economy will return to point A, after a period of inflation above the world level. During the transition back to point A, the real exchange rate appreciates because of the inflation differential, eventually fully undoing the real depreciation achieved through the initial devaluation. This is yet another case of long-run monetary neutrality. We knew all along that the long-run equilibrium is at point A, so the question was what would take us there. In the end, if we start from long-run equilibrium, all real variables must return to their initial values, which apply to the output gap and to the real exchange rate.

Another possibility, however, is for the central bank to devalue again. If it does so, it will see its competitive advantage again eroded by the inflation differential, and will have to devalue again, and again. This is the limited sense in which monetary policy independence is restored under a fixed but adjustable exchange rate regime. Through a succession of devaluations, the central bank can keep

---

[9]   Chapter 20 presents the working of such a regime.

[10] Why is capital flowing out? Answer: as IS moves left, it intersects the LM curve below the BP line. Ch. 10 explains this point in great detail.

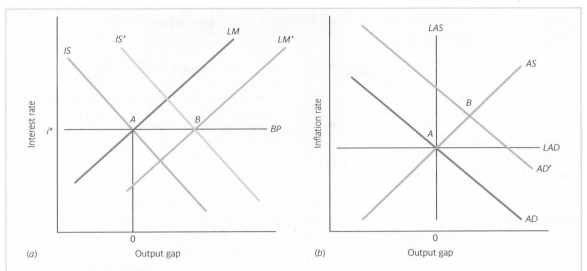

Fig. 13.6 A Devaluation

Starting from point *A* in panel (*a*), a nominal devaluation depreciates the real exchange rate and the improved current account shifts the *IS* curve to *IS'*. The associated monetary expansion moves the *LM* curve to *LM'* and the new short-run equilibrium occurs at point *B* in both panels. Panel (*b*) shows that inflation has now risen above the world level, which starts reducing external competitiveness. The ensuing deterioration of the current account shifts both the *IS* and *AD* curves back to the left. Eventually, the economy returns to point *A* in both schedules.

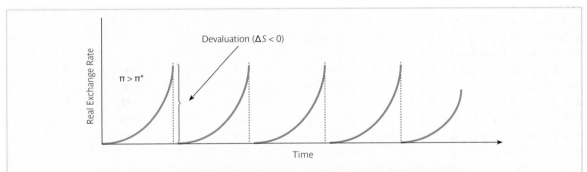

Fig. 13.7 Expansionary Monetary Policy under a Fixed Exchange Rate Regime

A devaluation is followed by inflation rising above the world rate. The initially depreciated real exchange rate starts appreciating again until it is brought back to the pre-devaluation level. The central bank may then devalue again the nominal exchange rate, which immediately depreciates the real exchange rate, triggering a new period of high inflation and real appreciation. In the end, monetary policy results in higher inflation and a succession of devaluations.

pushing temporarily real GDP above trend, but it will have to accept a higher inflation rate. The real exchange rate will depreciate abruptly at the time of each nominal devaluation, only to appreciate again, as Figure 13.7 illustrates. In the end, this strategy merely allows a country to opt for a different inflation rate from the one that prevails in the country to which the currency is pegged. Box 13.3 shows how such an arrangement operated between France and Germany for nearly two decades.

Box 13.3 Peaceful Coexistence with Different Inflation Rates: France and Germany

France and Germany have long been pursuing two contradictory objectives. They wanted to peg their exchange rates to each other but they had very different views about inflation. Germany, still remembering its devastating hyperinflation of 1922–3, was committed to very low inflation while France was more interested in using monetary policy to boost growth. The solution was a peg, first informal, then formal after the launch in 1979 of the European Monetary System, and finally the adoption of a common currency in January 1999. The peg was adjustable and indeed there were frequent realignments between these two currencies, with the franc being regularly devalued vis-à-vis the Deutschmark.

Figure 13.8 shows the evolution of the real exchange rate between France and Germany during this period. It is the real-life version of Figure 13.7: occasional depreciations of the franc vis-à-vis the Deutschmark appear as sharp drops of the real exchange rate, which then gradually appreciates back, until the next devaluation. The figure also shows that, after a severe crisis in 1993, the real exchange rate stabilizes. This reflects France's 'franc fort' policy. In preparation for the monetary union, France had then decided to effectively give up monetary policy independence, renounced devaluing its currency, and gradually managed to achieve an inflation rate similar to Germany's.

Fig. 13.8 The Real Exchange Rate Franc/Deutschmark, 1975–1998

The franc–Deutschmark exchange rate was generally fixed but adjustable during the period 1975–98. France's higher tolerance for inflation than Germany led to recurrent depreciations of the franc vis-à-vis the Deutschmark. Each depreciation was then followed by a real appreciation, until the next one.

13.3 Aggregate Demand and Supply under Flexible Exchange Rates

Under flexible exchange rates, aggregate demand reacts differently to inflation, because the roles of nominal money and nominal exchange rates trade places. The nominal money supply, endogenous under fixed exchange rates, is now exogenous and under the control of the central bank. The nominal exchange rate, in contrast, is no longer exogenously fixed, but is determined by market forces and is endogenous.

13.3.1 Aggregate Demand and the Complete System

The effect of inflation on demand

We ask: what is the effect of inflation when 'all else remains constant', which includes an unchanged monetary policy, defined as a constant rate of money growth? Figure 13.9 shows the effect of an exogenous increase in the rate of inflation from π to π'. The direct impact is to reduce the real money supply (M/P), hence a leftward shift of the LM curve, which after some time reaches the position LM' in panel (a).[11] As we know from Chapter 10, under flexible exchange rates, the position of the IS curve is endogenous because the exchange rate appreciates until, through its effect on the primary current account, the IS shifts to IS'. The new equilibrium is at point A', which shows that the effect of a higher rate of inflation is a decline in output. This output decline is required to bring money demand in line with the now lower real money supply. Reporting this result in panel (b) establishes that the short-run aggregate demand curve is downward sloping.

Under flexible exchange rates, the AD curve is downward sloping because a higher inflation rate with unchanged money growth reduces the real money supply. It represents aggregate demand because it captures the effect of a decline in the real money supply on demand once equilibrium is

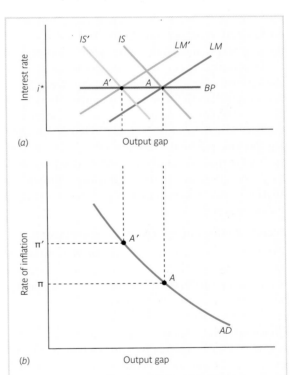

(a)

(b)

Fig. 13.9 *IS-LM-BP* and Aggregate Demand under Flexible Exchange Rates

The figure shows the effect of an increase in the rate of inflation on aggregate demand when the rate of nominal money growth remains constant (μ). Starting at point A with an inflation rate π, inflation rises to π'. This reduces the rate of real money growth and moves the LM curve to the left in panel (a). Demand is reduced (point A), hence the downward-sloping curve in panel (b).

[11] An implication of the purchasing power parity principle is that the higher inflation rate prompts the expectation of an exchange rate depreciation. Interest rate parity, as presented in Section 13.3.4, then requires that the domestic interest rate increases according to (13.1), and the BP line shifts upward. This slightly more involved treatment is not shown, but the qualitative conclusion is unchanged.

restored in the goods, money, and international financial markets. It is a short-run curve because, as long as domestic inflation exceeds the rate of nominal money growth, the real money supply keeps declining and the *LM* curve keeps shifting to the left.

Thus the short-run aggregate demand has the same shape under both fixed and flexible exchange rates, but for different underlying reasons. When the exchange rate is fixed, a higher inflation rate reduces demand through external competitiveness, not through the real money supply, which is endogenously supplied by the central bank through exchange market interventions. Under flexible rates, the situation is reversed. Competitiveness declines too, but not directly. The dominating influence on the real exchange rate is the behaviour of the floating nominal exchange rate, which appreciates as the shrinking real money supply tends to raise the interest rate and thus attracts capital inflows. Formally, when the nominal exchange rate is fixed ($S = \bar{S}$), the real exchange rate $\sigma = \bar{S}P/P^*$ increases because P increases faster than P^*. Under a flexible regime, the nominal exchange rate S must appreciate quite independently of P and P^*, until $\sigma = SP/P^*$ has risen enough to curtail aggregate demand to align the real money demand $L(Y, i)$ to a shrinking real supply $\bar{M}/P$.

Factors shifting the aggregate demand schedule

The *AD* curve shifts when any of the variables exogenous to the *IS-LM-BP* model changes. We need therefore to clarify which variables are endogenous and which ones are exogenous, and the exchange rate regime matters a great deal. Under flexible exchange rates, Chapter 10 shows that the *IS* curve is endogenously driven by the exchange rate to meet the *LM* and *BP* schedules. This means that neither fiscal policy, nor animal spirits, nor foreign output or any other exogenous change in demand can shift the aggregate demand curve. The aggregate demand curve shifts when either the *LM* or the *BP* curves do. Under flexible exchange rates, therefore, the growth rate of the nominal money supply $\mu = \Delta M/M$ is a key determinant of the position of the *AD* curve along with the foreign interest rate i^*, which determines the position of the *BP* line.

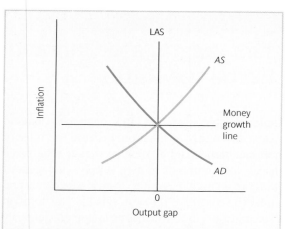

Fig. 13.10 Aggregate Demand and Supply under Flexible Exchange Rates
In the long run output is at its trend growth level (a zero output gap) and the money growth rate determines the rate of inflation. The figure depicts long-run equilibrium when the short-run aggregate demand and supply curves pass through the same point as the long-run schedules.

Inflation in the long run

In the long run, the long-run neutrality principle implies that inflation is determined by the rate of nominal money growth, which is set by the central bank. Ignoring trend growth, long-run inflation is simply equal to the growth rate of the nominal money supply: $\pi = \mu$.[12] This is shown in Figure 13.10 as the long-run aggregate demand schedule *LAD*. Note that this *LAD* schedule has the same shape as in the fixed exchange regime case, but that its position is no longer determined anymore by the foreign inflation rate.

The complete system

Figure 13.10 presents the complete system under flexible exchange rates. It includes the now-familiar short- and long-run aggregate supply curves as well as the short- and long-run aggregate demand curves. The figure depicts a long-run equilibrium: actual output is equal to trend output—a zero output gap—as required by the supply side, and inflation is

---

[12] If trend GDP growth is g, we can apply the reasoning in Box 13.1 to find that long-run inflation is $\pi = \mu - \eta g$.

set by money growth as required by the demand side. The PPP principle also allows us to infer the evolution of the exchange in the long run. The exchange rate makes up the difference between the domestic and foreign inflation rates. If the foreign rate of inflation is below the domestic rate, the exchange rate is depreciating; in the opposite case, it is appreciating ($\Delta S/S = \pi^* - \pi$).

13.3.2 Monetary Policy

Long run

The long-run effects of an expansionary monetary policy, i.e. of an increase in the rate of growth of the nominal money supply, are straightforward. Monetary neutrality implies that inflation will increase permanently, as will the rate of exchange rate depreciation ($-\Delta S/S$). The real side of the economy is left unaffected. In Figure 13.11, the economy moves from point A to point C and the vertical distance AC represents the increase in the money growth rate.

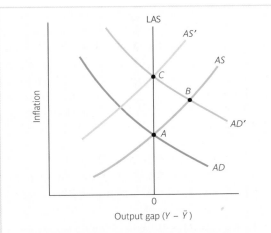

Fig. 13.11 Monetary Policy under Flexible Exchange Rates

Starting at point A, a monetary policy expansion shifts the AD curve rightwards to AD'. In the long run the economy will settle at point C, with GDP equal to trend output and the increase in inflation equal to the increase in the money growth rate. Short-run equilibrium occurs at point B. Thereafter core inflation tends to its long-run level and the economy moves from point B towards point C.

Short run

The expansionary effect of an increase in money growth is described in Figure 13.11 by the shift of the aggregate demand curve from AD to AD'. In the background—not shown here, but see Chapter 10—the LM curve shifts to the right and the IS curve follows as the result of a depreciating nominal exchange rate that boosts competitiveness and improves the current account. In the short run, the economy moves to point B: output is raised (and unemployment declines); inflation increases, but by less than the money growth rate; and therefore the real money supply still expands.

Transition

The transition will take the economy in steps from point B to point C. At point B, where output is above its growth trend level, the actual rate of inflation exceeds the core rate. What happens during the transition—and therefore the details of the trajectory—depends on the behaviour of the core rate of inflation. To the extent that it is backward looking, core inflation is sluggish; this is why, initially, the AS curve does not move and the economy reaches point B. Over time, as core inflation begins to track actual inflation, the short-run AS curve shifts upward and the economy moves from B towards C, along the curve AD'. As in the case of a fixed exchange rate regime, along the path from B to C, actual inflation always exceeds core inflation, while output declines as the real money growth rate is eroded by the rise in inflation.

Yet, core inflation has a forward-looking component which could anticipate that the long run is achieved at point C. If core inflation were purely forward looking, it would immediately adjust to the long-term inflation rate: the short-run aggregate supply curve shifts at once to position AS', the transition bypasses point B, and the economy jumps directly from point A to point C. In that case monetary neutrality occurs instantaneously, the dichotomy principle is verified at all times, and monetary policy loses its effectiveness. Two conditions are required for that to happen. First, core inflation must be entirely forward looking. Second, price- and wage-setters must be willing and ready to raise prices and wages to the full extent of the change in core inflation. The existence of either price or wage stickiness or of a backward component in core inflation is what makes the short run different from the long run.

In summary, an expansionary monetary policy increases output and inflation in the short run. In the long run, the effect falls entirely on higher inflation and not at all on output—this is the neutrality result under flexible exchange rates. In the short run, the backward-looking component of core inflation creates the non-neutrality needed for an output effect, while the forward-looking component tends to bring neutrality forward to the shorter run. The role of core inflation obviously requires closer scrutiny. This is the task of Chapter 16.

13.3.3 Fiscal Policy

From Chapter 10 we know that fiscal policy fails to move the *IS* curve, and therefore aggregate demand, because its effects are ultimately frustrated by the exchange rate reaction. A fiscal expansion leaks abroad because a real appreciation leads to a worsening of the primary current account. A fiscal contraction provokes a real depreciation which generates an increase in demand. For all practical purposes, the aggregate demand curve does not move.

13.3.4 Interest Rate Parity Revisited

Before looking at the behaviour of the economy under a flexible exchange rate regime, it may be useful to be more precise about the **interest rate parity** principle. This principle states that the domestic interest rate is equal to the foreign rate of return. Exactly what is the 'foreign rate of return' was left intentionally vague in Chapter 10. It is not just the rate of interest abroad, because foreign assets are denominated in the foreign currency, in which interest and principal are eventually paid out; the same applies to foreign currency borrowing. An appreciation of the euro in terms of dollars, for example, lowers the euro value of dollar assets and therefore reduces the return from holding them. This is why, when they compare interest rates in various countries, international investors must take into account the possible evolution of the currencies concerned. For example, when acquiring for, say, one year, a dollar asset, a European investor

must form a view of what will be the exchange rate between the euro and the dollar one year from now when she sells the asset and receives dollars that she will proceed to sell for euros.

In order to understand the interest parity condition we consider the following transaction. A large European bank borrows in euros and invests the proceeds in dollars for one year. At the end of the year, the bank will receive the principal and interest on its dollar assets, sell these dollars for euros, and pay back the principal and interest of its euro borrowing. Measured in euros, the cost of the operation is the euro interest rate i. The return is the dollar interest rate i^* *plus* the expected rate of appreciation of the dollar vis-à-vis the euro or, equivalently, *minus* the expected rate of appreciation of the euro vis-à-vis the dollar. Denoting by $\Delta S/S$ the expected rate of nominal appreciation of the domestic currency, this can be represented as follows:

Cost of borrowing euros (in euros): i
Return from dollar asset (in dollars): i^*
Return from dollar asset (in euros): $i^* - \Delta S/S$.

Of course, the bank does not know for sure what will happen to the euro–dollar exchange rate, so it must make a guess. But if the expected cost is less than the expected return, the bank will be willing to carry out this transaction, and will do so for very large amounts to make very large profits. In fact, all over the world, large financial institutions continuously monitor interest rates in various countries, seeking profitable opportunities of this kind. When they spot one, they immediately arrange for the deal, each of them for very significant amounts. Suppose that in the previous example, it is indeed the case that borrowing in euros and investing in dollars is generally seen as profitable because the former is lower than the latter:

$$i < i^* - \Delta S/S.$$

The immediate reaction of the international financial markets will be to borrow massively in euros, sell these euros for dollars, and invest in dollar-denominated assets. These massive capital inflows will have three immediate effects:

◆ A suddenly large demand for borrowings in euros will tend to raise the euro interest rate (i goes up).

◆ A suddenly large supply of funds in dollars will tend to lower the dollar interest rate (i^* goes down).

◆ Large sales of euros against the dollar will lead to an immediate depreciation of the euro vis-à-vis the dollar. But the markets also understand that in one year's time there will be large sales of dollars against euros, so they expect a stronger euro. Put differently, the markets now expect less of a depreciation, or more of an appreciation of the euro vis-à-vis the dollar ($\Delta S/S$ goes up or $-\Delta S/S$ goes down).[13]

Each of these steps makes the initial deal less appealing. Given the flows that international investors control, the immediate effect will be to eliminate the profit opportunity. Obvious deals of this kind never last for more than a few minutes,

at most. At all other times, which means nearly always, the euro interest rate must be equal to the dollar interest rate less the expected appreciation of the euro. This is the interest rate parity principle, now fully specified to account for exchange rate fluctuations; the modified interest rate parity condition is[14]

(13.8) $i = i^* - \Delta S/S.$

It can be interpreted as follows: if the domestic currency is expected to appreciate by, say, 5% over the next year, the foreign interest rate must be 5% higher than the domestic one. This higher interest return compensates for the expected capital loss that occurs if the foreign currency depreciates.[15] If instead a depreciation is anticipated, $\Delta S/S$ is negative and the domestic interest rate is higher than abroad.

13.4 How to Use the *AS-AD* Framework

This section illustrates how the complete system may be used to analyse important questions. It serves three main purposes: to illustrate the principles developed earlier; to develop familiarity with the framework; and to study some historical economic developments of general interest.

13.4.1 Supply Shocks

Supply shocks occur when production conditions are radically affected. They come in all shapes and forms but invariably create serious difficulties for policy-makers who are ill equipped to face the consequences. The reason is that the traditional demand-side policies are ineffective in this case while supply-side policies are economically complex and often politically unappealing.

The simplest example of an adverse supply shock is the sudden loss of factors of production, human or physical. This can be the result of natural disasters

or of wars. The economic transition from central planning to a market economy that occurred in Eastern and Central Europe after 1989 provides another example of an adverse supply shock. As illustrated in Figure 13.12, real GDP declined for a few years and then started to rise at a fairly brisk pace. The initial decline, the supply shock, was mainly due to the disorganization that set in as markets did not yet function while central planning had ceased to operate, and to the instantaneous obsolescence of the domestic production capacity once better foreign goods became available. Supply shocks can be favourable as well, for example an acceleration of technological advances. A current example is the information technology revolution that started in the mid-1990s and is still under way. Previous major episodes include the invention of electricity and of modern chemical products such as plastics.

---

[13] These two statements are equivalent because an appreciation is simply a negative depreciation, and conversely.

[14] The exact derivation of this condition as well as its modification for risk is presented in Ch. 19.

[15] In Ch. 10, we implicitly assume that $\Delta S/S = 0$.

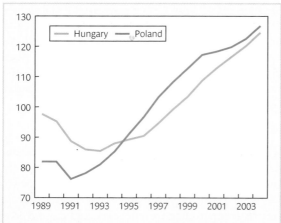

Fig. 13.12 GDP in Hungary and Poland, 1989–2004

Immediately after the collapse of central planning in 1990, GDP declined, but it then recovered and followed a fairly dynamic growth trend.

Note: GDP indices, 100 = sample average.
Source: Wyplosz (1999) and OECD.

The discovery of natural resources is also another instance of a favourable supply shock.

The oil shocks of 1973 and 1979 represent a turning point in post-war economic history. They marked the end of the rapid growth performance of most European countries and Japan, and were followed by markedly higher inflation and unemployment rates. Box 13.4 and Figure 13.13 show that, by the end of the 1980s, inflation had been rolled back, but in many countries employment and output growth have since remained significantly below the levels of the 1960s, the golden years. After a counter-oil shock in the mid-1990s, oil prices started again to rise sharply in 2000, and again in 2003 in the wake of the Iraq war. The *AD-AS* model was developed largely in response to these oil shocks, just as the *IS-LM* model was a response to the Great Depression.

A short-term policy dilemma

Supply shocks are represented by a shift of the aggregate supply curve. Typically the reason is an increase in production costs, which producers then pass on to their own prices. In Chapter 12, this was captured by the exogenous shock variable *s* in the aggregate supply equation:

(13.9) $$\pi = \bar{\pi} + a(Y - \bar{Y}) + s.$$

When the shock is unfavourable, i.e. when $s > 0$, the short-run aggregate supply curve shifts upward from *AS* to *AS'* as shown in Figure 13.14. The move from point *A* to point *B* represents stagflation, a combination of declining real growth and rising inflation. If the relative price increase is just a one-off event, the *AS* curve should soon shift back to

 Box 13.4 The Oil Shocks of the 1970s and 1980s

Major commodity prices started to rise in the early and late 1970s. While most of these increases were quickly reversed, nominal oil prices increased sixfold in two steps, with a partial reversal in 1986. The role of policy is highlighted by the choice of the exchange rate regime. At the time of the first shock, the industrial countries were trying to preserve a system of fixed exchange rates, including several European countries regrouped in the 'Snake' arrangement. Countries that were determined not to let inflation rise did not wish to maintain a fixed exchange rate with a more complacent rest of the world. Some countries, including Austria, Germany, Switzerland, and the Netherlands, opted for the low-inflation strategy; Japan, Italy, Spain, and the UK implicitly opted for the high-inflation approach; most other European countries adopted an intermediate stance with little or no policy reaction. Along the way, the international monetary system based on fixed exchange rates could not accommodate such policy divergences and collapsed.

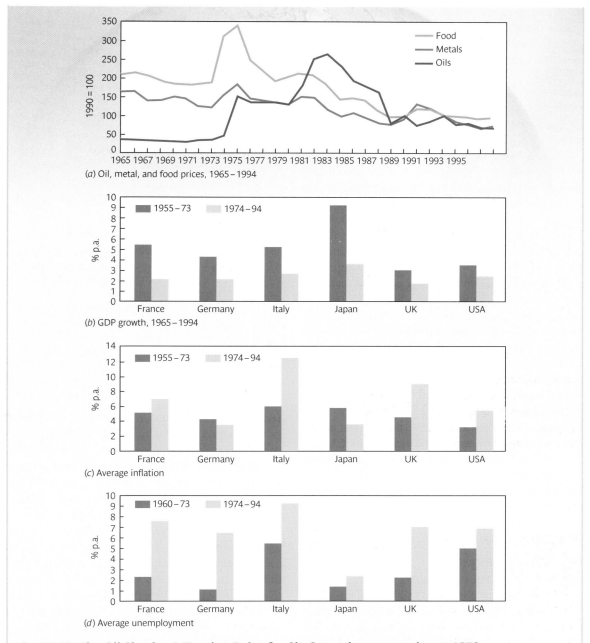

Fig. 13.13 The Oil Shocks: A Turning Point for Six Countries, pre- and post-1973

Panel (*a*) shows the prices of key commodities relative to the average consumer price index in the advanced economies. Real oil prices increased from 1973 until 1981, then declined significantly at the time of the counter-oil shock in 1986. Other commodity prices increased earlier, in 1971–2, but were quickly reversed, and in fact declined over the following decade. Panels (*b*)–(*d*) confirm that, with few exceptions, since the first oil shock of 1973–4 all key macroeconomic variables (growth, inflation, unemployment) have changed for the worse in OECD countries.

Sources: IMF; OECD, *Main Economic Indicators*.

its initial position.[16] This is optimistic, however. While the economy is at point B, workers unexpectedly face higher prices; quite likely, they will demand higher nominal wages and, if they succeed, the backward-looking component of core inflation $\bar{\pi}$ rises. This is why, even after the commodity price increase has been absorbed (when s goes back to zero), the AS curve is unlikely to shift back quickly.

Stagflation constitutes a serious policy dilemma for governments. One approach is to soften the blow on output and unemployment by adopting an expansionary policy (monetary or fiscal, depending on the exchange rate regime). Aiming at point C, and shifting the aggregate demand curve to AD' in Figure 13.14, hastens the return to trend growth but at the cost of higher inflation. Another approach is to prevent inflation from ever rising so that core inflation never changes. This calls for a prompt *contractionary* policy reaction, moving down the short-run aggregate demand schedule until it goes through a point like D. This reaction deepens the recession but, once the shock has worked itself through (and $s = 0$), the aggregate supply curve moves back to AS and the restrictive demand policy may be lifted to return to point A. The nature of the dilemma should be clear: the authorities can either aim at maintaining output and employment, but at the cost of higher inflation, or they can prevent a sharp inflationary impact, but at the cost of a low output and high unemployment. The reason behind this dilemma is also clear: macroeconomic management policies are demand-side policies and they are ill adapted to deal with supply shocks.

The exchange rate regime

The previous discussion makes it clear that a key issue is how core inflation reacts after the initial supply shock. Core inflation tends to increase because of its backward-looking component, but what about the forward-looking component? Much

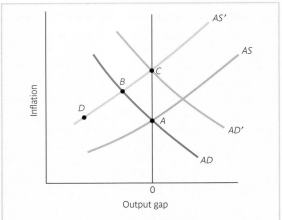

Fig. 13.14 An Adverse Supply Shock
An adverse supply shock shifts the AS curve up to AS'. The economy undergoes stagflation as it moves from point A to point B. If the authorities decide to avoid a fall in output and a rise in unemployment, they can adopt expansionary demand-side policies and drive the economy back to long-run equilibrium at point C. If instead they decide to prevent inflation from rising, they can adopt contractionary demand-side policies and aim at point D.

depends on which long-run equilibrium is expected to be reached eventually. If the authorities are known or are expected to aim at point D in Figure 13.14, the forward-looking component is likely to support this policy. If wage negotiators are convinced that inflation will be kept under control, they see the jump at point B as strictly temporary and keep core inflation at the pre-shock level. The aggregate supply schedule promptly returns to AS and the economy's trajectory will be from A to B and back to A. If instead wage negotiators expect an accommodating policy that aims at point C, core inflation will rise and permanently shift the AS curve to AS', even after the shock has passed. The trajectory will be from A to B and beyond, higher and to the left of B along the new AD' curve. However, since we have a negative output gap, core is above actual inflation, so the AS curve will eventually start shifting back towards AS', even though the one-off supply shock is over. The economy winds up at point C.

---

[16] A supply shock like a one-off increase in oil prices directly affects the price *level*, not its rate of *increase*, unless these prices keep increasing again and again. Normally, once they have reached a new higher level, the impact is passed once into higher goods prices. While the *level* of these prices remains higher, inflation is not directly affected any more.

Under flexible exchange rates, the central bank determines the position of the *LAD* line. The authorities can choose the long-run inflation rate and decide whether point *A* or point *C* will be eventually reached. This is not the case with a fixed exchange rate regime where the position of the *LAD* line depends on the 'foreign' inflation rate. In the presence of a serious supply shock, a fixed exchange rate regime can be maintained only among like-minded countries which have compatible views of how they will react. In Europe, for instance, the oil shocks of the 1970s and 1980s seriously strained the European Monetary System as different countries adopted different strategies. The adoption of a common currency, which floats freely, means that this decision is now in the hands of the European Central Bank. While the old danger of intra-European exchange rate turbulence is ruled out, policy disagreements remain. Following the rise of oil prices in 2003–4, ECB has been criticized by some governments as being too tight and by others as being too lax.

Lessons from supply shocks

Three general lessons can be drawn. First, an unfavourable supply shock is bad news. It adversely affects growth, unemployment, and inflation at the same time, in contrast with the Phillips curve trade-off. Second, demand management instruments are not appropriate for a supply shock. When the aggregate supply curve moves up and to the left, demand management cannot deal with both inflation and output. Demand-side policies must make the difficult choice between taking the shock as an increase in inflation or as a drop in output with higher unemployment. The appropriate response should be supply-side policies, aiming at bringing back the aggregate supply schedule as soon as possible to its initial position. This is not easy. The best hope is to shape the forward-looking component of core inflation and to try to 'disconnect' the backward-looking component. This requires a clear and credible signal from the authorities that they are determined not to accommodate the shock. Third, the exchange regime becomes crucial. A fixed exchange rate can be maintained only among countries that adopt the same strategy.

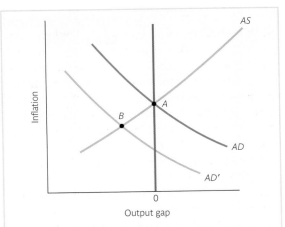

Fig. 13.15 An Adverse Demand Shock

An adverse demand shock is represented by a leftward exogenous shift of the short-run aggregate demand curve. The economy moves from point *A* to point *B*. In principle, the government has instruments at its disposal—monetary or fiscal policy, or both—which could restore the *AD* curve to its original position. This was the standard policy response of the 1960s. During the 1990s, however, the reaction has been remarkably subdued in European countries.

13.4.2 Demand Shocks

Exogenous shifts in demand are easier to deal with. Most of them are the result of macroeconomic policy actions, fiscal or monetary policy depending on the exchange rate regime. Other examples are exogenous events, like the sharp decline of stock prices in 2000–2, which was followed by a worldwide slowdown. Yet another example is German reunification, the source of an unexpected demand surge during the first half of the 1990s.

In Figure 13.15, an adverse demand shock is represented by a leftward exogenous shift of the short-run aggregate demand curve from *AD* to *AD'*. The economy moves from point *A* to point *B*: inflation declines and output falls below its trend level. In principle, the government has the required instruments at its disposal—monetary or fiscal policy, depending on the exchange rate regime—that could restore the *AD* curve to its original position. In the 1960s, this was the standard policy response.

Box 13.5 **Transatlantic Differences in 2000 – 2004**

Stock markets all but crashed worldwide in mid-2000, a distant reminder of the Wall Street events that ushered the Great Depression. Soon afterwards, growth started to stall around the world. Then came 11 September 2001, the terrorist attacks and the ensuing wars in Afghanistan and Iraq, which many feared would undermine confidence and lead households to save more and consume less, and firms to cancel investment projects. The ball landed squarely in the court of policy-makers: how would they react in the face of a sizeable demand shock? The contrast between Europe and the USA is striking. Both allow their exchange rates to float, so their central banks can use monetary policy. Figure 13.16 shows that the US Federal Reserve quickly lowered the interest rate and, as growth was not reacting, continued relentlessly, nearly reaching the minimum of 0%. The European Central Bank moved more slowly and much less aggressively. At the same time, the US Federal Government adopted a very expansionary fiscal policy stance, bringing the budget from balance to a deficit of more than 5%. European governments, on the other hand, tried to contain their deficits. As a result, growth returned to the USA in 2003, and very vigorously so, while it remained sluggish in Europe.

Why these differences? The US authorities do not harbour many qualms about the effectiveness of macroeconomic demand management policies. Under the

view 'that's all we've got anyway', they moved forcefully. The European authorities wavered. They expressed fears that inflation would rise, that public debts were too high, that macroeconomic policies do not work well. The European Central Bank continuously stresses that achieving its objective of 'medium-run' price stability is the best contribution that it can make to sustained growth and regularly voices doubts about using monetary and fiscal policy to speed up growth.

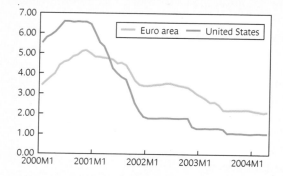

Fig. 13.16 Short-Term Interest Rates in Euroland and in the USA, 2000 – 2004
When growth slowed down in 2000, the US Federal Reserve aggressively lowered its interest rates while the European Central Bank moved with considerable caution.
Source: IMF.

Since the early 1990s, however, the reaction has been remarkably subdued in European countries.

There are different reasons for this reluctance. After a decade dedicated largely to erasing the inflation scars from the oil shocks (bringing core inflation down), most countries felt that the results had to be consolidated. This meant that monetary growth could not be allowed to rise again. Another policy achievement of the 1980s was the generally successful control over public indebtedness. Most governments felt that their budget constraint precluded any decisive use of fiscal policy to counteract a weakening of aggregate demand.[17] Finally, we

have seen that the rational expectation hypothesis implies that policy effects are greatly reduced. While the hypothesis is not generally taken literally, many economists and policy-makers accept the view that short-run macroeconomic policy is not very effective and prefer to focus on the long run. Box 13.5 presents a striking contrast between the European Central Bank and the Federal Reserve Board in the USA.

13.4.3 Disinflation

An important policy question, faced by many countries, is how to deal with a high rate of inflation. High and lasting inflation can only be the consequence of an excessively high rate of growth of the nominal money supply, so the cure must be to

[17] Ch. 16 provides more details on governments' reluctance to use their demand management instruments. Ch. 15 studies the public debt situation.

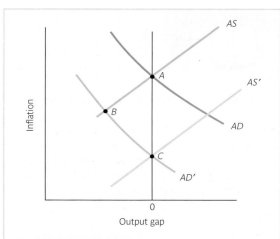

Fig. 13.17 **Disinflation**

Disinflation aims at bringing the economy from point A to point C. Using demand-side policies implies adopting contractionary monetary or fiscal policies, pushing the aggregate demand curve from AD to AD'. The short-run equilibrium at point B explains why disinflation is usually painful: it requires a period of low output and high unemployment. Long-run equilibrium is achieved at point C when the short-run aggregate supply curve has shifted to AS'. The speed of this shift depends on the time taken by core inflation to catch up with lower actual inflation.

slow down money growth. How it is implemented very much depends on the exchange rate regime.

Under flexible exchange rates, the central bank can control the rate of nominal growth, so the solution is technically simple, but painful as shown in Figure 13.17. We start from point A, which we assume to be a long-run equilibrium, which implies that nominal money growth is equal to the high inflation rate—we are on the LAD line—and that actual and core inflation are equal—we are on the LAS line. If the central bank reduces the nominal money growth rate, bringing it below the rate of inflation, the real money supply (M/P) starts declining. In the IS-LM-BP model (not shown), the LM curve shifts to the left, the real exchange rate appreciates, the current account worsens, and demand declines. This is captured by the leftward shift of the short-run aggregate demand curve from AD to AD'. The short-run effect of this disinflationary policy corresponds

to point B: inflation declines but so does output, and unemployment rises. At point B actual inflation is below core inflation so eventually core inflation will be revised downward and, over time, the short-run aggregate supply curve will shift downward until it reaches the position AS'. At point C a new long-run equilibrium is reached and the disinflation is complete. The cost has been a period of negative output gap and high unemployment.

Under a fixed and adjustable exchange rate regime, high and lasting inflation is only possible if the exchange rate is regularly depreciated, as explained in Section 13.2.4. Bringing inflation down requires a change in monetary policy. If the fixed exchange rate regime is to be retained, this means doing away with depreciations. In that case, we know that the LAD line is set by the foreign inflation rate, so it is essential to peg the exchange rate to the currency of a country where inflation is a suitably low. The peg becomes the anchor that will deliver disinflation. Since, initially, inflation is higher at home than abroad, this policy means a continuing real exchange rate appreciation. In the IS-LM-BP model (not shown), the IS curve shifts to the left, capital flows out, and the money supply starts to slow down. The resulting decline in aggregate demand is represented by the leftward shift of the short-run aggregate demand curve from AD to AD' in Figure 13.17. Then the logic is the same as under the flexible exchange rate regime. Core inflation must start declining to recognize the lower actual inflation rate and the economy will eventually settle at point A on the LAD line corresponding to the foreign inflation rate. Here too disinflation requires a period of negative output gap and high unemployment.

The interesting question is: how long does it take to move from point B to point C, and how much output is lost along the way? The **output cost of disinflation** is lower the faster the AS curve comes down. That, in turn, depends on the speed at which core inflation adapts to a declining inflation rate. The backward component of core inflation slows down the speed at which the AS curve shifts, while the forward-looking component accelerates the adjustment. In periods of disinflation, therefore, it would be helpful to give more weight to the forward-looking component, possibly even

Box 13.6   Wage Negotiations: The Time Dimension

In most European countries and in the USA, wage negotiations are *staggered* over a year or more. One wage negotiation takes into account the previous one, and may even anticipate the next one. Employees do not want to be bettered by other employees. Employers do not want to be underpriced and must hold their labour costs in line. In contrast, in Japan wage negotiations are *synchronized*. They take place every year at roughly the same time, the so-called 'spring offensive' (*shunto*). Each industry opens up bargaining, but closely monitors the state of play elsewhere. When one bargain is struck, it sets the trend and all the others follow quickly. For a time, wage negotiations in northern Europe were centralized and therefore highly synchronized. Even when they are staggered, some negotiations are *trend-setting*: they result in similar agreements later on and sometimes even trigger readjustments to previously reached ones, thus injecting a dose of synchronization. With wage staggering, aggregate nominal wages (the average of all nominal wages) move slowly, which retards the return to equilibrium unemployment. The *AS* curve will appear flatter. With full synchronization, average nominal wages are stable between negotiations, and then jump. This implies a steeper *AS* curve. The implications for the economy are profound: either a quick return to the equilibrium unemployment rate if the real wages are set right, or a prolonged departure if they are set incorrectly.

The situation is different in economies where inflation is high and has been so for a long time. There it is common to have mandatory or mutually agreed **indexation** schemes for wages. Brazil was particularly advanced in this regard, indexing virtually *all* nominal prices, including house rents, corporate balance sheets, taxes, and public utilities rates. Such indexation schemes can often reduce the staggering considerably, with the same effect as an increase in synchronization of wage-setting.

Although wage indexation removes some of the costs of high inflation to households and firms, it has serious adverse side-effects. First, indexation generally perpetuates any real wage gain achieved. This gives an incentive to any group of wage-earners to be the first to bid for higher wages. The result is that all groups rush to be first, as much to protect themselves as to achieve a head-start. Second, indexation reduces both public and government support for anti-inflation policies. This is why Germany, ever since its famous hyperinflation in the 1920s, has made indexation illegal. The third drawback is that indexation makes disinflation costlier in terms of unemployment. When inflation is on the way up, nominal wages trail behind prices: real wages are reduced and labour demand is robust. When inflation is on the way down, wages indexed on past inflation trail actual inflation: real wages rise, firms' profits are squeezed, and unemployment rises. This is why most European countries with legal or simply widespread indexation clauses eliminated them in the 1980s, much against the will of trade unions. Fourth, indexation eliminates downward real wage flexibility as real wages are at least constant unless there is a sharp burst of inflation. The lack of flexibility is a source of unemployment when an adverse supply shock occurs.

---

shutting off the backward-looking component. The backward-looking component depends on wage- and price-setting institutions, an issue examined in Box 13.6. The forward-looking component is often referred to as the 'psychological' nature of price- and wage-setting, but it can be influenced by policy institutions.

Wage negotiators may have opposing incentives in stating their expectations. It may be good bargaining tactics for workers to argue that inflation is high, while employers prefer to predict declines in the rate of inflation. Jointly, however, employers and employees have an incentive to be as close as possible to target, for errors may be costly in terms of competitiveness and profitability. As they aim at disinflation, the authorities have a strong interest in convincing wage negotiators that inflation will surely decline, since this will accelerate the downward movement of the *AS* curve. One solution is to credibly use the exchange rate as an anchor. To do so, the authorities must demonstrate that they will not let the exchange rate depreciate again. This is why a number of countries have adopted **hard pegs**, a variety of fixed exchange rate arrangements that makes it illegal to devalue.[18] If the exchange rate is not fixed, it is the credibility of the central bank as an inflation-fighter that becomes crucial. This is why a number of countries have given formal independence to their central banks, instructing them to aim at price stability; many independent central banks have adopted the **inflation-targeting strategy**, an approach that requires that they announce the inflation rate that they intend to achieve and that they explicitly and publicly tie their actions to the target, and to the target only.

One measure of the output cost of disinflation is the **sacrifice ratio**. It compares the cumulated increase in the rate of unemployment with the reduction in inflation achieved during that period. For example, the Phillips curves of Figure 12.6 show disinflation in Euroland and the UK over the period 1980–6. In both countries the unemployment rate rose significantly; the corresponding sacrifice ratios over this period were roughly 2.5 percentage points of inflation for 1 point of unemployment for Euroland, compared with a ratio of 2 : 1 for the UK.

Summary

1 The macroeconomy is analysed as the interplay of aggregate demand and aggregate supply. This framework emphasizes the distinction between the short run and the long run, when output returns to its trend growth path.

2 The short-run aggregate demand curve is downward sloping. Under fixed exchange rates, an increase in inflation above the foreign rate erodes external competitiveness and reduces total demand for domestic goods. Under flexible exchange rates, for a given growth rate of the nominal money supply, an increase in the inflation rate lowers the rate of growth of the real money stock, and hence has a contractionary effect on aggregate demand.

3 In the long run, inflation is restricted to be equal to foreign inflation under fixed exchange rates. Under flexible rates, long-run inflation is determined by the rate of growth of the nominal money supply.

4 Only under flexible rates can the monetary authorities set the money growth rate. Some independence can be achieved under fixed exchange rates by repeated devaluations or revaluations.

5 Under fixed exchange rates, fiscal policy can affect aggregate demand and output. The effects of a fiscal policy action are temporary, however. In the long run output must be back on trend and anyway the government's budget constraint prevents a permanently expansionary fiscal policy.

6 A fiscal expansion initially raises the output level at the cost of a higher rate of inflation. Over time, as core inflation rises and the unavoidable retrenchment of fiscal policy occurs, demand returns to trend output.

7 Under fixed exchange rates monetary policy is ineffective. This is also the case for fiscal policy under flexible exchange rates.

8 Under flexible exchange rates, a monetary expansion initially raises output and inflation. Over time, inflation continues to increase, eroding the real money supply and bringing output back to its trend growth path.

9 An adverse supply shock simultaneously lowers output and raises inflation. Demand management policies are ill equipped to deal with a supply shock. They may cushion the fall in income at the cost of more inflation, or reduce

[18] This is the strategy adopted, for example, by Argentina in 2001 and by Bulgaria in 1997. In both cases, it worked, although Argentina's arrangement collapsed in 2001. By then, however, inflation was negative!

the inflationary impact at the cost of a deeper fall in output and more unemployment.

10 Disinflation requires reducing the rate of monetary growth when the exchange rate is freely floating or sticking to the peg under a fixed exchange rate regime. It can be costly

in terms of lost output and above-equilibrium unemployment.

11 The faster core inflation adjusts, the lower the costs of disinflation. This calls for adopting credible institutions that can convince wage negotiators that the disinflation policy is 'serious'.

🔑 Key Concepts

- ◆ purchasing power parity
- ◆ *LAD* line
- ◆ short-run vs. long-run general equilibrium
- ◆ aggregate demand curve
- ◆ stagflation
- ◆ interest rate parity

- ◆ output cost of disinflation
- ◆ hard pegs
- ◆ inflation-targeting strategy
- ◆ sacrifice ratio
- ◆ indexation

❓ Exercises

1 Use the *AD-AS* model to trace out the *short-run* effect under both fixed and flexible rate regimes of: (i) a one-off increase in government spending; (ii) a permanent increase in money growth.

2 Consider the *AD-AS* model where the initial situation is not a long-run equilibrium, for instance where the economy starts with a negative output gap. What happens next without any government intervention under fixed exchange rates? Under flexible exchange rates?

3 Assume that PPP and the interest rate parity conditions are both satisfied. What can you conclude about the domestic and foreign interest real rates?

4 Assume that supply–side shocks dominate. What can you predict about the correlation between inflation and the output gap? Same question when demand shocks dominate. When would you expect to see a Phillips curve?

5 Use the *AD-AS* and *IS-LM-BP* to study the short- and long-run effects of an increase in foreign inflation under a fixed exchange rate regime.

6 Under fixed exchange rates, use the *IS-LM-BP* and *AD-AS* models to analyse the effects of a combined tight fiscal policy and expansionary monetary policy.

7 Under flexible exchange rates, use the *IS-LM-BP* and *AD-AS* models to analyse the effects of a combined lax fiscal policy and tight monetary policy.

8 What are the effects of a counter-oil shock when oil prices suddenly decline?

9 A government wants to use monetary policy under a flexible exchange rate to keep actual GDP above its trend growth rate for ever. In the *AS-AD* diagram, show graphically the consequences of such a policy.

10 Assume that core inflation is entirely forward-looking and that expectations are rational. What are the effects of fiscal policy (under fixed exchange rates) and monetary policy (under flexible exchange rates) on output and inflation? Consider both cases of expansionary or restrictive policies, at your discretion.

➔ Essay Questions

1 'Expansionary policies rely upon fooling people.' Comment.

2 Why does adding the supply side partly undermine the usefulness of demand management policies?

3 Why are supply-side policies more appealing than demand-side policies. What kind of supply-side policies can you envision?

4 'Sluggish expectations are helpful when inflation is rising but troublesome when inflation is declining.' Evaluate this assertion and imagine policy implications.

5 Experience seems to suggest that dealing with an oil shock with restrictive policies is more desirable than resorting to expansionary policies. Why could that be so?

Business Cycles

14.1 Overview 332

14.2 Stylized Facts about Business Cycles 333
  14.2.1 The Duration and Magnitude of Cycles 333
  14.2.2 Correlation with Output over the Cycle 337
  14.2.3 Leading and Lagging Indicators 337
  14.2.4 Relative Variability 339

14.3 Deterministic and Stochastic Interpretations of the Business Cycle 341
  14.3.1 Business Cycles as an Endogenous Phenomenon 341
  14.3.2 Deterministic Cycles: The Example of the Multiplier-Accelerator 341
  14.3.3 Stochastic Cycles: The Impulse-Propagation Mechanism 343

14.4 Sticky Price Business Cycles 346
  14.4.1 Impulses and Propagation in the *AS-AD* Framework 346
  14.4.2 Identifying Demand and Supply Shocks and their Propagation 347
  14.4.3 The Contribution of Demand and Supply Shocks 349

14.5 Real Business Cycles 349
  14.5.1 Productivity Shocks as Impulses 349
  14.5.2 Propagation Channels in Real Business Cycles 351
  14.5.3 Optimality Properties of the Cycle 352

14.6 Taking Stock of the Two Theories 352
  14.6.1 Productivity, Real Wages, and Employment 353
  14.6.2 Money, Credit, and the Cycle 354

  Summary 355

Almost all of the phenomena of economic life, like many other processes, social, meteorological, and others, occur in sequences of rising and falling movements, like waves.

—Eugen E. Slutsky

14.1 Overview

Economies tend to grow over time, but they grow in an uneven fashion. They tend to fluctuate around their long-term trends, as shown in Figure 10.1. Just as Chapter 3 studied trend growth and neglected shorter-run fluctuations, this chapter focuses on fluctuations around trend growth. The tendency for an economy to behave in a cyclical fashion has been considered a key puzzle of economic life for centuries, going as far back as the biblical observation that seven years of feast are followed by seven years of famine. It has long been observed that these patterns of expansion and contraction in activity, or **business cycles**, occur with some regularity. A recession does not necessarily mean negative growth, however. For fast-growing countries like South Korea and China, a year of 4–5% growth is sometimes considered a slump!

Many questions come to mind when thinking about business cycles. Is there such a thing as a 'typical' cycle? What is its frequency? Are cycles a result of purely predictable, or deterministic factors, or are they random in nature? Does each period of expansion sow the seeds of an unavoidable future recession? Conversely, is it the case that **recessions** are invariably followed by **booms**, if one is willing to wait long enough? Which aspects of economic life are subject to cyclical movements and which ones seem unaffected by boom and bust? This chapter begins with some stylized facts about the business cycle. Economic forecasters and policy planners intently study the economic scene to detect signals of future macroeconomic developments. They watch a number of variables that tend to move systematically with, or even anticipate, the business cycle. Especially important are **turning points**, when the economic cycle reaches a **peak** or a **trough**. Firms which correctly anticipate the end of a recession will hire more workers and invest in additional capacity ahead of the upturn, in order to have ample goods to sell. Firms which correctly foresee the end of a boom can slow down or cancel hiring and investment plans, and thus avoid more costly adjustments later on.

This chapter's goal is to explain business cycles. Previous chapters have given us most of the tools we need. Yet, while the *IS-LM* and *AS-AD* models are designed precisely to explain deviations of GDP from trend, more is needed. First, it is useful to track the behaviour of variables besides GDP—unemployment, prices and inflation, wages, firms' profitability, interest rates, etc. Second, the *IS-LM* and *AS-AD* frameworks allow us to study the effect of exogenous changes (e.g. in the money supply, or in entrepreneurial spirits), but is there something systematic in these factors themselves? Can they themselves be explained as endogenous phenomena?

In fact, there are two ways of thinking about business cycles. One is that business cycles are largely predictable, self-renewing phenomena, much like the mythical perpetual motion machine. Section 14.3 describes what would be needed for that to happen and concludes that it is highly unlikely. A second, more fruitful, insight conceives of the economic system as a black box, which receives stimuli at one end and transforms them into business cycles at the other. This 'impulse-propagation' mechanism approach is now generally accepted among business cycle researchers as the most fruitful way of proceeding, and is the subject of the rest of the chapter.

The biggest challenge for macroeconomics is to identify the primary source of stimuli which drive the cycle—the impulses—and to determine how they are transmitted—the propagation mechanism. Here macroeconomists often disagree. The two premier contending views correspond to the distinction introduced in Chapter 11 between price stickiness and flexibility. Section 14.4 presents the sticky price view, which can be seen as an extension of ideas introduced in Chapters 11–13. Section 14.5 explains the alternative case of flexible prices, which is often called the theory of **real business cycles**. The last section summarizes the current state of thinking on the two competing paradigms.

14.2 Stylized Facts about Business Cycles

We began our study of growth in Chapter 3 by identifying a number of 'stylized facts'. This strategy will be useful in this chapter as well. We will begin by identifying features that are common to business cycles over time and across countries. Business cycles are usually studied using quarterly data, in order to reveal enough details within the time period—usually just a few years—that a typical cycle takes to unfold.

14.2.1 The Duration and Magnitude of Cycles

Panel (a) of Figure 14.1 presents the path of GDP in the UK since 1961, as well as an estimated **trend** which 'smooths out' the uneven movements of real GDP. These fluctuations are even more evident in panel (b), which presents the deviations of actual from trend GDP, or **detrended** GDP, magnifying the deviations visible in the upper panel. Cycles seem to be recurrent, with two to three years above trend, two to three years below. When the economy turns down from its peak, the recession phase starts. As it runs up from a trough, this is the time of recovery, leading to an expansion.

Stylized Fact No. 1: In advanced economies, real GDP growth fluctuates in a recurrent but irregular fashion, with an average cycle length of five to eight years.

Although business cycle episodes tend to be similar, Figure 14.1 shows that they are far from identical. For example, the 1976 recovery was short-lived, leading to a 'double-dip' in 1977 following the 1975 recession. Conversely, the recovery that followed the early 1980s recession was long-lived. This irregularity makes it a delicate exercise to pinpoint peaks and troughs in the business cycle. In the USA, the task has long been performed by the National Bureau of Economic Research (NBER), which appoints a business cycle committee of independent economists. They declare as a peak the quarter that immediately precedes two consecutive quarters of decline in GDP. Similarly, a trough immediately precedes two consecutive quarters of positive growth. In Europe, the Centre for Economic Policy Research (CEPR) in London has recently begun to date business cycles for the Euro-area, using a more elaborate procedure.[1]

Table 14.1 presents a few descriptive statistics for business cycles in several countries.[2] The average

---

[1] www.cepr.org/Data/eurocoin/
[2] Using an estimated trend similar to that shown in Figure 14.1, we identify recessions as periods consisting of four or more consecutive quarters with GDP below trend and in which there were at least two quarters of negative growth during or preceding the period. The trough is judged as the quarter with the lowest GDP in the below-trend period, on the basis of undetrended data.

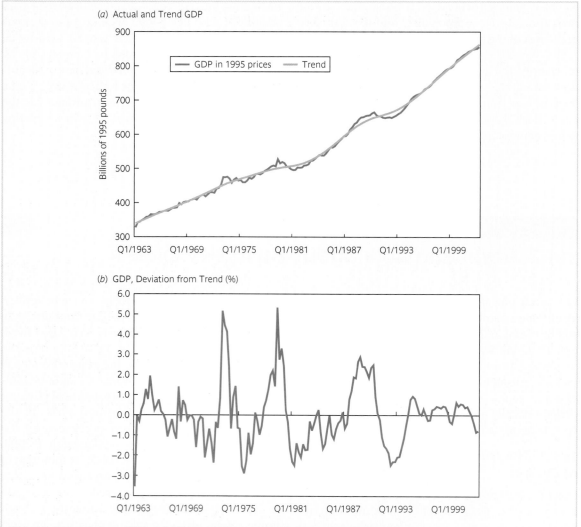

Fig. 14.1 Actual and Trend GDP and Detrended GDP, UK, 1963 – 2002

Panel (a) shows the evolution over time of actual and trend real quarterly GDP in the UK. Panel (b) displays the series after it has been detrended, or separated from its trend.
Source: OECD.

peak-to-peak cycle length is about thirty quarters or 7.5 years, with large differences in minimum and maximum length. Japan stands apart. It has undergone fewer cycles than the other major OECD countries. In fact, Japan has been on a continuing slow-growth phase from the early 1990s to 2003. While these are the cycles most widely monitored and referred to as business cycles, a number of different cyclical fluctuations in economic activity have long fascinated researchers. Box 14.1 describes some of these cycles.

Popular discussions of economic conditions emphasize short-run fluctuations associated with business cycles, to the point that cycles can have significant political repercussions, including bringing governments down. Yet on average these

Table 14.1 Descriptive Statistics of Business Cycles, 1963–2002

	No. of completed cycles	Average cycle length (quarters)	Max. cycle length (quarters)	Min. cycle length (quarters)	Average deviation from midpoint (%)
UK	4	21.5	25	19	4.2
France	3	28.0	38	14	2.0
Germany	5	19.0	27	11	3.8
Italy	5	20.2	40	10	2.2
Japan	2	46.5	73	20	4.0
USA	4	31.3	42	17	3.4

Source: OECD *Main Economic Indicators* database, authors' calculations.

Box 14.1 Famous Cycles

Business cycles, like comets, bear the names of their discoverers. Simon Kuznets (1901–85) was a Russian-born US economist who received a Nobel Prize for his work on growth. Russian economist Nikolai Kondratieff (1892–1931?) developed his theory of long-wave cycles in the 1920s before he was arrested and disappeared; the official Soviet Encyclopaedia then wrote about his work: 'this theory is wrong and reactionary.' It was also in the 1920s that Joseph Kitchin (1861–1932), a South African statistician and gold trader, uncovered his own more rapid cycles of 2–4 years' periodicity, which are associated with inventory movements, bank clearings, and wholesale prices. Clement Juglar (1819–1905), a nineteenth-century French physician, first studied cycles in human births, deaths, and marriages before turning his skills to interest rates and credit conditions. These Juglar cycles—which involve fluctuations of investment spending, GNP, inflation, and unemployment—are perhaps the closest thing to the business cycle that we will study in this chapter.

Interestingly, one of the most robust and regular cycles in economic activity is the seasonal cycle, which coincides with the seasons of the year. Movements of output in agriculture, manufacturing, construction, and tourism have obvious seasonal components which sometimes swamp business cycle fluctuations in magnitude, as do patterns in overall output associated with bank holidays, summer and winter weather, and harvests.

fluctuations represent only 2–5% of trend GDP from peak to trough. Movements of GDP around its trend are clearly dwarfed by the evolution of the trend itself, as Figure 14.1 amply illustrates. Thus, the second stylized fact:

Stylized Fact No. 2: Measured relative to average GDP and to the growth process, the amplitude of business cycle fluctuations is small.

To detect common aspects of business cycles, we will make use of **Burns–Mitchell diagrams**. These diagrams give a visual summary of the average behaviour of macroeconomic variables over a typical business cycle, measured in relation to (as a deviation from) their respective values at the cyclical peak.[3] Figure 14.2 displays these 'reference cycles' for real

3 Named after US economists Arthur Burns (1904–87) and Wesley Mitchell (1874–1948), two of the most influential empirical researchers on the 'trade cycle' in their time. They developed this technique at the NBER in the 1940s and 1950s. Their work was severely criticized in 1947 by Dutch-born Chicago economic theorist and econometrician Tjalling Koopmans (1910–86) as 'measurement without theory'. His attack turned several generations of economists away from the descriptive approach developed by Burns and Mitchell. A half-century later, Burns and Mitchell are making a comeback of sorts.

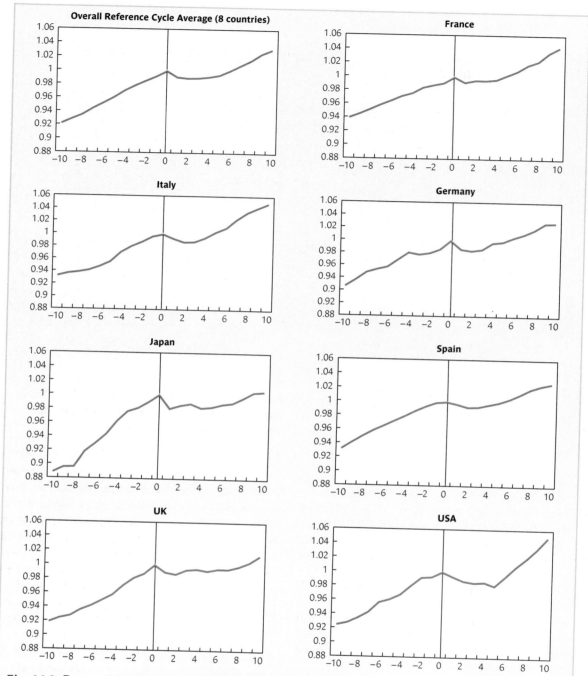

Fig. 14.2 Burns – Mitchell Diagrams for Real GDP, 1964 – 2002

The Burns – Mitchell procedure can be described as follows. First, for each country, cyclical peaks over the period are identified. Second, within a standard 'business cycle window' of 20 quarters (10 before the peak, 10 afterwards), GDP is normalized relative to its cyclical peak. Third, real GDP is averaged across all identified business cycle episodes. The figure displays this average for each country and, in the last graph, for the average of all eight countries (Canada not shown). Note that the scale differs across countries, reflecting higher trend growth rates over the period.

Source: OECD, *Quarterly National Accounts*, authors' calculations.

Table 14.2 Business Cycle Correlations of Macroeconomic Variables with Output, 1968–2002[a]

	Consumption	Investment	Government spending	Exports	Imports	Prices	Inflation
EU	0.86	0.90	−0.15	0.85	0.94	−0.45	0.30
Japan	0.71	0.89	−0.03	0.47	0.64	−0.15	0.18
USA	0.88	0.95	0.04	0.32	0.75	−0.75	0.15

[a] Correlation coefficient of seasonally adjusted and detrended values using the Hodrick–Prescott filter; see WebAppendix for details.

Source: OECD *Main Economic Indicators* database

GDP in eight OECD countries, as well as their overall average. Note that the data have not been detrended, and as such are free of manipulation. Consistent with Stylized Fact No. 2, the figures reveal the importance of the growth trend, even at the short horizon of business cycles. Business cycles do appear to be similar across countries; for example, the average recession lasts two to five quarters in all countries examined, which is much less than the average expansion (see Table 14.1). This is an encouragement to search for regularities in other variables, too.

14.2.2 Correlation with Output over the Cycle

The behaviour of GDP is used to identify business cycles, but what can we say about other important macroeconomic variables? Are they systematically affected by the cycle? Which ones tend to be **procyclical**, moving in the same direction as GDP, and which ones are **countercyclical** instead? Or are they seemingly independent of the cycle, or **acyclical**? One way of answering these questions is to look at the degree of covariation, or co-movement, of each variable with GDP.[4] Table 14.2 presents correlation coefficients of output with other macroeconomic

variables in Europe, Japan, and the USA after they have been detrended. Private domestic spending —consisting of consumption, investment, and imports—is procyclical. Public spending is quite smooth and acyclical: it would be countercyclical if the government were systematically offsetting movements in private spending, procyclical if it were stimulating it. This is robust enough to be a stylized fact:

Stylized Fact No. 3: The components of private expenditures are procyclical, while on average government consumption is acyclical.

14.2.3 Leading and Lagging Indicators

The correlations reported in Table 14.2 only tell us which variables move together simultaneously. If one variable systematically leads or lags another, contemporaneous correlation may be nil and yet an important link may still exist. The Burns–Mitchell diagrams in Figure 14.3 display the average cyclical behaviour of important macroeconomic variables for the UK, France, Germany, Italy, and the USA. The vertical line indicates the peak of the average reference cycle for GDP over all the countries. The figure shows that some variables tend systematically to peak ahead of, and others systematically to trail behind, real output. For example, the degree of capacity utilization, investment in inventory, real share prices, and real money balances are examples of **leading indicators**. They tend to predict the emergence of recessions and expansions. Other variables, such as unemployment and inflation, tend to be **lagging indicators**. Interest rates are an example of a **coincident indicator**.

---

4 The concept of correlation is introduced informally in Ch. 1. Two variables are statistically correlated when they exhibit a tendency to move together, and this tendency is summarized by the correlation coefficient. Procyclical variables would have positive values of the correlation coefficient near +1; countercyclical variables would have negative correlation coefficients with output near −1; acyclical variables would have correlation coefficients near 0.

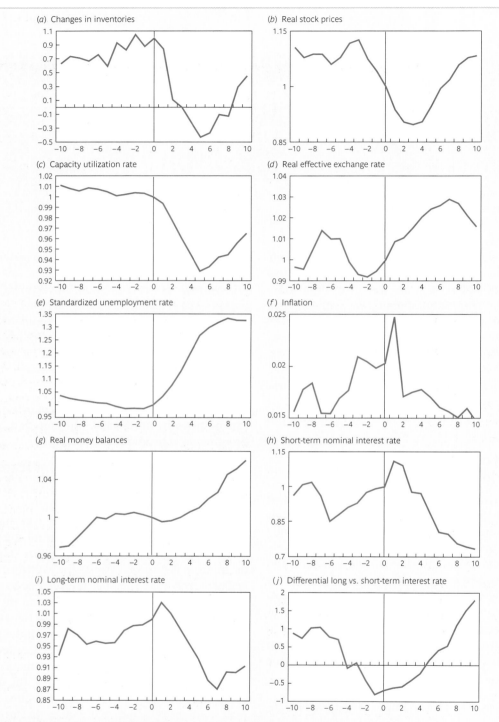

Fig. 14.3 Leading and Lagging Indicators, 1968–2002

These Burns–Mitchell diagrams show the evolution of key economic variables averaged over eight countries (Canada, France, Germany, Italy, Japan, Spain, UK, and USA) and over each country's business cycles. The vertical line corresponds to the cyclical peak (of output). Leading indicators tend to change direction in advance of the cyclical peak (changes in inventories, real stock prices, capacity utilization, and real money balances) while coincident and lagging indicators confirm a tendency already observable in output movements (unemployment, interest rates, inflation).

Sources: OECD, *Quarterly National Accounts, Main Economic Indicators*; IMF, *International Financial Statistics*, authors' calculations.

Table 14.3 Variability of Key Macro Variables over the Cycle, 1964–2002[a]

	GDP (%)	Consumption	Investment	Government purchases	Exports	Imports	Prices (GDP deflator)
EU	0.95	0.86	2.52	0.53	2.44	3.07	0.94
Japan	1.18	0.81	2.43	0.71	3.28	4.44	0.65
USA	1.61	0.80	2.68	0.77	2.68	3.12	0.54

[a] Variability is measured as the standard deviation of seasonally adjusted and detrended values using the Hodrick–Prescott filter; see Appendix for details.

Source: OECD *Main Economic Indicators* and *National Accounts* databases.

Stylized Fact No. 4: Some variables systematically lead GDP over the cycle (inventories, capacity utilization, stock prices, real money balances), while others (inflation, unemployment) systematically lag behind. Others (interest rates) are coincident.

Our knowledge of the macroeconomy can account for many of these regularities. For example, capacity utilization (panel (c) in Figure 14.3), a measure of production, tends to decline roughly two quarters before a cyclical peak, i.e. before that of GDP, which measures spending and income. How can production and spending differ from each other? When spending exceeds production, inventories of finished goods are sold to make up the difference. When output exceeds spending, inventories are accumulated, and this is the message conveyed by panel (a) of Figure 14.3.[5] Thus, moving towards a cyclical peak, firms begin to satisfy demand by selling from inventories. In contrast, near the trough, firms start restocking inventories in anticipation of a recovery. A similar logic can be applied to total investment spending. As the cyclical peak approaches, forward-looking firms reduce spending on new productive equipment, which is not needed in a recession; conversely, anticipating rising demand, they begin expanding capacity in advance of cyclical troughs.

[5] Inventories are goods produced but not yet sold as well as goods in process and intermediate goods used in production. In the National Income Accounts (see Ch. 2), inventory changes are counted as part of investment, so additions to inventories represent positive investment.

Financial variables are frequently useful leading indicators. The analyses of the last three chapters make it easy to understand why real money balances could help predict output. According to panel (g) of Figure 14.3, the real money supply starts to decline six months to a year in advance of the onset of a recession. Similarly, panel (b) suggests that real share prices start declining three to four quarters in advance of a downturn. Since real stock prices are a measure of Tobin's q, it is easy to see why they are a leading indicator: financial markets also anticipate the next phase of the cycle and, for example, expect poorer profitability during the downturn phase. On the other hand, the real exchange rate in panel (d) contains less clear evidence of a systematic relationship. Yet this is consistent with our theoretical analysis of the exchange rate in the open economy in Chapter 10, since monetary and real shocks can have different implications for the behaviour of the real exchange rate, as can the exchange rate regime itself.

14.2.4 Relative Variability

Another feature of business cycles is how much key economic variables move over the cycle relative to each other. Table 14.3 indicates several regularities across countries. At least for the USA and Japan, prices are less variable than output, which is consistent with the 'Keynesian assumption' that was introduced in Chapter 10. In Europe, prices appear absolutely and relatively more variable, which probably has to do with the openness of individual European economies as well as a history of higher inflation. Consumption is smoother than output, output is smoother than investment expenditures,

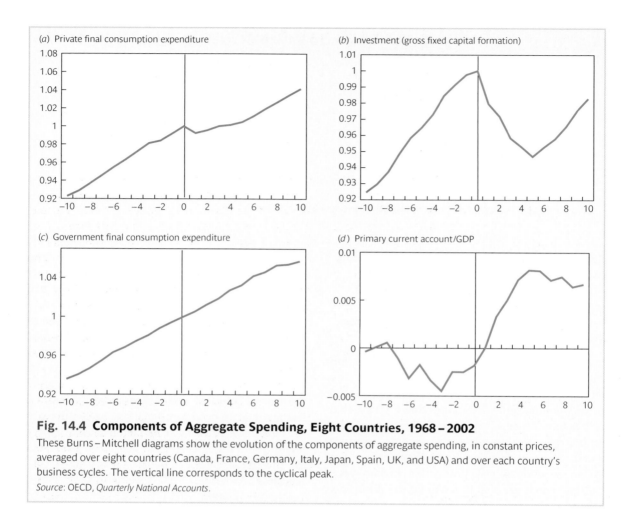

Fig. 14.4 Components of Aggregate Spending, Eight Countries, 1968 – 2002

These Burns – Mitchell diagrams show the evolution of the components of aggregate spending, in constant prices, averaged over eight countries (Canada, France, Germany, Italy, Japan, Spain, UK, and USA) and over each country's business cycles. The vertical line corresponds to the cyclical peak.

Source: OECD, *Quarterly National Accounts*.

and trade (exports and imports) represents the most unstable component of GDP. Figure 14.4, which presents the components of GDP in Burns–Mitchell format, confirms that investment spending and the current account are the most volatile. We have already seen the high volatility of inventory investment in Figure 14.3. In comparison, private consumption and government purchases of goods and services are relatively smooth. We conclude this discussion with the following stylized fact:

Stylized Fact No. 5: Investment—especially inventory investment—is more volatile and consumption less volatile than GDP. Exports and imports are highly variable, while government purchases are acyclical.

The fact that consumption is less volatile than GDP is consistent with the consumption–smoothing principle established in Chapter 6; the volatility of investment is a consequence of its forward-looking nature, as captured by Tobin's q. One surprising feature of Figure 14.4 is the smoothness of government final spending on goods and services. Two main factors account for the acyclical nature of government purchases. First, as a policy variable, government purchases are likely to be employed countercyclically, rising to reduce a recession and declining during expansions. Second, a large component of government consumption is the wages and salaries of civil servants, which also tend to be smooth over time.

14.3 Deterministic and Stochastic Interpretations of the Business Cycle

14.3.1 Business Cycles as an Endogenous Phenomenon

Why should economic fluctuations occur in a seemingly endless and systematic way? The long-held belief that cycles occur with perfect regularity can be dismissed by examining the data. Yet the list of stylized facts shows that cycles do not unfold in a completely random fashion, either. They exhibit important regularities and seem to follow an internal logic. This tension lies behind all theories of the business cycle. The question to answer is: does the cycle sow the seeds of its own reproduction, and if so, how? Might it be possible that cycles go on reproducing themselves, just like the rising and falling of the tides? This would be the case if the economic system constantly generated forces that successively speeded it up and then slowed it down. It turns out that it is quite possible to imagine how this can come about.

One necessary condition, which applies to any explanation of business cycles, is some systematic delay in economic responses to changing conditions. For example, the consumption function links current spending to current income and wealth. This may just hold for consumers' intentions, but they may take time in transforming that into effective action. This is the so-called **Robertson lag**. It is equally plausible that output does not rise immediately to meet increases in demand: the behaviour of inventories shows that firms initially supply additional demand by running down inventories, the so-called **Lundberg lag**.[6] In what follows both of these lags will be useful for studying mechanisms behind the business cycle.

14.3.2 Deterministic Cycles: The Example of the Multiplier-Accelerator

In the end, we expect GDP to depend on its own past—in fact, in a fairly rich and complex way. The WebAppendix shows how the *AS-AD* model indeed displays this pattern. To motivate this idea using a much simpler example, we study the so-called multiplier-accelerator model, which played an important role in the early development of ideas about business cycles.[7] The model ignores the price level, the monetary sector, the government sector, and the role of expectations, among other things. The model is only sketched in this section; a formal framework is presented in Box 14.2 and the WebAppendix.

As its name suggests, the main elements of the multiplier-accelerator model are the spending multiplier introduced in Chapter 11, which translates exogenous changes in demand into changes in total final demand, and the accelerator principle presented in Chapter 6, which relates the level of investment positively to changes in GDP. Consumption in period t, C_t, responds to income with a Robertson lag:

(14.1) $$C_t = a_0 + a_1 Y_{t-1},$$

where a_0 and a_1 are positive constants, with a_1 representing the marginal propensity to spend out of income with $0 < a_1 < 1$. Investment behaves according to the accelerator principle:

(14.2) $$I_t = b_0 + b_1(Y_{t-1} - Y_{t-2}),$$

with both b_0 and b_1 positive. Again, a Robertson lag is operative here. According to (14.2), for investment spending to exceed b_0, output must increase. Since there is no government or foreign sector, the

---

[6] Named respectively after the British economist D. H. Robertson (1890–1963) and the Swedish economist Erik Lundberg (1907–87).

[7] This model was developed by Paul Samuelson of MIT and John Hicks from Oxford, both Nobel Prize laureates, as well as the American economist Lloyd Metzler (1913–80).

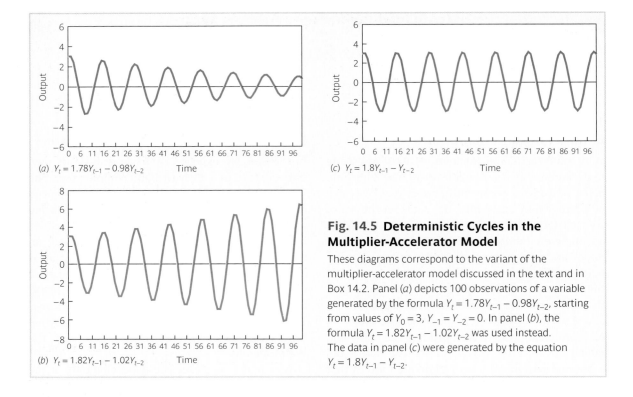

(a) $Y_t = 1.78Y_{t-1} - 0.98Y_{t-2}$ Time

(c) $Y_t = 1.8Y_{t-1} - Y_{t-2}$ Time

(b) $Y_t = 1.82Y_{t-1} - 1.02Y_{t-2}$ Time

Fig. 14.5 Deterministic Cycles in the Multiplier-Accelerator Model

These diagrams correspond to the variant of the multiplier-accelerator model discussed in the text and in Box 14.2. Panel (a) depicts 100 observations of a variable generated by the formula $Y_t = 1.78Y_{t-1} - 0.98Y_{t-2}$, starting from values of $Y_0 = 3$, $Y_{-1} = Y_{-2} = 0$. In panel (b), the formula $Y_t = 1.82Y_{t-1} - 1.02Y_{t-2}$ was used instead. The data in panel (c) were generated by the equation $Y_t = 1.8Y_{t-1} - Y_{t-2}$.

model is closed by the GDP identity $Y_t = C_t + I_t$, which after substituting (14.1) and (14.2) can be written as

(14.3) $Y_t = (a_0 + b_0) + (a_1 + b_1)Y_{t-1} - b_1Y_{t-2}$.

Equation (14.3) is called a **difference equation**. It traces out an endogenous dynamic path of output Y, given its past values and the constants a_0 and b_0. Only when the model is at rest in a steady-state equilibrium ($Y_t = Y_{t-1} = Y_{t-2}$), are dynamics absent. Figure 14.5 presents the dynamic paths of output of three difference equations, all of the form of equation (14.3), but for different values of a_1 and b_1.

In panel (a), the economy exhibits cycles that die out over time, or are **damped**. The response of the model to deviations from its steady-state equilibrium is to make these deviations ever smaller. In panel (b), the cycle is **explosive**: when consumption and investment react strongly to past GDP, each step takes the economy further away from its equilibrium. The last and most interesting is panel (c) in which $b_1 = 1$. In this case, the economy oscillates for

ever around equilibrium, but never reaches it. This is the case of **undamped oscillations**. Under these conditions, business cycles can recur in a systematic, never-ending fashion, like self-perpetuating cycles. This example illustrates the deterministic view of the business cycle.

Box 14.2 explains in more detail how the structure of the model is translated into the model's dynamic behaviour. As might be expected, a more detailed description of the behaviour of aggregate demand and aggregate supply is associated with even richer dynamic patterns. Could it be, indeed, that what we observe is the consequence of a pendulum-like motion started some time far back in the past and self-perpetuating ever since?

For two reasons, the answer is no. First, cycles produced by deterministic models are too regular to be consistent with Stylized Fact No. 1. Second, the overwhelming majority of cycles generated by deterministic difference equations either die down or explode, which is in clear contradiction with the endless recurrence of business cycles. Recurrent

Box 14.2 The Multiplier-Accelerator Model in More Detail

The model in the text, in which both consumption and investment react with a one-period (Robertson) lag to output and output changes, respectively, led to equation (14.3), sometimes called the reduced form of the model. It takes the form of a difference equation of second order, since it contains variables lagged up to two periods.

It is often useful to solve difference equations like (14.3), that is, to express them as a function of time only. First note that the value of output in the steady state—when $Y_t = Y_{t-1} = Y_{t-2}$—is given by

$$\bar{Y} = (a_0 + b_0)/(1 - a_1),$$

which can be thought of as the autonomous spending $(a_0 + b_0)$ times the multiplier $1/(1 - a_1)$, which is greater than one. The solution of difference equations like

(14.3) take the form $Y_t = k_1\lambda_1^t + k_2\lambda_2^t$, where λ_1, λ_2, k_1, and k_2 are constants, and depend on a_0, b_0, a_1, b_1, and the initial values of Y. The crucial parameters λ_1 and λ_2 are the roots of the quadratic equation

$$\lambda^2 - (a_1 + b_1)\lambda + b_1 = 0.$$

It can be shown that the solution to (14.3) will be oscillatory if $(a_1 + b_1)^2 < 4b_1$, and will be dampened or explosive, depending on whether λ_1 and λ_2 are smaller or larger than unity in absolute value. In the oscillatory case, this condition is equivalent to whether b_1 is greater or less than one. Three cases of this model are shown in Figure 14.5. In the first example, $b_1 = 0.98$, in the second, $b_1 = 1.02$, and in the third—the only case with truly perpetual cycles—$b_1 = 1$.

---

cycles such as the last panel of Figure 14.5 require a precise constellation of the economy's characteristics (in this particular example, $b_1 = 1$). Most economists believe that such an exact combination is a highly improbable explanation of business cycles. This opens the way for an alternative approach.[8]

14.3.3 Stochastic Cycles: The Impulse-Propagation Mechanism

A more plausible explanation starts by asking a question. In the previous section, the economy oscillated because it started away from its stationary-state equilibrium; but what displaced it out of the stationary state in the first place? Suppose an economy were constantly subject to random disturbances, or shocks. These might originate in demand (e.g. alternating optimistic and pessimistic entrepreneurial animal spirits or the consumer mood, or

policy actions) as well as supply (e.g. exceptionally bad or good crops and natural disasters; important inventions or discoveries like the steel furnace, railways, electricity, or computers, as well as minor ones; social unrest). The list of potential shocks is endless. Like drops of rain generating ripples on a lake, these shocks constantly buffet the economy, moving it away from its former position.

These shocks, often referred to as **impulses**, change the demand or supply conditions in the economy. Once randomly disturbed, the economy embarks on the kind of deterministic adjustment described in the previous section, until the occurrence of the next shock. The **propagation mechanism** transforms, or cumulates, impulses into oscillations. Whether the oscillations are damped or not is not essential to the story, since old oscillations are constantly being replaced by new ones corresponding to new shocks. In contrast to the previous section, it is unnecessary to search for the unlikely existence of a self-perpetuating cycle. In this vision of the business cycle shown in Figure 14.6, it is sufficient to accept the view that an economy is regularly buffeted by endless series of shocks, and never really settles down to its stationary state. The rest of this chapter follows on this lead,

---

[8] The example given in the text was a linear model. It is true that more general, non-linear models are capable of delivering more exotic and irregular dynamic patterns. Under certain parameter constellations, the results are so irregular as to be called chaotic. Nevertheless, the criticism continues to apply that the range of parameters for which business cycle-like behaviour is generated is limited.

Box 14.3   Computers, Scientists, and Business Cycles

The discovery that purely random events can be responsible for cycles was made independently by Slutsky and Frisch in the 1930s. Evidence that such events can generate cycle-like behaviour typical of actual economies was not forthcoming until the late 1950s with the first computers. Frank Adelman, a nuclear physicist, and his wife Irma, an economist, studied an economic model developed by Lawrence Klein, the 1980 Nobel laureate from the University of Pennsylvania, and Arthur Goldberger of the University of Wisconsin. (This model consisted of twenty-five equations summarizing the most important macroeconomic relationships in the US economy.) First, the Adelmans found that the Klein–Goldberger model could not generate a cycle on its own (a deterministic cycle), because the fluctuations were dying down as in Figure 14.5(a). Yet, when perturbed by random shocks, it produced data that had the same statistical properties as actual US business cycles. They concluded that:

Ever since the path breaking article of Frisch on the propagation of business cycles, the possibility that the cyclical movements observed in a capitalistic society are actually due to random shocks has been seriously considered by business cycle the-

ories. The results we have found in this study tend to support this possibility . . . The agreement between the data obtained by imposing uncorrelated perturbation upon a model which is otherwise non-oscillatory in character is certainly consistent with the hypothesis that the economic fluctuations experienced in modern, highly developed societies are indeed due to random impulses. (Adelman and Adelman 1959: 620)

The Adelmans simulated, or solved, their model 100 years into the future on an IBM 650 and were proud that 'computations for one year could be made during an operating time of about one minute'. Now that simulations take seconds or less on a laptop, this approach has become routine. Much effort has gone into improving and enlarging the models and the algorithms used for simulations. More recently, Robert E. Lucas of the University of Chicago and 1995 Nobel Prize laureate in economic sciences, made this research strategy explicit:

Our task as I see it . . . is to write a FORTRAN [a programming language] program that will accept specific economic policy rules as 'input' and will generate as 'output' statistics describing the operating characteristics of time series we care about, which are predicted to result from these policies.

which is the cornerstone of modern business cycle theory.[9]

How likely is it that purely random impulses working their way through the economy actually generate the kind of behaviour corresponding to our earlier stylized facts? Can shocks which continuously move the economy away from its steady state and followed by the cyclical response shown in Figure 14.6 actually explain business cycles? Box 14.3 recalls how this question received an affirmative answer at the dawn of the computer era. Random shocks can even transform the rather

Fig. 14.6 The Impulse-Propagation Mechanism

Random shocks hit the economic system, which reacts by generating business cycles. The cycles result from the averaging or accumulation of these random disturbances over time.

[9] The discovery that cycles can be generated from purely random factors was made in the late 1920s and early 1930s by the Russian Eugen Slutsky (1880–1948) and the Norwegian Ragnar Frisch (1895–1973), who was awarded the first Nobel Prize in 1969. Slutsky was a researcher at the Conjuncture Institute in Moscow during Stalin's dictatorship and was unable to publish this discovery until eight years later when his work was finally translated into English.

boring multiplier-accelerator model into realistic cycles. In panel (a) of Figure 14.7, 200 purely random shocks drawn over time are plotted.[10] Such

[10] Such a random variable which is identically and independently distributed is often called white noise. White noise has the property that current and past values contain no information helpful in forecasting future values.

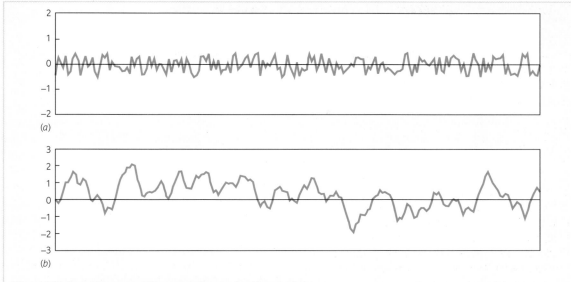

Fig. 14.7 Impulses and Propagations: An Example

Panel (a) depicts 200 observations of a random variable, ε_t. Panel (b) displays data from panel (a) after they were transformed, or 'filtered', by the formula $Y_t = 1.3Y_{t-1} - 0.4Y_{t-2} + \varepsilon_t$, starting from a given Y_0 and Y_{-1}. This 'filter' has the ability to mimic a true data series.

observations—the impulses—could represent a succession of unforeseeable events, big or small. Panel (b) shows what happens when these shocks are 'filtered' through a propagation mechanism; in this case we use the example of the multiplier-accelerator model described in Box 14.2. The result is a succession of artificial business cycles which resemble the UK data presented in Figure 14.1(b). Although the impulses themselves are not cyclical, the transformed variable exhibits irregular, periodic movements similar to business cycles.

This impulse-propagation mechanism is the dominant way of thinking about business cycles because it accords well with the stylized facts. Since they are random, the shocks will typically generate cycles of different sizes and magnitudes, as in Stylized Fact No. 1. If many of these impulses are related to permanent technological innovations, not only will they trigger cycles, but in the long run they will also cumulate into a process of unending growth. This is consistent with Stylized Fact No. 2: in the long run, the growth process (the accumulation of positive shocks) dwarfs business cycles (the

reaction to individual productivity and other shocks).[11]

Some of the most important questions remain unanswered, however. First, what is the exact nature of these impulses? Second, what is the impulse-propagation mechanism? We have used a simple example to show that such a mechanism is plausible. Yet this is not good enough: the objective is to show that the 'shocks' correspond to well-known disturbances. A good business cycle theory is one that can also replicate the key stylized facts discussed at the beginning of this chapter.

Two competing approaches to thinking about the impulse-propagation mechanism have been developed. The first follows the Keynesian tradition of sticky prices and takes the *AS-AD* framework as its point of departure; it is presented in the next section. The second asks whether cycles may exist when all prices are perfectly flexible; it is studied in Section 14.5.

[11] Ch. 18 revisits the issue of innovations and low-frequency growth cycles.

14.4 Sticky Price Business Cycles

14.4.1 Impulses and Propagation in the *AS-AD* Framework

Chapter 13 showed how the *AS-AD* model can help us understand the determinants of output and inflation in the short and long run. It can also be used to study business cycles. The point of departure is to identify the shocks as factors that shift either the *AS* or *AD* curves. **Demand shocks** shift the *AD* schedule, while **supply shocks** affect the position of the *AS* curve. Both demand and supply shocks can be positive or negative. Positive shocks, for example, move the relevant schedule rightwards.

The multiplier-accelerator model of the last section showed that lags in economic relationships are the central source of dynamics. This is also true in the

AS-AD framework. Lags exist for various reasons: slow responses of demand to income and of supply to demand imply that the *AD* schedule reacts gradually to demand disturbances. The supply side may also be a source of **persistence**, if core inflation only gradually catches up with past inflation.

As an example, consider a permanent increase in money growth in a system of flexible exchange rates. Furthermore, we will assume that core inflation is simply equal to last period's inflation. The cycle triggered by this disturbance is tracked down in Figure 14.8. (A formal analysis is provided in the WebAppendix to this chapter.) For simplicity, we start with an economy already in a stationary state at point A.[12] The monetary growth expansion

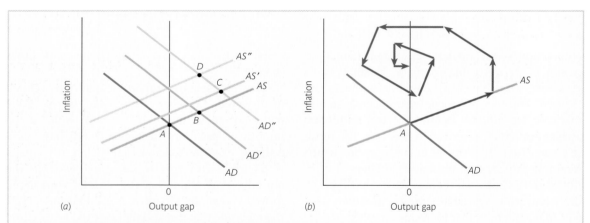

Fig. 14.8 The Propagation Framework in the *AS-AD* Model

In this example, the initial impulse is an increase in the rate of money growth. In panel (*a*), from its initial stationary equilibrium at point *A* the economy first moves to point *B*, as the *AD* curve begins to respond to the monetary impulse. Gradually, core inflation increases in response to actual inflation, and the *AS* curve—whose position depends on core inflation—slides to *AS'*. Further lagged responses of demand to money growth result in gradual shifts of the *AD* curve towards *AD"*, bringing the economy to point *C*; further movement in core inflation towards actual inflation moves the *AS* schedule towards *AS"* (point *D*). Because output has begun to decline, the *AD* curve begins a descent. As inflation declines, core inflation follows and the *AS* curve also moves downwards. The economy follows a loop of the kind exhibited in panel (*b*).

[12] This is simpler because there is no cycle under way that would interfere with the one under study.

takes the economy to point *B* in panel (*a*), with an increase in both output and inflation. Owing to demand lags, the initial shift of the *AD* curve to *AD'* represents only an initial, partial, response. For a time, the *AD* schedule will continue to move rightwards towards *AD"*. Indeed, the lagged response of output means that the longer-run shift of the *AD* curve always exceeds that of the short run and that, as output rises, the *AD* keeps moving to the right.

At the same time, the *AS* curve shifts upward as core inflation gradually catches up with the actual inflation rate. Over time, the economy moves towards point *C*. With actual output in excess of its trend level, inflation catches up and eventually overtakes money growth.[13] This implies that the real money stock starts declining and with it output. Declining output means that the *AD* curve begins to move leftwards. Actual inflation then starts to decline, followed by core inflation and a downward shift of the *AS* schedule (not shown). Pursuing this reasoning, it appears that the adjustment will be characterized by the 'loops' shown in panel (*b*), with alternating periods of output above and below equilibrium level—i.e. business cycles.

14.4.2 Identifying Demand and Supply Shocks and their Propagation

The example of the previous section shows how the *AS-AD* framework can be used to explain business cycles. The next step is to identify the characteristics of cycles, as predicted by the *AS-AD* framework. This naturally points to a distinction between demand and supply shocks. The case studied in the previous section—an increase in money growth—is an example of a demand shock. Is the theory's prediction, that demand shocks lead to loops of the type depicted in Figure 14.8, borne out by the facts?

The case of German unification, seen from the perspective of West Germany, provides an easily

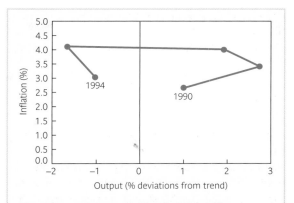

Fig. 14.9 A Demand Shock: The Effect of German Unification on West Germany, 1990–1994

German economic and monetary unification occurred in 1990. Spending by former East German households, firms, and governmental authorities increased dramatically, and most of this demand fell on West German producers. The figure traces out the effect on West German GDP—measured as a deviation from its trend—and rate of inflation.

Sources: OECD National Accounts; Main Economic Indicators.

identified demand shock.[14] While output in the East was collapsing, consumption, investment, and government spending by East German residents was rising rapidly. Consumers who had been repressed for several decades and anticipated an increase in their future incomes met West German banks eager to attract new customers, especially as none of them was indebted. This also applied to local governments, which loaded up on new infrastructure and equipment. Most of this spending went to West German firms, which were poised to satisfy this extra demand.

Figure 14.9 shows that the outcome was indeed a counterclockwise loop. The initial demand was accommodated without significant inflationary pressure. After two years of expansion, the tell-tale signs of overheating emerged: increasing nominal wage demands by unions, high-capacity utilization rates, etc. In the end, the German central bank (the

---

[13] How do we know this? We know that, as long as money growth exceeds inflation, the real money stock *M/P* rises. In the long run, the economy returns to trend GDP and the demand for money roughly returns to its initial value (since $M/P = \mathcal{L}(Y, i)$ and both *Y* and *i* approximately return to their initial levels). For *M/P* to return to its initial level, inflation must exceed money growth at some point.

[14] For East Germany, it was more likely a mixture of negative demand and supply shocks.

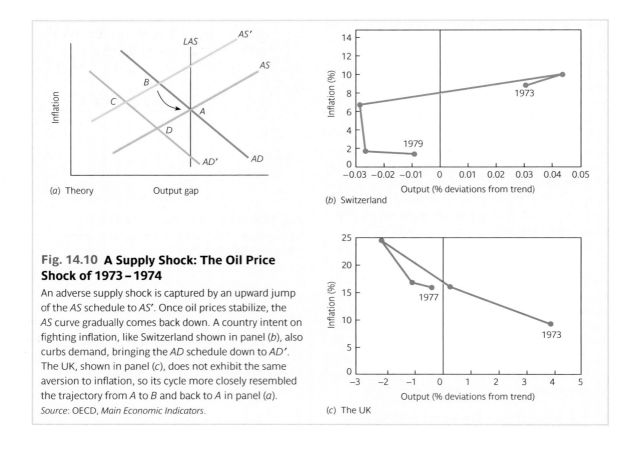

(a) Theory

(b) Switzerland

(c) The UK

Fig. 14.10 A Supply Shock: The Oil Price Shock of 1973–1974

An adverse supply shock is captured by an upward jump of the AS schedule to AS′. Once oil prices stabilize, the AS curve gradually comes back down. A country intent on fighting inflation, like Switzerland shown in panel (b), also curbs demand, bringing the AD schedule down to AD′. The UK, shown in panel (c), does not exhibit the same aversion to inflation, so its cycle more closely resembled the trajectory from A to B and back to A in panel (a).

Source: OECD, Main Economic Indicators.

Bundesbank) refused to allow any further money growth. By allowing market interest rates to rise, and by raising the discount and Lombard rates several times, the Bundesbank effected a prompt return to non-inflationary conditions.

The second example traces an economy's reaction to a supply shock, the first oil price increase in 1973–4. Panel (a) of Figure 14.10 shows the theory. The AS curve shifts up to AS′ because the cost of a major input, energy, abruptly rises. Without any policy reaction, the shock moves the economy from point A to point B. Thereafter, once the initial burst of cost increases is absorbed, the AS curve moves back to its initial position—but only gradually so, since core inflation is on the rise, trailing actual inflation. Similarly, with a reduced GDP, the AD curve also moves down, so that the return is shown as the curved trajectory from B to A. If instead the

authorities decide to fight the inflationary implication of the oil shock and tighten up demand, the AD curve shifts leftwards to AD′ and the economy moves from B to C and will return to point A via point D, for example.

Panels (b) and (c) give two examples of reactions to the oil shock. Panel (b) shows that the Swiss National Bank adopted an explicitly anti-inflationary strategy. After the shock, in 1974 inflation increased and output continued to grow as it completed the expansion phase started a few years before. But then, restrictive demand policies provoked a sharp recession followed by a gradual decline in inflation—the overall cycle matching trajectory ABCD in panel (a). In contrast, authorities did not fight inflation in the UK, which was already high at the time: panel (b) depicts a loop similar to the ABA trajectory in panel (a).

14.4.3 The Contribution of Demand and Supply Shocks

With plausible lags on both the demand and supply side, the *AS-AD* framework can broadly explain patterns observed in actual business cycles. The results of this analysis are consistent with an impulse-propagation interpretation of business cycles, operating through the sticky price framework developed in Chapter 13. In the next section we consider an alternative interpretation.

An important feature of the *AS-AD* analysis is the distinction between demand and supply shocks. To think about cycles—and how to deal with them— it helps to know which types of shock are more frequent. Table 14.4 presents estimates for the importance of these shocks in five of the G7 countries. Two kinds of demand shock were identified in this study: (1) monetary shocks, which are related to exogenous changes in monetary policy, and (2) real demand shocks, reflecting public (fiscal) policy, private spending behaviour, or foreign demand via the current account.[15] According to this study,

Table 14.4 Decomposition of the Variance of GDP, 1979:1 – 1993:4 (%, 1 year after shock)

Country	Demand	Supply	Money	Total
Canada	54	34	12	100
France	19	80	1	100
Germany	66	31	3	100
Italy	40	51	10	100
Japan	11	87	2	100
UK	32	64	4	100
USA	20	71	8	100

Source: Gerlach and Smets (1995).

monetary shocks are less important while demand and supply shocks are predominant. At the same time, there are significant differences from country to country.

14.5 Real Business Cycles

14.5.1 Productivity Shocks as Impulses

The *AS-AD* framework implies that business cycles are propagated because prices are sticky; they take time to adjust, and during that time, nominal demand shifts have effects as predicted by the *IS-LM*

model of Chapters 10 and 11. Does this mean that business cycles are impossible when prices are perfectly flexible? This is the challenge undertaken by the **real business cycle (RBC) theory**, which argues that business cycles can be viewed as a market-clearing, equilibrium phenomenon. The challenge is provocative. As Chapter 11 shows, an economy with fully flexible prices is perfectly dichotomized, even in the short run, and departures from the long-run *AS* (*LAS*) schedule are impossible. In that case, the only shocks that affect the real economy are supply shocks, which shift the *LAS* schedule. To the extent that monetary and fiscal policies do not affect the *LAS* line, they are irrelevant. At the same time, if the economy is always on its long-run supply schedule,

---

[15] How this is done is somewhat technical. The authors identify the shocks by defining them in terms of their short- and long-run effects on real GDP: demand shocks do not have permanent effects (they do not affect the *LAS* schedule); supply shocks have both temporary and permanent effects (both the *AS* and *LAS* schedules shift); monetary shocks have neither instantaneous nor permanent effects. (It takes time for money to affect output and it leaves the *LAS* schedule unchanged.)

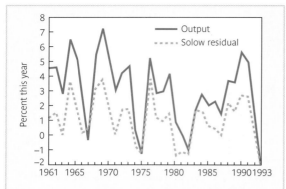

Fig. 14.11 The Solow Residual and GDP, Germany, 1961 – 1993

Growth in total factor productivity, as measured by the Solow residual, is strongly correlated with output. To some extent, the movements in total factor productivity growth appear random.

Sources: OECD; Statistisches Bundesamt; authors' calculations.

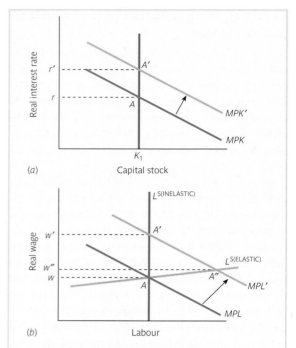

Fig. 14.12 A Productivity Shock

A productivity shock raises the marginal productivity of capital and labour. In the short run, the stock of capital is unchanged and the real interest rises. When aggregate labour supply is inelastic ($L^{S(\text{INELASTIC})}$), the labour supply curve is vertical so the effect on productivity gain is to raise the real wage rate without any change in employment. When aggregate labour supply is elastic ($L^{S(\text{ELASTIC})}$), the response is a small changes in wages with larger fluctuations in employment.

the propagation mechanism of the *AS-AD* model is shut down: real GDP simply moves randomly in response to random supply shocks. So it would seem that such an economy would be free from cyclical tendencies.

The hallmark of RBC theory is the emphasis of propagation mechanisms besides those related to price stickiness and the dynamics of core inflation. It starts by focusing on supply shocks related to the production technology: the main source of impulses is new discoveries, inventions, product innovations, or process improvements. These shocks alter the productivity of factors of production, change the environment of economic agents, and cause them to change their behaviour.

Figure 14.11 shows movements in total factor productivity—as measured by the Solow residual—in the case of Germany. The Solow residual, introduced in Chapter 3, is the percentage change in output minus a weighted average of growth in labour and capital inputs, where the weights are the respective factor shares of labour and capital respectively. In the RBC framework, shifts in total factor productivity—technology shocks—are the exogenous impulses that hit the economy.[16] The propagation mechanism assumed in the RBC theory

can be linked to the paradigm of Robinson Crusoe developed in Chapters 5 and 6. In fact, the RBC approach is frequently associated with more advanced versions of the growth theory presented in Chapter 3.

Figure 14.12 illustrates the initial impact of a favourable temporary productivity shock. In the

---

[16] In the sticky price interpretation, fluctuations of the Solow residual—which is highly correlated with real GDP—are endogenous and constitute one of several manifestations of a normal business cycle.

first instance, it raises the marginal productivity of both capital and labour. Given the stock of capital, the rate of return on capital rises.[17] In panel (a) labour supply is inelastic—the labour supply schedule is vertical—so the real wage rises. Output goes up since the same amounts of capital and labour are now more productive. On the demand side, wealth rises because both wage and profits are higher, so consumption also increases.

14.5.2 Propagation Channels in Real Business Cycles

How does the RBC approach translate the shock into a cycle? The RBC identifies two main channels. The first propagation mechanism involves physical capital. The increase in marginal productivity of capital provides an incentive to accumulate more. At a given real interest rate, we now have MPK > r. (Alternatively, Tobin's q increases). The build-up of capital takes time, and contributes to a higher output level along the way. Since the technology shock is temporary, its passing will mark a decline in the productivity of capital, triggering a process of decumulation and a fall in productive capacity back to the initial level. The result is a flexible-price business cycle.

The second propagation mechanism is related to the other factor of production, labour. One feature of the previous story is unappealing: if labour supply is inelastic, there is no change in employment over the cycle. This contradicts evidence that employment and unemployment fluctuate a lot, suggesting that aggregate labour supply is elastic. In that case, productivity shocks will be accompanied by changes in the supply of labour, and the overall response of output will be reinforced. For this channel to work, we need a good reason for the aggregate elasticity of labour supply to be so high.

The primary determinant of the slope of labour supply, as Chapter 4 showed, is the contemporary leisure–consumption choice: each period a worker

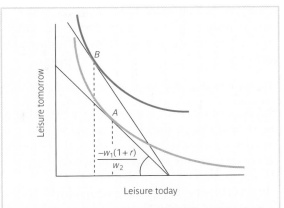

Fig. 14.13 Intertemporal Substitution of Leisure
Robinson Crusoe decides on his work effort by comparing, in present value terms, the wage today w_1 and tomorrow $w_2/(1 + r)$: the slope of his 'budget line' is the ratio of these wages. The combination of an increase in both today's wage w_1 and the real interest rate triggers substitution (work more today, less tomorrow) and income (work less today and less tomorrow) effects. In this particular case, Robinson reacts to a temporary wage increase by enjoying less leisure and working harder today, and taking more leisure tomorrow.

decides whether to work, earn money, and consume —or to enjoy leisure. Our conclusion, backed by empirical evidence, was that the supply of labour is quite inelastic at the household level. A flat aggregate labour supply curve would only result from the aggregation of different households (see Figure 4.4).[18] In addition, the RBC approach emphasizes another channel: the intertemporal choice between leisure today and leisure tomorrow.

This choice is represented in Figure 14.13 and resembles Robinson Crusoe's choice of consumption over time analysed in Chapter 6. Preferences are represented by indifference curves, and express the trade-off that workers perceive between leisure today, ℓ_1, and leisure tomorrow, ℓ_2. Ignoring profits and other financial wealth, Robinson's 'budget

---

[17] If the same shock affects the whole world, the world real interest rate is likely to rise. If it affects only one country, the real interest rate can still rise temporarily even if the nominal interest rate cannot change when the exchange rate is fixed: expected inflation absorbs the difference.

[18] In principle, a flat collective bargaining curve would achieve the same result, but the RBC approach has generally avoided considering these forms of market imperfections.

constraint' is determined by wealth Ω, which in turn is determined by wage income, i.e. today's wage plus the discounted value of tomorrow's wage:

(14.4) $\Omega = w_1(\bar{L}_1 - \ell_1) + [w_2/(1+r)](\bar{L}_2 - \ell_2)$

The slope of this constraint is $-w_1(1+r)/w_2$, that is, the ratio of today's wage w_1 to the present value of tomorrow's wage $w_2/(1+r)$. As usual, the optimum choice is where the indifference curve is tangent to the budget line.

A productivity shock that is temporary will raise today's wage w_1 and the real interest rate. This in turn will have two effects. A higher wage and a higher real interest rate mean a steeper budget line; work effort is worth more today relative to tomorrow. (Put differently, leisure today is more expensive than leisure tomorrow.) The substitution effect means that Crusoe works harder today. The income effect, in contrast, implies that Crusoe works less in both periods, since with the same work effort more leisure can be afforded in both periods. If the substitution effect dominates the income effect, the labour supply schedule in Figure 14.13 is elastic and more labour is supplied.

This is the second propagation mechanism of the RBC theory. A favourable productivity shock leads workers to supply more labour today, so GDP rises over and above the direct productivity effect of total factor. In the following period, workers 'cash in' and work less; as labour supply is reduced, GDP decreases. All of that occurs without invoking any wage or price rigidity.

14.5.3 Optimality Properties of the Cycle

RBC theory offers an alternative view of business cycles. Technology and other factors shift the production function out and raise the productivity of capital and labour. This causes firms to increase the stock of capital and workers to supply more labour. These reactions of the factors of production during the upswing phase of the cycle amplify the direct effect of the productivity impulse. More interesting, in a second stage, GDP declines as capital is decumulated and workers enjoy leisure or households incurring high costs of going to work stay at home. These cyclical responses are optimal for all concerned. It is the best that agents can do, and there is no (involuntary) unemployment and no lost opportunities. This interpretation stands in sharp contrast to the sticky price interpretation, which stresses unemployment and inefficient utilization of resources in recessions.

Thus, one important conclusion of the RBC approach—and one that is disturbing for many economists and therefore highly controversial—is that it is impossible to use demand management policies to improve matters in the macroeconomy. Indeed, a striking implication of the RBC theory is that it is not even desirable to smooth out the business cycle, since by definition both households and firms are doing the best they can, given changing constraints, so there is nothing to lament. Deep recessions, for example, are seen as the economy's best response to severe adverse productivity shocks. In Chapter 16 we shall return to this important issue in more detail.

14.6 Taking Stock of the Two Theories

The previous sections introduced two self-contained, internally consistent accounts of how impulses—shocks to demand, supply, or both—are translated via a propagation mechanism into business cycles. The *AS-AD*, or sticky price, account of business cycles relies on disequilibrium in markets—prices do not adjust immediately to changing demand and

supply conditions. In contrast, the RBC theory views the rising and falling tides of economic conditions as an equilibrium response to productivity shocks. It studiously avoids the terms 'demand' and 'supply', since in the RBC framework shocks to technology affect both simultaneously, and economic agents are fully aware of this. Most

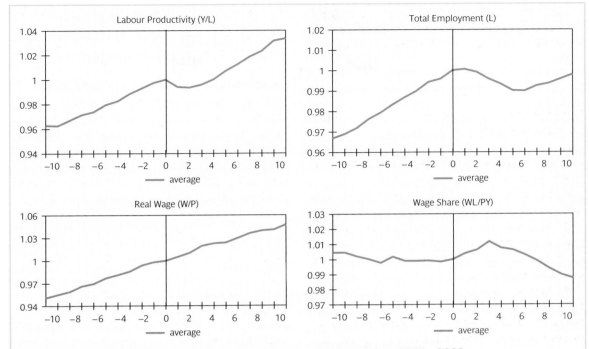

Fig. 14.14 Cyclical Patterns in the Labour Market, G8 Countries, 1965 – 2003

In the eight countries considered (Canada, France, Germany, Italy, Japan, Spain, the UK and the USA), labour productivity and employment are strongly procyclical and coincident. Real wages are acyclical, while the wage share is countercyclical and lagging.

Source: OECD National Accounts; Quarterly Labor Force Statistics; Main Economic Indicators, 1965 – 2003. Japan excluded from wage share calculations.

important, it is argued that agents have exhausted all possible means of making themselves better off, so policy has no role to play.

Where do we stand? How do the theories match up with the facts? The following sections assess some of the evidence.[19]

14.6.1 Productivity, Real Wages, and Employment

Additional stylized facts about the labour market over the business cycle can be used to sharpen the debate. Figure 14.14 shows the cyclical behaviour of labour productivity, employment, the real wage,

and the wage share for several OECD countries. Labour productivity—the ratio of output to employment—is procyclical and a coincident indicator. Employment is also procyclical. On the face of it, these facts are good news for the RBC view and a potential weakness of the *AS-AD* framework. With diminishing returns, given that the stock of capital cannot change much during a cycle, the marginal product of labour (and thereby the average product for all workers) should decline when production and employment increase. The RBC theory provides a plausible interpretation. If business cycles are driven by productivity shocks, then upswings necessarily coincide with periods of high productivity. High productivity plus intertemporal substitution of leisure or a flat aggregate supply curve then explain why labour demand and supply both rise during the upswing.

[19] To save space, we do not use our graphical apparatus (*IS-LM*, *AS-AD*, demand and supply as in Fig. 14.12) to explain every point. Careful readers will find it useful—indeed, an excellent exercise—to check their understanding by drawing their own graphs and reproducing the arguments.

However, the extreme volatility of total factor productivity seen in Figure 14.11 is suspect. Neither labour nor capital is always fully employed by firms. Because dismissal costs are positive and human capital is often firm specific, firms avoid firing employees immediately in downturns, even though production is reduced; workers are often asked to perform tasks less related to the direct production process, such as maintenance, building improvements, painting, and cleaning. During the expansion phase, there is a reserve of workers' effort which can be tapped. The same argument applies to the stock of capital. Indeed, capacity utilization is not constant over the cycle (see Figure 14.3). The stylized fact of procyclical total factor productivity might therefore be due to a faulty measure of inputs: in recessions labour is employed but not in directly productive activities—we say it is hoarded—and it is gradually put back to more directly productive use in the upturn that follows. Similarly, capital is not discarded but used less intensively in downturns, leading to underestimation of its productivity in these periods. The extreme procyclical behaviour of the Solow residual may therefore reflect hoarded factors of production.

Another interesting feature of Figure 14.14 is that real wages are acyclical.[20] Since the wage share is the ratio of real wages to labour productivity, it follows that the wage share—the proportion of total value added paid out in labour costs—is countercyclical.[21] Panel (d) confirms that the wage share promptly rises once the peak of the cycle has passed. Given its emphasis on intertemporal substitution of labour, the RBC approach now fares poorly: the procyclicality of employment is predicated on procyclical wages. Even if real wages were mildly procyclical, a very high elasticity of intertemporal substitution or labour supply would be required to explain the observed employment response. As noted in the previous section, most available data on individual behaviour point to inelastic labour supply, at least for heads of households. To the contrary, the small responsiveness of real wages to labour market conditions favours the sticky price view, and also represents evidence for the view that real wage rigidity is the source of involuntary unemployment.[22]

14.6.2 Money, Credit, and the Cycle

The direct relevance of money and credit for the business cycle has been an issue for a long time in macroeconomics. It is interesting that, while the real business cycle idea has gained momentum only since the early 1980s, the difficulty of associating business cycles with money and credit was evident to another keen observer, Karl Marx, who wrote:

Among other things, the superficiality of political economy becomes apparent when it assigns a causative role to the expansion and contraction of credit, which is really only a symptom of boom and bust of the industrial cycle. Just as heavenly bodies constantly repeat their revolutions once set in motion, so it is with production as soon as it is hurled into its pattern of expansion and contraction. Effects become for their part causes, and alternating conditions of the process, which constantly reproduce themselves, take on a periodic form. (Marx 1867: i, ch. 23)

Keynes himself was less than convinced that monetary conditions were always relevant for business conditions, arguing articulately in the **General Theory** that interest rates may not fall sufficiently in recessions to offset the negative effect on investment spending of a spell of bad 'animal spirits' among businessmen.

As noted above, the RBC admits no role for money in causing the business cycle. This is because the AS curve is always vertical, and money is neutral in the short run. We saw however, in Figure 14.3, that the real money stock is procyclical and in particular a leading indicator. In the sticky price business cycle (AS-AD) model, this is consistent with money growth leading and causing booms. It is not, however, consistent with the fact that nominal and real

[20] Inspection of the individual countries reveals no distinguishing patterns; in some cases there is weak evidence of procyclicality, in other cases, weak countercyclicality.
[21] The wage share is $WL/PY = (W/P)/(Y/L)$.

[22] RBC theorists counter that the reason is that job contracts do not usually provide for flexibility in the number of hours worked: they are rather of the all-or-nothing variety, i.e. work the normal work-week or don't work at all. If individual labour supply responses are 'discontinuous', with individuals shifting from zero hours to a fixed normal work-week and back, this might explain the high aggregate elasticity of employment observed.

interest rates are procyclical and coincident. Indeed, in the *IS-LM* framework, a money supply impulse is expected to work on output via declining interest rates. Procyclical money and interest rates can be reconciled in the sticky price world if the primary impulses to the cycle come from the real demand side (spending, fiscal policy, the current account). In that case, an increase in demand-led GDP is accompanied —or even led—by an increase in demand for money that is passively supplied by the central bank. Indeed, private spending—investment and inventory accumulation in particular—is both procyclical and leading (Stylized Fact No. 4). In addition, forward-looking variables are likely to react more forcefully to expectations (the stock market and other indicators of consumer sentiment). This explains why investment and spending on durable goods are so volatile. In recent years, new generations of models stressing the instability of the real demand side— some using techniques pioneered by RBC theorists —have had some successes in reconciling the *AS-AD* model with the facts.

Does such evidence seal the debate in favour of the sticky price view? Certainly not! The RBC view is that credit and money demand are passive, expanding with the economy but without any notable influence on real variables. This is also consistent with the coincident and strongly procyclical behaviour of interest rates in Figure 14.3, which the *AS-AD* framework can explain only if shifts to the underlying *IS* curve predominate, and if monetary policy works with a lag. After long focusing on technology, RBC researchers have begun to explore other disturbances to the economy, including fiscal policy, tastes, and institutions. A convergence of the two approaches may be on the horizon.

In the end, a central issue remains the flexibility of the price level. Evidence indicates that prices— measured as aggregate indices—do appear to be rigid in the short run. It is this element of realism that is lacking in the RBC theory of macroeconomic fluctuations and limits its acceptance by a wide spectrum of the economics profession, despite its intellectual rigour. While realism is not an essential element of a good macroeconomic model, this particular detail has such wide-reaching implications that it would appear essential to include it, or at least to explain why it is unimportant.

❗ Summary

1 Real output in economies tends to grow, but in a fluctuating, unsteady manner. Cyclical fluctuations of 5–10 years' duration are known as business cycles. They seldom deviate by more than 2–5% of output from average, and yet are assigned considerable significance in modern industrial societies.

2 Fluctuations in output are accompanied by fluctuations in many other macroeconomic variables. Some lead, some lag, and most are coincident.

3 Components of GDP exhibit differing degrees of volatility, which confirms that the economic forces behind them are different. Private consumption is smoother than investment, and exports and imports are perhaps the most volatile of all for small open economies.

4 Two theoretical approaches have been used to study business cycles: deterministic cycles, and stochastic cycles. The more modern and widely accepted view is that cycles represent the accumulation of random shocks over time.

5 The impulse-propagation mechanism transforms purely random shocks into more regular fluctuations. Crucial to the mechanism is the existence of lags in responses of some key variables to their determinants.

6 The *AS-AD* framework—which rests on the assumption that prices are sticky in the short run—is one example of an impulse-propagation framework. It rests on lags in the response of demand to GDP and of core to actual inflation.

This view emphasizes the distinction between demand and supply shocks.

7 The real business cycle theory offers an alternative to the sticky price interpretation of business cycles. Random, exogenous productivity shocks are the underlying impulses that are propagated through two main channels: capital accumulation, and the intertemporal substitution of leisure.

8 Both interpretations of the business cycle have strengths and weaknesses. The *AS-AD* framework has difficulties explaining procyclical product-

ivity and procyclical interest rates. Yet it can account for the high variance of employment and the apparent short-run rigidity of nominal prices and real wages.

9 The RBC theory is ill equipped to account for high fluctuations in employment despite the acyclical or only mildly cyclical behaviour of real wages. Most problematic for RBC theory is its assumption that prices are perfectly flexible and that fluctuations represent society's best response to a changing environment which cannot be improved upon.

Key Concepts

- business cycles
- booms, recessions
- turning points
- peak, trough
- trend, detrended
- Burns – Mitchell diagram
- procyclical, countercyclical, acyclical
- leading and lagging indicator
- coincident indicator

- Robertson and Lundberg lags
- difference equation
- damped, explosive, undamped oscillations
- impulses-propagation mechanism
- demand shocks
- supply shocks
- persistence
- real business cycle theory

Exercises

1 Using the *AS-AD* diagram, trace graphically the dynamic reaction of an economy under fixed rates to a permanent decline in the foreign rate of inflation.

2 Why is the path of government spending on goods and services—judging either from the correlation coefficient or from the Burns–Mitchell diagrams—so smooth and uncorrelated with output?

3 Trace the effect of a positive technological shock on the *AS-AD* model with constant monetary and fiscal policy. Contrast this with the effect of the same shock in a real business cycle model as described in the text.

4 Suppose shocks to the price of oil predominated in an economy during a particular period. What would the *AS-AD* model predict for the sign of the correlation between output and inflation?

How does your answer depend on the policy response?

5 Flip a coin fifty times, recording the outcomes in the order they occur (e.g. heads, tails, tails, heads, tails, etc.) by assigning the value +1 to heads, −1 to tails.

(a) Now construct a data series according to the formula $x_t = 1.3x_{t-1} - 0.5x_{t-2} + \varepsilon_t$, for $t = 1, 2, \ldots 50$, where ε_t is the outcome of the flip. (Assign the value 0 to the initial conditions x_0 and x_{-1}.) How many cycles do you observe?

(b) How does your answer to question (a) change if you use instead the formula $x_t = 1.3x_{t-1} - 0.9x_{t-2} + \varepsilon_t$. Can you explain the difference?

(c) Now compute the coin-flipping exercise using $x_t = 1.3x_{t-1} - 0.3x_{t-2} + \varepsilon_t$. What do you notice about the behaviour of x over time? Can you explain what is going on here?

6 In Figure 14.4, PCA appears on average to be a leading indicator and is countercyclical, meaning that the primary current account begins to deteriorate before the peak is reached.

(a) Given the evidence from Figures 14.3 and 14.4, which components of aggregate demand best account for this fact? Why does the cyclical behaviour of the PCA depend on whether cycles are synchronized or not at home and abroad, i.e. whether we reach our peak at the same time as do our main trading partners?

(b) In the Burns–Mitchell diagram below, (West) German net exports exhibit a clear divergence from the 'average' pattern displayed in Figure 14.4; i.e. they lead the cycle in a procyclical fashion. How might the sticky price view of the business cycle explain this fact? Can you think of a real business cycle interpretation of procyclical net exports?

7 The spread between long and short-term interest rates (the so-called term structure of interest rates) has a marked cyclical character. Judging from Figure 14.3, the spread seems to be countercyclical, that is, it falls in booms and rises in recessions. Which of the two interest rates do you think is doing most of the work in moving the

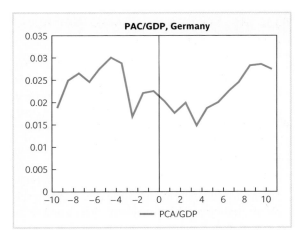

spread around, and why? How would you explain the slight leading indicator quality of the spread evident in panel (j)?

8 In the decade 1995–2004, Germany grew in real terms at a remarkably sluggish pace of roughly 1.3% per annum, compared with 2.2% for France and 2.5% for the UK. Many analysts claim that the culprit is a lack of German domestic demand, and point in particular to consumption, which has hardly increased over the period. Some have even argued that years of wage moderation in Germany have taken income out of the pockets of households and have contributed to the problem and that a sharp wage increase would reverse this trend, stimulating aggregate demand. Discuss this argument critically, using the AS-AD model, as well as other aspects of the macroeconomy you have studied to date.

9 In Figure 14.14, real wages are evidently acyclical. How can the RBC theory account for this fact if labour markets are constantly clearing? How can the sticky price view of the cycle account for this fact?

10 Measured labour productivity is highly procyclical, as can be seen from Figure 14.14. How can this help explain the behaviour of the wage share over the cycle? Why are procyclical hours and employment a problem for sticky price models of the business cycle? Could you imagine ways of 'fixing' the theory to account for this important stylized theory?

➲ Essay Questions

1 Explain why Keynesians support the endogenous cycle view while neoclassics favour the real business cycle interpretation.

2 Looking at Figure 14.1, cyclical fluctuations seem of limited importance, while a small difference in trend growth eventually makes a considerable difference for the standard of living. And yet, the media, policy-makers, and even voters seem to be fascinated by business cycles and display limited interested in long-term growth. Discuss this apparent paradox.

3 'Recessions represent a useful cleansing phase. This is when poorly managed and inefficient companies disappear, freeing resources for better managed and more efficient firms.' Comment.

4 Are there reasons to believe that modern business cycles are more pronounced than those of pre-industrial times?

5 It is often asserted that, if prices and wages were fully flexible, there would be no business cycles. Evaluate this possibility. Is it desirable?

PART VI

Macroeconomic Policy

15 Fiscal Policy, Debt, and Seigniorage *361*
16 The Limits of Demand Management *383*
17 Supply-Side Policy *407*
18 Economic Growth: Theory and Policy *435*

Macroeconomics originated as a field largely because of its proximity to policy-making. Part V has shown how, in theory, macroeconomic policies can prevent recessions, unnecessarily high unemployment, and inflation. Part VI explores the limits of demand management—ranging from the government's budget constraint to the interactions of private expectations with policy effectiveness—and the role of politics in policy-making. It also develops the principles of supply-side policies, the possibility of altering incentives to work, save, and produce, and how this affects the long-run capacity of the economy.

Fiscal Policy, Debt, and Seigniorage

15

15.1 Overview *362*

15.2 Fiscal Policy and Economic Welfare *363*
15.2.1 Provision of Public Goods and Services *363*
15.2.2 Redistributive Goals: Equity versus Efficiency *364*

15.3 Macroeconomic Stabilization *365*
15.3.1 Consumption and Tax Smoothing *365*
15.3.2 Output and Employment Stabilization *366*
15.3.3 Automatic Stabilizers *367*
15.3.4 How to Interpret Budget Figures *370*

15.4 Deficit Financing: Public Debt and Seigniorage *373*
15.4.1 The Public Debt with No Growth and No Inflation *373*
15.4.2 The Public Debt with Growth and No Inflation *374*
15.4.3 The Public Debt with Growth and Inflation *376*

15.5 Three Ways to Stabilize the Public Debt *376*
15.5.1 Cutting the Deficit *376*
15.5.2 Seigniorage and the Inflation Tax *377*
15.5.3 Default *378*

Summary *379*

Chancellor: In my old age I have been freed from pain.
  Listen and look at this portentous bill
  Which has made welfare out of all our ill:
  'Be it known to all men who may so require;
  This note is worth a thousand crowns entire.
  Which has its guarantee and counterfoil
  In untold wealth beneath imperial soil.
  And this is hereby a substitute approved
  Until such time as the treasure can be moved.'
Emperor: And do my people think it negotiable?
  Do army and court take it for pay in full?
  Strange though I think it, I must ratify it.

Steward: To collect those fluttering notes, one couldn't try it;
  Once issued, they are scattered in a flash.
  The Exchanges stand wide open for the queue
  Where every bill is honoured and changed for cash—
  Silver and gold—at a discount it is true.
  And then to butcher, baker, pub it goes,
  Half the world only seems to think of stuffing;
  While the other half in brand new clothes goes puffing.
  The clothier cuts the cloth, the tailor sews.
  Long live the Emperor! Makes the cellars gush
  In a cooking, roasting, platter-clattering crush.

—Goethe, *Faust*, trans. L. MacNeice

15.1 Overview

Governments play an important role in our economic lives. Especially in Europe, they are big, and have been growing bigger for most of the post-war period. Table 15.1 shows that governments in the European Union spend close to half of GDP, leaving the other half to the private sector. What do they spend their money on? A large part, about one-third of GDP, consists of transfers, subsidies to individuals

Table 15.1 **General Government Spending and Finances: EU, USA, and Japan, 2004**

	EU	USA	Japan
Total spending (% of GDP)	47.7	35.8	39.1
Public consumption[a]			
as % of GDP	20.4	14.8	17.2
as % of private consumption	35.8	21.4	31.2
Budget surplus (% of GDP)	−2.2	−4.2	−7.8
Gross debt (% of GDP)	72.5	65.7	164.1

[a] EU—2002.

Source: OECD.

(health and unemployment insurance, poverty alleviation). Transfers represent income redistribution from the haves to the have-nots, from the lucky ones to the needy ones, expressing a sense of solidarity among citizens and a rejection of excessive inequalities. Governments are also big consumers, constructing roads, purchasing buildings and the services of public employees, and much more. Of course, to pay for all that, they raise taxes, capturing close to half of GDP. Governments are not known to be particularly strict in managing their budgets. Deficits are frequent, and most governments are heavily indebted to the private sector and foreigners. While European countries have consolidated their budgets in recent years, on average public debt still represents nearly three-quarters of a year's GDP, and in some countries, such as Belgium and Italy, the stock of public debt still exceeds a full year of national output.

All of this may well be justified, but then it may not. This chapter looks at the economic functions of governments and how they fulfil their tasks. Do governments have an economic role to play at all? This question has been debated since time immemorial between right, left, and centre, between partisans of laissez-faire and interventionists. In this chapter we focus on two economic functions of governments: the microeconomic function, which includes the provision of **public goods** and services and income redistribution, and the macroeconomic function, which aims at stabilizing aggregate activity.

As already noted, governments often find themselves running budget deficits. Like anyone who spends more than they earn, they must then borrow and they accumulate a debt. This process is inherently explosive, since more debt means more debt service, hence the need to borrow more. But governments also have a unique feature: they can usually borrow from their central banks, which print money to 'buy' the public debt, as did Mephistopheles in Faust. This unique privilege, based on their monopoly right to create legal tender, is called **seigniorage**. It provides relief to the government when in need to borrow, but it eventually means fast money growth and inflation. Another privilege that some hard-pressed governments find hard to resist is to default, partially or totally, on the public debt. Private agents also default now and then, but the consequences are drastic, including jail sentences and the closing down of businesses. None of that applies to governments when they default. A confiscation of their creditors' wealth can be made perfectly legal. Fortunately, this most radical solution is only resorted to in times of national emergency.

15.2 Fiscal Policy and Economic Welfare

15.2.1 Provision of Public Goods and Services[1]

Governments 'produce' goods and services, mostly for collective consumption. Why are they involved in such an activity? The two main reasons is that some goods are fundamentally public goods while others are produced under increasing returns.

The particularity of public goods is that they cannot be appropriated for individual consumption; once they are available for one, they are available for all. This applies, for example, to law and order, defence, public gardens, or foreign affairs. In addition, some public goods exhibit a special characteristic: their use by one person benefits others. This is called an **externality**. A good example is education. All of society benefits from mass literacy; for example literate workers, who are on short supply in some poor countries, interact more effectively, which raises their productivity. Indeed, there is considerable evidence that economic growth is powerfully enhanced by the population's education level, which is called **human capital**. The generic feature of collective goods is that they cannot be appropriated

by anyone—think of law and order, for instance—and therefore cannot be sold. For this reason, private producers would not produce them, and if they are needed, governments must step in.

Futhermore, the existence of externalities implies that individuals would only buy what they need personally, overlooking the benefits to others. In general, they would buy less than is desirable for society as a whole. For example, if no one else knows how to write and read, my own incentive to pay to learn is close to nil. This is why basic education is not only public and free, but also compulsory. Police protection is another example. Security could be privately organized, but safe streets benefit all, whether they pay for it or not; in practice, only better-off, homogeneous neighbourhoods could afford to set it up. Society has an incentive to combat lawlessness on a wider scale than do individuals interested only in protecting their own safety.

A similar reasoning applies to the case of goods produced under increasing returns. One example is the usage of streets: the cost of paving and maintaining a road is roughly the same whether there are few or many users. Streets could be private and their use charged to users. This would undoubtedly relieve

---

[1] Ch. 15 further examines the characteristics of public goods.

traffic congestion in cities, but perhaps too much. Each of us could react to street tolls by reducing our movements to the point where the cost per remaining user would lead to the curtailment of street provision in some areas, in the end hurting everyone.

While there is a strong justification for *some* government consumption, there is no clear-cut border between goods and services that can be provided only publicly and those that could be provided privately. The absence of unequivocal criteria for deciding what should be publicly provided explains why there is much soul-searching on the issue. In many countries, debates continuously resurface concerning such cases as education (private schools and universities exist alongside public education), social security (health and retirement insurance are increasingly often privately provided), and utilities (highways are built and run by private companies; electricity and telephone networks are privately owned and operated).

15.2.2 Redistributive Goals: Equity versus Efficiency

A fundamental result from microeconomics is that **productive efficiency**—the optimal use of available productive resources—is achieved when each factor of production is paid its marginal productivity. This may result in a very unequal distribution of income and wealth. Indeed, we observe the coexistence of much individual wealth alongside grinding poverty. While this outcome may be efficient from a productive point of view, an altogether different logic emphasizes that human beings have similar basic needs that should be met under all circumstances. Equity or fairness is often seen as a requirement for society to be cohesive and stable. Yet equity and efficiency often work against each other; there is a fundamental **equity–efficiency trade-off**.

Governments can and do reduce inequalities. Progressive income taxes reduce the differences in post-tax incomes. Taxes levied on the better-off pay for transfers to the worse-off. In fact, a significant part of public spending is dedicated to income redistribution. Table 15.2 shows the size of transfers, both as a share of GDP and as a proportion of total government outlays. In some countries, this is the single largest item in the government budget. Not

Table 15.2 **Government Transfers, Various Countries, 1960 and 2004**

	Transfers as % of GDP		Transfers as % of government outlays	
	1960	2004	1960	2004
Austria	14.8	31.8	51.8	62.2
Belgium	12.7	30.5	44.8	61.9
Denmark	7.6	35.4	35.1	65.6
Finland	9.0	30.7	41.6	62.7
France	16.3	33.2	53.5	61.7
Germany	14.1	30.7	50.2	63.4
Greece	5.3	22.2	30.6	48.1
Ireland	9.6	18.4	38.7	54.6
Italy	11.2	28.8	45.4	60.6
Japan[a]	4.5	15.1	34.5	38.6
The Netherlands	8.6	25.4	n.a.	53.2
Portugal	3.7	25.8	24.5	55.0
Spain	2.9	22.7	23.1	57.3
Sweden	8.6	37.7	32.2	64.4
UK	9.0	26.2	30.7	62.1
USA[a]	6.0	15.4	24.4	43.1

[a] Accounting practices for transfers in the national accounts were changed in 1995 and may lead to a downward bias for the 1960 figure.

Source: European Economy, OECD, *Economic Outlook*.

surprisingly, different countries deal differently with the equity–efficiency trade-off. Sweden and the Netherlands seem to place more weight on equity than Japan or the USA, for example.

There is a trade-off however: income redistribution for the sake of equity has disincentive effects. Highly paid—and presumably highly productive—people may reduce their work effort in response to heavy taxation, or may even move abroad. On the other hand, those who receive transfers from the state may find it pointless to work hard for little net reward.[2]

---

[2] The topics of incentives and taxation are treated in Ch. 17.

15.3 Macroeconomic Stabilization

Table 15.3 Budget Balances, Various Countries, 1975–2004 (% of GDP)

	1975	1980	1985	1990	1995	2000	2004	Average 1975–2004
Austria	−2.4	−1.7	−2.6	−2.4	−5.3	−1.5	−1.1	0.1
Belgium	−5.4	−9.5	−10.2	−6.8	−4.3	0.1	0.2	1.6
Denmark	−1.3	−2.4	−1.4	−1.0	−2.3	2.5	1.9	1.9
Finland	4.6	3.3	3.2	5.1	−3.9	6.9	2.9	1.7
France	−1.6	0.0	−3.0	−2.1	−5.5	−1.4	−3.3	−0.4
Germany	−5.8	−2.9	−1.1	−2.0	−3.3	1.1	−3.3	−0.1
Greece	−2.9	−2.6	−11.6	−15.9	−10.2	−1.9	−0.7	−0.4
Ireland	n.a.	−11.7	−10.3	−2.8	−2.1	4.5	−1.2	−0.5
Italy	−12.4	−7.1	−12.7	−11.8	−7.6	−0.7	−2.8	−1.1
Japan	−2.0	−3.2	−0.6	2.0	−4.7	−7.4	−7.8	−1.6
The Netherlands	−2.4	−3.8	−3.2	−5.3	−4.2	2.2	−2.0	0.6
Norway	4.9	4.7	9.7	2.5	3.4	15.0	10.7	3.3
Spain	0.1	−2.6	−7.0	−3.9	−6.6	−0.6	−0.2	−0.9
Sweden	2.7	−4.0	−3.7	3.7	−7.4	3.4	1.2	−0.5
UK	−4.4	−3.3	−2.9	−1.6	−5.8	3.9	−2.2	0.0
USA	−5.2	−2.6	−5.1	−4.3	−3.1	1.4	−4.2	−0.4

Note: Surplus (+) or deficit (−).

Source: OECD, *Economic Outlook*.

Providing public services and redistributing income does not imply that total government spending systematically exceeds revenues. The government could perform its microeconomic functions without running budget imbalances, it only needs to raise enough tax revenue. As Table 15.3 shows, however, significant surpluses and deficits are the rule rather than the exception. Why do governments go through such gyrations in their accounts? This section shows that there are good reasons for this. In short, the second function of public budgets is to stabilize aggregate income and spending, which also results in stabilizing employment.[3] To achieve these goals, governments dissave in bad years and save in good years, just like many people do. That public imbalances can be justified does not mean that they always are, however.

15.3.1 Consumption and Tax Smoothing

A general fact of life is that people dislike fluctuations in their consumption levels; as a result, in bad years they borrow to sustain the previously reached level, and during good years they pay back and, if possible, save for the rainy day. The citizens' desire for **consumption smoothing** applies to their consumption of public goods and services as well, and it is the responsibility of governments—and a determinant of their electoral success—to provide a steady flow of

---

[3] The link between output and unemployment is given by Okun's law, which is presented in Ch. 12.

public goods and services. To do so, like individuals, governments have to borrow and save, depending on the economic situation. This is the more so that government income is very sensitive to cyclical fluctuations; tax revenues fall when peoples' incomes decline, simply because taxes are usually set as a percentage of income. There is even more to that. Taxes reduce individuals' incomes and, therefore, their private consumption possibilities. Changing the tax pressure—taxing less in bad years and more in good years—cushions private net incomes. **Tax smoothing** is the normal companion to consumption smoothing.

This principle has a central implication for the conduct of fiscal policy. If a series of bad years reduces the country's income, which is also the tax base, the government's best course of action is not to maintain the budget in balance. Rather, in order to enhance its citizens' welfare, it should endeavour to maintain a steady flow of public goods and services, and finance the tax revenue shortfall by borrowing.[4] Conversely, a few particularly good years during which taxable income rises should not be used to raise government consumption temporarily, but to increase its own savings. Acting on behalf of the public at large, a government should behave like any economic agent, meeting temporary income disturbances by saving or borrowing, within the limits of its budget constraint. Box 15.1 applies the principle of tax smoothing to the controversial case of Germany's unification.

Budget deficits met by public borrowing increase the public debt. Figure 15.1 shows how public debts (as a percentage of output) have evolved over the past century. Debts rise, sometimes spectacularly, during wars and decline afterwards. Wars are periods of unusually high public expenditure, yet they are rarely expected to last very long. The tax-smoothing principle seems to have been applied here (even if some countries eventually defaulted on part of their debts). Similarly, the oil shocks

of the 1970s were met in many countries by debt accumulation.

15.3.2 Output and Employment Stabilization

A cyclical downturn means that personal incomes decline temporarily. The laissez-faire view is that, facing a temporary income fluctuation, individuals should borrow and/or save to smooth their consumption pattern, with government playing no particular role. This prescription would be correct if all individuals could indeed borrow during a recession. Credit rationing, however, changes the situation.[5] Individuals who cannot borrow, or cannot borrow as much as they need, are unable to smooth out their consumption. Not only are they hurt, but their declining demand deepens the slowdown through the demand multiplier effect. This effect is illustrated in Figure 15.2 where, starting from long-run equilibrium at point A, a recession occurs, which is captured by the leftward shift of the aggregate demand curve from AD to AD'. Under fixed exchange rates, the government can use fiscal policy to stop this process. To keep the curve in its AD position and prevent the move from point A to point B, it either increases its own spending or provides tax relief. In effect, the government borrows on behalf of its credit-constrained citizens. Conversely, a demand boom provides the government with the opportunity to run a budget surplus and pay back the debt accumulated during previous downturns. These are examples when the government leans against the wind and conducts **countercyclical fiscal policies**.

The fact that unemployment rises during recessions provides another rationale for countercyclical fiscal policies. The mere increase in unemployment is not a justification for active fiscal policies. If unemployment rises because its equilibrium level has permanently increased, the economy will eventually settle along its long-run aggregate supply schedule and demand management is bound to fail. Attempts to keep unemployment below equilibrium through fiscal expansions will only lead to more public debt. However, short-run fluctuations

---

[4] S. 15.3.4 returns to this issue from an international perspective. Public sector borrowing can be done domestically or abroad. Globally, a country with a temporary fall in income must borrow. As a first approximation, it does not matter whether it is the private or the public sector that borrows abroad.

[5] Ch. 6 explains the mechanism and importance of credit rationing.

Box 15.1 Tax Smoothing after German Reunification

When he endorsed swift reunification early in 1990, Chancellor Helmut Kohl promised that there would be no new taxes for West Germans. Yet the former East Germany entered the Federal Republic with precious little dowry, a hugely inefficient productive sector, a large external debt (mostly to West Germany), poor infrastructure, and considerable environmental liabilities. In the eastern states, output fell by about 50%, unemployment —official and unofficial—rose to about 30%, and state-owned enterprises needed cash to stay afloat until they could be sold. From a budgetary viewpoint, the eastern provinces required massive public spending but could not contribute much to the financing. The pressure on the federal budget is apparent in Table 15.4 and continues to amount to roughly €75 billion per year. Yet this evolution is best regarded as temporary. Within a decade or two the eastern provinces will have very good prospects of catching up with the West. In the face of a temporary shock, tax smoothing calls for accumulating public debt and limiting tax increases, possibly borrowing abroad as well through current account deficits. Yet as the full costs of reunification were tallied many have begun to question how much of the obligations of the eastern states are temporary. Kohl's successor, Schröder, and his finance minister Eichel have come under public pressure to stem the rise of the national debt and close the external deficit, even if there are good economic reasons to put up with it.

Table 15.4 Fiscal Implication of German Reunification (% of GDP)

	1988	1989	1990	1991	1992	1993	1994	1995	1996	1997	1998	1999	2000[a]
Goverment expenditures	46.3	44.8	45.1	46.4	47.2	48.5	48.2	48.8	49.9	48.6	47.7	47.8	47.2
Budget surplus	−2.2	0.1	−2.0	−3.3	−2.6	−3.2	−2.4	−3.3	−3.4	−2.6	−2.0	−1.9	−1.9
Gross public debt	43.4	41.0	43.2	41.3	44.4	50.1	50.2	60.5	63.0	63.6	63.1	63.3	63.0
Current account	4.5	4.9	3.4	−1.0	−0.7	−0.5	−1.1	−0.8	−0.2	−0.1	−0.2	−0.9	−0.5

[a] OECD-Projection.

Source: OECD, *Economic Outlook*.

in unemployment around its equilibrium rate occur because price and wage rigidities prevent an optimal utilization of available resources. Counter-cyclical fiscal policy may be a corrective device to keep unemployment close to its equilibrium level, and output near its trend growth path. Sustaining aggregate demand with public spending when private demand weakens, or directly boosting private demand with tax relief, has the potential to limit the size of business cycles.

15.3.3 Automatic Stabilizers

We have argued that there are good reasons for governments to use their budget to smooth income and consumption. Interestingly, when a government refrains from using discretion to vary public spending and tax revenues, its budget automatically leans against the wind. Public budgets tend to go into surplus during upturns and into deficits during recessions. To see why, we separate out spending from revenues. Public consumption is largely unaffected by cyclical fluctuations, but transfers and tax revenues are systematically affected by economic conditions. Some transfers are explicitly linked to the state of the economy; this is clearly the case of unemployment benefits since spending depends on the number of recipients. Similarly, when incomes and spending rise, tax collection

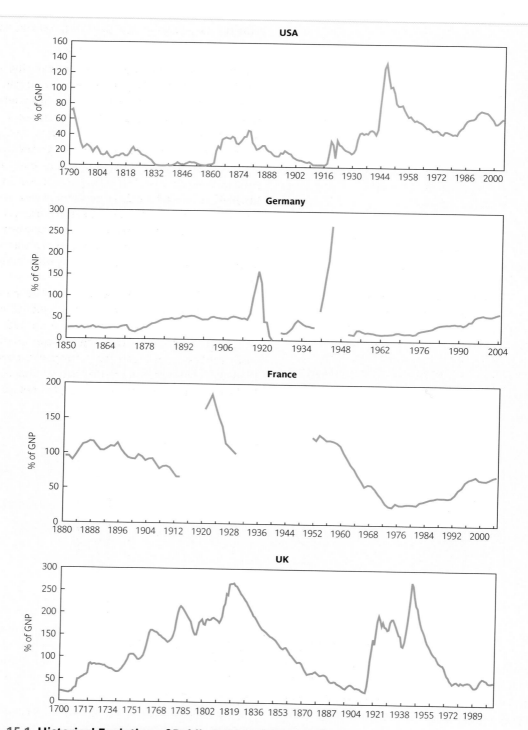

Fig. 15.1 Historical Evolution of Public Debts in Four Countries

The UK had a debt-to-GDP ratio of over 100% in 1855, a legacy of the Napoleonic wars. During the First World War the British debt rose to about 200%, and during the Second World War to 300%. The war efforts are also visible for the USA (including the Civil War).

Source: OECD, *Economic Outlook*; IMF, http://pages.stern.nyu.edu/~rsylla/.

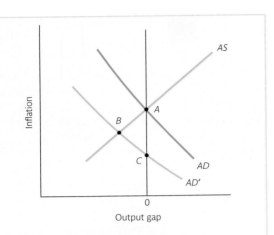

Fig. 15.2 Stabilization Policies

When demand exogenously falls, the economy moves from point *A* to point *B*. In the absence of stabilization policy, the economy will eventually move to point *C*. Fiscal policy can be used to speed up a return to trend output at point *A*, or even to prevent the *AD* schedule from shifting.

automatically increases, and conversely during economic slowdowns. The reason is that nearly all taxes are set as *rates* applied to incomes or spending. Figure 15.3 confirms that net taxes, i.e. taxes less transfers from the government to the private sector, are strongly procyclical—they move in the same direction as output. In the end, given the budgetary process described in Box 15.2, public spending is little—if at all—affected by business cycles, transfers are countercyclical, and taxes are procyclical; the budget balance is therefore automatically procyclical.[6] Only if the government takes explicit steps to alter its budget can the cyclicality of public budgets be avoided.

Summarizing, we have seen that, when an economy slows down, the budget deficit will normally increase, or its surplus will shrink or even shift into deficit. This automatic lowering of taxes amounts to an implicit fiscal expansion. Conversely, a better-than-expected economic performance reduces the budget deficit or increases the surplus because of

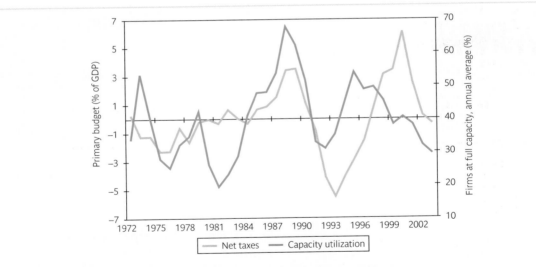

Fig. 15.3 Cyclical Behaviour of Net Taxes in the UK, 1972–2003

When the economy enters into a slowdown (the rate of capacity utilization declines), tax receipts fall and transfers rise usually with a lag of a year or two. Taxes net of transfers are procyclical.

Source: OECD, *Economic Outlook*.

---

[6] The budget balance is *G* + *TR* – *T*, where *G* is public spending on goods and services, *TR* are transfers and *T* are tax revenues. *G* is not cyclical, *TR* is procyclical, and *T* is countercyclical. Net taxes are *T* – *TR*, and are countercyclical. (Note that if *T* is countercyclical, –*T* is procyclical.)

Box 15.2 **The Budgetary Process**

All democracies follow roughly the same budgetary process. Once a year, the government presents a budget to its parliament, which then debates on—and sometimes amends—each item before voting on it. One part of the budget concerns spending by the various ministries or departments; the other part concerns tax revenue. The parliament approves tax rates, literally hundreds of them, from VAT to income, from petrol to corporate profits or property. While spending authorizations are set in amounts (say, euros) and are therefore immune to changes unless the law is amended, tax receipts in euros are uncertain, depending upon how much is to be taxed at the set rates. This is why parliament cannot decide exactly what the deficit or surplus will be. Instead, it is presented with a forecast of GDP which underlies a forecast of tax receipts and the associated deficit or surplus. It is well understood that economic conditions will settle the matter as the fiscal year goes on. In general, most governments have a tendency to forecast high

growth, large tax receipts, and small deficits, since such forecasts are not binding and make the authorities look good, at least for a while. It takes an unusually good year to have a better budgetary outcome than announced, while a moderate slowdown may easily result in large 'unexpected' slippages. The year 2003 is a case in point. It was a difficult year, with a growth performance significantly worse than expected; by late 2001, most forecasts anticipated a healthy growth performance. As time passed by, the outlook darkened, and it continued to worsen throughout the year. Table 15.5 shows the forecasts produced twice a year by the OECD. Initially, its estimates of budget outcomes were mostly on the optimistic side, and they remained so quite late. The exception is Spain, which achieved a better growth performance than the other countries. Italy also came out better than expected, but this was the result of 'exceptional measures' designed to conceal a worse deficit.

Table 15.5 **Expected and Realized Budgets in 2003 (% of GDP)**

Forecast time	December 2001	June 2002	December 2002	June 2003	December 2003	Actual
France	−1.4	−1.8	−2.5	−3.3	−4.0	−4.1
Germany	−1.8	−2.1	−2.6	−3.3	−4.1	−3.9
Italy	−1.1	−1.3	−2.8	−2.8	−2.7	−2.4
The Netherlands	0.7	−0.3	−0.3	−2.0	−2.4	−3.0
Spain	0.0	0.0	0.1	−0.2	0.1	0.3

Source: OECD, *Economic Outlook*, and *Eurostat*.

enhanced tax income for the government, a contractionary fiscal policy of sorts. In the end, we see that exogenous shifts in private demand are automatically cushioned—but not completely offset—by budgetary shifts: these are the so-called **automatic stabilizers**. They work in the absence of any policy action: simply by enacting the budget as approved by the parliament, the government finds itself conducting a countercyclical fiscal policy, dampening both recessions and expansions.

15.3.4 **How to Interpret Budget Figures**

With automatic stabilizers in place, the budget is partly endogenous. Policy choices plan a surplus or a deficit, but economic conditions determine the outcome. This is why raw budget figures do not always fully reveal the government's intentions and can be misleading. Table 15.1 shows that most countries underwent budget deficits in 1975 and 1980. Did this reflect a collective enthusiasm for expansionary policies? Quite to the contrary, these years coincided with the post-oil-shock recessions and the associated deterioration of public finances. Norway, an oil-exporting country, provides a neat counter-example: it underwent a boom and tax revenues were further boosted by oil taxes.

The endogeneity of budgets means that it is not straightforward to determine whether the stance of fiscal policy is tight or easy. A growing deficit may signal an explicit government decision to respond to a cyclical downturn, but it may as well reflect the automatic worsening of the budget as the economy slows down. This is bothersome, not just for observers and analysts, but for the government as well. How can it know that its response is appropriate if it does not even know what its effect on the budget is?

Any budget law—which authorizes a given level of spending and set all tax rates—includes an estimate of the expected balance, explicitly based on a forecast of GDP for the corresponding year. In Figure 15.4 the schedule FP (for fiscal policy) corresponds to such a budget law, i.e. spending and tax rates are taken as exogenous. The positive slope

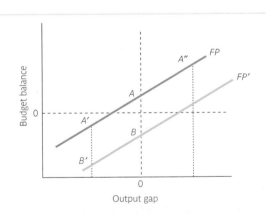

Fig. 15.4 Endogenous and Exogenous Components of Budgets

The line FP describes how the actual budget responds to cyclical fluctuations of output about its trend for a given fiscal policy stance. The move from line FP to line FP' describes a more expansionary policy stance. The cyclically adjusted budget is measured assuming a zero output gap. For fiscal policy stance FP it is given by point A, and for FP' by point B.

represents the working of the automatic stabilizer: given the amount of spending and the tax rates approved by the parliament in the budget law, an increase in the output gap—a rate of growth of GDP in excess of its trend growth rate—improves the budget balance because tax revenues grow; conversely, the budget balance deteriorates when the output gap declines. For instance, if the budget law assumes that the economy will be on trend during the corresponding fiscal year, it predicts the budget surplus indicated by point A. If the actual growth outcome is not as good as expected, point A' shows that the budget will end up in deficit.

What if the government decides to react to the budget deterioration by increasing spending or cutting taxes? This discretionary action is captured by a shift of the budget schedule, which moves to FP'. This schedule lies everywhere below FP, simply because the higher spending level or lower tax rates imply that, for any output gap, the new budget surplus will be lower than the previous one. What then does this fiscal expansion mean for the budget balance? If the economy does not respond to the fiscal boost during the fiscal year and the output gap remains the same as the one corresponding to point A', the budget deficit will widen, as shown at point B'. If, on the contrary, the fiscal expansion manages to limit the slowdown, the budget will be described by a point on the FP' schedule, somewhere up and to the right of point B'. For example, if the fiscal expansion succeeds in keeping GDP on trend, the new situation is described by point B.

The figure reveals why it is difficult to interpret budget figures. Suppose, for instance, that last year's situation is described by point A and that, in the present year, the outcome corresponds to point B'. We observe a sizeable worsening of the budget balance. Is it due to a fiscal expansion or to an economic slowdown? Both, in fact, but how do we know the role of each contributing factor? This is the question that we need to deal with.

The procedure is to ask what the budget balance would be if real GDP were on its trend path. The corresponding budget balance, which is constructed to be free of cyclical effects, is called the **cyclically adjusted budget**. Figure 15.4 considers two budget laws, represented by the schedules FP and FP'. The corresponding cyclically adjusted budgets are represented by points *A* and *B*, respectively. The distance *AB* is a measure of the fiscal relaxation corresponding to the shift from *FP* to *FP'*. In general, actual budget outcomes are not equal to the cyclically adjusted budget because the GDP is not at its trend level. Looking at the budget law represented by *FP*, it is easy to see that a positive output gap implies an actual budget surplus larger than the cyclically adjusted surplus: compare points *A* and *A''*.

Cyclically adjusted budgets are routinely calculated and discussed. For example, the European Stability and Growth Pact, designed to impose fiscal discipline within the monetary union, initially considered only actual budget outcomes, but the emphasis is increasingly shifting to structurally adjusted balances. The difference between the two budget measures is illustrated in Figure 15.5, which displays changes between 2000 and 2003. All countries that appear to the left of the vertical line have seen their budgets deteriorate. All those that appear above the horizontal line have actually tightened their fiscal policies. Very few of them have managed to reduce the actual deficit or improve the surplus, because of the marked cyclical downturn that has been felt nearly everywhere.

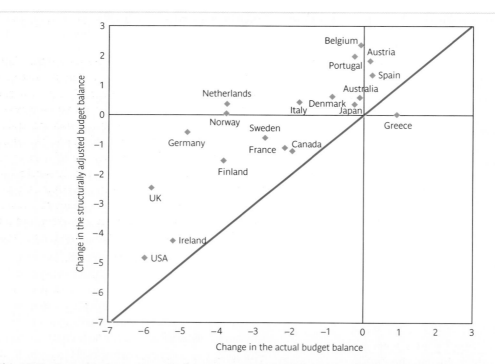

Fig. 15.5 Changes in Actual and Cyclically Adjusted Budget Balances from 2000 to 2003 (% of GDP)

The horizontal axis shows the change of the actual budget balance, the vertical axis displays the change in the cyclically adjusted budget balance, comparing 2000, a year of generally high activity level, and 2003, a slowdown year in many countries. In the north-east quadrant, for example, the actual budget deteriorates while the structural budget surplus increases (or the deficit is reduced): fiscal policy is contractionary and yet the actual budget surplus declines (or the deficit increases); the reason is that the output gap has fallen, dragging down the actual budget in spite of the government's effort to contain the deficit. More generally, all points above the diagonal correspond to cases where the slowdown contributes to a worsening of the actual budget, over and above the actual stance of fiscal policy. The case of the USA is quite striking: fiscal policy has been massively relaxed as the increase in the structural deficit indicates, and this has been accompanied by an even larger worsening of the actual deficit.

Source: OECD, *Economic Outlook*.

15.4 Deficit Financing: Public Debt and Seigniorage

Table 15.6 Gross Public Debt, Various Countries, 1970–2004 (% of GDP)

	1970	1980	1990	2000	2004
Austria	18.8	36.1	57.2	66.8	65.8
Belgium	63.3	76.2	129.1	109.6	98.6
Denmark	n.a.	47.0	70.8	54.3	47.8
Finland	n.a.	13.8	16.6	53.5	44.9
France	n.a.	30.1	39.5	65.4	71.2
Germany	17.9	31.1	41.5	60.5	66.5
Greece	18.8	22.8	79.6	106.2	98.7
Ireland	n.a.	n.a.	94.2	39.3	31.4
Italy	41.3	63.3	112.8	124.3	118.3
Japan	11.9	54.3	68.3	133.0	164.1
The Netherlands	49.7	45.4	77.0	55.8	52.7
Norway	41.5	38.9	29.2	30.0	20.0
Spain	n.a.	19.9	48.8	72.4	62.6
Sweden	29.7	46.1	45.7	64.2	58.3
UK	77.6	54.3	44.4	51.5	51.9
USA	49.2	45.2	66.6	58.8	65.7

Source: OECD, *Economic Outlook*.

Table 15.6 reveals a disquieting evolution: in almost every OECD country, public debts are very large.[7] They have grown during the 1970s, sometimes during the 1980s. Yet the intertemporal budget constraint prevents the permanent accumulation of public debts. At some point, budget deficits must be closed and turned into surpluses. But the evolution during the 1990s shows that this has not yet happened in several countries where the public debt has continued to rise. It is no surprise, therefore, that **debt stabilization** has emerged as a central concern. This section examines the debt stabilization issue. It allows us to understand the forces that lie behind the debt accumulation process, the challenge of stopping this unsustainable evolution, and what happens if it is not done.

15.4.1 The Public Debt with No Growth and No Inflation

Let us start with the easiest case where the central bank does not finance the public deficits, so that we can ignore the role of seigniorage. It is logical, then, to assume that inflation is nil, so we do not need to worry about the distinction between nominal and real variables. The government budget deficit is the sum of the primary deficit—the excess of purchases G over net tax receipts T—and of debt service—the (real) rate of interest r times the existing debt stock B. To finance the deficit, in the absence of monetary financing, the government must borrow and issue new debt ΔB. This observation can be formalized as

$$(15.1) \quad \underbrace{\Delta B}_{\substack{\text{debt} \\ \text{accumulation}}} = \underbrace{\underbrace{G - T}_{\substack{\text{primary balance} \\ \text{deficit}}} + \underbrace{rB}_{\substack{\text{debt} \\ \text{service}}}}_{\substack{\text{total budget} \\ \text{deficit}}}.$$

The overall budget deficit ΔB is sometimes called net public borrowing requirement. If the overall budget is in deficit, the government must borrow ($\Delta B > 0$), if it is in surplus, the government can retire some of its existing debt or accumulates assets ($\Delta B < 0$).[8]

---

7 The table presents gross debts. In contrast, net debt takes into account the state's assets. Net debt figures exist but are considered unreliable because of the difficulty in determining the value of state assets.

8 It is important to note that B represents the net public debt, which is the government's gross debt less its assets. The reason is that the government should normally receive interest from its asset holdings, which tends to reduce the overall budget deficit, exactly in the way debt service tends to increase the deficit.

Table 15.7 Net Debts and Primary Budget Balances, 2004[a] (% of GDP)

	Net debt in 2004	Actual primary budget surplus in 2004	Required primary surplus:[b]	
			to stabilize absolute size of debt	to stabilize debt/GDP ratio
Belgium	89.9	5.1	4.9	2.5
Germany	52.4	−0.2	3.3	1.7
Ireland	31.4	−1.1	1.6	0.8
Italy	93.9	1.5	5.9	3.0
The Netherlands	41.8	0.3	2.6	1.3

[a] These are forecasts produced in 2003 by the OECD.
[b] The required surplus assumes a 5% real interest rate and a 2.5% real GDP growth rate.

Source: OECD, *Economic Outlook*.

A striking implication of this way of looking at the public accounts is that the debt accumulation process can easily become explosive, as seems to have been in case in several countries. The reason is that, the higher the existing debt B, the higher is debt service rB, and therefore the larger the deficit and the need to accumulate more debt. Even when the primary budget is balanced ($G - T = 0$), the overall budget is in deficit and the debt continues to grow; in this case, the government keeps borrowing to pay interest on the existing debt, which means more indebtedness. Spontaneously, debt tends to accumulate at the rate r.[9] This feature of indebtedness is general and applies to any debt, be it public or private, domestic (i.e. held by domestic residents) or external.

To halt the accumulation of its debt, the government must run a permanent primary surplus large enough to provide enough resources to service the existing debt without having to rely on borrowing. Formally, we ask what must happen to have $\Delta B = 0$ in (15.1). It is easy to verify that we then have:

(15.2) $T - G = rB$
    primary   debt service
    budget surplus

[9] The tendency for the debt to grow at the rate r can be seen by looking at (18.1) when the primary budget is balanced: then, $\Delta B = rB$ or $\Delta B/B = r$, which is the growth rate of the public debt.

Stabilizing the debt level can be a formidable task. The longer the government puts off the day of reckoning, the larger the debt becomes, and the larger is the surplus ultimately required to stabilize it. This observation is illustrated in Table 15.7, which presents net debt levels and primary budget balances (as a ratio to GDP, more on that later) for a sample of countries. The third column gives the primary surplus needed to stabilize the net debt at its 2004 level, assuming a real interest rate of 5%. Of the countries shown, only Belgium fulfilled this requirement in 2004. In some cases—Germany and Italy—doing so would have required a considerable tightening of public finances. Fortunately, the following sections show that this debt stabilization criterion is excessively stringent, because it ignores both growth in GDP and the possibility of monetary finance.

15.4.2 The Public Debt with Growth and No Inflation

No one would seriously compare the indebtedness of the USA with that of France and Sweden. The ability to service, or pay for, the debt is obviously related to the country's economic size. This is precisely why all the data presented so far have been in terms of ratios to GDP, and why the appropriate objective should be to stabilize the ratio of debt to GDP rather than the debt level itself.

Box 15.3 Debt-Deficit Arithmetic

Growth, no Inflation. In order to study the evolution of the debt–GDP ratio, we divide the annual budget account (15.1) by real GDP and, with a little bit of calculus (see the WebAppendix), we find that the debt–GDP ratio increases with the budget deficit (as a share of GDP) and debt service on the debt–GDP ratio adjusted for GDP growth rate (g):

(15.3) $$\Delta\left(\frac{B}{Y}\right) = \frac{G - T}{Y} + (r - g)\frac{B}{Y}.$$

As long as the real interest rate exceeds the growth rate, the debt process is explosive. Note, however, that it tends to grow at the rate $r - g$, lower than r as implied by (15.1). For a given ratio of the primary deficit to GDP, more debt means more deficit and greater borrowing requirements. The primary budget surplus required to stabilize the debt–GDP ratio is found as follows:

(15.4) $$\Delta\left(\frac{B}{Y}\right) = 0 \text{ when } \frac{T - G}{Y} = (r - g)\frac{B}{Y}.$$

If the rate of interest r is below the GDP growth rate g, the debt–GDP ratio can be stabilized while running a budget deficit. Fast-growing countries have this possibility of outgrowing their deficits.

Growth and Inflation. In the presence of inflation, money has to be accounted for. The WebAppendix shows how budgetary accounts are modified to recognize that the deficit can be financed by both new debt issues and the creation of additional monetary base M0:

(15.5) $$\Delta\left(\frac{B}{Y}\right) + \frac{\Delta(M0/P)}{Y} = \frac{G - T}{Y} + (r - g)\frac{B}{Y}.$$

Stabilizing the debt–GDP ratio now requires an even smaller primary budget surplus, or can even be achieved with a primary deficit if enough monetary base is created:

(15.6)

$$\Delta\left(\frac{B}{Y}\right) = 0 \text{ when } \frac{T - G}{Y} = (r - g)\frac{B}{Y} - \frac{\Delta(M0/P)}{Y}.$$

This distinction assumes greater importance when one recognizes that GDPs grow secularly over time. Box 15.3 shows formally how the debt accounts change when we look at ratios to GDP. Beyond the arithmetic details, the important changes can be simply grasped. When we look at the evolution of the debt–GDP ratio, we can think of a 'race' between the numerator—the real debt level—and the denominator—real GDP. The faster the real GDP grows, the less the ratio increases. The debt itself may well increase in level and yet decline as a ratio to GDP; all it takes is for the GDP to rise faster than the debt level.[10] By the same token, in a growing economy, were the stock of the debt to remain stable as in the case studied in the previous section (see (15.2)), the debt-to-GDP ratio would vanish over

time. Since the real debt tends to grow at the rate r and the GDP grows at the rate g, the debt-to-GDP ratio tends to rise at the rate $(r - g)$. When the GDP growth rate exceeds the real interest rate, a balanced primary budget is sufficient for the debt–GDP ratio to shrink. When the real interest rate exceeds the economy's growth rate, the debt process is explosive; yet, the primary surplus required to stabilize the *ratio* of the debt to GDP is significantly smaller than the primary surplus required to stabilize the *level* of the debt, precisely because GDP growth helps contain the increase in the debt–GDP ratio. This is illustrated by the last column in Table 15.7, assuming a 5% real interest rate and a 2.5% real GDP growth rate. Even then, except for Belgium, none of the countries listed there was stabilizing its debt–GDP ratio in 2004.

These results help us understand why debts increased so much in the 1970s and 1980s. Over the 1960s and early 1970s, in most countries real GDP growth exceeded the real interest rate. For example, real interest rates in the UK during the period

---

[10] The rate of growth of the debt-to-GDP ratio B/Y is:

$$\frac{\Delta(B/Y)}{B/Y} = \frac{\Delta B}{B} - \frac{\Delta Y}{Y},$$ a formula previously encountered when

looking at the real money supply in Ch. 8. It shows that the ratio declines when the real debt grows at a lower rate than the real GDP.

1960–80 averaged 0.9% while real growth was 2.4%. Under such conditions, budget deficits need not result in a growing debt–GDP ratio. The debt accumulation process was not explosive, at least relative to GDP, a fact that probably encouraged complacency about deficits and debts. In contrast, over the period 1980–95, UK real growth hardly changed (2.4%), while real interest rates averaged 4.7%! The debt process became explosive and required prompt and vigorous action. Several countries failed to adjust quickly enough.

15.4.3 The Public Debt with Growth and Inflation

Inflation is a way of further relaxing the budgetary stringency required for debt stabilization. Monetary financing of the deficit occurs when the central bank purchases part of the public debt, either directly from the Treasury or indirectly on the money market. To pay for it, the central bank simply issues additional monetary base M0, a process some-times called seigniorage.[11] Naturally, greater use of seigniorage results in faster money growth (via the money multiplier effect) and, eventually, higher inflation. Formally, the role of seigniorage can be seen when the budget account (15.1) is modified to recognize that any increase in the nominal monetary base $\Delta M0$ provides real resources to the government. Since the real value of seigniorage is $\Delta M0/P$, the account is rewritten as:

$$(15.7) \quad \underset{\text{new debt}}{\Delta B} \quad + \underset{\substack{\text{seigniorage}}}{\Delta/(M0/P)} = \underset{\substack{\text{primary} \\ \text{deficit}}}{G-T} \quad + \underset{\substack{\text{interest} \\ \text{payments}}}{rB.}$$

Seigniorage is a cheap source of financing; it severs the link that makes the debt process explosive because little or no interest is paid on the monetary base.[12] But the explosiveness is simply transferred elsewhere, into inflation. All hyperinflationary episodes can be linked to a government's attempt to break away from its budget constraint. Hyper-inflations end when governments close their deficits, or when central banks stop financing them.

15.5 Three Ways to Stabilize the Public Debt

What are the options open to a government that wants first to stabilize an exploding debt–GDP ratio? There are three, and only three, known ways of achieving that objective: (1) cutting the deficit and achieving the required primary surplus, either by reducing public spending or by raising taxes; (2) financing deficits by money creation (monetization); (3) defaulting on some or all of the existing debt. All three amount to different forms of taxation: standard taxation in the first case, taxing those who happen to hold nominal assets (money, and nominal bonds) in the second case, and taxing those who own Treasury debt in the last case.

15.5.1 Cutting the Deficit

Deficit reduction is the virtuous road to debt stabilization. Politically, though, it is also the hardest to implement. Public spending benefits interest groups that resist cuts, for example government employees who will fight for their jobs or road construction companies that want to keep their business going. Raising taxes is notoriously unpopular. And yet,

---

[11] This expression finds its origins in the medieval practice of local lords who had the power to mint coins and used it to reduce—debase—their gold content. In a similar fashion, governments exploit the monopoly power of the central bank in creating the medium of exchange to acquire valuable resources from the private sector. Modern

seigniorage too is just another form of taxation, because the authorities exchange money, which is costless to produce, against goods and services: it is as if these goods and services were just taken away.

[12] Ch. 9 describes monetization of government deficits in more detail.

Box 15.4 Euroland and the Stability and Growth Pact

When a country has its own currency, it can use seigniorage to finance at least part of its deficits. Once it has joined the monetary union, this source of financing is lost, as is the ability to determine the domestic inflation rate.[13] The consequences for national fiscal policies are profound. First, the debt stabilization requirement becomes more stringent, as a comparison of (15.1) and (15.7) shows. Second, if the debt accumulation process is allowed to explode, with the inflation route closed the government will only have the possibility to default. The spectre of such an occurrence has greatly worried the founding fathers of the European monetary union and prompted the adoption of two measures. First, admission to the monetary union is restricted to countries that fulfil some criteria of good budgetary behaviour. Second, once a member, each country is subjected to

the Excessive Deficit Procedure. This procedure has been defined by the Stability and Growth Pact. In brief, the pact sets limits on the size of annual budget deficits, which are not allowed to exceed 3% of GDP. Should a country exceed this limit, it is given an initial 'early warning' and must then take prompt corrective action. Failure to correct the situation exposes the country to a fine. For the reasons presented in Section 15.3.3, during the 2000–3 slowdown many countries exceeded the 3% limit. In late 2003, the fine procedure should have been triggered against France and Germany, but real politics took over and the pact has been 'suspended', a decision that has subsequently been found illegal by the European Court of Justice. While the Stability and Growth Pact has not been adhered to, it has still restrained most governments, as can be seen from Figure 15.5.

---

deficit reduction has been the solution chosen and achieved in several European countries. As can be seen from Figure 5.9 and Table 15.3, countries with some of the most serious debt problems—Belgium, Denmark, Ireland, and Italy—have turned their primary budgets around. The recent European consolidation can be attributed largely to the adoption of the monetary union, as explained in Box 15.4.

15.5.2 Seigniorage and the Inflation Tax

Inflationary finance reduces the debt burden in two ways, already explained in Chapter 9. The first is

seigniorage. While not trivial, seigniorage income is too limited to be a major factor in large debt stabilizations. The second effect is the **inflation tax**, which is levied on nominal assets. Most public debts take the form of nominal non-indexed bonds. When prices rise, the nominal value of the debt remains unchanged but its real value is eroded, and debt-holders suffer a capital loss. The inflation tax is just the mirror image of this loss: the reduction of the real value of the debt is a gain for the government.

Seigniorage and the inflation tax go hand in hand. Seigniorage leads to money growth and therefore to inflation and debt relief via the inflation tax. Naturally, the inflation tax applies only to debt issued in local currencies. In addition, the tax works only if inflation is unexpected. The reason is that, when debt-holders anticipate inflation, they demand a nominal interest rate which compensates them for the expected erosion of the principal. The nominal interest rate rises in line with expected inflation, leaving the real interest rate unchanged.[14] In that case, the bondholders do not

---

[13] There is still money creation at the union's level, a source of seigniorage. Indeed, the European Central Bank must turn its profits back to the member countries. What is crucial is that the decision on how fast to let the money base grow, and therefore on how much seigniorage will be collected, is not in national hands anymore. It is entirely in the hands of the ECB, which is formally independent, constitutionally required to aim at price stability, and legally prevented from assisting governments in directly financing their budgets. For a detailed account of the fiscal policy restraints that countries wishing to join the European monetary union have to accept, see R. Baldwin and C. Wyplosz, *The Economics of European Integration*, McGraw Hill, 2003.

[14] This is the Fisher principle studied in Ch. 8.

suffer any cost and governments do not profit from inflation.

This result can be seen in a different way. In the budget accounts, (15.1) for example, it is the real interest rate that matters. For the inflation tax to work, the real interest rate must fall, otherwise the real cost of servicing the debt remains unchanged. When inflation rises unexpectedly and quickly enough, nominal interest rates on long-maturity assets cannot be modified as they are contractually fixed for the whole life of the asset. This explains why *ex post* real interest rates are just the mirror image of inflation.

To a fiscally undisciplined government the inflation tax may seem like an easy way to escape its debt obligations scot-free. It is not as painless as it looks, though. When inflation rises, newly issued bonds must serve higher nominal interest rates. In addition, lenders become suspicious and do not agree to long-term loans. As the maturity of the debt shortens, the government must constantly issue new bonds to pay back its maturing debt, and it must then pay the new higher nominal interest rate. If the debt accumulation process is still not stabilized, the government must again unexpectedly jack up the inflation rate, which will soon lead to higher nominal interest rates, calling for yet another increase in inflation, and so on. This is exactly how hyperinflations get under way. Through the inflation tax, hyperinflations do succeed in wiping out nominal assets and therefore in eliminating the public debt, but then hyperinflations must be stopped, and stopping a hyperinflation can be very costly. This is why it is an option only used under extreme political situations. It is no surprise that most hyperinflation episodes occur during (Congo in the 1990s) or after wars (Germany, Greece, Hungary after the First World War), or in troubled times (several Eastern European countries at the time of the collapse of the communist regimes) when the government is too weak to enforce fiscal discipline.

In the end, monetary financing of the deficit is just another form of taxation, like excise, income, or consumption taxes. It operates by reducing the value of the money base (the central bank's liability) and of the public debt (the Treasury's liability). Inflationary finance is a tax on money and bondholders.[15]

15.5.3 Default

The most brutal way of stabilizing the debt is simply to repudiate it. Except for post-war or post-revolution periods (when the blame can be put on exceptional circumstances or previous regimes), only governments under very severe stress resort to default. This can be outright default, which is always perceived as a major breach of confidence and leaves long-lasting scars on the reputation of governments; Box 15.5 describes the Italian experience in the Fascist era. On the other hand, it can be seen as a form of taxation, one that affects bondholders, much as inflation does. Indeed, partial default is exactly equivalent to a tax on bond income. If, for example, a government reduces the value of its debt by half, this is the same as imposing a 50% tax on interest and repayment of the principal.

The issue of default has different implications when the debt is owned by foreigners. Thus far, it has been implicitly assumed that the public debt was held by residents. In that case, debt accumulation or stabilization amounts to a redistribution of income across generations, between those who are taxed now and those who will be taxed in the future. When debt is owned by foreigners, the situation is different. As Chapter 5 shows, honouring external debt implies transferring resources to the rest of the world. This requires running a current account surplus, i.e. spending less than is earned. On the other hand, once it has defaulted on its external debt, a country cannot borrow abroad for a few years. During that period of 'international pariah status', the country cannot run a current account deficit. Comparing the two situations, honouring the debt requires a current account surplus, possibly for decades, while defaulting only requires a balanced current account, usually for a few years. This explains why sovereign nations are often more willing to default on the external than on the domestic debt when the going gets rough.

---

[15] More generally, inflation redistributes wealth from borrowers to lenders when the assets are nominal, i.e. set in money terms and not indexed to a price level.

Box 15.5 Mussolini and the Public Debt[16]

Italy emerged from the First World War with a large debt and a sizeable budget deficit. Between 1923 and 1926, having eliminated all political opposition, Mussolini re-established near budget balance and brought the debt–GDP ratio down by reducing spending and raising taxes (Table 15.8). Yet, concerned that the debt was too short in maturity, and therefore vulnerable to market conditions, in November 1926 the government imposed a mandatory conversion of debt of less than seven-year maturity into fixed-rate (5%) longer-term bonds. In 1934, these bonds were again forcibly converted into 25-year loans bearing a 3.5% interest. The first conversion is estimated to have resulted in a partial default of 20%, the second one in a loss of 30%. After these moves, the government found it very hard to undertake new borrowing. It was forced to cease issuing short-term debt in 1927 and paid a premium estimated at 2–3% on borrowing from banks.

 **Table 15.8 Public Finances in Italy, 1918–1928**

	1918	1922	1924	1926	1928
Tax revenues as % of public spending	23	46	90	100	90
Debt–GNP (%)	70.3	74.8	65.1	49.7	53.8

Source: Alesina (1988).

❗ Summary

1 One fundamental purpose of fiscal policy is to provide public goods and services. The boundary between what has to be produced publicly and what can be produced privately is not clear-cut.

2 A second function of fiscal policy is the redistribution of income and the alleviation of inequities that may be generated by the market mechanism. Doing so, however, may lead to inefficiencies.

3 A third function is to use the budget to offset temporary or cyclical fluctuations. This is done by running deficits in bad years—financed by borrowing—and surpluses in good years—to repay the previous borrowing.

4 Countercyclical fiscal policy has three main benefits: tax smoothing, private consumption smoothing, and private income maintenance.

5 The fact that in bad years some citizens cannot borrow on their own provides a justification for fiscal policy to step in and support private consumption smoothing.

6 If prices and wages are not fully flexible, fiscal policy can be used to stabilize demand, either directly through government spending, or indirectly through taxation by reducing fluctuations in private sector incomes.

7 When they vote on the budgets, parliaments set public spending levels and tax rates. During a recession (respectively, an expansion) tax receipts decline (resp. increase), leading to a deficit (resp. a surplus). As a result, the budget acts as an automatic stabilizer.

[16] This box draws on Alesina (1988).

8 The operation of the automatic stabilizer makes it difficult to interpret changes in the budget. The cyclically adjusted budget balance provides a way of disentangling the endogenous response to cyclical fluctuations from exogenous discretionary government actions.

9 Indebtedness is an inherently explosive process. When the primary budget is balanced and the debt is positive, it is necessary to keep on borrowing merely to service existing debt. The real debt accumulates at a rate given by the real interest rate.

10 To stabilize the level of the real debt, in the absence of money financing and real growth, the government must run a primary budget surplus equal to the interest charge. The longer it waits, the larger will be the debt and the interest burden that it faces, and the larger the required primary budget surplus.

11 In a growing economy, stabilizing the ratio of debt to GDP is a less stringent condition than stabilizing the absolute debt level. The required primary surplus is proportional to the difference between the real interest rate and the real GDP growth rate. Not only is this smaller than the real interest rate, it may well be negative, thus allowing permanent primary deficits.

12 Monetary financing reduces the debt burden for two reasons. Seigniorage provides resources directly to the government, virtually free of charge. As money growth eventually leads to inflation, the real value of nominal debt declines.

13 The inflation tax can be collected, however, only if inflation is unexpected. Otherwise the nominal interest rate rises, which protects lenders.

14 In addition to lowering the deficit—through spending cuts or tax increases—or resorting to money finance, debt can be stabilized by defaulting. This drastic form of taxation considerably hurts a government's reputation.

15 As long as the public debt is held by residents, debt stabilization or reduction implies income redistribution within the country. When part of the public debt is held by non-residents, stabilization requires a net transfer by residents to the rest of the world. A default redistributes wealth in the opposite direction.

🔑 Key Concepts

- public goods
- seigniorage
- externalities
- human capital
- productive efficiency
- equity – efficiency trade-off
- consumption smoothing

- tax smoothing
- countercyclical fiscal policy
- automatic stabilizers
- cyclically adjusted budgets
- debt stabilization
- inflation tax

❷ Exercises

1 Are bank notes and coins part of the public debt? Should they be? Why or why not?

2 The budget law sets public spending at €11,000 m. and the tax rate that applies to all incomes is 25%. Last year's GDP was €40,000 m. and the forecast is that it will grow by 3%. What is the budget balance set by the law? What will happen to the balance if the economy does not grow at all?

3 A country growing at a rate of 3.5% has a debt–GDP ratio of 40%. What is the primary budget surplus that keeps this ratio constant when the real interest rate is 2%? When it is 6%?

4 Suppose the debt–GDP ratio is 100%, growth is 3% per annum, and the real interest rate is 5%.

(*a*) What is the primary government budget surplus (as a percentage of GDP) that can stabilize the debt–GDP ratio?

(*b*) How does your answer change if interest rates fall to 2%? If growth falls to 1%?

5 The demand for (real) central bank money, the source of seigniorage, declines with the rate of inflation. Suppose, as an example, that this demand (in billions of euros) is given by:

π	0%	1%	2%	5%	10%	20%	25%	50%
$M0/P$	1,000	905	819	607	368	135	82	7

Seigniorage is a tax applied to this demand, whose rate is just the rate of inflation. Compute seigniorage as a function of the inflation rate. (Hint: an inflation rate of 5% corresponds to a tax rate equal to 0.05.) Which inflation rate maximizes seigniorage?

6 Figure 15.5 determines four quadrants (ignoring the diagonal). Characterize and comment on the situation in each quadrant.

7 The budget balance is –300 and GDP is 20,000. Potential GDP, however, is 20,600. Compute the structurally adjusted budget using the following information:

- Public consumption is not cyclical
- Transfers operate as follows: $TR = 13,000 - 0.5^*Y$
- Taxes are: $T = 2,000 + 0.3^*Y$

8 Consider a country where the public debt stands at 60% of GDP. The real interest rate is 3% and the trend growth rate is 2%. In the absence of seigniorage, what is the primary budget required to stabilize the debt level? The debt–GDP ratio?

9 Why does a primary surplus in excess of what is found in (15.2) imply that the public debt will eventually disappear? Why does a primary surplus in excess of what is found in (15.4) imply that the public debt will eventually disappear as a fraction of GDP?

➜ Essay questions

1 List all the public services that you can imagine. In each case, examine whether they can be privately provided.

2 'The national debt is a great scam, because it will never be repaid.' 'The national debt is irrelevant because we owe it to ourselves.' Comment.

3 The European Central Bank is constitutionally forbidden to lend directly to governments, i.e. it cannot purchase Treasury bonds directly from member governments. Yet it conducts open market operations, which may involve acquiring Treasury bonds on the markets. How do you evaluate this arrangement?

4 Critics of the Stability and Growth Pact argue that it prevents the operation of the automatic stabilizers during cyclical downturns. The propon-

ents respond that the way to deal with the pact is to run structurally adjusted surpluses. Explain and comment.

5 Between 1990 and 2004 the Irish public gross debt has fallen from 94% to 31% of GDP. Collect data on Irish budgets and growth during this period to explain this remarkable evolution. (Possible sources: OECD *Economic Outlook* database, Ireland's Finance Ministry's website: **www.finance.gov.ie**/)

6 Debt stabilization is controversial. One view is that it requires running balanced budgets, irrespective of the possible cyclical implications. Another view is that it is far better to use fiscal policy to support rapid growth. Evaluate these arguments.

The Limits of Demand Management

16.1 Overview *384*

16.2 Policy Activism and Demand Management: What are the Issues? *385*
16.2.1 Neoclassics and Keynesians: The Debate Made Simple *385*
16.2.2 Rational Expectations *386*
16.2.3 Unemployment: Is it Always at Equilibrium? *387*
16.2.4 Uncertainty and Policy Lags *388*
16.2.5 The Costs of Inflation *390*

16.3 Macroeconomic Policy and Expectations *393*
16.3.1 The Lucas Critique *393*
16.3.2 Reputation and Credibility *393*

16.4 The Institutions of Policy-Making *394*
16.4.1 Fiscal Policy *394*
16.4.2 Central Bank Credibility *396*
16.4.3 Rules versus Discretion *402*

16.5 Politics and Economics *402*

Summary *404*

The ideas of economists and political philosophers, both when they are right and when they are wrong, are more powerful than is commonly understood. Indeed the world is fuelled by little else. Practical men, who believe themselves to be quite exempt from any intellectual influences, are usually the slaves of some defunct economist.

—J. M. Keynes

As an advice-giving profession we are way over our heads.

—R. E. Lucas Jr.

16.1 Overview

Since Keynes, the possibility of ironing out the business cycle by clever macroeconomic management has inspired politicians and policy-makers. Despite the theoretical possibility of demand management developed in past chapters, there are many reasons to be cautious. The sceptical tone of this chapter reflects an ongoing reappraisal of what macroeconomic policy can actually achieve. The rise in inflation, unemployment, and public indebtedness in the 1970s, as well as the painful medicine applied in the early 1980s, have left a bitter taste and little stomach for experimenting again with policy activism. Doubts about the general efficacy of demand management are not confined to theoretical consideration; there is also increasingly less confidence that governments are capable of using macroeconomic policies systematically to smooth out aggregate fluctuations.

The age-old controversy between **neoclassical** and **Keynesian** economists has evolved considerably ever since Keynes launched his celebrated attack in 1936. Arguments have been adduced by each side to the debate, only to be undermined by new counterarguments. Yet, in spite of an apparently rising degree of sophistication, similar themes keep resurfacing. Four of them have dominated the landscape.

The first one concerns a relatively narrow and technical issue, but it has wide-ranging implications for economic policy. At stake is the speed at which goods and labour markets clear, depending on the degree of nominal wage and price rigidity in an economy. Chapter 11 shows that if all prices adjust rapidly, the economy is better left alone. If instead they are slow to adjust, we face a policy trade-off between inflation and real economic performance. In such a world, even if the trade-off is temporary, there is a place for demand management policies.

The second theme concerns expectations. How do expectations of inflation, leading to the concept of core inflation developed in Chapter 12, relate to government policy or exogenous events? Shifts in policies affect expectations and, through expectations, agents' behaviour. If agents fully see through the authorities' intentions and constraints, macroeconomic policies become largely useless. In the words of Chapter 13, if core inflation is entirely forward looking the economy never leaves the long-run aggregate supply schedule. Similarly, if forward-looking markets impose budget constraint on governments and force them to promptly reverse deficits, the aggregate demand curve cannot be shifted.

The third theme concerns the quality of government and national institutions. So far we have asked what governments can do to deal with business cycles. But we never questioned their good intentions or their ability to carry out the analysis. Real-life governments may differ from the ideal view that they are well intentioned and omniscient. As they face the electorate, they may be tempted by quick fixes that please important pressure groups. They may not like what economists tell them, if only because it runs against their political interests. Thus, even if macroeconomic policies can be used to improve things, as Keynesians argue, it may be better that governments refrain from using these instruments, as recommended by neoclassical economists.

The fourth theme can be seen through the prism of expectations. Expectations look to the future, but the future is unbounded. When a government announces its intentions for the next year or two, or for the next legislature, we still need to ask: and what happens afterwards? What are the government's next intentions, or the next government's intentions? The impossibility of long-term commitments may have deleterious effects; total freedom to carry out policy actions that can result in high inflation or exploding public debts may be destabilizing today's expectations. The response is the setting up of rules, institutions, and practices dedicated to establishing and maintaining credibility. A new trade-off emerges between rules, which anchor the future but limit freedom of action, and discretion, which permits policies to deal with unforeseen events but creates its own uncertainties.

These ideas inevitably lead us into the realm of politics, as we require an understanding of how present and future governments act and react to each other. If voters care about economic policies, politicians will need to address this concern to stay in power. In short, so far we have taken economic policies as exogenous; we now have to worry what motivates these choices and, in a way, to make them endogenous.

16.2 Policy Activism and Demand Management: What are the Issues?

16.2.1 Neoclassics and Keynesians: The Debate Made Simple

Ever since the publication of *The General Theory* in 1936, a fierce debate has raged between those who had embraced the Keynesian way of thinking about the macroeconomic short run, called Keynesians, and those who defend the classical framework of flexible prices and rely on the inherent self-corrective nature of the economic system. The latter group, known as neoclassics, initially put much emphasis on the role of money and monetary developments while de-emphasizing the usefulness of fiscal policy. Many disagreements, which persisted into the late 1960s, were focused on arcane issues such as the slopes of the *IS* and *LM* curves and the endogeneity of the money supply. These issues have since been resolved. The debate partly revolved around the question of nominal price rigidity, but there is now near-complete consensus that prices and wages are sticky, with remaining disagreements concerning the rate of inflation.

The debate is illustrated in Figure 16.1. Starting from point A, an expansionary policy (monetary policy under flexible exchange rates, fiscal policy under fixed exchange rates) takes the economy first to point B, and then to point C, where the effect is entirely absorbed by a permanently higher rate of inflation, ratified by a proportional exchange rate depreciation. The move from B to C depends on the speed at which the short-run AS curve shifts. This in turn depends on how core inflation reacts to actual inflation. Quick adjustment means a fast move from A to C, in which case policy only creates inflation, at best with a fleeting boost to GDP. In that case, if the economy always remains on its long-run aggregate supply schedule LAS, a superior solution is to aim at point D, where inflation is low. In this view, the move from A to D is very rapid and low inflation can be achieved at little or no output cost. This is the neoclassical perspective.

Keynesians do not think that the economy is always on its LAS schedule and are interested in

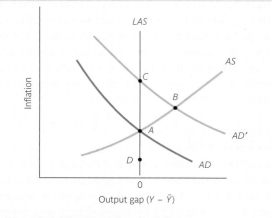

Fig. 16.1 The Neoclassical Case

A monetary expansion moves the economy from point *A* to point *B* in the short run and to point *C* in the long run. If deviations from trend *T* are short-lived, the move is actually from point *A* to point *C*, which is not really helpful. It is more desirable to aim at point *D*, where inflation is low.

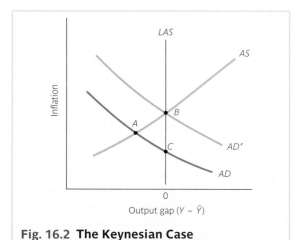

Fig. 16.2 The Keynesian Case

When the economy is below trend at point *A*, waiting for prices to adjust to reach point *C* may take a long time. A monetary policy boost takes the economy promptly back to full employment at point *B*.

situations like the one corresponding to point *A* in Figure 16.2, where output is below its trend level, and unemployment is above its equilibrium level. By construction, at point *A*, actual inflation is below its core rate. Over time, core inflation will decline and the short-run *AS* curve will shift downward until point *C* is reached. In the Keynesian view, this adjustment may take a very long time, during which unemployment is high and output is forgone. This means frustration among the unemployed, and inefficiency as productive resources remain underutilized. The preferred solution for Keynesians is to pursue an expansionary policy, shifting the aggregate demand schedule to *AD'* and bringing the economy swiftly to point *B* where things would settle.

The disagreement boils down to a simple question: can the economy stay away from the long-run aggregate supply schedule for a long time? Put differently, how quickly does the short-run *AS* shift to bring the economy to rest on the vertical *LAS*? Neoclassics argue that these shifts occur too fast for policy to make much of a difference and, anyway, policy is not needed if GDP is never far from its

growth trend. They assert that the forward-looking component of core inflation far dominates the backward-looking component. Keynesians disagree. It is remarkable that so sharp a divergence about the desirability of policy actions arises from an apparently narrow dispute concerning what seems to be a point of detail. Indeed, it is possible to agree on the entire analysis of demand and supply—as presented in Chapter 13 and recalled here—and yet disagree on every aspect of economic policy simply because there is some doubt about the speed at which the *AS* curve shifts.

16.2.2 Rational Expectations

The speed at which the *AS* curve shifts depends on the relative importance of the forward-looking component of core inflation. This raises the question of whether this component is good enough in correctly anticipating the developments that will determine the future inflation rate. For a while, Keynesians argued that people learn slowly about events and therefore adjust their expectations very gradually. Put differently, the forward-looking component is really driven by the past and is not providing information that fundamentally differs from the backward-looking component.

Neoclassical economists achieved a great victory when they argued that the only consistent way of thinking about expectations is to treat them as rational. The **rational expectations** hypothesis posits that people do not make systematic errors. They may occasionally underestimate future inflation, and then overestimate it, but on average they get it right. If they do, and if the forward-looking component of core inflation dominates, then the *AS* curve will move fast and, on average, right. Two implications follow. First, on average, the economy will always be close to, if not exactly spot on, the *LAS* schedule. Second, the only departures from the *LAS* schedule will be the result of random expectation errors, which does not provide much room for policy to play a useful role. Indeed, in that case policy must rely entirely on surprises and errors. If surprises can be engineered now and then, they cannot be systematic, simply because there is no such thing as a systematic surprise. As for expectation errors, they can only be exploited by policymakers if they know better than the public at large, but then the solution is for the government to share its knowledge, which is what democracy would call for.

The strength of the rational expectation hypothesis is that any alternative description of the formation of expectations must assert that people make systematic mistakes, for instance that people always underestimate inflation when it is rising. This is a hard case to argue. In any country, there exists a large number of forecasting companies that sell their services to firms, trade unions, the media, and even the government. The value of their services is that they are right, or at least not systematically wrong. And, as they all compete for the same customers, you would assume that those that are systematically wrong would eventually go bankrupt.

Granting that point, Keynesians respond that it is misleading to think of core inflation only as expected inflation. Even if all agents perfectly anticipate the future, they may have signed nominal contracts that lock them into prices and nominal wage increases that are based on rationally

expected inflation, but at some earlier period in time. Thus, when inflation deviates from these older expectations, there will be some interval of time when agents can do little or nothing about their errors. During that interval, which can be long-lasting, the economy deviates from trend output.

16.2.3 Unemployment: Is it Always at Equilibrium?

The Keynesian view associates unemployment and recession with the underutilization of resources, when output and employment are below their equilibrium levels. Chapters 4 and 12 decompose unemployment at any point in time into a structural or equilibrium component, and a part due to cyclical fluctuation around equilibrium. The first panel of Figure 16.3 shows that the British unemployment rate has fluctuated very widely over a century, ranging from under 3% at times in the early 1900s, the 1950s, and 1960s, to almost 25% of the labour force in the early 1930s. Do these joint fluctuations mostly reflect changes in equilibrium or are they deviations from a reasonably stable equilibrium rate? Put differently, do the periods of high unemployment correspond to severe supply shocks, or are they the effects of demand shocks that call for demand management?

A comparison with other countries reveals a strikingly similar evolution. For example, the second panel of Figure 16.3 shows that Germany too underwent high unemployment in the 1920s and 1930s, the result of a difficult recovery from the Second World War, followed by the Great Depression, both symptoms of insufficient demand. Unemployment was low in the last decades of the nineteenth century, when the industrial revolution ushered in rapid technological progress, an obvious supply shock. Unemployment was also low during the post-war boom of the 1960s and early 1970s, when both demand and supply were buoyant. The late 1970s and the 1980s were characterized in both countries by a sharp increase in unemployment, the result of the oil shocks—supply-side shocks—followed by restrictive demand policies designed to bring inflation down. In the 1990s and early 2000s, the two countries parted ways: unemployment in the

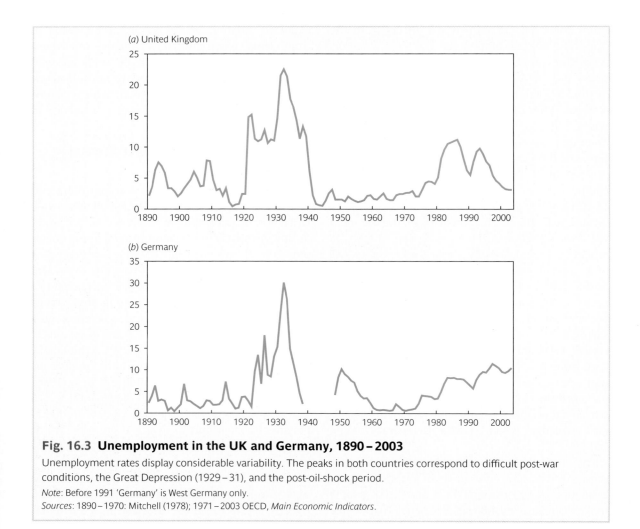

Fig. 16.3 Unemployment in the UK and Germany, 1890–2003

Unemployment rates display considerable variability. The peaks in both countries correspond to difficult post-war conditions, the Great Depression (1929–31), and the post-oil-shock period.

Note: Before 1991 'Germany' is West Germany only.

Sources: 1890–1970: Mitchell (1978); 1971–2003 OECD, *Main Economic Indicators*.

UK has fallen to below 5%, while it remains stubbornly high in Germany. This reflects a different evolution of equilibrium unemployment. It remains high in Germany where labour markets remain highly rigid, while Britain has harvested the long-run effect of reforms enacted by Thatcher in the 1980s and maintained by all successor governments.

This broad overview illustrates that both supply and demand shocks occur periodically. Most of the time these are just reasonably small shocks, as can be seen from Figure 16.3. The larger, widespread, and long-lasting shocks described above are events that strike contemporaries and deeply affect economic thinking. When demand-side shocks prevail,

as in the 1920s and 1930s, and possibly the 2000s, Keynesian ideas gain currency. Conversely, neoclassical views prevail at times of supply-side shocks, as in the 1980s. And yet, both are right or, more precisely, each view holds one part of the truth.

16.2.4 Uncertainty and Policy Lags

The other battlefront between Keynesians and neoclassics concerns the ability of governments to conduct policy effectively. Even if markets do not function perfectly, a case has to be made that governments can improve the situation. That markets fail to adjust because many prices are set in advance, as Keynesians argue, does not necessarily imply that governments may be able to offset the effects of nominal rigidities. The same uncertainty or incomplete information that prevents markets from making the best possible use of available resources may also plague government actions. Why should policy-makers have a better ability than markets to deal with uncertainty? And what if governments too make mistakes? When they set prices wrong, private agents—firms, wage negotiators —have a strong incentive to promptly discover their mistakes and take remedial action. It is not obvious that governments face the same incentives or, even if they do, that they can react as fast.

Indeed macroeconomic economic policy is plagued by a number of lags. First comes the **recognition lag**, the time it takes to discover that some policy intervention is called for. Then governments need time to formulate policy, the **decision lag**. Depending on the government structure, this can be coupled with an **implementation lag**, as ministries must originate and parliaments must pass legislation. Even if implemented quickly, policies take time to produce their effects. This is especially true of monetary policy. It takes several months before the easing of money market conditions and depreciating exchange rates have an impact on real activity. To make matters even worse, the duration of this **effectiveness lag** is quite variable.

This is why neoclassics assert that the best policy is to do nothing at all. If uncertainty is the main problem, they argue, the best that governments can do is not to make matters worse by injecting additional uncertainty. If the government has no information advantage over the private sector, it might even do more harm than good by trying to stabilize the economy. If it does know better—a dubious assumption—there is no guarantee that policies will be implemented in time and achieve the stated objectives. Figure 16.4 illustrates this debate. The dark line represents the path of output subjected to business cycle fluctuations if the economy were just left to itself. A perfectly thought-out and implemented policy would begin to stimulate the economy just when it is nearing a peak so that, given the various lags described above, its effects come into play just at the time it is needed. Similarly, it would turn restrictive just when the

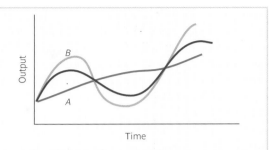

Fig. 16.4 Lags and Demand Management Policy

The dark line shows the business cycle arising from fluctuations in aggregate demand in the private sector. A demand management policy correctly implemented would smooth out the fluctuations (curve A). If there are significant effectiveness lags, the government may need to enact these measures well in advance of the turning points in the cycle. If instead the government reacts passively, it may simply reinforce the cycle (curve B).

trough is passed, so as to moderate the strength of the upturn. Ideally, the outcome would be curve A. Now add uncertainty about the recognition, decision, implementation, and effectiveness lags. In the worst case, we face the risk of achieving curve B: the stimulus planned for the downturn affects the economy exactly when it is coming out of the recession while restraint comes into play just when the economy has peaked. Here, policy makes things worse!

In order to avoid this outcome, governments must enter the forecasting business, either generating their own 'in-house' predictions or employing outside consultants to help. In practice, national policy-makers use the indicators of business conditions discussed in Chapter 14 and displayed in Figure 14.3. For example, real stock prices and real money balances are relatively reliable leading indicators, and anticipate downturns by roughly four to six quarters. Another leading indicator is the differential, or spread, between interest rates on debt of private corporations and 'safe' government bonds; when the spread increases significantly, a recession tends to be in the making. Capacity utilization, changes in inventory stocks, and investment spending plans also prove useful in the forecasting game, offering somewhat less lead time. The very fact that the lead time of these indicators is frequently only a year to eighteen months suggests that keeping ahead of the cycle is difficult. At the same time, the problem may not always be as severe as supporters of laissez-faire would like us to think.

16.2.5 The Costs of Inflation

Figure 16.2 provides an example of how the Keynesian approach to demand management can lead to higher inflation. Unless contractionary policy is pursued with the same vigour as expansionary policy, demand management policies can easily display an inflation bias. Maybe, this is an acceptable priority. Couldn't lower joblessness and higher output outweigh the inconvenience of permanently higher inflation? Indeed, the cost of inflation is another source of disagreement between Keynesians and neoclassics. Inflation is undesirable, yet it is surprisingly difficult to explain why. Here is a list of concerns.

Income and wealth redistribution

Inflation has important redistributive effects. To start with, inflation often distorts relative prices. When prices rise rapidly, even small differences in rates of increase of particular goods or of wages can lead to dramatic relative price changes. Typically, real wages stay ahead, which hurts firms' profitability, eventually deterring investment and harming growth. Those on fixed incomes and limited political clout, such as pensioners or dole recipients, do not keep up. Real exchange rates tend to swing widely in high inflation environments, shifting income between local and foreign producers, and between the local producers of traded and non-traded goods since exchange rates strongly influence traded good prices but leave non-traded good prices relatively unaffected.

In addition, inflation redistributes wealth. In contrast to real assets (real estate, durable goods, foreign exchange, precious metals), the value of nominal non-indexed assets is eroded if inflation comes as a surprise which is not factored into the agreed nominal rate of return, as explained in Chapter 15. When real interest rates become negative, wealth shifts from lenders to borrowers. Hyperinflations, in particular, can leave a legacy that survives many generations: seventy-five years on, Germans still consider inflation as an absolute evil.

Uncertainty and the value of price signals

Prices play a signalling role: they tell producers what and how to produce, consumers what and how to consume, whether to save, etc. In all cases, what matters is not absolute but relative prices, that is, what one particular good costs in terms of others. A correct interpretation of (relative) price signals is crucial to the efficiency of a market economy. It turns out that high inflation usually means more variable inflation. The more variable inflation is, the less confidence firms and households have in what they observe. Firms and households then tend to underreact to true relative price signals, confusing movements in the price level with changes in relative price. Evidence for the distortionary effect of inflation is given in Figure 16.5. Panel (a) documents the positive link between inflation level and variability. Panels (b) and (c) show that a more uncertain inflation is associated with more variable real wages and unemployment, an indication that nominal fluctuations may have real effects. When the efficient functioning of the price mechanism is attenuated, overall productivity declines, eventually resulting in lower growth and higher unemployment. Indexation may worsen the situation because it tends to freeze the hierarchy of all relative prices and to lock in real rigidities.

The value of money

The answer to income and wealth redistribution is indexation. If all nominal values—all prices and wages, but also nominal interest rates, asset prices and the exchange rate—are indexed, the losers are simply those who hold money, which, by definition, is not indexed. The losses suffered when the value of money declines steadily—more frequent trips to the bank—may seem trivial. Yet examples of hyperinflation in history show that the consequences can be highly disruptive. Box 16.1 describes these costs and explains the concept of an ideal or 'optimal' rate of inflation.

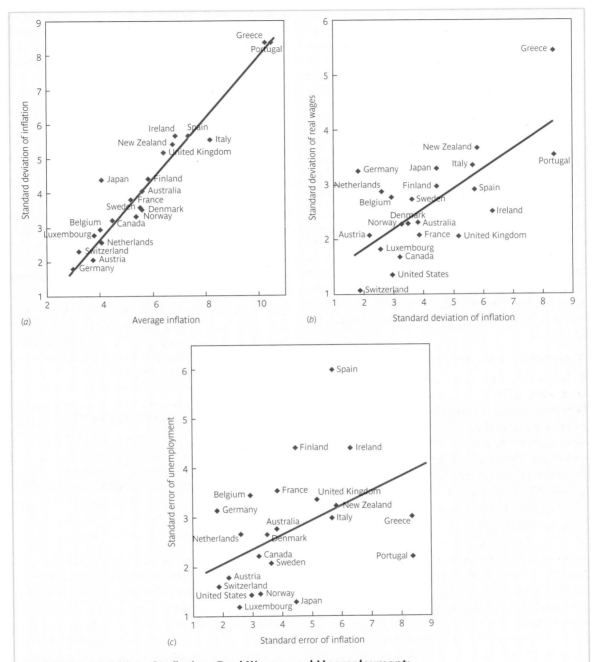

Fig. 16.5 Variability of Inflation, Real Wages, and Unemployment: All OECD Countries, 1960–2003

Comparing across all OECD countries over forty years, it appears that higher inflation is accompanied by more volatile prices (partial correlation = 0.84). The other associations are less strong but still significant: more volatile inflation is accompanied by more volatile real wages (partial correlation = 0.35) and more volatile inflation is accompanied by more volatile unemployment rates (partial correlation = 0.24).

Sources: IMF; OECD, *Economic Outlook*; Bureau of Labor Statistics.

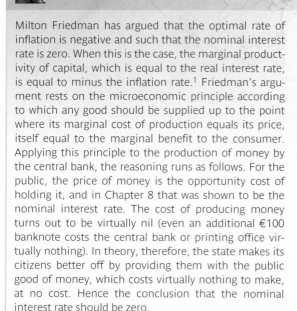

Box 16.1 Optimal Inflation

Milton Friedman has argued that the optimal rate of inflation is negative and such that the nominal interest rate is zero. When this is the case, the marginal productivity of capital, which is equal to the real interest rate, is equal to minus the inflation rate.[1] Friedman's argument rests on the microeconomic principle according to which any good should be supplied up to the point where its marginal cost of production equals its price, itself equal to the marginal benefit to the consumer. Applying this principle to the production of money by the central bank, the reasoning runs as follows. For the public, the price of money is the opportunity cost of holding it, and in Chapter 8 that was shown to be the nominal interest rate. The cost of producing money turns out to be virtually nil (even an additional €100 banknote costs the central bank or printing office virtually nothing). In theory, therefore, the state makes its citizens better off by providing them with the public good of money, which costs virtually nothing to make, at no cost. Hence the conclusion that the nominal interest rate should be zero.

Friedman obviously has a point. Money is expensive and its cost is most evident when inflation is very high; in such episodes, the demand for money all but vanishes. But his prescription has never been taken up, for good reasons. To start with, deflation means that goods and services will be cheaper tomorrow than today; why buy anything now when prices will be much lower next year? This pattern has been visible in Japan recently, as it suffered a prolonged slump for the decade of the 1990s. More importantly, a fact of life is that all goods and services are taxed, so why should money be treated any differently? Inflation is a tax, and has a role to play alongside all other taxes. In fact in many countries where tax collection is weak, because of the costs of setting up a non-corrupt administration, inflation is one of the very best sources of tax revenues that can be tapped. For these countries, it may be efficient to have significant inflation. In the developed countries, tax collection is not a problem so money should simply be taxed like all other goods, following the principles of optimal taxation.[2]

In recent years, many central banks have adopted the **inflation targeting strategy**, which involves revealing what they think is a desirable objective; see Section 16.3.1. Their thinking is that inflation is acceptable when people stop worrying about it. Table 16.1 presents their targets for 2003. Typically, these central banks aim at inflation rates around 2%. This is also the rate identified by the European Central Bank as the limit of price stability.

Table 16.1 Inflation Targets Set by Inflation-Targeting Central Banks in 2003

	Australia	Brazil	Canada	Chile	Colombia	Czech Republic	Hungary
Inflation target	2–3% 'central tendency'	8.5%	1–3%	2%–4%	6%	2%–4%	3.5% ± 1%
	Iceland	Israel	Rep. of Korea	Mexico	New Zealand	Norway	Peru
Inflation target	2.5% ± 1.5%	1–3 %	3% ± 1%	3%	1–3%	2.5%	2.5% ± 1%
	Phillippines	Poland	South Africa	Sweden	Switzerland	Thailand	United Kingdom
Inflation target	4.5–5.5%	less than 4%	3–6%	2% ± 1%	less than 2%	0–3.5 %	2.5% ± 1%

Source: A. Fracasso, H. Genberg and C. Wyplosz (2003) 'How Do Central Banks Write?', *Geneva Report on the World Economy*, Special Report 2, CEPR. London.

[1] The argument that the marginal productivity of capital should be equal to the real interest rate is a standard result from microeconomic theory; it is presented in Ch. 6. The real interest rate r is the nominal interest rate i less the inflation rate π, i.e. $r = i - \pi$. When $i = 0$ we have $r = -\pi$.

[2] The basic principle is that taxes should be spread over all goods and services and that the tax rates should be inversely related to the ease with which people cut down their spending on any good when its price rises (the price elasticity). For example, the optimal tax rate on petrol is high because people keep using their cars almost irrespective of petrol prices. By the same token, food should be heavily taxed, but here equity kicks in as an obvious other consideration. Money could be treated as food.

16.3 Macroeconomic Policy and Expectations

The paramount role of expectations in shaping many economic decisions has been stressed in Part II. Consumption and saving, investment, price- and wage-setting, and asset allocation are all sensitive to perceptions of the future. Among the most watched-after developments are possible future policies. In fact, tomorrow's (expected) policies may be more important than current policies in shaping today's actions by firms, consumers, and financial investors. This opens up a fascinating range of issues that are examined in this section.

16.3.1 The Lucas Critique

We know that current consumption is driven by wealth and current disposable income. Wealth, in turn, is the present value of future net incomes. Wealth is not observable because it depends on private expectations and because many of its components—chiefly human capital—are not explicitly valued by markets. In contrast, the link between consumption and disposable income, discussed in Chapter 6, can be observed directly. This link takes wealth as given and, as long as wealth changes slowly, it is an acceptable approximation. But sharp changes in wealth are bound to disrupt previously established patterns linking current consumption and disposable income. Since wealth depends on agents' expectations, shifts in these expectations can have dramatic effects. For example, a temporary tax reduction affects current disposable income, but leaves wealth largely unchanged, which means little effect on consumption. However, if believed to be permanent, the same tax reduction will increase wealth and boost consumption.

The point is general. It underlies the **Lucas critique**, which asserts that past behaviour of economic actors can be a poor guide for assessing the effects of policy changes.[3] The actions of private agents are driven less by the current behaviour of the government than by perceptions of its general rules of conduct, called the **policy regime**. For this reason, reactions of the public and financial markets to economic policy actions cannot necessarily be predicted by past behaviour.

One implication of the Lucas critique is that governments are on safer grounds when planning small steps within a given policy regime. Regime changes may trigger hard-to-predict private reactions. This can be interpreted as yet another argument against policy activism, and in any case it is a good reason for governments to be cautious. Another implication is that policy-making must combine current actions and binding commitments for the future. The following sections develop this general view.

16.3.2 Reputation and Credibility

When the government announces a policy change, private agents tend to react with suspicion. This is not necessarily because governments are untrustworthy, but because they are widely seen as political animals that react to short-run changes in electoral prospects. The result is that policy actions often suffer from poor **credibility**. The result? The private sector does not react as the authorities were hoping, or wishing, and the policies are at best ineffective, at worst counter-productive. When the effects of policy actions differ from those promised, the government's credibility further declines, triggering a vicious cycle of ill-fated policies and sinking trust.

Establishing credibility cannot be done on the cheap. For example, in order to bring inflation down from point B to point C in Figure 16.2, the monetary authorities must be willing to spend quite some time at point B, where output is depressed. Another, quite different example involves tax policy. Reducing the corporate profits tax is a way of encouraging investment and therefore future growth. Figure 16.6 reproduces the firm's investment decision presented in Chapter 6. A tax reduction shifts the

---

[3] This principle was first established in 1976 by Robert Lucas Jr., a leader of the Chicago school and Nobel Prize laureate. The Lucas critique has radically changed the way macroeconomists think about policy and its effects on the economy.

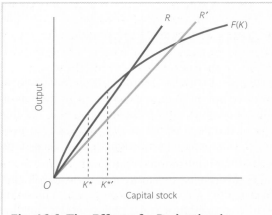

Fig. 16.6 The Effect of a Reduction in Corporate Taxes

A reduction of corporate profit taxation reduces the required pre-tax rate of profit. As the ray *OR* shifts to *OR'*, the optimal capital stock rises from *K** to *K*'*, with a corresponding increase in output.

capital? If firms suspect such a policy, they will simply pocket the tax cut and ignore the initial incentive. It is essential therefore for the government to promise that future taxes will not affect already installed capital. This promise is not credible, however, for when the capital is in place, the government's best course of action is to renege and tax.

These are just two examples of the wider phenomenon called **time inconsistency**. A broad range of policies are time inconsistent: policies that appear optimal today (low inflation, reduced taxes on corporate profits, no taxation on installed capital) are not optimal later on, especially after agents have adjusted their behaviour accordingly.[4] If a course of action is time inconsistent, it is not credible, because the private sector will not consider it likely to be implemented. What is left is always less desirable, for example a high rate of inflation and less capital accumulation.

What can be done to turn things around and create a virtuous cycle? The key insight is that promises are not believable unless they are backed by some explicit and visible commitments. Commitments, in turn, generally require an institutional backing. This is the recent trend in macroeconomic policy-making, and it has already had a very significant impact in many countries. We now review some of these developments.

ray describing the cost of capital from *OR* to *OR'*. This provides incentives for firms to accumulate more capital, from *K** to *K*'*. But firms must ask themselves how the government will meet its intertemporal budget constraint once it has reduced corporate profit taxes. Could it be that the government, later on pressed to close the budget deficit, will change its mind and tax already installed

16.4 **The Institutions of Policy-Making**

16.4.1 **Fiscal Policy**

One of the surprising implications of the Lucas critique is that a fiscal expansion—contrary to the usual expectation under a constant policy regime—might have *contractionary* effects. The case could

arise if, for example, an increase in government purchases is perceived by households as permanent. The government budget constraint requires that higher public spending be matched in present value by higher taxes, which cut into private

---

[4] Time inconsistency is a very general phenomenon, which applies to many fields besides economics. A son will promise to drive carefully if lent his parents' car; a person in prison always pledges not to engage in unlawful activity if released

early; politicians promise the moon if elected. All of these promises are time inconsistent. The risk is that only time-consistent solutions, which are less desirable for all involved, are adopted: no son is lent a car, no inmate is released early, and politicians are never trusted.

wealth.[5] Lower private wealth, in turn, leads to less private spending. If the reduction in private spending more than offsets the increase in public spending, it becomes possible that a fiscal expansion will be met by a negative effect on aggregate demand.[6] In effect, the private sector interprets the current increase in public spending as a first step towards fiscal relaxation which will, in the end, require severe tax increases that will cut into personal disposable income and therefore wealth. The fall in perceived wealth, and in private spending, may be considerable, and can overwhelm the current expansionary effect of a fiscal policy change.

Conversely, a fiscal contraction could be expansionary if households, previously pessimistic about the government's ability to deal with its budget deficits and rising indebtedness, associate current spending cuts with a lasting fiscal relief and infer a significant increase in their wealth. This intriguing possibility seems to characterize stabilization episodes in Denmark, Ireland, Portugal, Spain, and Sweden during the 1980s, in which fiscal contractions were accompanied by strong economic expansions. These so-called non-Keynesian effects of fiscal consolidation are presented in Box 16.2.

Whether expectations play such a radical role or not, there is little doubt that fiscal policy actions cannot be designed without paying attention to what happens after. The key idea is that the public is aware of the government's intertemporal constraints, which is an implication of the Ricardian equivalence concept studied in Chapter 5. That chapter concludes that, while not strictly verified in practice, Ricardian equivalence cannot be entirely dismissed.

A first implication for fiscal policy is that the public needs to be reassured that the government will not resort to heavy taxes in the future. Such a fear hurts growth in many ways. It discourages spending because it reduces wealth through the perception that future incomes will suffer. It also deters investment in human and physical capital, two of the key

sources of long-term growth.[7] Another implication is that governments need to convince the public that future deficits will not be allowed to mushroom into an unsustainable public debt. If the governments fail to persuade the public, the expectation that drastic actions will have to be eventually taken later on will set in. As Chapter 15 shows, these actions must take the form of higher taxes of one form or another: either explicitly through direct taxation or implicitly through inflation or default. Yet another implication is that, much as a fiscal consolidation can be expansionary, an expansionary fiscal policy can fail to achieve its aim and could even be contractionary.

The general conclusion is that governments need to commit themselves to a future course of action. As we have seen, such commitments may carry little credibility when a time inconsistency problem is involved. A complicating factor is that a government cannot commit its successors, especially as some of them are likely to be from opposing political parties. The situation would seem hopeless were it not for the possibility of establishing institutions that address these fears. The first of them is the existence of regular elections, which makes it possible to sanction governments that misbehave. Constitutions also typically include safeguards that protect the citizens from government abuse, for example outlawing retroactive taxation.

The current trend is to search for institutional arrangements that limit the use and misuse of fiscal policy. The general idea is to adopt rules that commit the budget to an understandable and verifiable approach. Euroland's Stability and Growth Pact is an example of a tight rule, which has proven to be too tight to be enforced at all times, see Box 15.4. The British government has adopted its own 'Fiscal Rule' which limits deficits to the size of public investments. Other fiscal rules which commit to primary budget surpluses have been adopted in Brazil and Chile in the early 2000s.

In the USA, although there is no binding rule at the federal level, budget rules exist in forty-nine of the fifty continental states (the exception being Vermont). No-deficit rules exist in thirty-six states. In

---

[5] This discussion is related to the Ricardian equivalence principle presented in Ch. 5.

[6] Graphically, the *IS* and *AD* curves shift to the left, not to the right.

[7] Ch. 18 presents long-term growth.

PART VI MACROECONOMIC POLICY

Box 16.2 Non-Keynesian Effects of Fiscal Consolidation

The *IS-LM* analysis predicts that a fiscal consolidation, designed to durably reduce or eliminate the budget deficit to stabilize the public debt, should have a contractionary effect. This is why a number of governments hesitate to undertake what they believe will be an unpopular measure, even though they know that current deficits are unsustainable. The evidence that some fiscal consolidations have been followed by an expansion has opened the puzzling possibility of 'non-Keynesian effects'. That fiscal consolidations can be made expansionary means that governments stand to hit a political jackpot! The question is how to do it. There is much debate about whether there is such a thing as the non-Keynesian effect of fiscal consolidation, yet both theory and some evidence makes this a distinct possibility. The theory is outlined in the text; it rests on expectations. The evidence is intriguing. The study from which Table 16.2 is drawn examines all episodes of fiscal consolidations in the European Union during the period 1970–2002. It identifies forty-nine such episodes and finds that, for about half of them, the output effect is not clearly contractionary. The table lists those episodes where the output effect can be classified as expansionary under a number of criteria. It seems that favourable non-Keynesian effects are more likely when the debt level is high, and when the stabilization takes the form of expenditure cuts rather than tax increases. Both characteristics are very much what theory predicts. High debts mean that the day of reckoning is not far off, which may well lead the private sector to be concerned by impending drastic actions that hurt their perception of wealth. Cutting spending means that the stabilization will not take the form of tax hikes, which may have been previously anticipated and were weighing on expectations of future disposable incomes.

Table 16.2 Episodes of Expansionary Fiscal Consolidations in the European Union

Country	Year of expansionary consolidation
Belgium	1985
Denmark	1983–4
Germany	None
Greece	1987
Spain	1986
France	None
Ireland	1987–8
Italy	1976–77, 1993
Netherlands	None
Austria	None
Portugal	1986
Finland	None
Sweden	1983
UK	1997

Source: Gabriele Giudice, Alessandro Turrini and Jan in 't Veld (2003), 'Can Fiscal Consolidations be Expansionary in the EU? Ex-Post Evidence and Ex-Ante Analysis', Economic Paper No. 195, European Commission.
http://europa.eu.int/comm/economy_finance

nine states only the automatic stabilizer is allowed to operate in that budgets must be balanced on average, allowing deficits in bad years to be repaid in better times. In twenty states, either the government or the legislature must adopt a budget balanced *ex ante*, not *ex post*. Similar, although less restrictive, rules exist for the German *Länder*.

16.4.2 Central Bank Credibility

Central banks face some of the most serious time-inconsistency problems. The value of money rests on the assumption that it will be kept in short supply by the central bank, despite occasional incentives to allow the printing press to pick up speed. One incentive is the revenue from seigniorage. History shows that this temptation is often difficult to resist. Furthermore, surprise inflation reduces the value of the public debt, and highly indebted treasuries often ask their central banks to help out. How to commit central banks not to fall victim to such temptations? Recent changes are based on the idea that good institutions can do the trick.

Table 16.3 Central Bank Independence Reforms

Australia	None	Italy	1998
Austria	1999	Luxembourg	1999
Belgium	1993	The Netherlands	1998
Canada	None	New Zealand	1990
Denmark	None	Norway	None
Finland	1998	Portugal	1998
France	1994	Spain	1994
Germany	None	Sweden	1999
Greece	1997	Switzerland	2000
Japan	1998	United Kingdom	1998
Iceland	2001	USA	None
Ireland	1998		

Source: Sven-Olov Daunfeldt and Xavier de Luna (2003), 'Central Bank Independence and Price Stability: Evidence from 23 OECD-countries', The Swedish Research Institute of Trade (HUI).

Central bank independence

A first major change has been the granting of formal independence to central banks. The evolution in the OECD countries is documented in Table 16.3. As explained in Chapter 13, entrusting monetary policy to unelected officials establishes a distance between the electoral concerns of governments and a cool-blooded analysis of the economy's needs. Figure 16.7 relates the economic performance of the OECD countries to a measure of the degree of economic independence of central banks.[8] Panel (a) shows that where the central bank is more independent inflation tends to be lower. What about the output–inflation trade-off? From panel (b) it can be seen that there is no link between economic growth and the degree of central bank independence. The two panels together have a clear implication: by granting its central bank a large degree of independence, a country achieves low inflation at no cost in terms of long-run growth. This result is consistent with a vertical long-run AS curve. In the

end, an independent central bank's main asset is its credibility. This provides a clear incentive for it to aim at a low inflation rate, and in the long run the economy will then settle in the lower portion of its LAS schedule. Some means of establishing central bank independence are presented in Box 16.3.

Inflation targeting

A second major change, already mentioned, is the adoption of the inflation targeting strategy. A growing number of central banks follow this strategy. They announce the inflation rate that they wish to achieve in, say, two years, they publish their own forecast of inflation at the same horizon, and then explain their decisions as a reaction to any discrepancy between expected and target inflation. This policy regime is both transparent and easy to understand, two characteristics that boost the central bank's credibility. Adopting a fixed exchange rate regime is another way of committing the central bank to a verifiable strategy. Indeed, if the peg is adhered to, the central bank has little or no leeway. The problem is that pegs are hard to enforce for very long and indeed most fixed exchange rate regimes include a realignment escape clause, which undermines their credibility.

Stabilizing hyperinflations

Hyperinflations—when the *monthly* rate of inflation exceeds 50%—are traumatic events. They are also interesting because they can uncover economic mechanisms that are less easy to detect under normal conditions. A key aspect of hyperinflations is that core inflation becomes entirely forward looking with an increasingly shorter time horizon. Hyper-inflations have been observed in a number of countries over the past century, and some of these cases are reported in Box 16.4. Sustained, significant surges in the inflation rate accompanied the end of central planning in Poland, Serbia, Russia, Ukraine, and Belarus. One of the best-known historical examples of hyperinflation is that of the Weimar Republic (Germany) in the period 1922–3. Table 16.5 shows the price index and associated rate of inflation in Germany as well as the money stock during that period. In just one month, October 1923, the price index rose by 29,720%. This makes for a *daily* average increase of about 19%, and it could well

[8] Ch. 9 presents an alternative measure of central bank independence.

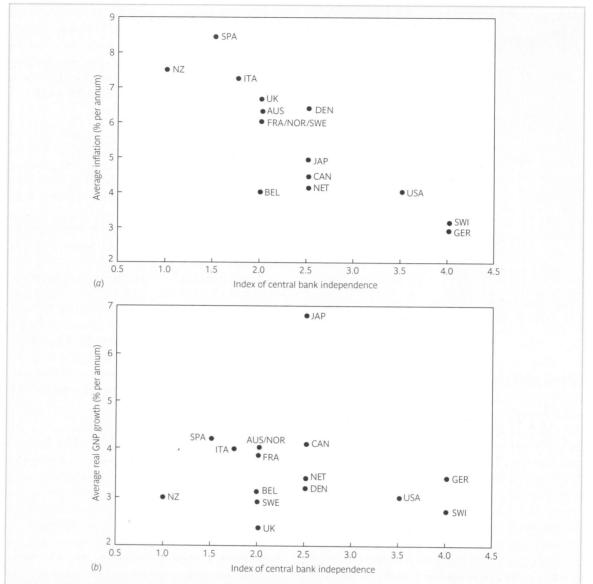

Fig. 16.7 Inflation, Growth, and Central Bank Independence

Both charts link an index of central bank independence to the inflation and GDP growth performance of OECD countries over the period 1955–88. Panel (*a*) exhibits a clear relationship: inflation is lower the more independent the central bank. Panel (*b*) fails to reveal any link between independence and GDP growth: independence delivers low inflation at no cost.

Source: Alesina and Summers (1993).

Box 16.3 The Nuts and Bolts of Central Bank Independence[9]

The autonomy of a central bank depends on its political independence and its economic freedom of manoeuvre. As a central bank is vested with important authority and serves the public interest, it must be subject to some measure of democratic control. The line between democratic control and political interference is a thin one, though. **Political independence** depends upon such aspects as the way in which central bank governors and boards are appointed. Long terms of appointment, with no possibility of early dismissal, offer more independence than terms with no set limit so that dismissal can occur at any time. Non-renewability of the term in office removes the incentive to please politicians. Current arrangements are described in Table 16.4. For example, the board members of the European Central Bank are appointed for eight-year, non-renewable terms, while governors serve a minimum of five years with a renewal option; presidents of the National Central Banks are chosen according to national practice. Although governments often insist on being represented on the policy-making boards, they no longer exert direct influence on monetary policy decisions. When conflicts arise, precise procedures contribute to greater autonomy. In Denmark and the UK, there are no legal avenues for resolving disagreements between the central bank and the government, which effectively means that the government can impose its will. In Euroland, the European Central Bank is not obliged to obtain approval for policy decisions, although they must present their policies to the European Parliament at regular intervals and accept the non-voting presence of the Finance Ministry of the country which holds the EU presidency.

Economic independence depends on the practical aspects of daily operations. For example, the central bank may be able to restrict its lending to the Treasury. Yet, as open market operations can be the back door for financing budget deficits, in Euroland, the central bank is not allowed to participate in auctions for Treasury bills or to purchase new government debt. Of course, the ECB and all central banks will always be subject to pressure from finance ministries since interest rates determine the financing costs of governments. Another important aspect is who decides on exchange rate policy, since

 Table 16.4 Terms of Central Bank of Governors and Boards

Canada

Governor appointed by finance minister for 3-year term, renewable

Board appointed by government for 3-year term, renewable

Germany

President appointed by federal president for 8-year term, non-renewable

Council members appointed by federal president for 8-year term, renewable

Netherlands

President appointed by government for 7-year term, renewable

Governing board appointed by government for 7-year term, renewable

UK

Governor appointed by government for 5-year term, renewable

Switzerland

Directorate of 3, appointed by council for 8-year term, renewable

USA

President appointed by senate for 4-year term, renewable

All board members (including president) appointed for 14-year term

European System of Central Banks (Maastricht Treaty)

President appointed by EC Council for 8-year term, non-renewable

Executive board members (up to 5 in addition to president) appointed by EC Council for 8-year term, non-renewable

Council includes board members and governors of National Central Banks, each with terms of at least 5 years, renewable

Source: Roll et al. (1993), central bank communications.

---

[9] This box owes much to the work of Grilli et al. (1991).

Box 16.3 (*continued*)

money supply, interest, and exchange rates cannot be set independently. In Euroland, the exchange rate is decided by the council of ministers of the Euroland countries, but this rare limit on ECB's independence has yet to be tested.[10] Yet another distinction concerns the decision of the inflation target when its exists. The ECB enjoys **goal independence**: while its mandate is to achieve and maintain price stability, it is for the bank itself to decide what price stability exactly means. The ECB

has announced that it aims at a 'positive rate of inflation that does not exceed 2% in the medium run'. Other central banks, e.g. the Bank of New Zealand and the Bank of England, are given the inflation objective by the Minister of Finance. For example, the Bank of England has been instructed to aim at a rate of 2%, and must explain in writing any deviation of more than 1%. These banks are free to decide how to aim at the objective; they are **instrument independent**, not goal independent.

Table 16.5 **German Hyperinflation: Money, Prices, and Inflation, January 1922 – October 1923**

	Currency (Jan. 1922 = 1)	Prices (Jan. 1922 = 1)	Inflation (% per mont)
January 1922	1	1	1
January 1923	16	75	189
March 1923	45	132	−12
May 1923	70	221	157
July 1923	354	2,021	386
August 1923	5,394	25,515	1,262
September 1923	227,777	645,946	2,532
October 1923	20,201,256	191,891,890	29,720

Source: Holtfrerich (1986).

have been double or triple that amount on some days. Failing to adjust wages or prices for just one day would have meant economic ruin. Under such conditions, nominal rigidities—which arise because it is costly to change prices too often—disappear entirely. Table 16.5 shows that money, prices, and the

exchange rate in Germany moved tightly together during the hyperinflation, indicating that neutrality held on a monthly basis.

To defeat a hyperinflation, a lasting, credible reduction of money growth is required. There is no getting around this. The problem is that, if governments have gone down the route of hyperinflation, it is probably for serious reasons, which are all likely to involve acute political weakness. It is unlikely that mere announcements of lower monetary growth—or higher interest rates—will suffice to convince the public that the episode is over; rather, a policy regime change is necessary. First and foremost, stopping a hyperinflation requires fiscal austerity. Several examples which confirm this conclusion are given in Box 16.4. Closing

[10] It is interesting to note during the 1990s, the fiercely independent Deutsche Bundesbank, the German central bank, was 'trumped' twice by politicians: the first case was German economic and monetary union, and second, European Monetary Union. In 1990 it argued against a swift monetary unification with East Germany, then against the one-Deutschmark-for-one-Ostmark conversion rate. In the end, it bowed to the government's wishes. Thus, even the considerable freedom enjoyed by such institutions can be modified if public demand for such a change is sufficiently high.

Box 16.4 Fiscal Austerity and Stopping Hyperinflations

Uncontrollable budget deficits are at the root of all hyperinflations. The linkage between budget deficits, public debt, and money growth was described in Chapter 15. When the inflation rate rises to hyperinflation levels, the government finds it difficult to raise real resources via taxes, since taxpayers often intentionally postpone paying taxes and thereby reduce or eliminate their real tax burden. In the final stages of a hyperinflation, the entire deficit, and sometimes the entire budget, is financed by seigniorage, i.e. central bank credit. This new credit is matched by high-powered money growth and becomes the fuel for inflation, in line with the monetary neutrality principle according to which, in the long run and ignoring trend growth, the rate of inflation π is equal to the rate of money growth μ. Formally, if the real budget deficit is $(G - T)$ and, if it is entirely financed by money creation, we have $\frac{\Delta M0}{P} = (G - T)$, so the inflation rate is given by

$$\pi = \mu = \frac{\Delta M0}{M0} = \frac{G - T}{M0/P} = \frac{(G - T)/Y}{M0/PY},$$

which is just the ratio of the real deficit to real monetary base, both as fractions of real GDP. (Note that the denominator is endogenous and likely to *decline* as hyperinflations intensify.) Successful policies which ended hyperinflations share the feature that they credibly closed the budget deficit, even if in a number of creative ways:

Germany (1921–3): Monetary reform (the Rentenmark): 1 new Rentenmark = 10^{12} old paper marks; new central bank (Rentenbank) with binding limits on the volume of banknotes and lending to government; balanced government budget; dismissal of 25% of all government employees and 10% of civil servants discharged; a slight rise in unemployment in 1924.

Austria (1921–3): Establishment of an independent central bank forbidden to finance deficits with banknote advances; banknote issue backed by gold, foreign earnings assets, and commercial bills; currency reform, austerity budget, and new taxes; substantial increase in

measured unemployment from September 1922 to March 1923.

Hungary (1922–4): New central bank prohibited from lending to government except on security of gold or foreign bills; gold reserves imposed; budget balanced by late 1924; less substantial increase in unemployment than in other episodes.

Poland (1922–3): New central bank; 30% reserve backing of notes (gold and foreign assets) beyond which backing of silver and bills of trade required; quick government moves to balance the budget; currency reform which imposed fixed gold content. Rise in unemployment by 50%; later loss of discipline by the central bank, deterioration of foreign exchange rate and price level.

Bolivia (1985–6): Exchange rate pegged by government using reserve loan from the IMF; nominal wage freeze; balanced budget; new valorized (inflation-proof) taxes introduced. Substantial increase in unemployment; output decline of 30%; real interest rates remained at double-digit levels for several years thereafter.

Israel (1985): Sharp cut in the budget deficit from 17% to 8% of GDP; US dollar exchange rate stabilized; new independence for the central bank, and a dramatic reduction in growth. Sharp rise in unemployment.

Poland (1990): Sharp cut in subsidies; sharp devaluation of currency followed by peg to US dollar; credit from central bank to government severely restricted. Unemployment rose from nil to 10%, output fell by some 10%, and real wages fell sharply.

Russia (1995): Move by the government to finance its deficit through borrowing directly from the markets (Treasury bills were created under the name of GKO) and the central bank committed the exchange rate to a crawling peg vis-à-vis the dollar with narrow bands of fluctuations, called the 'corridor'. GDP fell by about 10% between 1994 and 1997 while inflation declined from 130% to 11%.

Sources: Sargent (1982); Dornbusch and Fischer (1986); Berg and Sachs (1992).

the budget deficit and bringing down the rate of money growth represent a dramatic combination of restrictive policies. The result is guaranteed, eventually, as long as this policy is rigorously pursued.

16.4.3 Rules versus Discretion

Whether they bind fiscal or monetary policy actions, rules have the merit of preventing time-inconsistent actions, or at least to limit their scope. A vivid description of rules often refers to 'binding the hands' of the policy-maker. Rules, however, may also prevent governments from taking actions that are desirable. Tight fiscal rules may block the automatic stabilizer mechanism. In the midst of a recession, when net taxes decline, such a rule imposes spending cuts or tax increases, i.e. contractionary policies which deepen the recession. This is precisely what happened in Europe in 2002–4 when an economic slowdown pressed many members of the Euro-zone against the 3% deficit limit set by the Stability and Growth Pact, as described in Box 15.4. The British fiscal rule, which is less tight than the Stability and Growth Pact, has not been seriously tested yet. It is open to interpretation, which might make it too flexible.

Similarly, the decision to use of the exchange rate as an anchor for monetary policy is often softened by the possibility of occasional adjustments. If the adjustments are too frequent, many of the expected benefits are eroded. If adjustments are completely prohibited, as with currency boards, they become too rigid, as the Argentine case described in Box 10.4 illustrates. In Europe, the European Monetary System was used flexibly in the early 1980s, and it failed to impose monetary discipline in several countries. It was then used rigidly, eschewing realignments for several years, but then was nearly dismantled as currency crises almost wrecked it in 1993.

In general, if the rules are very rigid, they are bound to be counter-productive or to be overlooked under adverse conditions. If they are too soft, they differ little from full discretion. The room for manoeuvre is very narrow and there is much soul-searching under way. This concerns both fiscal and monetary policy.

The monetary policy solution has been to move beyond simple rules and to establish institutions with adequate incentives. Central bank independence, along with a clear price stability objective, possibly backed by the inflation targeting strategy, seems to have worked well over the past decade. As a result, inflation is now generally low and yet most central banks have enough room to deal flexibly with business cycles. The reason for this apparent success is that the independent experts in charge of central banks enjoy considerable discretion regarding the use of the monetary policy instrument but have little leeway in terms of the objectives that they have to achieve.

16.5 Politics and Economics

So far, governments have been described as well-meaning entities which care about the welfare of the country. A very different approach is to think of governments as being run by politicians who care about getting elected and staying in power. Policy then becomes endogenous to both economic and political circumstances, and, reciprocally, economic circumstances are partly shaped by policy actions. The loop is closed and provides interesting, if not always encouraging, insights into the role and function of demand management policies. In particular, this view suggests that demand management policies are not used to stabilize the economy but, on the contrary, that their abuse by politically motivated governments is a source of business cycles. Why should governments ever do that? Two explanations are possible.

If governments care first and foremost about their own good fortunes, they will use macroeconomic policies to boost their re-election prospects. The

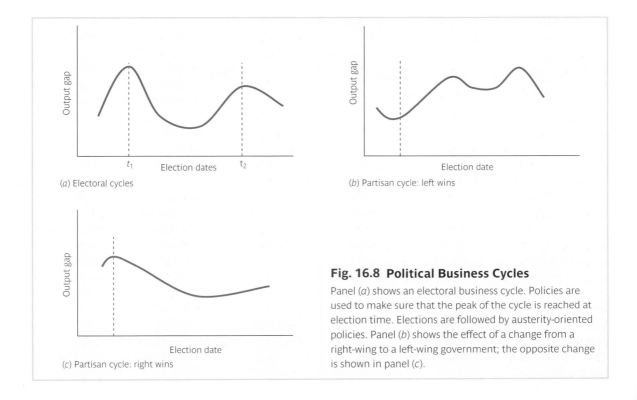

(a) Electoral cycles

(b) Partisan cycle: left wins

(c) Partisan cycle: right wins

Fig. 16.8 Political Business Cycles

Panel (a) shows an electoral business cycle. Policies are used to make sure that the peak of the cycle is reached at election time. Elections are followed by austerity-oriented policies. Panel (b) shows the effect of a change from a right-wing to a left-wing government; the opposite change is shown in panel (c).

outgoing governments will make sure that the economy is booming and employment is high on Election Day. Naturally, this might soon be followed by inflation so, in the aftermath of its election, the government will proceed to tighten its policies. Panel (a) of Figure 16.8 shows the prediction from this view of **electoral business cycles**.

A different view is that, when in power, a political party pursues a partisan agenda. This agenda can be motivated by ideology or by the coalition of interests that back the party. At any rate, the **partisan business cycle** view predicts that changes of party in power result in policy changes that generate their own cycles. It is customary to describe left-leaning governments as being Keynesian and right-leaning governments as being neoclassical. Then, if a left-leaning government replaces a right-leaning government, we should expect to see GDP growth initially increase and unemployment decrease, all of this possibly at the expense of rising inflation and deficits, which will require a contractionary correction, followed by yet another

expansion, etc. This pattern is shown in panel (b) of Figure 16.8. The opposite political shift, from left to right, is expected to generate policies that focus more on price stability and are less activist, as shown in panel (c).

The existence of **political business cycles** is not firmly established. The evidence in favour of electoral cycles is stronger than the evidence in favour of partisan cycles. There are good theoretical and empirical reasons to be sceptical.

The general view that governments can manipulate their macroeconomic instruments to achieve political gain on Election Day runs sharply against the forward-looking view developed in Section 16.3. Citizens who care about the future should see through government attempts. They should understand, for instance, that a boom designed to blossom on Election Day will be followed by restrictive policies soon afterwards. Not only should they not be impressed but also they could be expected to vote against a government that actually destabilizes the macroeconomy.

Fig. 16.9 Partisan Politics

Voters' views are spread over the range of ideologies and political preferences. To be elected, a party needs to collect a majority, its own supporters *plus* the median voter.

Similarly, the idea that partisan governments can use macroeconomic policy to favour interest groups is not as straightforward as it may seem. Presumably voters span the whole spectrum of opinions, as symbolically shown in Figure 16.9. To be elected a party must gather support from all the voters that share most its views *plus* the '**median voter**' in the centre. This median voter, who holds the key to electoral success, does not hold right- or left-wing views, so why should there be a shift in policies? The only reason is that the median voter is being seduced first and cheated upon next. This would explain both partisan policy swings and the non-re-lection of a government that has served the interests of its constituencies at the cost of incurring the median voter's wrath. The other possibility is to form coalitions of left- and right-wing parties

that shun the centrist electorate. In that case, the equilibrium of the extremes could still deliver policy stability.

In practice, the view that left-leaning governments are Keynesian while right-leaning governments are neoclassical may be an outdated oversimplification. As noted above, in times of dominating supply-side shocks, the pendulum shifts towards the neoclassical view, with the opposite shift in times of dominating demand-side shocks. The late 1990s, a period of rising popularity of the neoclassical views, witnessed the emergence of the 'third way' among left-leaning parties in a number of countries (New Labour in the UK, Schröder in Germany, Clinton in the USA, etc.) while right-leaning parties have adopted the 'compassionate Conservative' image championed by Bush and Chirac.

Finally, the type of rules and institutions developed to deal with expectations, as described in Section 16.4, means that the possibility to use demand management tools for short-run political advantage has to be significantly curtailed. For one, the granting of a large degree of independence to central banks effectively shields monetary policy from such pressure. Fiscal policy, which involves parliaments, remains politicized, but rules limit the room for manoeuvre.

❶ Summary

1 While demand management policies can in principle smooth business cycle fluctuations, recent experience and economic principles suggest caution.

2 Neoclassics and Keynesians mostly disagree on the *degree* to which actual prices and markets achieve efficient allocation of resources and optimal satisfaction of individual needs. Neoclassics contend that market-clearing is a good first-order approximation, and that markets are

closer to perfection than governments. Keynesians consider that markets suffer from a host of imperfections and that economies can suffer from persistent underutilization of resources.

3 Uncertainty plays an important role in the debate. For Keynesians, it means that private decisions are taken with imperfect knowledge of future conditions. This results in wrong pricing and resource allocation decisions. For neoclassics, uncertainty means that policy mistakes are as

likely to make matters worse as they are to improve them. Keynesians want discretion in policy-making, whereas neoclassics favour rules.

4 Because expectations crucially shape private behaviour, limited policy changes may not affect private behaviour patterns, while changes in regime policy may alter them abruptly. The Lucas critique implies that policies that look good given the past may turn out to deliver very different outcomes from those desired.

5 Time inconsistency arises when the policy plans that are best today become less desirable at a later stage. This represents a powerful incentive for governments to renege on promises once the private sector has acted in the belief that the promises will be carried out. Time-inconsistent policies are not credible.

6 There are two ways of making time-inconsistent policies credible: legally binding rules and reputation. Rules invariably restrict policy discretion and activism. Reputation requires that governments refrain from actions even if they are, at the time, desirable.

7 Monetary policy is a fragile instrument because of severe time-consistency problems. This has led central banks to seek rules (independence) that establish credibility. Independent central banks tend to be associated with lower inflation rates.

8 In reality, citizens have different interests and opinions. Real-life governments are not necessarily well meaning, but instead care mainly about being re-elected. This may lead some governments to use economic policy in a politically opportunistic way.

9 Political business cycles may take the form of expansionary policies being introduced just before elections, to be followed by corrective contractionary policies after elections. Partisan business cycles may result from the alternation of governments that defend the interests of their constituencies.

☻ Key Concepts

- neoclassics, neoclassical economics
- Keynesians, Keynesianism
- activist policies
- rational expectations
- recognition, decision, implementation, and effectiveness lags
- inflation targeting strategy
- Lucas critique

- policy regime
- credibility
- time inconsistency
- political business cycles
- partisan business cycles
- median voter theorem
- political/economic independence
- market-clearing

❓ Exercises

1 Describe the lags that affect economic policy-making and their consequences for the effectiveness of: (*a*) fiscal policy; (*b*) monetary policy.

2 What are the costs of inflation? Are there any advantages of inflation? If so, what are they?

3 Monetary policy works through either the interest rate or the exchange rate. Do you think that the effectiveness lag differs according to the exchange rate regime? If so, explain why and how.

4 Imagine a sudden and unexpected wave of high wage settlements. What would be the likely solutions proposed (*a*) by a neoclassic? (*b*) by a Keynesian? Argue their cases.

5 Describe how elections can be won in a two-party system? In a three-party system?

6 Why are the non-Keynesian effects of fiscal consolidation based on more than the forward-looking Ricardian equivalence?

➔ Essay Questions

1 Why, in a democracy, should not governments use better information to carry out political surprises?

2 What institutions can be imagined to deliver better fiscal policies? Can the example of central bank independence be used as a blueprint for fiscal policy institutions?

3 Can activist demand management policies affect equilibrium unemployment?

Supply-Side Policy

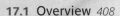

17

17.1 Overview *408*

17.2 Market Efficiency and Equilibrium Output *409*
17.2.1 The Benchmark of Efficiency: Perfect Competition *409*
17.2.2 Competition in Product Markets *410*
17.2.3 Competition in Labour Markets *410*
17.2.4 Market Failures and Overall Market Efficiency *411*

17.3 Improving the Effectiveness of Goods Markets *414*
17.3.1 Dealing with Externalities *414*
17.3.2 Taxation and the Provision of Public Goods *415*
17.3.3 Dealing with Malfunctioning Markets *417*

17.4 Improving the Efficiency of Labour Markets *420*
17.4.1 Heterogeneity and Incomplete Information *421*
17.4.2 Imperfect Contracts and Labour Market Regulations *423*
17.4.3 Incentives and Taxation *426*
17.4.4 The Political Economy of Labour Market Reform *427*

Summary *432*

For almost twenty years now, European unemployment has been a major social problem and the sign of underutilized resources at a time of unfilled needs. . . . Faced with such a prospect, European economists cannot remain silent.

—Jacques Drèze and Edmond Malinvaud

17.1 Overview

In the last chapter, we explored the role of demand management in macroeconomic policy-making. Recessions are costly in terms of unemployment and lost output; recovery from these recessions can be accelerated by well-chosen activist policies. Yet some have concluded that no policy is better than a misguided activist one. Since the economy returns to its long-run path anyway, they claim, demand policy can do more harm than good. All the same, most governments do make use of demand policy, and some rather frequently at that.

An alternative or even a complementary policy to demand-side management is to increase the pro-

ductive potential of an economy, irrespective of the state of aggregate demand. Policy measures which raise the long-run or potential GDP ($\bar{Y}$) are known as **supply-side policies**. This is shown in Figure 17.1, which plots on the horizontal axis output Y itself, rather than its deviation from potential output $(Y - \bar{Y})$. Successful supply-side policies raise potential GDP from $\bar{Y}$ to $\bar{Y}'$ faster than if were it left to the normal process of economic growth. The attractiveness of such policies is that they bypass the uncomfortable trade-off between output and inflation. In the short run, more output and lower inflation are possible as the economy moves from A to A'.[1] Similarly, policies inimical to the supply-side reduce $\bar{Y}$, causing higher inflation in the short run and higher unemployment in the long run.

This chapter surveys supply-side policies and assesses their effectiveness. One general conclusion is that, regardless of their effectiveness, supply-side policies do not produce immediate miracles. They may increase incentive to raise production; they may be aimed at improving general efficiency; they may require some sectors to decline and free resources for other, more valuable uses. All these measures take time to work, five to ten years, or even longer.

We examine three broad approaches to increasing the economy's long-run potential. First, good supply-side policy should aim to make markets as efficient as possible; and when markets fail that test, government intervention can improve matters.

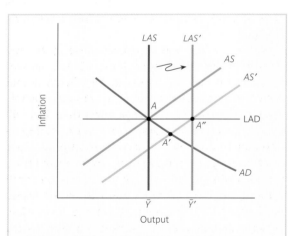

Fig. 17.1 The Macroeconomics of Supply-Side Policies

Supply-side policies aim at mobilizing productive resources to increase equilibrium output. Shifting the aggregate supply curve yields both more output and less inflation in the short run (point A'). In the longer run, inflation returns to its previous level (as indicated by the long-run aggregate demand schedule) but output is permanently higher.

---

[1] Note that the short-run effect of the shift is a reduction in the rate of inflation, as the new short-run and long-run AS curves shift rightward. For a given rate of monetary growth the inflation rate returns to its previous level (point A''); see Ch. 13.

This was also the message of Chapter 15. Second, given that governments are already interfering in the market place for both good and bad reasons, they should strive to minimize the negative impact of their intervention. One example is regulation; another is taxation; yet another is subsidy policy. Third, unemployment remains a deep concern in much of Europe where roughly 10% of the labour force is out of work. Yet in the most recent decade, the United Kingdom, the Netherlands, Denmark, Ireland, Finland, and Sweden have proved that unemployment need not be a curse. Even if the political resistance is strong, all of Europe can share in these successes, and we review how.

17.2 Market Efficiency and Equilibrium Output

17.2.1 The Benchmark of Efficiency: Perfect Competition

Adam Smith (1723–90), perhaps the most famous economist of all time, claimed in his book *The Wealth of Nations* that efficient resource allocation was best left to the market system. One of the greatest achievements of modern economics has been to confirm that, under ideal conditions, market economies achieve optimal employment of resources.[2] What are those ideal conditions? Most importantly, markets must 'work', prices must be free to adjust, there must be sufficient competition, and 'externalities' identified in Chapter 15 must be absent. Not surprisingly, these ideal conditions are unlikely to be met in practice. If this is the case, governments can intervene to improve the use of resources and achieve a larger level of output in the economy.

An important example is the labour market, studied in Chapter 4. Consider Figure 4.7. Firms' demand for labour is described by the downward-sloping marginal product of labour (MPL); firms hire labour to the point at which its marginal productivity equals the real wage. Similarly, workers supply hours of work until their opportunity cost—leisure—outweighs the real wage. The market-clearing equilibrium point A can be seen as an ideal state.

Increasing employment beyond point A in Figure 4.7 reduces the MPL below what workers are willing to work for. Reducing employment below A would raise the MPL above the real wage necessary to motivate labourers to give up their free time. Put differently, if wages are above the market-clearing level, firms would restrict employment and workers would increase their supply, resulting in involuntary unemployment. If real wages are too low, firms demand more man-hours than workers are willing to supply.

Why would the real wage ever move to its equilibrium or **market-clearing** level $\bar{w}$? The answer is: competition. Very unrealistically, imagine that hours of work are traded in a perfectly flexible market. If a firm offers a wage lower than $\bar{w}$, it will not attract as many workers as it seeks. Competition among firms will lead some to improve their offer. As they succeed in luring workers from their previous jobs, other firms will have to respond with yet a higher offer. Competition will bid up wages until they reach the market-clearing level. Conversely, imagine that the workers initially ask for a wage above $\bar{w}$. Some will not find a job, or not be able to work as many hours as they wish. Forces of competition will trigger a decline in the wage as unemployed workers underbid those who have jobs, eventually driving wages to point A.

That point A represents an ideal state is a general principle: for an economy to achieve the optimum allocation of resources, all markets must clear. Either all prices are right and all productive resources are fully employed, or none of them is and

---

[2] In the 1950s, Nobel laureates Kenneth Arrow of Stanford and Gerard Debreu of Berkeley showed how Adam Smith's intuition could be rigorously established. They identified the conditions under which a market economy delivers the socially optimal allocation of resources.

underutilization and inefficiency spread throughout the economy. Economists tend to be split into two camps on this issue. Some are convinced that markets are naturally efficient, so there is no need for governments to interfere. This is the **laissez-faire** view. Others believe that few markets meet the high standards set forth by Adam Smith. The existence of **market failures**, when and where they can be identified, provides a justification for government intervention. Note, however, how cautiously this statement is worded. Interventions are only justified if two conditions are met: first, they should be limited to clearly identified market failures; second, they should be targeted directly at the market failure to avoid creating additional distortions of their own. We next identify several generic market failures and the associated range of interventions.

17.2.2 **Competition in Product Markets**

When several firms compete with each other in the same market, they are under constant pressure to adapt the price and design of their product to the desires of the consumer—otherwise they will disappear from the screen. They will try to operate as efficiently as possible, and in doing so perform the function society wants them to: allocate available resources to their most efficient uses. And that was what Adam Smith predicted.

Competition, however, can be painful. Every economic agent wants to protect herself from competition. Firms strive to acquire a premier position in the market at the expense of their rivals, thereby earning substantial profits aptly called **economic rents**. How do they do this? Firms normally strive to establish some monopoly power, or market dominance, by exploiting increasing returns or by differentiating their products. When production exhibits increasing returns to scale, larger firms can squeeze out smaller firms by producing more and thus reducing their costs; eventually a few of them survive and dominate the market (think of the market for automobiles). Firms can also try to stunt competition by preventing others from entering their markets. Most means of maintaining dominance in a market are prohibited; threats against competitors and extortion are illegal. Yet it is standard practice for producers to spend significant amounts of money

creating brand names and convincing consumers that their products are different. If customers like consuming products which are different—or merely believe that they are—they will be willing to pay more for them. Firms use clever marketing as a means of obtaining and defending this monopoly power, and the amounts spent on product differentiation are evidently justified by the resulting profits. Product differentiation thrives on individuals' desire for variety in the market place.

Measures which increase competition and thereby economic output are generally referred to as **competition policy**. Competition policy can take a number of forms. In many countries, monopolies are regulated or supervised closely. Firms are seldom allowed to acquire excessive shares of their markets. Collusion in the form of cartels and price-fixing schemes are illegal. More recently, governments have also limited the ability of firms to dominate their input and output markets. The famous Microsoft court case is an attempt to limit the power of this firm. Similarly, the UK government has separated electricity generation from electricity distribution and the EU Commission has moved in this direction at the Community level with respect to both electricity and gas transmission. More generally, as European integration proceeds, antimonopoly powers are being transferred to Brussels, which now monitors market shares at the EU level. Some interesting cases of EU competition policy are discussed in Box 17.1.

17.2.3 **Competition in Labour Markets**

Workers also try to avoid competition, and labour markets are frequently characterized by non-competitive behaviour. For one, labour supply is intimately linked with the human condition, and competition among workers for jobs is often considered inappropriate, in bad taste, or even unethical. Second, wages are often set in bilateral negotiations, and trade unions are seen as protecting interests of employed workers in a vulnerable situation. An alternative perspective sees trade unions as monopolists with high real wages in mind.[3] With high real wages, labour demand is low and

---

[3] The analysis of trade unions is developed in Ch. 4.

Box 17.1 **EU Competition Policy and National Preferences**

Economists have a particular affinity for competition because it leads to efficiency in production. For obvious reasons, this enthusiasm is rarely shared by producers in non-competitive markets, where large profits may be at stake. Yet policy-makers and consumers may also be sceptical. Especially in the European Union, where cultures and traditions are defined by national boundaries, there may be reservations that unbridled competition might destroy or weaken national identities. It may be difficult indeed to discern the difference between respect for consumer preferences and restraint of trade. The latter means less competition, less efficiency, and lower output and employment.

Examples of this dilemma facing the EU abound. In a highly publicized case involving beer quality in the late 1980s, Germany was taken to the European Court of Justice, which has the final say in matters of competition policy. Since 1516, Germany had produced the golden beverage according to the *Reinheitsgebot* ('beer purity law'), which restricted the content of beer to four ingredients (water, yeast, malted barley, and hops). Such strict regulation of beer quality does not exist elsewhere in Europe. This law was used to exclude 'impure' foreign beer which did not meet the exacting standards of the *Reinheitsgebot*. The European Court of Justice found that beer brewed using rice and other ingredients should be permitted, while allowing German brewers to market their beer as conforming to the previous regime. Many years later and despite the new import rules, national tastes prevail; most German beer drinkers continue to drink German beer. Similarly, Italians now must have a choice between *grani duro* pasta and that made with other wheat varieties; French cheese consumers can try Danish *blø* if they wish. The consumer, in theory, is better off.

Still, the *Reinheitsgebot* case raises a number of interesting questions. Should the EU forbid the import of beef from the USA, which may be treated with hormones or antibiotics? Should genetically modified plants be allowed? Should imports of foreign 'culture'— in particular, audio and video recordings—be limited? Should a minimum price of books in bookstores be guaranteed, as in France, Germany, or Austria? Such regulations are usually justified using non-economic arguments; the question remains whether these truly outweigh their economic costs.

equilibrium unemployment high. If a majority of trade union members accept this trade-off, they will press for an outcome that is not efficient. In a similar way, firms like to control or even reduce competition on labour costs, and firms are frequently organized in employers' associations. These associations take decisions that are usually binding also for members, and may be followed by non-members (usually smaller firms). If labour and management set wages in collective bargaining without considering the interest of non-member workers, typically the unemployed, and of non-member firms, the level of competition is reduced, and the economy is less efficient. This subject is picked up in Section 17.4.

Competition in labour markets is not limited to labour unions and management. A number of practices by professional associations—of lawyers, doctors, and architects for example—also restrict the supply of labour and raise wages. Limitations on inter- national immigration can be interpreted as the ultimate restriction of competition for labour. Because so many political and sociological issues are associated with immigration, it would be premature to advocate open borders for everyone on purely economic grounds. Yet it remains true that immigration is efficient, usually increasing GDP enough to compensate any losers in the receiving country. Box 17.2 gives more details.

17.2.4 Market Failures and Overall Market Efficiency

The goal of supply-side policy is to improve the functioning of markets. In general this means intervening where the market has failed. This was already the message of Chapter 15, which looked at—temporary—demand failures which call for demand-side policies that speed up the elimination of these failures. Here we look at structural failures,

Box 17.2 The Supply-Side Economics of Immigration

Because labour is so abundant relative to capital in developing countries, many, many people there are very, very poor. In India, for example, GDP amounts to roughly €1–2 per day. Many Indians are highly educated and would readily migrate to Europe where the hourly wage might average €20–5 per *hour* or even more. Even those without exceptional skills but who are able-bodied and willing to work could compete with the less skilled. Almost on a weekly basis, we hear of Kurds, Chinese, Vietnamese, and Indians who are apprehended while trying to penetrate EU borders. Most of these people are not seeking political asylum as much as economic betterment; one can hardly blame them. Is it economically efficient to keep these people out?

The analysis of Chapter 4 suggests that it is not, and Figure 17.2 shows why. Two labour supply curves are drawn, one corresponding to that of the natives only, without the immigrants. The second curve to the right is the sum of the natives *plus* the newly arrived migrants. For the moment, the labour demand curve is assumed unchanged by migration; it represents the marginal product of labour. For a given wage level, the area under the curve and above that wage represents total profits earned by firms in the economy. In Figure 17.2, profits are thus *AWB* before the migrants arrive. When they do, the aggregate labour supply curve shifts outward, wages decline from *w* to *w'* and employment rises from *L* to *L'*. Total GDP rises by the amount *BLL'D*, the sum of the additional marginal products of the newly employed.

So if immigration is economically efficient, why all the fuss? First, the distribution of the increase in GDP is not shared by all: profits rise by *WBDW'* and the migrants earn *CDL'L''* but wages of native workers have declined from *WBLO* to *W'CL''O*. Only if the demand curve shifts

out—which may occur if there is new investment by natives, or if the immigrants themselves bring capital with them—is this situation likely to be remedied. Second, immigrants may place demands on infrastructure and the social safety net which they have not helped to pay for. Finally, although economists certainly understand the efficiency of immigration, other sociological aspects may be more important: mankind's complex tribal, if sometimes crude and primordial, instincts.

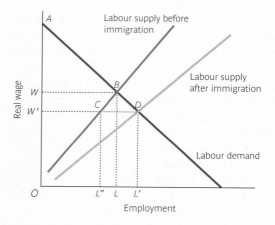

Fig. 17.2 The Supply-Side Economics of Immigration

The consequence of immigration is to shift total labour supply outward. In the new equilibrium, wages decline from *W* to *W'* and employment increases from *L* to *L'*. While GDP rises unambiguously by *BLL'D*, this gain is not evenly spread: the income of capital increases from *AWB* to *AW'D*, migrants now earn *CDL'L''*, while the income of natives declines from *WBLO* to *W'CL''O*.

which call for supply-side policies that could aim at eliminating the failures. But many of these failures simply cannot be eliminated; they are in the nature of things. Supply-side policies may help by reducing the extent and the impact of these failures. We start by looking at the generic origins of 'natural' market failures, which we group in four categories.

Externalities

An externality occurs when someone's action inevitably affects others. A good example is pollution: when a firm dumps its waste in a river, those who live or work downstream suffer and may have to spend resources to purify the water that they drink. The market alone apparently cannot redress the wrong. It turns out that it can, provided **property rights** are well defined and that it is not too costly to enforce these rights.[4] If, for example, the law specifies that everyone has a right to clean water, it is the polluting firm that will have to spend resources to clean up the water. In facing this situation, the firm will adopt cleaner production processes. Alternatively, it will offer to indemnify those who live downstream to prevent them from taking the case to court (where it would probably lose anyway). Conversely, the law could specify a right to pollute. Then the costs would be borne by the people who live downstream, who would pay for cleaning the water, or offer money to the firm for it to reduce its disposal or adopt other production processes. The second solution may seem unfair, and it is. The point here is that, once property rights have been established, the market will deliver spontaneously the best possible outcome given the presumption that nature makes it impossible to produce without creating waste.

Externalities can be **positive**. This is the case when one's actions provide others with a better outcome. One example is putting flowers in your windows: you pay the price and passers-by enjoy the sight at no cost. A general conclusion is that not enough is produced when activities generate a positive externality. Since you bear the costs of putting flowers on your balcony, you balance the price and the benefit (your pleasure). Putting out even more flowers might actually raise society's pleasure, but you have no incentive to do so. Pollution is a good example of a negative externality. Market incentives are for producers of **negative** externalities to generate too much of these for the social optimum.

Any externality which is transmitted by market prices is called a **pecuniary externality**. Assigning property rights and creating a market is often enough to solve the problem. But other, inherently **non-pecuniary externalities** are more challenging. An example is training and education. Better trained people share their knowledge with co-workers and their own children. Thus their knowledge has a value for society at large and, if they are not compensated, they will not accumulate as much human capital as is optimal from the standpoint of the economy. For this reason, society has an interest in stepping in, and subsidizing education. In Chapter 18 we will see how externalities involving education, law and order, and health can influence long-run growth. We look at the policy implications in Section 17.3.1 below.

Public goods

Public goods like parks, clean air, or information are special: they are non-rival, meaning that consumption by one does not make them less available to others, and they are non-excludable, meaning that, when they are available, everyone can use them freely. As a consequence, no one can be charged for using them, and they must be provided by the state. Law and order is an externality, but it is also a public good. Just imagine a society where it is not provided, or insufficiently provided: economic activity collapses and poverty spreads, as has been the case in countries torn by civil wars, like Liberia or Somalia.

Increasing returns

Some industries are characterized by increasing returns to scale. We have excluded that possibility in earlier chapters because it creates new problems. A good example is railways. A railway that just serves two cities will only be used by people living in or going to these two cities. If it includes a vast network, the link between the same two cities will be used by many more people, many of whom will only pass through these two cities. The larger the network, the more valuable is each of its sections, and the larger the profits to be earned from each section. Left to the market, competition will lead to a **natural monopoly**, with just one company owning all of the network. But we know that, once it has established itself, a monopoly will tend to charge too much, resulting in the socially inefficient use of its product. There is a need for the state to intervene, in this case by granting monopoly rights to a company—which can be public—in exchange for a regulation which will prevent monopolistic pricing.

---

[4] This result is known as Coase Theorem, named after Ronald Coase, a US economist who received the Nobel Prize for his work on the importance of property rights in a market economy.

Information asymmetries

It is a simple observation that we know more about ourselves than others. This information asymmetry plays a pervasive role in all sort of markets. Traders often hide information that may reduce the price they can get for their goods; just think of the seller of a used car. Financial traders make profit by reacting faster than their competitors to new information, so they will naturally tend to hide their true motives. In the first case, the market can easily dry up. In the second case, one trader's move, if badly interpreted by the others, can trigger a stampede; this is what often lies at the root of financial crises. Here again, we face a fact of nature, with serious economic implications. The state has a role to play, for example by prescribing what information must be provided by sellers of used cars or by forcing financial firms to disclose much information that they would prefer to keep for themselves.

Even die-hard free marketers recognize that markets are subject to failures, that these failures may have serious implications for economic performance, and that only the state can solve most of the associated difficulties. Should the state intervene and solve all market failures? Here economists disagree. Some, for example the public choice school led by Nobel Prize winners Friedrich Hayek and James Buchanan, maintain that, when it intervenes, the state does more harm than good. Others view state intervention as unavoidable, especially in modern societies where economic interactions can be quite complex and thus potential conduits for the diffusion of adverse effects of market failures. It is fair to say that in no country does the state completely refrain from intervening, for the right or wrong reasons. We look at supply-side policies directed at goods markets in Section 17.3, and at labour markets in Section 17.4. Many market failures not only affect the level of output, but also growth rate. In Chapter 18 we consider those policies that are mainly directed at enhancing growth. Similarly, we set aside for Chapter 19 those policies that deal with financial market failures.

17.3 Improving the Effectiveness of Goods Markets

17.3.1 Dealing with Externalities

The basic principle is to internalize the externalities, meaning make those that create an externality bear its costs or the benefits. In the pollution example above, this is achieved by making clean water a right. This principle is illustrated through a few important examples which have recently received prominent attention.

Human capital accumulation

The first example, also mentioned in Section 17.2.4, is investment in **human capital**. It is one of the most crucial factors of economic development. Human capital is acquired at school, of course, but also at work. In addition school years may well be spread over a lifetime to allow people to update their depreciating capital and learn about newly acquired knowledge. One person's knowledge benefits society in a myriad ways: it helps co-workers, of course, but better-educated people can make better decisions in everyday life—including to take better care of themselves and their children, or how to vote with a better understanding of what is at stake. An individual's return from human capital is believed to be significantly smaller for the individual than for society. If she invests with only her individual return in mind, she will underinvest regarding what is justified by the broader social return. This why society has a great interest in encouraging people to invest in more human capital than they would spontaneously. Free and compulsory education has been the first response to this externality. Subsidizing traineeship in firms or continuing education further the same goal. Further, unemployed people tend to see their human capital depreciate. This provides an additional justification for measures that reduce the duration of unemployment spells and for the active labour market policies described in Box 17.5 below.

Law and order

Law and order has all three characteristics of a market failure: it is an externality, it is subject to increasing returns to scale, and it is a public good. It is an externality since everyone benefits from others being honest. Investment in physical and human capital is threatened when crime robs people and firms of their assets, and will be less than desirable in the absence of law and order. It is subject to increasing returns to scale, since commonly accepted and enforced law works better than when everyone sets their rules and practises self-enforcement. Private protection, the spontaneous market response to the absence of law and order, is inefficient; it also accentuates the effect of inequality, as rich people can better defend themselves than poor people. Law and order is also a public good, since it is non-excludable and non-rival. Thus, on all three grounds, leaving law and order to the market results in a massive failure. Indeed, from time immemorial, one of the key attributes of any political power has always been the provision of law and order.

Health

Health is obviously a private 'good'. Everyone enjoys good health. It is also a source of externality. People with poor health do not work well and are often absent, so their productivity is reduced. If they are not paid while sick, they can become destitute, relying on society's generosity, or resorting to criminal activity to survive. Sicknesses can also be contagious, a vivid example of externality. Health can be provided privately, and it is so in many countries. Private health programmes generate inequalities, and most people think that it is unacceptable that rich people receive better treatment than poor ones. But, in addition, because of the externalities that it generates, privately provided health is inefficient, as everyone will only spend up to the point where their (marginal) benefit equals marginal cost. This is why most countries have established systems of social security and enforce compulsory medical examinations and vaccination. A healthy society is a rich society. Causality undoubtedly runs from wealth to health, but it also runs in the opposite direction.

17.3.2 Taxation and the Provision of Public Goods

The provision of public goods

Public goods are special because they naturally are non-rival and non-excludable. Being non-excludable, public goods cannot be charged to their users. A toll booth can be installed at a bridge's entrance, but what price should its owner charge? Non-rivalry means that the marginal cost of their use is very small; thus the price ought to be low. But fixed costs can be large (a bridge is very expensive to build!), so how can the producer be compensated? In addition, a bridge is a natural monopoly if it is the only one in the vicinity. If the owner charges a high price and makes large profits, market competition will lead to the multiplication of bridges next to each other, a very inefficient outcome. Markets just cannot cope with such failures; public goods need to be provided collectively (free bridges), or their provision needs to regulated (privately built bridges are generally subject to strict regulations, including pricing and quality of service).

Public goods are pervasive: transportation and amenities, but also justice and police, passports, defence, and diplomacy, etc. In each case, there is a market solution, but it is inefficient as not enough —sometimes none at all—would be privately provided. And in each case, the insufficient provision of the public goods would greatly impair economic activity, possibly leading to the breakdown of other, well-functioning markets. This is why the provision of public goods is a fundamental supply-side policy. The more efficient the provision, the more productive the economy will be. Efficiency means that public goods are produced at the lowest possible cost—which also involves issues of corruption—as further discussed in Section 17.3.3. It also requires that resources be collected to finance the production of public services, an issue to which we now turn.

Taxation

Once a society has agreed to let government perform certain public functions, public resources need

Box 17.3 **The Deadweight Loss from Taxation**

Why is any tax a source of market distortion? Figure 17.3 shows the general case of a tax paid as a percentage rate of the value of the activity (an *ad valorem* tax). Under perfect competition, the demand curve describes the marginal utility of a representative consumer for the good, and the supply curve describes the marginal cost of producing it. At point *E*, where the two curves intersect, the consumer at the margin is willing to pay exactly what the producer requires; perfect competition achieves the social best. Taxes alter the situation: the price paid by the buyer must differ from the after-tax price received by the seller. The new supply curve *S'* shows that the producer receives only a fraction of the market (relative) price. At the new market equilibrium point *D* the price is higher and the amount consumed and produced is lower. Both consumers and producers are worse off.

What are the losses to an economy from **distortionary taxation**? Figure 17.3 gives us the answer. The loss to consumers of not enjoying the price *OG* is given by *ADEG*. This can be thought of as consumers' willingness to pay above the market-clearing price, or **consumer surplus**. At the same time, the lower price (net of tax) to producing firms means that firms will lose profits on goods they would have sold at cost lower than the no-tax price. The existence of these profits is due to the fact that the supply curve is upward sloping. This second area *BCEG* is known as **producer surplus**. This consumer and producer surplus are not lost entirely. Despite the price rise, purchases of *AD* will still occur. The tax income from an *ad valorem* tax is given by the rectangle *ABCD*. This leaves the two triangles, *DEF* and *CFE*,

which represent lost consumer and producer surplus, or deadweight loss to society.

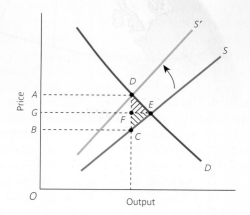

Fig. 17.3 The Effect of Taxation

Taxes drive a wedge between the price faced by the buyer and the price charged by the seller. Here a sales tax (e.g. VAT) shifts the supply curve upward. The new equilibrium occurs at point *D*, with less output, a higher buying price (distance *OA*), and a lower selling price (*OB*) than at the tax-free equilibrium point *E*. Tax revenue for the government is measured by area *ABCD*, the quantity sold times the tax rate (the difference between the two prices). Consumers, who could buy quantity *GE* at price *OG*, suffer a 'welfare loss' measured by the area *ADEG*. Similarly, producers suffer a loss represented by the area *GECB*. Of these two losses—area *ADECB*—the government receives *ABCD*. What is left, the triangles *DEF* and *EFC*, represent, respectively, lost consumer and producer surpluses—deadweight losses—arising from the tax.

to be raised in order to pay for them. This is done through taxation of final goods and services, factors of production, and other activities. Taxation generally distorts markets by driving a wedge between the cost of producing goods and services and the price paid by the consumers. This effect is described in Box 17.3. Yet, in order to provide public goods, the government must raise taxes and accept the associated distortions. Still, it should do so in the

least inefficient way. The **Ramsey principle of public finance** states that this is achieved by spreading taxes as widely as possible and by taxing most heavily those goods with the most inelastic (i.e. steepest) demands and supplies. Implementing this principle is politically contentious. Each producer stands to be hurt when a tax is applied to its production —because the producer surplus is reduced, see Box 17.3—and therefore lobbies hard to obtain as

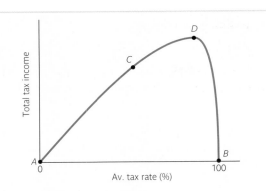

Fig. 17.4 The Laffer Curve

When the average tax rate is 0% there is no tax income (point *A*). When it is 100%, tax income is also likely to be zero (point *B*). At intermediate tax rates, there is some tax income, e.g. at point *C*. By continuity, the Laffer curve assumes a hump-shaped relationship between tax income and average tax rates. The maximum tax intake occurs at point *D*.

low taxes as possible. Tax reforms always bring diverse coalition of private interests that often succeed as the silent majority that stand to benefit from them remain inactive.

Non-distortionary taxes do not affect economic behaviour. An example would be lump-sum taxes levied on individuals without any reference to incomes, wealth, or spending, or taxes levied unexpectedly on past incomes and wealth so that it is too late to react. For this reason, non-distortionary taxes are appealing to governments. In practice, however, retroactive taxation is considered unfair precisely because it takes people by surprise. Lump-sum taxes are also unpopular, as Mrs Thatcher's fateful experience with the poll tax in 1990 showed. As a result, nearly all taxes are distortionary.

Because distortionary taxes move the economy away from its first-best equilibrium, it is entirely conceivable that higher tax rates actually result in *lower* tax yields. This effect is sometimes called the **Laffer curve** and is depicted in Figure 17.4.[5] This

curve describes a theoretical relationship between *total* government tax revenues on the vertical axis and the *average* tax rate (the ratio of tax receipts to GDP) on the horizontal axis. The tax rate ranges from 0 to 100%; at a 0% rate, tax revenue is nil (point *A*); when the tax rate reaches 100%, no one is likely to work or produce at all so tax receipts are also nil (point *B*). At intermediate tax rates, tax receipts are positive, as at point *C*. The hump-shape of the curve indicates that the tax rate distorts the economy so much that beyond some tax rate, taxable income *declines* faster than the tax rate increases. The threshold point *D* corresponds to the average tax rate for which tax receipts are at a maximum. Any rate of taxation to the right of point *D* is inefficient because the same tax income can be raised with a lower tax rate, i.e. less distortion. The Laffer curve is not taken too seriously for policy purposes, since its most important detail is unknown: the location of point *D*. In the early 1980s, Laffer claimed that the USA had passed this point; when the USA did cut tax rates, tax revenue actually declined.

17.3.3 Dealing with Malfunctioning Markets

The solution to market failures is not always to produce public goods and services. In fact, it is increasingly being recognized that private producers tend to be more cost-efficient than publicly owned ones, provided that they be adequately regulated. In this section we look at monopolies and review some prominent examples of the **privatization** process and of how regulation operates.

Monopolies

Markets characterized by increasing returns tend to evolve to a situation where a very few firms buy out or eliminate the others. When only one firm survives, it is a monopoly. Once it has achieved that position, its incentive is to charge high prices, and possibly to stop innovating and let its goods quality decline. When just two or three dominate, they have incentives to agree among themselves to raise prices and lower competition in terms of quality and innovation. This is called collusion. Thus, in the presence of increasing returns, markets evolve spontaneously to a situation where competition is

---

5 Economist Arthur Laffer, then from Chicago, is reported to have been influential in persuading President Reagan to cut taxes in the early 1980s.

Box 17.4 Privatization, Deregulation, and the European Telecommunications Boom

In the early 1990s a number of European countries, led by the UK and later by Germany, began to privatize and deregulate their telecommunications industries. These had been the domain of the national postal systems, which had moved slowly to introduce new technologies and continued to charge high prices for services which cost little at the margin to produce. In effect, the Europeans were doing little more than recognizing the successes of the USA in the early 1980s after the break-up of the monopoly ATT (American Telephone and Telegraph) and the resulting deregulation of long-distance telephone service. The Europeans went farther than the Americans, however; by agreeing on a pan-European standard for wireless technologies and wireless application protocols, they created a common market for an activity which obviously involves massive external

effects. They also intensified direct competition with local telecom service provision, which remains a local monopoly in most countries.

The deregulation of telecoms in Europe has led to visible positive supply-side economic effects. The telecom industry has not only been a source of value added and income growth for Europeans, but also hundreds of thousands of new jobs. Most importantly, consumers have benefited. Table 17.1 shows the extent to which prices for these telecommunications services have fallen in Germany. More recently, the public auction of third-generation mobile communication radio frequencies heralds the combination of these technologies with the internet, and promises the introduction of new products and services that the old national postal services could never have offered.

Table 17.1 Telecommunications Prices in Germany, 1995–1999

	1995	1996	1997	1998	1999
All telephone services	127.1	128.9	124.0	122.4	108.4
All trunk line systems	117.1	120.9	118.2	117.4	104.6
by service:					
Fixed fees	90.5	99.5	99.2	99.8	100.0
Call-by-call fees	137.8	137.6	133.0	131.0	108.3
Local	80.3	93.1	93.1	93.6	99.4
National Long Distance	216.4	201.0	185.7	187.6	110.4
International Long Distance	236.3	212.8	212.2	188.8	159.4
All cell phone systems	236.0	201.3	157.9	144.0	114.4
by user type:					
Infrequent usage users	317.8	244.9	147.4	133.7	119.8
Low usage users	244.9	202.3	153.3	142.3	114.2
Average usage users	199.3	186.3	167.1	149.5	113.2

Source: German Federal Statistical Office.

insufficient to match the principles of market efficiency. Examples of industries prone to increasing returns include cars and aeroplanes, transports and telecommunications.

One response is to regulate these industries. Governments step in and either break down the monopolies (e.g. the ongoing deregulation in the

electricity, telecommunication, and airline industries), or prevent mergers, and actively fight against collusion. Because competition increasingly takes place at the world level, such anti-trust and anti-collusion policies are often conducted at the supranational level. In Europe, the European Commission has been granted wide authority in that area. For instance, it has blocked several mergers between international giants and imposed pro-competition conditions on others.

Privatization

In many countries, the other response to market failures, especially the existence of natural monopolies, has been to set up state-owned companies that would not seek to exploit their monopolistic power. This has been the case of railways, electricity generation and distribution, water distribution, telecommunications, etc. Starting in the early 1980s in Europe, the performance of these state monopolies has been found wanting. The prices that they charged were regulated, and based on their costs, but who controlled the costs? Suspicion grew that, in the absence of competition, these firms were not particularly interested in producing at the lowest possible cost. The infamous monopolistic rent was not captured in the form of private profits, but in the form of slackness in production, poor quality of service, technological backwardness, and sometimes comfortable salaries and other advantages. The contrast between Europe and the USA, which relied to a much lesser extent on publicly owned companies, had become glaring.

The response has been a wave of privatization, still under way. Once a company had become private, it was interested in expanding across borders. The presence of state-owned monopolies in some countries prevented the entry of foreign competitors, while allowing the national company to expand abroad, clearly an unfair situation. This is why the Single Act of 1992 has given the European Commission the right to force national governments to privatize most of their state-owned monopolies and to open their markets to foreign competition. Ten years down the road, the process is still far from complete, a testimony of how entrenched the interests are. Box 17.4 recalls the successful privatization process in the telecommunications industry. This process has freed a dynamic force for economic growth and job creation.

Regulation

Regulation is often the best response when markets are not well behaved. Financial markets are essential for economic growth, since banks and financial intermediaries collect savings to finance investment by firms and public deficits. Yet financial markets are often considered with suspicion, partly because of markets' tendencies to undergo violent crises, a manifestation of the asymmetric information problem. In response, they are regulated. Banks are forbidden to take excessive risk, because depositors cannot effectively monitor their banks and stand to lose part of their savings if the bank collapses. Financial operators also face legal restraints on the risk that they can take, in an effort to limit the occurrence of financial crises.

That regulation affects nearly every aspect of economic life reflects how widespread market failures are, but also a tendency of the state to do too much. Asymmetric information explains why food labels, airline services, or driving licences are regulated. Yet the regulation of store closing times in much of Europe, tree-felling in Germany, or chimney-sweeping in Switzerland might be a step too far, possibly protecting private interests at the expense of the public good.

Subsidies and industrial policy

For a variety of non-economic reasons, many countries operate elaborate systems of subsidies which shield certain firms and industries from the discipline of the market. Table 17.2 displays the evidence for some OECD countries. Subsidized firms can sustain losses and avoid adjusting to changing economic conditions. In doing so, they keep resources (e.g. labour) employed, but inefficiently. They do not face the full cost of their operations (part of the costs are charged to taxpayers), or else the factors of production are paid more than their true marginal productivity.[6] In fact, they may even keep factor prices artificially high and hurt productive activities that are not subsidized.

Public ownership of firms is another form of subsidization. Unlike private firms, state-owned enterprises (SOEs) rarely face demanding shareholders

---

6 For example, after the oil shocks, a reduced world demand for tankers and the emergence of competitors in Asia (Japan, Korea) combined to create major difficulties for European shipyards. The UK, Germany, France, and many other countries reacted by subsidizing their shipbuilding companies. In the end, the costs became too large and the situation too hopeless for the subsidies to be maintained. While the subsidies did save jobs for a few years, they did so in a very inefficient way.

Table 17.2 Subsidies in Various Countries (% of GDP)

	1975	1990	2002
Belgium	2.59	1.66	1.56
France	2.17	1.81	1.25
Germany	1.77	1.76	1.46
Italy	2.61	1.88	0.99
The Netherlands	1.12	2.25	1.54
Spain	0.65	1.06	1.15
Sweden	2.39	3.48	1.60
USA	0.47	0.44	0.31

Source: OECD, *Economic Outlook*.

and are almost never shut down. When they lose money, they generally receive public resources. This may come either as an explicit subsidy from the government to cover the loss, or as a loan to the company at interest rates unavailable to other firms. SOEs operate in virtually every major industry in Western Europe.

Most countries regard certain economic activities as indispensable for strategic or political reasons. These include defence-related industries such as steel, energy, high technology, aircraft, and ship-building. As many of these activities exhibit increasing returns to scale, governments often try to guarantee that the firms are large enough. This is often the underlying logic behind **industrial policies**. Industrial policies amount to official backing of national corporations or whole industries. This takes the form of subsidies, public orders, and trade policies. **Trade policies** include tariffs on foreign goods, quotas on imports, export credits financed at concessionary rates, and procurement policies whereby domestically produced goods are chosen over cheaper foreign ones, not to mention 'buy domestic goods' campaigns.

The ultimate effect of these policies is to raise prices above competitive levels. Consumers or taxpayers make up the difference. Once again, the principle that prices reflect efficient production costs is violated. Supply-side considerations have led to a reassessment of strategic requirements. The European Single Act (1992) bans most trade policies mentioned above for intra-European trade. Yet industrial and trade policies survive, often conducted at the EU rather than national level, with such celebrated examples as Airbus and Ariane. More recently, private European banks have complained that state savings banks and their parent entities enjoy hidden subsidies in the form of government guarantees. EU competition authorities have demanded that these be privatized or at least set on equal footing, singling out the German *Sparkassen* and the *Landesbanken*. These institutions respond that they represent the only means of achieving blanket availability of banking services in remote, rural areas, and provide financing for projects that private banks generally shun. As the issue of state aids becomes increasingly political, it assumes the aspects of national preferences discussed in Box 17.1.

17.4 Improving the Efficiency of Labour Markets

The last section established that product markets can fail and require government action. The same applies to labour markets, but doubly so. Besides the obvious human dimension—that individuals and their well-being are associated with labour supply, wages, and unemployment—it turns out that a number of aspects of labour markets make them fundamentally different from markets for fish, steel, or tomatoes, even under ideal conditions. In this section a number of these differences will be explored. To the extent that policy-makers recognize these special aspects of labour markets, they can design policies which can keep the equilibrium rate of unemployment low and the level of output high.

17.4.1 Heterogeneity and Incomplete Information

One of the most striking facts about labour markets is the degree of turnover, or the rate of flow between the states of the labour force shown in Figure 4.14. For example, Chapter 4 noted that annual inflow into and outflows out of unemployment are frequently larger than the stocks of unemployment at any given point in time. The high rate of in- and outflow points to two important aspects of labour markets: heterogeneity of labour and incomplete information about its quality.

First, neither workers and the labour hours they supply nor the jobs at which they work are identical; we say that workers and jobs are heterogeneous. A trivial example of heterogeneity lies behind the turnover noted in Table 4.6, which is concentrated among young, female, and unskilled workers. Even in high labour turnover countries like the UK or USA, it turns out that most workers stay at a given job for a very long time. High turnover is frequently a transient phenomenon in the life cycle which is more characteristic of newcomers to the labour market, and reflects a complicated process of 'picking and choosing'.

Second, because workers and jobs can be so different, or heterogeneous, information is likely to be incomplete. Even with the help of modern technology such as the internet, it is still impossible to know about all jobs on offer at any point in time; it may be necessary to search harder to find the most attractive jobs. Some employers do not actively advertise job openings and may open a position only after meeting an acceptable candidate. Workers must decide on accepting a job or searching further without knowing what may lie ahead. Most likely, they will have had some employment experience in the past, which guides their expectations concerning pay and work conditions; the offers they can expect in the future may not always correspond to patterns in the past. For example, it is a fact that computer operators—workers who once programmed and serviced large mainframe computers—were highly trained and well-paid professionals in the 1970s and 1980s. As personal computer and networking technologies became dominant, the demand for this occupation shrank dramatically. Those who lost their job may have had difficulties finding a similar one at pay similar to that in the past. Similarly, a job and the employer who is deciding how to fill it have particular needs and expectations which may not be met by every applicant, but in times of tight labour markets it may not be easy to find the dream candidate.

It is for this reason that unemployment must be interpreted carefully. To the extent that the unemployed are really 'unemployed resources', they represent a lost opportunity and a reason that trend GDP is lower than it could be. Indeed, Chapter 4 gave a number of reasons why workers ready to work at current wages are unable to do so. Yet unemployment also contains some elements of efficiency. Those who have lost their jobs involuntarily through lay-off or plant closure frequently possess industry- or firm-specific human capital which would be wasted or unutilized were the worker forced to accept the first new job that came along. A crude indicator of the 'efficiency' of **job matching** in a given labour market is the extent to which jobs openings—called vacancies—and job-seeking, unemployed workers coexist at the same time in a labour market. Because job descriptions and worker qualifications are often specific, one can speak of a job-matching process. Forcing jobs and workers together indiscriminately would certainly not be efficient.

The extent of mismatch in the labour market is summarized by the **Beveridge curves** of Figure 17.5. Named to honour the work of British economist William Beveridge in the 1940s, Beveridge curves relate unemployment and vacancy rates in an economy over time. Movements in the north-west and south-east directions are associated with the business cycle: firms offer fewer jobs and unemployment is higher in recessions, while the vacancy rate rises and the unemployment rate declines in economic expansions. The *position* of the Beveridge curve, on the other hand, indicates the longer-run efficiency of job matching in labour markets. The coincidence of a large number of vacancies with high unemployment—a Beveridge curve far away

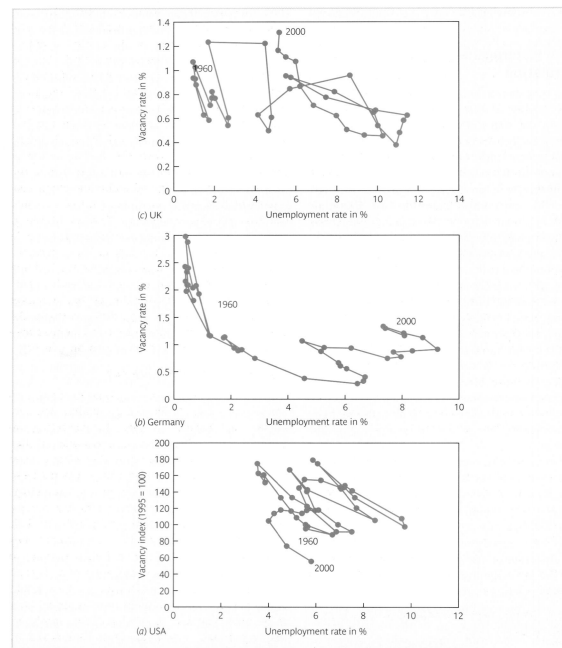

Fig. 17.5 Beveridge Curves in the UK, Germany, and the USA, 1960–2000

The Beveridge curve is the empirical inverse relationship between vacancies and unemployment. In a recession vacancies tend to decline and unemployment increases. The more efficient is the job-matching process—the way unemployment workers and unfilled job vacancies are matched—the closer to the origin the Beveridge curve is. Over the past thirty years, the Beveridge curve seems to have shifted outward in several European economies, although not in the USA. In the UK, the curve is now shifting back, the result of numerous labour market reforms.

Sources: OECD, *Economic Outlook*; Eurostat.

from the origin—suggests that workers are either badly informed, or unable to take up the offers for lack of mobility or adequate skills, or unwilling to change and adapt. The Beveridge curve seemed to shift away from the origin in the mid-1970s, suggesting increasingly inefficient or mismatched labour markets—in fact, a rise in the equilibrium rate of unemployment. In the USA, this shift was of temporary duration; it has been much longer-lasting in the UK, while in Germany, the return to the earlier position has been very slow, if at all present.

Shifting the Beveridge curve towards the origin —put differently, reducing the unemployment rate at any level of vacancies—can be good supply-side policy. For policy-makers, it simply means implementing measures which improve the job-matching process. One is to improve information on job openings by increasing the number and effectiveness of job agencies. Recent advances in networking technology have made it possible for unemployed seeking work to know about job offers all over a country—as long as they are posted. Second, the adaptability of workers' skills may be enhanced via job retraining programmes. This means giving workers whose skills are unwanted or obsolete new ones which are in demand. Another possibility is to increase workers' and firms' geographical mobility, for example by making the housing market more efficient or providing subsidies to firms in search of new locations. In recent years, countries have begun to make more use of **active labour market policies**, which is nothing but the creative and flexible use of all of the measures already mentioned and more—as opposed to the passive policy of simply paying out unemployment benefits. Box 17.5 gives some details on the Nordic approach to labour market policy.

17.4.2 Imperfect Contracts and Labour Market Regulations

Because of their social and political aspects, labour markets are often heavily regulated. Regulations cover a wide range of aspects: paid holidays, the length of working days and weeks, safety standards, works councils, union representation, and other facets of the employment relationship. These regulations may often have efficiency costs and

sometimes seem only marginally motivated by good economic arguments. The columns of Table 17.4 report the relative severity of the most common types of labour market regulations in OECD Europe.

Besides the problem of imperfect information noted in the last section and that of imperfect competition discussed in Section 17.2, a number of economic factors have led governments to regulate labour markets, sometimes strictly. Again, most of them have to do with the special nature of the labour relationship, and are a response to the impossibility of writing and enforcing labour contracts which specify all possible events which could occur, as well as all responses to those events (nor is it particularly efficient, given what lawyers would charge to write such contracts!). The enormous complexity of the world of affairs and the inability or unwillingness of workers to deal with it may lead to exploitation; leaving the rest to the market may disadvantage workers in particular situations. For that reason, governments have often stepped in—although not always in the most appropriate way.

Imperfect mobility and regulation

One situation of possible exploitation relates to worker mobility. Mobility of demanders and suppliers is a central mechanism for correcting imbalances in a perfectly competitive market: if they feel they are getting a bad deal, they simply move elsewhere. In labour markets, things may not be so simple: the suppliers of labour are human beings. Mobility means changing jobs, an industry, occupation, or residential location, and people by their very nature tend to be immobile. Furthermore, they may even *value* their 'immobility', preferring to take a pay cut or even risk unemployment to stay put.

Under certain circumstances, an employer might try to exploit this immobility. For example, after the employment relationship has begun, employers may try to take advantage of the employed by lowering their real wages. In perfect market situations, the worker would simply leave the firm, and look elsewhere, incurring mobility costs. In advanced economies these costs may be rather significant, and this may not be a desirable mechanism. One way to prevent this is to impose minimum wages; another is to extend union contracts to

Box 17.5 **Active versus Passive Labour Market Policies**

Despite a number of adverse shocks in the past decade, the Nordic countries continue to boast the world's lowest unemployment rates, proving that generous but strictly administered unemployment benefit programmes are consistent with 'European' solidarity with the unemployed. In Sweden, unemployed workers may claim benefits for roughly 300 days of unemployment. Unlike most countries, however, at the end of this period benefits are not renewed. Instead, a position in a job training programme is offered. Employment offices may even require that an unemployed person move to another city. Refusal can, and sometimes does, result in

termination of benefits. As a result, the Scandinavian countries spend less on unemployment benefits and more on active labour market policies, i.e. programmes involving direct job creation, targeted job subsidies, retraining, relocation of families away from distressed regions, and special programmes to get young people started. In general, the unemployed are supervised more closely and kept in touch with the labour market. Table 17.3 gives details. In relative terms, Nordic countries spend more on active labour market policies than other Western European countries, while maintaining much lower long-term unemployment rates.

Table 17.3 **Scandinavian Labour Market Programme Expenditure, 2002 (% of GDP)**

	Denmark[a]	Finland	Norway	Sweden
Active measures				
Labour market training	0.86	0.3	0.05	0.29
Youth measures	0.1	0.17	0.01	0.02
Direct job creation	0.15	0.14	n.a.	n.a.
Total active programmes	1.58	1.01	0.86	1.41
Passive measures				
Unemployment compensation	1.37	1.53	0.53	0.92
Early retirements	1.67	0.53	n.a.	0.01
Total passive programmes	3.04	2.06	0.53	0.93
Total	**4.62**	**3.07**	**1.39**	**2.34**
Long-term unemployment rate[b]	1.52	3.79	0.77	1.79

[a] Data are for 2000.
[b] 6 months and over.

Sources: OECD, **www.sourceoecd.org/content/html/index.htm** (Employment Outlook and Main Economic Indicators database).

uncovered workers and firms in the sector.[7] Similar arguments are often invoked to justify work-week and work-time regulations, job protection, and rules concerning job safety.

[7] Minimum wages are also, if not primarily, imposed for reasons of equity in income distribution. For example, if the elasticity of labour demand is thought to be low at low wages, then raising the minimum wage does little harm while increasing the income of the lowest-income working families, putting more value on employment.

Regulation of dismissal

A related argument has been invoked for regulations of dismissal 'without cause', i.e. not due to malfeasance or misbehaviour on the part of the worker. Lay-offs for reasons related only to the business cycle are associated with uncertainty and economic dislocation. In many European countries, prior notice of termination of employment must be given to workers—during which time the employee remains on the payroll and represents a cost to the

Table 17.4 Measures of the Strictness of Labour Market Regulation (2 = most strict, 0 = least strict)

	Working time regulations	Regulation of limited-time contracts	Job protection legislation	Minimum wage regulation	Aggregate index
Euro area					
Austria	1	1	1	0	3
Belgium	0	1	1	1	3
Finland	1	1	1	1	4
France	1	1	1	2	5
Germany	1	1	1	1	4
Greece	2	1	2	2	7
Ireland	2	0	2	0	4
Italy	1	2	2	2	7
The Netherlands	1	0	1	1	3
Portugal	1	1	1	1	4
Spain	2	1	2	2	7
Memo: Arithmetic Average	**1.1**	**0.9**	**1.3**	**1.1**	**4.4**
Other EU					
Denmark	0	0	0	0	0
Sweden	1	2	1	1	5
United Kingdom	0	0	0	0	0
Other OECD					
Norway	1	2	1	0	4
Switzerland	1	1	1	0	3
United States	0	0	0	0	0

Source: IMF *World Economic Outlook* May 1999.

firm. 'Social plans' are often required for large-scale redundancies, in which the exact list of employees is decided using criteria like age, family status, and re-employability. Severance payments are often legally mandated for workers dismissed for economic reasons. While common in EU countries, job protection is by no means the norm in the OECD, with the USA and UK offering examples of countries where 'employment at will' contracts prevail.

While severance regulations make it difficult for firms to reduce employment in the short run, they also increase the effective cost of labour to firms. In doing so, they make firms more reluctant to hire in good times, precisely because they worry about consequences in bad times. Firms will tend to use the 'intensive' margin more often (overtime, conversion of part-time into full time) before hiring new individuals. The third column of Table 17.4 reports a ranking of the degree of 'job security' provisions provided in a number of industrial countries. It is noteworthy that countries in which youth unemployment rates are high tend to have the most restrictive dismissal laws.

As the economy becomes increasingly subject to global influences and technological advances, employment relationships have changed fundamentally in nature. They have become less likely to involve lifetime relationships, and are more likely at some point to be 'restructured' or reoriented towards fully new areas of activity. Severance rules of the type described inhibit the growth of new firms as well as the expansion of existing ones. As the pressures for more flexible employment grow, firms have become increasingly creative in finding ways to undo the intended effects of the legislation. For example, they may chain several short-term contracts together for the same employee, or hire workers from temporary help agencies, shifting the burden to others. In the end, it may be worth considering market solutions in which workers accept to work under 'employment at will' for a wage premium, allowing firms to pay for additional flexibility while preserving employment protection.

17.4.3 Incentives and Taxation

The social safety net

The social safety net refers to the system of transfers and benefits designed to help the disadvantaged and vulnerable in society. These include unemployment benefits, social welfare, old-age pensions, early retirement, health insurance, and disability benefits. A large gap divides European countries, which transfer between 20% and 30% of their national income to individuals or firms, from the USA, Japan, and Switzerland, which transfer only 10–15%. This might lead a casual observer to conclude that high European unemployment is a product of the 'social welfare state', which puts weight on solidarity but at the cost of productivity and economic efficiency. Yet it is too hasty to claim that Europeans have erred too far in the direction of social protection, in comparison to the rest of the OECD. The high level of transfers observed in Europe is to some extent a *response* to high unemployment, which may have other underlying causes. At the same time, these transfers—in the form of unemployment benefits, welfare, and premature retirement and disability pensions—take the pressure off workers and firms to adjust to a changing world economy. The greatest danger is that the safety net becomes a trap, leading to long-term unemployment.

It is useful to use the tools developed in Chapter 4 to help think about the adverse effects of the safety net on incentives. The social systems of most countries share two institutional features. First, poor or unemployed people receive transfers—income maintenance programmes or unemployment benefits—from the state. Second, income taxes are progressive: the rate of taxation increases as income rises. Taking up a job not only means receiving a salary, but also paying taxes if the salary is high enough, and thereby losing eligibility for income maintenance programmes. It is conceivable then that people can be financially worse off by taking a job, not to mention incurring a loss of leisure, and possibly some activity in the underground (shadow) economy. Implicitly, these people face an effective marginal tax rate—considering the overall effect of work on their income—in excess of 100%. Box 17.6 shows how safety net programmes may lead to a **welfare trap**, inducing people to remain unemployed or stay out of the labour force, thereby reducing the productive potential of the economy. Recent experience of 'work-to-welfare' in the USA indicates that the incentive aspect is important for bringing workers on social assistance back to work.

Labour taxation

Because labour is so important in any economy, it is natural to expect governments to tax it. Perhaps because the Ramsey principle of public finance (Section 17.3.2) is so compelling, labour is one of the most highly taxed 'commodities'. As Box 17.7 explains, not only is labour subject to income taxes paid by households, but also to a number of social security contributions by both employees and employers. It is also natural to expect that labour taxation might influence the demand for labour, with higher taxes raising the real cost of labour faced by firms, leading to lower employment in the sector that pays the tax.[8] Table 17.5 shows the rate of taxation on labour in various countries in its various guises. Despite high unemployment, little effort has been made so far to alleviate the tax burden placed on the labour market.

---

[8]   This qualification is important. If some type of labour is untaxed, demand, employment, and wages may rise when labour taxes rise elsewhere. The obvious example is the underground economy, which always thrives when labour taxes are high.

Box 17.6 Crusoe Caught in the Safety Net

In Figure 17.6 Crusoe is faced with a time line (budget constraint) which is no longer strictly linear. This is because when not at work at all ($l = \bar{\ell}$), he receives a transfer of T from the government—unemployment benefits, welfare, or other payments associated with the social safety net. Moreover if Crusoe works a little bit, he loses benefits by exactly the amount of his additional income —an effective marginal tax rate of 100%. This is representative of the current situation in many European countries. Since Crusoe loses a euro of benefit for every euro he earns in work, the budget line is flat up to the point at which Crusoe receives T, whether he works or not. Crusoe values leisure, so it is hard to see why he would accept part-time work in this regime. Unless the after-tax wage is high enough, Crusoe is unlikely to work.

Figure 17.6 also shows the impact of reducing the effective marginal tax rate from 100% to some lower rate which is nevertheless higher than that for someone already in work and not receiving welfare payments, holding T constant. As the tax rate declines, the budget line for the household becomes steeper; at some point Crusoe can make himself even better off than he was at A, by choosing point B. In doing so his income is added to the tax base and contributes to higher GDP. The effect can be intensified if the carrot (the lower effective marginal tax rate) is combined with a stick (lowering T), although this type of reform is politically difficult to implement.

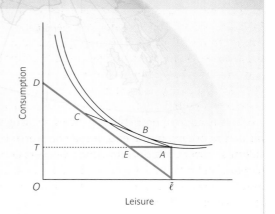

Fig. 17.6 Incentives and the Social Safety Net

In a social welfare system with benefit T when out of work but with 100% marginal tax rate, the individual depicted in this figure chooses not to work (point A), because no net additional income results from modest increases in labour supply, starting at zero. The budget constraint is $\bar{\ell}AED$. If the individual is allowed to keep some additional income (changing the budget constraint to $\bar{\ell}ACD$) the individual can improve her well-being by working (point B). The most important problem with lowering the effective marginal tax rate to unemployment benefit and welfare recipients is the cost to the state, which can be considerable.

Yet this net effect depends on the elasticity of labour demand and supply. If collective labour supply is relatively inelastic—perhaps reflecting the inelastic labour supply of households—the burden of the tax will fall primarily on wages, and employment will be relatively unaffected. In Europe, however, wages are set in collective bargaining, leading in all likelihood to a flatter collective labour supply curve. Under these conditions, high labour taxes might reduce employment significantly, and be associated with a large loss of consumer and producer surplus.[9] In the very long run the elasticity of

labour demand is likely to be very high, since firms may simply move to other locations where labour costs are lower. It is for this reason that the integration of European economies is forcing a harmonization of taxation across national boundaries, with or without explicit government co-ordination.

17.4.4 The Political Economy of Labour Market Reform

Unemployment is generally regarded as a curse of modern market economies, and remains the subject of intense political discussion. In Europe, unemployment levels have been high for almost three decades. In addition, it was seen in Table 4.4 that, in contrast to the USA, European unemployment has risen steadily over successive business cycles.

---

[9] Ch. 4 provides more details on the collective labour supply curve; producer and consumer surplus are defined and discussed in Box 17.3.

Table 17.5 Labour Taxation in 2003 (% of GDP)

Country	Total tax receipts	Fraction of total tax receipts due to:			Highest rate of personnal income tax
		Income tax	Social security contributions		
			Employee	Employer	
Euro area					
Austria	45	8	14	23	50
Belgium	55	21	11	24	52
Finland	45	20	5	20	53
France	48	9	9	29	58
Germany	51	17	17	17	51
Greece	35	0	12	22	40
Ireland	24	10	4	10	42
Italy	46	14	7	25	46
Luxembourg	32	7	12	12	39
The Netherlands	36	6	19	10	52
Portugal	32	4	9	19	40
Spain	38	10	5	23	45
Other EU					
Denmark	43	32	11	1	59
Sweden	48	18	5	25	57
United Kingdom	30	14	7	8	40
Switzerland	30	9	10	10	39
Czech Republic	43	8	9	26	
Hungary	46	13	9	24	40
Poland	43	5	21	17	40
Other OECD					
Australia	24	24	0	0	
Canada	31	18	6	7	46
Japan	24	6	9	10	50
New Zealand	20	20	0	0	
Norway	37	19	7	11	
United States	30	15	7	7	42

Source: CESIfo.

Unemployment represents underutilized labour resources; if this underutilization is not the conscious choice of households, it is involuntary and represents a supply-side problem. As the leading quote at the beginning of this chapter indicated, an important challenge for the nations of Europe is to address this issue, perhaps using the ideas and concepts developed here.

Suppose there is agreement—among policymakers, at least—that labour markets should be

Box 17.7 Taxes and the Labour Market in Europe

Labour taxes can be grouped into three classes: income taxes, social insurance charges paid by employers, and social security contributions by the employees. All three can be added up, as they either reduce the workers' net receipts and thus affect the supply of labour, or increase the cost of labour and reduce demand. They are usually not called taxes, but 'contributions' to funds for unemployment benefits, national health insurance, retirement and pension benefits, disability insurance, solidarity with various causes including low-cost housing and special retraining programmes, etc. Let τ_F be the employer's wage tax rate, let W be the wage of the employee before his own income taxes and employee social security contributions, let τ_W be the tax rate of contribution of the employee, and let τ_P be the personal income tax rate. The take-home pay for the worker after taxes will be $W_{\text{take home}} = (1 - \tau_W)(1 - \tau_P)W$, while the cost of labour to the firm is given by $W_{\text{labour costs}} = (1 + \tau_F)W$. As a result, the effective labour cost is equal to the takehome pay multiplied by the factor $\dfrac{1 + \tau_F}{(1 - \tau_W)(1 - \tau_P)}$,

which is often called the **labour tax wedge**. Holding $W_{\text{take home}}$ constant, increases in the tax wedge increase labour costs and reduce the demand for labour. In addition to all this, workers also pay income tax on their take-home salary, which may be progressive, or increase at the margin as taxable income itself rises.

Does high labour taxation necessarily lead to high unemployment? Not at all: it depends on how the supply of labour or the collective bargaining system reacts. Equilibrium unemployment rate will remain unchanged only if after taxes wages fall by exactly the amount of tax—that is, if workers shoulder the entire burden. But the collective labour supply curve will not be vertical in general; households may find it attractive at high taxes to work less, work in the underground economy, or take overtime pay in the form of a holiday (leisure), as is often done in Scandinavia. It is thus likely that such high taxes make hiring labour unattractive, and that a reduction of such taxes could increase employment. The problem for governments is how to replace the revenue that is lost.

reformed. How should a country go about it? Several problems arise with simply 'deregulating'. First, many companies that had wanted to reduce employment under the old regime will take advantage of deregulation, and lay-offs may actually increase in the short run. In most European countries, the political consequences of such a move are severe enough to make reform unthinkable. Second, an issue of *time consistency* arises.[10] Suppose a firm that would like to hire more employees expands its employment in response to deregulation. At this point, a government seeking approval with job-security-conscious voters may reimpose the dismissal regulations, 'trapping' such firms at higher employment levels. Firms will anticipate this, with the sad result that no new workers will be hired, despite deregulation! Governments will need to precommit themselves to a 'no-reregulate' regime before employers are convinced.

It is also true that an overwhelming majority (90–5%) of workers are employed, so that their domination over the unemployed might even be regarded as democratic, and is mitigated by unemployment benefits in any case. Governments frequently find it difficult to reform labour market institutions because their interventions are often regarded as interference in the collective bargaining process. One noteworthy approach is that followed by Spain, which has a serious structural unemployment problem. Since the mid–1980s, temporary contracts for workers have been permitted, with some restrictions.[11] Such contracts allow firms to hire workers without restrictions on a limited-time, contractual basis. As a result, roughly four-fifths of all new employment in Spain since

[10] Time consistency is discussed in Ch. 16.

[11] For example, firms were not allowed to 'roll over' the same worker in a series of short-term contracts. Naturally, employers have devised numerous loopholes to deal with this restriction.

the late 1980s has been under such limited-time contracts. This response suggests that firms are willing to hire more workers when job security obligations are absent. Second, young people have been the primary beneficiary of such reforms, which has helped relieve the youth unemployment problem so acute in Spain. Finally, increasing the relative number of workers who have jobs with less protection seems to increase the consensus for broader reforms which followed. By increasing the power of the insiders, labour market reform became more palatable.

In general, the political economy of labour markets may be the most important element determining success or failure of reforms. Efforts to increase the attractiveness of part-time work have often been blocked by unions, who see their bargaining power diluted by new employees unlikely to be members. Work-sharing proposals which increase the cost of labour are resisted fiercely by employer associations. Recent successful reforms in France have shown that management and labour often put many different elements on the negotiating table, trading reduced working time and relief on labour charges for flexibility, wage moderation, and reform of the unemployment benefits system.

Box 17.8 provides more detail on the extremes of labour market reform strategies. In rare cases, such as Britain under Margaret Thatcher, unions have been reformed against their will by democratically elected governments, with much social tension. The other extreme, in the Netherlands, was engineered in classic corporatist fashion, with the active involvement of unions, management, and the government. While both approaches involve radically different levels of social consensus and cohesion, they have one important aspect in common: they both required about a decade to bear fruit, as well as the patience of the electorate to stay the course until the benefits were realized.

 Box 17.8 Bust 'em or Trust 'em? Trade Unions and Reform in the UK and the Netherlands

At the end of the 1970s, both the United Kingdom and the Netherlands faced similarly distressing economic conditions. Both had high rates of unemployment and low growth in economic output. The root of the unemployment problem in both countries seemed to be that real wages had got out of hand, exceeding wage growth warranted by growth in total factor productivity. In the UK, a Tory government led by Prime Minister Margaret Thatcher took the position that the system needed to be changed. Her programme, which was passed by Parliament with much resistance, was a radical overhaul of the UK collective bargaining system. In a series of open confrontations, she limited trade unions' ability to disrupt the workings of the economy. New legislation limited wide immunity enjoyed by unions from civil suits to those directly involving industrial action, and forced unions to elect their officials in secret balloting. In the decade 1980–9, union membership in the UK declined by 21% and union density declined from 50.7% to 41.5%. Over the same period unemployment declined considerably, as seen in Figure 17.7. Although condemned at the time by many academic economists, Thatcher's reforms evidently did reduce equilibrium unemployment significantly in the UK in the years which followed.

In the Netherlands, a radically different approach was chosen. In 1982, in a widely publicized agreement reached by labour and management at Wassenaar, unions consented to moderate real wage growth in both private and public sectors and management agreed to expand part-time employment. While not officially part of the agreement, the government followed with tax breaks for part-time jobs as well as cuts in public sector employment and wages. Most important, tax rates on labour were reduced, blunting the net impact of real wage moderation on households' incomes. In the years that followed, real wages in the Netherlands grew much more slowly than in neighbouring EU economies, as Figure 17.7 indicates. In fact, Dutch real wage behaviour in the 1990s more closely resembles that of the United States than neighbouring Germany! The employment growth and decline in unemployment which later followed in the Netherlands seems to confirm that wage moderation is one important element of a successful labour market reform package, but need not require 'union busting', the radical dismantling of collective bargaining mechanisms.

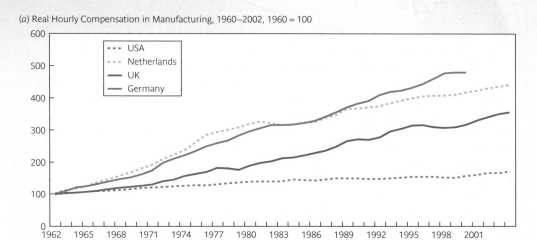

(a) Real Hourly Compensation in Manufacturing, 1960–2002, 1960 = 100

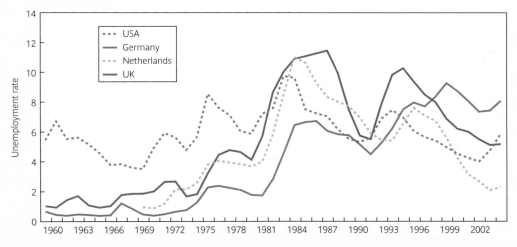

(b) Unemployment Rates, 1961–2002

Fig. 17.7 Real Wages and Unemployment in the UK, the Netherlands, Germany, and the USA, 1960–2002

The recent experience of the UK and the Netherlands strongly suggests that equilibrium unemployment declined in the late 1980 and early 1990s, in contrast to Germany. Much of this improvement can be linked to real wage moderation since the early 1980s. In the UK, this moderation was accomplished by reducing union power significantly. In the Netherlands, it was the outcome of a broad agreement between labour unions and employer associations, with the tacit and sometimes active support of government.

Sources: Eurostat, OECD, United States Department of Labor.

❶ Summary

1 Supply-side policies are appealing because, in contrast to demand-side policies, they do not imply a short-run trade-off between unemployment and inflation. They increase output permanently at any given level of inflation and economic growth, and may even increase the rate of growth itself.

2 One principle underlying supply-side policies is that markets do not function perfectly. By removing market imperfections, the economy's overall output and productivity can be enhanced.

3 There are three main sources of market failures: externalities, increasing returns to scale, and asymmetric information.

4 Externalities occur when someone's economic activity has an effect, positive or negative, on others. Positive externalities imply that one does not recognize the benefits to society of one's actions, and will undertake less than is socially desirable. Negative externalities imply that one does not recognize the costs to society of one's economic actions, and will undertake too much of them. Pecuniary externalities are solved once property rights are ascertained. Non-pecuniary externalities require government interventions.

5 Increasing returns lead to monopolies. Some monopolies are natural, inherent to the task itself. The solution used to be state ownership. Increasingly, state monopolies are privatized and government interventions take the form of regulations.

6 Asymmetric information occurs when one's actions are not known to others. It may lead to inefficient outcomes. Regulation can be designed to alleviate this problem.

7 Public goods that are non-rival and non-excludable tend not be privately provided. Governments can and should step in, and provide these goods which can be highly productive.

8 Taxation is necessary to pay for the operation of government. It is also a source of inefficiency because it drives a wedge between the price paid by the consumer and the price received by the producer, reducing demand and supply.

9 Because the operation of governments requires resources with alternative uses in the private sector, supply-side considerations call for limiting public spending to the production of goods and services that cannot be produced by the private sector. There is much debate on the correct size of government.

10 Governments often subsidize firms and industries. Although the objective of subsidies is to protect firms, they remove the incentive to compete, and ultimately cost jobs. State ownership has similar effects. The supply-side response is to cut down on subsidies and to privatize.

11 High structural unemployment is a supply-side problem. It arises as a result of labour market distortions, some of which are due to private agents and others to interventions of government.

12 Eliminating structural unemployment is possible by better management of labour taxation, severance regulations, labour relations, and the social safety net. Active labour market policies can help prevent the emergence of long-term unemployment.

13 Labour market reforms are highly politicized and controversial. Because the beneficiaries of reform are usually in the minority, their interests may be difficult to protect. Broad-based reforms almost always require give and take of the involved parties. Whether conflictual or consensual, reforms require time—as long as a decade—to have a measurable effect.

🔑 Key Concepts

- supply-side policies
- market-clearing
- laissez-faire
- market failures
- economic rents
- competition policy
- property rights
- pecuniary and non-pecuniary, positive and negative externalities
- natural monopoly
- human capital
- Ramsey principle of public finance

- distortionary taxation
- consumer and producer surplus
- Laffer curve
- privatization
- industrial policies
- trade policies
- job matching
- Beveridge curve
- active labour market policies
- welfare trap
- labour tax wedge

❓ Exercises

1 What is the difference between active and passive labour market policies?

2 Why are supply-side policies both more promising and more difficult to implement than demand-side policies?

3 What is an unemployment trap? How does it work?

4 Why does immigration policy represent a supply-side policy? Why is it so controversial?

5 According to the Ramsey principle of public finance (see Box 17.3), on which would you levy higher taxes, jewellery or petrol? Labour income or capital income?

6 It is often alleged that the Laffer curve is more likely to be relevant in countries with a large underground economy. Explain. How might the underground economy contribute to the 'unemployment trap' described in Box 17.6?

7 Chapter 7 discussed the 'Dutch disease', the reaction of the real exchange rate to an increase in domestic wealth associated with a resource discovery. In the case of Britain and Norway, both countries enjoyed the benefits of the North Sea oil discoveries of the 1970s. Norway subsidized its exporting industries as a response, while Britain used the resources to help balance the budget and therefore pay for transfers and government spending. Why might a subsidy be good supply-side economics in this case?

8 It is sometimes claimed that overtime working contributes to the unemployment problem. In particular, hiring and firing costs make it more attractive to pay current workers to work more (the intensive margin) than to hire more workers (the extensive margin). Furthermore, tax provisions may shield overtime income from normal labour taxation. How might reform of overtime

working be difficult under these conditions? Can you think of reform measures that might encourage fewer overtime hours?

9 Show diagramatically how shifting out the collective labour supply curve—using the six panel diagrams of Chapter 10—can lead to increased output.

10 Trace through the macroeconomic effects, in the short and long run, of a policy that reduces equilibrium output (for example, an increase in labour taxation). Under what conditions could this lead to a permanent increase in the rate of inflation? (Hint: use the *AD-AS* framework developed in Chapter 13.)

➔ Essay Questions

1 'A cut in income taxes in Europe would have significant supply-side effects.' Comment.

2 Why do some countries find it easier to carry out reforms than others?

3 How would you try to convince workers that they would globally benefit from lower employment protection?

4 Taxes are distortionary but they finance public goods. How would you appraise a proposal for severely cutting public services in order to reduce tax distortions?

5 Identify an economic rent that you find particularly objectionable and think about ways of eliminating it.

Economic Growth: Theory and Policy

18

18.1 Overview *436*

18.2 Growth and Complementary Inputs *437*
   18.2.1 Convergence and Complementary Inputs *437*
   18.2.2 Human Capital *438*
   18.2.3 Public Infrastructure *439*
   18.2.4 Is it Enough? A Sufficient Condition *440*

18.3 Growth, Knowledge, and Innovation *441*
   18.3.1 Knowledge as a Public Good *441*
   18.3.2 Patents *442*
   18.3.3 Technical Innovations *444*
   18.3.4 Product Variety *446*

18.4 Growth and the Economic Environment *446*
   18.4.1 Property Rights *446*
   18.4.2 Peace *448*
   18.4.3 Stable Economic Environment *449*
   18.4.4 Openness to Trade *450*
   18.4.5 Health *450*

18.5 Growth and Politics *452*
   18.5.1 Democracy and Growth *452*
   18.5.2 Inequality and Growth *452*

   Summary *454*

No one could have ever intended to deny that technological change is at least partially endogenous to the economy. Valuable resources are used in the pursuit of innovation, presumably with some rational hope of financial success. The patent system is intended to solidify that hope, and thus attract more resources into the search for new products and processes.

—Robert M. Solow

18.1 Overview

This chapter returns to long-run growth, the topic which motivated our first analysis of the macro-economy in Chapter 3. There, the Solow model identified three sources of **economic growth**: population growth, capital accumulation, and technological progress. An important conclusion of this analysis was that neither population growth nor capital accumulation can explain continuing advances in standards of living that have been observed in the past two centuries. Evidently, technological progress is the engine of growth. But what is technological progress? And can anything be done to harness or accelerate this formidable source of economic prosperity? This chapter delves more deeply into these fascinating issues which lie on the frontiers of economic research.

In the Solow model, population growth and capital accumulation cannot sustain economic growth on their own because both labour and capital are subject to diminishing marginal returns. Technological progress is the engine of growth because it is assumed never to exhaust itself: it increases exogenously irrespective of what happens. This assumption is unsatisfactory. Technological progress is the result of costly efforts at research—producing knowledge—and development—making that knowledge work for us. Research and development (R&D) in turn is an economic activity in its own right. So why doesn't R&D fall victim to decreasing returns? To answer that question, it helps to keep in mind how Chapter 3 concluded: it showed an example where growth perpetuates itself simply because marginal productivity of capital does not fall. This is our point of departure here: as we explore technological progress, we open up the hunt for possible sources of non-decreasing marginal productivities.

First, we extend our description of the productive system, captured by the aggregate production function, in three ways. To start with, labour is not homogeneous: some workers are highly skilled, others much less so. This leads us to introduce additional factors of production: human capital (skills acquired on the job or through investment in education, and kept in use through good health care) and public infrastructure. Section 18.2 explores the convergence hypothesis according to which poor countries eventually catch up with the richer ones.

Second, we recognize that technological progress is the outcome of costly efforts which must be rewarded in some way or another. Section 18.3 examines how knowledge can be thought of as an economic good, albeit with unique features. The analysis begins with the recognition that growth is a collective undertaking. Traditional economics assumes that the pursuit of self-interest is sufficient to promote the collective well-being. But introspection tells us this need not be the case. In many ways, we all depend on each other through channels which are not mediated by markets. In previous chapters, an externality was said to arise when one agent's actions have an implication, positive or negative, on other agents' well-being and behaviour, yet there can be no market price reward.

As Chapter 17 pointed out, externalities can be positive or negative: in either case, if left to themselves, markets may not lead to the optimal outcome. In the case of knowledge creation and related activities which have positive effects on growth, do we know whether these contributions to economic activity will be remunerated sufficiently? Will the inventor of the next wonder drug or telecommunications device reap some rewards for the hard work, or will copycats steal the idea? To this end, societies establish **property rights** over ideas for some limited time, enforce them with judicial systems, and generally seek to encourage entrepreneurial activity essential to research and development.

Finally, for some reasons, some people are excluded from this collective undertaking. Poverty exists everywhere in the midst of plenty. Does growth reduce poverty? And is poverty a threat to growth? More generally, the political system of a nation influences, and is influenced by economic growth. Especially for the poorest countries of the world these issues are of an existential nature and will be taken up in Section 18.4.

18.2 Growth and Complementary Inputs

18.2.1 Convergence and Complementary Inputs

In the Solow model, prosperity in the steady state is determined by two factors: (1) the saving rate and (2) the state of technology, which is represented by the production function. Low incomes per capita result from insufficient capital accumulation, presumably for lack of adequate saving, destruction by war or natural disaster, or the absence of a functioning market economy. Countries with similar technologies and savings rates should, however, have the same steady-state income per capita. Moreover, those starting from a low per capita GDP should accumulate capital per capita faster than wealthy economies and thereby eventually catch up. This is the **convergence hypothesis**.

The central prediction of the convergence hypothesis—that the poorer a country initially is, the faster it subsequently grows—can be tested. Figure 18.1 plots the average growth rate over the period 1960–97 of 102 countries against their per capita GDP in 1960. Panel (a) of the figure, which looks at a large number of developed and developing countries, is not too encouraging. However, panel (b), which presents the same data for twenty-three advanced countries alone, offers more convincing support for the convergence hypothesis. While standards of living among the wealthier countries are

converging, many poorer countries seem to be 'stuck' with low per capita GDP and low or even negative growth.

It is not easy to account for the continuing economic malaise of poor countries. Low savings alone cannot explain the dramatic differences that we observe in reality. As long as state-of-the-art technology is available in all countries and if capital is free to move, investors (multinational firms, financiers) could move resources to countries where capital–labour ratios are low and, therefore, returns on investment ought to be high. As a result, capital–labour ratios (k) should be equalized across countries. This process may take some time, of course, but a process of convergence towards the similar capital–labour ratios and therefore per capita GDPs should occur. Plainly, it hasn't.[1] The

---

[1] Nobel laureate Robert Lucas of Chicago has estimated that if India and the United States had the same production function, the marginal product of capital in the former should be 58 times the marginal product in the latter! In his words, 'If this [Solow] model were anywhere close to being accurate, and if world capital markets were anywhere close to being free and complete, it is clear that, in the face of return differentials of this magnitude, investment goods would flow rapidly from the United States and other wealthy countries to India and other poor countries. Indeed, one would expect *no* investment to occur in the wealthy countries in the face of return differentials of this magnitude' (1990: 92).

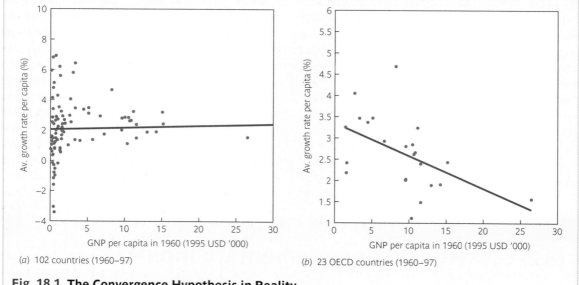

(a) 102 countries (1960–97)   (b) 23 OECD countries (1960–97)

Fig. 18.1 The Convergence Hypothesis in Reality

Panel (a) shows no relationship between the per capita growth rate between 1960 and 1992 and initial per capita GNP, for a sample of 102 countries. Poor countries do not seem to catch up. However, when the sample is restricted to 23 OECD countries, as in panel (b), the convergence hypothesis is supported.

Sources: The World Bank, *World Development Indicators*.

poorer countries' inability to close the income gap represents a massive challenge to the international community, and to economics as well. It questions the basic assumption that free markets benefit all. It also casts doubt on the validity of the Solow growth model. At the very least, it suggests that there is something systematic at work that the model does not take into account. Indeed, the two-factor production used in Chapter 3 may be too simple.

One strategy towards explaining persistent poverty in developing countries is to adapt the convergence hypothesis to include other influences —complementary inputs—which are not explicit in the Solow model, in particular the education level of the population and the level of public infrastructure. When this is done, the convergence hypothesis tends to do better when confronted with the facts.

18.2.2 Human Capital

Just as firms acquire capital for producing goods and services, individuals can expend time, energy, and money to acquire knowledge. This activity ranges from going to school, learning a skill, or taking a training course. Acquisition of knowledge is an investment, and will be undertaken when it pays to do so. It is for this reason that one speaks of investment in human capital. Better-trained and educated workers tend to be more productive, and more productive workers can earn higher wages. Furthermore, more educated workers tend to enhance the productivity of other factors. Skilled workers are better at operating complex machines, and may be used to manage other labourers and organize the production process. Thus, it makes sense to think of production as combining not only physical capital K and hours of work L, but also third input, human capital H. The economy's production function becomes:

(18.1) $$Y = A F(K, L, H)$$

Much of the reasoning of the Solow model in Chapter 3 can be repeated using this expanded version of the production function. Like physical capital, human capital can be accumulated and is subject to depreciation. Accounting for human capital yields non-trivial conclusions: human capital contributes to output per capita, so countries which invest more in education and training tend to be better off in the long run. Furthermore, as a complementary factor of production, human capital increases the marginal productivity of other factors. Yet this is not enough for our purposes: if the production function (18.1) is subject to constant returns to scale, so that the marginal product of human capital is decreasing,[2] long-run growth rates in economies with low and high 'savings' rates in human capital will still be the same.

While education is a key factor of growth, a number of puzzling issues remain which prevent drawing immediate conclusions. To start with, as any investment, education pays off later. Unlike many investments, human capital involves no collateral, or assets which can be pledged in case repayment of the loan is impossible. While firms can raise money from banks, stock markets, or their owners to buy equipment, many people cannot pay for their own education, especially in poor countries. The usual response is that governments provide public education, along with scholarships for poorer students. Yet, if the returns from education come in the form of better salaries, should the state provide public money for private benefit? The answer may still be yes, if human capital creates externalities. It should be obvious that being the only one who knows how to read in a country is less useful, both privately and collectively, than if many other people also know how to read and write.

Externality thus explains why governments should provide resources for education, but it raises a new perplexing question: my education helps me get a better life through a better salary, but it also benefits my co-workers, so how do I get the incentive to invest enough to match their own interests as well? Free education is not enough, since years in school are years without any salary. Compulsory education is one answer. Social status, a non-pecuniary reward, is another one.

If externalities are present, human capital may no longer be subject to decreasing returns in the aggregate, even if any given individual perceives diminishing returns at the margin. At the individual level, there is only so much to be gained from another year at school. Collectively, the existence of an externality may alter this conclusion: if all citizens study longer and better, the marginal productivity of human capital overall may not decline. This would open up the possibility of self-sustaining growth described in Section 3.6.

It would also explain a key puzzle. Decreasing marginal productivity means that the reward to human capital should decline with its quantity.[3] Thus human capital should be better paid in less developed countries where it is less abundant. While it is true that elites in poor countries may enjoy a better relative position than in developed countries, educated people continue to migrate from poor to rich countries, not the other way round. The reason is that they benefit from the externality of human capital. At the collective level, human capital may not face diminishing marginal productivity.

18.2.3 Public Infrastructure

A second missing factor is public infrastructure, a type of public good already discussed in Chapter 15, which includes streets, public transport, telecommunication, postal service, airports, systems of water distribution, electricity provision, and sewage treatment, etc. Public infrastructure contributes directly to production, much like any other form of capital. Firms use roads and telephone lines much as they use their own machines and lorries. At the aggregate level, the production function can be further augmented to include this stock of public capital K^G:

---

[2] If the production function is subject to constant returns to scale in all inputs, it must be the case that the marginal productivity of each input taken individually is decreasing. The reason is that otherwise, adding more of one input would keep production rising at least as fast. Then adding the other input at the same rate would have production rising even faster, i.e. increasing returns to scale.

[3] This is an implication of microeconomics principles: optimally, factors of production should be paid their marginal productivity.

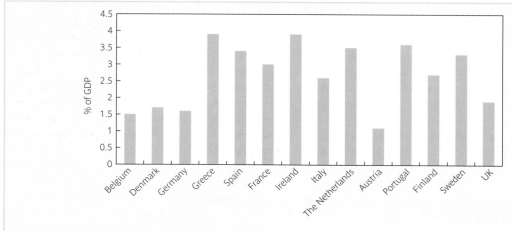

Fig. 18.2 Public Investment Spending, 2004

Public capital accumulation is shown as a percentage of GDP. Wide variations are visible across countries, partly reflecting privatization of infrastructures.

Note: These are forecasts by the European Commission.

Source: European Commission, *Public Finances in EMU*, 2003.

(18.2) $Y = A\,F(K, L, H, K^G)$

This obvious observation, however, raises a number of interesting questions. Public infrastructure is not free. While this is also true for private physical capital, there is a crucial difference. Firms carefully evaluate the balance of costs and benefits from acquiring more equipment. Because infrastructure is a public good paid with taxes, it is virtually impossible for the government to evaluate the benefits that accrue in millions of ways to millions of users. Moreover, policy-makers rarely reap the benefits of productive spending directly; at best, they will enhance tax revenues in the future, and they may not be in power to claim credit for the growth effects which accrue several years later. Figure 18.2 shows the amounts that European governments spent on capital accumulation in 2004.

A number of difficulties may arise in getting the level of spending right. First, governments might underinvest because other uses of taxpayers' money are more politically rewarding, or because pressures to cut the budget force spending cuts. Second, the government might spend too much on infrastructure because political lobbies for public works defend this budgetary item. Growth may be held back for lack of adequate infrastructure in the first case, because of excessive taxation in the second case. In order to reduce the risk of such slippage, one solution is to privatize: over the last decade, the production of electricity, telephone, water, railways, etc. has been spun off to the private sector precisely for that reason.

18.2.4 Is it Enough? A Sufficient Condition

If human capital and infrastructure are subject to the same decreasing returns as capital and labour, then human capital and infrastructure investment cannot explain sustainable differences in growth rates across different economies. We just have a richer description of production, but the curse of the Solow model still applies: countries with the same savings rates and technology will converge to the same steady state.

This need not be the case, however. One particular firm's investment may have beneficial effects on other firms. For example, investing in computerized production may allow other firms to reduce costs by agreeing to common standards. Similarly, the fact that many people are literate, or computer literate, allows each of them to work more effectively with the others. An important implication is that while investment by one firm may be subject to declining productivity, if similar investments are also carried out by other firms, overall productivity may not be declining after all. This is the concept of externality that the great English economist Alfred Marshall once hypothesized, and which has been encountered in previous chapters.[4] The striking implication is that this makes it possible for growth to be driven endlessly by the accumulation of production factors—physical capital, human capital, and infrastructure—as long as they are not subject to aggregate decreasing returns to scale. As a result, we do not need to think of technology as the exogenous—meaning an unexplainable black box—source of growth. This was the message from Section 3.6. Now we can explain advances in productivity and **growth** has become **endogenous**.

18.3 Growth, Knowledge, and Innovation

18.3.1 Knowledge as a Public Good

In the production function above, the state of technology is captured by the A.[5] Change in this factor means technological progress, the fact that more is produced with the same use of factors of production. In Chapter 3, technological progress is shown to be the only permanent source of growth, and it is taken as exogenous. This is not very satisfactory and our aim is to now examine what can drive technological change. In particular, we investigate the role played by the accumulation of knowledge. Knowledge is a very particular good indeed. In particular, it is a public good. Public goods are generally identifiable when they are either **non-excludable**, meaning that the consumer of a good cannot legally or physically prevent others from consuming it at the same time, or **non-rivalrous** when the consumption of a good by one person does not affect others' ability to enjoy it. Table 18.1 shows how different goods can be classified according to the extent to which they possess these two characteristics.[6]

Knowledge is both non-excludable and non-rival. It is non-excludable because, once it has been produced, it tends to be freely available. In the form of education or TV and radio programmes, knowledge is also non-rival; the consumption by one person does not preclude someone else from consuming (or using) it at the same time. Because knowledge can be used over and over again, it will not reach diminishing returns. Mathematical results from ancient times (e.g. how to compute the area of a circle) have been put to such extensive use since they were discovered that they could well be among the most productive investments ever![7] This last observation

---

[4] Chs. 15 and 17.

[5] More generally, technological progress can be represented in many forms. The standard production function can be generalized to $Y = A_1 F(A_2 K, A_3 L)$, with the terms A_1, A_2, and A_3 bearing the names 'Hicks-neutral', 'Solow-neutral', and 'Harrod-neutral technical change' respectively.

[6] Ch. 15 has already examined some aspects of public goods.

[7] Professor DeLong of Berkeley has described the fascinating example of the 'technology' of icons, cursors/pointers, double-clicking, and windows. This paradigm for working with information was developed by the Xerox Corporation in their Palo Alto research facility in the 1970s, before personal computers and the mouse were even invented. Apple was able to convert the technology into a usable system and Microsoft, Intel, and other companies were able to make enormous amounts of money on what was essentially a free technology. He writes: 'The net result? Large benefits to the economy and the society in terms of expanded productivity growth from the work carried on at Xerox's Palo Alto Research Center in the 1970s. But barely a cent returned in revenues to Xerox from this particular drain on its cash flow. Companies that are in business to make money will not long spend a great time and effort on such research projects that do not boost productivity and revenues, even if they boost industry productivity and revenues manifold. Thus there is every reason to believe that the private sector tends to underinvest in research and development.' *Source:* J. Bradford DeLong (1997), 'What Do We Really Know about Economic Growth?', **www.j-bradford-delong.net**.

Table 18.1 **Non-rivalrousness and Excludability: A Taxonomy of Goods**

	Rivalrous	Non-rivalrous
Excludable	Most conventionally marketed private goods	Police protection, patented Inventions, copyrighted material, subscription cable television programming
Non-excludable	Parking spaces, public tennis courts, beaches and park benches, congested highways	National defence, good weather, radio/television programming, internet, knowledge

is crucial: we have seen that the accumulation of capital cannot be the source of ongoing growth because this factor of production exhibits diminishing marginal returns. Now we foresee that knowledge can be the secret behind endless growth.

However, the problem with non-excludable goods is that their producers will not generally be sufficiently compensated for their efforts. This is why street cleaning services and public parks, which are also non-excludable, must be supplied publicly. Does this apply to knowledge as well? Indeed, a great deal of research—especially basic research—must be funded by government or non-profit institutions. But then, the problem encountered with public infrastructure arises with knowledge as well: it is difficult if not impossible to determine the proper level of public financing of research. To make things even more complicated, research is inherently uncertain and often entails very long gestation periods; it is a risky undertaking. This all makes it very possible that not enough is spent on an activity that is obviously not politically attractive and yet, over the long haul, may be an essential source of increases in standards of living.

Summing up these important arguments, we have reached three conclusions. First, knowledge is unlikely to face diminishing returns. It seems to be one recipe for endless growth. Second, since it is impossible to imagine all the uses that can be made of any piece of knowledge, we will never be sure that we spend enough on its production. Third, if we want to encourage the privately funded supply

of knowledge, we need to imagine ways of making it profitable, and that means reducing its non-excludability. The next section takes up this idea.

18.3.2 Patents

A **patent** is a legal right granted to exclusive commercial use of an invention, normally for a limited period of time. While not generally granted to ideas *per se*, patent protection is reserved for inventions which are sufficiently novel and wide-reaching. They limit the non-excludability of these additions to our knowledge for a number of years.[8] With the possibility of obtaining a patent, investing in R&D can pay off. For some period, the holder of the patent can charge prices which are at least high enough to cover the costs of the research and development of the product. But there is a side-effect: patents confer monopoly power to discoverers and thus allow them to charge much more than development costs. In one sense, monopoly is bad, since it allows the seller to set prices above the competitive level, and thus discourages demand. Patents indeed hinder the full exploitation of useful knowledge. In another sense, patents offer powerful incentives to researchers. Without them knowledge would not increase and economic growth would come to a halt. The border between fair remuneration and

---

[8] Patents are similar to copyrights, which safeguard artistic expression from plagiarism or outright duplication, and trademarks, which recognize exclusive use of a name or symbol to distinguish a firm's product in the market place. Art and trademarks can be seen as a form of knowledge.

Box 18.1 Protecting and Punishing Monopolists

To many people, Bill Gates is a bad, mean monopolist. Monopoly rights belonging to the Microsoft Corporation have made him into one of the richest men in the world, since virtually every computer in the world is equipped with its computer software products. Perhaps this is why many cheered when the US Department of Justice and the European Commission initiated lawsuits against Microsoft. The lawsuits, however, were not about monopoly power derived from legal patents and **copyrights**. They were related to Microsoft's allegedly heavy-handed efforts at stifling or even eliminating new competitor products and services. While Microsoft has made it possible for hundreds of millions of people to use computers for work and pleasure, history and innovations must continue. New innovators will continue to improve computers' software, and should be encouraged to do so. Herein lie the troubles of Bill Gates: his company was accused of using his monopoly power to stifle potential innovators.

Microsoft's encounter with justice is reminiscent of an equally famous trial pitting the US Justice Department against International Business Machines (IBM) in the late 1970s. At the time, IBM dominated the computer hardware industry: PCs didn't exist, and there was hardly a competitor which could produce powerful mainframe computers the way IBM did. The charge was very similar: IBM was accused of using its dominant position to eliminate new competitors. In the end, IBM argued that it retained its lead only thanks to its ability to innovate, and was hard-pressed to do so because of

pressure from the competition. IBM won twice: the case against it was dismissed and its argument was soon proved correct as it lost ground to competition, especially with respect to small portable computers and networking machines. In relative terms, it is today a shadow of its former self. Microsoft too has avoided the stiff consequences that its critics were wishing to be imposed. Whether it will soon become a minor player remains to be seen.

An altogether different story involves the pharmaceutical industry. Most wonder drugs are indeed patented, and their inventors reap massive profits. What makes the case different is that drugs are paid for by health insurance, private or public. Insurance agencies agree with the pharmaceutical industry on 'fair' prices, which exceed the marginal cost of producing the drugs by a factor commonly believed to be ten or more. Pharmaceutical firms claim that this is the only way for them to recoup the huge costs of R&D. Critics call the industry's profits excessive, but find it difficult to find solid evidence to back their claim. They correctly note that a significant part of humanity cannot afford these drugs and die or are permanently incapacitated as a result, a fact most recently underlined by the global AIDS epidemic. Even more troubling is the absence of priority in the pharmaceutical research community to develop drugs which could eliminate tropical diseases, such as malaria, which kill or cripple hundreds of thousands. These diseases are ignored because they affect primarily poor people in poor countries with no ability to pay for the R&D costs.

exploitation of monopoly power is arbitrary and subject to considerable legal wrangling. Box 18.1 recounts two famous cases.

This is why, even if patent protection confers monopoly power on the inventors, it may be a necessary evil for promoting the production of knowledge and thus for economic growth. If the widely shared benefits of knowledge production are not reflected in their compensation, researchers will not deliver as much innovation as is socially desirable, if only because too few bright students will choose this career. Viewed this way, it is perhaps less objec-

tionable that successful innovators derive extra profits from their temporary monopoly power.

It is worth noting that patents are yet another example of the time-inconsistency problem discussed in Chapter 16. *Ex ante*, patent rights can tempt both entrepreneurs and researchers to create knowledge and to embed it in new applications. After an invention is patented however, the owner of the patent will charge a high price, possibly even higher than normal costs would warrant. From the perspective of the agreement, this is legitimate, of course, and tolerated for the most part. On the other hand, given that the invention has become public knowledge, it is easy to see that governments have an *ex post* incentive to abrogate the patent agreement. This would clearly make everyone better off in the short run.[9] Wisely, however, governments generally avoid reneging on their promise. If they did, they would score a short-term gain but then research and development would come to a standstill, since the promise of a patent would no longer be credible.

18.3.3 **Technical Innovations**

Long waves

Innovations add to our stock of knowledge but they come in many forms and shapes: new ideas (e.g. Newton's painful discovery of gravity), new techniques (electricity, the steam and combustion engines, computers), or new processes (float glass, household appliances, the internet). How do these major discoveries really occur?

One view is that discoveries appear more or less randomly. R&D produces innovations, some big, some small, continuously restarting growth by boosting the existing technology.[10] Another view, initially proposed by Harvard economist Joseph Schumpeter, is that big discoveries tend to be associated with waves. Figure 18.3 shows the average annual rate of increase in total factor productivity, the term *A* in (18.2). It shows a sharp acceleration in the UK and the USA early on in the twentieth century, which continues until the early 1970s. This wave is often associated with a succession of great inventions in the latter part of the nineteenth century: electricity, engines, petro-chemistry, pharmaceuticals, telephone, radio, etc. According to Schumpeter's vision of innovations, major innovations were bunched in their occurrence but diffused slowly over the

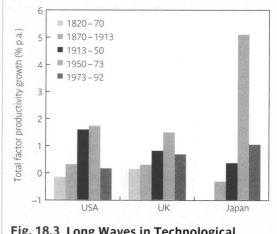

Fig. 18.3 Long Waves in Technological Progress

Sustained increases in technological changes seem to come in long-lasting waves.

Source: Maddison (1995).

following decades, rather than years. Figure 18.3 also shows that the wave did not hit Japan until much later, a question that we take up further in this chapter.

To explain why innovation came in **long waves**, Schumpeter puts the entrepreneur at centre stage. When growth slows, profits decline and some enterprising managers react by investing more in risky R&D projects. More research effort eventually pays off, producing a number of innovations that emerge more or less simultaneously, all within a decade or two. What happens next is that, as profits rise spectacularly, fierce competition sets in. Competition takes two forms: improvements and **imitation**. Both chip at the monopoly power of the original innovators, eating into their profits and reducing their ability and desire to pursue vigorous R&D. Technological progress slows down, ending the big wave of accelerated growth. As profits gradually decline, a new generation of entrepreneurs emerge and prepare the next long wave.

This view claims to explain the pattern observed in the industrial revolution. The long cycles once observed and studied by Kondratieff (see Box 14.1) constitute an interesting interpretation, but one that cannot be taken as a well-established fact;

---

[9] An excellent example is the growing number of anti-AIDS drugs, which have cost millions to develop but frequently considerably less to produce. Some developing countries have threatened or even started to manufacture and distribute these drugs, explicitly violating property rights. Recent concessions of pharmaceutical corporations (and the rich economies which host them) to supply drugs cheaply to developing countries can be seen as an attempt to regain control of their eroding intellectual property.

[10] This view is similar to that of the real business cycle theory of cyclical fluctuations discussed in Ch. 14.

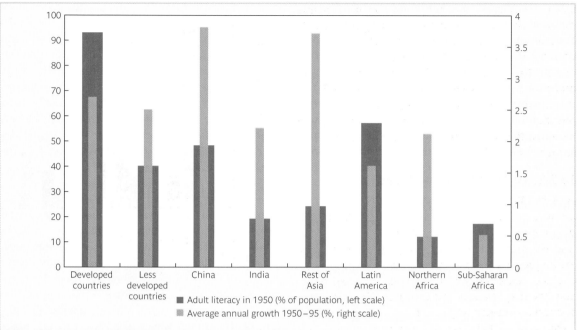

Fig. 18.4 Human Capital and Growth, 1950–1995

The figure displays average annual growth over the period 1950–95 and the literacy rate (percentage of adult population that is literate) in 1950. Extreme cases (developed countries vs. sub-Saharan countries) seem to indicate that low human capital is associated with faster growth. Causality could go both ways. One should not forget, however, that many factors other than human capital affect growth, so just looking at a figure like this one may make a link look weak while it is in fact quite strong.

Source: Richard A. Easterlin (2000), 'The Worldwide Standard of Living Since 1880', *Journal of Economic Perspectives* 14(1).

there haven't been enough of them to serve as convincing evidence. Yet some features of the long wave theory are attractive. The kind of competition that sets in following a wave of innovation explains both the long **diffusion** process and its eventual petering out. It is especially intriguing now that some claim that the information technology revolution is triggering a new wave of accelerated growth, as discussed in Box 3.4. At any rate the long wave theory provides support for the view that innovations diffuse slowly; it takes time to challenge Ford or Microsoft, but the challenges do come and will ultimately be successful in eroding the market positions of the monopolists. It also illustrates the role patents can play in encouraging R&D and their tendency to create entrenched monopolistic powers.

Interaction with human capital

Transforming innovations into production processes requires skills, often new skills. For this reason, diffusion is often slowed down by the necessity of building up new human capital. This process, in turn, depends on human capital already accumulated, the quality of the education system, and its ability to adopt and transmit new knowledge.

Human capital is a linchpin for any theory of growth which is based on inventions and innovation. Not only does it raise current productivity, it also helps the diffusion of innovations. Figure 18.4 shows that countries at each end of the spectrum of human capital (measured quite imperfectly by the literacy rate) achieve widely different performances. One interpretation is that a low stock of human capital hampers growth. Another interpretation is that causality runs the other way, that poor countries cannot afford accumulating much human capital, given the costs of education systems. We need not choose between these two interpretations, because they may *both* be correct at the same time. Taken together, they suggest the existence of **poverty traps**: poor countries cannot invest enough in human capital, which in turn hinders growth. For the same reasons, individuals too can be trapped in poverty, even in developed countries, which provides a justification for means-tested scholarships.

Multinationals and learning by doing

Finally, it is often believed that multinational corporations serve as a channel in the diffusion of innovations. This view is based on the phenomenon of **learning by doing**, whereby people and firms improve their knowledge on the job. When a multinational establishes a production unit in a developing country it usually brings with it a technology invented in its home country. Individuals who work in such establishments acquire the technology and can subsequently create their own firms based on the new technology, or migrate to other firms which can then tool up.

This possibility should be kept in mind when considering the controversies that surround multinational corporations. They are often criticized for shifting production to low-cost countries, thus taking away jobs from their home countries while offering much lower wages in the developing countries where they settle. The multinationals' response is that they create jobs in the developing countries, which means future customers for the goods produced elsewhere, and that their profits usually accrue to shareholders in the home country. An argument which they seldom make, which might be the most convincing from a *social* perspective, is that they contribute to convergence by accelerating the diffusion of innovations and thus the transfer of knowledge.

18.3.4 Product Variety

Another form of innovative activity arises when firms develop new variations of their products which are different from previously available ones, for either real or perceived reasons. Most but by no means all of these innovations are related to consumer goods. The introduction of a new automobile model or a grape varietal, a newly opened restaurant, or the annual waves of *prêt-à-porter* and *haute couture* all represent innovations for which consumers are willing to pay measurable amounts. In many cases, the increase in diversity makes the consumer better off, sometimes the new products themselves represent fundamental innovations for which needs still have to be developed or invented. To the extent that consumers are willing to pay an ever higher price, these types of innovation also represent growth potential for an economy.

18.4 Growth and the Economic Environment

18.4.1 Property Rights

A recurrent theme is that growth is driven by investment in both physical and human capital. As emphasized in Chapter 6, capital accumulation is a bet on the future: it requires spending now for future, uncertain returns. It is often taken for granted that firms' ownership of their equipment will be unquestioned both today and in the future, and that individuals will be able to use the skills that they acquire. In both cases, we assume that property rights exist, are clearly defined, and systematically enforced. This assumption is generally borne out in many countries, but not universally so, and probably not for most of humanity.

Property rights usually require precise legislation or constitutional provisions which guarantee that individuals and firms cannot be dispossessed of their belongings, unless they violate the law and even then, only after due process. The concept of property rights is not restricted to merely retaining one's belongings. In the extreme case, it would guarantee that one's possessions can always be used as intended and disposed of, under all circumstances. Such absolute property rights are rarely observed: landowners are rarely allowed to build 'the house of their dreams' without the implicit or explicit permission of their residential area. More relevant for economic growth, property rights are denied if a firm is taken over by the state, say, to produce weaponry against the will of its owners. Nationalizations, which occurred in France as recently as the early 1980s, similarly violate property rights, even if the owners are compensated, because they break the link between investment and its intended use. Nationalizations are an example of retroactive legislation, enacted after the original investment was carried out. They damage the fabric of trust between capital owners and the government, which depends on productive economic activity to finance its activities.

At the individual level, property rights should be extended to human rights. Being arbitrarily sent to jail, or being barred from some jobs, prevents one from using one's human capital. Mere threats of imprisonment or assassination also deny property and human rights. As long as individuals are not guaranteed the freedom to exercise all (reasonable) activities as they wish, independently of their sex, race, political opinions, or religious beliefs, their property rights are not established.

It is easy to see why property rights are a precondition for long-run economic growth. If investors cannot be sure they will own their investments in a country, why bother to invest there? Even if the rate of return on capital in other, wealthier countries is lower, a lower risk of expropriation or arbitrary restriction of property rights may tip the balance in their favour. And if investment is held back, so will be future growth. This elementary proposition is far from being universally accepted. Box 18.2 briefly looks at the case of communist regimes which explicitly reject private ownership of means of production. More generally, property rights are routinely denied by arbitrary, undemocratic regimes and by wars, both civil and international.

The relationship between property rights, broadly defined, and growth is more complicated than meets the eye. There is powerful evidence that rich and fast-growing countries tend to be democratic,

 Box 18.2 Growth in Communist Countries

In its unrecanted form, communism holds that private ownership of capital leads to never-ending concentration of wealth in a few hands, while workers are maintained at the subsistence level of existence. To avoid this, communism set about collectivizing ownership of production means, in effect by nationalizing large private firms, and in some countries even by banning small ones as well. In several countries, collective ownership was extended to land and housing.

What is left of incentives to work, invest, and innovate under such a system? In a system of central planning, communist regimes offered a combination of carrots (incentives) and sticks (penalties). Firm managers negotiated production plans with the central planning office, and were provided with the necessary means, equipment, and salaries. Both managers and workers were also offered various incentives to produce more: more money, medals, better housing, and honours. Underperformance was punished, sometimes harshly so.

How did it work? Figure 18.5 shows that, up until the early 1970s, the growth performance was good, certainly on a par with Western Europe. Part of the reason was catch-up after the war destruction, in the East as in the West. But then things turned sour, much worse than in Western Europe. Most countries experienced two decades of negative growth rates, an extraordinary failure. Central planning simply did not work, and brought the collapse of the communist regimes. The odd man out is China: a poor performance over the first period, followed by fast growth. Part of the story is the gradual relaxation of central planning, accompanied by the introduction of private ownership. But another part of the story seems to be the strict discipline imposed by the regime, a puzzling observation.

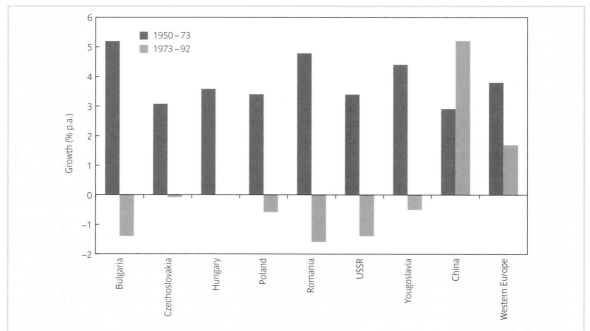

Fig. 18.5 Growth Performance under Central Planning
The good performance over the first 25 years has been followed by a catastrophic decline over the following two decades. China stands out as a different and puzzling story.
Source: Maddison (1995).

law-abiding, and peaceful, but it is not clear what comes first, economic well-being or property rights. One view is that property rights are a prerequisite for sustained economic growth, another view is that affluence makes basic freedoms and property rights more desirable. It could well be that each aspect strengthens the other, generating either virtuous circles of growth and better-established rights, or vicious circles leading to poverty traps which combine economic stagnation and the absence of property (and human) rights.

Indeed, there are cases of countries which embarked on a stable, often fast growth path while enjoying limited property and human rights: the communist countries, Pinochet's Chile, or some countries of South-East Asia. Conversely, it can be argued that some countries visibly fail to grow because property rights are non-existent. A sobering example is sub-Saharan Africa, which has grown by a mere 1.5% (GNP per capita) over the

years 1965–97, while the world's overall growth over the same period stood at 50.9%. This average performance conceals a wide disparity, depending on the policy regime as Figure 18.6 shows.

18.4.2 Peace

The other main threat against property rights is wars, which destroy both physical and human capital. If wars are occasional, the catch-up process sets in once they are over. The reason is clear: expected peace encourages investment. This was the experience of Europe after 1945, enjoying rapid growth while building supra-national institutions (the common market, the European Court of Justice, monetary union) and peace-enhancing mechanisms (NATO, the Organization for Security and Cooperation in Europe) to reduce the risk of renewed conflict.

On the other side, Africa has been devastated by wars, mostly civil wars, as states inherited from

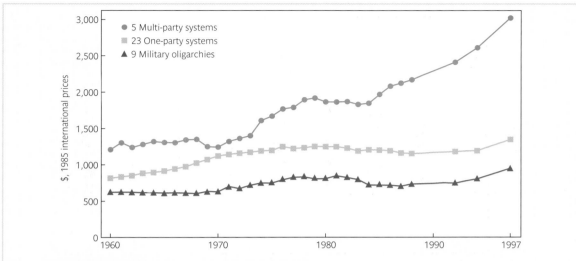

Fig. 18.6 Real GDP per capita in Sub-Saharan Africa

The five countries with democratic political regimes (Botswana, Gambia, Mauritius, Senegal, and Zimbabwe) display a much better growth performance than countries with one-party systems. Countries with military regimes have stagnated.

Source: Benno Ndulu and Stephen O'Connell (1999), 'Governance and Growth in Sub-Saharan Africa', *Journal of Economic Perspectives*, 13(3).

colonial times have tried to come to grip with ethnic diversity. For example, the index of ethnic fractionalization stands at 67.6% in sub-Saharan Africa, and at 32.7% on average in the other developing countries.[11] Besides the obvious material destruction, investment is held back and human capital declines through the emigration of wealthy and powerful elites. Figure 18.7 establishes an unmistakable link between growth and property rights, where the latter is measured by a legal index of the rule of law prevailing in the country.

18.4.3 Stable Economic Environment

Individual property rights and peace are important aspects which can further economic development. They do not, however, represent the whole story. Other elements of the economic environment must also be right to attract investment, especially for-

---

[11] This index reports the probability that two people randomly chosen in a country belong to two different ethnic groups.
Source: Paul Collier and Jan Willem Gunning (1999), 'Why Has Africa Grown Slowly?', *Journal of Economic Perspectives*, 13(3).

eign direct investment. Beyond property rights, the legitimate scope of government and its taxation behaviour should be directed towards establishing stability and continuity, rather than interrupting it. Even in democracies it is possible for governments to change frequently—with shifting coalitions of smaller parties, for example—and this may lead to constantly changing tax and expenditure policy. This type of uncertainty, especially if it applies to the taxation of physical or human capital, may deter longer-term projects from being undertaken.

The same applies to the inflation rate. It was shown in Chapter 16 that high and variable inflation rates tended to weaken the allocative function of prices and thus the efficiency of the economy. Since inflation is like a tax, it will tend to dull incentives to invest in productive activities and force firm owners to focus more on avoiding its effects.

Governments which understand this will take action to bind their successors to time-consistent policies. This may take the form of constitutional amendments, borrowing from abroad in foreign currency at long maturities, or the establishment of central bank independence. Currency boards and

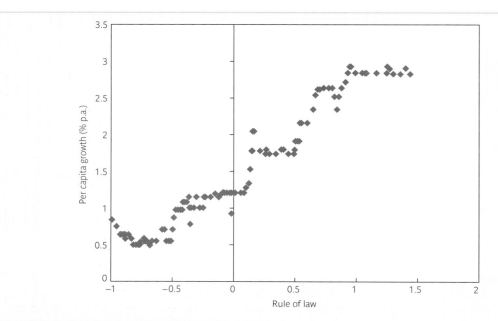

Fig. 18.7 Rule of Law and Growth, 1960 – 1998

Based on a large sample of countries, the figure relates average economic growth over nearly four decades with an index measuring how well the rule of law applies. The index ranges from –2.5 (complete breakdown) to +2.5 (perfect legal protection). It includes political corruption, likelihood of government repudiation of contracts, risk of government expropriation, quality of bureaucracy, and overall maintenance of law. The figure sends a very strong message: the better is the rule of law enforced, the faster a country grows. Note the beneficial effect only sets in after some minimal threshold.

Source: William Easterly (1999), 'On Good Politicians and Bad Policies: Social Cohesion, Institutions and Growth', The World Bank.

dollarization—representing the abdication of monetary policy in the most extreme way—are particularly striking examples of how countries have attempted to solve this problem.

18.4.4 Openness to Trade

Growth and openness to international commerce are known to be positively related. Countries which have large trade exposure—measured as the ratio of exports plus imports to GDP—tend to have faster GDP growth rates. The experience of more open Western European countries, and especially the Asian Tigers of the last two decades, suggests that open economies grow faster, all things considered. This faster growth can be attributed to a number of possible effects. First, closed economic systems can often impede the transfer of knowledge, effectively excluding some individuals from what should be a non-excludable good. Openness allows for ideas

to flow more easily across national boundaries. Second, openness means increased competition from abroad. Domestic producers cannot rely on protection to shield their market positions from the threat of imports. They must constantly remain at the 'edge' of new developments. To use the terminology of Section 18.3, this requires either innovation or imitation; either will have positive effects on productivity and growth.

18.4.5 Health

An important aspect concerning human capital accumulation is health. Where health services are poor (or access is limited to the richest segment of the population), life expectancy is low. This obviously reduces incentives to invest in human capital, but also can affect the productivity of otherwise healthy individuals in a negative way, and even lead to outmigration of wealthy elites.

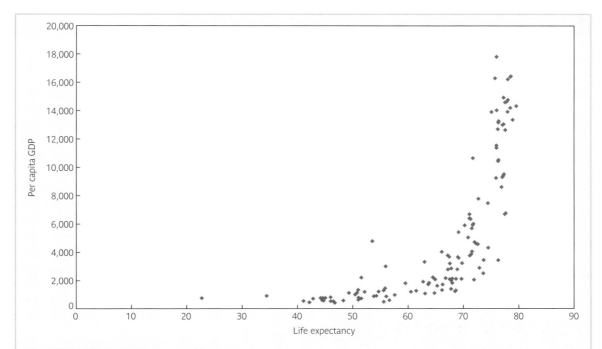

Fig. 18.8 Life Expectancy and Income

In a cross-section of nations, life expectancy declines dramatically at low to moderate income levels. It is difficult to believe that general health conditions do not influence investment decisions, especially in skills and education. At the same time, the demand for health depends on income.

Source: David Bloom, David Canning, Bryan Graham, and Jaypee Svilla (2000), 'Out of Poverty: On the Feasibility of Halving Global Poverty by 2015', CAERE Discussion Paper No. 52, Harvard Institute for International Development, January.

As with other issues the issue of causality arises immediately: does health cause income, does income cause health, or both? Figure 18.8 shows that the relationship between income and life expectancy is positive, but by no means linear. The richest countries have achieved roughly equal life expectancies, but deep inequalities appear at lower income levels. In general, life expectancy declines dramatically with income. Not only is life expectancy shamefully low in the very poorest countries, but the growth benefits from improved human condition in these countries are likely to be shamefully high. In large parts of the world, existing medicines could cure endemic sicknesses, but people cannot afford them. The AIDS disaster in Africa is a tragic example of a vicious circle in which poverty shortens life expectancy, which further cripples incentives to invest in human capital and future growth.

18.5 Growth and Politics

18.5.1 Democracy and Growth

The relationship between democracy and economic growth is a controversial one. Democracy, we would presume, is conducive to a better growth performance, for all the reasons reviewed so far: property rights, economic and political stability, health, etc. Yet democracies are not perfect institutions. The rule of majority does not preclude actions against minorities, including some that violate property and human rights. Such actions may include legal pressure on 'the rich', ranging from nationalizations to heavy taxation, both of which discourage investment. At the same time, well-organized lobbies in many democracies enable wealthy minorities to exert disproportionate influence on decision-making.

It is also frequently claimed that democracies are incapable of the self-imposed current sacrifices necessary for sustained economic growth. Some salient examples are increasing the savings rate to accumulate capital for future generations, restructuring of economic activity which implies the painful decline of some sectors (farming and mining for example), reform of the social safety net and labour market regulations, and migration towards cities which is accompanied by some degree of social and family dislocation. The political difficulties faced by democracies to face up to such painful changes has fed claims that only dictatorships are capable of suppressing opposition to changing conditions long enough for growth to take hold. In their view, democracy is a luxury that only rich societies can afford.

Yet this conclusion is certainly tenuous. Only democracies have the legitimacy to guarantee property rights essential for investment in human and physical capital (see Section 18.4). As the next section notes, inequality is harmful to growth, and inequality is better tolerated when the political regime receives legitimacy from a majority of citizens. It is even argued that such legitimacy is necessary to carry out the deep reforms that accompany sustained growth. Dictatorships can impose changes, for a while; eventually the changes themselves —which may be desirable from an economic viewpoint—become as unacceptable as the dictatorship itself, and may be swept away in painful revolutions. Finally, democracies rarely go to war with each other.

Sadly enough, the evidence on democratic institutions and growth remains inconclusive. For every study that finds a positive role for democracy in fostering growth, another fails to detect such an effect. At least, there is no evidence that democracy harms growth. An interesting piece of evidence is Japan's performance as shown in Figure 18.3: Japan embarked on a high growth path in the second half of the twentieth century, after it had adopted democratic institutions.

18.5.2 Inequality and Growth

A hump-shaped relationship between inequality of income and wealth was first reported by Nobel laureate Simon Kuznets in 1955. The 'Kuznets curve' depicted in Figure 18.9 states that, starting from an

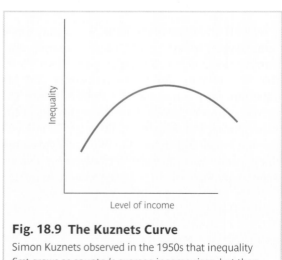

Fig. 18.9 The Kuznets Curve
Simon Kuznets observed in the 1950s that inequality first grows as country's average income rises, but then declines. This relationship is sometimes known as Kuznets's law.

initially low level of development, growth seems to proceed with increasing inequality and then the relationship reverses itself, and inequality declines.

Many theories have been put forward to explain the Kuznets curve. Some relate the creation of high-productivity jobs to the transition from agriculture to industry. Early in that phase, industrial jobs are poorly paid, which is why inequality increases. Then, as industry matures it offers better salaries and then the development of the service sector further works toward more equality. Others assert that a low initial stock of physical and human capital inevitably provides large rewards to the happy few (i.e. the owners). As the stock of capital rises, its marginal productivity declines, and so do the rewards. In addition, better-off societies seem to be more concerned with equality than growth. As a result, taxation becomes more progressive and transfers explicitly aimed at reducing inequality become more widespread.

Over nearly five decades, the Kuznets curve has survived numerous statistical challenges and appears to be robust. Once again, as with property rights and democracy, we face the question of what comes first, the chicken or the egg: is it inequality that affects growth, or the other way round? Could there be too much insistence on inequality? One view is that fast growth requires sufficient incen- tives for would-be entrepreneurs: measures which compress income distribution, like redistributive taxation and social norms, dull these incentives and eventually hurt growth. On the other side, the accumulated evidence is clearly that inequality harms growth. Three main explanations have been advanced.

First, politics interacts with redistribution. While high inequality preserves incentives for entre- preneurs, it can backfire. When income is very unequally distributed, majorities will tend to vote for redistribution. In a democratic system, at least, it appears better to avoid severe inequalities. This seems to be the approach adopted in northern Europe. Second, if credit markets do not function, then inequality will prevent a large fraction of the population from investing in human capital, which reduces if not eliminates their chances of becom- ing entrepreneurs, which has a cost to society as a whole. Finally, high levels of inequality tend to generate social unrest in the form of envy, self-arranged redress, and crime. As general insecurity rises, property rights decline. The standard response, to increase police and fill up jails, may alleviate the threat to property rights, but it represents spending that could be better used in a more peaceful society. It also requires taxation which, again, may hurt entrepreneurs.

ⓘ Summary

Most of the arguments developed in this chapter are summarized and quantified in Table 18.2. The table presents estimates of the effect on average annual growth of a range of factors.

1 Catch-up (convergence). Starting below steady state in a Solow model, a country should be accumulating capital, both physical and human, more rapidly, as well as adopting new technologies. The table indicates that the economic backwardness is closed at a rate of about 2.5% per year (the higher is initial GDP, the less it subsequently grows).

2 Human capital. People's knowledge, ranging from basic literacy to sophisticated skills, represents an additional factor of production. Table 18.2 measures the effect of investment in education, the average number of years spent in secondary or higher education by males.[12] Raising the population's schooling by one year is found to speed up growth by a spectacular 1.2% per year.

3 Health. A one-year increase in life expectancy at birth raises average growth by a whopping 4.2%. The effect is likely to come through investment in human capital and, more generally, work effort. This effect is unlikely to be important in rich countries where it is retirement that limits the length of active lifetime. It may be crucial in the poorest countries where few people ever reach retirement age.

4 Fertility. The negative effect of the rate of fertility (the average number of children per woman) seems related to two main effects: capital widening as in the Solow model, and time spent by mothers in child rearing instead of economic production.

5 Public consumption. Reducing public consumption by 10% of GDP raises growth by 1.4%. This measure does not include productive spending, such as public infrastructure. The negative effect probably corresponds to the corresponding high public employment, which tends to be inefficient and invite corruption, as well as to the necessary tax collection, which acts as a disincentive to savings, investment, and innovative activity.

6 Rule of law. Lasting, credible property rights are a precondition for investment in both physical and human capital. Going the full way from the worst to the top ranking raises growth by 2.9% annually.

[12] An important clarification: this does not mean that female schooling is unimportant, even if the study reported here does not detect any clear *direct* effect. Quite to the contrary, female schooling is usually found to be more socially productive than male schooling, but this effect is considerably more complex, and mostly *indirect*. In many developing countries, female school attendance is much lower than for males, so a little effort produces large effects. Also better-educated females make better mothers, with considerable impacts on children's education, health, and, more widely, approach to life. Female education also affects fertility.

Table 18.2 **What Drives Growth? Some Estimates**

Factor	Effect on average annual growth rate
Initial GDP	−2.5
Education	1.2
Life expectancy	4.2
Fertility rate	−1.6
Government consumption	−1.4
Rule of law	2.9

Source: Robert J. Barro (1997), *Determinants of Economic Growth*, MIT Press.

🔑 Key Concepts

- **economic growth**
- **property rights**
- **the convergence hypothesis**
- **endogenous growth theory**
- **non-excludable, non-rival**

- **patents, copyrights**
- **long waves**
- **diffusion, imitation**
- **poverty traps**
- **learning by doing**

❓ Exercises

1 Why is the acquisition of human capital called an investment, like the acquisition of physical capital?

2 What prevents the private production of goods: non-rivalry or non-excludability?

3 Like physical capital, knowledge and human capital depreciate. Explain.

4 'Retroactive legislation raising income tax will have much worse adverse effects than retroactive legislation raising property taxation.' Comment.

5 Do you expect high inflation to affect long-run growth? If so, how and why?

6 Why must knowledge not be subjected to diminishing returns if it is to be a permanent source of growth?

7 Why is it generally the case that patents are granted for a limited period of time?

8 Figure 18.1 shows that convergence is taking place among rich countries and not between rich and poor countries. How would you use the principles developed in this chapter to explain this fact?

➔ Essay Questions

1 What is the link between property rights and investment in both physical and human capital?

2 Why, in your view, does much of Africa seem unable to grow and eradicate poverty? Would higher amounts of aid help, and if so, how?

3 'Wars are as much a symptom as a cause of under-development.' Comment.

4 Describe the many ways in which corruption stunts growth.

5 The European Union has adopted in 2001 the Lisbon Strategy, with the aim of making of Europe 'the most dynamic, knowledge based economy in the world by 2010, an economy that can create sustainable economic growth with more and better jobs and greater social cohesion'. Find the associated measures on: **http://europa.eu.int/comm/lisbon_strategy/index_en.html**, and evalaute them in the light of the principles developed in this chapter.

PART VII

Asset Markets and International Financial Architecture

19 **Asset Markets and Macroeconomics** *459*
20 **The Architecture of the International Monetary System** *491*

Markets for financial instruments are a ubiquitous feature of economic life, but are they really important, or merely a distracting side-show? What function do these markets really have? How are they organized, both within and between nations? Is there a role for establishing rules of play, especially when troubles in the financial system of one country spill over to others? The concluding part of the textbook studies these issues and connects them with our primary interests, how economies grow and fluctuate over time.

Asset markets are important because they determine crucial variables: the interest rate, the valuation of firms big and small, the wealth of households, the price of risk, the relative value of national monies. Chapter 19 studies the principle characteristics of asset markets and how they relate to macroeconomic relationships explored up to this point. Special reference is made to the nominal exchange rate.

The globalization of financial relationships is here to stay; in principle this should make us all better off, but recurrent crises make us wonder about the net impact on our lives. Thus, financial markets are not allowed totally free reign, and are usually regulated. This is also why, as presented in Chapter 20, the international monetary system is constantly being built and rebuilt. Its history is reviewed and the recent debate on the 'international architecture' summarized.

Asset Markets and Macroeconomics 19

19.1 Overview *460*

19.2 How Asset Markets Work *460*

19.2.1 Facts about Asset Markets *460*

19.2.2 Functions of Asset Markets *462*

19.2.3 Information and Market Efficiency *465*

19.2.4 The Interest Parity Conditions *466*

19.3 Linking Asset Markets and Macroeconomics *470*

19.3.1 Bond Prices and Interest Rates *470*

19.3.2 Stock Prices *473*

19.3.3 Nominal Exchange Rates and National Money Markets *473*

19.3.4 Market Efficiency or Speculative Manias? Implications for Macroeconomics *475*

19.4 Exchange Rate Determination in the Short Run *479*

19.4.1 The Exchange Rate as an Asset Price *479*

19.4.2 Money and Goods Market Equilibrium *482*

19.4.3 The Monetary Approach: The Case of Flexible Prices *483*

19.4.4 Overshooting with Rigid Prices *484*

Summary *486*

19.1 Overview

From Tobin's q to interest and exchange rates, we have often encountered prices which are determined in financial markets. It should be clear by now that asset prices deeply influence the macroeconomy: they affect wealth and spending, the cost of borrowing and investments, and the exchange rate, which lies at the heart of trade and financial flows. These prices share a number of unique features. They determine the value of **assets**, the various forms in which wealth is held. These prices are set in markets which are quite different from goods markets, not only because they are impersonal—transactions are almost never face to face—but also because they exhibit a high degree of volatility. They often appear driven by the whims of traders whose preoccupation is with very short-term gains, without much concern for the impact of their actions.

What really sets assets apart from other goods is that they are durable; they are not consumed, but stored for later disposal. Their value is not in today's use, but in their resale price. For this reason, they are driven entirely by the future. Almost by definition, the future is uncertain, so assets are almost always risky. Another fairly general characteristic of assets is that they tend to be traded on large markets.

This chapter offers a unified treatment of asset prices and markets, with some emphasis on exchange rates. We start by describing asset markets and explaining some of their key features. They are big because they deal in stocks, not flows. They are fast-moving because profit opportunities are huge, but dissipate in seconds. They put a price tag on a special but essential economic factor, uncertainty. We then look at the asset prices encountered in many of the earlier chapters: bond prices, interest rates, stocks. We explore why markets sometimes embark on apparently senseless behaviour, producing successive phases of exuberance and bust. And we close the chapter with a more detailed treatment of exchange rates. There, the main aim is to deal with the apparent paradox that exchange rates, which determine competitiveness in trade, are driven by financial considerations. The answer leads us to separate the short from the long run; we find that the short run is financial and the long run is real.

19.2 How Asset Markets Work

19.2.1 Facts about Asset Markets

A number of aspects establish the fundamental uniqueness of asset markets. First, unlike goods and services which are bought for consumption and perishable in some sense (fruits don't last long, cars and computers get outdated, and services are produced while they are consumed) assets are durable. This distinguishing characteristic, plus the fact that they can be held with negligible storage costs, are two reasons that financial assets are a premier vehicle for saving. They can be bought now and sold later, either when the time comes to use savings for consumption or when they are exchanged against other assets to cash in profit or avoid a loss.

Second, in contrast with markets which trade in *flows* of goods or services, financial markets are markets for *stocks*. While trade on any given day involves only a fraction of existing assets, the whole stock of assets can be dumped on the market at very short notice, if the owners so desire. This explains the size and potential volatility of financial markets. For example, in September 2000 the stock of shares

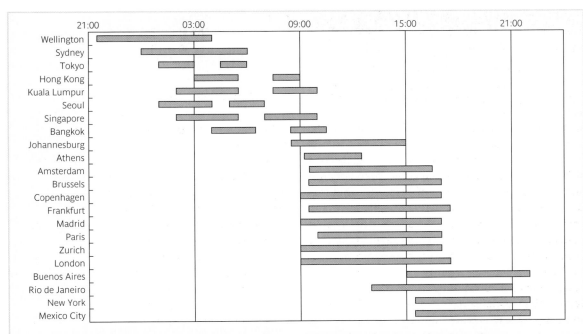

Fig. 19.1 Trading Hours of Stock Markets around the World, Greenwich Mean Time
Stock markets are located around the world. As the world turns, some market somewhere is open, processing new information and pricing assets accordingly.
Source: Deutsche Börse.

outstanding in DaimlerChrysler Corporation was about 1 billion shares. On an *average* day in the nine months preceding, about 3.5 million shares were traded, one-third of one per cent of the stock. Yet the number of shares transacted could vary from a few hundred thousand to potentially more than the entire stock outstanding—if stocks change hands several times. Similarly, the market for foreign exchange involves daily volumes which stagger the imagination: on an average *day*, it is estimated that roughly 1.2 trillion dollars worth of foreign exchange is traded, mostly in dollars, euros, and yen. This represents about 15% of *annual* GDP of the United States or Europe!

Third, financial markets are typically well-organized trading systems dealing in standardized assets that can be traded in large quantities with ease. In earlier times, the markets were oriented around physical presence of market participants in a trading hall, or exchange. The action was dominated by shouting, gesticulating traders wading through seas of hastily scribbled papers. Today, most markets are computerized, and market participants are linked through telecommunication lines from terminal screens virtually anywhere in the world. The World Wide Web has created a single, global market in stocks and other financial instruments, with traders constantly in touch with market activity. As Figure 19.1 shows, at any moment in time, twenty-four hours a day, some financial market is open somewhere in the world, and any individual in the world with access to a telephone may trade on it. This is perfect competition!

These characteristics require that the usual demand and supply analysis be adapted in two ways. First, looking at the flow of transactions can be misleading. The annual supply of savings by households represents a mere flow increment to their stock of wealth. Newly created assets—from newly printed money to new shares of a company—are indistinguishable from existing ones and, at any moment, trading involves both new and old assets. At any time holders of assets can decide to sell their holding, or buyers can emerge interested in acquiring the existing stock. This is why the market for assets is very different from the market for goods. In the goods market, it is demand for and supply of flows that must be balanced; in asset markets, prices move to clear the demand for and supply of the whole stock. Second, durability means that a key concern of market participants is the future value of each asset that they hold. After all, in contrast to non-durable goods that are promptly consumed, assets are acquired for keeps, not for immediate enjoyment.[1] Thus, asset markets are necessarily forward looking and must face considerable uncertainty.

The potential unloading of huge stocks on the market and the intrinsic presence of uncertainty explains why financial markets can be so very volatile. In a matter of minutes, changing expectations, or mere rumours, can radically alter demand and supply, swelling the volume of trade, or drying up markets. Prices, which equate demand and supply on a second by second basis, can therefore swing widely. This reasoning applies not just to strictly defined assets (stocks, bonds) but to any durable object that can be (relatively) easily stored and sold—artwork, commodities, or contracts for the delivery of goods which may not yet exist at some time in the future (such as oil, electricity, wheat, or pork bellies). In fact, all these durable goods are traded on markets (oil in Rotterdam, wheat and pork bellies in Chicago) which resemble those for financial assets.

19.2.2 Functions of Asset Markets

The intense activity associated with asset markets combined with the often phenomenal profits of market participants create the impression that financial markets are gambling casinos with little economic purpose. Far from it, markets for financial assets perform three essential economic functions.

The first is to bring together borrowers and lenders. The second is to put a price on the future and on uncertainty. The third is to allow participants to control the risk they are exposed to. In what follows these functions are explored in more detail.

Intermediation

Financial markets are the meeting place for millions of households and firms who want to shift resources intertemporally—either saving or borrowing—or intratemporally—from one form of asset or liability to another. But most individuals do not deal directly on asset markets. This is not only because the quantities they desire to trade are small, but also because transacting in asset markets requires a great deal of expertise. To avoid these problems, they can act indirectly through **financial intermediaries**. Financial intermediaries channel resources from savers to borrowers and investors, and help solve the 'double coincidence' problem that arose in Chapter 8 with respect to goods and services. Like money, financial intermediaries divorce the act of saving (deferred consumption) from the act of investment (creation of physical productive capacity).

As a result, dealings in asset markets tend to resemble wholesale markets involving professional traders, who accept and execute large orders on the basis of mutual trust and charge each other relatively small fees. For example on foreign exchange markets, an average trade is in the order of €5 million; going from pounds sterling to euro and back again involves a transaction cost of around 0.05% or about €2,500. Similar fees are charged for large transactions involving stocks or bonds. In return for a fee, intermediaries place orders for several smaller customers at once, or may even 'make a market' by maintaining a large inventory which they can sell from or add to. In this way, intermediaries themselves become asset-holders.

Allocation of risk

The price of the future—or the rewards for waiting—is the interest paid by borrowers, as explained in Chapter 5. By setting interest rates, financial markets price the future. Bonds, which are loan contracts, represent fixed payment streams in the future; the price of these payment streams defines the relevant

---

[1] Well, Shylock seemed to enjoy his assets, but then he was a bit odd.

interest rate. Shares, which are partial ownership of companies, promise dividend payments which must be in line with interest rates, if they are to be sufficiently attractive to be held. But assets are inherently risky because they are held for future sale. Borrowers can default—totally or partially—on bonds, and dividends depend on firms' profitability, and firms can even go bankrupt. Asset-holders therefore look for ways to reduce their exposure to risk. They are willing to accept some risk in exchange for better returns, but to some degree only, and they wish to protect themselves from catastrophic events such as a collapse of prices. Not all asset-holders are equally **risk averse**, and their horizons also differ. This leads us to another function of financial markets: to price risk and allocate it to those who are most willing to bear it.

Just as it is possible to protect ourselves against the costs of car accidents, house fire, unemployment, and death by purchasing insurance, it is possible to use asset markets to insure against financial uncertainty. This is done through diversification, the holding of a mix of several different assets. Box 19.1 explains how diversification works. In

Box 19.1 Risk Diversification

'Don't put all your eggs in one basket' is folk wisdom. The principle is remarkably simple: if you pool many risky outcomes, the result can be much less risky than any of the outcomes taken individually. Under some conditions, averaging mightily removes variability. Consider the following, simple example. The return from 'Investments' A and B depend on independent flips of a coin. In either case, 'heads' means receiving €100, 'tails' means receiving nothing. On average, if repeated many times, either investment yields €50; we say that its *expected value* is €50. Now compare either of these two 'investments' with a new one, C, which is simply one-half of A plus one-half of B. The expected value of C remains €50 but its *variability* is lower. To see this, list the four possible outcomes: A = heads/B = heads, which pays €100, A = heads/B = tails and A = tails/B = heads which each pays €50, and A = tails/B = tails which pays nothing. Taken individually, A or B pay €100 or nothing; in the form of C, an investor receives €50 with one chance out of two, leaving the probabilities of the extreme returns of €100 or nothing to just one chance in four. Diversifying A or B by holding a bit of each seems to have reduced the risk.

The diversification effect is even greater when the two investments tend to move in opposite directions (in the language of statistics: when they are negatively correlated). Consider the case when the returns from A and B are decided by the same coin flip: 'heads' means A pays €100 and B nothing, while 'tails' means A pays nothing

and B delivers €100. As before, A and B have the same expected value and same volatility, but now C pays €50 in *all* cases; diversification has eliminated risk completely. What fully eliminates the risk in this example is that A and B are the exact opposite of each other: one pays off when the other does not. This property is called perfectly negative correlation. It is a special case of the general proposition that pooling negatively correlated assets is the way to reduce riskiness. This is what diversification is all about.

Finally, consider a third example: a single flip of a coin determines that both A and B either yield €100 or nothing. This is a case of perfectly positive correlation. The composite investment C (half of A and half of B) does not reduce risk at all, it offers exactly the same yields as A and B taken separately.

Financial markets are at their best when they pool assets which are negatively correlated, a property described as different risk characteristics. Diversification can reduce the riskiness of investors' portfolios, but it cannot eliminate it (unless the risks are perfectly negatively correlated, which occurs extremely rarely). If much of the risk is macroeconomic (business cycles, policy actions), risk cannot be diversified much. Foreign assets, however, are likely to have different characteristics. This creates a strong incentive to pool markets across national borders, the key reason for the existence of globalized financial markets.

Box 19.2 The Price of Risk

Return to the first example of Box 19.1. Investments *A* and *B* have the same expected value, €50. How much would you be willing to pay to acquire either investment? Most people are risk averse, and they would rather get €50 for sure than buy a risky investment with the same expected value. (Those who don't care and would pay €50 are said to be risk neutral; risk lovers would pay even more than €50 for the thrill.) If you are willing to pay, say, €48 for *A*, the risk premium is €2 or 4% of the risk-free price. If total demand and supply of that asset are equated at €48, then the risk premium represents the market price of risk. Since *B* has the same characteristics, it should also be priced at €48. What about investment *C*? It has the same expected value as *A* and *B*, but is less risky. An investor would be willing to pay more for investment *C* than for either *A* or *B*. If the market price is, say, €49, the risk premium on the new asset is only €1 or 2%. Note that diversification not only reduces risk, it also reduces the price of risk. Facing less risk, investors prefer the new asset. The issuers of the assets *A* and *B* are also happy, as they pay a lower risk premium. This is how diversification is an efficient way of spreading the risks of individual assets in the market.

Now consider the second example of Box 19.1, when a single flip of a coin produces two opposite investments *A* and *B*. We found that the composite investment *C* is riskless, and it should sell for €50, with no risk premium. We say that all the risk has been diversified away, which benefits both the sellers and the buyers of investments *A* and *B*. In the third example where *A* and *B* are perfectly positively correlated, there is no diversification at all and the composite asset *C* should sell for €48, with no reduction in the risk premium.

Finally, for a more realistic example, suppose that you pay now, but the coin is flipped only in a year's time. Above and beyond the risky gamble, any investor will expect to receive interest for the time the money was parked in the investment. Compensation for risk in this case can be expressed as a premium added to the risk-free interest rate available on say, a government bond. Suppose that, as before, the 'investment' has an expected value of €50 and the market currently prices it at €46 *today*; suppose further that the risk-free rate is 3%. Then the risk premium can be computed as 5.7% (the total expected rate of return ((€50 − 46)/€46 = 0.08696 = 8.7%) minus the risk-free rate (3%)).

fact, many financial firms offer diversification to their customers by proposing ready-made funds, a mix of well-chosen—negatively correlated—risky assets. They can vary the riskiness of these portfolios and accommodate different tastes of their customers. 'Funds of funds' have also been proposed to achieve further diversification.

Pricing of risk

Risk can be reduced, but cannot be fully eliminated. Someone must be willing to bear some risk. The way to convince people to bear risk if to offer them compensation. This compensation is called a **risk premium**. It means that the rate of return, or the total payouts of an asset divided by its price, increases with the riskiness of assets. Box 19.2 describes how and why.

Both borrowers—issuers of stocks and bonds—and lenders benefit from the existence of financial

markets. Taken in isolation, each investment is risky and would have to pay a high yield to attract wary savers. Enter the picture financial intermediaries, banks and other specialized institutions, which pool these individual risks by offering home-made funds to savers. The borrowers pay lower risk premiums, the lenders bear less risk, and the intermediaries collect a fee. Because diversification tends to be more complete when more assets are involved, the best services tend to be offered by the major financial centres dealing in stocks of companies from all over the world. This is precisely why asset trading tends to concentrate in few places and also why worldwide electronic trading is growing so fast. Stock market trading volume, or turnover, is often mind-boggling for the average citizen, which leads to a frequent misperception of financial markets as a sophisticated version of

Las Vegas. Yet concentration and volume is the consequence of the endless search for diversification to the benefit of all, whether they are lenders or borrowers, and whether they are large or small.

19.2.3 Information and Market Efficiency

Asset prices reflect the collective judgement of market participants. This judgement, in turn, is based on all the information collected by market participants. The information concerns each single asset, its underlying value and future performance. It is a hallmark of properly functioning financial markets that participants are engaged in a never-ending search for profit opportunities, either for their customers or for their own accounts. Both the amount of money at stake and the speed at which information flows make it unlikely that opportunities not involving additional risk will be left unexploited for any significant period of time. Markets which satisfy this condition—that publicly available information cannot earn consistently above-average returns—are said to be **efficient**.

A more precise definition of market efficiency is that prices fully reflect all available information.[2] Market efficiency requires two things: that markets use all available information about the future, even if costly; and that they process information correctly, i.e. based on principles that are not systematically contradicted by the facts, nor do they make systematic mistakes. Efficiency in markets implies that there are no opportunities for easy profit. If such an opportunity existed, it would be immediately spotted and eliminated by adequate buying and selling, bringing prices in line. This **no-profit condition** implies a tight link between asset prices. To see how, we start with riskless arbitrage and then consider the no-profit condition in the presence of risk.

Arbitrage

Arbitrage concerns operations which do not involve additional risk.[3] It is customary to distinguish three types of arbitrage: yield arbitrage, spatial arbitrage, and triangular arbitrage.

Yield arbitrage concerns two similar assets which happen to offer different returns. Strictly speaking, it applies to riskless assets, like Treasury bills, but it is sometimes applied to risky assets which bear similar risk (like assets A and B in Box 19.1). Consider the following example: two riskless government bonds, which otherwise have the same attributes, offer different rates of interest, or yields. Holders of the less attractive bond will sell in favour of the one with the superior yield. In fact, the entire stock of the less attractive bond could be put up for sale. As the higher-yielding bond becomes more expensive and the lower-yielding bond becomes cheaper, the implied yields converge (recall the relationship between bond prices and bond yields from Chapter 5). Arbitrage prevents such pricing misalignment from occurring: yield arbitrage imposes identical returns for identical assets.

Spatial arbitrage concerns the same assets traded in different locations. For example, large commercial banks borrow from each other at the interbank interest rate. If the interbank rate in two cities were to diverge, enterprising banks present in both cities would immediately borrow in the cheaper market and lend in the dearer one. To see that spatial arbitrage forces the convergence of yields and prices, Figure 19.2 looks at three-month nominal interest rates on DM interbank deposits in Germany and in London's offshore market. One would expect that, with capital mobility and negligible risk differences, the yields should be virtually identical; in the past fifteen years this is indeed the case.

Triangular arbitrage applies mostly to foreign exchange markets and is possible when the relative

---

[2] The idea of market efficiency is related to the rational expectations hypothesis introduced in Ch. 5. Rational expectations assume that agents do not make systematic forecasting errors. Market efficiency applies this concept to markets and price-setting.

[3] In financial market jargon, this distinction is not always so clear. For example, traders who search for information on corporate takeovers in order to take a position in the stock 'in play' are sometimes called risk arbitrageurs. Technically, this is a contradiction in terms: if a takeover is called off, the 'risk arbitrageur' may be left holding a great deal of stock and may suffer a large loss.

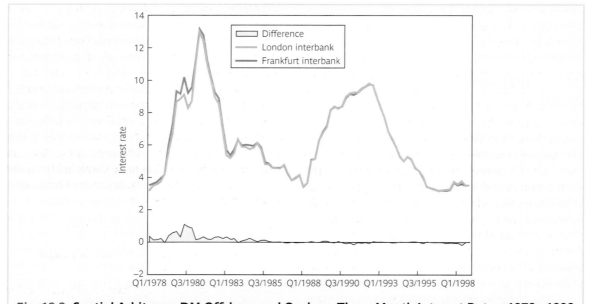

Fig. 19.2 Spatial Arbitrage: DM Offshore and Onshore Three-Month Interest Rates, 1978–1998

With a brief exception in the period 1979–81, when controls were operative, capital mobility seemed complete between offshore and onshore financial centres. Spatial arbitrage has been near-perfect, equalizing interbank interest rates on DM interbank transactions in Frankfurt and London.

Source: IMF.

prices of three—or more—currencies are not consistent with each other. If the euro costs one US dollar and one euro costs 8 Danish krone (DKR), then the DKR/$ rate must be (DKR8/€)/($1/€) = 8 DKR/$. Otherwise limitless profit would be possible by buying the euro where it is cheap and selling it where it is more expensive. Figure 19.3 displays this example.

19.2.4 The Interest Parity Conditions

An important application of the notion of market efficiency is the interest parity condition that has already been presented in Chapters 10 and 13. Here we revisit this important relationship, injecting more detail and realism, in particular by taking account of the presence of risk. This leads to two versions of the condition: covered interest parity, an example of riskless yield arbitrage, and uncovered interest parity, which allows for risk.

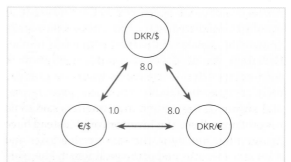

Fig. 19.3 Triangular Arbitrage

When two exchange rates among three currencies are known, the exchange rate between the remaining pair of currencies is given by triangular arbitrage. In the absence of transactions costs, any discrepancy between purchasing a currency directly and acquiring it using a third currency is eliminated.

Covered interest parity (CIP)

This arbitrage condition is based on the comparison of returns from a domestic and a foreign asset with similar risk characteristics. For example, an investor in the UK can obtain an annual rate of interest i on riskless British Treasury bills issued in sterling at home and i^* on equally riskless bills issued in euros. The two investments are not equivalent, since the sterling value of the euro may change over the investment period, thereby altering the total return measured in sterling for the euro-denominated investment. Let the price of the pound in euros at the beginning of the year be S_t. By selling one pound at the beginning of the year, a British investor obtains S_t euros that she can invest for one year to receive $(1 + i^*)S_t$ at the end of the year. This is a completely certain return, since both the interest i^* and exchange rate S_t are known at the beginning of the year, but it is in terms of euros, and the exchange rate in the next period is uncertain. The investor can eliminate all risk by signing a contract at the beginning of the year to sell $(1 + i^*)S_t$ euros against pounds at the end of the year. Such a **forward contract** specifies the exchange rate at which this sum will be converted from euros to pounds: it is the one-year ahead **forward exchange rate**, denoted F_t. The forward exchange rate corresponds to a transaction which implies a delayed delivery of the currency; it is to be distinguished from the **spot exchange rate** S_t, which implies immediate delivery. Thus the British investor can be certain that for every pound invested this way, she will receive $(1 + i^*)S_t/F_t$ pounds at the end of the year. Because the forward contract eliminates all exchange risk, the foreign investment is said to be **covered** or **hedged**. The investor could instead have invested her money in the safe sterling asset and receive $(1 + i)$ at the end of the year, which is equally riskless since the interest rate is known when the decision is made. Arbitrage guarantees that the two returns must be equal. The result is the **covered interest parity condition**, which can be formally written as:

(19.1) $(1 + i) = (1 + i^*)S_t/F_t$

A useful approximation of the CIP condition can be found by arguing a bit more loosely. The British

investor will compare the domestic interest rate i on one hand, and the return on the foreign investment, on the other hand. The return on the foreign investment comes in two parts: the foreign interest rate i^* less the forward depreciation of the euro—measured as the interest rate in percentage terms—which is also the appreciation of sterling, $(F_t - S_t)/S_t$, called the forward premium. Indeed, if the forward value of the pound is higher than its spot value, the pound value of the euro investment loses in value; this capital loss has to be deducted from the euro interest rate. Formally, it can be shown that an approximation of (19.1) is

(19.2) $i^* = i - \dfrac{F_t - S_t}{S_t}$.

        interest rate = interest rate − forward premium
        in UK   in Euroland

A positive premium means that the forward value of sterling in terms of euros is higher than its spot value, i.e. that sterling is 'stronger' forward than spot. In that case, the euro interest rate i^* has to be higher than the sterling interest rate i to make up for the euro forward weakness. The WebAppendix further develops the concept of the forward premium.

Uncovered interest parity (UIP)

What happens when the investor does not eliminate exchange risk by engaging in a forward contract? Indeed, she can sell sterling spot at rate S_t, invest in euros for a year, and wait until the end of the year to buy back sterling at the then prevailing spot exchange rate S_{t+1}. This is risky, though, because no one knows at the beginning of the year what the exchange rate will be by year's end. What appeared to be a good deal may turn out disappointing if the euro depreciates vis-à-vis sterling, leaving the investor with fewer pounds than expected. Of course, the euro can appreciate unexpectedly, and the deal will turn out to be terrific. Leaving her foreign investment open or unhedged, the investor takes a risk, and this will involve a risk premium as explained in Box 19.2.

To examine the new situation, we start by assuming that the investor is risk neutral, so that the risk premium is zero. The strategy is the same as before, except that the euro investment will not be sold at the end of the year using the forward rate F_t agreed upon earlier, but at the prevailing spot exchange rate S_{t+1}. Going through the same reasoning, the expected return in pounds from one pound invested in euros is $(1 + i^*)S_t/_tS_{t+1}$, where $_tS_{t+1}$ is the end-of-year exchange rate as expected at the beginning of the year. A one-year investment in pounds still yields $(1 + i)$. The no-profit condition for a risk-neutral investor implies that both returns are expected to be equal. This gives the **uncovered interest parity (UIP)** condition, which can be written formally as:

$$(19.3) \qquad (1 + i) = (1 + i^*)(S_t/_tS_{t+1})$$

return in UK = expected return in Euroland

which can be approximated conveniently by:

$$(19.4) \qquad i = i^* - \frac{S_{t+1} - S_t}{S_t}.$$

interest rate = interest rate – expected appreciation
in UK   in Euroland   of sterling

The UIP simply asserts that rates of return are equalized across countries once expected exchange rate changes are taken into account. On the left-hand side of (19.4) we have the one-year pound interest rate; on the right-hand side we have the euro interest rate less the expected capital gain or loss from changes in the sterling–euro exchange rate, expressed in percentage terms, for the same one-year maturity. Expectations cannot be observed directly, but the UIP provides an implicit measure of what the market expects. If interest rates in Britain are higher than in Euroland $(i > i^*)$, then the euro is expected to appreciate (i.e. sterling depreciates, and the expected rate of sterling depreciation is given by the difference in observed interest rates: $(S_{t+1} - S_t)/S_t = i^* - i < 0$). To be willing at all to hold pound-denominated assets with a lower interest than euro-denominated assets, investors will expect a capital gain as compensation. If euro-rates are higher, the UIP implies that sterling is expected to appreciate vis-à-vis the euro.

The uncovered interest parity condition can be modified to accommodate risk aversion by allowing for a risk premium that the British investor will require to hold euro-denominated assets:

$$(19.5) \qquad i^* = i + \frac{S_{t+1} - S_t}{S_t} + \psi_t.$$

interest rate = interest rate + expected   risk
in Euroland   in UK   appreciation   premium
                            of sterling

where ψ_t stands for the risk premium which makes a UK investor indifferent between investing in Euroland and staying at home. Turning things around, we can *define* the risk premium as the deviation from the uncovered interest parity condition, which can vary over time:

$$(19.6) \qquad \psi_t = (i^* - i) - \frac{S_{t+1} - S_t}{S_t}.$$

risk premium = interest   – expected appreciation
               differential

We have looked at the situation from the point of view of a British investor who seeks to be compensated for the risk of holding euro-denominated assets. At the same time, European investors are likely to hold British assets; they face the same type of exchange risk, but the other way round: all things equal, they too would require a premium on euro-denominated assets, i.e. a negative ψ. So, British investors want a positive risk premium, Euroland-based investors want it negative; what is the end result? As always, the answer is given by the market. In the end, the risk premium will be such that it exactly balances all these demands and supplies from Britain, Euroland, and elsewhere. As these demands and supplies vary, so will the risk premium, which is known to be volatile and usually small because for any British investor taking the action described above we are likely to find a Euroland-based investor doing the same. Clearly, the risk premium is a complicated phenomenon whose full treatment is beyond the scope of this textbook.[4] All we need to understand is that the existence of a risk premium ψ_t (which can be positive or negative) means that we should not expect the uncovered parity condition to hold exactly. It will be true up to a—generally volatile—risk premium.

---

[4]   Finance theory (the Capital Asset Pricing Model or CAPM) states that the risk premium is determined by the correlation between the asset's return and the return from the world portfolio.

The bid–ask spread

The risk premium takes another interesting form. To carry out the various operations described above, investors 'go to the market'. There they need to find a counterpart, someone interested in doing exactly the same operation, for the same amount, but in reverse. This is extremely unlikely, so the market would be useless were it not for the presence of **market makers**. Market makers are usually big financial institutions that have an interest in keeping the market **liquid** at all times, meaning that every desired operation can be carried out instantly. They stand ready to satisfy any demand, buying or selling any amount—up to a reasonable ceiling, which can be as high as €1 million—that appears on the market. Each market maker specializes in certain trades, e.g. the euro–sterling exchange rate or bunds (the debt of the German government). Of course, as they do so, they provide a service. They also take a risk; for example, selling forward sterling for euros represents a commitment to deliver sterling upon **maturity** of the forward contract, which means buying sterling on the spot market at a rate presently unknown. The investor who buys a forward contract gets rid of risk, passing this risk on to the market maker. Quite naturally, the market maker needs to be compensated for both the service and the risk. This takes the form of a **bid–ask spread**.

The bid–ask spread is familiar to anyone who has travelled abroad and has bought currency at an exchange booth. There, as on all foreign exchange markets, exchange rates are quoted in pairs: a lower 'bid' price for those who want to sell the foreign currency, and a higher 'ask' price for buyers. The difference is the market maker's profit. The bid–ask spread in wholesale foreign exchange trading is currently quite small—roughly 0.2% on a five-million euro transaction between euros and sterling. Yet it can be much higher for currencies which are inherently risky, or are thinly traded. Box 19.3 gives a nice example of how a bid–ask spread evolved over time for the Ostmark, the money of the German Democratic Republic, the communist German country which disappeared from the European map after German unification in 1990.

 Box 19.3 The Short-Lived Market for Ostmarks

Even before the Berlin Wall fell on 9 November 1989, trade in the East German currency, the Ostmark (OM), was significant, and DM quotes for OM were published daily in major West German newspapers. After this historic date, volume increased by an order of magnitude as East Germans tried to convert their savings into harder currency. It remained unclear until March 1990 that monetary unification would occur, implying automatic conversion of OM currency and bank deposits into DM. The conversion rate of one DM for one OM applying to a part of East Germany's holdings and one for two for the rest—resulting in an average estimated by the Bundesbank at 1.8—was first officially suggested in March. It was then formalized as part of the state treaty of monetary and economic union between the two German states in May 1990.

Considerable uncertainty characterized this period. Furthermore, before the Berlin Wall opened, the markets were relatively thin and trade was exclusively a Western business. This is reflected in the bid–ask spread which stood at more than 30% in early 1989, as seen in Figure 19.4. As the situation became clearer, trade moved to the streets of East and West Berlin and most banks entered the game. With the decision to establish a monetary union between West and East Germany by July 1990—in effect, replacing OMs with DMs—uncertainty declined, and so did the spread.

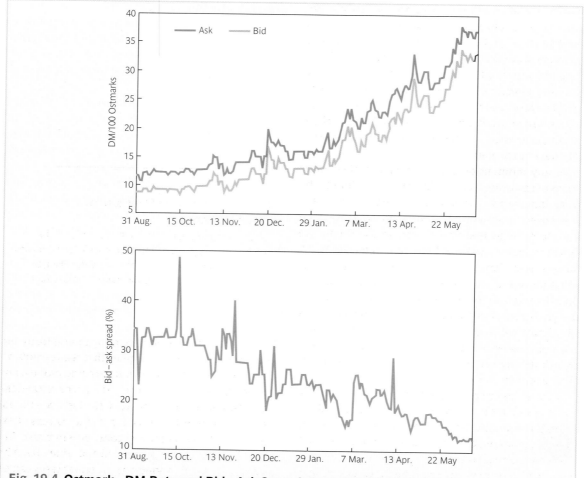

Fig. 19.4 Ostmark – DM Rate and Bid – Ask Spread, August 1989 – June 1990

As monetary union approached, the risk involved in holding Ostmarks, the currency of the vanishing German Democratic Republic, declined. This is reflected in the bid – ask spread, which fell significantly.

Source: Burda and Gerlach (1993).

19.3 Linking Asset Markets and Macroeconomics

19.3.1 Bond Prices and Interest Rates

The term structure of nominal interest rates

The interest rate is the price of the future. In Chapter 9, we saw that the central bank determines the short-term nominal interest rate—for loans overnight up to one month duration—by altering the supply of liquidity to the economy. Yet most borrowers are interested in the real interest rate and in longer maturities, as most commercial loans range from one to ten or more years. To have an impact on economic conditions, monetary policy must also affect longer-term real interest rates. The other channels of monetary policy are the exchange rate, which affects external competitiveness, and asset prices which affect private wealth. We now examine the links between short-term nominal interest rates, the exchange rates, the long-term real interest rate, and the value of shares and bonds, all of which are determined in financial markets. Again, the central theme is the no-profit condition of efficient markets.

At any moment of time, financial markets offer loans of maturities ranging from the very short to the very long term. The associated rates on interest, converted at annual rates, map out what is called the **term structure of interest rates**. From the lender's perspective, a loan of longer maturity means less liquidity, since repayment generally does not occur until the loan matures. Naturally, this is a riskier commitment. For the borrower, longer maturity is a longer-term commitment that the funds will remain at his disposal. To compensate the lender, interest rates bear a risk premium which increases in maturity, all other things equal. This is shown in Figure 19.5.

Short-term interest rates change frequently, especially because monetary policy can change. If short-term interest rates are expected to increase over the next two years, for example, the longer-term rates will have to rise too. To see why, notice that a two-year loan can be arranged in a number of ways: one loan of two years maturity, or two successive one-year

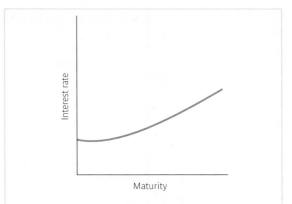

Fig. 19.5 The Term Structure of Interest Rates

Lenders require a higher return for committing their funds to long-term loans. Borrowers value long horizons for the use of their loans and are therefore willing to pay a higher interest rate as the maturity of the loan increases.

loans, or a series of twenty-four one-month loans, etc. The no-profit condition implies that these combinations are equivalent ways of borrowing money, and should impose the same cost to the borrower and the same reward to the lender, with due account for risk. If the interest rate is expected to increase next year, then the two-year rate must also increase, but today. The reasoning applies to all maturities. Box 19.4 formally shows that long-term interest rates can be seen as averages of the current and expected future

Box 19.4 The Term Structure of Interest Rates

The term structure of interest rates combines maturity and risk premiums (which makes rates higher, the longer their maturity) with the expectations hypothesis which is based on the no-profit condition. Consider a long-term interest rate of L years' maturity. Ignoring the maturity and risk premiums, it is equivalent to a succession of one-year loans which are 'rolled over'. If the annualized interest rate on the long-term loan is i^L, the return is $(1 + i^L)^L$ (compounding annual rates). If the one-year interest rate expected to prevail t years from now is i_t^e, where the

superscript e denotes an expectation, the return from a succession of such loans is $(1 + i_1)(1 + i_2^e) \ldots (1 + i_t^2)$ $\ldots (1 + i_L^e)$. The no-profit condition implies that these returns should be equal. As a first approximation, this equality states that the long rate at time t, i_t^L is an average of expected future short rates, possibly plus a risk premium ψ_t^L:

(19.7)
$$ i_t^L = \frac{\sum\limits_{i=1}^{L} i_{t+i}^e}{L} + \psi_t^L $$

Table 19.1   Bond Prices and Yields

Description of the payment stream	Price in euros given yield i:	Yield given price P
A. One-year pure discount bond paying 1 euro:	$1/(1+i)$	$1/P - 1$
B. Two-year pure discount paying 1 euro in 2nd year	$1/(1+i)^2$	$1/P^{1/2} - 1$
C. Ten-year discount bond paying 1 euro in 10th year	$1/(1+i)^{10}$	$1/P^{1/10} - 1$
D. Bond paying a coupon each year of C euro for 2 years plus payment of 1 euro in 2nd year ($C < 1$)	$X/(1+i) + (1+X)/(1+i)^2$	$[4P(C+1) + C^2]^{1/2}/2P - (1 - C/2P)$
E. Consol paying 1 euro per annum, forever	$1/i$	$1/P$

rates than can be chained to deliver an equivalent loan. Then the maturity and risk premiums come on top. The result is that the central bank's actions, both current and anticipated, affect interest rates at all maturities. This explains why the bond markets are so intensely interested in what central banks are up to!

Bond prices

Lending is a job normally performed by banks, but loans can also be directly organized by large borrowers in financial markets. In that case, they take the form of bonds, i.e. recognition of debt by the borrower along with a schedule of payments concerning both interest and the principal. Bonds can then be traded like any other asset. But what determines the price at which bonds sell? The bond price represents the present discounted value of the payments agreed upon at the time when the bond was issued. The resulting inverse relationship between bond prices and interest rates was discussed already in Chapter 5, and is shown in Table 19.1 for some types of bonds. Bond A is the simplest case of a bond of one-year maturity. Its price is $P = 1/(1 + i)$ and, with some manipulation, the interest rate can be expressed in terms of the price as $i = (1 - P)/P$. More complicated bonds, involving coupons and longer yields to maturity cannot be expressed as neatly as Bonds B, C, and D (!), and require the use of a computer. The last example E is the 'ultimate bond' or **consol**: it exists forever, in principle, and is called for that reason a **perpetuity**. With few exceptions, only governments are in a position to make such a promise. But such debt has been issued in the past

(and has existed for a long time!) in the United Kingdom. For consols, the interest rate and price move inversely and equiproportionately.[5] This is only approximately true for all other bonds.

Real interest rate arbitrage in the long run

The UIP conditions, with and without a risk premium, link nominal interest rate at home and abroad and embody the tight linkages implied by international financial integration. Does the arbitrage argument extend to the *real* interest rate, which is decisive for intertemporal decisions? Intuitively, one might expect an arbitrage opportunity to arise if real interest rates across countries—with similar risk characteristics—differed significantly. It turns out that the purchasing power parity condition (PPP)[6] does imply that real interest rates at home and abroad will be equal although, like PPP, this is likely to hold only in the medium to long run.

This **real interest parity** condition follows from the UIP, e.g. in the form of (19.3). Rearranged, this means that the interest rate differential is equal to the expected exchange rate appreciation of the domestic currency. But in the medium to long term, relative PPP implies that the future rate of depreciation is equal to the future inflation differential:

---

5   The consol formula is: $P = 1/(1 + i) + 1/(1 + i)^2 + \ldots + 1/(1 + i)^n + \ldots = [1/(1 + i)][1 + 1/(1 + i) + \ldots + 1/(1 + i)^n + \ldots]$. The second term is the infinite sum of a geometric series. This implies that $P = 1/(1 + i)\{1/[1 - (1/1 + i)]\}$ which can be simplified to the result in the table.

6   Purchasing power parity is presented in Ch. 8. The relative version is employed here.

(19.8) $(S_{t+1} - S_t)/S_t = \pi^*_{t+1} - \pi_{t+1}.$

If forecasts of inflation at home π^e_{t+1} and abroad π^{*e}_{t+1} are consistent with PPP, the definition of the real interest rate[7] $r_t \equiv i - \pi^e_{t+1}$ and $r^*_t \equiv i^* - \pi^{*e}_{t+1}$ along with (19.8) and (19.4) imply:

(19.9) $r_t = r^*_t.$

This relationship is called the **international Fisher equation**. As it is based on relative PPP, it is at best a medium- to long-run proposition. Nevertheless, it is a useful benchmark for evaluating long-term foreign investment strategies, as it implies that the real rate of interest should be largely the same in all countries and is independent of the evolution of exchange rates.

19.3.2 Stock Prices

Shares in firms, or stocks as they are often called, are held by households or their intermediaries, and are issued by firms to acquire resources for capital expenditure. Stocks are risky assets because they represent a claim to a share of profits in the issuing firm after costs—wages, interest payments, rent, taxes, and other expenses—have been paid. How are stocks valued? Once again, we make use of the no-profit condition, comparing now a riskless Treasury bill with a constant real yield r per annum and a traded share in a company which pays all its profits (in real terms) out at the end of each period as dividends d_t. The hitch is that, while the Treasury bill pays a fixed yield, the yield or rate of return on the stock investment consists of the dividend plus possible capital gains or losses when the share price changes. If q_t is the share price at the beginning of period t, the rate of return on the company share is the dividend yield, d_t/q_t, plus the anticipated capital gain, $(q_{t+1} - q_t)/q_t$ (a gain if $q_{t+1} > q_t$, a loss if $q_{t+1} < q_t$). The no-profit condition implies that both assets have the same yield over period t:

(19.10)

$$r = d_t/q_t + (q_{t+1} - q_t)/q_t$$

yield on Treasury bills = dividend yield + capital gain

$\underbrace{\qquad\qquad\qquad\qquad\qquad}_{\text{total return on shares}}$

[7] The Fisher equation is introduced in Ch. 8.

which can be transformed into:

(19.11) $q_t = \dfrac{d_t + q_{t+1}}{1 + r}$

Today's stock price q_t is equal to the present discounted value of the dividend in the period, plus that of the next period's price q_{t+1}. A theme which recurs constantly in the study of financial markets, expectations of the future price drives today's stock price.

Can this be the end of the story? If q_{t+1} depends on q_{t+2} in the same way that q_t depends on q_{t+1}, we can substitute (19.11) for itself in an endless process of telescopic recursion. Will such an endless repetition converge to anything sensible? It turns out that, in the case studied, if the stock price doesn't grow faster than the real interest rate r, the current stock price is indeed well defined, and is given by:

(19.12) $q_t = \displaystyle\sum_{i=0}^{\infty} \left(\dfrac{1}{1+r}\right)^{i+1} d_{t+i}$

which expresses the current stock price (in real terms) as the present discounted value of expected future earnings only: the role of the future price disappears. The market values a company on the basis of what it is expected to earn, now and in the indefinite future.[8] The formula (19.12) is called the fundamental valuation of an asset, and can be found in many applications of financial economics, including the next one, the nominal exchange rate. Stock prices can rise suddenly when market expectations of future profits rise, for example, in times when new technologies are developed. Later in this chapter, we address the question whether stock prices always reflect rational pricing of future company profits.

19.3.3 Nominal Exchange Rates and National Money Markets

The nominal exchange rate and relative liquidity conditions in national money markets

The exchange rate can be thought as the relative price of national monies. Much as share price

[8] What is the relationship between this and Tobin's q used in Ch. 6? Tobin's q is the ratio of the share price (q here) to the replacement cost of installed capital.

changes affect the return on stocks, the exchange rate affects the opportunity costs of holding various currencies, and assets denominated in these currencies. Indeed, we have already encountered the interest parity condition (19.2) which bears a telling resemblance to the share price equation (19.10). The interest parity condition builds a bridge between the exchange rate and liquidity conditions in domestic money markets, represented by their respective nominal interest rates.

This section extends the analysis of Chapter 11, in which the domestic nominal rate was compared by financial investors at home and abroad with some 'required foreign rate of return', designated by i^* but not described in much further detail. In this chapter, using the interest parity condition, we have already decomposed the 'required foreign rate of return' as the foreign nominal interest rate i^* less the expected rate of appreciation of our currency (equivalently, plus the expected rate of depreciation of the foreign currency). We now consider the consequences of that decomposition.

The UIP condition without risk aversion (19.2) can be rewritten as

$$(19.13) \qquad S_t = \frac{(1 + i_t)}{(1 + i_t^*)} S_{t+1}^e$$

The current spot exchange rate S_t is now determined by domestic and foreign interest rates and by the market's current *expectation* of next period's exchange rate S_{t+1}^e. Like all asset prices, the nominal exchange rate is *forward looking*. What happened before is irrelevant: bygones are bygones and the exchange rate is not tied to its past. It is totally free to jump to any level warranted by current or expected future conditions. Especially important is the implication that an appreciation anticipated in the future shows up *immediately* in the current exchange rate.

As with stock pricing in the previous section, equation (19.13) determines the exchange rate in terms of itself in the subsequent period: S_t is driven by the expectation of S_{t+1} which itself is driven by the expectation of S_{t+2}. To keep things simple, we now ignore uncertainty, and therefore the difference between actual and expected values of the exchange rate, as in the previous section. Inserting

into (19.13) the similar expression linking S_{t+1} to S_{t+2}, we find:

$$S_t = \frac{(1 + i_t)}{(1 + i_t^*)} \frac{(1 + i_{t+1})}{(1 + i_{t+1}^*)} S_{t+2}^e,$$

and, repeating the operation n times:

(19.14)

$$S_t = \frac{(1 + i_t)}{(1 + i_t^*)} \frac{(1 + i_{t+1})}{(1 + i_{t+1}^*)} \frac{(1 + i_{t+2})}{(1 + i_{t+2}^*)} \cdots \frac{(1 + i_{t+n})}{(1 + i_{t+n}^*)} S_{t+i}^e.$$

As with stock prices, the current exchange rate reflects all current and future interest rates at home and abroad, and its own long-run value. This expression shows just how important expectations of the future are for the present. Even events far into the future can have a large impact on today's exchange rate. This is why exchange markets—and asset markets in general—are so concerned with information. Even remote future events affect the present.

While not yet providing a complete theory of exchange rate determination, the discussion shows that relative conditions in national money markets are essential for understanding how macroeconomic conditions influence nominal exchange rates. It shows how the anticipation of tight monetary policy at home in the future (i is expected to rise) can lead to an appreciation today (S increases).

An apparent contradiction resolved

There is a subtle question, however, which often trips up those trying to understand (19.14). Suppose interest rates at home rise unexpectedly. According to (19.14) an appreciation should result; yet we know from UIP that higher interest rates at home should be associated with a *depreciation* of our currency (S falling). The confusion may be further exaggerated if one explains the initial appreciation by capital inflows. Is this a contradiction?

The contradiction is only apparent, once we recognize that we implicitly assume that the exchange rate does not change in long-run (we hold S_{t+n+1} constant in (19.14)). The two ways of reasoning are reconciled in Figure 19.6. As the domestic interest rate rises i above the world rate i^*, the exchange rate appreciates temporarily, but is expected to depreciate back to its initial value. As required by UIP, an expected depreciation of the domestic currency (a capital loss) offsets the interest rate advantage at

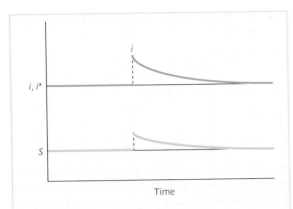

Fig. 19.6 **An Increase in the Domestic Interest Rate**

When the domestic interest rate (*i*) rises above the world interest rate, uncovered interest rate parity requires that there be an expected exchange rate depreciation. Given an unchanged expected long-run nominal exchange rate, the exchange rate must appreciate now in order to generate that expected depreciation.

home. *Holding the future expected exchange rate constant*, the only way for the current exchange rate to depreciate in future periods is to appreciate *now*. Over time, the exchange rate will indeed depreciate back to its long-run level. Importantly, capital movements are not necessary as long as asset returns are equalized. All that is necessary is that markets change the price. In highly integrated and efficient financial markets, this happens almost instantaneously.

The fundamental determinants of the nominal exchange rate

The 'cumulated' interest parity condition (19.14) states that the exchange rate is determined by present and future interest rates and is anchored by its long-run value. The exchange rate **fundamentals**, therefore, are those variables that influence the current and future domestic and foreign interest rates as well as the long-run exchange rate. Domestic and foreign economic conditions—as captured by the *IS-LM* and *AD-AS* frameworks—drive domestic and foreign interest rates. The fundamentals thus include present and future monetary and fiscal policies at home and abroad.

We can now see the link between the present short-run 'financial market' view of the exchange rate and the long-run or 'relative price of goods' view elaborated in Chapter 7. There we saw that the nation's intertemporal budget constraint determines the long run value $\bar{\sigma}$ of the real exchange rate, defined as $\sigma = SP/P^*$. Given the price levels $\bar{P}$ at home and $\bar{P}^*$ abroad expected to prevail in the long run, the long-run value of the nominal exchange rate is $\bar{S} = (\bar{\sigma}\bar{P}^*)/\bar{P}$. Now, in (19.14) we can always let the horizon extend far enough for S_{t+n+1} to correspond to $\bar{S}$, leaving us with the following expression:

(19.15)

$$S_t = \frac{(1+i_t)}{(1+i_t^*)}\frac{(1+i_{t+1})}{(1+i_{t+1}^*)}\frac{(1+i_{t+2})}{(1+i_{t+2}^*)}\cdots\frac{(1+i_{t+n})}{(1+i_{t+n}^*)}\bar{\sigma}\frac{\bar{P}^*}{\bar{P}}$$

This expression indicates that the current nominal exchange rate S_t depends on three sets of fundamentals:

• the path of future domestic and foreign interest rates, therefore all relevant economic conditions affecting the interest rate (as captured by the *IS-LM* framework): monetary and fiscal policies, foreign demand, etc.;

• the real exchange rate $\bar{\sigma}$ needed to meet the nation's intertemporal budget constraint, therefore the foreign debt and the country's competitive position;

• The level of prices $\bar{P}$ and $\bar{P}^*$ at home and abroad far into the future, therefore present and future inflation, both at home and abroad.

The list of fundamentals becomes long because of the ubiquitous role of the exchange rate in the relative price of goods and assets. In light of this, it is easy to understand why exchange markets react to a very broad range of indicators.

19.3.4 Market Efficiency or Speculative Manias? Implications for Macroeconomics

The efficient markets hypothesis poses something of a paradox: if markets are efficient, we shouldn't have to work very hard to obtain information on assets: the market has done it for us already! The current price of bonds, stocks, foreign exchange, and other financial instruments should represent a consensus based on information available to traders in the market. If stock prices decline today, we do not really need to find out why: the market has already processed the relevant information and drawn the correct implications. As a corollary, it is unlikely that anyone will outperform the market consistently. Reports of investors systematically beating the markets are more likely a sign of good luck than much else. For every winner we hear about, there are as many losers, who have disappeared from the market either because they ran out of money or because they were dismissed by their bosses. Using this line of argument, Nobel laureate Milton Friedman argued that speculation cannot be destabilizing: those traders who are responsible for pushing asset prices away from their 'fundamental' prices given by equation (19.12) are those who buy high and sell low. If prices return to their fundamental values, these destabilizing traders should consistently lose money and ultimately exit the market.

At the same time, some studies do turn up statistically measurable deviations from market efficiency. For example, if stock prices decline today, there is a tendency for them to revert over time to their previous values. This could imply that markets overreact to news, and that the markets may not be fully efficient. Yet why doesn't anyone buy these 'oversold' assets when it is profitable to do so? This would restore the price to its fundamental value immediately. The answer may lie in risk aversion, the fact that too few traders are willing to take positions and hold them long enough for this to occur. In this case, the deviation from the fundamental value may be consistent with the absence of profit opportunities, *given that the risk involved in correcting it has its own price*: the expected 'profits' are insufficient to compensate for the riskiness of betting against the irrational price. Betting against the market involves considerable risk, and deviations from fundamental values can get worse before they get better.

How and why might asset prices deviate from their fundamental values? It is always tempting to write off financial markets as irrational and prone to fads. But there are often more satisfying accounts which can be illustrated with two examples. One of them is the coexistence of professional traders and inexperienced amateurs. The other is the phenomenon of rational speculative bubbles.

Noise traders

In the first example, only a subset of traders are informed and have access to information about the true underlying value of assets, whereas the remainder are **noise traders** who act on limited 'noisy' information. These noise traders can be either irrational or simply misinformed, and they behave accordingly. The result is that they systematically lose money to the informed traders. Noise traders arrive continuously on the scene, with new ones replacing those who systematically lose and quit in disgust, so that there are always some of them around. Despite perfectly efficient and rational behaviour on the part of the professionals, stock prices may again diverge from their fundamental value for long periods of time.

Bubbles

The second account of deviations from efficiency is the presence of **speculative bubbles**, persistent deviations of asset prices from their fundamental values. To see how bubbles may arise, consider the share valuation example from Section 19.3.2, which resulted from a no-profit condition (19.10) between the share and the real interest rate r. Let us assume for simplicity that the real dividend is fixed forever at d. The fundamental value is:

$$\bar{q} = \sum_{i=0}^{\infty} \left(\frac{1}{1+r} \right)^{i+1} d = \frac{d}{r}.$$

It is constant and satisfies the no-profit condition equation (19.10), since $\Delta q = 0$. The puzzling observation is that an infinity of other paths of prices also satisfy (19.10). Consider the case where the stock price is higher than $\bar{q}$. With a constant dividend, the dividend/price ratio is now smaller than in the case of the fundamental value. For the no-profit condition to be satisfied, the right-hand side of (19.10) must remain equal to the real interest rate r. This is possible only if the share price is expected to rise tomorrow: the expected capital gain offsets the inferior rate of return provided by the dividend. Thus an overvalued share (when its price exceeds its fundamental value) calls for a continuing increase in price, further and further away from

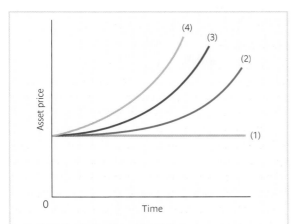

Fig. 19.7 Possible Stock Price Paths

Path (1) is the fundamental value of the asset. The price of the stock is equal to the present value of the dividend d, which is assumed constant, so it satisfies the arbitrage condition. Paths (2), (3), and (4) also satisfy the arbitrage condition, but are explosive bubbles.

the fundamental. Any price today can thus be validated by its subsequent evolution. Figure 19.7 plots possible evolutions of the share price over time, for given r and d. Only one initial price does not 'explode', and it corresponds to the fundamental value.

The non-fundamental paths, which are exploding without any apparent fundamental justification, are self-fulfilling: prices rise because they are *expected* to, without violating any market efficiency condition. The apparently inexorable growth of the share price is called a speculative bubble: a bubble because it keeps growing until it bursts, speculative because its growth is due to the expectation of future capital gains. A bubble is rational in the sense that it will continue to grow as long as traders believe that the bubble will continue to grow, validate market expectations, and offer the 'normal' return.

There is a catch, however: bubbles eventually burst. Why? Because if an asset price were to grow indefinitely, it would eventually exceed the world's wealth, becoming too expensive for anyone. And if no one can afford it, its price must decline. But the logic of a bubble is that its price must be expected to grow for a very long time—in principle, forever. If there is a known date at which the price will stabilize, the situation will unravel. When the price stabilizes, (19.10) shows that, with $\Delta q/q = 0$, the asset price must be equal to its fundamental from that point on. In the period just before the price stabilizes, for it to be a bubble, the price must be expected to rise, and therefore to be below the fundamental value. This is a contradiction, however, with the earlier observation that the price of a bubble is always above its fundamental. So the period just before stabilization of the price cannot be *below* the fundamental, it can only be *at* the fundamental. Working backwards, it is easy to see that the same reasoning applies all the way to the present: there can be no bubble that is anticipated to stop growing. So bubbles grow for a while but rational traders know that they will eventually burst and they stand ready to jump. As in a game of musical chairs, someone eventually can't move fast enough, and gets burned.

Bubbles may appear bizarre, because they have all the features of economic rationality and market efficiency, save for the end. Economists still debate whether bubbles really exist; and some wonder if they do not have some efficient aspect. Box 19.5 and Figure 19.8 review a famous historical bubble-like episode in Holland's seventeenth century. One does not have to go that far back in history, however, to find suspicious episodes: the run-up of the world's stock markets before the crashes of 1929, 1987, and 1989, the explosion of property prices in the UK and Scandinavia in the late 1980s, and in Ireland in the late 1990s. In each of these instances, reports by contemporaries indicate that market participants were convinced that the boom would continue. In each case, the bursting of the bubble was followed by serious economic dislocation. Most recently, the advent of the 'new economy' ushered in by the information technology revolution was touted as the end of economics as we know it, a technological 'golden age'. For an impartial observer, however, it looks more like a confirmation of 'plus ça change . . .'. The breathtaking ascent of high-tech stock prices in the late 1990s, followed by an equally sharp decline which occurred in 2000–1, is reminiscent of a bubble (see Figure 19.9).

Box 19.5 **Tulipmania**[9]

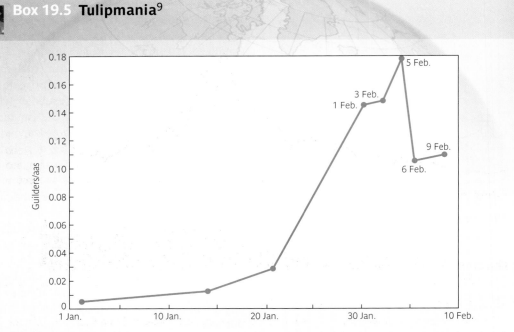

Fig. 19.8 Tulipmania, 1637

History has given us several instances of price behaviour that looks like speculative bubbles. In Holland, the price of rare tulip bulbs during the seventeenth century rose by extraordinary rates within a month's time, only to collapse thereafter.
Source: Garber (1990).

The bubble involved tulip bulbs with non-negligible fundamental value because they were of exotic varieties. Yet they became exorbitantly expensive. Figure 19.8 displays the price of tulip bulbs in the first two months of 1637, when they increased by over 3,000%, and then collapsed sharply. For example, the price of the Switser variety is reported to have fallen to one-twentieth of its 2 January 1637 price.

In one of the most authoritative accounts of the Tulipmania episode, Charles MacKay (1852) wrote:

The demand for tulips of a rare species increased so much in the year 1636, that regular marts for their sale were established on the Stock Exchange of Amsterdam, in Rotterdam, Harlem, Leyden, Alkmar, Hoorn, and other towns. Symptoms of gambling now became, for the first time, apparent. The stock-jobbers, ever on the alert for a new speculation, dealt largely in tulips, making use of all the means they so well knew how to employ, to cause fluctuations in prices. At first, as in all these gambling mania, confidence was at its height, and everybody gained. The tulip-jobbers speculated in the rise and fall of the tulip stocks, and made large profits by buying when prices fell, and selling out when they rose. Many individuals grew suddenly rich . . . Nobles, citizens, farmers, mechanics, seamen, footmen, maidservants, even chimney-sweeps and old clotheswomen, dabbled in tulips. People of all grades converted their property into cash, and invested it in flowers. Houses and lands were offered for sale at ruinously low prices, or assigned in payment of bargains made at the tulip mart. Foreigners became smitten with the same frenzy, and money poured into Holland from all directions. The prices of the necessaries of life rose again by degrees; houses and lands, horses and carriages, and luxuries of every sort, rose in value with them, and for some months Holland seemed the very antechamber of Pluto.[10]

---

[9]   Part of this description is taken from Peter Garber's (1990) survey of the Tulipmania boom.

[10]   Pluto was the ancient Greek god of wealth.

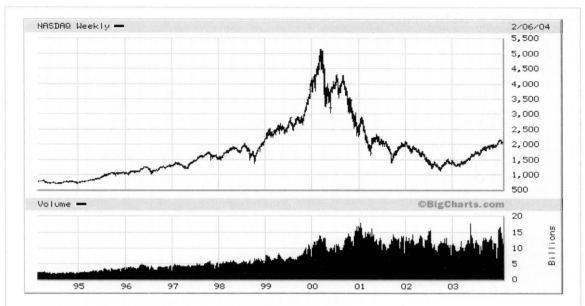

Fig. 19.9 The Rise and Fall of NASDAQ Stocks, 1996 – 2003

NASDAQ stands for the National Association of Securities Dealers Automated Quotation (system). It is the US stock exchange that specializes in high-technology companies, especially personal computers, telecommunication, and the internet. After more than quadrupling in value over the period 1997 – 2000, the NASDAQ index collapsed just as spectacularly by more than 60% from its all-time peak.

Source: www.bigcharts.com

19.4 Exchange Rate Determination in the Short Run

19.4.1 The Exchange Rate as an Asset Price

In the long run, as the relative price of goods, the real exchange rate's role is to move the current account and to enforce the intertemporal budget constraint. Chapter 7 shows how its behaviour is driven by real forces such as the country's net asset position and wealth, its productivity, world tastes. This view does not, however, fit the short run, as Figure 19.10, which presents day-to-day changes of the nominal $/€ rate, makes abundantly clear. Sharp changes are often followed by movements of similar magnitude in the opposite direction The variability of nominal exchange rates is often remarkably high, with daily changes of ±1% or more per day commonplace. (A daily change of 1% corresponds to an annual compounded return of more than 3,000%.) With sticky prices, these nominal fluctuations also characterize the real exchange rate in the short run. This is not the pattern that we expect from relative prices, but one that matches asset prices. In the short run, therefore, we think of the nominal exchange rate as the relative price of currencies. This section pursues

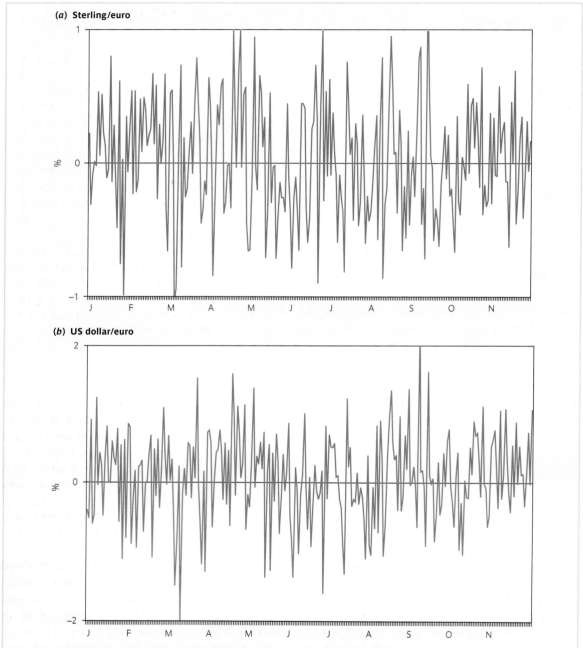

Fig. 19.10 Daily Changes of the Dollar/Euro Exchange Rate in 2003

Day-to-day variability of the nominal exchange rate is considerable. Sharp changes in one direction are frequently undone on the following day.

Source: European Central Bank.

Box 19.6 Mussa's Stylized Facts and the Asset Behaviour of Exchange Rates

In 1979, Michael Mussa, at the time professor at the University of Chicago, assessed the first half-decade of floating exchange rates after the end of the Bretton Woods system.[11] His observations, which remain true today, can be summarized in the following stylized facts:

1 On a daily basis, changes in floating foreign exchange rates are largely unpredictable.

2 On a month-to-month basis, over 90% of exchange rate movements are unexpected, and less than 10% are predictable.

3 Countries with high inflation rates have depreciating currencies, and over the long run the rate of depreciation of the exchange rate between two countries is approximately equal to the difference in national inflation rates.

4 Countries with rapidly expanding money supplies tend to have depreciating exchange rates vis-à-vis countries with slowly expanding money supplies. Countries with rapidly expanding money demands tend to have appreciating exchange rates vis-à-vis countries with slowly expanding money demands.

5 In the longer run, the excess of domestic over foreign interest rates is roughly equal to the expected rate of appreciation of the foreign currency. On a day-to-day basis, however, the relationship is more tenuous.

6 Actual changes in the spot exchange rate will tend to overshoot any smoothly adjusting measure of the equilibrium exchange rate, the real exchange rate predicted by the analysis of Chapter 7.

7 The correlation between month-to-month changes in exchange rates and monthly trade balances is low. On the other hand, in the longer run, countries with persistent trade deficits tend to have depreciating currencies, whereas those with trade surpluses tend to have appreciating currencies.

this lead. It provides an account of the short run—hour by hour or month to month—and then reconciles the interpretation of the exchange rate as the relative price of goods with that of the relative price of monies. Our goal is to explain the stylized facts listed in Box 19.6.

Like any other asset price, the exchange rate is a forward-looking variable. The exchange markets are continuously absorbing and assessing news regarding political conditions, releases of economic data, and pronouncements by government ministers, central bankers, bank analysts, prominent businessmen, gurus, etc. After the fact, much of this 'news' will be amended, made more precise, or disavowed if not actually proved wrong. In the meantime, however, it influences crucially the evolution of the exchange rate. This provides an explanation of the pattern shown in Figure 19.10. News—both genuine facts and rumours—moves the exchange rate up one

moment, and down the next. The fact that the 'news' component is so much more important than expected depreciation or appreciation deriving from UIP is consistent with the second stylized fact cited in Box 19.6. In practice, predictable trend changes—such as a return to PPP, a well-understood need to depart from PPP, or simply the changing profile of already expected interest rates—represent a relatively small part of short-term exchange rate movements.

When a variable changes randomly from period to period, it is said to follow a **random walk**.[12] In that case, the only change between its value today and its value tomorrow will be white noise, a random shock which can be as much positive as it can be negative and on average zero. Thus, the best next-period forecast of a variable that evolves as a random

[11] Ch. 20 discusses briefly the Bretton Woods system in more detail.

[12] Formally, a variable x_t follows a random walk when it evolves as $x_t = x_{t-1} + u_t$ where u_t is a 'white noise' (i.e. with expected value of zero and serially uncorrelated). At time $t - 1$, the best forecast of x_t is x_{t-1}.

walk is simply its current value. Surprisingly, perhaps, this most naive forecast often turns out to be the best one, indeed, this is the first stylized fact in Box 19.6. What about the fundamentals, then, are they useless? The next section attempts to rehabilitate them.

19.4.2 Money and Goods Market Equilibrium

As we need to clearly separate out the short and the long run, it is convenient to collapse time into two periods, today (period 1), and the indefinite future, that is, the long run (period 2). We also assume that output is constant at $\bar{Y}$.[13] Recall the *LM* curve which describes the money market equilibrium condition in each period $t = 1$ and 2:

$$(19.16) \qquad \frac{M_t}{P_t} = L(\bar{Y}, i_t).$$

Start with the short run, period $t = 1$, and assume for the time being that the long-run exchange rate S_2 is given. Given the nominal money supply M_1, money market equilibrium imposes a positive relationship between the current exchange rate and prices represented in Figure 19.11 by the upward-sloping *MM* schedule. To see why, imagine that the price level increases. This reduces the real money supply, so money demand must decline too. This requires that the nominal interest rate rises. Since the foreign interest rate i^* is taken as constant, UIP implies that the domestic interest rate i_1 increases only when the exchange rate is expected to depreciate. As we consider that the future exchange rate S_2 is constant, the current exchange rate must appreciate.[14] This is quite sensible: the excess demand for money that follows a price increase prompts domestic residents to borrow abroad; the ensuing capital inflow leads to an appreciation.

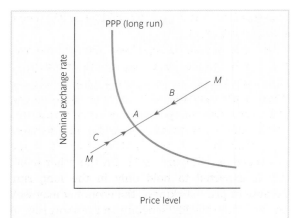

Fig. 19.11 General Equilibrium

Money market equilibrium implies a positive relationship between the exchange rate and the price level, the *MM* schedule. For a given nominal money stock, a price increase reduces the real money supply. Demand is equilibrated with supply by an increase in the interest rate which triggers an exchange rate appreciation. The long-run equilibrium in the goods market is characterized by PPP. This in turn implies an inverse relationship between the exchange rate and the price level, the PPP schedule. Equilibrium in the money market holds continuously, so positions off the *MM* schedule are not possible. In contrast, PPP is valid only in the long run—under some conditions—so in the short run, positions off the PPP schedule are possible. Long-run equilibrium occurs at point A, with equilibrium in both money and goods markets.

---

[13] This assumption makes a lot of sense in the short run since GDP does not change much from day or day. In the long run, GDP goes back to its trend growth path, and we simply overlook growth.

[14] This may look tricky, but it is quite simple. We want $(S_2 - S_1)$ to decrease—an expected depreciation—and S_2 is given, so it is S_1 that must change and it must increase for $(S_2 - S_1)$ to decrease.

This reasoning can be formalized by inserting the UIP condition (19.4) in the money market equilibrium condition (19.16) for period 1:

$$(19.17) \qquad \frac{M_1}{P_1} = L\left(\bar{Y}, i^* - \frac{S_2 - S_1}{S_1}\right).$$

Now we ask what determines the long-run exchange rate S_2. In the long run, goods market equilibrium is characterized by relative PPP, i.e. a stable real exchange rate. If prices abroad are constant, the real exchange rate remains unchanged as long as the exchange rate and the price level move in the opposite direction: any increase in the price level must be met by an equiproportional depreciation. This is represented by the PPP schedule in Figure 19.11.[15]

Now that we are equipped with these two schedules, we note that the money market is always in equilibrium, in both the short and long run. So the interest rate—and the exchange rate via UIP—must instantaneously jump to a level that guarantees equilibrium between money supply and demand. As a result, the economy is always located on the MM schedule of Figure 19.11. On the other hand, PPP is expected to hold only in the long run; because of price stickiness, the economy may well be away from the PPP schedule in the short run. In the long run, however, PPP reasserts itself and the economy must be at point A.

In the short run, point C below the PPP schedule corresponds to an **undervalued** exchange rate; either the nominal exchange rate is undervalued, or the price level is too low and there is an excess demand for domestic goods. Over time, the price level must rise or the exchange rate must appreciate. The long-run equilibrium in the goods market is restored as the economy moves up along the MM schedule. Conversely, at point B above the PPP schedule, either the exchange rate is **overvalued** or prices are too high. Because they are too expensive relatively to foreign competitors, domestically produced goods are in excess supply and their prices tend to be falling. The return to equilibrium requires a combination of declining prices and exchange rate depreciation.

19.4.3 The Monetary Approach: The Case of Flexible Prices

Starting from long-run equilibrium at point A in Figure 19.12 (so that $S_1 = S_2$ and $i = i^*$), we consider a once-for-all unexpected 5% increase in the money supply. Long-run neutrality implies that the price level must increase and the exchange rate must depreciate, both by 5%, proportionately to the money supply. This is why the MM schedule shifts

[15] The PPP schedule corresponds to $S = \sigma P^*/P$ where σ is the real exchange rate, assumed to be constant in the long run. Formally, it is a hyperbola. If a shock causes the long-run equilibrium real exchange rate to change, the PPP schedule shifts: outward in the case of real appreciation, inward in the case of a real depreciation.

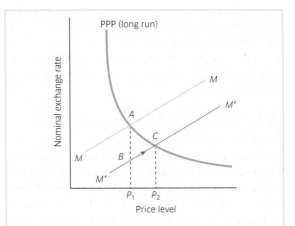

Fig. 19.12 Overshooting

An increase in the money supply shifts the money market equilibrium schedule down and to the right, from MM to M'M'. The new long-run equilibrium obtains at point C, the intersection of the PPP schedule (long-term goods market equilibrium) line and M'M'. In the short run, with sticky prices, only the exchange rate can move. The economy jumps to point B to maintain money market equilibrium. As point B lies below the PPP schedule, there is excess demand for domestic goods, and prices will start to rise. Over time, rising prices reduce the real money supply, pushing up the interest rate and therefore requiring an exchange rate appreciation as we move from B to C. As point B is below point C, the exchange rate initially overshoots its long-run level. This overshooting creates an excess demand for domestic goods and puts upward pressure on prices.

down and to the right to M'M'. The long-run equilibrium is at point C.

What about the short run? We assume first that prices are perfectly flexible, the neoclassical assumption. Then the goods market is always in equilibrium, and the economy is always at the intersection of the PPP and MM schedules. Neutrality occurs in the short run, and the economy immediately jumps from point A to point C. This result is known as the **monetary approach** to exchange rate determination. It says that *all* movements of the nominal exchange rate are due to changes in the nominal money supply. If money increases by 5%, both the price level and the exchange rate increase by 5% also. This provides an interpretation of

Box 19.7 Overshooting and Undershooting in the *IS-LM* Framework

The *IS-LM* framework allows us to consider the case—treated formally in the WebAppendix—where output varies. In Figure 19.13, we start from long-run equilibrium at point *A* (so $i = i^*$ and $S_t = {}_t S_{t+1}$). As in Section 19.3, we interpret i^* strictly as the foreign interest rate *only*. The increase in the money supply shifts the *LM* curve rightward to *LM'*. This depresses the domestic (nominal and real) interest rate and is met by a depreciation which shifts the *IS* curve to the right because of the gain in competitiveness. If spending is not too sensitive to the real interest rate (through investment) and to the exchange rate (through the current account), the *IS* curve shifts only to *IS'*. At point *B*, the domestic interest rate is below the world level and there must be a compensating expectation of exchange rate appreciation: the exchange rate overshoots. If spending is very sensitive to interest and exchange rates, the *IS* curve shifts further to *IS"* and the economy is at point *C*. The interest rate is *above* the world level; the exchange rate is expected to depreciate afterwards so it jumps less than, rather than more than, its long-run change: now there is undershooting. In both cases, the interpretation is the same: with sticky prices, an increase in the money supply creates an excess supply of money, so that output must rise to restore equilibrium. (With flexible prices, the real money supply remains unchanged as the price level rises in the same proportion as the nominal money stock.) If demand does not rise enough (point *B*), the interest rate must decline on impact, and there is overshooting. If demand is very responsive, it boosts output so much that the interest rate must rise, and there is undershooting.

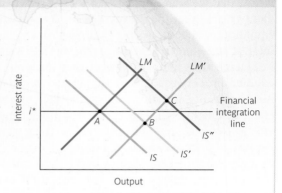

Fig. 19.13 Overshooting and Undershooting in the IS-LM Framework

Starting from full equilibrium at point *A*, an increase in the money stock brings the *LM* curve to *LM'*. As the nominal interest rate falls, the nominal exchange rate depreciates. With sticky prices, the real exchange rate depreciates, shifting the *IS* curve to the right. With a small shift (*IS'*) at point *B*, the domestic interest rate is still lower than abroad: the exchange rate must be expected to appreciate, hence an overshooting depreciation. With a larger shift (*IS"*) at point *C*, the exchange rate undershoots: since the domestic interest rate exceeds the world level, the exchange rate is rationally expected to further depreciate and is therefore below its long-run level.

Stylized Fact No. 3 in Box 19.6, which states that countries with high inflation rates have depreciating currencies. Yet if prices are sticky in the short run, the monetary approach will fall short of being a full explanation of nominal exchange rate behaviour, at least in the short run.

19.4.4 Overshooting with Rigid Prices[16]

What happens, then, if the price level is rigid in the short run, moving only slowly to eliminate goods

---

[16] The overshooting result was first established by Rudiger Dornbusch from MIT in 1976.

market imbalances and deviations from the equilibrium real exchange rate? We already know that, in the long run, prices recover flexibility and a 5% increase in the money supply remains described by point *C*. In period 1, however, the price level remains unchanged at P_1. At the same time, money market equilibrium must be maintained so, in Figure 19.12, the economy must jump instantaneously on to the new schedule $M'M'$. With prices unable to move in the very short run, the task of keeping the money market in equilibrium is performed by the nominal exchange rate which takes the economy immediately to point *B*. Over time, the price level adjusts and the economy will move up along *MM* from *B* to *C*.

A key feature of short-run point *B* is that it lies *below* long-run point *C*. The nominal exchange rate overshoots its long-run level, depreciating by more than the 5% warranted by the money stock increase. From *B* to *C*, overshooting is gradually eliminated as the exchange rate appreciates, while the price level rises to its new higher equilibrium level. That the exchange rate overshoots its equilibrium value is exactly Stylized Fact No. 6 in Box 19.6: actual changes in spot rates tend to overshoot any measure of the equilibrium exchange rate.

Box 19.7 provides an interpretation of over-shooting using the *IS-LM* framework. Figure 19.14 shows the evolution over time of the interest and exchange rates and of the price level in the more general case when there are more than just two periods. Once the money supply has increased, initially the interest rate must decline to maintain equilibrium in the money market. This raises demand for domestic goods. In response, the price level rises gradually towards its higher long-run level. The lower interest rate must be compensated by an expected appreciation. In the long run, the exchange rate will have moved from its initial value S_0 to S_1, which is 5% lower. In the short run, the exchange rate must jump below its long-run value: it *over*depreciates in order to appreciate thereafter. As the price level rises, the real money supply declines and the interest rate increases. A rising interest rate, in turn, coincides with an appreciating exchange rate. Figure 19.14 provides the background for Stylized Fact No. 4 in Box 19.6, which links depreciation rates in the long run to monetary growth. Money increases 'tend' to lead to depreciations, but overshooting may blur the picture as the initial depreciation is followed by a partially offsetting appreciation.

Overshooting shows that persistent deviations of real exchange rates from their equilibrium values, or **misalignments**, are possible, even with rational expectations. This would be impossible if goods prices were perfectly flexible. The overshooting result implies that monetary disturbances can

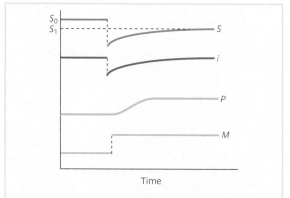

Fig. 19.14 Overshooting over Time
The nominal money increase eventually leads to an equiproportionate change in the price level—which rises—and in the exchange rate—which depreciates. Thus, we expect the nominal exchange rate to settle eventually at the level S_1, below its initial value S_0. Initially, with sticky prices, the money supply increase pushes interest rates down. This requires that the exchange rate be expected to appreciate, hence an initial overshooting undervaluation, i.e. a jump below S_1.

move the exchange rate away from PPP, *even in the absence of real disturbances*. This in turn affects consumption, the allocation of resources, firms' profitability, real wages, and the current account. Movements in the real exchange rate may also occur, of course, in response to real disturbances. Real disturbances, related to differences across countries in the rate of technological advances, tastes, or government policies, might be judged to be less frequent. Figure 19.15 shows the effective nominal and real exchange rates for the three major currencies: the US dollar, the euro, and the Japanese yen. Fluctuations are sizeable (some 50% over periods of two to three years is not uncommon) but occur in the form of long swings around a fairly steady mean. Strikingly, nominal and real exchange rates move closely together, which is an indication that prices are sticky and that monetary forces play an important role in the short-run determination of the real exchange rate.

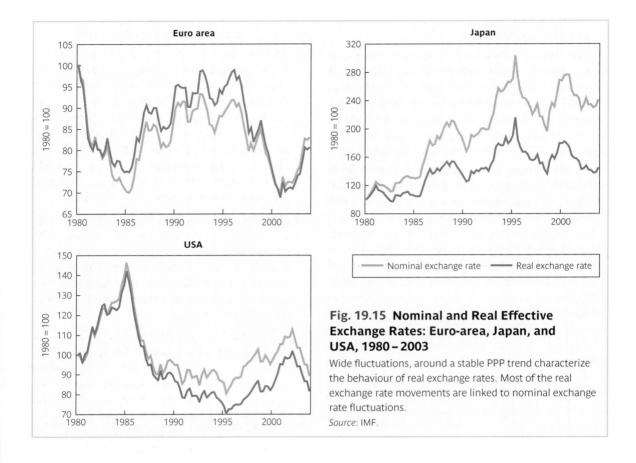

Fig. 19.15 Nominal and Real Effective Exchange Rates: Euro-area, Japan, and USA, 1980–2003

Wide fluctuations, around a stable PPP trend characterize the behaviour of real exchange rates. Most of the real exchange rate movements are linked to nominal exchange rate fluctuations.

Source: IMF.

❶ Summary

1 Asset markets put a price tag on the future and on risk. They allow households and corporations to decide on saving and borrowing without having to gather the whole array of uncertain information that affects their own future. They allow those savers who are most willing to bear risk to do so, at minimum cost.

2 While financial intermediaries can be thought of as intervening on financial markets on behalf of their customers, in fact most of the transactions correspond to trade among intermediaries.

3 Financial assets are traded with ease in large well-organized markets, they are durable, and they are cheap to store. Financial markets continuously balance the demand and supply of asset stocks, not just the flow increments to the stocks that are created each period. For stocks to be held voluntarily, returns among similar assets—similar in terms of risk and maturity—must be equalized.

4 The no-profit condition is a characteristic of efficient financial markets. In the absence of risk-taking, it takes the form of arbitrage. A good example of arbitrage is the covered interest parity condition: when capital is internationally mobile, a higher domestic interest rate is matched by a forward exchange rate premium.

5 In the presence of uncertainty and undiversifiable risk, the no-profit condition implies that expected returns are equalized up to a risk premium which rewards risk-averse agents for bearing risk. A good example of the no-profit condition is the uncovered interest parity condition: when capital is internationally mobile, an expected exchange rate depreciation should be compensated by a higher domestic interest rate, and conversely.

6 Markets are efficient when they gather all the available information and treat it to the point where prices reflect fully what is known and the risks attached to any single asset. The evidence on market efficiency is mostly favourable, in spite of phenomena such as speculative bubbles or noise trading.

7 If both uncovered interest parity and purchasing power parity conditions hold, real interest rates are equalized worldwide. Since PPP holds at best in the long run, real interest rate equalization is only a medium- to long-run proposition.

8 Exchange rates are forward-looking variables. An implication is that the uncovered interest parity condition determines today's exchange rate as a function of today's interest rates and the expected exchange rate next period.

9 Today's exchange rate is linked to present and future interest rates at home and abroad, and to the spot exchange rate far along in the future. The link takes the form of a chain of present and future uncovered interest parity conditions. All that is at present known about the future is reflected in today's value of the exchange rate. Changes in the exchange rate occur primarily because new information arrives, including revisions of expectations about the future.

10 The long- and short-run views of the exchange rate are not inconsistent. Real factors that drive the long-run real exchange rate are present in today's nominal exchange rate. The long-run exchange rate is the *anchor* that guides the path of future expected exchange rates and relates it to the current value.

11 The forward-looking aspect of the exchange rate explains why its behaviour closely resembles a random walk, since new information arrives randomly. This makes it hard to see the link between the exchange rate and its fundamentals which are typically considerably less volatile. Yet, they are present via the market's expectations of their future expected values.

12 With prices sticky in the short run, an increase in the money stock leads to an exchange rate depreciation which overshoots its long-run value. All other things equal, an increase in the stock of money leads in the long run to changes of the same proportion in the exchange rate and price level.

⊕ Key Concepts

- ◆ assets
- ◆ financial intermediaries
- ◆ risk aversion
- ◆ risk premium
- ◆ no-profit condition
- ◆ arbitrage, no-arbitrage condition
- ◆ covered interest parity (CIP)
- ◆ forward contract, forward exchange rate
- ◆ spot exchange rate
- ◆ hedged
- ◆ uncovered interest parity (UIP)
- ◆ market maker
- ◆ market liquidity

- ◆ maturity
- ◆ bid – ask spread
- ◆ term structure of interest rates
- ◆ consol, perpetuity
- ◆ real interest parity
- ◆ international Fisher equation
- ◆ fundamentals
- ◆ noise traders
- ◆ speculative bubbles
- ◆ random walk
- ◆ monetary approach
- ◆ undervaluation, overvaluation
- ◆ misalignment

❷ Exercises

1 Explain why the bid–ask spread can be thought of as the price of risk.

2 Assets markets are considerably more volatile than goods market. Asset markets balance stocks while goods market balance flows. What is the link between these two observations?

3 Consider three assets A, B and C with uncertain outcomes depending on three possible future states of the world:

  State of the world 1: A: €50; B: €100; C: €0
  State of the world 2: A: €0; B: €50; C: €100
  State of the world 3: A: €100; B: €0; C: €50
Is it possible to fully diversify risk?

4 Ten-year bond yields are 5.2% in Denmark compared with 4.8% in Euroland. Yet Denmark currently fixes its exchange rate to the euro. Does this necessarily represent an opportunity for pure arbitrage or risky yield arbitrage? Why or why not?

5 Suppose the interest rate for one-year Treasury bond is 5% per annum, and for a Treasury bond of two-year maturity, 7% per annum. By an arbitrage argument, at what rate could you lend in one year's time over a maturity of one year? Describe your trading strategy.

6 Insider trading occurs when some traders have superior private information which they use to 'beat' the market. In most countries, insider trading is forbidden on stock markets but not in exchange markets.

(a) Is it self-evident that insider trading on stocks should be banned? (Hint: think in terms of market efficiency.) Why do you think that insider trading is generally illegal?

(b) Why do you think that insider trading is not prohibited in foreign exchange markets?

7 Suppose that you could buy and sell US dollars for €1 and euros for ¥120, but that at the same time the dollar–yen rate was ¥115.

(a) What strategy would you pursue to take advantage of this 'money pump'? What would be the likely effect of the market's recognition of its existence?

(b) The example given in the previous problem ignores the bid–ask spread. How would your answer change if the bid–ask spreads were: $0.99–1.01/a, ¥118–122/a, and ¥113–117/$?

8 Assume prices are flexible. Using the apparatus introduced in Section 19.4, explore the short- and long-run implications for the exchange rate (British terms), prices, and interest rates of: (a) a permanent contraction of the money supply; (b) a permanent, exogenous increase in output; (c) a permanent, exogenous decline in the foreign price level.

9 (*formal*) Consider the example of a speculative bubble in the text (Section 19.3.4). Now imagine that while, as before, there are two assets, investors no longer have perfect foresight. The private asset can be purchased at variable real price q_t and pays a fixed real dividend d. Now, however, there is a probability s that in the following period $q_{t+1} = 0$ (i.e. the bubble will burst), and a probability $(1 - s)$ that it can be sold at $q_{t+1} > 0$. Investors are risk-neutral and equate the rate of return on the government 'safe' asset r with the expected rate of return on the private asset.

(a) Write down the arbitrage condition.

(b) Solve for the 'non-exploding' value of current q_t.

10 A small open economy with perfect capital mobility is characterized by the following equations:

$$M_t/P_t = 0.5\bar{Y} - 30{,}000[i^* - (S_{t+1} - S_t)/S_t]$$
$$i_t = i^* - (S_{t+1} - S_t)/S_t,$$

with $\bar{Y} = 8{,}000$ and $i^* = 0.04$.

(a) Draw the MM curve when $M_t = 2{,}000$ and $S_{t+1} = 1$, limiting yourself to the cases where P_t and S_t are positive. Show what happens when M_t rises to 3,000.

(b) In the long run, purchasing power parity holds so that $\sigma = SP/P^*$, with $\sigma = 1$ and $P^* = 0.5$. Show the PPP curve.

(c) What is the long-run price and exchange rate equilibrium when $M_t = 2{,}000$? When $M_t = 3{,}000$?

(d) Compute the short-term nominal exchange rate when M_t changes unexpectedly from 2,000 to 3,000, assuming that S was initially at its long-run equilibrium level.

⮕ Essay Questions

1 What are the conditions needed for a financial market to be efficient? Are they likely to be met in practice?

2 Why can exchange rate volatility create difficulties for trade in goods and services?

3 People have bad opinions of financial markets seen as a source of illegitimate enrichment for already wealthy people. How would you dispel this view?

4 Financial traders are often young people, who manipulate huge amounts of money and receive impressive salaries. How can you explain this?

The Architecture of the International Monetary System

20

20.1 Overview *492*

20.2 History of Monetary Arrangements *493*
20.2.1 The Gold Standard and How It Worked *493*
20.2.2 The Inter-war Period *496*
20.2.3 The Bretton Woods System of Fixed Exchange Rates *497*
20.2.4 The European Monetary System *501*

20.3 The International Monetary Fund *504*
20.3.1 IMF Assistance and Conditionality *504*
20.3.2 Special Drawing Rights *504*
20.3.3 Surveillance *505*

20.4 Currency Crises *506*
20.4.1 Crises, crises *506*
20.4.2 First Generation Crises *508*
20.4.3 Further Generation Crises *510*
20.4.4 Contagion *513*
20.4.5 Supervision *514*

20.5 The Choice of an Exchange Rate Regime *514*
20.5.1 The Old Debate: Fixed vs. Flexible Exchange Rates *515*
20.5.2 The New Debate: Financial Liberalization *515*
20.5.3 Monetary Unions, Currency Boards, and Dollarization *519*

Summary *521*

When we understand that Lombard Street is subject to severe alternations of opposite causes, we should cease to be surprised at its seeming cycles. We should cease too, to be surprised at the sudden panics. During the period of reaction and adversity, just even at the last instant of prosperity, the whole structure is delicate. The peculiar essence of our banking system is an unprecedented trust between man and man: and when that trust is much weakened by hidden causes, a small accident may greatly hurt it, and a great accident for a moment may almost destroy it.

—Walter Bagehot (1873)

20.1 Overview

The decade of the 1990s was the decade of currency and banking crises. The first outbreak was in Europe, when the Exchange Rate Mechanism of the European Monetary System fell victim to a speculative attack in the late summer of 1992, and all but collapsed in 1993. The spectre of financial crisis moved on to Mexico in late 1994. It reappeared in Thailand in mid-1997 and spread all over South-East Asia over the next six months, ravaging the area's banking systems. It returned to Russia and Brazil in 1998, leaving few countries untouched. Some leading banks and financial institutions in the USA, Japan, and Europe were badly shaken, some even went bankrupt. The international community did not stand idly by: tens of billions of US dollars were injected via the **International Monetary Fund** to put a stop to the crises, which spread like a modern-day plague. In the aftermath, the Fund faced fierce criticism, accused of being too harsh and intrusive by some, of perpetuating bad practices and lost causes by others, or of pouring too much money into lost causes. The international financial system was declared in need of a complete overhaul, but nothing happened as calm returned and the sense of urgency waned. Then Argentina defaulted on massive loans after the collapse of its famed currency board arrangement. In 2002 massive pressure led to a sharp fall of Brazil's currency, just because a left-wing president was about to be elected.

The international monetary world is a dangerous place. It is also changing. The emerging economies, formerly poor countries catching up with the developed world, are joining the bandwagon of globalization, a process both hailed and feared. And yet, many of the questions being debated are old ones. What exchange rate regime to adopt? Should capital movements be restrained? How to balance the relationship between the developed North and the poor South? What role for international financial institutions like the IMF and the World Bank? The present chapter revisits these old questions, and some new ones as well, with a fresh look. We have learned a great deal over the last decade, both about the theory of exchange rate crises and about the practice of exchange rate regimes.

Section 20.2 provides a quick overview of the history of the international monetary system, if only to help us understand the current situation. Section 20.3 describes in some detail the role and structure of the IMF, the linchpin of the present system. The crises of the 1990s are presented and interpreted in Section 20.4, paving the way for the perennial question of the appropriate exchange rate regime. The current debates are reviewed in Section 20.6.

20.2 History of Monetary Arrangements

20.2.1 The Gold Standard and How It Worked

For centuries, both domestic and international trade was carried out with gold and silver. Metallic monies were used for thousands of years because, as explained in Chapter 8, they were easily recognizable and acceptable by others. Being scarce, metal was a reasonably stable store of value; not easily subject to manipulation, it was a reliable medium of exchange. National currencies as we know them did not exist. Progressively over the nineteenth century, banknotes started to circulate alongside gold and silver. These notes were a promise to pay the bearer in precious metal. They were as good as the name of the issuer, mostly his honesty in not issuing more notes than he had precious metal. Initially at least, the notes were issued by private bankers, who often failed to exercise adequate self-discipline. As a result the banknotes were not always fully backed by metallic reserves, which led to occasional banking crises. This is one reason why central banks were created, and why they displaced private banks as issuers of paper money. Central banks were formally required to hold close to 100% gold or silver to back their issues of banknotes. These notes were convertible into gold, coins, or bullion at the holder's request, and conversion was indeed routine. With close to 100% backing, banknotes simply represented another, more convenient way of holding gold or silver.

The resulting arrangement, known as the **gold standard**, lasted from 1879 to 1914, less than forty years (see Box 20.1), and collapsed one month before the outbreak of the First World War. The gold standard era is sometimes nostalgically associated

---

 Box 20.1 Bimetallism and Gresham's Law

It was only at the end of the nineteenth century that gold became the premier international medium of exchange. For centuries, silver and gold had competed against each other. **Bimetallism**, as the system was called, established a fixed parity between gold and silver, and coins in both metals were usually accepted for all transactions, both nationally and internationally. The relative value of gold and silver was set by international agreements, which were occasionally called into question as new discoveries of either metal threatened to upset the parity. Troubled times then followed with the operation of **Gresham's law**. This principle states that the currency (metal) that is more valuable (in non-monetary markets) than its official rate stops circulating: 'bad money chases out good.'[1]

Partly because silver became more plentiful, bimetallism ceased to exist in Europe in the 1870s. The last major countries to defend bimetallism formed the Latin Monetary Union in 1865, setting a parity of 15.5 ounces of silver for 1 ounce of gold. This union consisted of Belgium, France, Italy, and Switzerland. (For this reason all save Italy adopted the 'franc' as the name of their national money.) In the USA, where a central monetary authority was absent, bimetallism survived for a longer time. The final blow occurred when the newly created German state switched to gold and unloaded large amounts of silver on the free market. The risk of complete gold loss in a world under a gold standard forced the remaining countries to abandon bimetallism entirely.

---

[1] Living in the sixteenth century, Sir Thomas Gresham had been in charge of royal finances, then became a foreign exchange trader in Antwerp until he created the Royal Exchange, better known today as the London Stock Exchange. It is sometimes argued that the gold standard in the UK was an artefact of Isaac Newton's decision in 1717 to undervalue silver in terms of gold; within little time, Sir Isaac had only gold on his hands.

with the fast growth and rapid industrialization of the time, and is regarded as a great economic success story. This 'success', in turn, is often attributed to the gold standard's automatic adjustment mechanism. In fact, the gold standard was not without problems, nor were these adjustment mechanisms as automatic as is often believed. But it remains a benchmark and, in many respects, new developments like monetary unions and currency boards (studied in Section 20.5.3) attempt to re-create some of its most desirable features. So it is well worth a hard look.

Domestic operation of the gold standard

In principle, the gold standard was a simple affair. Money was gold. Demand was stable, driven by the need to carry out everyday transactions. Supply too was quite stable; even large discoveries amounted to small disturbances, for the amounts brought out (the flows of newly coined gold) were small in comparison to existing stocks. The role of the monetary authorities was merely to establish and guarantee the gold content of their own currencies, the gold exchange rate.

International operation of the gold standard

Fixed Exchange Rates. Pegging a currency's value to gold fully determined all exchange rates vis-à-vis other gold currencies. For instance, if the Dutch guilder was set at the price of 50 per ounce of pure gold (the usual weight reference) and sterling was set at £25 per ounce, the guilder was worth £0.5. If the exchange rate were to decline to £0.4 (a depreciation of the guilder relative to sterling), it would make sense to purchase gold in the Netherlands with guilders, ship it to the UK, tender it to the Bank of England in exchange for sterling, and, finally, convert sterling into guilders. For every 100 guilders tendered in the Netherlands for gold, the transaction would yield 2 ounces of gold, sold in the UK to acquire £50. Selling these sterling balances against guilders at the 0.4 exchange rate would yield 125 guilders, a 25% profit! Such a prospect was sure to trigger large sales of sterling and large purchases of guilders in the exchange markets, promptly appreciating the guilder's value back to its only sustainable sterling value, £0.5. To be sure, the example ignores transaction costs, especially

the cost of transporting the gold across the sea.[2] Once these are accounted for, the exchange rate can move a little bit from the gold-implied parity, leaving a **band of fluctuation** within which it is not worth undertaking the buying, selling, and shipping. These bands were known as 'gold points', and are similar to exchange rate intervention bands employed in modern fixed exchange rate systems. They implied margins of fluctuation of about 1%.

Endogenous money supply. Being the way to settle exchanges, nationally and internationally, gold was freely flowing as the counterpart of payment imbalances. A country running a trade deficit would lose gold to its trading partners; the metal was physically shipped abroad to pay for the excess of imports over exports. The exported gold coins were then minted and coined in the currency of the surplus country. Thus, a trade deficit implied a shrinking money supply, a surplus meant an expanding money supply. This had two consequences. First, the reduction of the money supply in the deficit country led to higher interest rates and to a capital inflow; a capital account surplus financed the trade deficit. Second, higher interest rates tended to slow down economic activity and to depress prices, which improved the country's competitiveness and restored the trade balance. In the surplus country the process went in the opposite direction: balance of payment surpluses led to gold inflows, which raised the money supply and depressed interest rates. In the medium run, higher inflation would tend to reduce the surplus, as competitiveness is eroded (the real exchange rate appreciates). This symmetric process is the **Hume mechanism**, after the Scottish economist and philosopher David Hume who first described it.

The main benefits of the gold standard

The world has never seen, and probably never will see, a true pure gold standard. Still, some observers regret the passing of the gold standard. Why? First, the Hume mechanism had the virtue of credibility. Under a gold standard, monetary policy is entirely

---

[2] These transport costs are unnecessary if the participating countries are willing to acquire foreign currencies and swap them back at regular intervals—as was often the case in the heyday of the gold standard period.

Table 20.1 Inflation Rates in Five Countries, 1900–1913 (annual average rate of increase in GDP deflator, %)

France	Japan	USA	Germany	UK
0.9	2.8	1.3	1.3	0.9

Source: Maddison (1995).

determined by the stock of gold. In principle, it is out of the politicians' hands. Second, with the money supply naturally constrained by the availability of a rare resource, inflation is not likely to emerge on any significant scale. This is documented in Table 20.1. Third, there is no need for a particular country to be at the centre of the world monetary system, avoiding conflicts on which country that should be.

Limits of automatism

Despite these appealing aspects, the gold standard had its limitations. Sterling was the main currency, backed by the most developed financial centre, London. Britain had been on the gold standard longer than other countries, since 1819 when the Bank of England received its key statutes (Peel's Act). Furthermore, as the largest creditor country, Britain provided the rest of the world with sterling balances which often ended up as reserve currency held by other central banks.[3] Three consequences followed from Britain's hegemonic position. First, the Bank of England was able to set the interest rate for the rest of the world, but with its eye on British economic conditions. Second, the demand for sterling as a reserve currency allowed Britain to finance long-running balance of payments deficits, paid with sterling-denominated debt issued by the Bank of England. Britain could escape the automaticity of the Hume mechanism: its money supply was not declining because gold was not shipped to cover its deficits. Third, the widespread acceptability of sterling balances allowed the Bank of England to

maintain a ratio of reserves to deposits—known as 'the Proportion'—well below 100%; at the height of the gold standard late in the nineteenth century, the Proportion fluctuated between 30% and 50%. To the extent that its gold stock was shielded from the vagaries of the balance of payments and since the Proportion could vary, the Bank of England possessed considerable freedom to set its interest rate.

Britain was not the only country that tinkered with Hume's mechanism. Some countries actually imposed limits on gold exports and imports, as well as on minting and coinage. Many central banks accumulated sizeable reserves of foreign currencies, first and foremost in pounds sterling. Thus, the assumed link between metal and money supply was less than fully automatic. Furthermore, the gold reserves of the Bank of England eventually fell below the value of the Bank's liabilities towards other central banks, leading to an 'overhang' of unbacked British debt. It is something of a miracle that the overhang never threatened the credibility of external sterling liabilities.

The limits of a metallic standard

The automatic mechanism that is often considered as the main advantage of the gold standard does not come for free. It has a cost in terms of economic instability. And indeed the gold standard years typically display low inflation but greater output variability, in line with the trade-off between rules and discretion described in Chapter 16. If respected, the rules of the gold standard are very strict: the money supply is determined solely by the balance of payments, so macroeconomic adjustments must entirely be dealt with through wage and price changes. If wages and prices adjust slowly in a recession—that is a central message of Chapters 11 and 12—this adjustment process may take a long time. In the meantime, the economy 'goes through the wringer' of unemployment and recession.

Another problem is that the overall supply of gold depends on natural discoveries. Economic growth, on the other side, implies a continuously expanding demand for real balances. If gold discoveries do not match the demand needs, increases in the real money supply can occur only if the price level declines—i.e. the price of gold must rise. Figure 20.1

---

3 During the forty years preceding the First World War, some 20% of British savings were invested abroad.

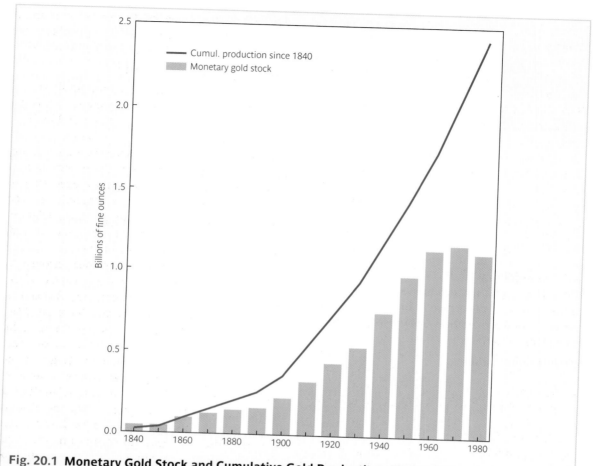

Fig. 20.1 Monetary Gold Stock and Cumulative Gold Production, 1840–1980
Although gold production has continued over time, its rate of increase has tapered off. At the same time, the demand for gold for industrial purposes has increased over the past hundred years. Perhaps not coincidentally, gold stocks held by central banks have remained flat for several decades.
Source: Cooper (1982).

shows that the gold supply has not been flowing regularly, with periods of scarcity coming on the footsteps of great discoveries in California, Alaska, and South Africa, as well as technological advances in mining and mineral processing. As these shocks were largely random, the money supply and the price level were hardly stable.

20.2.2 The Inter-war Period

Inter-war monetary arrangements can be conveniently arranged around three subperiods. The first ranges from the end of the First World War to the return to the gold standard in 1926. The gold standard was then maintained until 1931, and was followed by a period of managed float marked by competitive devaluations and a collapse of world trade as a consequence of the Great Depression.

The free float period (1919–1926)

In 1919 two countries, the UK and the USA, dominated the world monetary scene. During the First World War, USA remained on the gold standard, but the UK had suspended the mechanism and allowed the pound to depreciate by some 30%. Under the leadership of a young Chancellor of the Exchequer, Winston Churchill, Britain made the fateful decision to return to the gold standard at the pre-war parity. With strongly deflationary policies in place, the pound was brought back to its pre-war parity in 2001, but was still significantly overvalued because of the accumulated inflation since 1914. Germany and a number of other Central European countries returned to the gold standard only after experiencing and vanquishing their celebrated hyperinflations. France devalued the franc immediately after the war but underwent rapid inflation in the years 1922–6. Its return to the gold standard in 1926 after the Poincaré stabilization marked the return to the pre-war situation, albeit at a devalued parity.

Ephemeral gold standard (1927–1931)

The newly restored gold standard was a poor shadow of its predecessor. It had two competing centres, London and New York. Many currencies were badly misaligned; some were overvalued, like sterling; others were undervalued, like the French franc. Gold holdings became an ever smaller part of foreign exchange reserves as most central banks were accumulating dollar and pound balances. Free convertibility between banknotes and gold was suspended, and most central banks actively discouraged or prohibited the circulation of gold coins.[4] The Hume mechanism, was circumvented by sterilization operations. The vestiges of the system were the principle of currency convertibility[5] and fixed exchange rates.

When the Great Depression hit after 1929, the gold standard was already weak. With its overvalued currency, Britain was particularly vulnerable. Its gold reserves shrank quickly while France, with an undervalued currency, was accumulating gold and selling off its sterling balances. Soon Britain's official liabilities exceeded its gold reserves and it had to suspend convertibility in September 1931 and let sterling float. The gold standard was over.

The managed float (1931–1939)

Britain allowed the pound to depreciate sharply to about \$3.3/£, and a number of countries holding large sterling balances followed suit (Table 20.2). Formerly overvalued currencies became undervalued. At a time when all countries were struggling against the Great Depression, these devaluations were a tempting means of exporting the recession to other countries by achieving a competitive trade advantage. A gold bloc, including France, Belgium, the Netherlands, Italy, Switzerland, and Poland, was established to resist the temptation of retaliatory depreciations. The situation worsened seriously in 1933 when the USA, the remaining centre of the gold standard, imposed an embargo on gold exports, introduced exchange controls, and depreciated the dollar from \$20.67 to \$35 per ounce of pure gold. The *coup de grâce* was the dissolution of the gold bloc following the devaluation of the Belgian franc in 1935. 'Beggar-thy-neighbour' policies (competitive devaluations) followed, but were self-defeating since each country attempted to devalue vis-à-vis all the others. The next step was a 'tariff war': each country raised its tariffs to restrict imports, thus encouraging the substitution of domestically produced products. Imports declined but so did exports, as other nations followed suit. While the aim of boosting output failed, international trade collapsed as shown in Figure 20.2.[6]

20.2.3 The Bretton Woods System of Fixed Exchange Rates

The principles

Preparations for the **Bretton Woods conference** of July 1944 started long before the end of the Second World War.[7] The conference led to the creation

---

[4] In some cases, e.g. Britain, convertibility was possible only for large denominations, since the Bank of England restricted its conversion to bullion (as opposed to coins). The system is sometimes referred to as the 'gold bullion standard'.

[5] A currency is convertible when holders, both private and official, may exchange it without restriction. Convertibility does not necessarily imply a fixed exchange rate, since a floating rate system also allows participants freely to purchase and sell foreign exchange.

[6] Remember: $Y = C + I + G + X - Z$: *ceteris paribus*, reducing Z raises Y, but if X falls by the same amount, there is no net gain.

[7] Named after a small ski resort in the US state of New Hampshire. The conference considered two plans published in 1943, prepared for the USA by Treasury Secretary Harry White, and for the UK by John Maynard Keynes. The White plan eventually prevailed.

Table 20.2 Beggar-thy-Neighbour Depreciations, Various Countries, 1931–1938 (value of currencies as a % of their 1929 gold parity)

	1931	1932	1933	1934	1935	1936	1937	1938
Belgium	100.1	100.2	100.1	99.9	78.6	72.0	71.7	71.8
Denmark	93.5	70.3	55.8	50.0	48.5	49.0	48.6	48.1
France	100.1	100.3	100.0	100.0	100.0	92.4	61.0	43.4
Germany	99.2	99.7	99.6	98.6	100.3	100.1	99.7	99.6
Italy	98.9	97.4	99.0	97.0	93.0	82.0	59.0	59.0
Norway	93.5	67.2	62.7	56.3	54.5	55.2	54.7	54.1
The Netherlands	100.1	100.3	100.1	100.0	100.0	94.9	80.9	88.8
Switzerland	100.6	100.6	100.2	100.1	100.0	92.6	70.2	70.0
UK	93.2	72.0	68.1	61.8	59.8	60.5	60.0	59.3
USA	100.0	100.0	80.7	59.6	59.4	59.2	59.1	59.1

Source: League of Nations, *Statistical Bulletins*.

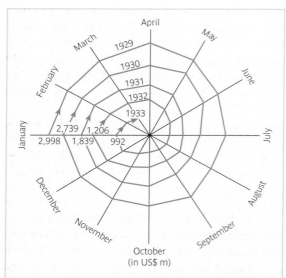

Fig. 20.2 The Decline of World Trade during the Great Depression

During the period 1929–33, the enormous increases in world trade that had been accomplished in the previous three decades were wiped out by a spiral of protectionist measures. This famous illustration by Professor Charles Kindleberger of MIT shows just how quickly trade wars can get out of hand.

Source: Kindleberger (1973).

of the International Monetary Fund (IMF). The new world monetary order was conceived as the antidote to the inter-war situation:

- Exchange rates were to be fixed; realignments required prior IMF approval.

- The IMF could provide loans as an alternative to devaluation for countries facing balance of payments difficulties.

- The dollar was the centre of the system. All countries officially declared a fixed parity, called a par or central value, vis-à-vis the US dollar, which itself pegged to gold directly. Currencies were allowed to deviate by no more than 1% from the par value.

- Exchange controls and tariffs were allowed only as temporary measures for the immediate post-war period.[8] In the event, full currency convertibility was only achieved in Europe in 1958, and a number of developing countries still have non-convertible currencies and capital controls.

Gold and the dollar

Officially, all currencies were defined in terms of gold. Yet, at the end of the Second World War, the

---

[8] Keynes was in favour of controls on short-term capital flows. The rolling back of tariffs was later entrusted to the GATT (General Agreement on Tariffs and Trade).

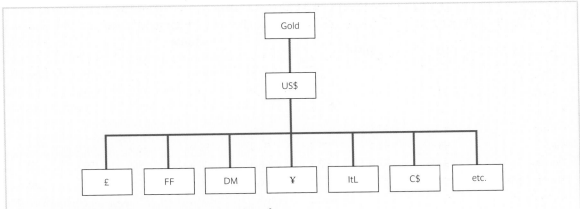

Fig. 20.3 The Three Layers of Bretton Woods
The three layers of the Bretton Woods system consisted of gold, the US dollar, and the other participating currencies. The USA declared a gold parity for the dollar, thereby pegging to gold. Intervention took place mostly in dollars, but implicit was the understanding that gold stood behind the dollars.

USA held about 70% of all gold reserves and was the only country credible enough to set a gold parity. With the US Marshall Plan providing them with dollar balances, the most obvious approach for the other countries was to declare a parity vis-à-vis the US currency.[9] The outcome was a *de facto* three-tier system, represented in Figure 20.3. Gold remained the fundamental standard of value, but for all currencies this was mediated by the dollar, hence the name **gold exchange standard** given to the Bretton Woods system. The system thus relied on the ability of the USA to maintain the declared parity of $35 per ounce of gold.

The International Monetary Fund

For a long while, the Bretton Woods system worked rather well. After a rash of post-war parity adjustments—including an unauthorized devaluation of the French franc in 1948—exchange rate stability prevailed. Trade expanded quickly and was easily financed by dollar balances, provided initially by the Marshall Plan, then by US trade deficits and the resulting capital flows. The IMF became the respected watchdog of the fixed exchange rate system. It developed an elaborate system of loans to countries suffering balance of payments difficulties.

Its resources were provided by member-country deposits, 25% in gold or US dollars—depending on the country's gold stock—and 75% in the country's own currency. The size of a country's deposit, based on its size in international trade, determines its **quota**. Quotas determine each member country's voting weight and its borrowing rights, and are set anew every five years.

Devaluations were in principle restricted to cases of 'fundamental disequilibria', balance of payments deficits not of a temporary (cyclical) nature. In order to help member nations avoid devaluation, the IMF made, and still makes, resources available for immediate lending—called 'purchase agreements' when effected and 'repurchase' when reimbursed. Each member country is eligible for immediate lending for up to its quota. Beyond that, lending becomes conditional: the IMF requests a formal agreement on specific policy steps and results designed to solve the 'non-fundamental' part of external disequilibria. This **conditionality** has become the central source of power of the IMF, and has survived the collapse of the Bretton Woods system.

The Triffin paradox and the collapse of the Bretton Woods system

As economies grew and international trade developed, more 'international money' was needed. Since the US dollar was the international money, more

---

9 The Marshall Plan was a massive aid programme for post-war Western Europe and Japan funded by the USA.

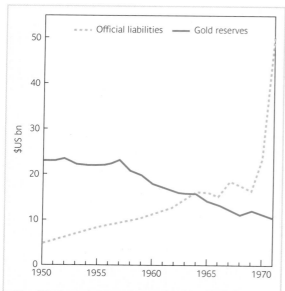

Fig. 20.4 US Official Liabilities and Gold Reserves, 1950–1970

As long as foreigners were willing to hold dollars, the USA could finance its large balance of payments deficits by increases in foreign holdings of official assets (dollars held by central banks). Yet the gold reserve of the USA declined over the entire period shown, as foreign central banks occasionally tendered their dollars for gold. Sometime in 1964, the stock of external official claims against the US gold exceeded the dollar's gold backing. At that moment, the credibility of the gold exchange standard was called into question.

Sources: Dam (1982); IMF.

A conjunction of economic and political events brought the situation to a climax. The Vietnam War and ambitious domestic social programmes (President Johnson's 'Great Society') led to increased public spending in the USA, which accelerated growth and inflation and deepened the current account deficit. At the same time, countries critical of the Bretton Woods arrangement began to protest loudly. French President de Gaulle publicly complained about the 'privilège exorbitant', which allowed the USA to use seigniorage to finance its political activities (the Vietnam War) and economic power (the acquisition of European corporations by US companies at the time). In a dramatic gesture, France began to swap dollars for gold in the mid-1960s, increasing its precious metal stock from $3.7 to $5.2 billion between 1964 and 1966.

The markets took notice. Anticipating an increase in the price of gold, they sought to buy it while it was still cheap. The response of the monetary authorities was to form the Gold Pool (Belgium, Italy, the Netherlands, Switzerland, West Germany, the UK, and the USA, with France inactive after 1967), an agreement to sell gold to maintain the $35/ounce parity. As the drain on official gold holdings accelerated, the Pool pulled out of the gold market and declared that they would henceforth trade gold only among themselves—would neither sell to nor buy from private parties—at the official price. The market price of gold rose substantially higher than the official parities. Tensions within the Gold Pool grew until President Nixon's historic decision to suspend the gold parity of the US dollar on 15 August 1971.

From the Smithsonian Agreement to Jamaica

The severing of the gold–dollar link destroyed a key component of the Bretton Woods arrangement, but the gold crisis was not the sole factor in its demise. Inflation had been rising in most countries in the late 1960s, but at increasingly different rates (Figure 20.5), challenging exchange rate parities that had remained unchanged since the late 1940s.[11] Speculative capital movements followed. Britain

dollars would have to be made available to the world economy. For internationally held dollar balances to grow, the USA must run balance of payments deficits, just as Britain did during the days of the gold standard. Inevitably, US official liabilities abroad must outgrow the country's gold reserves. Figure 20.4 shows that this happened in 1964. Yet at this point, the USA can no longer guarantee the gold value of the US dollar. This is the **Triffin paradox**,[10] a fatal weakness of the gold exchange standard.

---

[10] It is named after the Belgian economist Robert Triffin who identified the 'fundamental flaw' of the Bretton Woods system.

[11] The French franc was devalued in 1958; the Deutschmark and Dutch guilder were revalued in 1961.

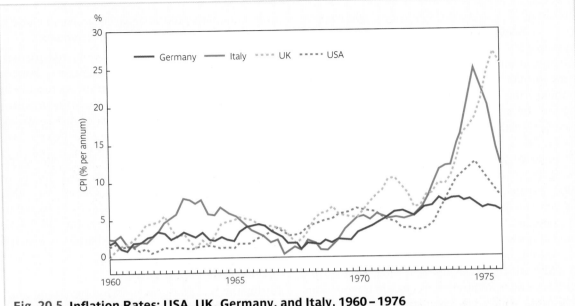

Fig. 20.5 Inflation Rates: USA, UK, Germany, and Italy, 1960–1976

Inflation rates during the Bretton Woods era moved closely together, which is characteristic of a fixed exchange rate regime. As soon as the system collapsed in 1971, inflation rates diverged sharply.

Source: IMF.

and Italy came under IMF conditionality in 1969. The pound was devalued in 1967, followed by the French franc in 1969, while the Deutschmark was revalued. The delinking of the dollar from gold opened the Pandora's box for further realignments. The credibility of the exchange rate system was severely damaged.

The last major effort to save the sinking ship was an agreement reached in December 1971 during a conference at the Smithsonian Institution in Washington, DC. The dollar was devalued vis-à-vis gold to $38 per ounce, yet remained inconvertible into gold, even among central banks. Some currencies were revalued, others devalued; the margins of fluctuations were enlarged from 1% to 2.25% around par value, while the European countries maintained a reduced (half) margin: this was the 'Snake' arrangement. By the end of 1972, the pound was floating, soon to be followed by the Swiss franc, the Italian lira, and the Japanese yen. In March 1973, the remaining 'Snake' members decided to float jointly vis-à-vis all other currencies including

the dollar within a wider 2.25% margin. France left, then re-entered, as did Italy; then both left again. Sweden and Norway joined informally. By 1975 the principle of fixed exchange rates was more or less dead, at least for the convertible currencies of the industrialized countries. In January 1976, the Jamaica agreement made official the new role of the IMF: from then on, it would be in charge of overseeing a world monetary system of increasingly flexible exchange rates.

20.2.4 The European Monetary System

For Europe, the Bretton Woods system had offered a convenient, if indirect, way of pegging their currencies to each other, and this arrangement had deepened economic ties within the Common Market, consisting of the member countries of the European Community (EC).[12] The demise of the

---

[12] The European Community is the predecessor of the European Union. The name change was officially decided in Maastricht in 1991.

gold exchange standard posed a problem with both economic and political implications. The response was the establishment of the European Monetary System (EMS) which began operation in March 1979. All nine European Community (EC) members at the time formally joined the EMS, but the UK deferred participating in the **Exchange Rate Mechanism** (ERM), the system of fixed exchange rates, until October 1990. With the exception of Sweden, all newer EC (henceforth EU) members (Greece, Spain, Portugal, Austria, and Finland) subsequently joined the ERM. After violent **speculative attacks** on the ERM parities in September 1992, Italy and the UK left the ERM; Italy rejoined in 1997. The ERM disappeared formally with the launch in 1999 of the **European Monetary Union** (EMU); a new EMS-II was established for EU member countries not part of EMU which nevertheless wanted to fix their exchange rates to the euro; its current members are Denmark, which has been given an exemption, and the countries that joined the EU in 2004.[13] EMS-II will be used as the gateway to EMU for new EU members.

Key features of the EMS

Three original features characterized the first version of the ERM:

+ *Bilateral Parities.* Exchange rates were fixed but adjustable. In theory at least, there was no special-status currency, like the US dollar under Bretton Woods. Fixity was defined as an official central **parity** between any pair of member currencies: a central rate, and a band of fluctuation initially set at ±2.25%, which was expanded to ±15% in August 1993, following a major exchange rate crisis.[14]

+ *Consensus Decisions.* A country could not alter its parity within the system unilaterally.

---

[13] At the time of writing, not all of them have yet joined the EMS, but all are expected to do so. Britain and Sweden have declined to participate in either the EMU or the EMS-II.

[14] Technically, the ERM parities were defined vis-à-vis the ECU, the forerunner to the euro, which was simply a basket of currencies of all EMS members. Bilateral parities were derived as cross rates implied by the central ECU parities. A special ±6% band was employed temporarily by Italy, the UK, Portugal, Spain, and Greece.

Realignments had to be agreed upon by every member. Despite the apparent restrictiveness of this rule, realignments are not infrequent.

+ *Mutual Support.* In order to defend the parities, member central banks were allowed to borrow virtually unlimited amounts from each other at very short notice. Prompt repayment was required —normally within forty-five days—but revolving credits were possible.

In practice, the German mark emerged as the central currency. The Bundesbank intervened mostly in US dollars, whereas the other members used EMS currencies more frequently. Germany appeared to manage its exchange rate vis-à-vis the US dollar, leaving it to the other central banks to manage theirs vis-à-vis the Deutschmark.

The four phases of the EMS

During the first phase, from its establishment until the mid-1980s, the ERM operated as a fairly loose system which tolerated member countries' diverse tastes for inflation. Realignments were frequent and undramatic, aimed at correcting deviations from purchasing power parity (PPP) resulting from persistent differences in inflation rates between participating countries.

The second phase, from the mid–1980s to 1992, was marked by the gradual emergence of the Deutschmark as the system's anchor currency. Realignments were successfully avoided from January 1987 to September 1992. All countries tried to emulate the mark's strong currency status and identified low inflation as the main objective of monetary policy. During this period, the EMS came to be perceived as a major success: the absence of any realignment for nearly six years was attributed to adroit policy co-ordination. Emboldened by success, the authorities proceeded to prepare a shift to a single currency: the result was the Maastricht Treaty adopted by EU heads of state late in 1991.

This period of tranquillity and optimism came to an abrupt end in the summer of 1992. During the subsequent third phase of crisis and turbulence, continuous upheaval rocked the ERM ship, and it nearly sank. Not only did several realignments occur in quick succession, but two currencies actually left the ERM to float on their own. Roughly a year later, in August 1993, the margins of fluctuation were widened to ±15%, and the fixed exchange rate system hardly differed from free floating.

The fourth and last phase of the EMS, which represented two decades of European monetary history, an 'ERM without teeth', was hastily designed in the wake of speculative attacks. With 15% wide bands, the situation was stabilized, allowing an orderly transition to EMU.

The impossible trilogy

With hindsight it is easy to understand why the ERM was under duress. The globalization of international financial markets brought near-perfect capital mobility with it, allowing investors and speculators to swap billions of short-term assets at the push of a button. A central bank which commits to fixing an exchange rate in effect becomes the ultimate market maker in the money market, and is obliged to accommodate at the set parity all transactions that the market does not. This commitment, as was made clear in Chapter 9, is inconsistent with an independent monetary policy.

The coexistence of fixed exchange regimes and capital controls is thus more than coincidental. Capital controls enable countries participating in fixed exchange rate arrangements to preserve some monetary autonomy. The countries that use capital controls tend to have higher inflation. Indeed, controls may be essential to organize orderly realignments in the face of market attacks.

These policy conflicts and dilemmas are summarized neatly as the **impossible trilogy**. This principle states that the following three aspects of a monetary system are jointly incompatible:

1 full capital mobility;
2 fixed exchange rates;
3 monetary policy independence.

They are, however, taken in pairs, feasible and have been observed throughout monetary history, and even today. The impossible trilogy is a direct implication of the Mundell–Fleming (IS-LM) framework: if capital is fully mobile, the interest rate is given exogenously by the foreign rate i^*, and the LM curve is given by cumulated net capital inflow.

This principle offers a powerful framework for reviewing the EMS experience. The early EMS was able to survive because of the presence of capital controls. During the first phase, it allowed for the coexistence of fixed exchange rates and some degree of monetary independence in the form of different inflation rates compensated for by periodic realignments. The second phase was an attempt to adopt the same monetary policy everywhere under German leadership. As long as economic conditions did not call for different policies, this was a relatively costless way to cope with the impossible trilogy. It is during that period that capital controls were dismantled. However, the shock of German unification and a worldwide recession in the early 1990s, which raised the costs of the loss of monetary policy independence, changed all that. The crises that followed correspond to the travails that go with ignoring the impossible trilogy. The solutions adopted—free floating in Italy and the UK, wide bands elsewhere—correspond to the abandonment of the fixed exchange rate.

Once capital controls are removed, the choice boils down to either a single monetary authority or a free float. The experience of 1992–3 shows that the temptation of monetary independence plays havoc with a fixed exchange rate arrangement. Politically, it was probably unavoidable that countries relinquishing monetary independence in a system of fixed exchange rates would challenge the Bundesbank's leadership, just as France challenged the American *privilège exorbitant* three decades previous. It is not surprising that the countries that pledged to abandon capital controls in the mid-1980s—Belgium, France, Italy, and Spain—soon thereafter proposed the creation of a European Monetary Union. Nor is it surprising that the Bundesbank initially expressed doubts about the urgency of taking a step which amounted to sharing its undisputed control over European monetary policy.

20.3 The International Monetary Fund

The influence of the IMF is probably stronger today than in the heyday of the Bretton Woods system, if only because it is now in charge of a system that is less internally inconsistent than before. In the post-Bretton Woods 'system', each country is free to choose its own exchange rate regime, and there is no agreed-upon international currency. Gold has long been 'demonetized', meaning that it is no longer a reference, and many countries have since sold large parts of their gold stocks.

20.3.1 IMF Assistance and Conditionality

Countries continue to occasionally face balance of payment problems, although they are somewhat different from the Bretton Woods era. In principle, countries are now free to depreciate their currencies in response to adverse shocks, and over the longer haul such policies can bring the current account back to levels consistent with an intertemporal budget constraint. Frequently, though, the authorities prevent their exchange rate from adjusting to shocks by intervening in the foreign exchange markets, sometimes with borrowed foreign exchange. Eventually they may exhaust their foreign exchange reserves. What can they do then? An obvious answer is to treat the causes, and not the symptoms of the crisis. Taking remedial action, usually moving away from undisciplined monetary and fiscal policies, requires time, however, and the house is burning. The solution is to call the IMF, the international fire-fighter.

When called upon in an emergency, the IMF proceeds in three steps. It first assesses the situation and makes recommendations to the authorities. Then comes conditionality: an emergency loan is made available and the troubled country commits itself to a number of policy actions. Finally, as the loan is being disbursed, typically in several instalments, the IMF monitors the implementation of the agreement and may suspend further disbursements if the country in question is violating its commit-

ments. In an average year, some ten to twenty standby loans are arranged.[15] The average volume of loans outstanding represents about 12% of world exports. In 2004, 182 countries were members of the Fund.

It is important to stress that the Fund's assistance is not a gift, but a loan, generally with a maturity of 1–4 years. The interest rate charged is slightly above the market rate to discourage using the Fund as a cheap source of money. Most private financial institutions deal only with sovereign borrowers in good standing with the IMF, so the Fund usually has a great deal of leverage over borrowing countries, which are generally excluded from the private capital market. This explains, of course, why countries in trouble turn to the IMF and are also willing to accept the conditions that it requests. Despite popular beliefs to the contrary, most countries actually pay back their loans. The reason is that the IMF has priority over all other creditors, and not repaying the IMF means being excluded from all other sources of international financing. Only a handful of 'pariah' countries have defaulted on IMF loans, and have to pay back when and if they want to re-enter the international financial arena. Most eventually do.

20.3.2 Special Drawing Rights

Despite having lost the official status it enjoyed in the Bretton Woods system, the US dollar remains the *de facto* means of payment for international trade and the foreign exchange reserve of choice at central banks. Although it is sometimes asked whether the euro might challenge or replace the US dollar, the more interesting question is: why should the international means of payment be any particular country's currency? In the late 1960s,

---

[15] Standby loans are made in emergency cases; the IMF offers a large menu of lending facilities tailored after particular needs. They can be seen at the IMF website: **www.imf.org/external/np/exr/facts/glance.htm**.

many countries lobbied for the creation of a new world currency, reviving an old idea which had been defeated at the Bretton Woods conference in 1946.[16] If the IMF could be transformed into the world central bank, it was thought, it could issue its own currency for all central banks to settle their payments, borrow from each other, and intervene on exchange markets. Unsurprisingly the USA, the Fund's largest shareholder—with a veto right—objected.

With the objective of increasing and stabilizing the supply of international liquidity, it was decided at the Rio Conference in 1967 to create the **special drawing right** (SDR). SDRs can be seen as a line of credit allocated by the IMF to each country in proportion to its quota defined above. Each member country can draw on its line of credit to obtain convertible currencies from the Fund. At the time of its conception, the SDR was valued at the rate of SDR 35 per ounce of gold, thus making it worth exactly US$1. The SDRs were not however backed by gold or dollars; just like money created by banks, SDRs are valued simply because they are accepted.[17]

After gold convertibility was suspended, the SDR's value was redefined as a basket of four currencies.[18] SDRs yield an interest rate—the weighted average of interest available on the four underlying currencies. Symbolically, the SDR is the IMF's unit of account. As a basket, it is less volatile than any of its components, which has made it convenient for other purposes. Some countries peg their exchange rate to the SDR. Private debt issues have been

denominated in SDRs, although technically they are just a basket of the constituent currencies. Some 9 billion SDRs were initially created in 1970, and more were subsequently added, the last time in 1981, to a cumulative total of 21.4 billion. A new allocation was decided in 1997.

20.3.3 Surveillance

The IMF is not just a firefighter; it is also a safety inspector. It continuously monitors the macroeconomic scene in each member country in order to detect possible risks to its currency and to keep abreast of the local situation, should an emergency arise. Surveillance takes several forms:

◆ Annual visits and evaluations (called Article IV consultations). The IMF's economic assessments and recommendations, once highly confidential, are now posted on the Fund's website (each country has the right to refuse the release of this information, but that is considered a bad signal).

◆ Twice a year, the IMF publishes the *World Economic Outlook* which outlines its views of the situation in member countries.

◆ For countries which are in difficult situations, the IMF conducts 'enhanced surveillance', which means more frequent evaluations and recommendations.

◆ For countries which have borrowed from the Fund, the so-called programme countries, the monitoring is more or less permanent, based on agreed-upon targets for policies and outcomes.

Each government knows that its policies are monitored and that the conclusions are presented to the Executive Board of the Fund. Box 20.2 explains how decisions are made. Surveillance is justified as a preventive means of avoiding disruptive policies that wrecked the world economy during the inter-war period. When countries pursue economic policies that are criticized by the IMF, this disapproval is noticed by the outside world and usually results in internal and external political and financial pressure, which can go far in correcting aberrant policies.

---

[16] The 'Keynes Plan' envisioned the creation of an international reserve currency, the bancor, which would play the role gold did in the old gold standard era, but which would be supplied by an international agency, i.e. not the United States.

[17] Hence the following quote by the economist Fritz Machlup: 'Now the forward-looking experts of the Fund and the negotiating governments have proved that their reputation for backwardness in economic thinking had been undeserved. All that matters for the acceptability of anything as a medium of exchange is the expectation that others will accept it. . . . Money needs takers, not backers' (quoted by Dam 1989: 152).

[18] The four currencies, and their weights in the basket, are the US dollar (44%), the euro (25%), the yen (9%), and the pound (12%), reflecting their international use. The weights are revised every five years.

Box 20.2 How the IMF is Managed

The ultimate authority is exercised by the IMF's Board of Governors which meets, in principle, once a year. The governors are the finance ministers or central bank governors of all member countries. Voting is in proportion to each country's quota. In practice, the Board of Governors delegates managing authority to the Board of Executive Directors. There are twenty-four executive directors, who reside at the IMF's headquarters in Washington and meet nearly every day. The largest-quota countries (the USA, the UK, Germany, France, Japan, Russia, and Saudi Arabia) have one executive director each, while the other executive directors represent several countries, grouped along regional lines. The Executive Directors select the Managing Director to run the professional staff.[19] All decisions are taken by the Board of Executive Directors who cast votes in the name of each country according to its quota. In this way the Executive Directors represent the interests of their countries, while the staff and the Managing Director represent the institution. Table 20.3 displays the voting rights of some countries.

Table 20.3 IMF Votes in January 2005 (%)

	Votes	Quotas (in millions of SDRs)
USA	17.14	37.15
Japan	6.15	13.31
Germany	6.01	13.01
UK	4.96	10.74
France	4.96	10.74
Italy	3.26	7.06
Saudi Arabia	3.23	6.98
Canada	2.99	6.37
The Netherlands	2.39	5.16
Belgium	2.16	4.61
Spain	1.42	3.05
Sweden	1.13	2.40
Industrial countries	62.57	134,803.60
Asia	10.26	21,725.50
Africa	5.31	10,744.50

Source: IMF, www.imf.org/external/np/sec/memdir/members.htm

20.4 Currency Crises

20.4.1 Crises, crises

Over the 1990s, the world has become globalized, meaning that trade and financial integration has accelerated, among other things. Long-standing trade barriers were brought down, as many countries (especially in Latin America and Asia) which had long protected themselves from international competition shifted gears and have become fierce competitors themselves. They also opened up their financial accounts, establishing full currency convertibility and allowing almost complete capital mobility. These liberalization moves were first met by successes: growth picked up, often led by exports and fed by very sizeable capital inflows. Figure 20.6 shows the case of Thailand, one of the East Asian Tigers.

Then something very ugly happened in many emerging market economies. Capital flows reversed

[19] A long-standing gentlemen's agreement is that the IMF's Managing Director is from Europe while the President of the World Bank is from the USA.

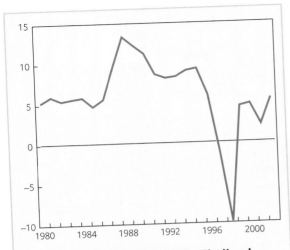

Fig. 20.6 GDP Growth Rate in Thailand

Growth picked up speed, and momemntum was carried by massive capital inflows in the 1990s. When these flows reversed direction in 1997, the currency collapsed and the economy went into a tailspin.

Source: World Bank and Bank of Thailand.

Boom-and-bust cycles share a number of common features. The boom starts with liberalization. It attracts foreign investment which feeds growth. Growth becomes too rapid to be sustainable, and soon inflationary pressures arise. The authorities, on the other hand, are so pleased that they overlook the growing overvaluation of the exchange rate; who wants to spoil the party with a devaluation? These easy years are usually characterized by unbounded optimism and laxity, and considerable risk-taking. Domestic banks have little trouble obtaining funds from abroad in foreign currencies and lend them on freely in domestic currency. Governments too often borrow abroad in foreign currency, getting better interest rates and betting on the continuation of the miracle. The IMF is either as optimistic as the local authorities, or is a voice in the wilderness as its danger warnings go unheeded. International investors marvel at their successes, but keep a critical eye on the situation.

Then something happens. The current account deficit deepens too much, or some miracle country elsewhere in the world stumbles. Then the investors move out faster than they came, accompanied if not preceded by local investors. The crisis erupts and output falls, often deeply. As Figure 20.6 illustrates, growth eventually returns, and often surprisingly fast. Yet the confidence of citizens in free markets has been badly shaken, governments have fallen, things may never be the same again. The remarkable thing is that things can get so bad after having been so good.

Why do crises occur, then? Crises are like automobile accidents: they seem to happen randomly and unexpectedly, but this is generally not the case. A first class of explanations maintains that dangerous drivers are more likely to have more accidents. Not only can we see the accidents coming, but we can do something to prevent them, either by sending bad drivers to school or by increasing the penalties for hazardous practices. This is the first generation theory of crises. Further theories are more subtle: they hold that crises can occur even among (almost) perfect, merely because they are *expected* to occur. While impeccable drivers may be reasonably immune to such accidents, most of the average ones may not be.

themselves, first slowly, then in a panic rush for the exit. The authorities scrambled to defend their currencies, quickly exhausted initially plentiful reserves, and then threw in the towel. The result was a string of massive depreciations (some on the order of 50%). Indebted local firms and banks which had borrowed in foreign currency, mostly dollars, saw their debts double overnight, making them effectively bankrupt. Domestic and foreign speculators sold the shares of indebted companies on the local stock markets and parked the proceeds in foreign exchange, doubling the pressure on the beleaguered countries. Many economies simply folded, plunging millions of bewildered people into unemployment and poverty.

Such **boom-and-bust cycles** are nothing terribly new. They have been observed in Chile in 1982, in Mexico in 1986 and again in 1995, in Thailand in 1997, from where it spread to Korea, Indonesia, and the Philippines, then on to Russia in 1998. It had also happened, in a milder way, in the UK in 1991 and in Finland and Sweden in 1992–3.

20.4.2 First Generation Crises

The first generation theory sees crises as the outcome of policies that are inconsistent with a fixed exchange rate regime. We already know from Chapter 11 that, with perfect capital mobility, monetary policy must be fully dedicated to the fixed exchange rate if that is the chosen regime. Not all governments recognize this point, however. They let the domestic money supply grow too fast, often because this looks like an easy way to finance a budget deficit. We know what happens next: interest rates decline and capital flows out. If the flow is not too large, because of limitations to capital mobility or because real-life markets are a bit more hesitant than theory claims, the authorities believe that they can have the cake and eat it too, expanding money domestically, buying it back on the foreign exchange markets to keep up the peg, and sterilizing to keep things going.

Figure 20.7 tells the story. Recall from Chapter 8 that the asset side of the monetary base is the sum of the central bank's foreign exchange reserves and domestic credit $(M = R + D)$. The policy mistake is for the central bank to intervene on the open market to increase the amount of domestic credit that it offers to commercial banks: this is the upward sloping trajectory of D. While supply rises, what happens to demand? It is is driven by the public's preferences, and leads to the familiar LM equilibrium condition:[20]

(20.1) $M = R + D = L(i)$

where we ignore the evolution of output, because it moves little over the weeks or days that lead up to a crisis. For the same reason we have assumed that the price level is constant and indexed it as $P = 1$. In this short horizon, therefore, money demand is only driven by the interest rate. What, then drives the interest rate? We know that, if capital is freely mobile, it must satisfy the interest parity condition.[21] This condition states that the domestic interest rate is equal to the foreign rate less the

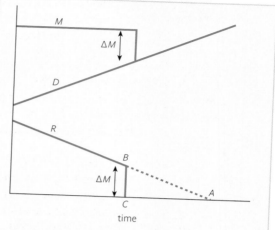

Fig. 20.7 First Generation Crisis
The central bank follows a policy of continuous expansion of the domestic component D of the money supply M. To keep the exchange rate constant it must intervene on the foreign exchange market and keep the money supply constant in face of a constant demand. Foreign exchange reserves R steadily decline, towards ultimate exhaustion. The attack occurs at point B, when reserves are just sufficient to absorb the sales of domestic money $\Delta M = BC$ induced by the expectation that, after the crisis, the exchange rate will float and depreciate continuously, raising the domestic interest rate and reduce money demand by ΔM.

expected rate of currency appreciation. Formally, it is written as:

(20.2) $i = i^* - \Delta S/S.$

As long as markets believe that the fixed exchange rate will be upheld, if only for just another day, the expected change in the exchange rate $(\Delta S/S)$ is nil, and the domestic interest rate i is equal to the foreign rate i^*. This implies that the demand for money stays constant. But how can the money supply stay constant, when the monetary authority is increasing domestic credit at the same time?

The formal, short answer is easily seen in (20.1): to keep the money supply M equal to the constant money demand $L(i)$, the central bank has to spend its reserves R at the same time as it expands domestic credit D. The more detailed explanation is as follows. The central bank attempts to expand the

---

[20] For simplicity, we treat money and monetary base as the same, or equivalently, look at the derived demand for the monetary base M0.

[21] This is the BP schedule in the IS-LM-BP model.

money supply by providing commercial banks with more money base M against more domestic credit D. But the public is not interested in acquiring more money ($L(i)$ is contant as long as i is constant), so the extra money is invested abroad. As money flows out, it puts pressure on the exchange rate, forcing the central bank to intervene, in effect reabsorbing the money base that it has created in the first place. This looks silly, and it is. It is the policy mistake that will lead to a crisis.

Figure 20.7 tracks the opposite evolution of domestic credit D and foreign exchange reserves R over time. For a while, foreign exchange reserves can be run down gradually. Yet this process cannot continue forever: one day the reserve stock is bound to be depleted. A reasonable central bank would stop its attempt at monetary expansion before it is too late, but here we study what happens if the central bank carries on its misguided policies. It is crucial to realize that when reserves are exhausted, the fixed exchange rate system must be abandoned for lack of ammunition. A naive extrapolation of this trend would point to A as the 'day of reckoning'. After that day, one might reason, inflation will rise, as will nominal interest rates (the Fisher principle, see Chapter 8) and the exchange will plummet as will the demand for money, as investors stampede out the door.

This reasoning is flawed, however! Market traders will not wait idly by until the exchange rate collapses. Indeed, the message of Chapter 19 is that they will anticipate this event. They understand that once the fixed exchange regime is abandoned—a certainty given the central bank's assumed determination to let D expand—the exchange rate will be floating, and depreciating, so ΔS will be negative. In this case, the interest rate parity condition predicts that the interest rate i must increase (see (20.2)). If the interest rate increases, the demand for money falls. Equation (20.1) even tells us by how much, say ΔM.[22] This reduction occurs as agents—called

speculators in this capacity—sell their own money for foreign currency, in effect signalling the onset of the crisis. Who buys the domestic currency? Only the central bank does, to honour its standing commitment to defend the parity under attack. To do so, it draws on its remaining stock of foreign exchange reserves. The fall in money demand ΔM is exactly matched by the loss of foreign exchange reserves ΔR.

We now see why the crisis is unavoidable and how it takes the form of a sudden sale of domestic ccurrency. The only remaining question is: when will the crisis occur? The decision is in the hands of the public. The would-be speculators know that a crisis will occur and must guess when to start running on the currency. Buy foreign exchange too late, after the exchange rate has already depreciated, and you suffer a capital loss. Buy foreign exchange too early, when the central bank can still defend its parity, and you gain nothing, only incurring the conversion costs. There is one good time to attack: it is represented by point B in Figure 20.7. This is when reserves reach the level ΔM, the correctly anticipated decline in the money supply post-attack. This is the last moment when everyone will be able to swap domestic for foreign money at the still fixed exchange rate. The crisis takes the form of a sudden sale of domestic money—a speculative attack —which provokes a dramatic fall in central bank reserves from point B to point C, where the reserves have been exhausted. With no reserves left, $R = 0$, the parity must be abandoned. Thereafter, by (20.1) $M = D$, will continue to grow while the exchange rate, now floating, continues to depreciate.

This simple story captures the essence of an exchange crisis. Two aspects are quite striking. First, while it might appear that it is the attack that causes the collapse of the exchange rate regime, nothing could be further from the truth. The exchange rate regime was doomed long before the crisis, its day of reckoning only delayed by the existence of a large enough stock of foreign exchange rate reserves. The attack merely determines the timing of the collapse. Second, no one is surprised. All was quiet before the storm, but it was deceiving. Everyone saw it coming and was just waiting for the right time to act. The crisis was fully anticipated. In

---

[22] Precisely, the money base will contract by $\Delta M = L(i^*) - L(i^* - \Delta S/S)$, since $L(i^*)$ is money demand before the crisis (when $i = i^*$) and $L(i^* - \Delta S/S)$ is money demand after the crisis when the domestic interest rate has risen to take into account the rate of depreciation once the exchange rate is floating after the crisis (remember that $\Delta S/S < 0$).

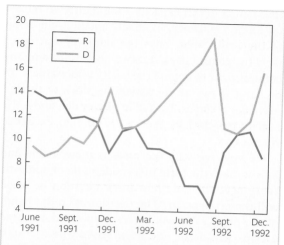

Fig. 20.8 British Foreign Exchange Reserves and Domestic Credit: The 1992 Crisis (£ billion)

The evolution of domestic credit and reserves in the months preceding the September 1992 crisis conforms well with the first generation theory of crises. Easy money (a rising volume of credit) made a crisis almost inevitable. As the Bank of England was maintaining its ERM peg, foreign exchange reserves were declining. What the monthly data do not show is the precipitous fall on 12 September, estimated by some at £20 billion. *Source*: IMF.

real life, of course, there is some uncertainty and things are not quite so clean—Figure 20.8 shows the evolution of British foreign exchange reserves and domestic credit in the run-up to the September 1992 exchange crisis—but the two conclusions remain valid.[23]

20.4.3 Further Generation Crises

First generation crises are the outcome of policies that are incompatible with a fixed exchange rate regime. Some might even say they are well deserved.

[23] This highly stylized model neglects—intentionally—a number of aspects which are possibly more realistic, but don't help us to understand the underlying mechanism. Economic growth, asymmetric information among traders, and uncertainty about central bank policy could all in principle be introduced. That we don't means that the underlying intuition survives these modifications. That is what makes a good model!

In contrast, there exist other descriptions of currency crises of a very different nature. Second and third generation crises share a common feature: they are **self-fulfilling**. They do not have to occur, but they do so, once it is expected that they will. The reasoning may sound circular, and it is. A simple variant of the previous example illustrates starkly how crises could be self-fulfilling. The central bank is now assumed to keep domestic credit D constant. The exchange rate peg is credible, as it should be; no one expects the exchange rate to change and the interest rate parity conditions indicate that the interest rate is constant. The demand for money is therefore also constant, as is the stock of foreign exchange reserves. The situation appears perfectly stable and could go on for ever, were it not for a sudden loss of confidence in the domestic currency, for reasons that are soon to be discussed. If such an exogenous loss of confidence occurs, domestic money is sold and the central bank is forced to spend its foreign exchange reserves to uphold the exchange rate peg. In the two panels of Figure 20.9 we assume that the resulting attacks exhaust the remainder of the central bank's reserves.

The crucial link in the chain of events is the market's expectation of the central bank reaction to the exogenous attack. If market participants anticipate that the central bank will maintain the money supply at its previous level by creating sufficient domestic credit, then the crisis will be vindicated *ex post*. This outcome is shown in panel (*a*). The money supply remains constant, but the central bank has lost its reserves and is unable to maintain a fixed exchange rate. There is, however, an alternative outcome. If the central bank does not increase domestic credit, the money supply contracts by the full amount of the attack, as seen in panel (*b*). In that case, the interest rate increases sharply, which makes domestic assets attractive to international investors, capital promptly flows back in and reserves are quickly replenished. The attack fails. If market participants are convinced that this is the case, an attack is pointless, and will not occur. Both outcomes are equally possible, both are in equilibrium.

Summarizing, if the market expects the central bank not to 'give in' to an attack by relaxing

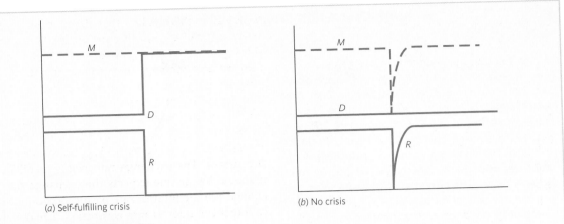

(a) Self-fulfilling crisis   (b) No crisis

Fig. 20.9 Self-Fulfilling Crises
The central bank has a policy fully compatible with the maintenance of a fixed exchange rate: domestic credit is kept constant. If a crisis suddenly occurs, it can behave roughly in two ways. In panel (a), the market believes the central bank will attempt to offset losses of reserves in foreign exchange market interventions to keep the money supply, and the interest rate, unchanged. The attack and its consequences vindicate the markets' view that the central bank will cave in to pressure. In panel (b) instead, the market believes that the central bank is much less likely to increase domestic credit, so the money supply falls by the full amount of foreign exchange market interventions. The interest rate increases, which attracts capital from abroad and replenishes the stock of reserves. The central bank proves its mettle, reserves are not exhausted, and the crisis does not occur. The aftermath for the real economy may, however, be quite painful.

monetary conditions, it will expect the interest rate to rise after the attack, and there can be no attack.[24] If, on the other side, the market correctly anticipates that the central bank will not let the interest rate rise, or at least not enough to attract a sufficient capital inflow, then any attack will be justified *ex post* by central bank behaviour. The attack is entirely self-fulfilling: it occurs because it is expected to succeed, even though pre-attack monetary policy was fully compatible with the fixed exchange rate regime. Reserves were not declining and the regime could have been maintained for ever. The weakness does not lie in *observed* policies but in the *expected* central bank reaction.

[24] This is especially true when one considers that many 'one-way speculators' often operate with near zero capital: the speculator borrows domestic money at the domestic rate and purchases foreign exchange at the rate believed to be overvalued, and then invests it at the foreign interest rate. When the attack comes, the debt is paid off using part of the capital gain. Nothing scares such a speculator more than a sudden rise in domestic interest rates, since that means painfully higher refinancing costs and often financial ruin. *Sic semper mercatoribus!*

Central to this story is the behaviour of the central bank when the attack takes place. Why should it ever behave as in panel (a), a clearly less desirable reaction than the one depicted in panel (b)? Herein lies the true explanation of self-fulfilling attacks: the central bank must fear the consequences of a sudden increase in the interest rate. Raising the interest rate is never free but, given the catastrophic consequences of a crisis, the cost of doing so must be even more forbidding. For that to be the case, there must pre-exist some **vulnerability** that makes the interest rate defence unappealing. Two broad categories of vulnerabilities have been identified.

◆ Second generation of crises: Macroeconomic vulnerabilities

A good example of second generation crises is the presence of high unemployment. A restrictive monetary policy is bound to worsen an already bad situation, to the point where the markets calculate that the central bank will prefer to let the exchange rate go. Another example may be a stock

Box 20.3   The South-East Asian Crisis of 1997–1998

In June 1997, pressure started to build on the baht, the Thai currency. On 2 July, the Bank of Thailand abandoned its peg, which was followed by an immediate 20% depreciation. Speculation immediately turned to the Philippines peso and to the Malaysian ringitt. The peso was allowed to float (within bands) on 11 July, the ringitt on 14 July. Next in the eye of the storm, the Indonesian rupiah too was left to float on 14 August. By mid-October, bowing to months of pressure, Vietnam widened the band of fluctuation of the dong, and the Taiwan dollar was devalued. Brazil and Argentina started to feel the pressure at the end of October, while the Bank of Korea started to intervene heavily in defence of the won. When it had to give up on 17 November, the won promptly fell by 10%, which triggered a new wave of attacks against the other currencies in the region (Figure 20.10). Stability finally returned when, following the other crisis countries, Korea reached an agreement with the IMF on 3 December, involving the largest ever loan. A conspicuous exception was Indonesia, where a political crisis was under way. The ringitt continued to collapse until President Suharto resigned in late May 1998; by then the ringitt had shed 75% of its initial value.

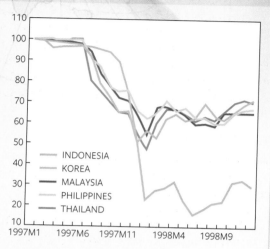

Fig. 20.10 Currency in Crisis (index 100 = January 1997)

The Thai currency was the first to fall in June 1997. The other Asian currencies soon followed, a spectacular case of contagion. When the dust settled, most currencies had lost a third of their initial value, the Indonesia ringitt being down by 70%.

Source: IMF.

---

market that is perceived to be too high and at risk of crashing. A sharp increase in the interest rate lowers stock prices (see Chapter 19) and could tip the whole market into an uncontrolled free-fall. Examples of second generation crises include Sweden in 1992, Mexico in 1995, Argentina in 2001.

◆ Third generation of crises: Balance-sheet vulnerabilities

A good example is the case of a highly indebted government, with a debt that is indexed to the interest rate. With debt service already high, a sharp increase in the interest rate raises debt service, increases the overall budget deficit, and sends the debt even higher, possibly to levels deemed unsustainable. More generally, when the government, banks, or firms have on their balance sheets liabilities which are indexed or in foreign currency,

they are extremely vulnerable, and this is bound to sap the central bank's resolve. Much the same applies. The East Asian crises of 1997–8, described in Box 20.3, provide examples of third generation crises.

The upshot is that self-fulfilling attacks can occur, but only if some underlying vulnerabilities exist already. The vulnerability is not lethal, as in first generation crises, but combined with an attack it makes the cost of a defence of the exchange regime unacceptably high. The existence of a vulnerability is not a guarantee that an attack will occur; it may or it may not, and if it does, it will succeed.

Self-fulfilling crises underline the importance of central bank credibility, a concept studied in Chapter 16. Even in the pre-existence of a vulnerability, a central bank may decide to resist any challenge to the existing regime, as in panel (b) of

Figure 20.9. If its determination is known, then there will be no attack. On the other side, a decline in central bank credibility may trigger an attack. The attack may succeed if the central bank's resolve has indeed declined, but it may fail if the perception was erroneous.[25] What is not clear is what triggers the attack, why it occurs in some vulnerable countries and not in others. All that is needed, it seems, is for some smouldering embers to fall on the powder keg.

20.4.4 Contagion

The striking spread of exchange crises in 1997–8 has rekindled interest in the **contagion** phenomenon. A number of observers have rushed to the conclusion that markets are too erratic to be left on their own and ought to be regulated.[26] The principles developed above provide three reasons for contagion. A good illustration is offered by the Asian crisis of 1997–8 which is described in more detail in Box 20.3.

First generation contagion: competitiveness

The Asian Tigers trade among themselves and export broadly similar goods to the developed countries. So, when the baht, the currency of Thailand, fell by 20%, the neighbouring Tigers lost a few teeth and claws. To recover the earlier competitiveness, they would need a painful decline of local currency prices and compressed profits, or an exchange rate depreciation. Thus trade competition works as a natural channel for contagion. This story is remarkably similar to the inter-war period described in Section 20.2.3.

Second and third generation contagion: learning to know central banks and vulnerabilities

Self-fulfilling crises can occur if doubts persist about a central bank's resolve in the event of a crisis. The collapse of the baht and of the fixed exchange regime in Thailand made two points.

[25] Note that the reasoning assumes that markets are behaving rationally. This stands in contrast with frequent explanations that appeal to unspecified 'psychological factors', hinting that markets behave irrationally. While not ruling this out, we prefer as economists to avoid explanations which lie outside our purview, even if this has its costs.

[26] The issue of capital controls, and of the Tobin tax, is taken up in S. 20.5.2 below.

First, it was readily apparent that banks and firms had borrowed huge sums of dollars, and that the banking system was weak. This made the country vulnerable to a depreciation, since many banks and firms would become bankrupt as dollar liabilities would sharply increase in local currency terms. Furthermore, the central bank was prevented from vigorously defending the baht, as high interest rates would induce loan defaults and similarly damage the banking system. Early reports indicated that the situation was similar elsewhere in the region.

Second, the Bank of Thailand was not in a position to resist the pressure. Having liberalized its financial account, it faced a massive exit of capital that had flowed in during the years of fast growth. Other countries in East Asia were in similar, if not identical positions. Thus a self-fulfilling crisis, long ruled out on the basis of the remarkable growth performance of the Asian Tigers, became distinctly possible. The Thai crisis provided the trigger.

Three features of this process are remarkable:

- 'Cheap talk' and 'life as usual' before the crisis. Local and international investors who know the situation are aware of both the vulnerability and limited resolve of the central bank. They are concerned, but no one moves, since moving alone would achieve nothing.

- Herd behaviour when the crisis hits. When the first spark flies, previously concerned investors see their worst fears confirmed. They do not wait to see how events unfold, they make the event by withdrawing their funds in a state of panic.

- 'I told you so', after the crisis. Once the crisis has occurred, the vulnerability that seemed, and was, benign *ex ante* becomes conventional wisdom.

International investors' duress

Many international investors were clearly surprised by the Thai crisis, and suffered losses as they engaged in fire sales, selling their local assets at any price. For a number of reasons, their best next reaction is to move out of other similar countries, thus spreading the virus:

- Many financial institutions, like pension funds and insurance companies, are limited in their holdings of risky assets in their portfolios. When

Thailand fell, Asian assets previously considered safe were suddenly considered riskier by rating agencies, and dumped *en masse* by institutional investors.[27]

♦ Individual asset managers are rewarded for doing better than the market. Most lost heavily in Thailand. Elementary prudence encouraged them to avoid the risk of future losses by promptly moving out of the region.

♦ The other investors, observing their colleagues' behaviour, come to suspect that they do not know the full story and that things are far worse than they thought. They too rush for the exit door.

20.4.5 Supervision

One conclusion from our post-mortem of the Asian crisis is that where there is smoke there is fire, but that fire may range from an innocuous cigarette in an ashtray to the stove burning out of control. Do you call the fire department (the IMF) in every case? To extend this metaphor: in the former case, there is no 'fundamental' reason for a speculative attack, but under certain conditions, speculative attacks can still occur, and are a surprise (unlike crises of the first generation, which are bound to occur). Could more supervision have helped? One noteworthy and surprising aspect of the Asian crisis was the extent to which sovereign governments were *not* direct contributors to the crisis. A cursory examination of the Tiger economies confirms that fiscal policy was prudent if not tight, monetary policy was under control, and the IMF evidently shared this view.

The big mistake Asian governments and central banks seem to have made was to guarantee dollar loans made by foreign banks to local private sector entities. By doing this, governments reduced the true level of foreign exchange reserves available for intervention, and wrote a blank cheque for bad lending by international banks. This also rendered their pristine fiscal positions a poor indicator of their true financial strength in a crisis. In any case, the world financial system was sailing in uncharted waters, and it was not clear what kind of supervision, if any, could avoid similar problems in the future.

Lacking an international bank supervisory agency, it seems that the best stop-gap solution to problems of financial architecture is to open the door a little bit wider, publish even more information—and do it on the internet—making it a bit more difficult for such situations such as East Asia in the 1990s to arise. In any case, it is unreasonable to expect the private sector to help much in this regard. One characteristic of asset traders is their strategic disincentive to disclose bad news, especially if its truth is not 100% guaranteed. Better to sit on negative information and wait and see. Disclosing it can make one the laughing stock of the market. In contrast, disclosing good news can never hurt—after one has taken the positive position in the asset, of course.

20.5 The Choice of an Exchange Rate Regime

Ever since the end of the gold standard, policymakers and economists have debated the choice of an exchange rate regime. The choice was perceived to be between fixed-but-adjustable exchange rates Bretton Woods style, or more or less freely floating rates. Fashions have come and gone, from Bretton Woods to Jamaica. Nowadays the pendulum seems to have swung back to a revival of pseudo-gold standard arrangements (monetary unions, currency boards, dollarization) which rely largely on the Hume mechanism. Prompted by the globalization phenomenon and recent crises, the debate has also raised the old question of the desirability of capital liberalization. This section reviews the old debate and moves on to the more recent ideas.

---

[27] The major rating agencies have been blamed for not foretelling the Asian crisis and hurriedly downgrading regional assets.

20.5.1 The Old Debate: Fixed vs. Flexible Exchange Rates

The case for flexible exchange rates

Two arguments favour flexible rates, and two criticize the case for fixed rates. They boil down to the view that it is better to leave the exchange rate to the markets than to the authorities.

- Exchange rate changes are needed to compensate for inflation differentials (the PPP principle). Fixed exchange rates can only be adjusted sporadically, which leaves long periods when they are misaligned. In addition, such realignments are easily predictable and lead to speculative attacks.

- Exchange rate changes are also needed to cope with shocks which alter external competitiveness, for example changing energy prices, the emergence of new competitors, etc. With a fixed exchange rate regime, either all prices have to adjust, or the exchange rate must be changed. With wage and price rigidity as a fact of life, the first solution can be protracted and painful, possibly requiring pressure on wages and prices to be brought about by the Phillips curve mechanism, i.e. unemployment.[28]

The case against fixed exchange rates is essentially that:

- We do not know with much precision what the equilibrium value of the exchange rate should be. Policy mistakes are likely to arise from ignorance, or from misguided political motivations.
- Fixed exchange rates are vulnerable to crises. As noted in Section 20.4.4, only those countries with impeccable credentials (no vulnerability, a highly credible central bank) may consider themselves immune to speculative attacks. All the others may be subject to a crisis, first, second, or third generation, with devastating consequences.

[28] In a famous metaphor, a key proponent of flexible rates, Chicago economist and Nobel Prize winner Milton Friedman noted that the shift to summer time can be achieved by having everyone adapt behaviour and do the same things an hour earlier, or by moving the clock ahead by one hour. The latter is much easier, he argued, than changing the habits of millions of people. Changing the exchange rate is easier than changing millions of prices.

The list of cases of exchange rate mismanagement is impressive. It starts with Britain's painful return to an obviously overvalued pre-First World War gold parity in 1925, to the dollar overvaluation that preceded the collapse of the Bretton Woods system, to numerous cases where thriving black markets indicate that the official parity is off the mark. More recent cases include the decisions of Italy and the UK to leave the European fixed exchange rate mechanism, the Asian crisis, and several crises in Latin America.

The case for fixed exchange rates

This is really a case against flexible rates, and against the view that markets do a better job than the authorities. The case is built on the observation that flexible exchange rates tend to fluctuate widely, too widely to be explained by inflation differentials or real disturbances. Two explanations are usually offered, which are not mutually exclusive:

- Overshooting implies that the exchange rate tends to move away from its equilibrium level.
- Exchange markets deal with considerable uncertainty with large payoffs when betting right, and large losses when wrong. This leads markets to move in fits and starts, imparting additional uncertainty and instability to the economy.

For good or bad reasons, most European countries have demonstrated a keen attachment to exchange rate stability since 1945. The fear has always been that exchange rate volatility would hurt intra-European trade and threaten the Common Market. The decision to create a monetary union may be seen as the last step in continuous efforts at keeping intra-European exchange rates stable.

20.5.2 The New Debate: Financial Liberalization

Capital controls: the pros and the cons

The process of financial integration, which began in the 1980s and accelerated in the 1990s, has become controversial, if only because it has been linked to the wave of currency crises in the emerging markets. One after another, developed and then developing countries have dismantled capital controls which were put in place at the end of the Second

Box 20.4 The Tobin Tax

Back in 1972 James Tobin, a Yale economist and Nobel Prize laureate, proposed to 'throw sand in the wheels of international finance'. He identified two main objectives, reducing exchange rate volatility and preserving the autonomy of macroeconomic policy (see the main text for the argument), and concluded that restraining capital movements was a worthy effort. The proposal was not well received; as Tobin recalls, 'It did not make much of a ripple. In fact, one might say that it sank. . . . I realize that I am opposed by a powerful tide. A wide-spread orthodoxy holds that financial markets know best, that the discipline they exert on central banks and governments is salubrious' (Tobin 1996).

Tobin claimed that capital movements ought to be slowed down. He was not in favour of the market-unfriendly, administrative restrictions in use at the time. He observed that the vast majority of foreign transactions involve round trips of seven days or less, speculative money which serves no investment or saving purpose. He argued that a single flat tax on every foreign exchange market transaction of very small size would deter the unproductive short-term trips without much affecting long-term capital movements which underlie productive foreign investment. Why? Investors compare the returns from any deal to the returns from holding safe assets, like government bonds. To do so, they compute profits and losses from any transaction in annualized terms. For example, a small tax of 0.1% per transaction implies a total cost of 0.2% for a round trip (invest, earn your profit, and bring it back). If the trip takes a year, it means an annualized cost of 0.2%. If the trip lasts less, say half a year, the annualized value of the tax about doubles. (The law of compounding applies, so it is a bit more but negligibly so.) As the horizon shortens, the annualized tax becomes very high, e.g. 10.9% on a week-long trip, see Table 20.4 below. Conversely, on very long-term investments, the tax becomes negligible.

Recently, the tax has undergone a revival among both serious economists and anti-globalization demonstrators. One of the new motivations is the tax revenue that its proponents expect, e.g. $300 billion annually with a 0.1% tax. Being an international tax, it could be used for international purposes: the UN and its agencies, NGOs, etc. It is felt, however, that should a Tobin tax be imposed, its yield would be many times smaller because the markets will organize themselves to minimize the volume of transactions, and also because they would migrate to safe havens—most likely a computer-laden ship in international waters.

Table 20.4 The Impact of a 0.1% Tobin Tax and the Holding Period of Investments

Holding period of investment:	1 day	2 days	1 week	1 month	6 months	1 year	5 years
Implicit tax (annualized basis)	55.2%	24.6%	10.9%	2.4%	0.4%	0.2%	0.04%

World War, and sometimes long before. The restrictions can take a variety of forms: outright prohibitions of export or import of money and other financial instruments, limits on such transfers, dual exchange markets (one fixed, for commercial transactions, one flexible for financial transactions), and, more recently, the Tobin tax which is described in Box 20.4. While capital controls are highly controversial, the principles involved are quite straightforward.

Critics of capital controls argue that restrictions to the free movement of capital prevent savers from getting the best available returns, and prevent firms from borrowing on the best possible terms. Saving and investment both suffer, with adverse effects on long-term growth. They further observe that, by isolating its domestic financial markets, a government can 'milk' them to finance its own budget deficits at costs lower than the international capital market would offer. Furthermore, when capital controls are effective, national interest rates cease to reflect the local economic situation. Since high and rising interest rates signal a worsening situation, they tend to discipline imprudent governments. Shutting down the signal offers relief to governments, but at the cost of a worsening situation in the future, possibly leading to a crisis on the way.

Those in favour of capital controls present three main arguments:

- First, following on an argument initially spelled out by Keynes, they claim that financial markets are unstable, prone to fads and panics. The result is volatility that is unjustified by underlying economic fundamentals, and is costly to firms and households.

- Second, following on the Mundell–Fleming result that full capital mobility prevents the use of monetary policy under fixed exchange rates, and makes fiscal policy impotent under flexible rates, they argue that restricting capital mobility restores the option of using demand management instruments. When applied to monetary policy, this principle is the impossible trilogy already discussed in Section 20.2.4.

- Third, saving is a source of growth if it is invested in productive uses like plants, machinery, schooling and training, etc. The proponents of capital controls note that the bulk of international capital movements are of a very short-term nature, even aimed at intraday trading opportunities, rather than long-term investment in human or physical capital.

The link with exchange rate regimes

The macroeconomic policy independence argument has a direct bearing on the debate on the choice of an exchange rate regime. The main weakness of fixed exchange rate regimes under full capital mobility is that in most cases they require the abandonment of an independent monetary policy. It requires some discipline for central bankers to give up any hope of influencing local monetary

conditions, and few central banks have lived up to the requirement.[29] As a result, fixed exchange rate regimes are prone to speculative crises and have shown rather limited survival ability.

The argument can be turned on its head, however. A direct implication of the impossible trilogy principle is that fixed exchange rate regimes are more likely to survive when capital controls are in place. A good example is Europe's EMS: it operated reasonably well in the 1980s until capital controls were removed by 1990; the system was badly shaken shortly thereafter in 1992. Thus the choice is not just between fixed and flexible exchange rates, but also involves the capital mobility regime. Countries which value exchange rate stability should not rule out restrictions on capital movements altogether. Similarly, countries which favour full capital mobility should not stick to a fixed exchange rate regime for too long. The question of fixed versus flexible exchange rates has become central to the accession process of transition countries, and it is reviewed in Box 20.5.

If full capital mobility is considered an inexorable evolution of economic relations, however, the fixed exchange rate option may be going the way of the hula hoop and bell-bottomed pants. The impossible trilogy means that monetary policy autonomy must be sacrificed, but few countries are prepared for such a step that may be difficult to defend on the domestic political front. Furthermore, the phenomenon of second generation crises suggests that it may take years, possibly decades, before the central bank has achieved a level of credibility which eliminates vulnerabilities. In the meantime, the threat of currency crises looms large. The **hollowing-out hypothesis** maintains that the choice of exchange rate regimes is no longer between floating rates and soft pegs—the traditional fixed-and-adjustable exchange rates—but between floating rates and hard pegs, regimes described in the next section. Critics of the hollowing-out hypothesis argue that soft pegs are still feasible, provided

[29] One excellent example is the central bank of the Netherlands after the mid-1980s, which almost dogmatically tracked German monetary policy until monetary union was implemented.

Box 20.5 **Exchange Rate Regimes in the Transition Countries**

One of the many fascinating aspects of the transition process in Central and Eastern Europe is the diversity of exchange rate arrangements chosen. Here are countries which face the same fundamental challenge: move from central planning to a market-based economy and integrate with the rest of the world, mostly Western Europe, and yet they diverge on a central issue, and often change track. Initially, the absence of market prices meant that the true value of the currencies was completely unknown, which would have argued in favour of letting the exchange rate float and find its equilibrium. But the absence of financial markets, and lack of knowledge to set them up quickly, largely closed that

option. Most countries elected to adopt a 'managed float' regime, which meant a floating exchange rate that was heavily controlled, fixed and adjustable rates in disguise. Some temporarily floated (Lithuania), others went to a currency board (Estonia and then Lithuania and Bulgaria), others fixed and then floated (Czech Republic, Poland, Russia), while others increasingly tightened up (Hungary). Similarly, capital liberalization has proceeded at different speeds, with a handful of countries moving quickly (Czech Republic, Poland). The diversity of solutions adopted is a testimony to the fundamental difficulty of choosing an exchange rate regime.

bands of fluctuations are large enough or the peg is allowed to vary (e.g. crawling pegs) to account for changing economic conditions.

Optimal sequencing

Back in the early 1950s, nearly all countries operated in strictly controlled environments. Many prices were fixed, some goods were even rationed, commercial banks were heavily regulated, and financial markets limited or non-existent. External controls regulated exports and imports, tariffs were heavy, and capital flows essentially forbidden. What a difference half a century can make! Liberalization seems an inescapable trend, and basic economic principles support this trend. On the other hand, liberalization has not always been an easy journey. The Asian crisis once more showed that there can be serious setbacks on the way. Is there a better way of liberalizing? The response is to adopt a proper **sequencing** of liberalization. McKinnon[30] has proposed an optimal order of sequencing. It is based on two main ideas. First, liberalization should start with the restrictions that are costliest in terms of economic efficiency. Second, some steps need to be taken before others to avoid inconsistencies.

◆ The first step should be the creation of well-functioning domestic goods markets: free prices and abolish rationing. It makes little sense to have free external trade if domestic trade is heavily constrained.

◆ The second step should be the gradual liberalization of international trade, starting with administrative measures (quotas on exports and imports), moving on to eliminating export tariffs, and then finally reducing import tariffs to avoid shocks to domestic producers.

◆ Soon after the first step, the domestic financial sector should be liberalized, under competitive conditions. Banks should be allowed to freely set interest rates on deposits and loans, to open branches as they see fit, and to choose the range of services that they offer their customers. Bank regulation and supervision should be developed in parallel to ensure the soundness of the banking system.

◆ Domestic financial markets come next. Bonds and stock markets are allowed to compete with the banking system to both collect savings and finance borrowing by firms and public entities. Here again, regulation and supervision must proceed in parallel to guarantee a proper functioning of naturally unstable markets.

[30] Ronald McKinnon, a Stanford economist, has also contributed to the theory of optimum currency areas.

Box 20.6 **The N − 1 Problem**

Take N countries with N currencies. There are N − 1 independent bilateral exchange rates, as Figure 20.11 illustrates: all the other bilateral rates can be retrieved from these N − 1 rates via triangular arbitrage. Now link these currencies together, either in a monetary union or just a system of fixed exchange rates. As N − 1 independent bilateral exchange rates are frozen, N − 1 central banks lose their independence, and the Nth remains free of policy constraints. In the Bretton Woods system, all central banks were pegging to the US dollar, leaving the Fed with the task of pegging the dollar to gold. In the EMS, no Nth country was designated, but the Bundesbank captured the Nth degree of freedom. In a monetary union, such as EMU, all N central banks lose their policy-making autonomy and a new central bank is created to manage the new currency.

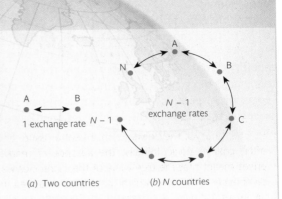

(a) Two countries   (b) N countries

Fig. 20.11 The N − 1 Problem

Two countries which decide to fix their exchange rate lose one degree of freedom. When N countries form a fixed exchange rate system, they commit N − 1 exchange rates, or N − 1 degrees of freedom. (All the bilateral exchange rates can be calculated from just the N − 1 rates shown in panel (b): all the missing arrows can be drawn.)

◆ External financial liberalization comes next. The Asian crisis well illustrates the risks of full capital mobility when the domestic financial sector is not functioning properly. Furthermore, the exchange regime must be appropriately adapted to changing circumstances, as rigidly fixed exchange rates are unlikely to survive capital mobility when full capital mobility is established.

20.5.3 Monetary Unions, Currency Boards, and Dollarization

The menu of exchange rate regimes has recently been enlarged. A number of countries have adopted new arrangements which were once regarded as curiosities. These 'hard pegs' differ from the soft pegs by the fact that they do not allow margins of fluctuations and that they rule out realignments (devaluations or revaluations). Hume's mechanism has made a comeback by eliminating discretionary monetary policy entirely and reducing central banks to the role of passive *bureaux de change*. Three varieties of hard pegs have been observed which are worth noting.

Monetary unions

A monetary union involves the irrevocable fixing of exchange rates and the abandonment of margins of fluctuation among a number of countries. In fact it means that individual currencies are no longer distinguishable, a common currency may be substituted. The immediate implication is that individual central banks lose any remaining autonomy, although one central bank is needed to manage the common currency. This is a special case of the **N − 1 problem** spelled out in Box 20.6. The union's central bank manages the overall money supply. Interest rates are the same across the union since money can flow freely. National money supplies are then determined entirely through the Hume mechanism.[31] If a country runs a balance of payments surplus, money is flowing in and the national

---

[31] It should be noted that the mechanism described here is somewhat more general than Hume's in the following sense: an expansion of the money supply need not require a trade surplus, but could also be achieved with a capital account surplus (an excess of private capital flows).

money supply rises; a deficit results in loss of money supply.

It might seem strange for independent countries to give up their currencies. In fact, it is the logical consequence of the impossible trinity: with full capital mobility, fixed exchange rates imply the loss of monetary policy autonomy. Yet, the threat of currency crises remains: the only way to eliminate that threat is to eliminate the currencies themselves. Since there is no real policy autonomy to lose, the system can only be strengthened. At the same time, however, there are costs of a monetary union: giving up monetary or exchange rate policy has its own consequences. In the end, it depends on the company a country chooses. The theory of **optimum currency areas** spells out criteria for creating a monetary union and is presented in Box 20.7.

The wave of capital account liberalization, when combined with the attachment of some countries to exchange rate stability, makes it attractive to move from a soft peg to a hard peg, hence the renewed appeal of monetary unions. Europe has adopted this scheme, which is described in the book's website. Previously, monetary unions had been established in French-speaking Africa and in the Caribbean Islands. Some think that this is the world's future.

Dollarization and euroization

Dollarization is the unilateral adoption by a country of the US dollar as sole legal tender, which can be thought of as a one-sided monetary union with the United States. It can involve the link to another currency, e.g. the euro. It is as close to the gold standard as a monetary system can be, without having gold itself circulate; it functions in the same way, including Hume's mechanism. It is another variety of hard pegs.

A number of countries never had their own currency: Panama and Liberia have been dollarized since their independence. Ecuador and El Salvador adopted the dollar in 2000 and 2001 respectively. Argentina flirted with the idea in 1999. Kosovo has euroized. One reason for dollarizing is the percep-

tion that a foreign central bank will do a better job at enforcing price stability than an indigenous one. Another reason is proven inability to come to grips with inflation, as in the case of Ecuador. If trade links with the country whose currency is adopted are intensive, it seems like a good idea. It remains, however, that the interest rate is driven by foreign economic conditions, which may be awkward.

Currency boards

Currency boards used to be the arrangement of choice in the British Empire. They have made a comeback, starting with Hong Kong in 1983, followed by Argentina in 1991, Estonia in 1992, Lithuania in 1994, Bulgaria and Bosnia-Herzegovina in 1997. Currency boards resemble dollarization, except that the local currency is maintained. The three key features of a currency board are the following:

- A fixed exchange rate is established vis-à-vis an anchor currency. The local currency is fully convertible into the anchor currency at that rate, with no limit.

- The local currency is fully backed by reserves. This is required to ensure full and unlimited convertibility.

- Currency boards often hold reserves of 105% or 110% of their liabilities, a precaution since most money is produced by commercial banks which are not restricted to 100% backing. In practice, it means that the high-powered money supply is entirely driven by the balance of payments via Hume's mechanism. Monetary authorities are completely passive.

With the exception of Hong Kong, currency boards have usually been adopted by countries which have long suffered high inflation and felt that there was no political will to establish a full-blown independent central bank dedicated to price stability. One transition country, Estonia, started off with a currency board, and its success at avoiding inflation has inspired Lithuania and Bulgaria.

Box 20.7 Optimum Currency Area Theory

A region constitutes an optimum currency area when its use of a common currency implies no loss of welfare.[32] The best way of thinking about it is to ask what is lost when the exchange rate instrument is abandoned. This becomes problematic when the union is buffeted by asymmetric shocks, i.e. shocks which hurt some members but not the others, for this is when the exchange rate is useful. Adjustment to asymmetric shocks must now take place through prices, which can be very painful. The theory looks for criteria which makes this adjustment unnecessary. Two main criteria have been suggested.

♦ Factor mobility. Consider the case when an adverse shock, for example a loss of competitiveness, hits a country. The country soon goes into a recession, and laments the loss of its exchange rate that could have been handy to restore its external competitiveness. If,

however, its factors of production could move out to more fortunate members of the monetary union, the pain would be spread out, and the common central bank could use the common external exchange rate to adjust optimally. If capital or labour or both are mobile there would be little cost in unemployment of factors, and the loss of internal (within the union) exchange rates would be trivial.

♦ No asymmetric shocks. Most of the shocks concern the world demand for and supply (competitiveness) of locally produced goods. If the members of the union produce a similar menu of goods, then the likelihood of asymmetric shocks diminishes. The same applies if the member countries produce a very diversified menu of goods; in that case a particular shock is likely to be of little import.

❶ Summary

1 International monetary arrangements initially arose from the need to provide international trade with easy means of settling transborder payments. For centuries, both domestic and international trade was carried out using gold and silver. On the other hand, the famed gold standard lasted less than forty years, from 1879 to 1914.

2 Taken literally, the gold standard implied a rigid monetary rule and a fixed exchange rate regime. By the Hume mechanism, a trade deficit caused a shrinking money supply, while a surplus meant an expanding money supply. Both processes act to equilibrate trade imbalances.

3 The evolution of the monetary system after the First World War can be seen as a series of ad hoc

responses to international crises and system inadequacies. In particular, the Bretton Woods system was designed to avoid the competitive devaluations of the inter-war period by establishing a system of fixed exchange rates based on the US dollar's link to gold. Nevertheless, this 'gold exchange standard' was not a gold standard in the strict sense.

4 The collapse of the Bretton Woods system was due to the internal inconsistencies of a system that required increasing amounts of international reserves to be provided by the USA, that were in theory convertible into gold. Large US balance of payment deficits in the late 1960s created a dollar overhang of official external liabilities which far exceeded the USA's gold assets.

5 The IMF fulfils two main roles. It exercises surveillance over member countries on a routine

---

[32] The seminal work on optimum currency areas is by Robert Mundell, the same economist who shaped the Mundell–Fleming *IS-LM* framework presented in Ch. 11.

basis. It provides emergency assistance to countries which face balance of payments difficulties. Its loans are conditional on the adoption and implementation of programmes designed to cope with the source of payment imbalances.

6 Currency crises can be divided into two types. First generation crises occur when domestic policies are incompatible with the exchange rate peg. They are usually anticipated. Second generation crises are self-fulfilling. They afflict central banks which appear vulnerable or uncommitted to an exchange rate target, or which have not acquired sufficient credibility. They may occur under these conditions, but do not have to.

7 Currency crises seem to be contagious for three reasons: first generation contagion through loss of competitiveness; second generation contagion when markets discover similar vulnerabilities or lack of central bank commitment; and investors' contagion when losses in one country prompt international players to withdraw from other countries which suddenly appear risky.

8 Capital liberalization brings about long-term benefits. But financial markets are prone to bouts of instability which may result in currency crises. In addition, full capital mobility severely restricts the ability to carry out macroeconomic policies (Mundell–Fleming).

9 The choice of an exchange rate regime involves various trade-offs. In the end, small open economies may favour some degree of exchange rate stability while larger countries may prefer to integrate themselves in the world economy at fluctuating real exchange rates.

10 The widespread shift to capital account liberalization has had the effect of sharpening the choice between floating and fixed exchange rates. Soft pegs are increasingly seen as dangerous, hence the fashion for hard pegs: monetary unions, currency boards, and dollarization.

☺ Key Concepts

- **International Monetary Fund (IMF)**
- **gold standard**
- **bimetallism**
- **Gresham's law**
- **band of fluctuation**
- **Hume mechanism**
- **Bretton Woods conference**
- **gold exchange standard**
- **quota**
- **conditionality**
- **Triffin paradox**
- **Exchange Rate Mechanism**
- **speculative attacks**
- **central parity; parity**

- **European Monetary Union (EMU)**
- **impossible trilogy**
- **special drawing rights (SDRs)**
- **boom-and-bust cycles**
- **first, second, and third generation theories of speculative attacks**
- **self-fulfilling attacks**
- **vulnerabilities**
- **contagion**
- **hollowing-out hypothesis**
- **sequencing**
- $N-1$ **problem**
- **optimum currency area**

❷ Exercises

1 Why can't beggar-thy-neighbour policies work? What is the difference with tariff wars?

2 Does the Hume mechanism work within a monetary union?

3 'Currency crises cannot be foreseen, markets attack as soon they expected a crisis.' Comment. In your answer, you may distinguish betweem first generation and self-fulfilling crises.

4 Draw the implications of the $N-1$ problem for the international monetary system and for regional exchange rate arrangements like the EMS.

5 Can self-fulfilling crises also affect the banking system?

6 'The developing countries cannot borrow in their own currencies. This puts them at permanent risk of a currency crisis.' Explain and comment.

⊙ Essay Questions

1 The poorer countries regularly propose that the IMF issue more SDRs and that they be distributed mostly to the poorer countries to support their development. The richer countries refuse, contending that this would be inflationary. What is your view?

2 It has been said that the Bretton Woods system was doomed from its start. Explain why. Could its demise have been avoided? How?

3 Is a return to the gold standard feasible? Desirable?

4 The ten new members of the EU are committed to fully free capital movements, join the ERM, and then become members of the monetary union. What do you think of this arrangement? What would be your own preferred arrangement?

5 The IMF is frequently accused of imposing tough policies on the countries that ask for its assistance. Evaluate this view.

Epilogue 21

21.1 The Keynesian Revolution *526*

21.2 The Monetarist Revolution *528*

21.3 The Rational Expectations Revolution *531*

21.4 Microfoundations of Macroeconomics *532*

21.5 Institutional and Political Economics *533*

21.6 Labour Markets *534*

21.7 Growth and Development *536*

21.8 Conclusions *537*

The ideas of economists and political philosophers, both when they are right and when they are wrong, are more powerful than is commonly understood. Indeed the world is ruled by little else. Practical men, who believe themselves to be quite exempt from any intellectual influences, are usually the slaves of some defunct economist.

J. M. Keynes, *The General Theory*, 383

Throughout this book, we have emphasized the usefulness of macroeconomics as a tool for understanding and improving the way the world works. To this aim, we have presented a unified treatment of the field, but have downplayed the historical evolution of ideas over the years as well as important controversies, past and present, which have accompanied these ideas. This neglect was intentional. Focusing on controversies can be fascinating, but it can also cloud the extent of agreement and common understanding, leaving the unsatisfactory impression that macroeconomics is too conflict ridden to be of any practical use. Once the basic framework is well understood, however, it is both interesting and illuminating to track the field's intellectual history. The concluding chapter of this textbook presents a highly compressed survey of the major steps of the field's development, the key players and the policy debates, with an emphasis on the European scene.[1]

21.1 The Keynesian Revolution

John Maynard Keynes, 1883–1946

Source: Copyright Hulton-Deutsch Collection/Corbis

The birth of macroeconomics is conventionally associated with the publication in 1936 by John Maynard Keynes of the *General Theory of Employment, Interest and Money*. Its influence has been phenomenal; some even claim that it changed more lives in the twentieth century than any other single work. Many factors explain this success.

The book came out towards the end of the Great Depression and can be seen, as often, the response of economic research to challenges of the time. To contemporaries who had witnessed the rapid rise of mass unemployment, the classical laissez-faire view looked factually wrong and almost immoral. Others had already moved in the same direction, but Keynes brought together many apparently disparate themes. The idea that prices do not necessarily clear at full employment had been put forward by the British economic Robert Malthus (1766–1834). Knut Wicksell (1851–1926) and his successors, who came to be known as the 'Stockholm School', had gone quite a long way toward what was to become the *IS* curve. Other economists—including Hjalmar Schacht who single-handedly vanquished the German hyperinflation in 1923 and later went on to become Hitler's Finance Minister—had long advocated deficit spending on public works during the Great Depression. But Keynes' attack was unique in many ways. The *General Theory* proposed a wholly new concept of equilibrium, even though it took decades to fully decipher what it really meant. It was a combination of scholarly analysis, strident criticism and practical policy recommendations that appealed to both theoreticians and policy-makers. Keynes did not just aim at fellow researchers, he frequently descended the ivory tower of academia to promote his ideas in the media where his reputation as a brilliant and provocative polemicist was well established.

---

[1] In preparing this chapter, we have benefited from very useful comments and suggestions from Charles Bean, Irwin Collier, Barry Eichengreen, Hans Genberg, Francesco Giavazzi, Guido Tabellini, and Jürgen von Hagen.

The truth is that Keynes was a man of many talents and, by 1936, of great experience as well. As a young economist during the First World War, he had worked in the UK Treasury, which he represented at the Versailles Peace Conference, until he undiplomatically quit. In *The Economic Consequences of the Peace*, he criticized the harsh reparations imposed on Germany, maintaining that Germany could not pay for the war and would be destabilized by the economic burden of the Treaty. His analysis turned out to be prophetic and established his reputation. The book also strained Keynes' relations with British government circles until the Second World War. His strident criticism of Chancellor Winston Churchill's decision to return the pound to its pre-war parity did not help in this regard. Maynard, as his friends called him, was also a charismatic intellectual leader. He assembled a group of brilliant economists at Cambridge University who went on to dominate the profession in Britain and beyond.

One important message of the Keynesian revolution was that fiscal policy can be used to fight recessions in particular when monetary policy is ineffective—either because expansionary monetary policy no longer lowers the nominal interest rate or when investment spending is depressed by bad 'animal spirits'. Deficit spending, as it was then called, was taken on board in many countries after the war, in effect becoming conventional wisdom. German-speaking countries too have been influenced by Keynesian ideas, but scepticism there has been present and, to this day, a large segment of the policy-making and academic establishments see them as dangerous. It is not unlikely that these views are linked to the role that deficit finance had in the hyperinflation of 1922-3. Germany's mistrust of Keynesian policies has found its way, in a subdued form, in the monetary union's Stability and Growth Pact and in the statements of the European Central Bank (ECB), in which fiscal deficits tend to be seen as a source of concern rather than as a potential means of output stabilization. In most of Europe, though, Keynesian ideas are very much alive, although their limits—described in Chapters 15 and 16—are generally well recognized.

Keynes' theory was not fully worked out. The *General Theory* is difficult to read; it frequently lacks precision and can be confusing. It fell upon his disciples to dot the i's. Most of the effort was conducted in his native Britain and in the USA, with some important contributions from Sweden and a few others, including the Polish economist Michal Kalecki (1899-1970), who had anticipated many of Keynes' ideas and went on to try to merge Keynesian and Marxist schools of thought.

Beyond clarifying Keynes' views, one task that his disciples had to grapple with was to reconcile the Keynesian construction with generally accepted theories. It soon emerged, indeed, that the attack on the 'classics', as Keynes labelled established economics, was not general and rested on the assumption that the price level is constant. This assumption was acceptable in situations of low employment, like the Great Depression, but was seriously at odds with post-war economic conditions, characterized by full employment and, later on, rising inflation. The necessary reconciliation effort, the neoclassical synthesis presented in Chapter 11, was carried out mostly in the USA, with Nobel Prize Laureate Paul Samuelson (1915-) and his MIT colleagues at the forefront, but also by Keynes' colleague in Cambridge, John Hicks (1904-89) and by Don Patinkin from Hebrew University in Jerusalem (1922-95).

European macroeconomists were not particularly productive during this period, with a few notable exceptions. Some Swedish economists, under the leadership of Assar Lindbeck (1930-), and their Norwegian colleagues developed a small open economy version of the Keynesian model. Nobel laureates Jan Tinbergen, from the Netherlands, and James Meade (1907-95), a student of Keynes' in Cambridge, also made major contributions in extending Keynes' framework to the small open economy case. Yet, the most achieved construction is the Mundell-Fleming model presented in Chapter 10. Interestingly, Marcus Fleming (1911-1976) was a British economist working in the International Monetary Fund. Robert Mundell (1932-) was undoubtedly inspired by the smallness and openness of his native Canada and of Switzerland, where he lived for a time.

An important implication of Keynesian economics was that countries as a whole could be a research subject. Today, it is hard to believe that pre-Keynesian economics was mostly preoccupied with sectors and firms, and had little to say about questions such as growth or employment.[2] In fact, aggregate data, like GDP, the unemployment rate, or the consumer price index, were sporadically collected and seldom the subject of great research interest. The rise of Keynesian economics prompted a vigorous effort at developing the relevant concepts and assembling the data. This effort started in the late 1930s at a time when most of the leading economists were either in the USA or in Great Britain. Unsurprisingly, therefore, the main contributions were developed in these two countries, with early pioneers such as Simon Kuznets (1901–85) from Columbia University and Richard Stone (1913–91), a Keynes student from Cambridge, both of whom eventually were awarded the Nobel Prize for this work. Once data were available, and with the advent of the first computers, economists have undertaken to build large-scale models that were meant to mimic the economy. Following early work by Italian-born Nobel Prize laureate Franco Modigliani, these large models have become stand-

ard fares in most finance ministries, international organizations, and economic forecasting companies where they are routinely used to produce forecasts and simulate the effects of policy decisions. Despite the subsequent decline of Keynesian economics, these models continue to exert considerable influence on day-to-day decisions by governments, banks, and businesses.

The neoclassical synthesis shows that the Keynesian equilibrium is a special case, which occurs when prices are sticky. Obviously, the next task was to explain how prices move, when they eventually do. This led to a search for what was known as the 'missing equation'. This equation was discovered as an empirical regularity by A. W. Phillips (1914–75) at the London School of Economics, see Chapter 12. This discovery prompted the next question: what is the theory behind the Phillips curve? Work on this question, mostly in the USA, was well under way just when the curve started to vanish. The disappearance of the Phillips curve, predicted by Friedman in the late 1960s, paved the way for the rise of the monetarists, a rival school of thought committed to exposing what was seen as fundamental flaws in Keynesian economics.

21.2 The Monetarist Revolution

**Milton Friedman,
1912 –**

Source: Copyright Hulton-Deutsch Collection/Corbis

---

[2] An important exception was the work of Gottfried Haberler (1900–95), who in 1937 published an important compendium of contemporary business cycle theories—with the important exception of Keynes', which Haberler later strongly criticized.

By the late 1940s, the Keynesian school had established a strong foothold in the USA, where most of macroeconomic research was conducted, but it never enjoyed total supremacy. The University of Chicago, in particular, remained a stronghold of the classics that Keynes had sought to dismiss. Keynesian ideas certainly attracted attention at Chicago; in the 1940s, Chicago economist Lloyd Metzler published an influential attempt to characterize Keynes' ideas formally. But the Chicago academic tradition must have seen a fundamental threat in Keynesian macroeconomics. It is thus not surprising that the 'Chicago School' led against the Keynesians an intellectual attack, eventually as successful as Keynes' own attack against the classics. Part of the success of the Chicago School is due to Milton Friedman, whose many talents matched those of Keynes himself.

Friedman combined extraordinary intellectual vigour, leadership charisma, government experience, and communication skills. Like Keynes, he spent the war years at the Treasury, the US Treasury in his case, where he contributed to the war effort. Like Keynes, he assembled a group of young economists, who regularly met in the 'Workshop in Money and Banking' and went on to rewrite macroeconomics. Like Keynes, he devoted much time and effort to popularize his ideas, writing a regular column in the US magazine 'Newsweek' and becoming a popular guest on television shows. And, like Keynes, he did not shy from contacts with politicians, providing advice to unsuccessful presidential candidate Barry Goldwater, as well as to the considerably more successful President Reagan and to Prime Minister Thatcher. Many of his Chicago associates became known as the 'Chicago boys' who achieved considerable—and still controversial—influence in South America and elsewhere.

Friedman pursued several ideas, all of which undermined the key building blocks of Keynesian economics. First, he was an unabashed defender of free markets, which Keynes was prompt to see as subject to failures. This led him to actively promote the view, long advocated by the Austrian-born economist Friedrich von Hayek (1899–1992), that governments are a threat to freedom, and not just in economic matters.[3] Friedman and his colleagues resuscitated the influence of the laissez-faire school, which had been shattered after the Great Depression.

Second, Friedman confronted Keynes' view that fiscal policy is a useful tool for macroeconomic stabilization and that monetary policy is useless.

The label 'monetarist', widely applied to the Chicago School, comes from this aspect of Friedman's work.[4] His *A Monetary History of the United States, 1867–1960*, written in 1963 jointly with Anna J. Schwartz (1915–), is generally regarded as a masterpiece which fundamentally changed the way we look at monetary policy. At the empirical level, this book attributes the Great Depression to bad monetary policy, in contrast with Keynes, who tended to blame procyclical fiscal policies. At the theoretical level, the book re-established the classic 'quantity equation' $MV = PY$, where V is the velocity of money. This equation, which was dismissed by the LM equation, brings home the neutrality of money: if velocity V and Y are taken as exogenous, the price level P is directly driven by money. In the classical view, Y is at full employment and V is constant, whereas in the Keynesian view Y is highly variable, P is constant and V depends on the interest rate.[5] Monetary neutrality, an old wisdom of classical economics discarded during the Keynesian heydays, was back and has not left us ever since. Its implications are profound; it now lies at the core of central banking, as explained in Chapter 9.

Third, in a careful study of consumption patterns in the USA, *A Theory of the Consumption Function*, a book published in 1956, Friedman argued that the Keynesian function $C = C(Y)$ had little theoretical foundation and questionable empirical validity. He put forward instead the permanent income hypothesis, which relates consumption to permanent income, or wealth, effectively reinventing the intertemporal analysis presented in Chapters 5 and 6, and previously explored by Yale economist

---

[3] Friedrich von Hayek (1899–1992), another Nobel Prize winner, was a prominent product of the Austrian School, which was disbanded in the late 1930s when the Nazis took over. Hayek moved first to the London School of Economics and in 1950 to Chicago, where he was a colleague of Milton Friedman.

[4] In a true gesture of modesty, Friedman is known to have given credit to Henry Simons (1889–1946) for founding the Chicago School.

[5] The debate was really about which assumption one is willing to make. There is no incompatibility between the quantity and LM equations: the LM equation $M/P = L(Y, i)$ can be rewritten as $M/P = l(i)Y$ if one assumes that output elasticity of money demand is 1, which means then that $V = 1/l(i)$. But the LM equation must be considered along with the IS equation to explain the interest rate, and with the AS curve to explain inflation, while the quantity equations is meant to the only equation that is needed to understand prices. The quantity equation is also known as the 'Cambridge equation', in deference to pre-Keynes Cambridge.

Irving Fisher (1867–1947). The important consequence of this work was to weaken the significance of the Keynesian multiplier and the view that fiscal policy can be a tool for output stabilization. Later on, the Keynesians restored some of the clout of the old consumption function by arguing that many consumers are credit rationed, as explained in Chapter 6.

Finally, in what may have been his greatest triumph, Friedman explained why the Phillips curve, then still considered as the missing equation, would vanish as soon as the authorities attempted to exploit the output–inflation trade-off. Not only did he restore the importance of expectations—and thus established the expectations-augmented Phillips curve—but he restated the long-run neutrality proposition—and thus invented the long-run vertical aggregate supply schedule. His work was published in 1968, and the Phillips curve went awry soon thereafter in the early 1970s. Not only were the Keynesians proven wrong, they were once more 'missing an equation', and monetarism became the new accepted wisdom, in academic circles first, among policy-makers next. It is important to note, however, that Edmund Phelps (1933–), from Columbia University in New York, who had reached the same result as Friedman and at roughly the same time, regards himself as Keynesian, see Chapter 12. Phelps essentially foretells modern economics, as presented in this book, which accepts the expectations-augmented Phillips curve as the missing equation, even if it means that there is no lasting trade-off between output and inflation.

In general, Europe was slow to recognize the power of the monetarists' attack, and did not contribute much to the research effort. In the UK, the academic establishment was dominated by Keynesians, most of whom refused to acknowledge that a major battle had been lost. The election of Mrs Thatcher changed all that. She brought in Friedman as an adviser, proclaiming that her government would follow the master's precepts, including rolling back government, pushing for wage stability by destroying the trade unions' grip on labour markets and, of course, a strict application of the monetary neutrality principle. She had been converted to monetarism by two close advisers

working in a think tank that she had created, the Centre for Policy Studies: Alan Walters (1926–), a British economist then working at Johns Hopkins University in the USA, and Patrick Minford (1943–), who had resisted Keynesian influence in his bastion at Liverpool University. When, early on during her first term, the scope of Thatcher's policy intentions became clear, 364 academic economists signed a manifesto that promised disaster if these policies were implemented. Two decades later, most of the signatories agree that 'we all are Thatcherites now'.

Elsewhere in Europe, the evolution was gradual, mostly the result of generation changes, as freshly graduated macroeconomists started to popularize either monetarist ideas or less orthodox versions of Keynesian economics. Still, in some countries like France, Keynesian ideas remain to this day the dominant reference in policy-making circles. Two French economists, Edmond Malinvaud (1923–) —who served for two decades as Head of the national statistical institute—and Jean-Pascal Benassy (1948–) had developed in the 1970s a disequilibrium interpretation of the Keynesian model. The particular feature of this interpretation, which has now been abandoned, is that it assumes that there can be lasting excess demand or supply in goods and labour markets.

In German-speaking countries, as mentioned above, Keynesian ideas never quite displaced the classical view, so there was no need for a monetarist counter-revolution. Economists and policy-makers saw the movement as a vindication of their own views, event though monetarism is considerably more subtle than classical economics. During the years of Keynesian domination, the flame of classical economics was carefully maintained at the annual Konstanz seminar, initially created by two early monetarists, the Swiss economist Karl Brunner (1916–89) who worked at Rochester University and Alan Meltzer (1928–) from Carnegie Mellon University in Pittsburgh.[6] The Konstanz Seminar still meets every year.

The Chicago school also contributed much to our understanding of the open economies. Much

---

6 The tradition at Konstanz is to display a flag that bears '$MV = PY$'.

of Mundell's work was produced when he was in Chicago, where he also trained a generation of international macroeconomists who developed the 'monetary approach to the exchange rate'. This approach shapes much of Chapter 19, including the stylized facts proposed by Michael Mussa (1944–) and the overshooting result of German-born Rudiger Dornbusch (1942–2002), both students of Mundell. Many others Chicago economists—including Mundell himself—worked at the IMF where they forged the Fund's doctrine and produced important work under the leadership of Dutch economist Jacques J. Polak (1914–).

Yet, Friedman's ideas have not always been widely accepted. One of his other major contributions is the intellectual defence of freely flexible exchange rates, as noted in Chapter 20. He gathered ammunition for this position while spending time in Paris in 1950 while at the US governmental agency which administered the Marshall Plan. At the time, he concluded that the European Common Market could not work with fixed exchange rates and he still maintains that the European Monetary Union is a mistake. This view still finds much support in the UK.

21.3 The Rational Expectations Revolution

Robert Lucas Jr., 1937 –

Source: The Nobel Foundation

Thomas Sargent, 1943 –

Source: New York University

The attack on Keynesian economics was not over yet. Another blow came with the rational expectations revolution. The expectations-augmented Phillips curve of Friedman and Phelps had left an important question unanswered: what drives expectations? Most economists thought of the expectations as gradually catching up with actually observed inflation, i.e. they were only taking account of what Chapter 12 defines as the backward-looking component or core inflation.

Although Phelps had made some headway in introducing the forward-looking component, the next major step was achieved in Chicago again where Nobel Prize laureate Robert E. Lucas Jr., a student of Friedman, spearheaded the rational expectations revolution.[7] Rational expectations are presented in Chapter 5 and 13, and further developed in Chapter 16. What Lucas and his colleagues[8] noted is that if the forward-looking component dominates and if expectations are not systematically biased, the Phillips curve is always vertical and systematic policy does not work. The conclusion was that monetary policy only affects output and employment if and only if it creates inflation surprises. Since creating short-lived surprises is not the way to conduct policy, the circle was closed. Friedman's contribution meant that fiscal policy is not helpful but that monetary policy is a powerful instrument, although one

[7] Lucas was not the first one to formulate this view. It was first advanced by a number American of economists from Carnegie Mellon University—they inspired Lucas who spent several years there before taking up a chair in Chicago—John Muth (1930–), Ed Prescott (1944–), and Finn Kydland (1943–).
[8] In particular Thomas Sargent (1943–) and Neil Wallace (1939–).

whose effects are eventually dissipated in inflation. The rational expectations revolution's message was that macroeconomic policies should not be used on and off with complete discretion. Instead, policy should obey rules and aim at establishing credibility for adhering at the rules.[9] This was not a complete vindication of the classic laissez-faire approach, but an indictment of Keynesian policy activism.

It is fair to say that the view that 'only unanticipated money matters' was not a big hit in policy-making circles. Indeed, it is hardly surprising that central banks explicitly reject the view that their role is limited to creating surprises. The empirical evidence is mixed, largely because expectations are difficult to observe.

21.4 The Microfoundations of Macroeconomics

Finn Kydland
1943 –

Source: Carnegie Mellon University

Edward Prescott
1940 –

Source: Federal Reserve Bank of Minneapolis

Because of its compelling logic, the rational expectations hypothesis attracted immense interest and opened the way for further innovations in other directions. Clearly, if it is appropriate to assume that expectations are rational, then why shouldn't all other economic decisions be rational as well? Researchers at 'freshwater universities' in the USA —Chicago, Minnesota, Rochester, Carnegie-Mellon and University of Pennsylvania—have established the microeconomic foundations of the consumption, investment, and primary account functions studied in Part II of this book. Some researchers even disassociate themselves completely from the

use of aggregate functions—giving in completely to the Lucas Critique discussed in Chapter 16. European economists from all countries—many after a sojourn in those US universities—are deeply involved in this research programme.

Insisting on the rigorous discipline of microeconomic foundations may be intellectually attractive, yet business cycles remain a fact of life that must be explained. This led neoclassical economists to the Real Business Cycles (RBC) research programme presented in Chapter 14. The aim of this effort is to show that models with flexible prices and fully rational agents—in brief, the Robison Crusoe story developed in Part II—can reproduce the key features of actual business cycles. The 'RBC school', inspired by the American Ed Prescott from Arizona University and Norwegian-born Finn Kydland from Carnegie Mellon University, has a significant following in Europe. Both won the Nobel Prize in 2004.

Despite the intellectual attractiveness of the RBC approach, it has not been an empirical success. Many of the most important stylized facts remain unaccounted for. Price stickiness simply appears to be a fact.[10] This opened up an opportunity for the New Keynesians, who were already at work on

---

[9] The preference of rules over discretion was first expressed by Milton Friedman in an essay written in the 1950s.

[10] This is hardly news! Milton Friedman and Anna Schwarz wrote extensively on long and variable lags with which monetary changes affect the price level. Even the old Scot David Hume (1711–76) was fascinated by the fact that gold inflows in seventeenth-century Spain had so little short-run influence on the price level.

their own response to the rational expectations revolution. Their main aim has been to show that price stickiness is not incompatible with microeconomic foundations and full rationality. New Keynesians have thus been able to produce a new synthesis, which fully rests on rational behaviour but deliver the traditional Keynesian results. Much of this work has been carried out at traditionally Keynesian 'saltwater universities' in the USA (Harvard, MIT, Yale, Princeton, Berkeley),[11] with some important contributions from Europe, e.g. Jordi Gali's (1961–) work at Pompeu Fabra University on the microfoundations for the expectations-augmented Phillips curve.

Interestingly, now accepting price stickiness, the RBC school has reached the same synthesis. A new consensus seems to be emerging and the line between Keynesian and non-Keynesian economists has become fuzzy. In the end, the *IS-LM* analysis is alive and well, even with microfoundations, though with many qualifications, as Chapter 11 makes clear. From the policy perspective, the view that fiscal and monetary policies can play a role as tools for output and employment stabilization is now generally accepted along with the recognition that the role of expectations requires much more prudence and care than the traditional Keynesians dared to admit, as explained in Chapter 16.

21.5 Institutional and Political Economics

Friedrich August von Hayek, 1889–1992

Source: Copyright Bettmann/Corbis

James Buchanan 1919–

Source: Photo courtesy of James Buchanan

Since the rational expectations revolution in the early 1970s, macroeconomics has managed to avoid further paradigmatic earthquakes. A number of innovations have occurred at the frontier between

economics and political science. This ongoing research programme starts from the obvious observation that policy actions are not taken in a vacuum, but by policy-makers, who are real-life politicians and keenly sensitive to public opinion as they seek re-election and power. In doing so, they need to calculate what will be the effects of their actions on the economy—the traditional macroeconomic question—and their voter's reactions. This theme is explored extensively in Chapters 15, 16, 17, and 18.

Once these questions are asked, it becomes clear that political systems matter a lot. We need to look at the respective influences of government and parliament, at the degree of independence of the central bank, and at the electoral rules. Here, the variety of institutions across Europe offers a unique source of observation. It comes as no surprise that European economists—some of whom are based in the USA—have often played a leading role in this area of research.

The roots of this new approach are both old and interesting as it has brought together some very different traditions. German-language economists

[11] Saltwater universities are located on the East and West coasts of the USA, while freshwater universities are inland, often close to the great lakes.

in the tradition of the Historical and Austrian schools have long explored these issues and their *Ordnungspolitik*—hard to translate but formally meaning 'policy of establishing or maintaining order', or more precisely, the institutional framework for economic activity—remains very influential in this part of Europe. With few exceptions,[12] however, these approaches did not exert much international influence, partly for language reasons, partly because they rejected formalization of their ideas. The same questions were explored independently by US-based economists of the 'Public Choice School', including Nobel Prize laureates James Buchanan (1919–) and Douglass North (1920–). Most economists associated with the public choice research programme consider themselves more aligned with the laissez-faire view.[13] Coming from a radically different perspective, New-Keynesian economists began to study why governments make policy mistakes, rather than simply criticizing them as do laissez-faire economists. They stress that sometimes policy-makers pursue bad policies because they have distorted incentives. Since incentives are determined by institutions, to improve policy-makers' incentives, institutional reforms may be needed. Important contributions have been made by Alberto Alesina, an Italian economist at Harvard University, Torsten Persson (1954–) from Stockholm University and Guido Tabellini

(1956–) from Bocconi University, among others. Finally, a few French microeconomists—brought together at Toulouse University by Jean Tirole (1953–) and Jean-Jacques Laffont (1947–2004) —have explored the question of incentives and decision-making under uncertainty. Their results are gradually percolating into macroeconomics, where they allow studying the interaction between policy-makers and the private sector.

This work indicates that the kind of differences that oppose laissez-faire advocates and interventionists are too blunt when stated as 'the government should stay out of economics' vs. 'governments must take responsibility for economic welfare'. There are some tasks that some governments can usefully perform and others cannot, and tasks of general interest that are better left to the markets. For example, fiscal policy may play a stabilizing role, but governments tend to suffer from a deficit bias, especially in political regimes where decisions are made by divided parliaments. Equally important is the realization that some economic policies cannot be improved unless the political institutions are first reformed. A good example is that central bank independence is generally a precondition for good monetary policy. Employment and growth are two further examples of the important innovations brought by this fundamental intuition.

21.6 Labour Markets

One of Europe's sad distinguishing features is the high rate of unemployment that has prevailed over the last two decades. In a number of reassuring cases, however, some—mostly smaller—European countries have been able to roll back unemploy-

ment. As Chapters 4 and 17 emphasize, the problem lies in labour market structures, institutions, and policies. Here again, comparison and analysis of the diversity of situations in Europe has offered a wealth of lessons about the nature of unemployment and the ways to deal with it. European economists have made significant progress, if only to develop a genuine understanding of their own labour markets that profoundly differ from those in the USA.

[12] Prominent examples are Bruno Frey (1941–) of Zurich and Roland Vaubel (1948–) of Mannheim University.
[13] Many members of the Public Choice School are part of the Mont-Pélerin Society, a group created by Friedrich von Hayek in Mont-Pélerin near Lausanne, Switzerland.

**Richard Layard,
1934 –**

Source: British Academy

**Stephen Nickell,
1944 –**

Source: Bank of England

Much of the pioneering effort has been conducted at the London School of Economics' Centre for Labour Economics led by Richard Layard (1934–) and Steve Nickell (1944–). Other important early contributors are Edmond Malinvaud (1923–), from France, Jacques Drèze (1929–) from the University Louvain-la-Neuve in Belgium, Herbert Giersch (1921–) from the University of Kiel in Germany, and Assar Lindbeck (mentioned above) who, together with Dennis Snower (1950–) from the University of London, developed the insider–outsider theory, according to which labour representatives defend the interests of the employed workers—the insiders—at the expense of those who are not employed—the outsiders. The overwhelming evidence is that labour market rigidities lie at the root of Europe's unemployment problem. This assessment is not much disputed today but was initially rejected by Keynesian economists, who blamed instead restrictive demand management policies. One way of simplifying the debate is whether the problem lies with a high equilibrium unemployment rate (the case of rigidities) or whether actual unemployment is kept above its equilibrium rate. Interestingly, monetarists always took the view that the equilibrium unemployment rate had risen. The diagnosis that structural problems are at the root of the unemployment problem in Europe is hardly disputed, except by a handful of die-hard Keynesians, and recognized by many governments.

This conclusion has triggered a search for appropriate solutions. Structural problems call for structural reforms, and reforms are always controversial. In the area of labour markets, the controversies are laden with emotional political and social undertones; in some countries deep ideological battles have resurfaced. The reason is simple, and is reminiscent of the problem of dynamic efficiency discussed in Chapter 3: to get to where we want to go, up-front sacrifices are necessary. Real wage moderation, cuts in unemployment benefits, reform of job protection and the deregulation of product markets may well hurt many individuals today, even if later ultimately leading to an increase in employment and GDP. Finding out how to convince and compensate the losers in reforms is the magic formula which smaller European economies seemed to have found. Several European economists are actively investigating conditions under which politically difficult economic reforms can be adopted. What has to be done is now subject to much agreement, with important detailed work carried out by the economic staff of the OECD and IMF. Some countries have implemented many of these measures, and unemployment has significantly declined. In others countries, governments have been too sensitive to even acknowledge the need for action.

21.7 Growth and Development

**Robert Solow,
1924 –**

Source: The Nobel Foundation

**Paul Romer,
1955 –**

Source: Hoover Institution

**Robert Barro,
1944 –**

Source: Hoover Institution

Much as our understanding of labour markets has greatly benefited from institutional economics, one of the most important—and more vexing—issues involving the wealth and poverty of nations has also been profoundly rethought. As explained in Chapter 3, research on the neoclassical growth model[14] conducted at MIT by Nobel Prize laureate Robert Solow, had two key implications: (1) capital is more productive where it is scarce and (2) the key source of sustained growth is unexplained—or exogenous—technological progress. Both implications were deeply unsatisfactory, and both have motivated important innovations to conventional growth theory.

[14] This theory is called neoclassical because it relies on standard microeconomic principles, much like neoclassical macroeconomics. But Bob Solow, as he is generally called, has been a leading and enthusiastic proponent of Keynesian economics.

As noted in Chapter 18, Robert E. Lucas Jr. challenged economists to explain why capital doesn't flow from rich to poor countries. Poor countries are characterized by low capital intensity and in theory must have a much higher marginal productivity of capital than rich countries. One important solution to his puzzle is that high productivity may be high in theory, but in fact is significantly reduced by the prevalence of poor institutions that allow corruption, instability, and war to discourage investment.

If technological change is exogenous, however, it is not possible to explain why institutions matter. In the mid-1980s, Paul Romer (1955–) from Stanford University showed how technological progress could be treated as endogenous. As explained in Chapters 3 and 18, the crucial step was to recognize that knowledge does not suffer from decreasing returns. This established a link with Lucas' question: education is an investment in human capital, and it is deterred by poor institutions exactly as investment in physical capital. This discovery allowed many others to explore the process of growth and economic development. Much empirical evidence has since been produced by Robert Barro (1944–) at Harvard University in collaboration with Spanish-born Xavier Sala-i-Martin (1963–) from Columbia University, with important contributions by many others, including French-born Philippe Aghion (1956–) from the University of London.

The result of this research has been a thorough reappraisal of underdevelopment and of policies that try to deal with extreme poverty in many parts of the world. The emphasis has shifted from earlier recommendations by the rich countries to 'do as we do' to try and encourage the establishment of better institutions that would provide political leaders in the poor countries with the incentives to adopt pro-growth policies. This literature has also profoundly affected the international financial institutions, in particular the World Bank and the regional development banks. The results are slow in coming but some important successes have been achieved. The same message also concerns the rich countries, especially Europe, which stopped catching up with the USA in the mid-1980s. The message is that reforms are needed to make the political system interested in supporting agents of change rather than established economic interests.

21.8 Conclusions

While economists are not detached from their own prejudices, it is crucial that they focus as much as possible on developing rigorous theories and conduct dispassionate evaluations of their policy implications. By and large, this is what economists have done. Controversies abound, but over time intellectual exchange and the search for unifying truths have brought economists closer together in an ever-increasing degree of agreement. For example, Patrick Minford (see above) was harshly criticized in the 1980s when he argued that high unemployment benefits discouraged unemployed workers from looking for new jobs. His former Keynesian critics have now accepted the view that unemployment benefits need to be structured in a way that reduces potential adverse effects on work incentives. In contrast to much of the public debate, professional macroeconomists see their field as an intellectual challenge to solve pressing problems, and not as an ideological exercise.

Macroeconomics was born in Europe as a revolt against classical economists in the wake of the Great Depression. Much of the ensuing research was carried out in the USA. These developments clarified the limits of Keynesian economics and eventually allowed a field to emerge, which is not yet fully unified but where controversies are now well understood and circumscribed. Prompted by problems of low growth and high unemployment, European economists have made important contributions that make macroeconomics a lively field with its own flavour. Although there is no such thing as European macroeconomics, a number of macroeconomic issues in Europe merit more attention than they receive in the USA. These range from the role of regulations, taxes and transfers in labour markets to the functioning of monetary unions. More than anything else, Europe consists of 'small and open' independent countries, and this fact sets it apart from the highly integrated states of the USA. If the last ten years of our textbook is any evidence, it is these differences which make macroeconomics in Europe so special.

Essay Question

Make your list of future Nobel Prize winners, and explain why you chose them.

References

Adelman, Irma, and Adelman, Frank (1959), 'The Dynamic Properties of the Klein-Goldberger Model', *Econometrica*, 27: 596–625.

Alesina, Alberto (1988), 'The End of Large Public Debts', in F. Giavazzi and L. Spaventa (eds.), *High Public Debt: The Italian Experience*, Cambridge University Press, pages 34–79.

—— (1989), 'Politics and Business Cycles in Industrial Democracies', *Economic Policy*, 8: 55–98.

—— and Summers, Lawrence (1993), 'Central Bank Independence and Macroeconomic Performance: Some Comparative Evidence', *Journal of Money, Credit, and Banking*, 25(2): 151–62.

Barro, Robert J. (1989), 'The Ricardian Approach to Budget Deficits', *Journal of Economic Perspectives*, 3(2): 37–54.

—— (1991), 'Economic Growth in a Cross Section of Countries', *Quarterly Journal of Economics*, 106(2): 407–43.

—— and Sala-i-Martin, Xavier (1995), *Economic Growth*, McGraw-Hill.

Baumol, William (1956), 'The Transactions Demand for Cash: An Inventory-Theoretic Approach', *Quarterly Journal of Economics*, 66: 545–56.

Berg, Andrew, and Sachs, Jeffrey (1992), 'Structural Adjustment and International Trade in Eastern Europe: The Case of Poland', *Economic Policy*, 14: 117–73.

Bloch, Laurence, and Coeuré, Benoit (1994), 'q de Tobin marginal et transmission des chocs financiers' ('Tobin's Marginal q and the Transmission of Monetary Shocks'), *Annales d'Économie et de Statistique*, 36: 133–67.

Booth, Alison (1995), *The Economics of Trade Unions*, Cambridge University Press.

Burda, Michael, and Gerlach, Stefan (1993), 'Exchange Rate Dynamics and Currency Unification: The Ostmark–DM Rate', *Empirical Economics*, 18: 417–29.

Chadha, Bankim, and Prasad, Eswar (1994), 'Are Prices Countercyclical? Evidence from the G-7', *Journal of Monetary Economics*, 34(2): 239–57.

Cooper, Richard (1982), 'The Gold Standard: Historical Facts and Future Prospects', *Brookings Papers on Economic Activity*, 1: 1–45.

Dam, Kenneth W. (1982), *The Rules of the Game*, University of Chicago Press.

—— (1989), *The Rules of the Game*, University of Chicago Press.

Danthine, Jean-Pierre, and Donaldson, John (1993), 'Methodological and Empirical Issues in Real Business Cycle Theory', *European Economic Review*, 37(1): 1–35.

De Gregorio, José, Eichengreen, Barry, Ito, Takatoshi, and Wyplosz, Charles (1999), 'An Independent and Accountable IMF', *Geneva Report 1*, CEPR.

Deutsche Bundesbank (2000), *Macro-Econometric Multi-Country Model: MEMMOD* Frankfurt Deutsche Bundesbank, June, p. 102.

Dolado, Juan, Kramarz, Francis, Machin, Stephen, Manning, Alan, Margolis, David, and Teulings, Coen (1996), 'The Economic Impact of Minimum Wages in Europe', *Economic Policy*, 23: 317–72.

Dornbusch, Rudiger, and Fischer, Stanley (1986), 'Stopping Hyperinflations Past and Present', *Weltwirtschaftliches Archiv*, 122(1): 1–47.

Ebbinghaus, Bernd, and Visser, Jelle (2000), *Trade Unions in Western Europe Since 1945*, Macmillan.

European Commission (2000), 'Industrial Relations in Europe', *Employment and Social Affairs*, Brussels.

Fair, Ray C. (1987), 'International Evidence on the Demand for Money', *Review of Economics and Statistics*, 69(3): 473–80.

Freeman, Richard, and Schettkat, Ronald (2002), 'Marketization of Production and the US–Europe Employment Gap', NBER Working Paper 8797, February.

Friedman, Milton (1968), 'The Role of Monetary Policy', *American Economic Review*, 58: 1–17.

Garber, Peter (1990), 'Famous First Bubbles', *Journal of Economic Perspectives*, 4(2): 35–54.

Gerlach, Stefan, and Smets, Frank (1995), 'The Monetary Transmission Mechanism: Evidence from the G-7 Countries', Centre for Economic Policy Research, Discussion Paper 1219, July.

Giavazzi, Francesco, and Pagano, Marco (1990), 'Can Severe Fiscal Contractions Be Expansionary? Tales of Two Small European Countries', in O. J. Blanchard and S. Fischer (eds.), *NBER Macroeconomics Annual 1990*, MIT Press, pages 75–111.

Goodhart, Charles (1988), *The Evolution of Central Banks*, MIT Press.

Gordon, Robert (2000), 'Does the "New Economy" Measure up to the Great Inventions of the Past?', NBER Working Paper 7833, August.

Grilli, Vittorio, Masciandaro, Donato, and Tabellini, Guido (1991), 'Political and Monetary Institutions and Public Financial Policies in the Industrial Countries', *Economic Policy*, 6(2): 341–92.

Holtfrerich, Carl (1986), *The German Inflation 1914–1923: Causes and EAects in International Perspective*, Berlin/New York: De Gruyter.

Homer, Sydney (1963), *A History of Interest Rates*, Rutgers University Press.

Kaldor, Nicholas (1961), *The Theory of Capital*, Macmillan.

Keynes, J. M. (1930), *A Treatise on Money*, Macmillan.

Kindleberger, Charles (1973), *The World in Depression*, University of California Press.

Lucas, Robert E. Jr. (1990), 'Why Doesn't Capital Flow from Rich to Poor Countries?', *American Economic Review*, 80(2): 92–6.

Maddison, Angus (1989), *The World Economy in the 20th Century*, OECD Development Centre.

—— (1991), *Dynamic Forces in Capitalist Development*, Oxford University Press.

—— (1995), *Monitoring the World Economy 1820–1992*, OECD Development Centre.

Marx, Karl (1867), *Das Kapital*, Vol. i, Dietz Verlag (1983).

Mitchell, Brian (1978), *European Historical Statistics*, Columbia University Press.

—— (1983), *International Historical Statistics*, Macmillan.

—— (1998), *International Historical Statistics*, Macmillan.

Neumark, D., and Wascher, W. (2003), 'Minimum Wages, Labor Market Institutions, and Youth Employment: A Cross-National Analysis', mimeo, Michigan State University, March.

Ritschl, Albrecht (2004), 'News from Tobin's q: Capital Markets were Efficient in 1929', Working Paper, HU 2004.

Rogoff, Kenneth (1998), 'Blessing or Curse? Foreign and Underground Demand for Euro Notes', *Economic Policy*, 26: 261–303.

Roll, Eric, Begg, David, Goodhart, Charles, and Wyplosz, Charles (1993), *Independent and Accountable: A New Mandate for the Bank of England*, Centre for Economic Policy Research.

Sahay, Ratna, and Végh, Carlos (1995), 'Dollarization in Transition Economies', *Finance and Development*, 32(1): 36–9.

Sargent, Thomas (1982), 'The End of Four Big Inflations', in R. Hall (ed.), *Inflation*, University of Chicago Press, pages 41–98.

Schneider, Friedrich, and Enste, Dominik (2000), 'Shadow Economies: Size, Causes, and Consequences', *Journal of Economic Literature*, 38: 77–114.

Summers, Robert, and Heston, Alan (1991), 'The Penn World Table (Mark 5): An Expanded Set of International Comparisons, 1950–1988', *Quarterly Journal of Economics*, 106(2): 327–68.

Tobin, James (1956), 'The Interest Elasticity of the Transactions Demand for Cash', *Review of Economics and Statistics*, 38: 241–7.

—— (1996), 'Prologue', in M. ul Haq, I. Kaul, and I. Grunberg (eds.), *The Tobin Tax*, Oxford University Press, pages ix–xvii.

Wyplosz, Charles (1999), 'Macroeconomic Lessons from Ten Years of Transition', in B. Pleskovic and J. E. Stiglitz (eds.), *Annual World Bank Conference on Development Economics*, The World Bank, Washington, DC.

Glossary

This glossary presents brief definitions of the key concepts listed at the end of each chapter. Numbers refer to the corresponding chapter(s).

absolute purchasing power parity (**8**): theory asserting that price levels are equalized across countries once they are converted into a common currency

absorption (**2**): total national (private and public) spending on goods and services

accelerator (**6**): the positive effect of an increase in GDP on the rate of investment

accounting identities (**2**): relationships linking macroeconomic magnitudes to each other by definition

active labour market policies (**17**): programmes involving direct job creation, targeted job securities, retraining, relocation of families from distressed regions, or special programmes to get young people started in the job market

activist policies (**16**): government policies which try to improve market outcomes by correcting market dysfunctions

acyclical (**14**): an economic variable is acyclical when it does not move systematically with aggregate output over the business cycle

aggregate demand (**1, 11, 12, 13**): the sum of planned consumption, investment, government purchases of goods and services, plus net export of goods and services (the primary current account)

aggregate demand curve (**13**): downward-sloping curve relating aggregate demand negatively to the rate of inflation

aggregate production function (**5**): a relationship linking total output to employed resources such as capital, labour, and other factors of production

aggregate supply (**12**): total volume of goods and services brought to market by producers at a given price level

aggregate supply curve (**12**): upward-sloping curve linking inflation to aggregate output supplied by firms

animal spirits (**6**): term referring to entrepreneurs' optimism and willingness to undertake risky investment projects

appreciation (exchange rate) (**7, 8, 13, 19**): a market-determined increase in the value of a currency (less of that currency must be relinquished to buy one unit of foreign currency); *see*: **depreciation**; **revaluation**

arbitrage (**11, 13, 15**): the simultaneous purchase and sale of assets of identical characteristics to earn a profit without risk-taking: **spatial arbitrage** responds to diverging asset prices across different market locations, **yield arbitrage** responds to differing asset returns, and **triangular arbitrage** to three asset prices that are not mutually consistent

augmented Phillips curve (**12**): a Phillips curve incorporating core inflation and allowing for supply shocks

autarky (**5**): the state in which a country operates when it does not trade with the rest of the world

automatic stabilizer (**15**): the economic mechanism that automatically cushions the impact of exogenous changes in aggregate demand, via the effect of income on saving decisions

average or unit costs (**12**): production costs per unit of output

balance of payments (2): a summary of all real and financial transactions of a country with the rest of the world

balance sheet (8): a statement of the financial position of a firm or other entity at a particular point in time, indicating its assets, liabilities, and net worth

balanced growth (3): term describing a steadily growing economy where certain key ratios remain constant, for example the capital–output ratio

Balassa–Samuelson effect (7): the observation that price levels in richer nations are systematically higher than in poor ones; attributed to higher non-traded goods price inflation in fast growing countries

band of fluctuation (20): the range within which the market value of a national currency is permitted to fluctuate by international agreements, or by unilateral decision by the central bank

bank reserves (9): the central bank liabilities (cash or central bank deposits) that commercial banks choose or are required to hold to meet demands of depositors and/or the requirements of regulators

battle of the mark-ups (12): the interpretation of the wage and price setting mechanism whereby firms set prices as high as possible over costs, including wages, while employees try to have wages grow faster than the inflation rate

beggar-thy-neighbour policies (11): policies, especially exchange rate policies, designed to divert domestic demand away from foreign goods and towards domestically produced goods

Beveridge curve (17): downward-sloping curve relating the unemployment rate to the vacancy rate; the position of this curve measures the efficiency of the job-matching process

bid–ask spread (9): in the foreign exchange market, the bid is the price at which one can sell foreign exchange (to some market maker); the ask is the price at which one can buy it on the market. The spread is the difference—usually quoted as a percentage—between the two prices

bimetallism (20): the use of both gold and silver as a commodity money standard

boom/recession (14): period of expanding/contracting aggregate economic activity

borrowing constraint (5): restrictions on borrowing arising from uncertainty about future incomes, which prevent agents from taking advantage of their intertemporal allocation of resources

Bretton Woods Conference (20): meeting held in 1944 and attended by officials from 45 nations to shape a new international money order after the Second World War

British terms (7): one of two ways of quoting the exchange rate, here in units of the foreign currency per one unit of domestic currency (e.g. US$1.52 for $1 for UK residents); *see also* **European terms**

bubbles (9): persistent deviations of asset prices from their fundamental values, or from widely held views about their fundamental values

budget line (5): the line expressing the resource constraint of households in consuming today and tomorrow, the slope is the negative of the gross interest rate.

Burns–Mitchell diagram (14): a diagram displaying the behaviour of macroeconomic variables over the typical business cycle as a deviation from their values at the cyclical peak

business cycles (1, 11, 12, 14): succession of periods of rapid growth and slowdown or decline in which output fluctuates around its long-run trend

capacity utilization (rate) (1): the proportion of installed equipment currently employed; higher rates occur during booms, lower rates correspond to recessions

capital (2): one of the factors of production; usually refers to plant, equipment, inventories, and structures

capital account (2): component of the balance of payments accounts that records financial transactions with the rest of the world

capital accumulation (3): the increase of the stock of capital, sometimes called net investment or net formation of capital. It differs from gross investment, which also includes the capital put in place to replace depreciated equipment

capital adequacy (9): minimum net worth banks are required to have as a fraction of total risky assets

capital control premium (19): the deviation from the covered interest parity arising from restrictions on capital movements

capital controls (11, 17, 20): restrictions on the movement of assets into and out of a country

capital – labour ratio (3): the ratio of the stock of capital to the use of labour

capital widening line (3): the straight line in the diagram of the Solow-model with population growth, which shows the investment per capita needed to maintain a constant per capita capital stock per unit per capita (in efficiency units)

central bank (9): a public or quasi-public agency with an explicit legal mandate to issue banknotes and other liabilities as legal tender

circular flow (2): the fact that each final sale of a good or service represents income to factors of production employed to produce it; similarly, income to factors of production is either spent or saved, while savings are used to finance final purchasers of goods by others

classical dichotomy (10): the situation pertaining when equilibrium values of nominal variables can be determined independently of real variables; the real side of eonomic activity (growth, unemployment, etc.) is affected only by technology and tastes

closed economy (10): an economy that does not trade with, borrow from, or lend to other countries

Cobb – Douglas production function (3): a particular form of the general production function linking output Y to capital K and labour L: $Y = AK^{\alpha}L^{1-\alpha}$

coefficient of variation (1): a measure of variability expressed as the standard deviation divided by the mean

coincident indicator (14): a macroeconomic variable which coincides with aggregate output over the cycle

collective labour supply curve (4): the link between the amount of man-hours that workers supply collectively (via wage negotiations or through their unions) and the real wage

collectively voluntary/individually involuntary unemployment (4): unemployment that is undesirable from the point of view of individual workers but accepted by them collectively as they trade off higher wages for fewer jobs

commodity money (8): forms of money that have intrinsic value in other uses, or derive their value from the commodity out of which they are made, chiefly gold or silver

competition policy (16, 18): policies aimed at decreasing monopoly power and increasing rivalry among sellers in markets

conditionality (20): requirements imposed by the IMF on member-countries' macroeconomic policies for obtaining certain types of loans

constant returns to scale (3): term describing a production function in which simultaneous equiproportional increases in the factors of production result in an equiproportional increase in output

consumer price index (1, 2, 12): an index of prices of a basket of goods representative of the consumption pattern of the 'average consumer', using fixed quantity weights in some base year

consumer surplus (17): the difference between the maximum amount that a consumer would be willing to pay for a specified quantity of good and what she must actually pay for it

consumption (2): goods and services produced and sold to households for the satisfaction of wants

consumption function (6): a symbolic way of stating that the aggregate consumption is positively related to aggregate wealth and, if a significant proportion of households is constrained in credit markets, to disposable income

consumption – leisure trade-off (4): the fundamental determinant of the labour supply decision: in order to consume, we need income and therefore we need to work, which means giving up leisure time

consumption smoothing (6, 15): optimal choice by households to smooth out the impact of temporary disturbances to income on consumption plans by either borrowing (in the case of a negative shock) or saving (in the case of a positive shock)

contagion (20): situation arising when one country devalues in a fixed exchange rate system, causing others to lose competitiveness and become candidates for devaluation, even if this was not initially justified

convergence criteria (20): set of conditions that must be met by countries wishing to join the European Monetary Union

convergence hypothesis (5): the hypothesis of a negative association between per capita growth and initial per capita GDP

coordination failure (1): situation occuring when agents (households, firms) fail to realize that their actions are interdependent, and that acting jointly might benefit all

copyrights (18): a legal right that prevents commercial usage by others of works like books, music, etc.

core or underlying inflation rate (12): the inflation rate taken into account during wage bargaining to anticipate future inflation or to recuperate losses from past inflation

corporatism (4): the degree to which trade unions, management, and governments work together to achieve macroeconomic objectives

correlation coefficient (1): a statistical measure, ranging from −1 to 1, which shows how closely two variables move together: a value of zero indicates the absence of correlation; a value of 1 indicates perfect positive correlation; a value of −1 indicates perfect negative correlation

countercyclical (14): term used to describe an economic variable when it is negatively correlated with the state of the economy; that is, it moves in the opposite direction to aggregate output over the business cycle

countercyclical fiscal policy (15): corrective device intended to keep the economy near its equilibrium level by increasing or decreasing aggregate demand via public spending or tax policies

covered interest parity (19): a no-arbitrage condition equating the difference between domestic and foreign interest rates to the forward exchange discount

credibility (16, 20): the degree to which authorities are believed by the public to take specific actions in response to disturbances; e.g. credible central bank is known not to tolerate inflation; *see:* **reputation**

credit rationing (6): a condition in loan markets in which there is excess demand for loans at the market interest rate

crowding out (11): mechanism by which an expansionary fiscal policy may in the end have little, no, or even a negative effect on aggregate output and income because other components of demand decline

current account (2, 3, 7): the sum of a country's trade in goods, services, and unilateral transfers with the rest of the world

cyclically adjusted budgets (15): budgets adjusted for the effect of the business cycle on tax revenues

damped, explosive and oscillating cycles (14): a time series is denoted to be damped (explosive, oscillating) if it displays diminishing (increasing, steady) cycles

debt stabilization (15): the process of arresting explosive growth in the debt–GDP ratio, usually achieved by cutting government expenditures and raising taxes

decision lag (16): time lag in policy effectiveness needed by government to formulate policy

decreasing returns to scale (3): describes a production function for which an equiproportional increase in the factors of production results in a less than equiproportional increase in output; *see also* **constant returns to scale** and **increasing returns to scale**

deflation (1, 13): a period of sustained decrease in the general price level, or more generally a sustained decline in the inflation rate

demand determined output (10): when suppliers produce whatever is demanded at a given price level

demand management (16): policy to keep the economy at its equilibrium level by correcting aggregate demand

demand shock (14): sudden increase or decrease in aggregate demand

demand side (1, 12): the analysis of spending decisions by economic agents

depreciation (capital) (2, 6): the loss of original value of a physical asset owing to use, age, and economic obsolescence

depreciation (exchange rate) (7, 8, 13, 19): a market-determined decrease in the value of a currency (more of that currency must be relinquished to buy one unit of foreign currency); *see*: appreciation, revaluation

depreciation line (3): the straight line in the diagram of the Solow-model without technical progress and population growth, which shows the investment per capita needed to maintain a constant capital stock per capita

derivatives (19): securities that derive their value from the behaviour of other underlying securities

derived demand (9): a demand for something which arises as a product of a demand for something else

desired demand function (10): total planned spending given the interest rate and real GDP

detrending (14): removing the trend in economic time series

devaluation (11, 13, 20): decision by the monetary authority to reduce the value of the currency; *see*: revaluation, appreciation, depreciation

difference equation (14): an equation relating the trajectory of a variable in the current period to past values in a linear fashion; e.g. $y_t = a_0 + a_1 y_{t-1} + a_2 y_{t-2}$

diffusion (18): the process through which discoveries are progressively adopted by various industries

diminishing marginal productivity (3, 5): the tendency that, as the inputs into production are increased, the increments of output will decline

discount lending or rediscounting (9): instrument of monetary control employed by the central bank when it lends reserves directly to commercial banks at the discount rate

discount rate (9): interest rate at which the central bank lends reserves to a commercial bank by discount lending or rediscounting

discounting (5): valuing future goods or money in terms of goods or money today; *see also* **intertemporal price**

disequilibrium (10): situation occuring when, at given output or interest levels, desired demand is not equal to supply

distortionary taxation (17, 18): *see*: **tax distortions**

diversification (19): purchasing several different assets to reduce risk to wealth caused by fluctuations in the value of any single asset

dollar shortage (20): a situation that was feared within member-countries of the Bretton Woods system in the 1950s, because the USA ran current account surpluses

dominated asset (8): an asset that bears a lower rate of return than assets of comparable riskiness

double coincidence of wants (8): a condition required for barter to take place, in which the type and quantity of goods offered by one trader match those desired by the other

durable goods (6): goods that yield a flow of services into the future

Dutch disease (7): the loss of competitiveness arising from a real exchange appreciation as a result of the discovery of natural resources

dynamic inefficiency/efficiency (3): an economy is dynamically inefficient when a reduction of current savings can make all generations better off; it is dynamically efficient when future generations can be made better off only by reducing consumption (i.e. increasing savings) today

economic agents (1): term used to denote decision-makers in an economy

economic growth (1, 3): secular increases in the output of an economy, usually measured by the annual growth in GDP per capita

economic independence (16): the central bank is not subject to restrictive rules regarding the way it conducts its operations

economic rents (17, 18): returns to factors of production that exceed the minimum amount necessary to keep those factors of production in operation

effective exchange rate (7): an index consisting of a weighted average of a country's exchange rates *vis-à-vis* its main trading partners

effective labour (3): a measure of labour input which accounts for not only the number of hours worked but also for the effect of technical progress on the productivity of those hours

effectiveness lag (16): time lag resulting from a slow or delayed impact of economic policies on real activity

efficiency wages (4): wages paid in excess of the marginal productivity of labour in order to induce sufficient effort on the part of the workers

employers' associations (4): organizations of employers which represent their interests, especially in collective bargaining

endogenous and exogenous variables (1): endogenous variables are explained by economic principles; exogenous variables, in contrast, are determined outside the system under study

endogenous growth (3, 18): an explanation of growth as the result of decisions taken by private agents in response to economic conditions, rather than in response to the exogenous evolution of technical progress

endogenous growth theory (18): in contrast with the theory of exogenous growth, which explains sustainable growth by exogenous technological advances, endogenous growth theory tracks down the sources of growth to the accumulation of factors of production, with particular emphasis on knowledge

endowment (5, 6): the exogenous resources that economic agents expect to have in the present and in the future

equilibrium GDP (10): the GDP level at which the desired demand for goods and services is equal to the supply

equilibrium rate of unemployment (4, 11): the unemployment rate that occurs when employment and unemployment stabilize, i.e. when aggregate demand for labour is met by aggregate supply. Because labour supply may not perfectly reflect individuals' preferences, this unemployment may in part be involuntary (structural unemployment), but it may also reflect the efficiency of the labour market (frictional unemployment)

equilibrium real exchange rate (7): the theoretical level of the real exchange rate (the nominal exchange rate doubly deflated by price indexes

at home and abroad) necessary to enforce the national budget constraint with the rest of the world

equity – efficiency trade-off (15): the fact that improving equity among society's members often has a negative impact on the economy's efficiency

European Central Bank (20): centre of a planned new European System of Central Banks

European Currency Unit (ECU) (20): the unit of account of the European Monetary System and the European Community, and the basis for defining the parities in the Exchange Rate Mechanism (ERM); consists of a basket of the EC currencies; *see:* **Exchange Rate Mechanism**

European Monetary System (EMS) (20): international agreement set up in 1979 to stabilize the exchange rates between the currencies of some EC countries

European Monetary Union (EMU) (20): the planned-for achievement, by 1999 at the latest, of a single common currency for the European Community

Eurosystem (9): the system of central banks consisting of the European Central Bank plus the twelve national central banks of the European Monetary Union

European System of Central Banks (20): system including the European Central Bank and national subsidiaries in an integrated system of European central banks

European terms (7, 18): one of two ways of quoting the exchange rate, here in units of domestic currency per one unit of the foreign currency (e.g. €0.8 or US$1 for residents); *see also* British terms

excess supply (10): a market situation in which the quantity supplied exceeds desired demand at prevailing prices

exchange market intervention (10): the central bank buys or sells its own currency against foreign currencies on the foreign exchange market in order to prevented unwanted exchange rate movements

Exchange Rate Mechanism (ERM) (20): the fixed exchange rate system of the European Monetary System

exchange rate regime (11): description of the exchange rate system adopted by a country: the exchange rate may be fixed, so that the central bank maintains the value of the domestic money in terms of another currency or group of currencies or it may be freely floating

export function (11): function representing part of a country's foreign spending and therefore following its fluctuations—the greater the foreign spending, the greater will be exports

externalities (5, 15, 18): activities that affect the welfare of economic agents not undertaking them directly

factors of production (1, 2): inputs in the production process, such as labour, capital, or land, which create value added (in contrast to intermediary inputs)

fiat money (8): money which the state declares to be legal tender although its intrinsic value may be little or nothing

final and intermediate sales (2): final sales refer to sales of goods and services to the consumer or firm that will ultimately use them; intermediate sales refer to producers who use and transform these goods or services as part of their own production of goods and services

financial account (2): net sales of foreign assets by private domestic residents (a purchase by domestic residents worsens the financial account balance, a sale improves it)

financial integration line (19): the line in the IS–LM diagram defining the domestic interest rate level consistent with financial integration in the world economy with full capital mobility

financial intermediaries (9): economic entities that collect funds from depositors and lend them to borrowers

financial intermediation (2): the channelling of savings by households by banks and other financial institutions to those willing to undertake physical investment

finding rate (4): the rate at which unemployed workers find a job, calculated as a ratio of job finds (per month or per year) to total unemployment

fiscal policy (13, 15, 16): the use of the government budget to affect the volume of national spending, or more generally to provide public goods and services, as well as to redistribute income

Fisher principle (8): the decomposition of the nominal interest rate (i) into the sum of the real interest rate (r) and the expected rate of inflation (π^e)

fixed capital formation (5): *see* investment

flows and stocks (2): a flow is an economic variable measured between two periods of time; a stock is a magnitude measured at a given time

foreign exchange interventions (2, 9): purchases and sales of foreign money in exchange for domestic money undertaken by monetary authorities

foreign exchange reserves (2): foreign currencies held by the monetary authority for the purpose of intervening in the exchange markets

forward bias (19): the difference between the expected future spot exchange rate and the corresponding forward rate

forward contract (19): a financial contract that arranges now, at an agreed-upon price, for a deal that will occur at a future date

forward exchange rate (19): an exchange rate agreed upon today for a currency exchange that will occur at a future date

forward market (19): the market for foreign exchange delivered and paid for at some point in the future but at a price agreed upon today

forward forecast error (19): the deviation of the forward rate from the realized spot exchange rate

forward premium or discount (19): price of a forward contract with respect to the spot price

frictional unemployment (4): unemployment resulting from individuals' changing jobs or entering the labour force

fundamental valuation (19): the value of an asset that is equal to the present value of future payments generated by the asset

fundamentals (7, 19): factors driving the exchange rate; the net external position, and determinants of the primary current account as well as monetary conditions and the degree of price rigidity: in general, the underlying real factors that determine the value of an asset

futures (**19**): contracts for future delivery of goods or financial assets, including **foreign exchange general equilibrium** (**1, 4, 7, 10**); a characterization of an economy that considers all markets and heirs impact on each other rather than a single market in isolation

GDP deflator (**2**): a (Paasche) price index for total value added of an economy, given by the nominal GDP divided by the real GDP (GDP valued at price of some base year)

general equilibrium (**10, 11**): condition of equilibrium applying simultaneously to several markets at the same time, recognizing the interdependencies between markets

GNP or GDP deflator (**2**): the ratio of nominal to real GNP or GDP, the rate of increase of which is a frequently used measure of inflation

goal independence (**16**): the central bank can freely define its precise policy objectives, usually within a broadly set mission

gold exchange standard (**20**): the system established at the Bretton Woods conference in 1944 whereby gold was the fundamental standard of value, but for all currencies the gold parity was mediated by the dollar

gold standard (**20**): a system whereby a country defines its monetary unit in terms of gold

golden rule (**3**): proposition that per capita consumption is maximized in a growing economy at the point at which the marginal product of capital is equal to the growth rate

goods market equilibrium (**10**): is the situation in which the desired demand equals supply

Gresham's Law (**20**): the proposition that a money which is more valuable than its official exchange rate will disappear from circulation: 'bad money chases out the good'

gross domestic product (GDP) (**1, 2**): a location-based measure of a country's productive activity, corresponding to the value added generated by factors of production, both local and foreign-owned, within a country

gross national product (GNP) (**2**): a measure of the productive activity of a country computed on the basis of the ownership of the factors of production

hedging (**19**): techniques used to protect oneself against foreign exchange fluctuations; more generally, any trading techniques used to eliminate risk

household labour supply curve (**4**): the number of hours a household is willing to work as a function of the wage per hour

human capital (**5, 6, 17**): the education, training, and work experience acquired by individuals

Hume mechanism (**20**): the process by which trade imbalances were equilibrated under the gold standard system: a trade deficit (surplus) implies a reduction (increase) in gold and money supply, which leads to higher (lower) interest rates, to capital inflows (outflows), and to falling (rising) prices improving (worsening) the country's competitiveness

hyperinflation (**1, 8, 13, 16**): term used to describe periods of extremely high inflation, usually when the monthly rate exceeds 50%

hysteresis (**4**): the failure of certain macroeconomic variables to return to their original values after the cause of the change is removed; temporary changes in certain variables lead to permanent changes in others

imitation (**18**): process whereby discoveries are copied by backward economies

implementation lag (**16**): time lag in policy effectiveness as a result of the time taken by parliaments and ministries to pass and originate legislation

import function (**11**): function representing part of domestic spending and therefore following its fluctuations: the greater domestic spending, the greater will be imports

impossible trilogy (**20**): the result that it is impossible to simultaneously operate a fixed exchange rate regime, allow full capital mobility and conduct an independent monetary policy

impossible trilogy (**20**): principle stating that, while pairwise compatible, full capital mobility, fixed exchange rates, and monetary policy independence are jointly incompatible

impulse-propagation mechanism (**14**): mechanism that transforms shocks (impulses) into irregular oscillations like the business cycle

income effect (**4, 6**): the portion of change in quantity demanded which is attributed to the change in real income that results from the price change

increasing returns to scale (3): a characteristic of the production function which occurs when a simultaneous equiproportional increase in the factors of production results in a more than equiproportional increase in output.

index (1): a number that has no dimension (i.e. is not expressed in units such as DM, tons, hours, etc.); it is usually set to take a simple value like 1 or 100 at a specific date

indexation (12): a provision in wage or other contracts by which nominal values are adjusted frequently to reflect changes in some price index and to maintain the real value of the contract's provisions

indifference curves (3, 6): a graphic representation of all possible combinations of two items that will yield equivalent utility (satisfaction)

industrial policies (18): these amount to official backing of national corporations or whole industries, taking on the form of subsidies, public orders, or trade policies

inflation differential (8, 16): the difference between the domestic and foreign inflation rates

inflation rate (1, 8): the rate of change of the level of prices, measured by some price index or deflator

inflation targeting (9): a policy approach taken by some central banks in which an inflation rate or band of inflation rates is explicitly and publicly announced

inflation targeting strategy (16): the central bank announces a target for the inflation rate that it aims to reach within 2–3 years, publishes its inflation forecast, and adjusts its policy in reaction to the difference between the target and the forecast

inflation tax (9, 15): real revenue that the government obtains by inflation. Inflation erodes the real value of nominal assets and therefore may improve financial condition of the government, reducing the value of its nominal liabilities

information asymmetry (8): a situation in which one party has better information than the other/s about the probability of an outcome, and all parties know it

insiders and outsiders (4): a distinction applied to workers who are already employed in a long-term employment relationships

installation costs (6): the costs of installing new productive equipment

instrument independence (16): the central bank is free to use its policy instruments as it wishes

interbank market (9): a wholesale market for money, which brings commercial banks together

interest rate (3, 5): payment for use of funds over a period of time; equivalently, the price of future income or goods in terms of present income or goods

interest rate parity (11, 13): the condition that interest rates are equalized across countries taking account of expected exchange rate changes

internal terms of trade (7): the ratio of traded to nontraded goods prices

international Fisher equation (19): uncovered interest parity and purchasing power parity imply that the real interest rates are equal across countries *ex ante*

International Monetary Fund (IMF) (20): an institution set up at the Bretton Woods conference in 1944 to promote international monetary co-operation and exchange rate stability, to establish a multilateral system of payments for current transactions, and to assist members facing balance of payments difficulties

intertemporal budget constraint (5): the relationship summarizing resources and opportunities available in the present and the future to a household for consumption; the present value of spending must be less than, or equal to, wealth

intertemporal price (5): the price of goods tomorrow in terms of goods today; how much we would be willing to pay for—or sell for—the good today for delivery at some future date

intertemporal trade (5): trade conducted by households and firms across time

interventionism (1): policy whereby a government supports, co-ordinates, and even controls certain aspects of private activity; *see*: **laissez-faire**

intramarginal interventions (20): interventions by central banks within the bands of fluctuation to try to dissuade markets that a realignment is under consideration

investment (5): the acquisition of productive equipment for later use in production; also called fixed capital formation

investment function (6): relationship between investment and its fundamental determinants: aggregate investment depends positively upon Tobin's q and GDP growth, and negatively upon the real interest rate

investment, gross and net (1, 2, 3, 4, 5): the acquisition of new productive equipment: gross investment comprises the total expenditure on new capital goods, including replacement of worn-out equipment; net investment represents addition to the capital stock

invisibles (2): trade in services between a country and the rest of the world

involuntary unemployment (4): unemployment that occurs when individuals are willing and able to work at the going wage rates but cannot find a job

IS curve (10): for given values of exogenous variables, the combinations of nominal interest rate i and real output (GDP) that are consistent with goods market equilibrium

job finding rate (4): the rate at which workers move from the state of unemployment to that of employment; *see*: separation rate

job matching (4, 17): the matching of job offers of firms' and unemployed workers

job separation rate (4): the rate at which workers move from being employed to being unemployed, because of quits, redundancies, or for other reasons

Keynesian assumption (10, 11): the assumption that the evolution of the price level is insensitive to aggregate demand in the short run

(Keynesian) demand multiplier (11): a ratio indicating the effect of increases in exogenous components of aggregate demand on total aggregate demand

Keynesian model (11): model based on the assumption that prices are sticky, at least in the short run

Keynesian revolution (1): the development of ideas and policies to deal with situations where price and/or wage rigidities lead to recessions; these ideas stand in opposition to (neo)classical economics, which holds that markets are able to take care of themselves

Keynesianism (10, 16): the view that government demand management policy should play a key role in macroeconomic policy: Keynesians hold that markets suffer from imperfections—for example slow clearing of labour and product markets—which are responsible for the occasional underutilization of resources

labour (1): factor of production, usually measured in man-hours, i.e. the total number of hours worked in a firm, an industry, or a country

labour and profit shares (1, 3): the labour or wage share is the fraction of total income paid to workers; the profit share is that going to the owners of capital

labour demand (4): the relationship linking the number of man-hours that firms wish to hire and the cost of labour

labour force (4): the total number of individuals who are either working or actively looking for a job

labour force participation (1, 4): the proportion of working-age people who are in the labour force

labour share (1): the fraction of national income or aggregate value added paid to labour as wages or other forms of compensation, including payments of firms to social insurance schemes on behalf of their employees

labour supply, individual and aggregate (4): the relationship linking the wage rate and the number of hours that employees are ready to work: aggregate supply refers to the overall behaviour of the labour force, while establishing that workers are interested in providing more working hours, and firms will want to use fewer man-hours, when the real hourly wage rate increases

labour tax wedge (17): the difference between labour's cost to firms and wages actually received by workers

Laffer curve (17, 18): the relationship between government tax revenues and the average tax rate: beyond some point, increases in tax rates are associated with decreases in tax revenues, because the distortionary effects outweigh the revenue gained

laissez-faire (**1**): term used to describe the view that properly functioning markets will deliver the best possible social outcome, and that intervention by the government in economic affairs should be rejected; *see*: **interventionism**

leading and lagging indicator (**14**): a macroeconomic variable which systematically leads (lags) aggregate output over the cycle

leakages (**11**): part of income not respent in the circular flow of income and expenditure, either as private savings, taxes, or imports

learning-by-doing (**18**): the on-the-job adoption of new technologies

legal tender (**8, 9**): money that is mandated by law to be accepted in the payment for goods and services

leisure (**4**): time spent not working

lender of last resort (**9**): the central bank, in its implicit commitment to protect bank customers by providing failing banks with sufficient monetary base to prevent collapse

life-cycle theory (**6**): theory that consumption choices are made with a planning horizon equal to the individual's expected remaining lifetime; that an individual will build up savings during working years and exhaust them during retirement years

LM curve (**10**): for given values of the exogenous variables and the price level, the combinations of real output (GDP) and interest rates for which the money market is in equilibrium

long-run aggregate supply (**12**): the vertical line in inflation–output space, showing that real and nominal variables do not influence each other in the long run

long waves (**18**): theories that identify the existence of very long cycles in economic growth, largely based on technological discoveries and their slow diffusion

Lucas critique (**16**): the hypothesis that households and firms incorporate perceptions of the policy regime in their behaviour; as a result, shifts in the policy regime can have fundamental effects on behaviour

Lundberg lag (**14**): assumption that output responds to spending with a lag, on the hypothesis that firms react initially to sudden changes in demand not by changing production, but by running down inventories

macroeconomics (**1**): the study of the aggregate or average behaviour of the economy, as opposed to microeconomics, the behaviour of individual households, firms, and markets

man-hours (**4**): a measure of labour input which is equal to the number of people employed times the average number of hours spent working

marginal cost of capital (**6**): the cost of an additional increment to productive capacity

marginal productivity of capital (**6**): additional output produced by employing an additional unit of capital in the production process

marginal productivity of labour (**4, 12**): additional output produced by employing an additional unit of labour in the production process

marginal rate of substitution (**6**): the rate at which one commodity can be substituted for another without changing the level of utility

market-clearing (**16**): term describing a market that works perfectly by equalling demand and supply at every instant

market efficiency (**19**): the property that asset prices reflect all the available information and risks attached to any single asset

market failures (**17**): when markets are not functioning as in theory, for example because competition is imperfect with dominant players or when all the relevant information is available to all market participants

market liquidity (**19**): a financial market is liquid when it is easy at all times to find counterparts when selling or buying assets. The opposite case is that of shallow markets

market maker (**19**): traders or institutions that stand ready to deal in a particular asset

market power (**12**): the ability for producers to set a price that differs from those of close competitors. This is trivially the case of monopolists but can also occur when producers are able to differentiate their products (often using brand names), thus creating some limited monopoly power. The limit is that excessive prices may lead consumers to choose another brand. In this case, we talk of monopolistic competition

mark-up pricing (12): the percentage by which a firm increases the selling price of goods above the average or unit costs of production

mathematical model (1): a list of equations formalizing postulated linkages between exogenous and endogenous variables

maturity (19): the length of time before an agreed-upon financial transaction will take place

median voter theorem (16): if voters' preferences are evenly spread along some dimension, then a political party's maximizing election strategy is to advocate policies that are most favoured by the median ('middle') voter

medium of exchange (8): currency or other objects used to pay for goods

menu costs (10, 11, 12): lump-sum costs incurred when adjusting a nominal price or wage

merchandise trade balance (2): the sum of exports less imports of merchandise goods for a country *vis-à-vis* the rest of the world over some time period

minimum wages (4): the lower bound set on wage rates that may be paid to workers, usually but not always by law

misalignment (19): a persistent deviation of the real exchange rates from its equilibrium value

misery index (1): the sum of the unemployment and inflation rates

mismatch (4, 18): situation arising when the labour market doesn't clear because workers and vacancies are of such different industrial, occupational, or location nature that not enough job matches can take place

model (1): a set of economic linkages, including the assumptions made in drawing up the list of endogenous and exogenous variables

Modigliani – Miller Theorem (5): the proposition that the way a firm finances its activities—either by issuing debt or equity shares (stock)—is irrelevant for the valuation of the firm

monetarism (16): ranging from the view that the quantity of money has the major influence on economic activity and the price level to the view that money affects only nominal—not real—variables, this multi-faceted school of thought

concludes that monetary policy is best used by targeting the rate of growth of the money supply; monetarists reject activist policies because of uncertainty, lags, and government incompetence

monetary aggregates (8): various definitions of the money stock, differing largely by their degree of liquidity

monetary approach (19): the view that, under stable-equilibrium exchange rates, all long-run movements of the nominal exchange rate are due to changes in the nominal money supply

monetary base (9): the sum of currency in the hands of the public and bank reserves

monetary economy (1, 10, 11, 12, 13): the part of the economy dealing with monetary and financial, nominal phenomena

monetary interdependence (11): term referring to the fact that, under fixed exchange rates, foreign monetary policy changes impact on domestic monetary conditions

monetary neutrality (8, 10): term used to describe the fact that money does not affect the real side of the economy

monetary policy (9): actions taken by central banks to affect monetary and financial conditions in an economy

monetary union (20): an agreement among sovereign countries to use a common currency

monetization (9, 15): open market purchases of Treasury bills by the central bank, or, more generally, the lending of the central bank to the government to cover its deficit

money demand function (9): the relationship between real money demand and its determinants: real GNP, the nominal interest rate, and the cost of bank transactions

money growth line (13): is a horizontal line corresponding to the rate of inflation controlled by the domestic monetary authorities under flexible exchange rates

money illusion (12): term used to describe the failure to distinguish monetary from real magnitudes

money market equilibrium (10): equality of the exogenous and the central-bank-controlled money supply and the money demand that corresponds to a particular output level and exogenous transaction costs

money market intervention (10): the central bank buys or sells assets—usually treasury bills or high-quality securities—in order to provide or reduce the money supply

money multiplier (9): the link between the monetary base and wider monetary aggregates

multiplier – accelerator model (14): model of the business cycle developed by Paul Samuelson in which the interaction of the accelerator principle of investment and the multiplier leads to cyclical behaviour

Mundell – Fleming model (11): the open economy version of the IS–LM model

N – 1 problem (20): in a fixed exchange rate system with *N* countries, the fact that *N* – 1 bilateral rates can be sufficient to determine all, leaving one degree of (monetary) independence

natural monopoly (17): occurs in industries exhibiting increasing returns (telecommunications, transport, etc.)

NDP (net domestic product) (2): in the national income accounts, GDP less depreciation

neoclassical assumptions (10): the view that prices adjust even in the short run, so that the economy is always dichotomized

neoclassical approach (10): model claiming that flexible prices clear all markets even in the short run

net exports (2): difference between the flow of domestic goods and services sold to foreigners and the flow of imported goods and services

net national product (2): a measure of national output which nets out the depreciation of productive equipment

net taxes (2): the government's tax income from households and firms after transfers have been subtracted

net worth (8): the difference between assets and liabilities listed in an institution's balance sheet, representing its value to the owners

neutrality of money/monetary neutrality (8, 10): the principle that the money supply does not affect real variables such as real output or unemployment, but rather the price level

no-arbitrage condition (19): the condition imposed on a model that arbitrage profits must be absent

no-profit condition (19): the requirement that it is not possible to make an obvious profit without taking associated risks on financial markets

noise traders (19): irrational or misinformed traders who cause deviations of stock prices from their fundamental value for a long time

nominal (1): a variable expressed in value or money terms, as opposed to 'real' terms (i.e. terms of goods)

nominal anchors (16): in stabilization programmes, the practice of setting or targeting one or more nominal variable—such as the exchange rate or nominal wages—in order to hasten return to the equilibrium level of output and to influence expectations

nominal exchange rate (7): the value of foreign currency in terms of domestic money

nominal interest rate (8): the interest rate as quoted on financial markets or by banks

nominal wage and price rigidity (12): the fact that, owing to menu costs, contracts, or customer relations, prices denominated in money do not react immediately to changes in demand, and thereby prevent output and employment from reaching their equilibrium levels in the short run

non-excludable goods (18): a good is non-excludable when making it available to one person makes it available to all. An example is knowledge (e.g. understanding gravity or why Newton got hit on the head by a falling apple)

non-rival goods (18): a good is non-rival when its usage by one person does not detract from others' usage. Examples are clean air or knowledge

non-traded goods (7): goods that are not easily traded

normative economics (1): economics that passes judgement or provides advice on policy actions; *see*: positive economics

numeraire (7): a benchmark good in terms of which all other goods are priced

objectives, targets, and instruments (9): categories used to describe central bank behaviour:

objectives are general goals (e.g. price stability or low inflation); **targets** are intermediate indicators useful for achieving objectives but not under direct control of central bank (money supply, exchange rate, longer-term nominal interest rates); **instruments** are directly under control of the central bank (refinancing rates for commercial banks, open market operations)

official account (**2**): net transactions performed by the monetary authority on the foreign exchange market (net sales of foreign exchange)

offshore markets (**19**): markets for assets denominated in a country's currency but located outside that country

Okun's law (**1, 12, 13**): the observed inverse relationship between fluctuations of real GDP around its trend growth path and fluctuations of the unemployment rate around its equilibrium level

oil shock (**12**): a sharp increase in oil prices

open market operations (**9**): transactions undertaken by a central bank which exchanges securities for its own liabilities; these operations have the effect of supplying reserves to, or draining them from, the banking system

opportunity cost (**5, 6, 8**): the value of a resource in its best alternative use

optimal capital stock (**6**): the stock of physical capital that maximizes the value of the firm, for which the marginal productivity of capital is equal to the marginal cost of investment

optimal currency area (**20**): a region for which no welfare loss is implied by the use of a common currency

option (call and put) (**18**): a contract that allows the owner to purchase (call) or sell (put) an asset at some predetermined price at or before some specified point in time

out-of-equilibrium conditions (**3**): conditions when a market is not equilibrium

output cost of disinflation (**13**): the sacrifice ratio, which compares the cumulated increase in the rate of unemployment with the reduction in inflation achieved over some period of time

output gap (**12**): temporary deviations of GDP from its trend or equilibrium level

output – labour ratio (**3**): the ratio of output to the labour used to produce that output

overall balance (**2**): sum of the current and financial accounts (including errors and omissions), which by double-bookkeeping is the mirror image of interventions by the monetary authorities

overshooting (**17**): situation arising when, in response to a disturbance that modifies its long-run level, the nominal exchange rate moves in the short run in the same direction but by a larger amount, to be eventually reversed

par or central value (**20**): the fixed official exchange rate declared by the monetary authority of a country

parallel currencies (**8**): currencies issued by private institutions or foreign countries that are used alongside domestic money

parity/central parity (**20**): defined as a fixed but adjustable exchange rate between any pair of countries; *see also* par or central value

parity grid (**20**): the complete set of central parities and margins of fluctuation in the EMS

partial equilibrium (**3**): the analysis of the determinants of equilibrium in a particular market, ignoring whether other markets are in simultaneous equilibrium

partial market equilibrium condition (**1, 4**): the equality of demand and supply in a particular market under study

partisan business cycles (**16**): business cycles resulting from the succession in power of parties with different economic priorities and preferred policies; *see:* **political business cycles**

patents (**18**): a legal right granted to exclusive commercial use of an invention, normally for a limited period of time

PCA function (**11**): function given by the difference between exports and imports and determined by domestic spending, foreign spending, and the real exchange rate

peak/trough (**14**): upper/lower turning point of a cyclical economic time series

pecuniary/non-pecuniary externalities (**17**): externalities that are/are not transmitted by the market's price mechanism

permanent income (6): the flow of income which, if constant, would deliver the same present value as the actual expected income path

perpetuity (19): a loan agreement with an infinite maturity

persistence (14): long-lasting effect of a shock hitting the economy

personal disposable income (2): household net income from all sources after taxes have been paid and transfers received

personal income/personal disposable income (2): total household income after income taxes and fines and fees have been paid; the amount that can be used for consumption or savings

Phillips curve (12): an empirical relationship linking the inflation rate negatively to the unemployment rate

physical capital (2): a factor of production consisting of durable inputs such as machines, buildings, computer hard and software, and physical inventories

Plaza and Louvre Accords (20): agreements from the mid-1980s between industrial countries on limiting exchange rate fluctuations

policy lags (16): the delays (recognition, decision, implementation, and effectiveness) between the occurrence of a situation calling for policy action and the ultimate effect of that action; may actually exacerbate rather than smooth economic fluctuations

policy mix (11): the joint use of monetary and fiscal policies

policy regime (11, 16): explicitly or implicitly established set of rules of governments

political business cycles (16): business cycles resulting from the use of macroeconomic policies to improve the state of the economy just before elections; *see*: partisan business cycles

political independence (16): the central bank is formally free from interference from the government or other public agencies

position (long or short) (19): a trader is long in a given currency when she owns, or has contracted to receive, that currency in the future; similarly, a trader is short when she has contracted to make payment in a foreign currency at some future time

positive economics (1): the description and explanation of economic phenomena; *see*: **normative economics**

poverty trap (3): a situation where a country cannot enter a phase of sustained growth

PPP (purchasing power parity) line (13): a horizontal line corresponding to the foreign inflation rate, because at fixed exchange rates purchasing power parity rules out permanent differences between domestic and foreign inflation

preferences (3): the way we describe an individual's behaviour when faced with alternative spending opportunities

present discounted value (5): the value of a stream of income or spending spread over time and valued at today's price; *see also* **intertemporal price**

price level (1): the average level of prices in an economy

price line (7): graphic description of the relative price of two goods

primary budget deficit (5): the budget deficit net of debt service (i.e. net of the payment of interest on the public debt)

primary current account (5): the current account less net interest payments (net investment income); alternatively, the difference between gross domestic product output and aggregate domestic spending when unilateral transfers are equal to zero

primary current account function (6, 7): the relationship linking the primary current account positively to the real exchange rate and negatively to the level of GDP or income

primary government budget surplus (5): the excess of government tax revenues over non-interest expenditures, or, equivalently, the excess of net taxes plus interest payments over government purchases of goods and services

private income (2): income to the private sector which remains after taxes have been removed from, and transfers have been added to national income (more precisely, GDP plus net factor income earned abroad)

privatization (1, 17): the sale or transfer of part or all of state-owned enterprises to the private sector

procyclical (14): an economic variable that it is positively correlated with the state of the economy; that is, it moves in the same direction as aggregate output

producer surplus (17): difference between the price that a producer actually receives for a given quantity of goods and the amount corresponding to the minimum price at which he would be willing to supply the same quantity

product differentiation (12): a strategy used by firms to make consumers perceive their products as different from those of their competitors. A good example are cola drinks

production function (3, 4, 5): theoretical relationship linking aggregate output to inputs of factors of production

production possibilities frontier (7): the curve depicting possible output combinations for a nation or region by the employment of its available production factors

productive efficiency (15): the optimal use of available productive resources

productivity growth slow-down (3): the downturn of total factor productivity growth observed since the mid-1970s despite the developments of new technologies

profit share (4): the proportion of GDP paid out to shareholders

progressive tax (17): tax system in which the tax rate is increasing with the (pre-tax) income level

property rights (18): rights to private ownership. The absence of effective enforcement of property rights stunts economic growth

public goods (8, 15, 18): goods and services that are provided free of charge and the consumption of which by one person does not prevent the consumption by another person (characterized by non-excludability and non-rivalry)

purchasing power parity (PPP) (7, 8, 13): principle asserting that the rate of nominal exchange rate depreciation is equal to the difference between the domestic and foreign inflation rates; a stronger (and less plausible) absolute form of PPP equates price levels across countries when expressed in a common currency

q-theory of investment (6): theory linking investment to Tobin's q, the ratio of firms' market value to the replacement cost of installed capital

quits (4): voluntary separations from jobs on the part of the employee

quota (IMF) (20): a country's voting and borrowing rights in the IMF, based on its initial deposit upon joining

Ramsey principle of public finance (17): principle that, for a given amount of revenue to be raised, goods with the most inelastic demands and supplies should be taxed most heavily in order to minimize overall loss of consumer and producer surplus in an economy

random walk (19): a variable that changes randomly from period to period, where the only change between its value today and its value tomorrow will be white noise and can be positive or negative

rate of capacity utilization (1): measure of the degree to which firms employ their plants and equipment; one indicator of cyclical conditions

rate of depreciation (6): the rate at which the capital stock loses economic value, either by becoming obsolete or by wear-and-tear, usually expressed as percent per annum

rational expectations hypothesis (5): hypothesis asserting that agents evaluate future events using all available information efficiently so that they do not make systematic forecasting errors

real (1): a variable expressed in volume, adjusted from its nominal counterpart to take account of inflation

real business cycle theory (14): theory of the business cycle which explains economic fluctuations primarily as a consequence of technology shocks assuming price flexibility

real consumption wage (4): the ratio of nominal wages to the consumer price index; a measure of the price of leisure (or the return to work) in terms of consumption goods

real economy (1, 10, 11, 12, 13): term referring to the production and consumption of goods and services, and the incomes associated with productive activities; *see:* **monetary economy**

real exchange rate (7): the cost of foreign goods in terms of domestic goods, defined as the nominal exchange rate adjusted by prices at home and abroad

real interest parity (19): the difference between domestic and foreign real interest rates, which is equal to the corresponding nominal differential less the expected inflation differential

real interest rate (8): the difference between the nominal interest rate and the expected rate of inflation

real wage rigidity (4, 12): rigidity arising when unemployment fails to cause real wages to decline

realignment (10): a change in a the official exchange rate parity

recognition lag (16): time lag in discovering that policy intervention is called for

relative price (7): the price of one good in terms of another, usually computed as the ratio of two nominal prices

relative purchasing power parity (8): situation occurring when the cost of the same basket of goods in different countries increases at the same rate once converted into a common currency

repurchase agreement (9): an open market operation by the central bank involving the purchase of securities from a commercial bank against bank reserves, with a commitment by the selling bank to buy the securities back after a pre-agreed interval of time; *see:* **reverse transaction**

reputation (16): the effect on the public of self-imposed rules by the government to refrain from some actions, even if at some point such actions are highly desirable

reserves ratio (9): the ratio of a commercial bank's reserves (vault cash or deposits at the central bank) to the total demand deposits it has issued

residual claimants (5): those who receive income from an enterprise after all other claimants have been paid

returns to scale (3): the impact on output of an increase in all inputs by the same proportion: if output increases equiproportionally, the production function is said to exhibit constant returns to scale; if output increases more or less than proportionally, we have respectively increasing or decreasing returns to scale

revaluation (11, 13, 20): decision by the monetary authority to increase the value of the currency; *see:* devaluation, appreciation, depreciation

reverse transaction (9): generally, a market intervention which is contractually linked to an offsetting transaction at some specified point in time in the future; *see:* **repurchase agreement**

Ricardian equivalence (5): hypothesis that the time profile of taxes needed to finance a given stream of government purchases has no effect on agents' intertemporal budget constraint and therefore on real spending and saving decisions; then public debt is not considered as private wealth

risk averse (19): behaviour characterized by a preference to avoid risk

risk neutral (19): behaviour characterized by an indifference to risk

risk premium (18, 19): compensation above and beyond the expected rate of return on an asset required by agents to hold it

Robertson lag (14): assumption that current spending is related to past income

rules vs. discretion (16): legal rules are established to rule out time-inconsistent discretionary government policies

saving (2): postponement of consumption using some part of disposable personal income

seigniorage (9, 15, 20): exploitation by the government of the monopoly power of the central bank to create money as a means of raising real resources

self-fulfilling attacks (20): exchange rate attacks that are not justified by the exchange rate fundamentals, but occur because, if they succeed, the authorities will relax monetary policy, proving the attack to be rational *ex post*

separation rate (4): the rate at which employed workers become unemployed per unit of time; *see:* job-finding rate

sequencing (20): principles that indicate in which order a country that has long prevented the normal operation of markets and has at least partially isolated its economy can remove existing restraints and integrate itself in the world economy.

severance payments (**4**): compensation, usually in the form of lump-sum cash payments, paid by employers to workers who are made redundant for economic reasons

small-country assumption (**11**): working assumption that real and financial conditions abroad are unaffected by domestic economic developments and that the 'foreign' rate of return is exogenous

small open economy (**10**): an economy that is affected by events abroad but that does not affect economic variables in the rest of the world

'Snake' (**20**): arrangement between EC countries during the final years of the Bretton Woods System to stick to a reduced (half) margin

soft budget constraint (**15**): expression used to describe the situation of state-owned firms whose losses are automatically covered by the government budget

Solow decomposition (**3**): the three-way decomposition of the sources of economic growth into capital accumulation, increase in labour utilization, and the Solow residual capturing technological progress

Solow growth model (**3**): a theory that analyses growth as being driven by exogenous technological change and the accumulation of factors of production

Solow residual (**3**): the part of GDP growth unexplained by the increase in factors of production and conventionally ascribed to technological progress

sovereign borrowing (**5**): borrowing undertaken by national governments vis-à-vis foreigners, usually in the form of bond issues or loans by international banks

spatial arbitrage (**19**): arbitrage that occurs when investors identify a divergence of prices of identical assets in different market locations; *see* arbitrage

special drawing rights (SDRs) (**20**): a reserve money created by the IMF in 1967 and allocated on the basis of quotas; used among central banks as an additional source of liquidity

speculative attacks (**20**): sudden loss of foreign exchange reserves of central banks, arising when exchange market participants anticipate an imminent devaluation

speculative bubbles (**19**): persistent deviations of market prices from their fundamental values

spot exchange rate (**19**): the exchange rate that applies to an immediate currency exchange

spot market (**19**): market in which transactions are for immediate delivery of good or asset purchased

stabilization policies (**15**): policies designed to stabilize aggregate income and spending as well as unemployment

stagflation (**12, 13**): periods when both inflation and unemployment increase

standard of deferred payment (**8**): a function of money which enables economic agents to fix terms of contracts involving payments

stationary GDP (**14**): the level of GDP that would in theory result after full adjustment occurs, in the absence of further shocks to the economy

steady state (**4**): a hypothetical state in which all variables have responded fully to exogenous changes in the environment

sterilization (**9**): actions undertaken by central banks to offset the impact of a foreign exchange intervention on the domestic money supply, usually a money market purchase or sale of securities in the same amount as the foreign exchange market intervention

sticky price business cycle theory (**14**): class of theories of the business cycle in which the rigidity of prices are of central importance

store of value (**8**): a function of money which enables economic agents to carry wealth from the present to the future

structural unemployment (**4**): unemployment arising as the result of a mismatch of demand and supply of labour; *see*: **mismatch**

stylized facts (**3**): regularities in macroeconomic data which guide economists in their search for models to account for economic phenomena

substitution effect (**4, 6**): the component of the total change in quantity demanded that is attributable to the change in relative prices

supply determined output (10): when the price level adjusts freely, so that general equilibrium is always found at the intersection of the IS and the goods supply schedule, then output is supply determined

supply shocks (12, 13, 14, 17): exogenous increases in non-labour production costs

supply side (1, 12, 17): the productive potential of an economy and the factors that determine its overall efficiency

swap transactions (19): exchange of sums of money of the same currency but on different terms, for instance selling francs for delivery now while simultaneously buying them back for delivery in three months' time

systemic risk (9): the risk of a generalized collapse of the banking system, arising because banks and financial institutions hold large amounts of each other's liabilities

tax distortions (15): effects on real behaviour arising from the wedge that taxes introduce between the price received by the provider of a good or service and the price paid by its consumer

tax smoothing (15): the proposition that a government should not change tax rates in response to temporary causes of budget deficits, but should borrow instead

technological progress (3): the contribution to economic growth of technological change, usually captured by the rate of increase of total factor productivity

term structure of interest rates (19): a curve that shows the interest rates for loans according to their maturity

terms of trade (7): the ratio between the price of exportables and the price of imports; measures how many foreign goods can be purchased with one unit of domestic output

time inconsistency (16): characterizes policies which, although optimal today, become less desirable at a later stage, especially after agents have adjusted their behaviour accordingly

Tobin's q (6): the ratio of the present value of the return from new investment to the cost of installed capital; often approximated as the ratio of share prices to the replacement price of equipment

total factor productivity (7): productivity in the production process that is attributable not to any particular factor of production, but to all; growth in total factor productivity is often measured as a weighted average of growth in average productivities of all factors of production

tradable goods (7): goods actually traded or potentially tradable with foreign countries

trade policies (17): policies designed to support a domestic product's sales through tariffs on foreign goods, or quotas on imports

trade union voluntary/involuntary unemployment (4): unemployment resulting from the fact that trade unions ask for higher real wages than if the market were perfectly competitive, which may be involuntary from the perspective of individuals

trade unions (4): organizations of workers formed for the purpose of taking collective action against their employers to obtain improvements of pay and other working conditions

transaction costs (8, 17): costs arising from transactions, especially financial transactions

transfers (2): direct payments by the government to individuals or firms not related to the provision of goods and services, e.g. subsidies, unemployment benefits, pensions

trend (1, 13): long-term tendency in a time series

triangular arbitrage (19): arbitrage requiring that the relative prices of three or more assets are consistent with each other; see: **arbitrage**

Triffin paradox (20): the inconsistency of the US dollar (a national currency) as a world reserve currency with its gold backing: in order for internationally held dollar balances to grow with the world economy, the USA had to run balance of payment deficits over time which eventually outstripped its gold reserves

turning points (14): times when economic cycles reach a peak or a trough

uncovered interest parity (UIP) (19): the condition that rates of return on assets of comparable risk are equalized across countries once expected exchange rate changes are taken into account

underground economy (2): economic activities from which income earned is not reported and therefore is untaxed

undervaluation/overvaluation (**7, 19**): a currency is undervalued/overvalued when its exchange is below/above its long-run equilibrium value, or the level consistent with its long-run fundamentals

undiversifiable risk (**19**): a risk that cannot be reduced by holding a mix of several different assets

unemployment (**4**): individuals without a job who are actively seeking work

unemployment benefit (**4**): financial assistance to those seeking a job but unable to find suitable employment

unemployment rate (**4**): the ratio of the number of unemployed workers to total labour force

unemployment stocks and flows (**4**): the stock of unemployment is the number of people willing to work but unemployed at a moment in time; flows refer to workers coming into unemployment (inflows) or to previously unemployed workers finding a job or leaving the labour force (outflows)

unit of account (**8**): a function of money which enables economic agents to express all prices in a common way

unpaid work (**2**): economic activity that is not paid for and is not accounted for in GDP

user cost of capital (**6**): the effective cost to a firm of using the production factor physical capital, including the opportunity cost of resources tied up in the capital, depreciation, changes in the value of capital, as well as tax treatment of these factors

utility (**6**): the satisfaction that a consumer derives from the consumption of goods and services

value added (**2**): increase in the market value of a product at a particular stage of production; calculated by subtracting the value of all inputs bought from other firms from the value of the firm's output

velocity of money (**8**): the number of times on average that a unit of money is spent during the measurement period (usually a year)

voluntary unemployment (**4**): the difference between total labour availability and the employment that would result from labour market equilibrium; reflects the fact that some people who are in the labour force do not wish to work at the current wage level

vulnerabilities (**20**): economic or financial conditions that make a self-fulfilling crisis possible

wage inflation (**12**): the annual rate of growth of nominal wages

wage share (**4**): the proportion of GDP paid out as wages

wealth (**2, 5, 6**): the sum of inherited assets or debts and the present value of current and future incomes

welfare traps (**17**): situations where public subsidies—part of the welfare state—discourage private activities and keep recipients dependent on welfare payments

yield arbitrage (**19**): arbitrage which applies to assets that are equivalent in terms of their risk characteristics; *see:* **arbitrage**

Index

absorption 32, 165–6, 232, 233, 541
accelerator principle 141, 147, 148, 541
  see also multiplier-accelerator model
accounting identities 22, 35, 541
active labour market policies 423, 424, 432, 541
activist policies 18, 384, 385–93, 532, 541
acyclical variables 337, 541
Adelman, Frank 344
Africa 448–9
  GDP 54, 449
  human capital and growth 445
  and IMF 506
  inflation 219
  investment rate 54
  seigniorage 219
  underground economy 28
  see also individual countries
aggregate demand 126, 232–7, 266, 304, 541
  disturbances 248, 252–3
  under fixed exchange rates 305–14, 316, 327
  under flexible exchange rates 315–17, 327
  and inflation 305–19, 327–8
  long-run 305, 308, 309
  short-run 305–7, 308, 315–16, 327
  see also AS-AD model
aggregate demand curve 304, 307–8, 309, 311, 315, 316, 323, 325, 327, 384, 541
aggregate production function 50–2, 61, 67, 436, 541
aggregate supply 126 n., 296–7, 304, 316, 541
  see also AS-AD model
aggregate supply curve 282, 285–6, 295, 296–9, 304, 311, 316, 320, 322, 387, 541
  long-run 286, 287, 304, 308, 316, 385, 551
  short-run 304, 308, 309–10, 312, 316, 320, 385, 386
Aghion, Philippe 536
Albania 121, 178
Alesina, Alberto 534

animal spirits of enterpreneurs 143, 232, 239, 354, 527, 541
anti-trust policies 418–19
appreciation
  exchange rate 39 n. 13, 154, 541
    and money demand 481
    nominal 193
    real 156, 163, 164, 166–7, 168, 232, 233, 234
arbitrage 243, 465–6, 472–3, 487, 541, 559
  spatial 465, 466, 541, 558
  triangular 465–6, 519, 541
  yield 465, 541, 560
Argentina 216, 402, 520
  exchange rates 250
  financial crisis 10, 492, 512
  income per capita 5
  inflation 250
Arrow, Kenneth 409 n.
AS-AD model 304, 319–27, 332
  and business cycles 345, 346–7, 349, 352, 354, 355–6
Asia
  financial crisis 10, 492, 512, 513–14
  GDP 54
  human capital and growth 445
  and IMF 506
  inflation 219
  investment rate 54
  seigniorage 219
  underground economy 28
  see also individual countries
asset markets *see* financial markets
asset prices 188, 460, 462, 476–9
  exchange rates as 479–82
  see also bond prices; stock prices
assets 180, 204
  dominated 177–8, 545
  durability of 460, 462
  fundamental valuation of 473, 547
  value of 460
Australia
  budget balances 372
  central bank 397
  consumption 33
  government purchases 33

  immigration 65
  inflation 391
  inflation targeting 392
  interest rates 117
  investment 33
  labour taxation 428
  prices 167
  unemployment 89, 391
  wages 89, 391
  youth employment/unemployment 89
Austria
  bank insurance 220
  budget balances 365, 372
  capital accumulation 440
  central bank independence 397, 398
  fiscal policy 396
  GDP 398
  hours worked 65
  hyperinflation 401
  income per capita 5
  inflation 391, 398
  labour market regulation 425
  labour taxation 428
  prices 167
  public debt 373
  trade unions 84
  transfer payments 364
  underground economy 28
  unemployment 91, 391
  wages 88, 391
Austrian National Bank 203 n. 4
autarky 104, 541
automatic stabilizers 367, 369–70, 379, 380, 541
Bagehot, Walter 492
balance of payments 14, 36–9, 40, 542
  deficit 39
  surplus 39
balance of payments (BP) line 243–4, 246, 249, 256–7
balance sheets 542
  consolidated 179–80, 203, 204
  and vulnerability to speculative attacks 512–13
Balassa-Samuelson effect 166–7, 542
Baltic States 28
  see also Estonia; Latvia; Lithuania

Banca d'Italia 203 n. 4
Bangladesh 5, 167
Bank of England 201, 203 n. 4, 214–15,
    400, 495
Bank of Japan 203 n. 4
Bank of Korea 512
Bank of New Zealand 400
bank reserves 203, 205, 223, 542
Bank of Thailand 512, 513
bankruptcy 120, 122
banks/banking 175, 180, 519
    consolidated balance sheets 179–80
    internet 187
    regulation 419, 519
    see also central banks; commercial
        banks
Banque de France 203 n. 4
Barings 223
Barro, Robert 115 n., 536
barter economy 177
base money see monetary base
Basle Committee 221, 222
battle of the mark-ups 290–1, 542
beggar-thy-neighbour policies 254, 497,
    498, 542
Belarus 28, 397
Belgium 65, 503
    accounting identity 35
    bank insurance 220
    budget balances 365, 372, 374
    capital accumulation 440
    central bank independence 397, 398
    currency depreciations 498
    fiscal policy 396
    GDP 47, 231, 398
    and gold bloc 497
    and IMF 506
    income per capita 5
    inflation 391, 398
    labour market regulation 425
    labour taxation 428
    and Latin Monetary Union 493
    money demand 184
    openness 10, 20, 231
    prices 167
    public debt 373, 374
    subsidies 420
    trade unions 84
    transfer payments 93, 364
    underground economy 28
    unemployment 89, 391
    wage share of value added 289
    wages 88, 89, 391
    women and employment 82
    youth employment/unemployment 89
Benassy, Jean-Pascal 530
Beveridge curves 421–3, 542
bid-ask spread 469, 542
bimetallism 493, 542
Bolivia 401
    ond prices 107, 185, 188, 472
    ıds

corporate 117
    pure discount 107
    Treasury 117
boom-and-bust cycles 507
booms 332, 542
borrowing 102, 104–24, 135–6
    constraints 118, 122, 542
    sovereign 121, 122, 558
Bosnia-Herzegovina 216, 520
Botswana 449
Brazil
    financial crisis 10, 492, 512
    fiscal policy 395
    GDP 231
    inflation targeting 392
    openness 231
    price levels 167
    underground economy 28
Bretton Woods Conference 497–8, 542
Bretton Woods System 497–501, 519,
    521
Britain see United Kingdom
British terms 153, 154, 542
Brunner, Karl 530
bubbles 476–9, 542, 558
Buchanan, James 414, 534
budget balances 365
    actual 371, 372
    cyclically adjusted 371–2, 380, 544
    primary 114, 115
budget constraint
    consolidated public and private
        114–16, 120, 122
    of the nation 120, 122
    public 113–14
    see also intertemporal budget
        constraints
budget deficit 362, 366, 367, 369, 379
    financing 373–6
    primary 113, 114, 116–17, 555
    reduction of 376–7
budget figures, interpretation of 370–2
budget line 74–5, 105, 114, 542
budget surplus 367, 369–70, 379
    primary 114, 555–6
budgetary process 370
budgets, endogenous and exogenous
    components of 371
Bulgaria
    and currency board arrangement 216,
        518, 520
    currency substitution 178
    growth performance 448
    money demand and inflation 192
    pyramid schemes 121
    underground economy 28
Bundesbank 203 n. 4, 312, 400 n., 502,
    503, 519
Burns-Mitchell diagrams 335–7, 542
Bush, G. W. 404
business cycles 6, 9, 11, 18, 49, 230,
    332–58, 542

acyclical variables 337, 541
and AS-AD model 345, 346–7, 352,
    355–6
coincident indicators 337, 338
countercyclical variables 9, 337, 544
and credit 354
damped 342, 544
deterministic 341–3
duration and magnitude of 333–7
as endogenous phenomenon 341
explosive 342, 544
flexible price 349–52, 355, 356
and impulse-propagation mechanism
    332–3, 343–7
inventory 11
and key economic variables 335–40
lagging indicators 337–9, 341, 346,
    355
leading indicators 337–9
long-wave 11, 335
and mark-up pricing 291–2
and money 354–5
optimality properties of 352
oscillating 342, 343, 544
peaks and troughs 332, 333, 555
political 402–4, 405, 555
procyclical variables 9, 337, 354, 355,
    356
and random shocks 343–5
real 333, 349–52, 353, 354, 356, 532–3,
    556
seasonal 335
sticky price 345, 346–9, 352, 354, 355,
    532–3, 558
stochastic 343–6
stylized facts about 333–40
turning points 332, 559
undamped oscillations 342
'Cambridge equation' 529 n. 5
Canada
    budget balances 372
    central bank independence 397, 398,
        399
    consumption 33
    demand multipliers 236
    GDP 33, 231, 349, 398
    government purchases 33
    and IMF 506
    income per capita 5
    inflation 391, 398
    inflation targeting 213, 392
    interest rates 117
    investment 33
    labour taxation 428
    openness 231
    prices 167
    unemployment 89, 391
    wages 89, 391
    women and employment 82
    youth employment/unemployment 89
capacity utilization 9, 337, 338, 339, 354,
    389, 542, 556

capital 542
  as factor of production 7, 47
  fixed capital formation 108, 547
  marginal cost of 139, 140, 145, 146,
    551
  secondary 222
  share of GDP 49, 63
  see also human capital; marginal
    productivity of capital (MPK);
    physical capital
capital accumulation 49–58, 62, 63, 64,
  66, 67, 436, 437, 440, 446, 542
capital adequacy 221–2, 543
Capital Asset Pricing Model (CAPM) 468
  n.
capital controls 248, 257, 503, 515–17,
  543
capital-effective labour ratio 61, 66
capital flows, international 243–6
capital intensity 48, 59
capital-labour ratio 48, 49, 51, 52, 53, 55,
  56, 58, 59, 60, 66, 437, 543
capital mobility 503, 506, 508, 517, 519,
  521, 522
capital-output ratio 48–9, 53, 54, 56, 66,
  141
capital stock 46, 48, 50, 51, 52–3, 55, 64,
  66, 67, 78, 109, 453
  depreciation 33, 34, 52–3, 55, 59, 60,
    62, 67, 109, 140–1, 545
  installation costs 144–5, 147, 148
  marginal cost of 139, 140, 145, 146
  optimal 138–9, 141, 144–5, 148, 554
  per capita 53
  replacement (user) cost of 141–2, 145,
    146, 148, 560
  resale value of 140
capital widening line 59, 61, 543
Carleton, Dennis 273
Cassel, Gustav 102
central banks 200, 203 n. 4, 223, 493,
  543
  assets 180, 181, 204
  balance sheet 180, 204
  credibility 396–402, 512–13
  and government financing 217–19,
    223
  independence of 219, 224, 327, 397,
    398, 399–400, 402, 404, 405, 534
  economic 399–400, 545
  goal 400, 548
  instrument 400, 549
  political 399, 555
  as lender of last resort 221, 224, 551
  liabilities 180, 181, 194, 204
  and the monetary base 203
  and monetary policy 200, 201–2,
    212–17
  and the money market 210–11
  and money supply 186
  see also Bank of England; Bank of
    Korea; Bank of New Zealand;
    Bank of Thailand; Bundesbank;
    European Central Bank (ECB);
    Federal Reserve; Swiss National
    Bank
Central and Eastern Europe 56–7
  currency substitution 178
  economic restructuring 165
  exchange rates 202, 245
  inflation 7, 9, 191–2, 202
  supply shocks 319, 320
  underground economy 28
  see also individual countries
centrally planned economies 56–7, 447,
  448
Centre for Economic Policy Research
  (CEPR) 333
Centre for Policy Studies 530
Chad 167
Channel Tunnel 111
Chicago School 528–9, 530–1
Chile 28, 213, 392, 395, 507
China 60
  economic growth 445, 447, 448
  GDP 47, 231
  literacy 445
  living standards 46
  openness 231
  prices 167
Chirac, Jacques 404
Churchill, Winston 527
circular flow diagram 30–3, 235–6, 543
classical dichotomy principle 271, 275,
  543
Clinton, Bill 404
closed economy 230, 543
Coase Theorem 413 n.
Cobb-Douglas production function 50, 141
  n.13, 543
coincident indicators 337, 338, 543
collateral 211
collective bargaining 83–7
  see also wage bargaining
collusion among monopolies 417, 418
Colombia 392
commercial banks 290
  assets 180, 204
  balance sheet 180, 204
  collapse of 220, 221
  deposit insurance 220
  liabilities 180–1, 194, 204
  and money creation 204–5
  and the money market 210–11
  regulation 220, 223
commodity monies 174, 543
commodity prices 294, 295, 298–9, 321
  see also oil prices
communications technology 6, 63
communist regimes 447, 448
competition 288
  in labour markets 410–11
  perfect 288, 409–10, 416
  in product markets 410
competition policy 410, 411, 543
computer technology 63
consols 107, 472
consumer price index (CPI) 26, 27, 74,
  182, 543
consumer relations, and price stickiness
  273
consumer surplus 416, 543
consumption 31, 32, 33, 40, 126, 127–37,
  340, 355, 362, 454, 543
  and disposable income 134–6, 137,
    148, 232, 233–4, 235, 393
  intertemporal and intratemporal 103
  and intertemporal trade 104–5
  life-cycle 129, 551
  optimal 127–9, 160
  permanent income 129, 529–30
  present discounted value of 106–7,
    148
  random walk theory of 130
  and real exchange rate 165–6
  and real interest rates 133–4, 137,
    148
  and savings 55–6, 67
  steady-state 55–6, 67
  today 105, 127, 128, 133–4
  tomorrow 105, 127, 128, 134
  and wealth 134–6, 137, 148, 232
consumption deflator 27
consumption function 127, 136–7, 148,
  232, 341, 529–30, 543
consumption-leisure trade-off 72, 73–6,
  97, 351, 543
consumption smoothing 129, 130–3,
  148, 233, 238, 340, 365–6, 379, 543
contagion phenomenon 513–14, 544
contracts
  credit 120–1
  forward 467, 469, 547
  labour 423–4
  and price stickiness 273
convergence hypothesis 436, 437–8, 544
coordination failures 11, 13, 544
copyrights 442 n., 443, 544
core inflation 292, 294–9 *passim*, 309–11,
  328, 329, 385–6, 544
  backward-looking component 295,
    309, 311, 323, 325, 531
  forward-looking component 295, 311,
    322, 323, 325–6, 384, 386–7, 531
  and the long run 295–6
  and supply shocks 320–3
corporate tax 34, 393–4
cost of living 11
costs
  average or unit 289, 541
  installation 144–5, 147, 148, 549
  labour *see* labour costs
  menu 273, 552
  non-labour 289, 293, 298
  production 282, 288–91, 293
countercyclical variables 9, 337, 544

covered interest parity (CIP) 466, 467, 487, 544
credibility 385, 544
   central banks 396–402
   of governments 393–4, 405
credit 106
   and business cycles 354–5
credit cards 176
credit contracts, international 120–1
credit rationing 118, 135–6, 366, 544
crowding-out effect 249, 544
currency boards 216, 245, 250, 449–50, 514, 518, 520–1
currency crises 10, 492, 506–14, 515, 518, 522
   contagion phenomenon 513–14, 522, 544
   first generation 507, 508–10, 513, 522
   second generation 511–12, 513, 518, 522
   self-fulfilling 510–13, 522, 557
   third generation 512–13
   vulnerabilities 511–13, 560
currency substitution 178, 193
currency/currencies 175, 203, 207
   convertibility of 497, 498, 506
   depreciation see exchange rate depreciation
   devaluations 251, 252, 312–13, 499, 501, 545
   as liability of central bank 180
   money multiplier with 208
   parallel 178, 208
   revaluations 251, 557
   single 502
   world 505
   see also Deutschmark; dollar; euro; exchange rates; Ostmark market
current account 37, 40, 544
   deficits 37, 39
   and oil shocks 132, 133
   surpluses 37, 39, 40
   see also primary current account (PCA)
Czech Republic 28, 131, 132, 166, 289, 392, 428, 518
Czechoslovakia 448
DaimlerChrysler Corporation 461
data 17–18
   and testing of theories 15
debit cards 176
Debreu, Gerard 409 n.
debt 108
   see also public debt
decision lags 389, 544
deflation 282, 544
de Gaulle, Charles 500
de-industrialization 164
DeLong, Bradford 441 n. 7
demand
   derived 209–10, 212, 545
   elasticity of 288
   xcess 238, 245–6

private sector 126–50
   see also aggregate demand; desired demand; desired demand function; labour demand; money demand
demand-determined output 272–5, 276, 306, 544
demand disturbances 248–9, 252–3
   fiscal policy and 309–12
   under fixed exchange rates 248, 257
   under flexible exchange rates 252–3
demand leakages 235–6
demand management policies 11, 323, 324, 327–8, 352, 384–406, 544
   see also fiscal policy; monetary policy
demand multipliers 235–6, 238, 256, 550
demand shocks 323–4, 346, 347–8, 349, 352, 544
   and unemployment 387–8
demand side 13, 544
demand (sight) deposits 174, 175, 180–1, 194
democracy and economic growth 452
Denmark
   accounting identity 35
   bank insurance 220
   budget balances 365, 372
   capital accumulation 440
   central bank independence 397, 398
   currency depreciations 498
   current account 132, 133
   GDP 47, 398
   hours worked 81
   income per capita 5
   inflation 391, 398
   interest rates 117
   labour market 424, 425
   labour share of income 8
   labour taxation 428
   monetary aggregates 182
   money demand 184
   and oil shocks 132, 133
   openness 10
   prices 167
   public debt 373
   Ricardian equivalence in 119
   stock prices 8
   trade unions 84
   transfer payments 93, 364
   unemployment 89, 391
   wage share of value added 289
   wages 88, 89, 391
   women and employment 82
   youth employment/unemployment 89
Denmark fiscal policy 395, 396
deposits, sight (demand) 174, 175, 180–1, 194
depreciation see capital stock depreciation; exchange rate depreciation
depreciation line 52, 53, 55, 56, 545
depreciation rate 52, 59, 140, 556

depression 4
   see also Great Depression
deregulation 418, 429
derived demand 209–10, 212, 223, 545
desired demand 233–4, 235, 237, 239, 266
desired demand function 233, 263, 545
detrending 333, 545
Deutsche Reichsbank 203 n. 4
Deutschmark 502
devaluations 251, 252, 312–13, 499, 501, 545
dictatorships 452
difference equation 342, 545
diffusion of innovations 444–5, 545
diminishing marginal productivity 50, 51, 52, 55, 60, 62, 66, 67, 77, 109, 545
direct credits to government 218
discounting 105, 107, 545
discretion versus rules 385, 402, 405, 557
disequilibrium 545
   goods market 245
   labour market 274, 276
   money market 188, 242
disinflation 324–7, 328
   output cost of 325–6, 327, 328, 554
dismissals 424–6
dollar 498–9, 500–1, 504
dollarization 178, 216, 450, 514, 520
dominated asset 545
   money as 177–8
Dornbusch, Rudiger 531
double coincidence of wants 177, 545
Drèze, Jacques 408, 535
Dutch disease 164, 545
dynamic efficiency/inefficiency 56–8, 67, 545
Eastern Europe see Central and Eastern Europe
economic agents 13, 545
economic growth 4–6, 46–69, 436–56, 536–7, 545
   and capital accumulation 49–58, 62, 436
   under central planning 447, 448
   and complementary inputs 437–41
   and democracy 452
   endogenous 65–6, 67, 441, 546
   and human capital 438–9, 440, 445–6
   and inequality 452–3
   and investment 46, 49–50, 52–4, 55, 58, 59, 66
   and knowledge 5–6, 46, 436–7, 441–6
   and population growth 5, 46, 58–60, 62, 67, 436
   and public infrastructure investment 439–40
   and rule of law 449, 450, 454
   and savings 49–50, 52, 53–8, 66
   and stability 449–50
   stylized facts about 47–9

and technological progress 6, 46, 60, 61–2, 63, 65–6, 67, 436, 441–6, 536
economic indicators
  coincident 337, 338, 543
  leading and lagging 337–9, 389–90, 551
economic rents 410
economic restructuring 165, 452
Ecuador 520
education 363, 414, 438, 439, 454
effectiveness lags 389, 546
efficiency
  labour market 420–31
  market 408, 409–31, 465, 475–6, 487, 551
  productive 364, 556
  see also dynamic efficiency/inefficiency
efficiency wages 88, 98, 546
Egypt 28, 167
El Salvador 520
electoral business cycles 403
emerging market countries 10
employers' associations 83, 87, 411, 546
employment 58, 64, 65, 96
  cyclical behaviour of 353–4
  equilibrium 78–80, 98
  incentives 426, 427
  separation and finding rates 90–3
  stabilization 366–7, 533
  youth 89
  see also jobs; unemployment
endogenous growth 65–6, 67, 441
endogenous variables 14, 15, 236, 238, 546
endowment 104, 105, 546
  of factors of production 72
entitlement effect 93 n.
EONIA (euro overnight index average) 211, 212
equilibrium 526, 528
  and the exchange rate regime 244–6
  GDP 234–5, 263, 546
  and international capital flows 243–6
  partial 244, 554
  see also equilibrium unemployment; general equilibrium; goods market equilibrium; labour market equilibrium; money market equilibrium
equilibrium unemployment 73, 94–7, 98, 286, 294–8 passim, 387–8, 535, 546
equipment, productive see capital stock; physical capital
equity-efficiency trade-off 364, 546
errors and omissions 38–9
Estonia 178, 216, 518, 520
Euro 18, 271, 272, 504
Euro-area 26
  balance of payments 37, 38
  central bank assets 181
  central bank independence 219
  consumption 33, 126

demand multipliers 236
  employment 58, 96
  exchange rates 153, 486
  government purchases 33, 126
  inflation 287
  interest rates 117, 324
  investment 33, 126
  labour market regulation 425
  labour taxation 428
  monetary aggregates 176, 182
  monetary base 207
  money supply 207
  population 58
  unemployment 287, 327
  wages 96
euroization 216, 520
European Central Bank (ECB) 201–2, 209, 323, 324, 377 n. 13, 527, 546
  independence of 399, 400
  interest rates 212
  open market operations 211
  'pillars' 202, 213
European Community (EC) 501
European Monetary System (EMS) 202, 216, 245, 312, 323, 402, 501–3, 517, 519, 531, 546
European Monetary Union 231, 245, 312, 377, 400 n., 502, 503, 515, 519, 546
European terms 154, 546
European Union 37
  accounting identity 35
  competition policy 411
  expansion of 10, 19
  openness 10
  unemployment 7
Eurosclerosis 96
Eurosystem (European System of Central Banks (ESCB)) 201, 399, 546
  consolidated balance sheet 203
Excessive Deficit Procedure 377
exchange controls 498
exchange rate depreciation 39, 154, 216, 483, 498, 507, 545
  and inflation 188, 193, 481
  and money supply 481
  nominal 193, 195, 252, 312
  real 155–6, 163, 168, 193, 232, 252, 312, 313
exchange rate determination 39
  with flexible prices 483–4
  monetary approach to 483–4, 552
  with rigid prices 484–5
  in the short run 479–86
Exchange Rate Mechanism (ERM) 245, 492, 502–3, 546
exchange rate regimes 231, 304
  choice of 514–21, 522, 547
  and macroeconomic equilibrium 244–6
  and supply shocks 322–3
exchange rate targeting 200, 201–2, 213, 216, 223

exchange rates 13, 14, 40, 460
  appreciation see appreciation
  asset behaviour of 479–82
  band of fluctuation 494, 502, 542
  crawling pegs 518
  devaluations 251, 252, 312–13
  effective 155, 168, 338, 339, 545
  equilibrium 481
  fixed 231, 236, 245
  flexible 236
  floating 40, 231, 245, 255, 256, 257, 496–7, 518, 522
  forward 467, 547
  hard pegs 326–7, 518, 519, 520, 522
  managed floating 245
  and market equilibrium 482–3
  misalignments 515, 552
  'news' component of 481
  overshooting and undershooting 483, 484–5, 515
  parity changes 251–2
  parity/central parity 502, 554
  realignments 252, 312–13, 515, 519, 557
  revaluations 251
  'Snake' arrangement 320, 501, 558
  spot 467, 481, 485, 558
  undervalued and overvalued 162, 483, 507, 560
  see also exchange rate depreciation; exchange rate determination; exchange rate regimes; fixed exchange rates; flexible exchange rates; nominal exchange rate; real exchange rate
excise taxes 34
exogenous variables 14, 15, 16, 236, 238, 546
expectations 15, 102, 103, 142, 239, 311, 384, 385, 393–4, 405, 533
expenditure 13, 362
  flow of 30–5
  see also consumption; government purchases; investment
export function 233, 547
exports 36–7, 161, 232, 233, 340, 355
  -GDP ratio 10
  net 32, 553
externalities 363, 412–15, 432, 436, 441, 547
  pecuniary and non-pecuniary 413, 432, 555
  positive and negative 413, 432
factor mobility see capital mobility; labour, mobility of
factors of production 7, 47–8, 72, 547
  see also capital; labour
Federal Funds Rate 212
Federal Reserve of the USA 201, 203 n. 4, 213
fertility rates 454
fiat money 179, 547

financial account 40, 547
  long-term and short-term 37–8
  private and official 37, 39
financial disturbances
  international 251, 255
  see also currency crises
financial intermediaries/intermediation
  31, 204, 462, 486, 547
financial liberalization 515–19, 522
  sequencing of 518–19, 558
financial markets 9–10, 13, 103, 230, 231,
  460–90
  demand and supply in 461–2, 486
  functions of 462–5
  liberalization of 519
  liquidity of 469, 473–5
  regulation of 419, 519
  uncertainty in 460, 462
  volatility of 460–1, 462
  see also foreign exchange market;
    money market; stock markets
financial (monetary) economy 9–10, 32,
  33
financial transactions 37–8
finding rate of jobs 91, 92–3
Finland 220, 507
  budget balances 365, 372
  capital accumulation 440
  central bank 397
  fiscal policy 396
  GDP 47
  income per capita 5
  inflation 391
  labour market 424, 425
  labour taxation 428
  money demand 184
  public debt 373
  trade unions 84
  transfer payments 93, 364
  unemployment 391
  wages 88, 391
  women and employment 82
fiscal policy 13, 18, 255, 379, 394–6, 404,
  527, 529, 533, 534, 547
  contractionary 394–5
  countercyclical 366–7, 379, 544
  and demand disturbances 309–12
  and demand shocks 349
  and economic welfare 363–4
  expansionary 249–50, 253, 254, 256,
    309–12, 318, 327, 394–5, 396
  under fixed exchange rates 249, 256,
    309–12, 327, 375
  under flexible exchange rates 254,
    256, 318, 517
  and *IS* curve 238–9, 284
  long-run effect of 309
  with rational expectations 311
  rules versus discretion 402
  short-run effect of 309
  and unemployment 14, 366–7
  Fisher, Irving 72, 104 n. 2, 106, 126, 530

Fisher principle or equation 191, 547
fixed capital formation 108, 547
  see also investment
fixed exchange rates 246–52, 255, 256,
  320, 397, 497, 503, 515, 522
  aggregate demand under 305–14, 316,
    327
  Bretton Woods System of 497–501,
    521
  and capital mobility 517, 519
  demand disturbances under 248, 257
  fiscal policy under 249, 256, 309–12,
    327, 385
  and gold standard 494
  hard pegs 326–7, 518
  and interest rate determination
    246–52
  monetary policy under 246–8, 254,
    313, 327, 508, 517
  money growth under 306, 325, 328
  and output 246–52
  and supply shocks 323
fixed prices *see* sticky prices
Fleming, J. Marcus 230, 527
flexible exchange rates 252–5, 256, 515,
  517, 531
  aggregate demand under 315–17, 327
  fiscal policy under 254, 256, 318, 517
  and interest rate determination 252–5
  monetary policy under 253–4, 255,
    257, 317–18, 327, 385
  money growth under 325, 327
  output and 252–5
  and supply shocks 323
flexible prices 262, 263, 268–71, 276
  business cycles and 349–52, 355, 356
  exchange rate determination with
    483–4
flow variables 22
Ford, Henry 126
forecasting 15–16, 103, 389–90
foreign direct investment 38
foreign exchange market interventions
  37, 216–17, 223, 247, 546, 547
foreign exchange markets 231, 461,
  465–6, 481
foreign exchange reserves 37, 39, 247,
  547
45° diagram 233–5, 263
forward contracts 467, 469, 547
France 18
  accounting identity 35
  bank insurance 220
  budget balances 365, 372
  budget (expected and realized) 2003
    370
  business cycles 335, 336
  capital accumulation 440
  capital-output ratio 48
  capital stock 64
  central bank independence 397, 398
  consumption 33, 134, 135

  currency depreciations 498
  economic growth 65
  employment 64, 82, 89
  exchange rates 314
  fiscal policy 396
  GDP 4, 16, 33, 34, 47, 65, 321, 336,
    349, 398
  and gold bloc 497
  government purchases 33
  hours worked 64, 76, 81
  and IMF 506
  incomes 5, 34, 134, 135
  inflation 12, 16, 314, 321, 391, 398,
    495
  investment 33
  labour market 425, 430
  labour share of income 8
  labour taxation 428
  and monetary union 493, 503
  money demand 184
  and oil shocks 321
  population 64
  prices 12, 167
  public debt 368, 373
  stock prices 8
  subsidies 420
  trade unions 84
  transfer payments 93, 364
  unemployment 87, 89, 91, 321, 391
  wages 76, 89, 391
  wealth 134, 135
  women and employment 82
  youth employment/unemployment 89
Freeman, Richard 81
freshwater economics 18
Frey, Bruno 534 n. 12
Friedman, Milton 129 n., 132 n. 6, 286,
  392, 476, 515 n., 529, 532 n.
Frisch, Ragnar 344 n. 9
fundamentals 473, 548
futures markets 103
Gali, Jordi 533
Gambia 449
Gates, Bill 443
general equilibrium 231, 244, 245,
  264–7, 276, 482, 548
  with flexible prices 263, 268–71
  short-run versus long-run 306–7, 308,
    309
  with sticky prices 263, 272–5
Georgia 28
German Democratic Republic (East
  Germany) 136, 137, 469, 470
Germany 18, 46
  accounting identity 35
  bank insurance 220
  budget balances 365, 372, 374
  budget (expected and realized) 2003
    370
  budget surplus 367
  business cycles 335, 336
  capital accumulation 440

capital-output ratio 48
capital stock 64
central bank independence 397, 398, 399
consumption 33
currency depreciations 498
current account 367
employment 64, 82, 89
exchange rates 298, 314
fiscal policy 396
GDP 4, 16, 29, 33, 34, 47, 65, 231, 321, 336, 349, 350, 398
government purchases 33
hours worked 64, 76, 81
hyperinflation 397, 400, 401
and IMF 506
incomes 5, 34
inflation 16, 219, 314, 321, 391, 398, 495, 501
investment 33, 143
labour market regulation 425
labour taxation 428
money demand 184
and oil shocks 298, 299, 321
openness 10, 231
output gap 285
population 64
prices 167
public debt 367, 368, 373, 374
reunification of,
    as a demand shock 347–8
    fiscal implications of 367
saving 112
seigniorage 219
subsidies 420
telecommunications 418
trade unions 84
transfer payments 93, 364
unemployment 87, 89, 91, 95, 285, 321, 387, 388, 391, 422, 431
vacancy rate 422
wage share of value added 289
wages 76, 88, 89, 391, 431
women and employment 82
youth employment/unemployment 89
Giersch, Herbert 96, 535
globalization 503
gold 11, 493, 496, 498–9, 500–1, 521
    demonetization of 504
gold bloc 497
gold exchange standard 499, 521, 548
Gold Pool 500
gold standard 493–7, 521, 548
    automatic mechanism of 495
Goldberger, Arthur 344
golden rule 55–8, 59, 62, 67, 548
Goldwater, Barry 529
goods market 230, 231
    aggregate demand and 232–7
    clearing 384
    disequilibrium in 245

excess demand in 238
excess supply and 238
and IS curve 237–41, 244, 256, 263, 264, 267
goods market equilibrium 234–5, 268, 276, 482, 483, 548
    and IS curve 237, 238, 256, 263, 264, 267
Gordon, Robert 63
government
    central bank financing of 217–19, 223
    credibility and reputation 393–4, 405, 557
    quality of 384–5
    size of, and real exchange rate 166
government intervention 11, 18, 534, 550
government purchases 32, 33, 166, 236, 238–9, 340
Great Depression 11, 221, 239, 273, 497, 529
Greece
    bank insurance 220
    budget balances 365, 372
    capital accumulation 440
    central bank independence 397
    fiscal policy 396
    inflation 391
    labour market regulation 425
    labour taxation 428
    money demand 184
    public debt 373
    trade unions 84
    transfer payments 364
    underground economy 28
    unemployment 89, 391
    unemployment benefit 93
    wages 88, 89, 391
    youth employment/unemployment 89
Greenspan, Alan 239
Gresham's law 493, 548
gross domestic product (GDP) 4–6, 22–35 passim, 40, 49, 398, 454, 548
    and aggregate demand 233–4
    capital share of 49, 63
    components of, by expenditure 33, 263
        variability of 126
    -debt ratio 374–6, 380
    definitions of 22–3
    deflator 24–5, 26, 40, 126, 167, 548
    detrended 333, 545
    equilibrium 234–5, 263, 546
    as flow variable 22
    labour share of 7, 8, 49, 63
    measuring and interpreting 26–30
    and money demand 183, 185, 186, 187, 189, 241–3, 256
    nominal 23–5, 26, 40, 158
    per capita 29, 46, 47, 52, 54, 59, 60, 65, 66, 437
    ratio of exports to 10

real 23–5, 26, 40, 47, 48, 54, 158, 186, 187, 238
    deviations from long-run trends 230
    and money market equilibrium 241–3
    and real money stock 183
    trend 4–5, 333, 335, 337
gross national product (GNP) 25, 548
growth theory 47–8, 67
Haberler, Gottfried 528 n.
Hall, Robert E. 130 n. 5
Hawtrey, R. G. 200
Hayek, Friedrich von 414, 529, 534 n. 13
health 415, 450–1, 454
hedging 467, 548
Hicks, Sir John 237 n., 527
high-powered money see monetary base
high-tech stock prices 477, 479
hollowing-out hypothesis 517
Hong Kong 28, 520
hot money 38
hours worked 50, 51, 52, 55 n., 58, 61 n., 63, 64, 65, 75, 76, 81
    see also man-hours
human capital 72, 363, 393, 452, 453, 548
    and diffusion of innovations 445–6
    and health 450–1
    investment in 414–15, 436, 438–9, 440, 452, 454
    marginal productivity of 439
human rights 448, 452
Hume, David 174
Hume mechanism 494, 495, 514, 519, 520, 521, 548
Hungary 10
    economic growth 448
    exchange rates 166, 216, 518
    GDP 320
    hyperinflation 401
    inflation 219
    inflation targeting 392
    labour taxation 428
    openness 10
    seigniorage 219
    underground economy 28
hyperinflation 4, 7, 9, 191–3, 218, 378, 390, 397, 400–2, 548
IBM 443
Iceland 167, 397
imitation 444, 548
immigration 46, 65, 411, 412
implementation lags 389, 548
import function 233, 548
imports 32, 36–7, 161, 232–3, 236, 340, 355
impossible trilogy principle 503, 517–18, 548
impulse-propagation mechanism 332–3, 343–7, 349–52, 355, 549
incentives, employment 426, 427
income 4–6, 29–30

capital share of 49, 63
and consumption 134–6, 137, 148, 232, 233–4, 235, 393
and demand, in goods market 235, 238
distribution of 7
flow of 30–5, 40
future 103, 129, 135
and inequality 452–3
labour share of 7, 8, 49, 63
and life expectancy 451
national (NI) 34
per capita 48, 52, 54, 437
permanent 129, 130, 555
personal disposable 33, 34–5, 134–6, 137, 232, 239, 393, 555
private 30–1, 556
real, and money demand 182–3
redistribution of 362, 363, 364–5, 379, 390, 453
temporary changes in 130
income effect 75, 97, 352, 549
indexation 292, 326, 390, 549
India 5, 46, 167, 445
indicators see economic indicators
indices
  stock market 7
  see also price indices
indifference curves 73–4, 85, 127–8, 159–60, 549
Indonesia 507, 512
industrial policies 420, 549
industrial revolution 5, 63, 444
inequality, and economic growth 452–3
inflation 7, 9, 11, 12, 14, 40, 154, 282, 283–99
  actual rate of 295–6, 297, 299, 309–11, 385–6
  aggregate demand and 305–19, 327–8
  and business cycles 338, 339
  costs of 390
  and exchange rate depreciation 188, 193, 481
  and Fisher principle 191
  long-run 188–91
  and money demand 184, 185, 192
  and money growth 188–91, 193, 200, 213, 317
  optimal rate of 390, 392
  and output 285, 296, 297, 299, 315
  redistributive effects of 390
  and unemployment 283–7, 294, 296, 297, 299
  wage 283, 560
  see also core inflation; disinflation; hyperinflation; stagflation; and under individual countries
inflation differential 193, 195, 549
inflation rate 7, 9, 14, 25–6, 549
  and economic stability 449
  and exchange rate depreciation 188, 193

expected 191, 195
  as procyclical 9
inflation targeting 200, 202, 213, 214–15, 223, 327, 392, 397, 402, 549
inflation tax 218–19, 223, 377–8, 380, 549
informal economy 28, 30
information, and market efficiency 465
information asymmetry 179, 220, 414, 432, 549
information technology 6, 63, 445, 477
infrastructure 5, 32, 438, 439–40
innovation see technological progress/innovation
insider-outsider theory 86, 535, 549
installation costs 144–5, 147, 148, 549
institutions, economic and political 18
instruments, monetary policy 201, 202, 554
interest rate parity 243–4, 256–7, 312, 318–19, 466–9, 474, 508, 549
  covered (CIP) 466, 467, 487, 544
  real 472–3
  uncovered (UIP) 467–8, 472, 474, 560
interest rates 13, 14, 102, 103, 114, 117–18, 200, 202, 231, 274, 275, 549
  and business cycles 338, 339, 354–5
  equilibrating role of 188
  under fixed exchange rates 246–52
  under flexible exchange rates 252–5
  general equilibrium determination of 265–6
  and investment 237, 238
  and money market equilibrium 241–3, 256
  and output 237, 238, 270, 274
  as procyclical 187, 356
  public versus private 114, 117–18
  see also nominal interest rates; real interest rates
International Business Machines (IBM) 443
international Fisher equation 473, 549
International Labour Organization (ILO) 82
International Monetary Fund (IMF) 492, 498, 499, 504–6, 522, 531, 549
  assistance 504, 522
  conditionality 499, 504, 522, 543
  quotas 499, 556
  special drawing rights (SDRs) 504–5, 506, 558
  standby loans 516
  surveillance 505
  voting 506
internet banking 187
intertemporal budget constraints 102, 113–14, 122, 549
  of consolidated private sector 110–13, 122
  and equilibrium real exchange rate 161–7

the firm and private sector's 108–13
  household's 104–8
intertemporal price 105, 549–50
intertemporal substitution 127, 128, 351–2, 353, 356
intertemporal trade 104–5, 550
interventionism 11, 18, 534, 550
intuition 17
inventories 337, 338, 339, 341, 389
investment 32, 33, 40, 67, 108, 126, 138–47, 239, 389, 550
  and economic growth 46, 52–4, 55, 58, 59, 66
  foreign direct 38
  and interest rates 109–10, 139–41, 142, 147, 237, 238
  marginal cost of 138, 146, 148
  marginal return on 145, 146, 147, 148
  net external position 163
  net return on 113
  opportunity cost of 109–10, 122, 138
  and output 141, 147, 148
  portfolio 38
  productive and unproductive 111
  q-theory of 142, 556
  and Tobin's q 141–7, 148, 232
  volatility of 340, 355
  and wealth 111
investment decision 108
investment function 127, 147, 148, 232, 237, 550
investment rate 32, 54
invisibles 37, 550
Ireland
  bank insurance 220
  budget balances 114, 115, 365, 372, 374
  capital accumulation 440
  central bank independence 397
  fiscal policy 395, 396
  GDP and GNP per capita 25
  inflation 391
  labour market regulation 425
  labour taxation 428
  money demand 184
  openness 10
  prices 167
  public debt 373, 374
  trade unions 84
  transfer payments 93, 364
  unemployment 89, 391
  wages 89, 391
  women and employment 82
  youth employment/unemployment 89
IS curve 246, 248, 249, 252, 276, 315, 550
  and goods market 237–41, 244, 256, 263, 264, 267
  movements along or shifts of 238–40
IS-LM model 244, 262, 263–4, 305, 332, 484, 503, 533
IS-LM-BP model 305, 306, 307, 309, 311–12, 315, 325

Israel 167, 178, 213, 219, 401
Italy
    accounting identity 35
    bank insurance 220
    budget balances 114, 115, 365, 372,
        374
    budget (expected and realized) 2003
        370
    business cycles 335
    capital accumulation 440
    central bank independence 397, 398
    consumer price index 26, 27
    consumption 33
    currency depreciations 498
    and exchange rate mechanism 515
    fiscal policy 396
    GDP 33, 47, 57, 321, 336, 349, 398
    GDP deflator 27
    and gold bloc 497
    government purchases 33
    hours worked 81
    and IMF 506
    income per capita 5
    inflation 321, 391, 398, 501
    investment 33, 57
    labour market regulation 425
    labour taxation 428
    and monetary union 493, 503
    money demand 184
    and oil shocks 321
    prices 167
    public debt 373, 374, 379
    saving 112
    subsidies 420
    trade unions 84
    transfer payments 93, 364
    underground economy 28
    unemployment 87, 89, 95, 321, 391
    wage share of value added 289
    wages 88, 89, 391
    youth employment/unemployment 89
Jamaica agreement 501
Japan 46, 452
    accounting identity 35
    budget balances 365, 372
    budget surplus 362
    business cycles 334, 335, 336, 337
    capital-labour ratio 48
    capital-output ratio 48
    central bank assets 181
    central bank independence 397, 398
    consumption 33, 337, 339, 362
    demand multipliers 236
    employment 64, 82
    exchanges rates 153, 486
    exports 337, 339
    GDP 16, 33, 47, 65, 231, 321, 336, 339,
        349, 398
    government purchases 33, 337, 339
    hours worked 64
    and IMF 506
    imports 337, 339

income per capita 5
inflation 16, 219, 282, 321, 337, 391,
    398, 495
interest rates 117
investment 33, 337, 339
labour taxation 428
monetary base 207
money demand 184
money supply 207
and oil shocks 321
openness 10
output-labour ratio 48
population 64
prices 167, 337, 339
public debt 362, 373
saving 112
seigniorage 219
technological progress 444
transfer payments 93, 364
unemployment 89, 95, 321, 391
wage share of value added 289
wages 89, 391
women and employment 82
youth employment/unemployment
    89
Jevons, William 177 n. 3
job matching 90, 94, 421-3, 550
jobs
    separation and finding rates 90-3,
        547, 550, 558
    see also employment
Johnson, Harry G. 304
Juglar, Clement 335
Kaldor, Nicholas 48
Kalecki, Michal 527
Keynes, John Maynard 11, 13, 134, 143,
    262, 273, 354, 384, 526-7
Keynes Plan 505 n. 16
Keynesian demand multiplier 235-6,
    238, 256, 550
Keynesian model/assumption 230, 231,
    232-3, 236, 256, 262, 263, 272-5, 276,
    306, 550
Keynesian revolution 13, 526-8, 550
Keynesianism/Keynesians 18, 384, 385-6,
    404, 405, 530, 550
Kitchin, Joseph 335
Klein-Goldberger model 344
knowledge
    and economic growth 5-6, 46, 436-7,
        441-6
    as non-excludable and non-rival 441
    as a public good 441-2
    see also technological
        progress/innovation
Kok, Wim 96
Kondratieff, Nikolai 335, 444
Konstanz seminar 530
Koopmans, Tjalling 335 n.
Korea, Republic of
    and currency crises 507, 512
    GDP 16, 231

inflation 16
openness 231
underground economy 28
Kosovo 520
Kuznets, Simon 335, 528
Kuznets's curve 452-3
Kydland, Finn 145 n. 21, 531 n. 7, 532
labour 550
    effective 61, 62, 66, 545-6
    as factor of production 7, 47, 72
    heterogeneity of 421
    mobility of 423, 521
labour costs 77, 95, 289-91, 299
    prices as mark-up on 290
    unit 289, 290-1
    see also wages
labour demand 72-3, 76-8, 85, 97, 264,
    270, 353, 550
    elasticity of 427
labour demand curve 77, 78, 79
labour force 6, 82, 550
    participation rate 75, 80, 82, 550
    women in 46, 64, 75, 80-1, 82
labour input 48, 51, 58-9, 61 n., 62, 63,
    64-5, 67, 109
    see also hours worked
labour market 72-100, 264-5, 273-5,
    288, 534-5
    active policies 423, 424, 432, 541
    clearing 384, 409-10
    competition in 410-11
    deregulation 429
    disequilibrium in 274, 276
    efficiency 420-31
    equilibrium 78-80, 94, 265, 267, 268,
        275, 276
    passive policies 424
    reform 427-31, 432
    regulation 423-6, 452
    states and transitions 90
labour productivity 76-8, 79, 288, 290,
    291
    cyclical behaviour of 336, 353-4
    see also marginal productivity of labour
        (MPL)
labour share 7, 8, 49, 63, 291, 293, 550
labour supply 72-6, 78, 79-80, 264,
    351-2, 353
    aggregate 76, 97, 550-1
    see also man-hours
    collective 95, 265, 270, 274
    elasticity of 351, 352, 354, 427
    household (individual) 76, 97, 270,
        274, 550-1
labour supply curve
    aggregate 75-6, 77
    collective 85-6, 97, 543
    household (individual) 74-5, 76, 77,
        97, 264, 548
labour tax wedge 429, 551
labour taxation 426-7, 428, 429, 432
labour unions see trade unions

LAD (long-run aggregate demand) line 305, 308, 309
Laffer curve 417, 551
Laffont, Jean-Jacques 534
lagging indicators 337–9, 341, 346, 355
laissez-faire 11, 13, 18, 366, 410, 529, 532, 534, 551
Laspeyres index 27
Latin America 178
  human capital and growth 445
  inflation 7, 9, 219
  seigniorage 219
  underground economy 28
  see also individual countries
Latin Monetary Union 493
Latvia 178
law and order 363, 413, 415
Layard, Richard 535
leakages 207–9, 551
  demand 235–6
learning by doing 446, 551
leisure 72, 97, 551
  consumption-leisure trade-off 72, 73–6, 97, 351, 543
  intertemporal substitution of 351–2, 353, 356
  relative price of 74
lender of last resort 221, 224, 551
lending 102, 104–24, 135
  central banks 211
    to government 217–19, 224
  commercial banks 203, 204–5
liabilities, banks 180, 181, 194, 204
liberalization, financial 515–19, 522
Liberia 520
life-cycle theory 129, 551
life expectancy 451, 454
Lindbeck, Assar 527, 535
liquidity 175, 469, 473–5, 551
literacy 445
Lithuania 178, 518, 520
living standards 5, 46, 48, 62, 67
LM curve 241–9 *passim*, 252, 256, 263–4, 269, 270, 276, 312, 315, 551
  see also IS-LM model
London Club 121
long wave theory 444–5, 551
LTCM (Long-Term Capital Management) 223
Lucas, R. E. Jr. 46, 344, 384, 437 n., 531, 536
Lucas critique 393, 405, 532, 551
Lundberg lag 341, 551
Luxembourg 82, 89, 165, 391, 397, 428
Maastricht Treaty (1991) 219, 502
Machlup, Fritz 505 n. 17
MacKay, Charles 478
McKinnon, Ronald 518
macroeconomics 551
  as a discipline 10–13
  methodology of 14–16
  ison, Angus 65

Malaysia 28, 248, 512
Malinvaud, Edmond 408, 530, 535
Malthus, Thomas Robert 60, 526
man-hours 48, 50, 51, 76, 77, 79, 551
manufacturing, labour share of income in 8
marginal cost of capital 139, 140, 145, 146, 551
marginal cost of investment 138, 146, 148
marginal cost of production 392
marginal productivity 51, 66
  diminishing 50, 51, 52, 55, 60, 62, 66, 67, 77, 109, 138, 264, 545
  non-declining 66
marginal productivity of capital (MPK) 55, 56, 59, 60, 62, 66, 67, 138, 139, 140, 144–5, 147, 148, 392, 436, 551
marginal productivity of human capital 439
marginal productivity of labour (MPL) 77–8, 83, 85, 88, 97, 353, 409, 551
marginal rate of intertemporal substitution 128
marginal rate of substitution 74, 551
marginal rate of transformation 158
marginal return on investment 145, 146, 147, 148
market-clearing 384, 404, 409–10, 551
market efficiency 408, 409–31, 465, 475–6, 487, 551
market failures 18, 410, 411–14, 551
market liquidity 469, 473–5, 551
market makers 469, 552
market power 288, 552
markup pricing 288–9, 290–3, 299, 552
Marshall, Alfred 441
Marshall Plan 499
Marx, Karl 72, 354
mathematical models 16, 552
maturity 469, 552
Mauritius 449
Meade, James 527
means of production, accumulation of 5
median voter theorem 404, 552
medium of exchange 552
Meltzer, Alan 530
menu costs 273, 552
merchandise trade balance 37, 552
Metzler, Lloyd 528
Mexico
  balance of payments 37, 38
  financial crisis 492, 507, 512
  inflation targeting 213
  price levels 167
  underground economy 28
microeconomics 11, 13, 127, 144–7, 532–3
Microsoft Corporation 111, 443
Minford, Patrick 530, 537
'missing equation' 528, 530

Mitchell, Wesley 335 n.
modelling 16, 552
Modigliani, Franco 129 n., 528
Modigliani-Miller Theorem 112, 113, 552
monetarists/monetarism 18, 528–31, 552
monetary aggregates 175, 176, 182, 201, 206, 223, 552
monetary base 203, 205, 218, 223, 247–8, 249, 250, 252, 552
  derived demand for 209–10, 212, 223
monetary base multiplier 206–7
monetary (financial) economy 9–10, 32, 33, 552
monetary interdependence 251, 552
monetary neutrality 182, 270, 271, 272, 275, 276, 286, 317, 401, 529, 530
monetary policy 13, 14, 18, 186, 200, 211–17, 284, 349, 404, 529, 531–2, 533, 552
  and exchange rate realignments 312–13
  expansionary 187, 249, 254, 256, 313, 317–18, 327, 527
  under fixed exchange rates 246–8, 254, 255, 313, 327, 508, 517
  under flexible exchange rates 253–4, 255, 257, 317–18, 327, 385
  independence 248, 249, 251, 255, 397, 503, 517–18, 534
  instruments 201, 202
  objectives 201
  reserve requirements as tool of 212
  rules versus discretion 402, 405
  targets 200, 201–2, 213–16, 223, 554
monetary shocks 349
monetary unions 514, 519–20, 552
  see also European Monetary Union; Latin Monetary Union
monetization 218, 376, 552
money 174–97
  balance sheet approach to 179–81
  and business cycles 354–5
  commodity 174, 543
  definitions of 174–5
  as a dominated asset 177–8
  economic functions of 177
  fiat 179, 547
  hot 38
  as medium of exchange 177
  neutrality of see monetary neutrality
  non-neutrality of 275
  as a public good 178–9, 194
  purchasing power 182, 191, 195
  real money balances 337, 338, 339
  speculative demand for 185
  as standard of deferred payment 177, 558
  as store of value 177, 558
  as unit of account 177, 560
  value of 390
  velocity of 184, 186, 529, 560

money creation 203–9, 376
and inflation 11
see also monetization
money demand 181–6, 194–5, 231, 270, 482, 508–9
elasticities of 183, 184
and exchange rate appreciation 481
and GDP 183, 185, 186, 187, 189, 241–3, 256
and inflation 184, 185, 192
nominal 184, 185, 191, 195, 202, 209
and nominal interest rates 183, 187, 188–90
and price level 181–2, 183, 184, 185
real 184, 185, 191, 201, 202, 266
and real income 182–3
money demand function 183–4, 185, 186, 190, 552–3
money growth
under fixed exchange rates 306, 325, 328
under flexible exchange rates 325, 327
and inflation 188–91, 193, 200, 213, 306, 317
money growth line 316, 553
money illusion 286, 553
money market 210–11, 216
disequilibrium 188, 242
relative liquidity conditions in 473–5
see also financial markets
money market equilibrium 209, 256, 266, 268, 276, 482–3, 484, 553
and *LM* curve 241–3, 244, 263–4, 482
long run 188–93, 195
short run 186–8, 195
money multiplier 205–9, 216, 223, 376, 553
money stock (M1) 179
nominal 182
real 182
and real GDP 183
money supply 200–26, 236, 247–8, 250–1, 252, 257, 508–9
and exchange rate depreciation 481
and gold standard 494
and *LM* curve 242, 243
nominal 186, 201, 243, 266, 270–1, 315, 324–5
and nominal exchange rate 483–4
and nominal and real variables 269–70
real 186, 243, 266, 270, 271, 315–16, 482
and interest rates 186, 187, 188–90, 274
moneyless society 175, 176
monopolies 417–19, 432, 442
collusion among 417, 418
natural 413, 432, 553
monopoly power 410, 443, 445
Mont-Pélerin Society 534 n. 13
Morocco 28

Mozambique 167
multifactor (total factor) productivity 63, 96, 350, 354, 444, 559
multinational corporations 446
multiplier-accelerator model 341–3, 346, 553
multipliers
demand 235–6, 238, 256, 550
see also money multiplier
Mundell, Robert 527, 531
Mundell-Fleming model 230, 245–6, 256, 503, 527, 553
see also IS-LM model
Mussa, Michael 481, 531
Mussolini, Benito 379
N – 1 problem 519, 520, 553
NASDAQ 479
National Bureau of Economic Research (NBER) 333
nationalization 447
natural resources, tradable 164
neoclassical model of flexible prices 262, 268–71, 276
neoclassical synthesis 262, 527
neoclassics 384, 385–6, 404
net domestic national product (NDP) 33, 34, 553
net worth 179, 553
Netherlands 18, 119
accounting identity 35
bank insurance 220
budget balances 365, 372, 374
budget (expected and realized) 2003 370
capital accumulation 440
capital stock 64
central bank independence 397, 398, 399
currency depreciations 498
current account 132, 133
employment 64, 82, 89
fiscal policy 396
GDP 47, 65, 231, 398
and gold bloc 497
hours worked 64, 81
and IMF 506
income per capita 5
inflation 391, 398
interest rates 189, 190
labour market 425, 430
labour share of income 8
labour taxation 428
money demand 184
and oil shocks 132, 133
openness 10, 231
population 64
prices 167
public debt 373, 374
saving 112
stock prices 8
subsidies 420

trade unions 84, 96
transfer payments 93, 364
tulipmania 478
unemployment 89, 93, 391, 430, 431
unpaid work 28
wage share of value added 289
wages 89, 96, 391, 430–1
women and employment 82
youth employment/unemployment 89
new economy 63, 477
New Zealand 93
central bank independence 397, 398
GDP 398
inflation 391, 398
inflation targeting 213
labour taxation 428
prices 167
unemployment 391
wages 391
'news' and exchange rate movements 481
Newton, Isaac 493 n.
Nickell, Steve 535
Nigeria 28, 167
Nixon, Richard 500
no-profit condition 465, 476, 487, 553
noise traders 476, 553
nominal exchange rate 152, 153–5, 193, 201, 240, 252, 269, 271, 282, 553
appreciation 193
depreciation 193, 195, 252, 313
effective 155, 168
fixed 236
as forward looking 474, 487
fundamental determinants of 475
and national money markets 473–5
overshooting and undershooting 483, 484–5, 554
as relative price of currencies 479, 481
undervalued and overvalued 483
variability of 479, 480
nominal interest rates 191, 195, 238, 354–5, 377, 378, 482, 553
long-term 338, 471
and money demand 183, 187, 188–90
and money supply 186, 187, 188–90
short-term 338, 471
term structure of 470–2, 559
non-excludable/non-rival goods 441, 442, 553
non-traded goods 155, 156–61, 163–6, 167, 168, 554
normative economics 15, 554
North, Douglass 534
Norway 371
bank insurance 220
budget balances 365, 372
central bank independence 397, 398
currency depreciations 498
GDP 47, 398
income per capita 5
inflation 391, 398

labour market 424, 425
labour taxation 428
money demand 184
oil fund 164–5
prices 167
public debt 373
trade unions 84
unemployment 391
unemployment benefit 93
wages 88, 391
women and employment 82
numeraire 158, 554
objectives, monetary policy 201, 554
official account 37, 39, 554
oil 164
oil price shocks 15, 96, 132, 133, 221, 287, 298–9, 320, 321, 323, 348, 366, 554
oil prices 16, 133
Okun's law 284–6, 293, 296, 299, 554
open market operations 210–11, 216, 554
openness 10, 230, 450
opportunity cost 554
    of investment 109–10, 122, 138
    and nominal interest rates 183
optimizing behaviour 126–7
optimum currency areas 520, 521, 554
Organization for Economic Cooperation and
        Development (OECD) 16, 82
    money, inflation, and exchange rate appreciation in the long run 189
Ostmark market 469, 470
output 4, 5, 48–9, 50–2, 66, 67, 109, 110, 274, 275, 298, 408
    demand-determined 272–5, 276, 306, 544
    equilibrium 409–14
        and desired demand 237, 239
        and labour market equilibrium 264–5
    under fixed exchange rates 246–52
    under flexible exchange rates 252–5
    general equilibrium determination of 265–6, 267
    and inflation 285, 296, 297, 299, 315
    and interest rates 237, 238, 270, 274
    and investment 141, 147, 148
    per capita 48, 53, 67
    stabilization 366–7, 533
    supply-determined 268–9, 276, 306, 559
    and unemployment 284–6, 297
    see also capital-output ratio; gross domestic product (GDP); output gap; output-labour ratio
output cost of disinflation 325–6, 327, 328
output-effective labour ratio 61, 66
output gap 284–5, 299, 308, 309, 310, 316, 322, 348, 554

output-labour ratio 48, 49, 51–6 passim, 58, 59, 61, 65, 66, 554
outsiders 86, 535, 549
overall balance 39, 554
Paasche index 27
Pakistan 167
Panama 520
Paris Club 121
partisan business cycles 403, 405, 554
patents 442–4, 445, 554
Patinkin, Don 262, 527
PCA function 156, 161, 233, 555
perfect competition 288, 409–10, 416
perpetuities 472, 555
persistence 346, 555
Persson, Torsten 534
Peru 28, 167
pharmaceutical industry 443, 444 n. 9
Phelps, Edmund 286, 530
Philippines 28, 507, 512
Phillips, A. W. 282, 528
Phillips curve 283–7, 296, 299, 515, 528, 530, 531, 555
    augmented 294–5, 296, 297–9, 530, 541
physical capital 32, 47, 351, 555
    see also capital stock
Polak, Jacques J. 531
Poland
    central bank assets 181
    consumption 136, 137
    and currency crises 10
    current account 137
    economic growth 57, 448
    exchange rates 166, 518
    GDP 57, 137, 230, 320
    and gold bloc 497
    hyperinflation 397, 401
    income 136
    inflation 219
    inflation targeting 213
    investment 57
    labour taxation 428
    openness 10, 231
    seigniorage 219
    underground economy 28
    wage share of value added 289
policy activism 18, 384, 385–93, 532, 541
policy lags 388–90, 555
policy mix 249–51, 254–5, 555
policy regime 393, 555
political business cycles 402–4, 405, 555
Ponzi, Charles 121
population 64
    and economic growth 5, 46, 58–60, 62, 67, 436
    and GDP per capita 59, 60
portfolio balance 185
portfolio investment 38
Portugal
    bank insurance 220
    budget balances 372

capital accumulation 440
central bank independence 397
fiscal policy 395, 396
inflation 391
labour market regulation 425
labour taxation 428
money demand 184
openness 10
trade unions 84
transfer payments 364
underground economy 28
unemployment 89, 391
wages 89, 391
women and employment 82
youth employment/unemployment 89
positive economics 15, 555
poverty 437, 438, 451
poverty trap 446, 555
PPP see purchasing power parity
precautionary motive 185
preferences 127, 159–60, 555
    household 73, 165–6
    national 411
Prescott, Edward 145 n. 21, 531 n. 7, 532
present discounted values 106–7, 555
price deflators 24–5, 27
price indices 25–6, 27, 40
    fixed-weight (Laspeyres index) 27
    variable weight (Paasche index) 27
    see also consumer price index (CPI)
price levels 11, 12, 27, 167, 168, 236, 555
    and general equilibrium 266
    and money demand 181–2, 183, 184, 185
    see also inflation
price line 158–9, 555
price stability 201, 213, 223
prices 11, 13, 23–6, 282, 288–93
    asset see asset prices
    bond 107, 185, 188, 472
    commodity 294
    and consumer relations 273
    and contracts 273
    general equilibrium determination of 265–6
    intertemporal 105, 549–50
    Law of One Price 167, 193
    mark-up 288–9, 290–3, 299, 552
    rigidity of 384, 385, 515, 553
    signalling role of 390
    see also flexible prices; relative prices; sticky prices; stock prices
primary current account (PCA) 120, 232, 240, 340, 555
    balanced 159–60
    and consumption smoothing 130–3
    deficits 120, 122, 156, 160, 161
    in the long run 161–3
    non-zero 160–1
    and real exchange rate 152, 155–6, 168
    surpluses 120, 122, 156, 160, 161, 232

primary current account (PCA) function 156, 161, 233, 555
privatization 417, 418, 419, 440, 556
procyclical variables 9, 337, 354, 355, 356, 556
producer price index (PPI) 27
producer surplus 416, 556
product differentiation 288, 410, 556
product variety 446
production
    and exchange rate depreciation 156
    hoarded factors of 354
    marginal cost of 392
    optimal 159, 160
production costs 282, 288–91, 293, 299
    average or unit 289, 541
    labour see labour costs
    non-labour 289, 293, 298, 299
production function 56, 108–9, 438, 439–40, 556
    aggregate 50–2, 61, 67, 436
    Cobb-Douglas 50, 141 n. 13, 543
    intensive 51–2, 53, 61, 62
    and labour demand 76–8
production possibilities frontier (PPF) 157–9, 160, 161, 163–4, 556
productive efficiency 364, 556
productivity
    multifactor (total factor) 63, 96, 350, 354
    traded versus non-traded goods 163–4, 168
    see also labour productivity; marginal productivity; marginal productivity of capital (MPK); marginal productivity of labour (MPL)
productivity shocks 349–51, 353, 356
profit 77, 141
    gross 30
profit share 550, 556
propagation mechanism see impulse-propagation mechanism
property rights 413, 437, 446–8, 452, 453, 556
the Proportion 495
Public Choice School 534
public debt 113–14, 116, 117, 122, 362, 363, 366, 368
    default 114, 363, 378, 380
    forgiveness 121
    with growth and inflation 375, 376
    with growth and no inflation 374–6
    monetization of 218
    with no growth and no inflation 373–4
    ratio of to GDP 374–6, 380
    servicing 113, 121, 163
    stabilization 373–9, 380
public goods 32, 363–4, 413, 415–17, 432, 439–40, 441–2, 556
    as non-excludable or non-rivalrous 441, 442, 553

public infrastructure 5, 32, 438, 439–40
public (state) ownership 419–20, 432
purchase agreements 499
purchasing power 182, 191, 195
purchasing power parity (PPP) 193, 305, 472, 481, 482, 483, 487, 515, 555, 556
    absolute 193, 541
    relative 193, 195, 557
pyramid schemes 120, 121
q-theory of investment 142, 556
quantity equation 529
quits 90, 556
quotas, IMF 499, 556
Ramsey principle of public finance 416–17, 556
random shocks 343–5, 346, 355
random walk 481–2, 556
    theory of consumption 130
rational expectations hypothesis 103, 311, 386–7, 465 n.2, 531–2, 556
Reagan, Ronald 529
real business cycle (RBC) theory 333, 349–52, 353, 354, 356, 532–3, 556
real economy 9–10, 32–3, 557
real exchange rate 152–70, 231, 232, 236, 240, 286, 306, 557
    appreciation 156, 163, 164, 166–7, 168, 232, 233
    and consumption 165–6, 234
    defined 153–4
    depreciation 155–6, 163, 168, 193, 232, 252, 312, 313
    effective 155, 168, 338, 339, 545
    equilibrium (long run) 152, 159, 161–7, 162–3, 163, 166, 168, 193, 546
    fundamental determinants of 163–6
    measuring 154–5
    misalignment 163, 485
    and net external investment position 163
    overvaluation/undervaluation 162
    and primary current account 152, 155–6, 168
    as relative price of non-traded goods 156–61
    in the short run 479
real interest parity condition 472–3, 557
real interest rates 105, 109, 152, 183, 186, 191, 195, 286, 352, 377–8, 470–1, 557
    and arbitrage 472–3
    and bond prices 107, 185, 472
    and business cycles 354–5
    and consumption 133–4, 137, 148
    and investment 109–10, 139–41, 142, 147
    and public debt 375–6
realism, and theory 14–15
recession 13, 332, 333, 352, 542
recognition lags 389, 557
redistribution 363, 364–5, 379, 390, 453

regulation
    of financial markets 419
    of labour markets 423–6
relative prices 74, 152, 156–61, 177, 232, 557
    equilibrium 160
    signalling role of 390
reliquification 192
repurchase agreements 211, 499, 557
reputation 393–4, 405, 557
reserve multipliers 206
reserve ratios 205, 206, 209, 212, 222, 223, 557
reserve requirements 205, 209, 212, 542
reserves, bank 203, 205, 223, 542
residual claimants 112, 557
returns to scale 51, 557
    constant 50, 51, 543
    decreasing 51, 544
    increasing 51, 413, 432, 549
revaluations 251, 557
reverse (repurchase) transactions 211, 499, 557
Ricardian equivalence proposition 115–19, 122, 395, 557
rigour 17
Riksbank 203 n. 4
risk
    allocation of 462–4
    pricing of 464–5
    systemic 220, 221, 559
risk aversion 463, 476, 487, 557
risk diversification 463–4
risk neutrality 464, 557
risk premiums 464, 467–8, 487, 557
Robertson lag 341, 343, 557
rolling over 211
Romania 28, 121, 448
Romer, Paul 536
rule of law 449, 450, 454
rules versus discretion 385, 402, 405, 557
Russia
    exchange rates 518
    financial crisis 10, 492, 507
    hyperinflation 191, 397, 401
    openness 10
    pyramid schemes 121
    underground economy 28
sacrifice ratio 327
Sala-i-Martin, Xavier 536
salaries 30, 34, 289
sales, final and intermediate 23, 30, 32, 40, 547
salt-water economists 18
Samuelson, Paul 527
Sargent, Thomas 531 n. 8
Saudi Arabia 506
saving-investment schedule 53, 59
savings 67, 102, 236, 557
    and capital accumulation 52
    corporate 112
    net 34

and economic growth 49–50, 52, 53–8, 66
private 9, 31–2, 112
net 32
savings rates 55, 66, 437, 452
dynamically efficient and inefficient 56–8
Schacht, Hjalmar 526
Schettkatt, Ronald 81
Schmidt, Helmut 284 n.
Schröder, G. 404
Schumpeter, Joseph 444
Schwartz, Anna 529, 532 n.
seigniorage 218, 219, 363, 376, 377–8, 380, 396, 401, 557
self-fulfilling attacks 510–13, 522, 557
Senegal 449
separation and separation rate from jobs 90, 91–2, 550, 558
Serbia 397
services 25, 163, 164, 167
share prices see stock prices
shocks
productivity 349–51, 353, 356
random 343–5, 346, 355
see also demand shocks; supply shocks
sight deposits 174, 175, 180–1, 194
silver 493, 521
Simons, Henry 529 n. 4
Singapore 28, 167
Single European Market 19
Slovakia 28
Slutsky, Eugen E. 332, 344 n. 9
small open economy 230, 558
Smith, Adam 409
Smithsonian Agreement 501
Snower, Dennis 535
social minima 87–8
social safety net 95, 426, 427, 452
social security contributions 428
Solow, Robert M. 436
Solow decomposition 65, 558
Solow growth model 46–7, 55, 59, 60, 62, 65–6, 67, 437, 438, 454, 536, 558
Solow residual 63, 65, 350, 558
sovereign borrowing 121, 122, 558
Spain
accounting identity 35
bank insurance 220
budget balances 365, 372
budget (expected and realized) 2003 370
business cycles 336
capital accumulation 440
central bank independence 397, 398
fiscal policy 395, 396
GDP 336, 398
and IMF 506
inflation 391, 398
labour market 425, 429–30
labour taxation 428
nd monetary union 503

openness 10
prices 167
public debt 373
subsidies 420
trade unions 84
transfer payments 93, 364
underground economy 28
unemployment 87, 89, 95, 391
wage share of value added 289
wages 89, 391
women and employment 82
youth employment/unemployment 89
speculative attacks 502, 514, 515, 558
speculative bubbles 476–9, 542, 558
stability, and economic growth 449–50
Stability and Growth Pact 372, 377, 395, 402, 527
stabilization 363, 365–72, 373–9, 380, 533, 558
stagflation 286, 299, 310, 320, 322, 558
state-owned enterprises (SOEs) 419–20, 432
steady states 49, 52–3, 55, 58–9, 62, 67, 558
sterilization 216–17, 223, 247–8, 558
sticky prices 230, 231, 244, 245–6, 256, 262, 263, 271, 276, 385, 528
business cycles and 345, 346–9, 352, 354, 355, 532–3, 558
exchange rate determination with 484–5
general equilibrium with 272–5
stock market index 7
stock markets 103, 461
stock prices 7, 8, 9, 141, 142, 143, 144, 147, 239–40, 473, 476–9
real 337, 338, 339, 389
stock variables 22
Stockholm School 526
Stone, Richard 22, 528
stylized facts 47–9, 559
subsidies 419–20, 432
substitution
currency 178, 193
intertemporal 127, 128, 351–2, 353, 356
marginal rate of 74, 551
substitution effect 75, 97, 352, 559
supply
excess 238, 546
see also aggregate supply; aggregate supply curve; labour supply; labour supply curve
supply-determined output 268–9, 276, 306, 559
supply shocks 293, 294, 298, 319–23, 327–8, 346–9 passim, 353, 559
and unemployment 387–8
see also oil price shocks
supply-side 11, 13, 559
supply-side policies 408–34

surplus
balance of payments 39
consumer 416, 543
producer 416, 556
see also budget surplus; current account surpluses
Sweden 18, 37
accounting identity 35
balance of payments 38
bank insurance 220
budget balances 365, 372
capital accumulation 440
central bank assets 181
central bank independence 397, 398
exchange rates 164
financial crisis 507, 512
fiscal policy 395, 396
GDP 34, 47, 231, 398
hours worked 76, 81
and IMF 506
incomes 5, 34
inflation 391, 398
inflation targeting 213
interest rates 117
labour market 424, 425
labour share of income 8
labour taxation 428
money demand 184
net external position 164
openness 10, 231
prices 167
public debt 373
stock prices 8
subsidies 420
trade unions 84
transfer payments 93, 364
unemployment 87, 89, 391
wages 76, 88, 89, 391
women and employment 82
youth employment/unemployment 89
Swindon 176
Swiss National Bank 203 n. 4, 348
Switzerland
central bank independence 397, 398, 399
consumption 33
currency depreciations 498
GDP 33, 34, 47, 231, 398
and gold bloc 497
government purchases 33
hours worked 81
income per capita 5
inflation 348, 391, 398
labour market regulation 425
labour taxation 428
and Latin Monetary Union 493
money demand 184
and oil shocks 348
openness 10, 231
prices 167
trade unions 84
underground economy 28

unemployment 7, 391
unemployment benefit 93
wages 391
systemic risk 220, 221, 559
Tabellini, Guido 534
targeting, monetary policy 200, 201–2,
213–16, 223, 554
tax returns 26, 29
tax smoothing 366, 367, 379, 559
taxes 13, 116, 117–18, 122, 236, 367,
369–70, 409, 432
ad valorem 416
corporate 34, 393–4
cyclical behaviour of 369
deadweight loss from 416
and disposable income 239
distortionary 118, 416, 417, 545
and economic stability 449
excise 34
income 428
indirect 33–4
and investment 239
labour 426–7, 428, 432
net 30, 369, 553
non-distortionary 417
progressive 364, 426, 453, 556
and provision of public goods 415–17
and supply shocks 293
value added (VAT) 26, 34
technological progress/innovation 140,
559
in banking and monetary control
223
diffusion and imitation of 444–5, 545,
548
and economic growth 6, 46, 60, 61–2,
63, 65–6, 67, 436, 441–6, 536
and labour demand 78, 79
long waves in 444–5
and supply shocks 350
and unemployment 79
telecommunications deregulation 418
terms of trade 559
internal and external 155, 549
terrorism 16
Thailand 10, 28, 492, 506, 507, 512,
513–14
Thatcher, Margaret 430, 529, 530
theory
and realism 14–15
testing of 15
time inconsistency problems 394, 405,
429, 443–4
Tinbergen, Jan 527
Tirole, Jean 534
Tobin, James 142 n.
Tobin tax 516, 517
Tobin's *q* 141–7, 148, 232, 240, 559
total factor productivity 63, 96, 350, 354,
444, 559
tradable/traded goods 155, 156–61,
163–5, 559

versus non-traded goods 156–7,
163–4, 168
trade
in assets 230
see also financial markets
intertemporal 104–5, 550
liberalization 518
openness to 10, 230, 450
trade policies 420, 559
trade unions 83–6, 96, 98, 410–11, 430,
530, 559
transaction costs 183, 187, 194, 559
transfer payments 30, 32, 34, 362, 364,
367, 426, 453, 559
see also unemployment benefits
transformation, marginal rate of 158
transition economies 7, 319, 518
trend GDP 4–5, 333, 335, 337
Triffin paradox 500, 559
tulipmania 478
Tunisia 28
Turkey 37, 38
Ukraine 10, 28, 191, 397
uncertainty 388–90, 404–5, 460, 462
uncovered interest parity (UIP) 467–8,
472, 474, 560
underground economy 26, 28, 176, 560
unemployment 6–7, 11, 13, 72, 73,
80–97, 273, 274, 409, 427–8, 515,
534–5, 560
actual 95, 97, 98, 296
and business cycles 338, 339
as countercyclical 9
and demand shocks 387–8
duration of 92–4
equilibrium 73, 94–7, 98, 286, 294–8
passim, 387–8, 535, 546
female 82
and fiscal policy 14, 366–7
frictional 90–1, 93, 94–5, 98, 547
and inflation 283–7, 294, 296, 297,
299
involuntary 83, 98, 276, 354, 428, 543,
550
and output 284–6, 297
and real wages 83
short-run fluctuations in 366–7
stocks and flows 91, 98, 421, 560
structural 94, 95, 98, 432, 558
and supply shocks 387–8
and technical change 79
voluntary 80, 98, 543, 560
youth 89
unemployment benefits 92–3, 94, 95, 98,
367, 426, 537, 560
unemployment policy 13
unemployment rate 6, 7, 327, 338, 560
and vacancy rate 421–3
unemployment trap 93
United Kingdom 18, 65
accounting identity 35
bank insurance 220

budget balances 114, 115, 365, 372
business cycles 335, 336
capital accumulation 440
capital–labour ratio 48
capital–output ratio 48
capital stock 64
central bank assets 181
central bank independence 397, 398,
399, 400
commodity prices 295
consumption 33
currency depreciations 498
current account 132, 133
demand multipliers 236
employment 64, 82, 89
exchange rates 153, 515
financial crisis (1992) 510
fiscal policy 395, 396
foreign exchange reserves 510
GDP 4, 6, 16, 33, 34, 47, 65, 231, 321,
333, 334, 336, 349, 398
government purchases 33
hours worked 64, 65, 76, 81
and IMF 506
incomes 5, 29, 34
inflation 12, 16, 287, 295, 321, 348,
391, 398, 495, 501
inflation targeting 213, 214–15
interest rates 117, 189, 190
investment 33
labour market 425, 430
labour taxation 428
monetary aggregates 176, 182
monetary base 207
money demand 184
money supply 207
and oil shocks 132, 133, 321, 322, 348
openness 10, 231
output–labour ratio 48
population 64
prices 12, 167, 295
public debt 368, 373
saving 112
taxes 369
technological progress 444
trade unions 84, 96, 430
transfer payments 93, 364
unemployment 87, 89, 91, 92, 95, 287,
295, 321, 327, 387, 388, 391, 422,
430, 431
vacancy rate 422
wages 76, 89, 391, 431
women and employment 82
youth employment/unemployment
89
United States 37, 65
accounting identity 35
balance of payments 38
budget balances 114, 115, 365, 372
budget surplus 362
business cycles 335, 336, 337
capacity utilization rates 9

capital-labour ratio 48
capital-output ratio 48
capital stock 64
central bank assets 181
central bank independence 397, 398, 399
consumption 33, 126, 337, 339, 362
currency depreciations 498
demand multipliers 236
employment 58, 64, 82, 89, 96
exchange rates 153, 486
exports 337, 339
Federal Funds Rate 212
Federal Reserve 201, 203 n. 4, 213
fiscal, policy 395–6
GDP 16, 33, 34, 47, 54, 65, 231, 240, 321, 336, 339, 349, 398
gold reserves 500
government purchases 126, 337, 339
hours worked 64, 76, 81
and IMF 506
imports 337, 339
incomes 5, 34
inflation 9, 16, 219, 321, 337, 391, 398, 495, 501
interest rates 117, 324
investment 33, 54, 126, 337, 339
labour market regulation 425
labour taxation 428
monetary aggregates 176, 182
monetary base 207
money demand 184
money supply 207
multifactor productivity 63
official liabilities 500
openness 10, 230, 231
output-labour ratio 48
population 58, 64
prices 167, 337, 339
public debt 362, 368, 373
saving 112
seigniorage 219

subsidies 420
technological progress 444
trade unions 85
transfer payments 93, 364
underground economy 28
unemployment 7, 87, 89, 91, 95, 321, 391, 422, 431
vacancy rate 422
wage share of value added 289
wages 76, 89, 96, 391, 431
women and employment 82
youth employment/unemployment 89
unpaid work 26, 28, 81, 560
unsterilized intervention 247
user cost of capital 141–2, 145, 146, 148, 560
USSR 448
utility 127, 560
value added 23, 24, 40, 560
wage share of 289
value added taxes (VAT) 26, 34
value subtracted 24
variables
acyclical 337, 541
countercyclical 9, 337, 544
endogenous and exogenous 14, 15, 16, 236, 238, 546
nominal 269, 270, 276, 282, 286, 304
procyclical 9, 337, 354, 355, 356, 556
real 269, 270, 276, 286, 304
Vaubel, Roland 534 n.12
Venezuela 28, 167
vulnerabilities, speculative attack 511–13, 515, 560
wage bargaining 95, 265
wage indexation 292, 326, 390
wage inflation 283, 560
wage negotiations 326
staggered, synchronized and trendsetting 326
wage share 289, 353, 560
wage shock 95

wages 14, 30, 34, 167, 282, 289–90, 352
efficiency 88, 98, 546
as mark-up on prices 290–1, 292, 299
minimum 88, 89, 98, 423, 424 n., 552
nominal 74, 269, 271, 273, 288, 290, 291, 299
rigidity of 384, 553
real (consumption) 49, 74, 77–8, 95–7, 98, 269, 270, 271, 273, 274, 286, 410–11, 557
cyclical behaviour of 353–4, 356
increases in 75, 79
and labour productivity 79, 291
reduction in 80
rigidity of 83–8, 354, 515, 557
and unemployment 83
Wallace, Neil 531 n. 8
Walters, Alan 530
war 448–9
Wassenar Accord (1982) 96
wealth 28–9, 105, 105–8, 112–13, 122, 141, 165–6, 239, 560
and consumption 134–6, 137, 148, 232, 529
inflation and redistribution of 390
inherited 108
and investment 111
liquid 175
private 116
and taxation 118
welfare trap 426, 560
wholesale price index (WPI) 27
Wicksell, Knut 175, 176, 526
women, in labour force 46, 64, 75, 80–1, 82
World Bank 536
yield 175
yield arbitrage 465, 541, 560
youth employment and unemployment 89
Yugoslavia 448
Zimbabwe 449